PSYCHOLOGY OF SPORT

Issues & insights

EDITED, WITH TEXT BY

A. CRAIG FISHER

Mayfield Publishing Company

Dedicated to those individuals who are
insightful enough to take an analytical look
at sport.

Library of Congress Catalog Card Number: 75-44698
International Standard Book Number: 0-87484-359-6

Manufactured in the United States of America
Mayfield Publishing Company
285 Hamilton Avenue, Palo Alto, California 94301

This book was set in Galaxy and Plantin by
Applied Typographic Systems and was printed and bound
by the George Banta Company. Sponsoring editor was
C. Lansing Hays, Carole Norton supervised editing, and
manuscript editors were Alice Rosendall and Lionel
Gambill. Michelle Hogan supervised production, and
the text and cover were designed by Nancy Sears.

Contents

10496

Preface

This book is designed to provide instructors and students in sport psychology courses with a learning instrument that combines the coherence and continuity of a textbook with the range of opinion, in-depth treatment of selected issues, and insight into research methods of a book of readings. To accomplish this, I have divided the vast area of sport psychology into four important and topical categories—Affiliation and Sport, Motivation and Sport, Aggression and Sport, and Personality and Sport. Major concepts and issues within each category are explained in the text and illustrated with articles drawn from psychology and physical education research journals, various other periodicals, textbooks, and previously unpublished presentations.

All major points of view are represented, and a continuum of difficulty permits the instructor a wide latitude in assigning readings. Mindful that every instructor has his own way of teaching a course, I have chosen the readings to provide breadth and variety to any of several possible approaches. The major sections need not be covered in the sequence in which they are presented here, nor do all articles need to be assigned. By judicious selection the material can be adapted to either an undergraduate or a graduate-level course.

Human behavior, in sport as well as in other areas of life, is complex. I have tried in this text to deal with that complexity without introducing either misleading superficiality or unnecessary complexities of presentation. I have simplified whenever possible, but I have not tried to give simple answers to complex questions.

ACKNOWLEDGMENTS

Special thanks are extended to those authors and publishers who gave permission to have their work included in this text. Their generous co-operation made possible the compilation of readings that is the backbone of the text.

I am grateful especially to Rainer Martens and Dean Ryan for their comments after reading the manuscript. Numerous alterations were made according to their suggestions, but in some cases I stubbornly resisted their wisdom. In those cases the errors and misinterpretations must be construed as mine.

The reserve librarians at Ithaca College provided invaluable assistance in tracking down foreign sources and correcting bibliographic citations. The text is more accurate and therefore more useful, thanks to their diligent efforts.

I am indeed grateful to Ithaca College for its financial support in defraying permission-to-reprint costs and to the administration and graduate faculty of the School of Health, Physical Education, and Recreation for their encouragement and especially their understanding during the writing and compiling phase. This support made the task easier.

Lansing Hays of Mayfield Publishing Company provided me with a concerned and dedicated editor, Carole Norton, and talented copy editors, Lionel Gambill and Alice Rosendall. Their efforts on my behalf are much appreciated.

I am deeply indebted to June Miles and Peg Moy for their painstaking efforts in typing the manuscript.

To the members of my family I express gratitude for their understanding of the great amount of time and single-minded purpose required to complete this book.

Ithaca, New York   A. Craig Fisher
October 1975

Affiliation

& sport

1

Affiliation & sport

1

To call man a social animal implies that his behavior is not wholly of his own choosing—that individuals can alter each other's behavior. These effects can be classified as (1) those caused by onlookers (*presence of others*), and (2) those derived from the group atmosphere (*cohesiveness*). Both effects are important in sport dynamics.

PRESENCE OF OTHERS

One need only read a newspaper or a sport periodical to see how fans affect sport performance. There is much conceptual literature indicating that audiences enhance performances requiring strength, endurance, or any kind of intense physical output. Morgan (1973) tells of a college distance runner who imagined an audience to sustain his endurance. In one instance when he was tiring he visualized his teammates urging him on to victory. Later in the race, when he was again feeling especially fatigued, he visualized his parents watching him run on television. The result was that he carried on and overcame the fatigue.

The belief exists, however, that certain kinds of audiences can inhibit performance. The home crowd does not cheer on the visiting team. This is doubtless one of the reasons the home team is usually favored to win in an otherwise even match. The audience tends to diminish the visiting team's performance.

Several questions arise from these accounts of group behavior and audience effects. What are the attributed effects on performance? Are these effects real? Phenomenologically, one would answer the second question in the affirmative, but what facts are available? Does the situation also hold true for learning as performance? Are there any modifiers that must be accounted for in understanding audience effects? Can these modifiers be isolated in laboratory experimentation, and can the effects of an audience be predicted in advance?

The events described here are classified under the heading of *social facilitation*. Although many of the original experiments conducted by psychologists dealt with motor performance variables, this trend did not continue. Thus it is left to sport psychologists to continue to explore the effects of the presence of others on the learning and performing of sport tasks.

Types of audiences

Before discussing the effects of audience facilitation and inhibition, it might first be fruitful to consider various types of audiences. The mere presence of other individuals who remain silent and offer no direct feedback is one category. These individuals are just physically present in the immediate environment. An audience could also actively relate to the learner or performer, and could be either supportive or threatening. In the former situation, positive feedback would take the form of applause, encouragement, and the like—this type of audience provides a degree of security. The threatening audience could be abusive in many ways. In both of these situations, there appears to be an assumption that the audience has some degree of knowledge about the tasks to be performed. It might seem rather ineffectual to be applauded by an audience that knows little of the intricacies of the action it is applauding.

Much of sport is highly competitive (consider some of the following locker-room slogans: ''Are you better than yesterday?'' ''Never be willing to be second best.'' ''When you're through improving, you're through!'' ''Be good or be gone!''). The athlete, whether novice or expert, is imbued with the notion that he should improve. This kind of improvement could be classified as self-improvement but in many cases standards are available against which actual performances can be compared. These standards might very well be set by an audience that is unseen but nonetheless felt. (Remember how Morgan's distance runner described the encouragement provided by imagined teammates and parents.) We might postulate that once an athlete achieves a reasonable skill level, he never again will perform in isolation. To that individual, performance must always be judged relative to standards imposed by an audience that is not now present—parents, peers, coaches, role models, and so forth.

There is one additional type of audience that must be mentioned, since much social facilitation research deals with this audience. This is the *coacting* audience. In group and team situations, athletes perform with other athletes. Coactors not only view—and perhaps interact with—others in various ways; they also perform the same task themselves. Knowing that others are pursuing a similar goal would seem to make a difference.

Audience–coaction effects

Two social facilitation paradigms have evolved as a result of continued experimentation to determine how the presence of others affects learning and performance. These two models are called *audience* and *coaction*. In assessing the effects of an audience, the experimenter manipulates the presence of passive spectators. (Sometimes the subject has an audience, sometimes he is alone.) (Researchers have used a passive audience to avoid having to equate the amount of active feedback to all subjects.) In the coaction paradigm, co-workers perform simultaneously and independently on the same task as the subject. It is important to make these distinctions so that the research can be correctly interpreted.

Seventy-five years of research findings have yielded conflicting results in both the audience and coaction effects on learning and performance. Even before delving into the major theoretical positions and assessing the effects of the presence of others, we can draw one conclusion. Davis (1969) stated that

Despite the fact that some research has failed to show that audiences produce a consistent improvement or decrement on some task . . . the great bulk of the evidence suggests that the knowledge that others are present or will soon be present to observe one's work does have a strong effect on performance [and probably on learning also]. . . . It should be evident by now that an individual performing before an audience is sometimes likely to "do better" than when alone and sometimes likely to "do worse," but is rather unlikely to be indifferent to the presence of others.

5

Robert Zajonc, in article 1.1, was able to make some sense of the conflicting experimental results and to see consistent findings. He linked the social facilitation paradigms to the Hull–Spence drive theory and contended that the mere presence of an audience acts as an arouser. Increased arousal leads to increased drive, facilitating the emission of dominant (most likely) responses. An audience has the ability to facilitate or inhibit *either* learning or performance, depending on the most likely response. In the early stages of learning a task, especially a complex sport skill, errors are many and performance is hampered by the presence of others. When the skill is well learned, however, performance is enhanced by an audience.

Zajonc provides a review of the literature on audience and coaction effects on learning and performance, much of which is derived from animal research. He points out the cues derived from coaction are important for their facilitating or inhibiting effects. In that event coactors become models for imitative learning. Although an audience may act as an arouser, Zajonc indicates that its effects may even be more complex than those normally attributed to arousers.

1.1 Social facilitation

ROBERT B. ZAJONC
University of Michigan, Ann Arbor

Most textbook definitions of social psychology involve considerations about the influence of man upon man, or, more generally, of individual upon individual. And most of them, explicitly or implicitly, commit the main efforts of social psychology to the problem of how and why the *behavior* of one individual affects the behavior of another. The influences of individuals on each others' behavior which are of interest to social psychologists today take on very complex forms. Often they involve vast networks of interindividual effects such as one finds in studying the

From *Science* 149(1965):269–274. Reprinted by permission of the author and the American Association for the Advancement of Science. Copyright 1965 by the American Association for the Advancement of Science.

process of group decision-making, competition, or conformity to a group norm. But the fundamental forms of interindividual influence are represented by the oldest experimental paradigm of social psychology: social facilitation. This paradigm, dating back to Triplett's original experiments on pacing and competition, carried out in 1897, examines the consequences upon behavior which derive from the sheer presence of other individuals.

Until the late 1930's, interest in social facilitation was quite active, but with the outbreak of World War II it suddenly died. And it is truly regrettable that it died, because the basic questions about social facilitation—its dynamics and its causes—which are in effect the basic questions of social psychology, were never solved. It is with these questions that this article is concerned. I first examine past results in this nearly completely abandoned area of research and then suggest a general hypothesis which might explain them.

Research in the area of social facilitation may be classified in terms of two experimental paradigms: audience effects and coaction effects. The first experimental paradigm involves the observation of behavior when it occurs in the presence of passive spectators. The second examines behavior when it occurs in the presence of other individuals also engaged in the same activity. We shall consider past literature in these two areas separately.

AUDIENCE EFFECTS

Simple motor responses are particularly sensitive to social facilitation ✻ effects. In 1925 Travis obtained such effects in a study in which he used the pursuit-rotor task. In this task the subject is required to follow a small revolving target by means of a stylus which he holds in his hand. If the stylus is even momentarily off target during a revolution, the revolution counts as an error. First each subject was trained for several consecutive days until his performance reached a stable level. One day after the conclusion of the training the subject was called to the laboratory, given five trials alone, and then ten trials in the presence of from four to eight upperclassmen and graduate students. They had been asked by the experimenter to watch the subject quietly and attentively. Travis found a clear improvement in performance when his subjects were confronted with an audience. Their accuracy on the ten trials before an audience was greater than on any ten previous trials, including those on which they had scored the highest.

A considerably greater improvement in performance was recently obtained in a somewhat different setting and on a different task (Bergum and Lehr, 1963). Each subject (all were National Guard trainees) was placed in a separate booth. He was seated in front of a panel outfitted with 20 red lamps in a circle. The lamps on this panel light in a clockwise sequence at 12 revolutions per minute. At random intervals one or another light fails to go on in its proper sequence. On the average there are 24 such failures per hour. The subject's task is to signal whenever a light fails to go on. After 20 minutes of intensive training, followed by a short rest, the National Guard trainees monitored the light panels for 135 minutes. Subjects in one group performed their task alone. Subjects in another group were told that from time to time a lieutenant colonel or a master sergeant would visit them in the booth to observe their performance. These visits actually took place about four times during the experimental session. There was no doubt about the results. The accuracy of the supervised subjects was on the average 34 percent higher than the accuracy of the trainees working in isolation, and toward the end of the experimental session the accuracy of the supervised subjects was more than twice as high as that of the subjects working in isolation. Those expecting to be visited by a superior missed, during the last experimental period, 20 percent of the light failures, while those expecting no such visits missed 64 percent of the failures.

Dashiell, who, in the early 1930's, carried out an extensive program of research on social facilitation, also found considerable improvement in performance due to audience effects on such tasks as simple multiplication or word association. But, as is the case in many other areas, negative audience effects were also found. In 1933 Pessin asked college students to learn lists of nonsense syllables under two conditions, alone and in the presence of several spectators. When confronted with an audience, his subjects required an average of 11.27 trials to learn a seven-item list. When working alone they needed only 9.85 trials. The average number of errors made in the "audience" condition was considerably higher than the number in the "alone" condition. In 1931 Husband found that the presence of spectators interferes with the learning of a finger maze, and in 1933 Pessin and Husband confirmed Husband's results. The number of trials which the isolated subjects required for learning the finger maze was 17.1. Subjects confronted with spectators, however, required 19.1 trials. The average number of errors for the isolated subjects was 33.7; the number for those working in the presence of an audience was 40.5.

The results thus far reviewed seem to contradict one another. On a pursuit-rotor task Travis found that the presence of an audience improves performance. The learning of nonsense syllables and maze learning, however, seem to be inhibited by the presence of an audience, as shown by Pessin's experiment. The picture is further complicated by the fact that when Pessin's subjects were asked, several days later, to recall the nonsense syllables they had learned, a reversal was found. The subjects who tried to recall the lists in the presence of spectators did considerably better than those who tried to recall them alone. Why are the learning of nonsense syllables and maze learning inhibited by the presence of spectators? And why, on the other hand, does performance on a pursuit-rotor, word-association, multiplication, or a vigilance task improve in the presence of others?

There is just one, rather subtle, consistency in the above results. It would appear that the emission of well-learned responses is facilitated by the presence of spectators, while the acquisition of new responses is impaired. To put the statement in conventional psychological language, performance is facilitated and learning is impaired by the presence of spectators.

This tentative generalization can be reformulated so that different features of the problem are placed into focus. During the early stages of learning, especially of the type involved in social facilitation studies, the subject's responses are mostly the wrong ones. A person learning a finger maze, or a person learning a list of nonsense syllables, emits more wrong responses than right ones in the early stages of training. Most learning experiments continue until he ceases to make mistakes—until his performance is perfect. It may be said, therefore, that during training it is primarily the wrong responses which are dominant and strong; they are the ones which have the highest probability of occurrence. But after the individual has mastered the task, correct responses necessarily gain ascendancy in his task-relevant behavioral repertoire. Now they are the ones which are more probable—in other words, dominant. Our tentative generalization may now be simplified: audience enhances the emission of dominant responses. If the dominant responses are the correct ones, as is the case upon achieving mastery, the presence of an audience will be of benefit to the individual. But if they are mostly wrong, as is the case in the early stages of learning, then these wrong responses will be enhanced in the presence of an audience, and the emission of correct responses will be postponed or prevented.

There is a class of psychological processes which are known to enhance the emission of dominant responses. They are subsumed under the concepts of drive, arousal, and activation (Duffy, 1962; Spence, 1956; Zajonc and Nieuwenhuyse, 1964). If we could show that the presence of an audience has arousal consequences for the subject, we would be a step further along in trying to arrange the results of social-facilitation experiments into a neater package. But let us first consider another set of experimental findings.

COACTION EFFECTS

The experimental paradigm of coaction is somewhat more complex than the paradigm involved in the study of audience effects. Here we observe individuals all simultaneously engaged in the same activity and in full view of each other. One of the clearest effects of such simultaneous action, or coaction, is found in eating behavior. It is well known that animals simply eat more in the presence of others. For instance, Bayer (1929) had chickens eat from a pile of wheat to their full satisfaction. He waited some time to be absolutely sure that his subject would eat no more, and then brought in a companion chicken who had not eaten for 24 hours. Upon the introduction of the hungry coactor, the apparently sated chicken ate two-thirds again as much grain as it had already eaten. Recent work by Tolman and Wilson (1965) fully substantiates these results. In an extensive study of social-facilitation effects among albino rats, Harlow (1932) found dramatic increases in eating. In one of his experiments, for instance, the rats, shortly

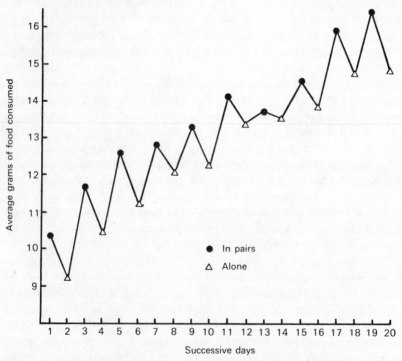

Figure 1 Feeding of isolated and paired rats. (From Harlow, 1932)

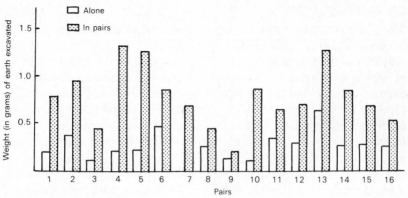

Figure 2 Nest-building behavior of isolated and paired ants. (From Chen, 1937)

after weaning, were matched in pairs for weight. They were then fed alone and in pairs on alternate days. Figure 1 shows his results. It is clear that considerably more food was consumed by the animals when they were in pairs than when they were fed alone. James (1953, 1960; James and Cannon, 1955), too, found very clear evidence of increased eating among puppies fed in groups.

Perhaps the most dramatic effect of coaction is reported by Chen (1937). Chen observed groups of ants working alone, in groups of two, and in groups of three. Each ant was observed under various conditions. In the first experimental session each ant was placed in a bottle half filled with sandy soil. The ant was observed for six hours. The time at which nest-building began was noted, and the earth excavated by the insect was carefully weighed. Two days afterward the same ants were placed in freshly filled bottles in pairs, and the same observations were made. A few days later the ants were placed in the bottles in groups of three, again for six hours. Finally, a few days after the test in groups of three, nest-building of the ants in isolation was observed. Figure 2 shows some of Chen's data.

There is absolutely no question that the amount of work an ant accomplishes increases markedly in the presence of another ant. In all pairs except one, the presence of a companion increased output by a factor of at least 2. The effect of coaction on the latency of the nest-building behavior was equally dramatic. The solitary ants of session 1 and the final session began working on the nest in 192 minutes, on the average. The latency period for ants in groups of two was only 28 minutes. The effects observed by Chen were limited to the immediate situation and seemed to have no lasting consequences for the ants. There were no differences in the results of session 1, during which the ants worked in isolation, and of the last experimental session, where they again worked in solitude.

If one assumes that under the conditions of Chen's experiment nest-building *is* the dominant response, then there is no reason why his findings could not be embraced by the generalization just proposed. Nest-building is a response which Chen's ants have fully mastered. Certainly it is something that a mature ant need not learn. And this is simply an instance where the generalization that the presence of others enhances the emission of dominant and well-developed responses holds.

If the process involved in audience effects is also involved in coaction effects, then learning should be inhibited in the presence of other learners. Let us examine some literature in this field. Klopfer (1958) observed green-finches—in isolation and in heterosexual pairs—which were learning to discriminate between sources of palatable and of unpalatable food. And, as one would by now expect, his birds learned this discrimination task considerably more efficiently when working alone. I hasten to add that the subjects' sexual interests cannot be held responsible for the inhibition of learning in the paired birds. Allee and Masure (1936), using Australian parakeets, obtained the same result for homosexual pairs as well. The speed of learning was considerably greater for the isolated birds than for the paired birds, regardless of whether the birds were of the same sex or of the opposite sex.

Similar results are found with cockroaches. Gates and Allee (1933) compared data for cockroaches learning a maze in isolation, in groups of two, and in groups of three. They used an E-shaped maze. Its three runways, made of galvanized sheet metal, were suspended in a pan of water. At the end of the center runway was a dark bottle into which the photophobic cockroaches could escape from the noxious light. The results, in terms of time required to reach the bottle, are shown in Figure 3. It is clear from the data that the solitary cockroaches required considerably less time to learn the maze than the grouped animals. Gates and Allee believe that the group situation produced inhibition. They add, however:

> The nature of these inhibiting forces is speculative, but the fact of some sort of group interference is obvious. The presence of other roaches did not operate to change greatly the movements to different parts of the maze, but did result in increased time per trial. The roaches tended to go to the corner or end of the runway and remain there a longer time when another roach was present than when alone; the other roach was a distracting stimulus.

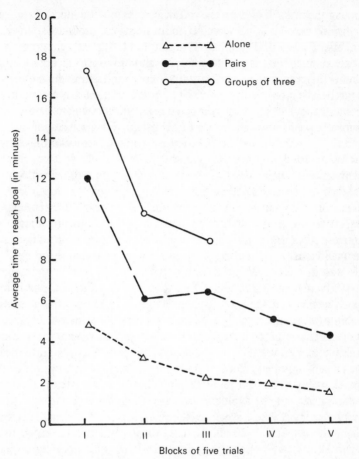

Figure 3 Maze learning in isolated and grouped cockroaches. (From Gates and Allee, 1933)

The experiments on social facilitation performed by Floyd Allport in 1920 and continued by Dashiell in 1930, both of whom used human subjects, are the ones best known. Allport's subjects worked either in separate cubicles or sitting around a common table. When working in isolation they did the various tasks at the same time and were monitored by common time signals. Allport did everything possible to reduce the tendency to compete. The subjects were told that the results of their tests would not be compared and would not be shown to other staff members, and that they themselves should refrain from making any such comparisons.

13

Among the tasks used were the following: chain word association, vowel cancellation, reversible perspective, multiplication, problem solving, and judgments of odors and weights. The results of Allport's experiments are well known: in all but the problem-solving and judgments test, performance was better in groups than in the "alone" condition. How do these results fit our generalization? Word association, multiplication, the cancellation of vowels, and the reversal of the perceived orientation of an ambiguous figure all involve responses which are well established. They are responses which are either very well learned or under a very strong influence of the stimulus, as in the word-association task or the reversible-perspective test. The problem-solving test consists of disproving arguments of ancient philosophers. In contrast to the other tests, it does not involve well-learned responses. On the contrary, the probability of wrong (that is, logically incorrect) responses on tasks of this sort is rather high; in other words, wrong responses are dominant. Of interest, however, is the finding that while intellectual work suffered in the group situation, sheer output of words was increased. When working together, Allport's subjects tended consistently to write more. Therefore, the generalization proposed in the previous section can again be applied: if the presence of others raises the probability of dominant responses, and if strong (and many) incorrect response tendencies prevail, then the presence of others can only be detrimental to performance. The results of the judgment tests have little bearing on the present argument, since Allport gives no accuracy figures for evaluating performance. The data reported only show that the presence of others was associated with the avoidance of extreme judgments.

In 1928 Travis, whose work on the pursuit rotor I have already noted, repeated Allport's chain-word-association experiment. In contrast to Allport's results, Travis found that the presence of others decreased performance. The number of associations given by his subjects was greater when they worked in isolation. It is very significant, however, that Travis used stutterers as his subjects. In a way, stuttering is a manifestation of a struggle between conflicting response tendencies, all of which are strong and all of which compete for expression. The stutterer, momentarily hung up in the middle of a sentence, waits for the correct response to reach full ascendancy. He stammers because other competing tendencies are dominant at that moment. It is reasonable to assume that, to the extent that the verbal habits of a stutterer are characterized by conflicting response tendencies, the presence of others, by enhancing each of these response tendencies, simply heightens his conflict. Performance is thus impaired.

AVOIDANCE LEARNING

In two experiments on the learning of avoidance responses the performances of solitary and grouped subjects were compared. In one, rats were used; in the other, humans.

Let us first consider the results of the rat experiment by Rasmussen (1939). A number of albino rats, all litter mates, were deprived of water for 48 hours. The apparatus consisted of a box containing a dish of drinking water. The floor of the box was made of a metal grille wired to one pole of an electric circuit. A wire inserted in the water in the dish was connected to the other pole of the circuit. Thirsty rats were placed in the box alone and in groups of three. They were allowed to drink for five seconds with the circuit open. Following this period the shock circuit remained closed, and each time the rat touched the water he received a painful shock. Observations were made on the number of times the rats approached the water dish. The results of this experiment showed that the solitary rats learned to avoid the dish considerably sooner than the grouped animals did. The rats that were in groups of three attempted to drink twice as often as the solitary rats did, and suffered considerably more shock than the solitary subjects.

Let us examine Rasmussen's results somewhat more closely. For purposes of analysis let us assume that there are just two critical responses involved: drinking, and avoidance of contact with the water. They are clearly incompatible. But drinking, we may further assume, is the dominant response, and, like eating or any other dominant response, it is enhanced by the presence of others. The animal is therefore prevented, by the faciliation of drinking which derives from the presence of others, from acquiring the appropriate avoidance response.

The second of the two studies is quite recent and was carried out by Ader and Tatum (1963). They devised the following situation with which they confronted their subjects, all medical students. Each subject is told on arrival that he will be taken to another room and seated in a chair and that electrodes will be attached to his leg. He is instructed not to get up from the chair and not to touch the electrodes. He is also told not to smoke or vocalize, and is told that the experimenter will be in the next room. That is all he is told. The subjects are observed either alone or in pairs. In the former case the subject is brought to the room and seated at a table equipped with a red button which is connected to an electric circuit. Electrodes, by means of which electric shock can be administered, are attached to the calf of one leg. After the electrodes are attached, the experimenter leaves the room. From now on the subject will receive ½ second of electric shock every 10 seconds unless he presses the red button. Each press of the button delays the shock by 10 seconds. Thus, if he is to avoid shock, he must press the button at least once every 10 seconds. It should be noted that no information was given him about the function of the button, or about the purpose of the experiment. No essential differences are introduced when subjects are brought to the room in pairs. Both are seated at the table and both become part of the shock circuit. The response of either subject delays the shock for both.

The avoidance response is considered to have been acquired when the subject (or pair of subjects) receives less than 6 shocks in a period of 5 minutes. Ader and Tatum report that the isolated students required, on the average, 11 minutes, 35 seconds to reach this criterion of learning. Of the 12 pairs which participated in the experiment, only 2 reached this criterion. One of them required 46 minutes, 40 seconds; the other, 68 minutes, 40 seconds! Ader and Tatum offer no explanation for their curious results. But there is no reason why we should not treat them in terms of the generalization proposed above. We are dealing here with a learning task, and the fact that the subjects are learning to avoid shock by pressing a red button does not introduce particular problems. They are confronted with an ambiguous task and told nothing about the button. Pressing the button is simply not the dominant response in this situation. However, escaping is. Ader and Tatum report that 8 of the 36 subjects walked out in the middle of the experiment.

One aspect of Ader and Tatum's results is especially worth noting. Once having learned the appropriate avoidance response, the individual subjects responded at considerably lower rates than the paired subjects. When we consider only those subjects who achieved the learning criterion and only those responses which occurred *after* criterion had been reached, we find that the response rates of the individual subjects were in all but one case lower than the response rates of the grouped subjects. This result further confirms the generalization that, while learning is impaired by the presence of others, the performance of learned responses is enhanced.

There are experiments which show that learning is enhanced by the presence of other learners (Gurnee, 1939; Welty, 1934), but in all these experiments, as far as I can tell, it was possible for the subject to *observe* the critical responses of other subjects and to determine when he was correct and when incorrect. In none, therefore, has the coaction paradigm been employed in its pure form. That paradigm involves the presence of others, and nothing else. It requires that these others not be able to provide the subject with cues or information as to appropriate behavior. If other learners can supply the critical individual with such cues, we are dealing not with the problem of coaction but with the problem of imitation or vicarious learning.

PRESENCE OF OTHERS AS A SOURCE OF AROUSAL

The results I have discussed thus far lead to one generalization and to one hypothesis. The generalization which organizes these results is that the presence of others, as spectators or as co-actors, enhances the emission of dominant responses. We also know from extensive research literature that arousal, activation, or drive all have as a consequence the enhancement of dominant responses (Spence, 1956). We now need to examine the hypothesis that the presence of others increases the individual's general arousal or drive level.

The evidence which bears on the relationship between the presence of others and arousal is, unfortunately, only indirect. But there is some very suggestive evidence in one area of research. One of the more reliable indicators of arousal and drive is the activity of the endocrine systems in general, and of the adrenal cortex in particular. Adrenocortical functions are extremely sensitive to changes in emotional arousal, and it has been known for some time that organisms subjected to prolonged stress are likely to manifest substantial adrenocortical hypertrophy (Selye, 1946). Recent work (Nelson and Samuels, 1952) has shown that the main biochemical component of the adrenocortical output is hydrocortisone (17-hydroxycorticosterone). Psychiatric patients characterized by anxiety states, for instance, show elevated plasma levels of hydrocortisone (Bliss et al., 1953; Board et al., 1956). (Mason, Brady, and Sidman, 1957) have recently trained monkeys to press a lever for food and have given these animals unavoidable electric shocks, all preceded by warning signals. This procedure led to elevated hydrocortisone levels; the levels returned to normal within one hour after the end of the experimental session. This "anxiety" reaction can apparently be attenuated if the animal is given repeated doses of reserpine one day before the experimental session. Sidman's conditioned avoidance schedule also results in raising the hydrocortisone levels by a factor of 2 to 4 (Lasagna and McCann, 1957). In this schedule the animal receives an electric shock every 20 seconds without warning, unless he presses a lever. Each press delays the shock for 20 seconds.

While there is a fair amount of evidence that adrenocortical activity is a reliable symptom of arousal, similar endocrine manifestations were found to be associated with increased population density (Thiessen, 1964). Crowded mice, for instance, show increased amphetamine toxicity—that is, susceptibility to the excitatory effects of amphetamine—against which they can be

17

Table 1 Basal plasma concentrations of 17-hydroxycorticosterone in monkeys housed alone (cages in separate rooms), then a room with other monkeys (cages in same room).

Subject	Time	Concentration of 17-hydroxycorticosterone in caged monkeys (*μg per 100 ml of plasma*)	
		In separate rooms	In same room
M-1	9 A.M.	23	34
M-1	3 P.M.	16	27
M-2	9 A.M.	28	34
M-2	3 P.M.	19	23
M-3	9 A.M.	32	38
M-3	3 P.M.	23	31
Mean	9 A.M.	28	35
Mean	3 P.M.	19	27

Source: Leiderman and Shapiro (1964, p. 7).

protected by the administration of phenobarbital, chlorpromazine, or reserpine (Lasagna and McCann, 1957). Mason and Brady (1964) have recently reported that monkeys caged together had considerably higher plasma levels of hydrocortisone than monkeys housed in individual cages. Thiessen found increases in adrenal weights in mice housed in groups of ten and 20 as compared with mice housed alone. The mere presence of other animals in the same room, but in separate cages, was also found to produce elevated levels of hydrocortisone. Table 1, taken from a report by Leidermann and Shapiro (1964) shows plasma levels of hydrocortisone for three animals which lived at one time in cages that afforded them the possibility of visual and tactile contact and, at another time, in separate rooms.

Mason and Brady also report urinary levels of hydrocortisone, by days of the week, for five monkeys from their laboratory and for one human hospital patient. These very suggestive figures are reproduced in Table 2 (Leidermann and Shapiro, 1964, p. 8). In the monkeys, the low weekend traffic and activity in the laboratory seem to be associated with a clear de-

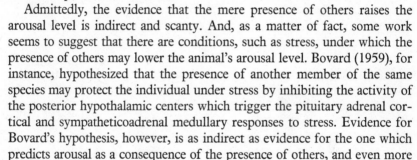

Table 2 Variations in urinary concentration of hydrocortisone over a nine-day period for five laboratory monkeys and one human hospital patient.

Subjects	*Amounts excreted (mg/24 hr)*								
	Mon.	Tues.	Wed.	Thurs.	Fri.	Sat.	Sun.	Mon.	Tues.
Monkeys	1.88	1.71	1.60	1.52	1.70	1.16	1.17	1.88	
Patient		5.9	6.5	4.5	5.7	3.3	3.9	6.0	5.2

Source: Leiderman and Shapiro (1964, p. 8)

crease in hydrocortisone. As for the hospital patient, Mason and Brady report, "he was confined to a thoracic surgery ward that bustled with activity during the weekdays when surgery and admissions occurred. On the weekends the patient retired to the nearby Red Cross building, with its quieter and more pleasant environment."

Admittedly, the evidence that the mere presence of others raises the arousal level is indirect and scanty. And, as a matter of fact, some work seems to suggest that there are conditions, such as stress, under which the presence of others may lower the animal's arousal level. Bovard (1959), for instance, hypothesized that the presence of another member of the same species may protect the individual under stress by inhibiting the activity of the posterior hypothalamic centers which trigger the pituitary adrenal cortical and sympatheticoadrenal medullary responses to stress. Evidence for Bovard's hypothesis, however, is as indirect as evidence for the one which predicts arousal as a consequence of the presence of others, and even more scanty.

SUMMARY AND CONCLUSION

If one were to draw one practical suggestion from the review of the social-facilitation effects which are summarized in this article he would advise the student to study all alone, preferably in an isolated cubicle, and to arrange to take his examinations in the company of many other students, on stage, and in the presence of a large audience. The results of his examination would be beyond his wildest expectations, provided, of course, he had learned his material quite thoroughly.

I have tried in this article to pull together the early, almost forgotten work on social facilitation and to explain the seemingly conflicting results. This explanation is, of course, tentative, and it has never been put to a direct experimental test. It is, moreover, not far removed from the one originally

19

proposed by Allport (1924). He theorized that "the sights and sounds of others doing the same thing" augment ongoing responses. Allport, however, proposed this effect only for *overt* motor responses, assuming that *"intellectual* or *implicit responses* of thought are hampered rather than facilitated" by the presence of others. This latter conclusion was probably suggested to him by the negative results he observed in his research on the effects of coaction on problem solving.

Needless to say, the presence of others may have effects considerably more complex than that of increasing the individual's arousal level. The presence of others may provide cues as to appropriate or inappropriate responses, as in the case of imitation or vicarious learning. Or it may supply the individual with cues as to the measure of danger in an ambiguous or stressful situation. Davitz and Mason (1955), for instance, have shown that the presence of an unafraid rat reduces the fear of another rat in stress. Bovard (1959) believes that the calming of the rat in stress which is in the presence of an unafraid companion is mediated by inhibition of activity of the posterior hypothalamus. But in their experimental situations (that is, the open field test) the possibility that cues for appropriate escape or avoidance responses are provided by the coactor is not ruled out. We might therefore be dealing not with the effects of the mere presence of others but with the considerably more complex case of imitation. The animal may not be calming *because* of his companion's presence. He may be calming *after* having copied his companion's attempted escape responses. The paradigm which I have examined in this article pertains only to the effects of the mere presence of others and to the consequences for the arousal level. The exact parameters involved in social facilitation still must be specified.

Even though Zajonc's proposition does not incorporate all that is known and reasonably speculated about social facilitation, it is a significant contribution. Davis (1969) acknowledges the import of Zajonc's work as follows:

> It is difficult to overestimate the importance of Zajonc's notion of socially originating arousal for organizing past results, guiding future research, and reviving interest in an obviously important but recently neglected area.

Martens (1969a) tested Zajonc's social facilitation hypothesis using a complex motor skill (coincident timing). Subjects were tested both in the alone condition (the experimenter was present, however) and in front of 10 spectators. The results of the study supported Zajonc's hypothesis for learning and performing. Subjects in the audience condition committed more errors early in learning and needed more trials to learn than the subjects in the alone condition. Once learning took place, however, the audience group performed better and more consistently than the alone group.

By administering a test of arousal (the Palmar Sweat Index, a measure of sweating on the palms), Martens was also able to conclude that the audience was a source of increased arousal. In most studies this possibility is not tested but is left to speculation.

In attempting to account for high anxious subjects learning faster than low anxious subjects in the presence of an audience, Martens mentions—among other possibilities—that "perhaps, as Wapner and Alper (1952) found, an unseen audience represents greater threat than an audience which is seen."

Kozar (1973) stated that the very nature of the content and teaching methodology of physical education and athletics dictates that learning and performance occur in the presence of others—teachers, coaches, classmates, teammates, opponents, and various kinds of audiences. This underscores the concern that individuals involved in teaching and coaching ought to have about the concept of social facilitation.

Although the mere presence of a passive audience has seemingly facilitated learning and performance of various motor tasks, can it be safely concluded that it was the mere presence that acted as the "cause" of behavior? Kozar contended that although the audience effects can be viewed as a source of arousal and drive, it may be that the audience is perceived as an evaluator of the performance. This is placing the power to facilitate in the mind of the subject and not in the body of the audience. This same point is made time and again throughout the psychological literature, whether it deals with personality, motivation, activation, aggression, or affiliation. The person's perception cannot be left out of the assessment of human behavior.

Subjects were assigned to one of three conditions—alone (not even the experimenter present), three supportive peers present, or three nonsupportive peers present. Findings did not support Zajonc's hypothesis relative to learning a complex motor task (stabilometer in this case). Subjects did not learn the task better in the alone condition, and Kozar speculated that the unseen audience was at work. This was prompted by the number of subjects who expressed concern about how their performance ranked relative to others in the same alone condition. The fact that there was no significant difference between the supportive and nonsupportive audience groups led the experimenter to conclude that perhaps the effect of the supportive audience was offset by the presence of many other (N = 49) coactors. These individuals could have critically evaluated the individuals' performances and judged their worth to the team effort. Kozar indicated that the instructions about the subject's group membership might have provided a degree of motivation for group performance and that this fact might have been the cause for the nonsignificant findings.

In an experiment designed to assess the effect of coaction on muscular endurance (by having subjects extend one leg and hold as long as possible under various audience conditions), Martens and Landers (1969) found that three coactors facilitated performance significantly more than one coactor or the alone condition. Perhaps a minimum number of individuals is needed to sufficiently arouse the subject to perform at a higher level.

In a design similar to that of Martens and Landers (1969), Les Burwitz and Karl Newell, in article 1.2 assess the effects of coactors on learning a novel motor task. They were interested in whether or not the mere presence of coactors influenced learning independently of any evaluative possibilities. Is it the presence of coactors that influences learning? Or is it the fact that coactors are in a position to evaluate one's performance? Even though attempts are made to reduce the chances for comparison between subjects, it is difficult to determine the evaluative potential of coactors in the mind of the performer.

1.2

The effects of the mere presence of coactors on learning a motor skill[1]

L. BURWITZ
University of Illinois, Urbana-Champaign

K. M. NEWELL
University of Illinois, Urbana-Champaign

This study determined the effects of the mere presence of 1 or 3 coactors on the acquisition of a novel motor skill. The performance of tetrads was significantly inferior to that of Ss (subjects) alone and in dyads. The findings were discussed in terms of Zajonc's social facilitation hypothesis and recent developments thereof.

Social facilitation research was atheoretical until Zajonc (1965) noticed a subtle consistency in the findings of previous research on audience and coaction effects. He placed the variable of the presence of others in the context of Hull-Spence behavior theory and suggested that an audience or co-workers enhanced the emission of dominant responses by increasing the individual's drive level. In short, Zajonc suggested that the emission of well learned responses was facilitated by the mere presence of others whereas the acquisition of new responses was inhibited. Recent studies of audience effects by Cottrell, Rittle, and Wack (1967) and Zajonc and Sales (1966) have obtained results consistent with Zajonc's proposal, and pertinent additional evidence has been reported by Martens (1969a) using a motor task.

Although the evidence has generally supported Zajonc's social facilitation hypothesis, Cottrell, Sekerak, Wack, and Rittle (1968) reported that while the presence of an audience enhanced the emission of dominant responses, the *mere* presence of others did not. Instead of the mere presence of others increasing drive level, Cottrell (1968) suggested that the perceived potential for evaluation by others leads one to anticipate positive or negative

From *Journal of Motor Behavior* 4(1972):99–102. Reprinted by permission.

[1]This investigation was supported in part by a research grant to the Motor Performance and Play Research Laboratory via the Adler Zone Center by the Department of Mental Health of the State of Illinois and by United States Public Health Research Grant No. MH-07346 from the National Institute of Mental Health. The authors gratefully acknowledge the assistance of P. Druker, S. Minkel, and A. Spiegel in data collection.

outcomes, and this anticipation of outcomes was a learned source of drive producing the social facilitation phenomenon.

Recently Klinger (1969) lent credence to the suggestion that the potential for evaluation was a necessary condition for social facilitation effects. He found the presence of a coactor, who could not evaluate the other Ss' (subjects') performance, did not improve scores on a vigilance task, although facilitation did occur when the coactor had access to the outcome of other Ss' performance. No experimental coaction findings have been reported where the evaluation potential has been removed in the learning of a task.

The aim of the present study was to determine the effects of coaction on the learning of a novel motor skill. Based upon the findings of Cottrell et al. (1968) and Klinger (1969) it was hypothesized that with potential evaluation and imitation conditions removed, there would be no significant difference in the performance scores between Ss who learned a motor task alone, in dyads, or in tetrads.

METHOD

Subjects. Ss were 108 male undergraduate students (average age 19 years) from an introductory psychology course who participated to fulfill a course requirement.

Task. The motor task used was essentially similar to a commercially produced game called "Roll-up." To perform the task S sat on a chair with the apparatus directly in front of him on a desk of normal height. He used both hands in manipulating 2 parallel inclined rods 18 in. in length to move a ball up a gradient toward him. Basically the skill involved opening the rods to allow the ball to gain sufficient speed to move up the gradient, without opening the rods so far that the ball fell through before it had a chance to reach the top of the incline. On falling through the rods the ball dropped into 1 of 7 holes which were equally spaced directly below the rods. The further up the gradient the ball was dropped the better the performance and the higher the score, with 7, 6, 5, 4, 3, 2, and 1 pt. being awarded in relation to the distance the hole was from the start position. If S started the ball up the gradient, but allowed it to roll back, a score of zero was recorded. Four pieces of "Roll-up" apparatus were used throughout the study.

Procedure. As Ss arrived at the experimental testing room they were randomly assigned to 1 of 3 coaction treatments (alone, dyad, or tetrad). A 3 × 9 factorial design with 3 levels of group size and 9 blocks of 10 trials each was used. Each of the 3 coaction cells contained 36 Ss.

In the alone condition, S learned the task seated at a table with E seated to the side and slightly behind. Ss in the dyad treatment sat opposite each other across a table 5 ft. wide, and were separated by a partition. The dyads were observed by an E seated to one side of the table. The tetrads sat along the side of one long table, with Ss 4 ft. apart. Again Ss were prevented from observing each other's performance by partitions while E observed from behind.

Five Es (3 male, and 2 female) were trained for the study and randomly assigned to treatments. E initially read suitable instructions to Ss according to the treatment condition, and each S was then allowed 2 practice trials. When testing began Ss recorded their own score immediately after each trial on the individual score sheet provided. In the dyad and tetrad groups, Ss began each trial after the signal "begin" from E, which was given only when all Ss in the room had recorded their previous score. In the alone condition, after having recorded their score, Ss could begin the next trial immediately.

RESULTS

Figure 1 presents graphically the data for the 3 coaction treatments over the 90 trials. Each point is the mean score averaged over the blocks of 10 trials. . . . Newman-Keuls test on the means of the 3 coaction conditions showed that Ss in the tetrad treatment (2.58) were significantly poorer than either the alone (3.26) or dyad. . . .

DISCUSSION

The significant coaction effect obtained in the present study failed to support the assertion that the potential for evaluation was a necessary condition for producing the social facilitation phenomena (Cottrell et al., 1968; Klinger, 1969). The present findings supported Zajonc's (1965) hypothesis,

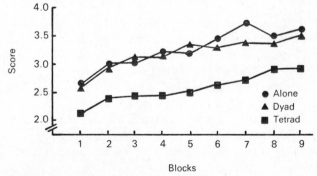

Figure 1 Coaction conditions by blocks

in that the influence of the *mere* presence of coactors was found to be significant.

There was no significant difference between the alone and dyad treatments, but both were significantly superior to tetrads. The results of this study suggested that, when the potential for evaluation was removed, the learned drive elicited by coactors was not sufficiently large to impair learning until the number of coactors was greater than 2. This assertion would explain why Klinger (1969) found no difference between the performance of alone Ss vs. Ss in the mere presence of 1 coactor, although he did find a difference between alone Ss and dyads who could evaluate each other's performance. The potential for evaluation appears to accentuate the group size effect.

The similarity between the performance of alone and dyads appeared to indicate that the mere presence of 1 coactor did not impair learning. It is feasible that confounding was caused by an E audience effect; that is, the mere presence of 1 coactor did impair learning but the presence of E inhibited the performance of alone Ss to a similar extent. Some support for this assertion was provided by Bergum and Lehr (1963) who found that Ss performing alone on a light-monitoring task were influenced by a 1-person audience.

The mere presence of a large enough group of coactors appeared to be a sufficient condition for social facilitation. This study points to possible differences in the social facilitation effects of the audience and coaction paradigms, with the potential for evaluation being perhaps a necessary condition to the former but not the latter, where it appears to merely accentuate group size effect.

A short time after Zajonc proposed his social facilitation hypothesis, Cottrell (1968) altered and extended the concept of increased drive due to the presence of others. Wheras Zajonc had postulated that increased drive was an innate characteristic, Cottrell proposed that the presence of others is a learned source of drive. Rather than being innate, drive is a function of the individual's social experiences. This position takes into account the individual's perception of the evaluative possibilities of the audience. Mere presence of others is not nearly as important as the potential positive and negative feedback derived from an audience. It is through social experiences that one is able to anticipate the effects of others, whether they be seen or unseen, few or many. It is this anticipation that results in the increased drive state. This latter position is reminiscent of the stand taken by Asch (1952) over two decades ago.

Reference to phenomenal facts would have revealed that one can at times feel close to others when physically alone, that one can be lonely or asocial when with others, and that the sheer putting of people in the same space does not have a constant meaning, even if we can describe exactly their number and the duration of their togetherness.

Cottrell's learned drive hypothesis has two important testable implications: (1) Coaction, by itself, is not effective in facilitating or inhibiting performance unless it induces rivalry in the individuals. Whether the presence of others is perceived as negative or positive is more important than the mere fact of co-working. (2) Both audience and coaction effects depend on the amount and kind of the individual's social experiences.

Cottrell's extension of Zajonc's position seems to have better enabled social facilitation "theory" to handle the so-called inconsistent findings without negating the acceptance of previous studies that supported Zajonc's original position. The learned drive concept also fits Schachter's (1959) finding that the presence of others can moderate the highly motivated individual by providing support and reassurance. Cottrell's position brings in an important concept of human behavior—that the social situation must be included in the equation.

Crabbe (1973) pointed out that no social facilitation research had been undertaken in sport psychology to clarify the Zajonc–Cottrell conflict over innate versus learned drive. He used preschoolers and second graders as subjects to investigate the conflicting hypotheses. If social experiences had been inconsequential, the subjects should respond similarly whether in the audience condition or in the alone condition. Crabbe's findings revealed that the rate of learning for the preschool subjects was lower in the presence of an audience (just the experimenter) than in the alone condition. This supported Zajonc's hypothesis. These results, however, were in direct opposition to those for the second-grade subjects. This does not support Zajonc's hypothesis. Taken together, these findings do not support the innate drive premise, that learning should have been better for both groups in the alone condition, but they could be interpreted as reflecting a possible greater social experience for the second grade subjects. Crabbe thus concluded that his findings generally supported the Cottrell hypothesis that motor performance is dependent on the child's social history.

Zander (1968) supports the idea that an audience has the potential to exert a powerful influence on an individual or a group of individuals. With reference to goal-setting and level of aspiration, Zander holds that performers set aspirations according to the expectations of observers. An audience would therefore be able to enhance performance by expecting good performance, or it could inhibit performance by expecting something less.

Kelley and Thibaut (1954) reviewed the effects of both kinds of situations (mere presence of others and coactors) and concluded that working in a social context results in

> (a) Greater quantity of work where physical output is involved, suggesting increased motivation to perform the task. (b) Lesser quantity or quality of work where intellectual processes or concentration are involved, suggesting that social stimuli are able to compete successfully with the task stimuli. (c) Inhibitions of responses and qualitative changes in the work, which suggest that the person somehow "takes account" of the others as he goes about his work, e.g., he has fewer idiosyncratic thoughts, exercises moderation in judgment, and gives more "popular" or common associations. (d) Greater variations through time in his output, indicating the presence of periodic distractions and/or the effects of working under great tension. (e) There is some evidence that these effects wear off as the person adapts to the social situation.

SOME INTERESTING SPECULATIONS

There are at least three additional issues that seem to be of sport interest. These are (1) audience characteristics, (2) performer characteristics, and (3) task complexity. Little evidence is available to do anything more than raise questions and speculate about the answers.

Audience characteristics

At certain times there appears to be a strong feeling of "stressful anticipation" prior to an athletic event. Spectators are buzzing and athletes appear to be nervously awaiting the beginning of the contest. The situation seems to be one of *contagion*—stress begets more stress and anticipation begets more anticipation. One would expect the effect on the athletes of this kind of audience to differ from that of the usual audience. Perhaps the audience is placing a great amount of stress on the athletes to win. What effect is this likely to have?

The sheer *size* of the audience might affect social facilitation. Would a football team that normally performs before 50,000 fans experience increased facilitation or inhibition if they performed before 100,000 fans? Or is there some point of diminishing returns?

Perhaps it is not the size that is important as much as the *social distance* of the audience. This refers to the emotional closeness between performer and audience (or a segment of the audience). One might speculate that the presence of those whom psychologists refer to as "significant others" (parents, girlfriend, boyfriend, peers) is far more important than the number of spectators present. The evaluations of parents and friends are probably more important to the athlete than those of others for two reasons: (1) the interrelationships between the athlete and parents and peers mean more and it is important to be seen in a positive vein, and (2) the evaluations of significant others are less transitory since they reside in the athlete's environment.

Does it matter how physically close (*proximity*) the audience is to the actual performance? In certain sports the audience sits so close to the athletes that a great number of observers could reach out and touch the players. Some arenas are built in such a fashion that the athlete feels the audience is nearly beside him. Would it be reasonable to speculate that an audience in close proximity to the athlete would have a greater potential for facilitation?

Performer characteristics

One of the omnipresent issues in the evaluation of human behavior is individual differences. Would a high anxious athlete be more susceptible to audience effects than a low anxious athlete? It seems likely that the *personality make-up* of the athlete would be somehow related to the audience–performer interaction. As we shall see in Part 4 of this text, however, the problems involved in personality assessment are enormous.

It would seem important to take into account the *skill level* of the performer when assessing audience effects. The athlete's proficiency could well be related to the concept of dominant responses as stated by Zajonc in article 1.1. The more highly skilled the performer, the greater the likelihood of correct responses being dominant. Would there be a straight-line relationship between the skill of the performer and facilitation effects, or would the relationship be curvilinear? Past a certain point in skill-learning—referred to as "well-learned"—would the audience lose some of its facilitating effect?

It is to these two performer characteristics—personality and skill level—that David Kohfeld and William Weitzel address themselves in article 1.3. They assess the importance of the peer group on a physical performance task—treadmill walking. The peer group's power in shaping behavior is well documented in social science research. How does this fact relate to physical performance tasks? The investigators were interested in delineating the personality characteristics of those individuals whose performance improved in the presence of peers. Kohfeld and Weitzel found support for the hypothesis that personality is related to task performance.

The most highly skilled performers received the greatest benefit from the presence of an audience of peers. Kohfeld and Weitzel interpret this fact as fitting Zajonc's and Cottrell's formulations of social facilitation.

1.3

Some relations between personality factors and social facilitation[1]

DAVID L. KOHFELD
Southern Illinois University, Edwardsville

WILLIAM WEITZEL
University of Minnesota, Minneapolis

The effects of audience presence on the treadmill performance of 85 soldiers were investigated. It was found that Ss walked faster in the presence of a peer group audience than when an experimenter was the only observer. Peer group facilitation was greater for Ss who scored relatively low on the Responsibility (Re), Good impression (Gi), Tolerance (To), Achievement via conformance (Ac), and Achievement via independence (Ai) scales of the California Psychological Inventory than for individuals scoring relatively high on these scales. The results also suggested that Ss who were most proficient at treadmill walking received greater benefit from peer group presence than did the less task-proficient individuals.

In a review of social facilitation studies, Zajonc (1965) concluded that the presence of spectators impairs the acquisition of new responses but enhances the performance of previously learned skills. This generalization apparently holds for both audience effects (the case where changes in behavior result from the presence of passive spectators), and coaction effects (behavior changes resulting from the presence of others engaged in the same activity as the subject). In view of several possible means of studying social facilitation (audience vs. co-action conditions; learned vs. unlearned responses), the present investigation was primarily concerned with studies of audience effects in which a well-learned behavior

From *Journal of Experimental Research in Personality* 3(1969):287–292. Reprinted by permission of the author and Academic Press, Inc.

[1]The variable-speed treadmill employed in this study was designed by George S. Harker, who also offered valuable assistance and encouragement to the first author during the course of the work. Data collection and tabulation were done by E. B. McClaskey, who served as *E* in the Experimenter Audience condition.

was utilized as the criterion variable. For example, Travis (1925) reported that subjects performed a pursuit rotor task with greater accuracy when an audience was present than when they worked alone. More recently, Fraser (1953) found that British Navy enlisted men made fewer errors during a vigilance task when the experimenter remained in the testing room. Bergum and Lehr (1963) also studied vigilance performance and reported that National Guard trainees correctly detected more signals when a Lieutenant Colonel or Master Sergeant would occasionally observe their performance. Clearly, these studies indicate that the presence of others can enhance task performance.

A noteworthy aspect of the aforementioned research is that no attempt was made to explain individual differences in susceptibility to audience presence. In Fraser's experiment, a comparison of the mean number of errors indicated superior performance when the experimenter was present, but only 7 out of 18 subjects contributed significantly to the main effect. An inspection of Travis' data reveals that only 10 out of 22 individuals improved their performance by 4% or more when an audience was present, the remaining 12 subjects showing little or no increase. Bergum and Lehr presented only group means to support their conclusions. In order to understand more fully the processes underlying the phenomenon of social facilitation, it would seem that greater emphasis should be placed on the responses of individuals to the presence of others.

The work of Ganzer (1968) appears to be a step in this direction. With serial learning as the criterion, he found that audience presence was more detrimental for high- than for low-anxious individuals, a result which is consistent with Zajonc's (1965, 1966) arousal interpretation of audience effects. Of more immediate concern for the present research is the implication that personality variables may correlate with social facilitation. Accordingly, the present study was designed to investigate the personality attributes of individuals who worked harder in the presence of a peer group audience than when an experimenter was the only observer.

METHOD

Subjects

Five consecutive groups of 13, 14, 20, 20, and 18 soldiers served as Ss. The program of experimentation was such that the groups were assigned to the laboratory sequentially; each group served in succession and there was no chance for social contact among the groups. For purposes of cross-validation, the data from Groups I–III ($N = 47$) were combined in order to make a comparison with data collected from the combined groups IV–V ($N = 38$). All Ss had just completed basic training and were in good physical condition.

Apparatus

A variable-speed treadmill was chosen for the present research for two reasons: (1) treadmill performance requires continuous involvement of the individual with the task, thus providing a dynamic situation where personality factors should be apparent, and (2) previous research has demonstrated that highly reliable measures of performance can be obtained from a treadmill whose velocity is directly responsive to the walker (Evans, 1961; Holmgren and Harker, 1967). The mechanism which regulated the velocity of the treadmill, and the equipment used to display and record S's walking speed were designed to give him as much latitude as possible in regulating his work output. Specifically, the treadmill drive consisted of a constant-speed motor with an electromagnetic clutch; variations in the voltage applied to the clutch resulted in concomitant changes in treadmill speed. S had continuous control over the clutch by means of a potentiometer device which was activated by his either moving forward or dropping back while walking on the treadmill. The potentiometer was calibrated to provide continuous acceleration or deceleration of the treadmill at the rate of 0.17 mph per 1 inch of S movement. Feedback of treadmill speed was provided to S by a meter registering mph, mounted at eye level. The voltage changes produced by a tachometer-generator which was coupled with the treadmill drive were fed into a voltage-to-frequency converter whose output was integrated and registered each minute by an electronic counter calibrated to read in mph.

Procedure

The same procedure was followed for each of the five groups employed in the study. The first three days of treadmill walking were devoted to task familiarization. During this time, Ss were given at least 5 minutes each day to practice accelerating and decelerating the treadmill, and to practice walking at various speeds, as indicated by the display meter. From the outset it was emphasized that at no time during the course of the experiment would running on the treadmill be permitted. E satisfied himself that each S had mastered the treadmill task before proceeding to the testing phase.

The next six working days involved Ss' walking for record. When S was performing in the Peer Group Audience condition, E informed him that he was being tested to see how well he could perform for a period of 10 minutes on the treadmill. That is, S was told that he had to work for 10 minutes, and it was up to him to walk just as fast as he could the whole time. During this time, at least six fellow Ss observed the walker as he performed. In addition, E recorded S's walking speed as the counter flashed it for each minute.

For the Experimenter Audience condition, S was given the same instructions as for the Peer Group condition, but was also informed that this was a practice session for which he would not receive a score. This procedure was followed in order to create the impression that S was completely on his own while performing in the absence of his peers. It was emphasized, however, that S should work as hard as he could during the Experimenter Audience sessions in order to remain in top physical condition. E was a middle-aged civilian technician who wore informal work clothing. During the Experimenter Audience sessions, unknown to S, the output of the electronic counter was fed into a printer which was completely hidden from S's view at all times. This allowed for a permanent record of S's walking speed to be taken while E casually observed the walker. Since preliminary work indicated that the schedule of audience conditions did not produce an order effect, the Peer Group condition was administered on days 1, 3, and 5; the Experimenter condition on days 2, 4, and 6.

RESULTS

Effects of audience presence

Figure 1 depicts mean walking speed as a function of Peer Group Audience vs. Experimenter Audience for Groups I-III. The points on the graph represent the means for minutes 1-10, averaged across Ss and the three sessions for each condition. It can be seen that the work output of the Ss was greater for the Peer Group Audience than the Experimenter Audience condition. Supporting this conclusion were the results of a Groups × Conditions × Sessions × Minutes analysis of variance which indicated the following significant sources of variation: Conditions, $F (1, 36) = 23.59, p < .001$; Groups, $F (2, 36) = 5.98, p < .01$; Sessions, $F (2, 72) = 6.69, p < .01$; Groups X Sessions, $F (4, 72) = 5.25, p < .01$; and Minutes, $F (9,324) = 3.18, p < .01$. The main effects due to Sessions and Minutes indicated that treadmill performance tended to decrease over time, both between and within sessions, respectively. The significant Groups effect resulted from

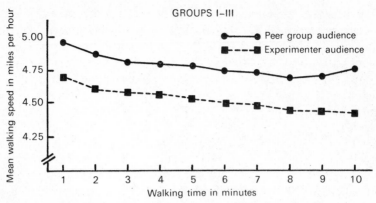

Figure 1 Groups I–III mean walking speed as a function of audience conditions

Group II walking fastest, Group I intermediate, and Group III slowest. The Groups × Sessions interaction was due to a more rapid decrease in mean walking speed over sessions for Group III than for Groups I and II.

Groups I–III correlational analysis

In line with the contention that individual differences are a critical aspect of audience effects, each S's audience scores were examined in relation to those of other Ss. It was apparent that some Ss walked faster than others under both audience conditions, a finding which was possibly due to individual differences in task proficiency rather than differences in Ss' disposition toward the audience conditions. It was also apparent that some individuals showed a relatively large dicrepancy between their Peer Group Audience and Experimenter Audience performances while other Ss displayed a more consistent output under both conditions. It seemed logical that this latter difference was more attributable to the differential effects of the audience conditions than to differences in walking ability. Accordingly, the difference between Ss' mean performance under the two audience conditions was chosen as a criterion measure with which to compare their scores on personality scales. Since a few Ss worked harder in the Experimenter Audience condition, thus yielding a negative difference score, an absolute value of 100 was added to the difference scores in order that all the criterion measures assume a positive value. A test for the reliability of these difference scores, employing the odd–even method for the consecutive minutes in each session (McNemar, 1957), produced an r of .93.

Table 1 Correlations between California psychological inventory scales and the treadmill performance criterion for two independent samples

CPI scale	Groups I–III ($N = 47$)	Groups IV–V ($N = 38$)
Responsibility (Re)	−.51**	−.29*
Good Impression (Gi)	−.41*	−.37*
Tolerance (To)	−.34**	−.45**
Achievement via Conformance (Ac)	−.33*	−.28*
Achievement via Independence (Ai)	−.32*	−.33*
Self-Control (Sc)	−.18	−.47**
Intellectual Efficiency (Ie)	−.33*	−.17
Socialization (So)	−.16	−.41**
Capacity for Status (Cs)	−.42**	−.06
Sense of Well-Being (Wb)	−.07	−.36*
Dominance (Do)	−.28*	.32*
Self-Acceptance (Sa)	−.13	.39**
Sociability (Sy)	−.27*	.23
Femininity (Fe)	−.14	.19
Psychological-Mindedness (Py)	−.23	.05
Flexibility (Fx)	−.11	.12
Social Presence (Sp)	.01	.13
Communality (Cm)	.07	−.12

*$p < .05$.   **$p < .01$.

Upon completion of treadmill testing each group was administered the California Psychological Inventory (CPI). Table 1 presents the *r*s of *S*s' CPI scores with the treadmill criterion. Examination of the Groups I–III correlations revealed a significant relationship ($p \leq .05$) between nine CPI scales and the criterion. The correlations obtained from Groups I–III looked promising; however, it was decided that the results should be replicated before attempting to interpret the correlational findings.

Cross-validation: groups IV–V
The data from Groups IV–V produced curves which were very similar to those depicted in Fig. 1. Again it was clear that *S*s worked harder in the

presence of an audience of peers, $F(1, 34) = 30.27, p < .001$. Other significant effects were due to Minutes, $F(9, 306) = 66.00, p < .001$, and to the Conditions X Sessions interaction, $F(2, 68) = 17.91, p < .001$. In view of the significant Conditions X Sessions interaction, the nonsignificant Sessions effect ($F = 1.20$) indicated that Ss had a tendency to increase their Peer Group Audience walking speeds over sessions while showing a commensurate decrease in Experimenter Audience performance.

The primary purpose of collecting data from Groups IV-V was to cross-validate the correlational data from Groups I-III. The reliability of the difference scores for the present sample was .86. Table 1 shows the correlation coefficients obtained from Groups IV-V. Cross-validation procedures were evaluated by comparing the rs for each CPI scale across the two samples. This was done by converting the rs to zs (McNemar, 1957, pp. 139-140). If the two zs for any scale were significantly different from each other, the hypothesis of equivalent rs across samples was rejected. The CPI scales in Table 1 were arranged into two categories: Responsibility (Re), Good impression (Gi), Tolerance (To), Achievement via independence (Ai), and Achievement via conformance (Ac) in category 1, and the remaining scales in category 2. The requirements for inclusion in category 1 were (1) the correlations for the two samples were not significantly different from each other, and (2) both of the rs for each scale were significantly greater than zero. Correlations in category 2 did not meet both of these requirements. The results of this analysis indicated that Ss who showed the smallest discrepancy between Peer Group and Experimenter Audience performance had a corresponding tendency to score high on five scales of the CPI.

DISCUSSION

The correlations between five CPI scales and the performance criterion supports the contention that personality differences are related to the effects of audience presence. Specifically, the relationship between Achievement via independence and Achievement via conformance (Ai and Ac) and the criterion suggests that individuals who placed relatively high value on achievement were inclined toward equal performance under both the Experimenter and Peer Group conditions. For the Responsibility (Re) and Tolerance (To) scales, it can be said that Ss who worked equally hard under both audience conditions tended to be more conscientious, dependable, enterprising, and tolerant (Gough, 1957). The correlation between Good impression (Gi) and the criterion indicated that Ss who were relatively more interested in the impression they made tended toward equivalent work output, regardless of who was watching them.

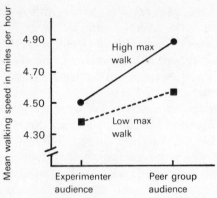

Figure 2 Mean walking speeds for High and Low Max Walk Ss as a function
of audience conditions

In a post-hoc attempt to describe further the type of person who is susceptible to audience presence, it seemed useful to examine the effects of the audience conditions on Ss who were highly proficient at treadmill walking as compared with those who were less proficient. Accordingly, the Ss were divided into two subgroups: (a) High Max Walk (Ss who were intrinsically more proficient at treadmill walking as measured by the maximum speed at which they could walk before breaking into a run), and (b) Low Max Walk (Ss who were least proficient at treadmill walking as measured by the same criterion). Figure 2 presents the mean walking speeds of the two subgroups for both audience conditions. It can be seen that both groups showed a significant increase in performance for the Peer Group condition, $F (1, 38)$ = 66.59, $p < .001$, a finding which supports Zajonc's (1965) notion that the presence of spectators enhances task performance. Of additional interest was the relatively greater increase in walking speed for the High Max Walk Ss than for the Low Max Walk Ss when working in the presence of the peer group as compared with the experimenter only. This result received statistical support from a significant Subgroups × Audience Conditions interaction, $F (1, 38) = 7.61, p < .01$. In terms of work output, it appears that Ss who were more proficient at treadmill walking received relatively greater benefit from the presence of a peer group audience than did the less task-proficient individuals. It is interesting to compare this result with Cottrell, Rittle, and Wack's (1967) recent finding that the presence of spectators had little effect on the performance of individuals who were highly proficient at paired-associates learning. The apparent contradiction in the results of these two experiments can possibly be resolved by noting that the present study examined task *performance*, whereas Cottrell *et al.* investigated the *acquisition* of responses. Accordingly, it is suggested that the presence of spectators may improve the task performance of highly proficient *S*s while having little effect on their acquisition of a task.

The nature of the relationship between audience conditions and work output deserves a word of further comment. Although a post-test questionnaire indicated that *S*s did not consider the scoring procedure to be important, some question remained as to whether the audience effects were confounded with that of *S*s' disposition toward scored (peer group) as opposed to "practice" (experimenter) performance. A recent pilot study (Kohfeld, 1968) in which 16 *S*s were conspicuously scored under both the Peer Group and Experimenter conditions may help to clarify this issue. In one phase of this experiment, the *S*s were instructed to walk as long as they could at 5.7 mph, their score being the amount of time they could endure at that speed. In order to compare the results with those of the present study, the performance measures in both experiments were converted to walking distances (speed × time). In the pilot study, it was found that *S*s walked 5% farther when the peer group was present than when *E* was the only observer. This value was quite comparable to the 6% difference obtained in the present study. Moreover, the pilot data indicated the following correlations between five CPI scales and the criterion: Re ($-.13$), Gi ($-.47$), To ($-.31$), Ac ($-.47$), and Ai ($-.53$). An inspection of Table 1 reveals that the *r*s are similar in direction and magnitude to those obtained in the present study. It seems reasonable to conclude that audience differences, and not scoring procedures, was the variable of paramount importance in both experiments.

In conclusion, the findings of the present experiment suggest that the social status or relevance of the peer group was greater than that of the experimenter alone. Furthermore, susceptibility to peer group status was apparently greater for *S*s who scored relatively low on the five personality scales than for individuals scoring relatively high on the scales. Broadly interpreted, it appears that people who work equally hard for both low and high status observers tend to possess certain positive personality attributes (Re, Gi, To, Ac, and Ai) to a greater degree than individuals who are more sensitive to the social status of their audience.

How big a part do *past experiences* play in mediating audience effects? Can athletes be conditioned to audience effects? Kelley and Thibaut (1954) stated earlier that some adaptation is possible but not much evidence of such conditioning is available.

Task complexity Sport skills span a range from simple to complex, at least superficially. Performance of any skill could again be related to the emission-of-dominant-responses concept. In such a skill as putting a golf ball into the cup from a distance of 20 feet, the dominant response for all persons is an "incorrect" one—that is, the putt is missed more often than it is made. Naturally, different skill levels will produce different effects. However, an audience can be expected to be detrimental to performance of sport skills when the incorrect response is dominant.

Although the research findings relative to social facilitation may seem contradictory at times, the postulates of Zajonc (1965) and Cottrell (1968) have influenced many of the present data.

In some instances the mere presence of others affected behavior, whereas in other situations only the potential to evaluate altered behavior. What seems likely is that the evaluative function of others exists in the eye of the performer. In other words, if the performer believes that others might be able to evaluate performance, then their presence may facilitate or inhibit task performance.

GROUP COHESIVENESS

Many factors comprise the sport success equation but none are quite so pervasive as the concept of cohesiveness. The following statements represent the oft-stated and much-believed relationship between success in sport and team cohesiveness:

In order for a team to be successful, it must be a tightly knit group of individuals and must exude a great amount of mutual attraction. Athletes must like and respect each other; coaches must also be members of this mutual admiration society. Individuals must strive for success, but this striving must be group-directed, for there is no place for the self-serving individual—"there is no I in TEAM." Coaches constantly try to foster the "we" feeling among all team members and to create a "family" atmosphere. Conflict destroys performance and is therefore antithetical to athletic success. Individuals who provoke conflicts and appear to be antagonistic to ideal group interactions must be eliminated if the team is to be successful—that is, winning. Although the reader could probably derive a definition of cohesiveness from the preceding comments, it might be more appropriate to take a look at the social psychologist's definition of the term.

Definition of cohesiveness

The technical term was introduced by Lewin in 1935 and defined by him in 1941. He spoke of forces attracting members to remain in the group and forces that drove members out of the group, and called the attracting forces "group cohesiveness." Most studies use a definition similar to Lewin's. The most commonly accepted phraseology seems to be that attributed to Festinger, Schachter, and Back (1950): cohesiveness is "the total field of forces which act on members to remain in the group." These definitions are still too general to have much meaning, however, since they lack preciseness.

Interpersonal attraction is the one basic tenet upon which cohesiveness is formulated. This point is evident in the definition by Lott (1961): cohesiveness is "that group property which is inferred from the number and strength of mutual positive attitudes among the members of a group." Certainly some degree of interpersonal satisfaction is essential for any group to form (without some mutual attraction there would be no group), but is interpersonal attractiveness synonymous with cohesiveness? Could an individual be attracted to a group for the purpose of achieving some goal that he could not achieve alone, a football championship, for instance? This is rather an asocial form of affiliation—the group members are important only for the purpose of achieving some personal goal. If this seems a reasonable possibility, then it is just as reasonable to assume that some individuals would be attracted to a group for purely social reasons. In this case, people would affiliate to satisfy needs that can be mediated only through interpersonal relations (Davis, 1969).

Consider for a moment the many reasons for becoming a team member. There might be an intense desire to be a winner in order to satisfy parental demands or to gain acceptance by peers. The athlete might be seeking approval, social support, prestige, or just friendship. Sport, by virtue of its lofty position in society, has the potential to satisfy the affiliation-seeking individual, whether the goal is social affiliation or task affiliation.

Several questions still need to be pursued before a proper perspective of cohesiveness can be gained:

What are some of these forces that attract individuals to groups?

How do the attraction forces combine?

Do different sources of attraction have some common effects or is each specific?

Is there a single value of cohesiveness that would incorporate all that is known about the concept?

Cartwright (1968) indicated that cohesiveness has been viewed from two different perspectives—as a dependent variable (cohesiveness as an effect) and as an independent variable (cohesiveness as a cause). To clarify these two points of view, Cartwright presented the following scheme for analyzing group cohesiveness.

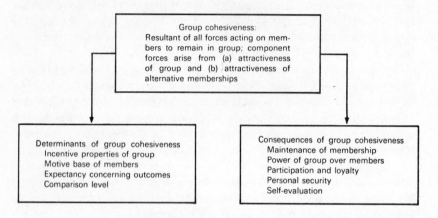

The determinants of group cohesiveness can be viewed as rewards and costs—there are positive and negative facets of attraction. Whether or not an individual becomes and remains a group member depends on the balance between the positive and negative forces. *Incentive properties of group* refers to the group's goals, programs, characteristics of its members, style of operation, and prestige. *Motive base for attraction* consists of the individual's needs that are mediated by the group (affiliation, recognition, approval, security). The *expectancy* that group membership will be either beneficial or detrimental is significant to the group's attractiveness. All potential group members have past experiences with groups and the *comparison level* indicates what outcomes should be derived from group membership.

In relation to the consequences of group cohesiveness, Thibaut and Kelley (1959) describe a very interesting aspect of the group's power over its members. Some groups retain their membership by ''negative cohesiveness.'' Although one might expect groups to disintegrate when the attraction forces are negative, there are some instances in which this does not occur. Individuals remain in such groups when restraints against leaving are too great. The group members comply with the demands of the group, but they themselves do not change their attitudes or values. This sounds like the situation described by the so-called football dropouts—Meggyesy (1971), Oliver (1971), and Shaw (1972). The complaint of these players was that football was dehumanizing them; they realized it but were powerless to do anything about it for a long time because of the hold the sport situation had on them. The restraints against leaving the sport (and for Meggyesy and Oliver a loss of thousands of dollars) were just too great.

Assessment of cohesiveness

Before summarizing some of the research findings, it is necessary to describe the various means of assessing cohesiveness. It should not be difficult to see that this construct has many dimensions (consider the many determinants), and therefore one should expect more than a simplistic method of assessment.

Cartwright (1968) briefly reviews the more commonly used measuring devices.

1. *Interpersonal attraction among members.* Various "friendship indexes" have been developed to assess the degree to which group members like one another.

2. *Evaluation of group as a whole.* Instead of assessing individual interpersonal attraction, this approach focuses on the entire group. Each member is asked to rate his liking for the group; for example, he may be asked, "How much benefit do you derive from the group?" "How attracted are you to the group members?"

3. *Closeness or identification with a group.* Scales of member identification have been constructed to measure the strength of the sense of belonging to a group.

4. *Expressed desire to remain in group.* Direct questions are asked about the strength of each member's desire to remain in the group, such as, "(a) Do you want to remain a member of this group? (b) How often do you think this group should meet? (c) If enough members decide not to stay, so that it seems this group might discontinue, would you like the chance to persuade others to stay?" (Schachter, 1951).

In article 1.4, a study of 144 intramural teams, Rainer Martens and James A. Peterson utilized a multidimensional approach to assess cohesiveness. They categorized their questions into three groupings: (1) evaluation of every other team member, (2) determination of the individual's relationship to the team, and (3) evaluation of the group as a whole. Basically, the questions were asked in those areas deemed significant by Cartwright (1968).

1.4

Group cohesiveness as a determinant of success and member satisfaction in team performance

RAINER MARTENS
University of Illinois, Urbana–Champaign

JAMES A. PETERSON
University of Illinois, Urbana–Champaign

The effectiveness of sport teams in competition is dependent upon many factors, one of which is the ability of individual members to work together. The coach often refers to this ability as teamwork, togetherness, or morale, while the researcher refers to it as group integration or group cohesiveness. Physical educators and coaches alike have long postulated that the most effective team is not necessarily composed from a combination of the best skilled individuals. The ability of individuals to effectively interact with teammates to obtain a group-desired goal has been recognized as contributing to team effectiveness. A commonly held assumption is that the higher the cohesiveness of a team the more effective it will be. The purpose of the present study was to investigate this assumption among intramural basketball teams. The problem was to determine if different levels of group cohesiveness affected the effectiveness and individual member satisfaction of these teams.

Lott and Lott (1965), in their review of the group cohesion literature, cite considerable research directed at the relationship between cohesiveness and performance. The conclusion reached by these reviewers is that the findings have been contradictory—i.e., in some situations a high level of cohesiveness was beneficial, while in other cases this same level of cohesiveness impaired performance. Lott and Lott state that:

It seems likely that in a task situation other variables such as the demands of the situation itself (instructions or job specifications), the standards of performance preferred by liked co-workers, and the degree to which sociability may interfere with the required behavior for a particular job, may be highly significant (p. 298).

The experimental literature concerning the relationship between cohesiveness and team performance for sport groups is also contradictory. Klein

From *International Review of Sport Sociology* 6(1971):49–61. Reprinted by permission.

and Christiansen (1966), Myers (1962), and Chapman and Campbell (1957) using basketball teams, rifle teams, and a novel motor task, respectively, have reported a positive relationship between the cohesiveness of these teams and their effectiveness. An equal number of studies, however, have found that increasing levels of cohesiveness among sport teams produced no increase in effectiveness or actually impaired effectiveness. Lenk (1966) cites several examples of highly effective olympic rowing teams having extremely low levels of cohesiveness. Fiedler (1953b, 1954) and McGrath (1962) have found that a high degree of cohesiveness often interfered with effective performance of basketball teams and rifle teams. To explain this apparent paradox, both McGrath and Fiedler have suggested that players on high cohesive teams may be more concerned with maintaining good interpersonal relations than with effectively playing basketball.

Certainly the need for further study as to the consequences of various levels of cohesiveness on the effectiveness of sport teams is obvious. However, another measure of the consequences that various levels of cohesiveness may have on participation is member satisfaction. It would appear that the degree of satisfaction individuals derive from participating in a sport with a particular group is of equal importance to the number of games won or lost. Therefore, the present study determined if different levels of group cohesiveness are partial determinants of member satisfaction as well as team effectiveness.

METHOD

Subjects and design

In cooperation with the Division of Intramurals at the University of Illinois, Urbana, over 1200 male university undergraduate students divided into 144 basketball teams were used as subjects. These teams participated in league play on the basis of their residential affiliation: fraternity (FRAT), men's residence halls (MRH), and men's independent associations (MIA). The members of each team, therefore, resided together and most had previously participated in intramural basketball together. Consequently, the members of a team were not unfamiliar with each other since a certain degree of social interaction had occurred previously.

A questionnaire instrument, used to assess each team's level of cohesiveness, was administered one day before the first league game of the spring intramural basketball program. Cohesiveness was assessed by a number of different questions. On the basis of these responses teams were categorized into low, moderate, or high cohesive teams. The number of games won was the measure of effectiveness. The degree of satisfaction was obtained from a questionnaire administered at the end of the season. Team effectiveness for the three levels of cohesiveness (using each measure of cohesiveness) was analyzed by a one-way analysis of variance disregarding the teams' residential affiliation. Member satisfaction was analyzed in a 3×3 factorial design. Each measure of cohesiveness trichotomized was the three levels of the first factor and the three residential organizations was the second factor.

Measurement of group cohesiveness

The most common nominal definition of group cohesiveness is Festinger's (1950). He defines cohesiveness as "the resultant of all the forces acting on members to remain in the group." Operationally defining this array of forces acting on members to remain in the group has not been very successful. As a result, the most prevalent approach for measuring group cohesiveness has been to assess the degree of interpersonal attraction between members of a group. Obviously interpersonal attraction does not constitute the only force acting upon members to remain in the group. Therefore, most previous research has operationally defined cohesiveness by measuring only one component of the nominal definition.

This arbitrary operational definition has been criticized by Gross and Martin (1952). They argue against the attempt by researchers to measure only one component of cohesiveness and, then, on the basis of the results obtained, make inference to the total concept. They suggest it is better to assess cohesiveness by a direct question to each member regarding the cohesiveness of the group. Rather than the researcher making an inference about the cohesiveness of a group on the basis of partial information, Gross and Martin advocate each member of the group making such an inference based upon his intimate aquaintance with the group.

In the present project a number of measures of cohesiveness which were suggested by previous research were used. The questionnaire was constructed in the form of a 9-choice alternative between two polarities. For example, to assess interpersonal attraction the following question was asked:

On what type of a friendship basis are you with each member of your team? If you know him very well and are good friends, rate him high on the scale. If you do not know him or are not good friends, rate him low on the scale.

1	2	3	4	5	6	7	8	9

Good friend   Not good friend

The questions asked were of three different types. Four questions assessed each team member's evaluation of every other member regarding: (a) the degree of interpersonal attraction, (b) contribution of each member based on his ability, (c) the contribution of each member based on being enjoyable to play with, and (d) the influence or power of each member. The second type of question asked each member to indicate his relationship to the team. The two questions of this type asked each member's opinion of: (a) how strong a sense of belonging he had toward the group, and (b) the value of membership on the team. The third type of question asked each member's evaluation of the group as a whole regarding (a) the level of teamwork, and (b) how closely knit the group was.

Procedure

Questionnaires were administered by four assistants supervised by the experimenter. Each team was contacted through the Division of Intramurals and asked to participate in the study. A time was arranged for each group to answer the questionnaire together. Once together the assistant had the names of every team member written and numbered on a poster visible to the entire group. Each member evaluated every other member according to the number assigned. Those individuals who could not attend the group meeting (a very small number) completed the questionnaire alone immediately before the first game.

All records of games won and lost were tabulated by the Division of Intramurals. The post-questionnaire was administered approximately two days after the last game of the season. All teams completed the season, even though a small number of individuals quit teams during the season.

The questionnaire data were transferred from IBM digital answer sheets to IBM computer cards. A mean for each question for each team was computed. The teams were then ranked for each measure of cohesiveness for each residential group and divided into the three categories: low, moderate, and high cohesiveness. This categorization of the eight cohesiveness questions then served as the three levels of the independent variable.

RESULTS

Team effectiveness

The one-way analyses of variance for the eight measures of cohesiveness are summarized in Table 1.

The first four questions assessed each member's rating of every other member in the group. None of the questions regarding interpersonal attrac-

Table 1 Summary of the analyses of team effectiveness variance for the eight measures of cohesiveness

Item	Df	Ms	F
Interpersonal attraction	2	0.65	0.28
Residual	141	2.29	
Contribution based on ability	2	0.44	0.19
Residual	141	2.30	
Contribution based on enjoyment	2	0.58	0.25
Residual	141	2.30	
Power of influence	2	3.01	1.33
Residual	141	2.27	
Sense of belonging	2	2.31	1.02
Residual	141	2.28	
Value of membership	2	16.86	8.15**
Residual	141	2.07	
Teamwork	2	7.26	3.29*
Residual	141	2.21	
Closely knit	2	6.33	2.86*
Residual	141	2.22	

*Significant at the .05 level.
**Significant at the .01 level.

tion, contribution based on ability or satisfaction or power significantly differentiated between successful and unsuccessful teams. The sense-of-belonging question also failed to show any differences between winning and losing teams.

The two questions designed to directly assess cohesiveness as a general construct—degree of teamwork and closeness—significantly differentiated between successful and unsuccessful teams. Figure 1 graphically illustrates the differences between the three levels of teamwork and closeness on the number of games won. For both cohesion criteria, a Newman-Keuls test (Winer, 1962) was used to determine the simple effects of the overall F. For the teamwork criterion, accepting the .05 level of significance, the high (2.89) and moderate (2.66) cohesive teams won significantly more games than the low cohesive teams (2.13). The difference between the high and moderate teams, however, was not significant. For the closeness criterion, the Newman-Keuls test revealed that high cohesive teams won significantly

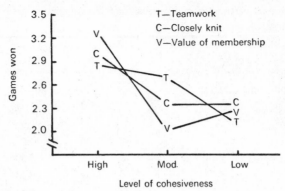

Figure 1 Number of games won for three different levels of cohesiveness based on three criteria

more games (2.96) than the moderate (2.46) and low cohesive teams (2.26). The difference between the moderate and low cohesive teams was not significant.

The most significant *F* value was obtained from the question regarding the "value of membership" each individual attributed to his basketball team. Those teams whose individual members attributed greater value in belonging to the group won significantly more games (3.26) than those with moderate (2.18) or low scores (2.27). The difference between the moderate and low teams was not significant for this criterion.

Individual member satisfaction

The post-questionnaire asked each individual to indicate how satisfied he was personally with playing on his team. A team mean was calculated which was the score used for the analysis of member satisfaction variance.

The eight analyses of variance on individual member satisfaction for each of the cohesiveness criteria are summarized in Table 2. Accepting the .05 level of significance, seven of the eight measures found significant differences on individual member satisfaction. The only item failing to show a significant difference was interpersonal attraction.

The Newman-Keuls procedure for a factorial design (Winer, 1962, p. 309) was used to determine the simple effects of the over-all significant *F*. For the contribution-based-on-ability criterion the Newman-Keuls test indicated that the teams rating themselves high on ability were significantly more satisfied (4.11)[1] than moderately-rated teams (4.58) and low-rated

[1]The lower the score the greater the satisfaction.

49

Table 2 Summary of analyses of member satisfaction for the eight measures of cohesiveness

Item	Df	Ms	F
Interpersonal attraction (A)	2	0.40	0.46
Residential affiliation (B)	2	0.35	0.40
A × B	4	1.36	1.56
Residual	135	0.87	
Contribution based on ability (A)	2	5.09	6.54**
Residential affiliation (B)	2	0.40	0.52
A × B	4	1.81	2.33
Residual	135	0.78	
Contribution based on satisfaction (A)	2	3.02	3.57*
Residential affiliation (B)	2	0.40	0.47
A × B	4	0.80	0.94
Residual	135	0.85	
Influence or power (A)	2	3.30	3.99*
Residential affiliation (B)	2	0.41	0.50
A × B	4	1.00	1.21
Residual	135	0.83	
Sense of belonging (A)	2	6.36	8.12**
Residential affiliation (B)	2	0.34	0.43
A × B	4	1.48	1.89
Residual	135	0.78	
Value of membership (A)	2	3.54	4.21*
Residential affiliation (B)	2	0.38	0.44
A × B	4	0.82	0.98
Residual	135	0.84	
Teamwork (A)	2	2.92	3.46*
Residential affiliation (B)	2	0.45	0.53
A × B	4	0.65	0.77
Residual	135	0.84	
Closely knit (A)	2	11.07	4.33*
Residential affiliation	2	6.57	2.57
A × B	4	1.93	0.76
Residual	135	2.56	

*Significant at the .05 level.   **Significant at the .01 level.

(4.78). The difference between the moderate and low-rated teams was not significantly different at the .05 level. The exact same pattern of significant differences was found for the contribution-based-on-satisfaction criterion. The mean for the high-rated group was 4.21, while the moderated group had a mean of 4.52, and the low-rated group had a mean of 4.74.

The Newman-Keuls test on the significant influence of power criterion revealed that the teams high on this measure were significantly more satisfied (4.24) than the low teams (4.79) while the moderate teams were also significantly more satisfied (4.43) than the low teams. The difference between the high and moderate teams was not significant.

For the sense-of-belonging criterion the high, moderate, and low teams each differed significantly from the other two groups. Unlike the other criteria, the high teams were most satisfied (4.10), but the low teams were next (4.51), while the moderate teams were least satisfied (4.88).

The teamwork criterion was the only measure in which the high cohesive teams were not the most satisfied. The Newman-Keuls test on this criterion indicated that the moderate teams were significantly more satisfied (4.26) than the low teams (4.77) and the high teams were significantly more satisfied (4.44) than the low teams. The difference between the moderate and high teams was not significant.

The closeness criterion found the very close teams to be significantly more satisfied (3.81) than the teams low in this criterion (4.83). The Newman-Keuls test on this criterion found no significant difference between the very close teams and the moderately close teams (4.30) and between the moderately close teams and the teams low in this criterion.

The value-of-membership criterion revealed that the teams who valued their membership the most were significantly more satisfied (4.16) than the moderate- (4.65) and low-rated teams (4.67) on this criterion. The difference between the low and moderate teams was not significant.

DISCUSSION

The results from the team effectiveness data are equivocal and focus upon the methodological problem of operatively defining cohesiveness. The general operational definitions were used: (a) each member rated every other member of the team on some component of cohesiveness—e.g., interpersonal attraction; (b) each member indicated his relationship to the team—e.g., value of membership; and (c) each member directly rated the cohesiveness of the group as a whole—e.g., level of teamwork. Our hypothesis that high cohesive teams win significantly more games than low cohesive teams was supported when assessing cohesiveness by the third approach and one question from the second approach. Results of the other measures of cohesiveness found no significant differences in games won between high and low cohesive teams.

The four components of cohesiveness assessed by the first approach were interpersonal attraction, contribution based on ability, contribution based on satisfaction, and influence or power. The questions concerning the contribution based on ability and satisfaction were used as additional indications of interpersonal attraction. The degree to which members of the team attributed power or influence to the group was the fourth component of cohesiveness. The nexus being that the more cohesive the team the greater its influence on the members. The failure of these measures to find any systematic variance between high, moderate and low cohesive teams as far as team effectiveness is concerned does not concur with previous research.

For example, Fiedler (1953b, 1954), Lenk (1966), McGrath (1962), and Veit (1968) have all suggested from their research that high levels of cohesiveness may be detrimental to effective performance. On the other hand, Chapman and Campbell (1957), Klein and Christiansen (1966), and Myers (1962) have found a positive relationship between cohesiveness and effectiveness. The sole operational definition of cohesiveness in each of these studies has been some form of interpersonal attraction. Our interpersonal attraction results (and the measurement of any component of cohesiveness) present a third finding, mainly that differences in interpersonal attraction among teams do not significantly affect team effectiveness.

Another portion of our results appeared ambiguous. The sense-of-belonging and value-of-membership questions were designed to measure each individual member's relationship to the team, and consequently, were expected to reveal similar results. This was not the case, however. The sense-of-belonging question did not differentiate between successful and unsuccessful teams, whereas the value-of-membership question found a very significant difference. Why the apparent discrepancy between two questions thought to assess the same phenomenon? One possible explanation is that sense of belonging seems to focus upon the individual's relationship with other members in the group and the status he has in the group. If this be the case, his status, which is really an indication of this relationship with the other members, may be a general evaluation of his interpersonal attraction toward the group. Possibly then the nonsignificant finding from the sense-of-belonging question is consistent with the interpersonal attraction results. The value-of-membership question, on the other hand, implies not only the importance of affiliating with the other members of the team, but with the goals and outcomes of the team. If the activities of the team are of intrinsic enjoyment to an individual even though he does not particulary feel a strong sense of commitment to that group, he may indeed value his membership while not having a strong sense of belonging.

The somewhat consistent pattern obtained from the different operational definitions lead us to the following conclusion. At the present time our knowledge of the operational measurement of cohesiveness is not sufficient to measure only certain components of cohesiveness and have it significantly discriminate between effective and ineffective teams. These data suggest that individual members are better able to integrate the components of cohesiveness to determine the level of cohesiveness present within a team.

In reviewing the previous relevant research we find no apparent explanation for the contradictory results; nor do we know why the previous research has consistently found differences between high and low cohesive teams when using interpersonal attraction as the criterion and the present study failed to find any difference. However, the significant results obtained in this study suggest that Gross and Martin's argument for a direct assessment of cohesiveness has merit.

Results of the analyses of individual member satisfaction showed that seven of the eight cohesion criteria significantly discriminated between satisfied and unsatisfied teams. These results suggest a circular relationship between satisfaction, cohesiveness, and success.

Those teams who are more cohesive are more successful, and teams which are successful have greater satisfaction from participation than unsuccessful teams. Greater satisfaction, in turn, leads to higher levels of cohesiveness, thus maintaining a circular relationship. In actuality, though, this cause–effect triangulation is bombarded with a number of other important factors that may influence this sequence of events.

In conclusion, we have found that when cohesiveness is directly assessed, it is an important determinant of team effectiveness. However, it is not contended that cohesiveness is the primary factor in successful basketball performance. The ability of the players and their opponents, the quality of coaching, the officials, and many other factors contribute to the effectiveness of a team. Our finding, however, does suggest that higher levels of cohesiveness are associated with greater success and satisfaction.

There is reason to believe that perhaps the best method of assessing each individual's attraction to a group is to ask the direct question: "How attractive is this group to you." The respondent places the group on a linear scale somewhere between "very great attractiveness" and "no attractiveness." It is interesting to note that Martens and Peterson (1971) found that cohesiveness, when thus directly assessed, was an important determinant of team effectiveness. Other measures of assessing cohesiveness revealed no such results.

Another assessment tool is the sociogram. This is another sociometric device to determine how much each group member likes the others. The sociogram provides a graphic representation of the lines of attraction among group members. It illustrates "stars," "isolates," "dyads," and "cliques." Niwa (1968) used the sociogram technique with 280 athletes from 20 sport clubs. He assessed cohesiveness on personal, mutual, and group levels, feeling that all three were important.

Almost all the research literature supports the assertion that cohesiveness is not a unitary trait. Gross and Martin (1952) state that studies using only one measure of cohesiveness are empirically deficient. Each of the various measures discussed in this section taps some elements appropriately identified as group cohesiveness, but intercorrelations between these elements are typically low:

> A standard all-purpose procedure for measuring group cohesiveness does not yet exist. This state of affairs, though disconcerting, is not really unexpected, for the development of measuring instruments cannot proceed much in advance of a basic understanding of the nature of the phenomena to be measured. Theory and measurement must advance together. Toward this end, we next [must] examine more closely the nature of the determinants of attraction to a group (Cartwright, 1968).

Determinants and consequences of group cohesiveness

Earlier, we discussed the relation to group attractiveness of four interacting sets of variables (incentive, motive, expectancy, and comparison level). We shall now examine several interesting variables that have been studied and that are relevant to the study of sport although not all the data are sport-derived.

Leadership Participatory (democratic) groups are generally but not always more attractive. One might suspect that for most sport groups a successful (winning) team dominated by autocratic leadership would be more attractive than an unsuccessful (losing) team that observes democratic practices. A study by Penman, Hastad, and Cords (1974) reveals that the more successful football and basketball coaches (from a sample of 30 head football coaches and 34 head basketball coaches from AA high schools in Minnesota and Washington) were more authoritarian. Perhaps, for many athletes, winning is prized more than affiliation and the autocracy of the sport scene is not perceived in a stifling or negative manner. In a sport such as football with its complex interactions among positions, perhaps a strong-willed autocratic coach or quarterback is a plus in the struggle for victory. The huddle is no place for the practice of participatory democracy.

In a report of a research study, Cammalleri (1973) asserts: "The pushy leader may be most destructive when good vibes and pulling together of members are crucial for the group's success." In a positive light, however, the study reported the greatest accuracy on a problem-solving question for groups with dictatorial leaders. What price success? When the group leaders were bossy, much aggression and hostility were evident and led to harsh interpersonal clashes. If such findings can be replicated in sport situations, then we can again ask whether winning is worth the cost and whether it should always take precedence over the friendly interaction of team members.

Success and failure   Research has made it clear that members of successful groups tend to like each other more than members of unsuccessful groups (Lott and Lott, 1965). However, little of this research was derived from sport groups, and it is with sport groups that inconsistency among findings is plentiful. Positive relationships between success and cohesiveness were reported by Klein and Christiansen (1969), Martens and Peterson (1971), and Landers and Crum (1971). Yet contrary findings were reported by Fiedler (1954), McGrath (1962), and Myers (1962). One study—Lenk (1969)—has even reported highly successful team performances in spite of open internal conflict. The reader ought to recall the problems of assessing cohesiveness and consider the possibility of some methodological problems, especially in view of the operational definition of the concept.

If goals are set too high and repeated task failure ensues, group attractiveness will probably be adversely affected. The key to understanding the effects of failure on group cohesiveness is to understand whether failure is due to lack of ability or to some external threat. Although, as stated previously, success generally engenders cohesiveness and failure generally breeds disintegration, it is also true that ". . . under certain conditions intermember liking follows shared failure, especially, we suggest, where the failure is perceived as arbitrarily imposed by an external source" (Lott and Lott, 1965). The official's decisions are often seen as unfair and prejudicial to those who lose a contest. If the athletes feel they were "done in" by an arbitrary judgment, then it is reasonable to expect that such a failure would not produce any reduction in team cohesiveness. In fact, if a consensus existed that a bad decision by an official had cost the game and this was supported by newspaper reports and television replays, then *increased* cohesiveness could mobilize the team against this common threat.

Two models of success causality require additional research for their extension and ultimate acceptability. The first is the *model of circular causation.* Teams that are more successful are more cohesive; therefore members are generally more satisfied with the group. The more they are satisfied, the more they pull together and the more they are successful. Martens and Peterson (1971) cautioned the reader that many factors impinge on the success–satisfaction–cohesiveness relationship. One should not be lulled into predicting success only from cohesiveness, or predicting cohesiveness only from success. The sport literature contains equivocal findings about this circular model.

Cratty (1973) describes the *moderation model.* This suggests that the most cohesive teams are those that experience a moderate amount of winning or losing. Team records such as 7–4 and 4–7 would be examples of these conditions. Such teams are supposedly undergoing a moderate amount of stress to keep winning and to avoid losing. This moderate stress level tends to produce greater team cohesiveness. Winning all the time is not challenging and losing all the time poses a threat to positive self-enhancement (Martens and White, 1975).

Performance and productivity   Findings relevant to the relationship between interpersonal attraction and task performance are contradictory. It appears that one must look past this apparent relationship to understand the determinants of task performance. Lott and Lott (1965) stated that "it seems likely that in a task situation other variables such as the demands of the situation itself (instructions or job specifications), the standards of performance preferred by liked co-workers, and the degree to which sociability may interfere with the required behavior for a particular job, may be highly significant."

Several studies report results compatible with the expected outcomes —that is, better task performance by compatible group members. However, there appears to be a reasonable explanation for the failure of some cohesive groups to produce high performance levels. It has been mentioned earlier that cohesive groups exert power over group members to conform to existing goal-oriented behavior. Both Berkowitz (1954) and Schachter et al. (1951) have shown that lowered production and poorer performance can be induced in highly cohesive groups. The question to ask here is whether the group is task-motivated (wants to get the job done) or affiliation-motivated (intermember attraction and friendships are all-important). Stogdill (1959) has suggested that group efforts spent on affiliation might be conceived as a reduction in the efforts to produce a high level of performance. In such a situation a negative relationship may exist between cohesiveness and performance.

Smith's (1968) study dealing with basketball players reveals results consistent with the above discussion. Task-cohesive groups had the highest productivity, but there appeared to be a negative relationship between social cohesiveness and group productivity. Supporting data can also be found in Fiedler's (1954) study with basketball teams and McGrath's (1962) research with rifle teams.

Cooperation and competition   As a result of the many studies of conflicts between boys at several camp settings, Sherif and Sherif (1953) concluded that competitive intergroup relations solidify group cohesiveness. Intragroup cooperation fosters intergroup competition, and at the same time promotes cohesiveness within the group. Myers's (1962) research with sport teams revealed similar results. In competitive teams the members pulled together and rated one another higher than in noncompetitive teams (teams that "competed" only against a set of standards).

From his research findings, Deutsch (1968) reported the following outcomes of cooperative endeavors: coordination of efforts, diverse contributions by group members, pressure to achieve, friendliness, favorable evaluations of the group and its efforts, and the feeling of having had favorable effects on fellow members. Cooperative organization of the group did not lead to greater interest, involvement, or learning.

It is possible, even probable, that groups can be cooperative and competitive at the same time. Consider a basketball team whose members cooperate toward the common goal of defeating opponents. Intragroup competition is invovled to the extent that two or three of the athletes are competing for the lead in scoring. Winning is important to the high scorers and they will cooperate to a degree, but they are not willing to be subservient to team goals. Lott and Lott (1965) reported that people will be more attracted to one another if they work for common rather than mutually exclusive goals. From his work in diverse industrial settings, Zander (1974) reinforces this idea:

> Organizational structures that emphasize and reward individual achievement tend to splinter rather than unify groups. Similarly, when a group exists mainly to determine how many dollars each member will take home in his pay envelope, as in group incentive plans, group pride may not develop at all.

The implications for sport groups seem obvious: interpersonal communication, friendliness, coordination of efforts, and group pride (the "we" feeling) appear to be disrupted if athletes see themselves competing for mutually exclusive goals. Some of these goals might be scoring leader, rebounding leader, and the "player of the game" award. If competition becomes the focus of every team practice with the result that there is always a winner and a loser, then we might question how much cohesiveness is being developed.

Group structure   How efforts are pooled in the group is of concern here. Groups can be classified as *coacting* (individual group members perform a part of the total task independently from the other members) and as *interacting* (individual group members are dependent upon one another for their performance). Cratty (1973) arranged athletic teams on a continuum from coacting only (bowling, golf, rifle) through coacting—interacting (swimming, football, track) to interacting only (basketball, soccer, ice hockey).

Interacting teams are dependent on each member's contribution but the team performance is not always the sum of individual performances. Sometimes the team performance is greater, sometimes less, than the sum of individual performances. Certainly a degree of coordination is necessary for optimum group performance. Teamwork (called means-interdependence by psychologists) is the common term for this coordination or interaction among team members. Nevertheless, there is much opportunity and necessity for role specialization within interacting teams, in terms of both skill performance (passer, catcher, tackler, blocker) and interpersonal relations (leader–follower). Cratty (1973) indicated that uniform high needs for achievement may not be all that desirable for interacting athletic teams if success is important. Some distinction, however, ought to be made between team achievement and individual achievement. Zander's (1974) work relative to this point was discussed earlier. Excessively high levels of intrateam competition may be detrimental to the cohesiveness of interacting teams. Performance depends on a coordinated team effort in which every player shares in the total performance; the more unequal the sharing, the less cohesive the team is likely to be.

Michael Klein and Gerd Christiansen, in article 1.5, investigate the relationship between several group variables and basketball team performance. They tested several hypotheses in a sequential fashion, using achievement motivation, group structure, and team interactions as the concepts that generated the postulates. They concluded that the interpersonal attraction between team members affected on-the-floor performance and was instrumental in determining whether or not a team was successful.

1.5 Group composition, group structure and group effectiveness of basketball teams*

MICHAEL KLEIN

GERD CHRISTIANSEN

The basketball coach has the following task: from twelve players belonging to one team, five are to be selected and permitted to be on the court at any one time. These groups of five are supposed to represent an optimal combination with regard to their goal, the victory. As a criterion for the decision as to which players shall be placed into a team combination, the coach usually acknowledges the effectiveness of the indi-

From *Sport Culture and Society: A Reader on the Sociology of Sport.* Edited by J. W. Loy and G. S. Kenyon. New York: Macmillan, 1969. Reprinted by permission of Macmillan Publishing Co., Inc. Copyright © 1969 by Macmillan Publishing Co., Inc.

*Translated by Dr. D. Elisabeth Kenyon from Michael Klein and Gerd Christiansen, "Gruppenkomposition, Gruppenstrultur und Effektivität von Basketball," in *Kleingruppenforschung und Gruppe im Sport, Kölner Zeitschrift für Soziologie und Sozialpsychologie,* 10 (1966), 180–191. This investigation was carried out with the friendly financial support of the German Sport Association.

vidual player's performance, which is determined according to certain indicators. This would, in part, suggest that those five players who hit the basket most often will be combined into a team of five persons. However, certain research results of sociology and social psychology indicate that the individual performance strongly varies according either to the situation or to the group structure in which it shall be actualized (see Homans, 1950; Rohrer and Sherif, 1951; Sherif and Sherif, 1953; Whyte, 1943).

It seems not of primary importance that the combination of a successful team consist of players who achieved a high level of individual performance effectiveness. Rather, it is important to investigate under what conditions the individual characteristics are effectively used to achieve the group goal. Such conditions result first from the group composition, i.e., the internal variation of individual characteristics, and second, out of structural peculiarities of the group.

For investigating the influence of group composition we used achievement motivation of the players as a criterion. That is, in order to actualize the effectiveness, a certain amount of achievement motivation within the team members must be present. We understand the term achievement motivation as a personality variable that expresses the relatively constant need to personally succeed in every game situation independent of the group task. Thus we assume that success of a group is dependent upon a group characteristic that is defined as the average achievement motivation of a particular group.

The average value of our criterion, "achievement motivation" still says nothing about the group as a unit, i.e., the variation of the characteristic within the group. It must be investigated now whether achievement of the group goal is more likely in groups which are homogeneous or heterogeneous with regard to achievement motivation.

M. E. Shaw (1960), R. L. Hoffmann (1959), and with N. F. Maier (1961) have found that there is a connection between heterogeneity of certain personality characteristics and efficiency in solving group problems. The results of these investigations lead one to believe that, although a certain level of average achievement motivation must be present, it is not necessary for all members to have equally high levels of achievement motivation.

Within groups which have a homogeneous achievement motivation it is not only important that such groups are composed in certain ways regarding their personal characteristics, it is also important that communication and consensus are present with regard to certain strategies to achieve this goal. The premise for communication and consensus of strategies is a high amount of cohesion within the group (see Berkowitz, 1954; Lott and Lott,

1961). Cohesion is said to be present when as high as possible a percentage perceives that the group is attractive. Thus "cohesion" would indicate that there are no severe conflicts within the group or contrary opinions about the strategy to achieve goals. This tells nothing about groups which have conflicts in other respects (see Lenk, 1965; 1966). It is certain only that a positive correlation between cohesion (as an indicator for consensus regarding strategies that achieve the goal of the group) and success of the group exists.

A further structural characteristic of groups which is important for the achievement of a commonly agreed upon group goal, consists of the consensus in the group regarding the distribution of roles, especially status consensus with respect to the member of the group who contributes the most to the achievement of the goal, namely that of the leader ("focused leadership"). The work of C. Heinicke and R. F. Bales (1953) supports our assumption that a great amount of "focused leadership" is related to group performance. Where consensus exists in the group concerning the distribution of roles, and especially status consensus concerning the leader, the variable "focused leadership" becomes a measure of the facilitation of the group task, as the team members can concentrate upon achieving the group goal.

Up to this point we have related group characteristics to success, which, with regard to the group goal, required conflictlessness and consensus within this group. On the other hand, it is possible that conflictlessness within the group can relate negatively to success. So, for instance, it is possible that the sociometric structure of friendship relationships conflicts with the optimal communication structure necessary for group success. Although characteristics such as cohesion and status consensus have no direct influence on the course of the ball during the game itself, it is believed of the inter-individual effects of the players have an immediate influence upon the course of the ball in the game and thus an indirect influence upon the success of the team. Within the game there must exist communication nets which distribute the information (here: balls) relevant for a quick and direct achievement of the goal; thus the efficiency of the team becomes possible. The assumption must be examined whether a communication structure for the performance of the group—set-up accordingly to the inter-individual affect relationships—is not optimal.

A communication net is assumed as the theoretical course of the ball which is provided for the group through structural conditions of the game itself (see also Schafer, 1966). In order to exclude these structural conditions of the game, this communication net is established as Basis One. The

alterations of the communication course which occurred under the influence of the sociometric influence of the group are normed (standardized)
on Element One. Now it must be determined whether the communication
net which was established in Element One is the optimum for the group to
achieve the goal and whether by this affect structure of the friendship relationships has a negative effect upon the success of the group.

METHOD

Within two top performing basketball teams each consisting of eight persons, a questionnaire for data concerning personality variables such as
aspiration and group variables, such as sociometric structure, cohesion, and
"focused leadership," was administered in February 1965, and in February
1966.

Within the first stage of the investigation, pass patterns, score totals,
pass failures, and aggressive acts were recorded by the protocol leader for
both teams during a total of 1200 game minutes in championship games of
the present season or during specially arranged practice or friendship games.

To eliminate the structural conditions of the game (for instance, the fact
that the ball distributor or the "post" receives the ball relatively more
often—see Schafer) or instructions of the coach (perhaps the invitations
to play more often with a certain person), the recorded data were standardized on Element One; i.e., the observed data were divided by the Basis One
expected data.

Within the second stage of investigation which studied seven persons
of one of the teams in March 1966, the situation was altered. This particular
team was chosen because it was very homogeneous with regard to characteristics such as age and individual achievement and ability. First, there
were only two consecutive age groups present within the team; second,
the individual ability of the team members with regard to technical skills,
shooting accuracy, speed, and physical condition was designated as absolutely equal.

Out of the seven persons in each case three played against three. This
procedure can be justified: (a) In such a basketball game there are always
only three persons interacting with each other. Every game move can be
broken up into all possible combinations of interaction among three persons;
(b) game structural conditions are eliminated; (c) the collection of data is
simpler and clearer; and (d) this kind of game was already known to the
team members through selection courses and regular practice sessions. Of
seven persons each was brought together with each other into triads, with
each combination playing against each combination. With seven persons

this yields 35 combinations and 70 games, of which in fact only 51 could be accommodated; thus the optimal figure of four games for each combination could not be attained. The teams played 41 three-minute games and 10 five-minute games. The games were normed on five minutes.

Before each game every player filled out a short questionnaire to acquire data on the "attractiveness" of the particular combination, "task-related leadership," "prediction of game result," and anticipated conduct of the partners.

The score differences of the games of each combination were totaled. Teams with a positive score difference were called successful teams; those with a negative score difference, unsuccessful teams.

Achievement performance

To measure this variable an aspiration index was used as proposed by L. Worrell (1959). The index compares the self-assessment of ability at present with the expected ability in the future. The greater the discrepancy between the two self-assessments of a person, the more likely the assumption is justified that the self-assessment of the future ability is unrealistic. In persons with an exaggerated aspiration level—based upon the Atkinson theory of aspiration level (1)—the tendency to avoid failure is greater than the tendency to achieve success. Thus, herewith a behavioral disposition to achieve little is assessed. A high score on the aspiration scale of Worrell means a low achievement motivation, and a low score, a high achievement motivation. We would like to propose that this aspiration index be used as an indirect method of measuring achievement motivation.

Homogeneity

For each group the difference between the highest and the lowest scores of achievement motivation was found. Thus the range of achievement motivation of the members of the group was used as an indicator of homogeneity. A high score means little homogeneity, and vice versa, a low score, high homogeneity.

Focused leadership

It was found by questioning who in the team contributes the most to achieve the goal. The modal value of those most motivated to succeed despite the competition can use their potential ability best. Therefore, we are dealing with persons with a high achievement motivation. Now groups with a common goal, composed of members who show this characteristic to a high degree, should have positive influence upon success.

63

Hypothesis: *The greater the average achievement motivation in a basketball team, the more it will be successful in play.*

Table 1 shows that, of the successful teams, the majority have high average achievement motivation, and vice versa, the unsuccessful teams show low average achievement motivation. Therefore, the results point in the expected direction.

Table 1 Average team achievement and motivation and team performance

Team performance	Average achievement motivation	
	High	Low
High	13	6
Low	5	11
Total	18	17

The relationship found answers only the question whether the members of basketball teams must have a certain task-specific personality characteristic for group success. But, disregarded here is the fact that in groups with a common goal, different contributions regarding the kind and extent of the activities are expected of the members in order to achieve the group goal. These different "role expectations" possibly demand a different degree of the task-specific personality characteristic. If, in basketball teams, all players have an equally high achievement motivation this might lead to difficulties in a quick and all-accepted role assignment during the game. Thus, the following hypothesis seems to be justified:

Hypothesis: *With regard to achievement motivation, heterogeneous basketball teams are more successful than homogeneous teams.*

Table 2 seems to confirm the relation proposed in the hypothesis.

Table 2 Composition of the teams according to achievement motivation and team performance

Team performance	Homogeneous teams	Heterogeneous teams
High	3	16
Low	13	3
Total	16	19

On grounds that groups with high homogeneous achievement motivation show unimpressive group performances, the hypothesis must be modified with respect to the connection between average achievement motivation and team effectiveness. The most effective are probably such teams that do show a high degree of average achievement motivation as a group characteristic but in which the degree of achievement motivation of the individual players varies.

It must be expected now that within those groups with heterogeneity with respect to the task-specific personality characteristic, fewer conflicts concerning the role assignment prevail than in homogeneous groups. From Table 3 it can be gathered that a connection between group composition and consensus concerning role distribution in the group does exist. The consensus about the role distribution in the group is measured here by status consensus concerning the person who contributes most to achievement of the goal.

Table 3 Composition of the teams according to achievement motivation and status consensus

Status consensus	Homogeneous teams	Heterogeneous teams
High	2	14
Low	15	14
Total	17	18

It can be assumed that status consensus about the role distribution facilitates interactions within the group and thus is a prerequisite to the success of the group.

Hypothesis: *Teams with high status-consensus play more successfully than teams with low status-consensus.*

Status consensus concerning role distribution does not only contribute to a better performance of the group, but also leads to greater cohesion of the group as the study of Heinicke and Bales (1953) has shown. This is probably the result of the ease of interactions within the group and the decrease of status conflict (Festinger, Schachter, and Back, 1950). It can be assumed that under the stated conditions the group is more attractive for the members. Attractiveness of the group is most often used in the literature as a criterion for cohesion.

Table 4 Status consensus and team performance

Team Performance	Status Consensus	
	High	Low
High	14	5
Low	2	14
Total	16	19

In groups with a common goal and clear role differentiation with regard to this goal, cohesion facilitates effectiveness of the group, since argument concerning strategies to achieve the goal can be achieved easier in cohesive groups.

Hypothesis: *A positive relationship exists between the cohesion of a team and its effectiveness.*

Table 5 Cohesion and team performance

Team performance	Cohesion	
	High	Low
High	13	6
Low	7	9
Total	20	15

Summarizing it can be established: the distribution of personality variables in task-oriented groups apparently is not a sufficient prerequisite for achievement of groups. In groups where interactions of the members are the means of achieving a mutual goal, the structure of the group decides whether the individual performances lead to group success or not.

So far no assertions have been made about the sequence of interactions during a game. During the game the course of the ball is the institutionalized form of the course of interaction. In order to be able to give statements about the direct course of the game it is assumed that a team will be more successful the quicker or the more direct the success is sought. It is presumed that for each attack there is an optimal ball course for success. These optimal game moves can be done only if each player has the chance to be given the ball when standing in a favorable position. This assumption is expressed in an hypothesis:

Hypothesis: *Teams are most successful when each player gets an equal number of passes.*

To test this hypothesis, first of all four variables, yet equally strong team combinations, of one team against different opponents, but equal times against equally strong opponents (team strength measured by league membership and position therein), were evaluated according to distribution of passes and success (score differences) for each sixty game-minutes. A value of 1.0 for the distribution of passes would herein mean an equal distribution.

Table 6 Distribution of passes and success

	Passes	Success
Combination 1	0.87	+ 18
Combination 2	0.72	+ 8
Combination 3	0.64	+ 5
Combination 4	0.47	− 12

Thus it can be determined that different combinations of the same team distribute balls differently wherein that combination which comes closest to the value 1.0 plays the most successfully and that combination which is farthest away from 1.0 plays the most unsuccessfully. In view of this finding, we suggest that different communication stages can be explained by different affect structures within the team combinations, which are operationalized through the sociometric selections. To test the assumption the following hypothesis was formed:

Hypothesis: *Interactions during the game situation (herein defined as passes) appear more often among team members who have elected themselves mutually in a sociometric inventory than among team members who have not elected themselves or have rejected themselves.*

To test this hypothesis three-way combinations were formed during training such that a sociometric couple and an unchosen player were always combined. Passes were then recorded when they originated from one member of the pair. From 1100 observed passes 748 (68 per cent) went to the sociometrically chosen player, and 352 (32 per cent) went to the unchosen player.

Thus it is justified to retain the hypothesis in that form. Yet, is we do not wish to be satisfied with the mere establishment of what was asserted in the hypothesis, we must investigate a few conditions under which alterations appear.

Hypothesis: *Sociometrically rejected team members are given the ball more often than sociometrically isolated ones.*

To test the hypothesis 380 passes in five-member teams were counted in which each two sociometric pairs and one isolate were present. Everyone had the chance to get 76 passes. Eighteen passes or 23.7 per cent of those statistically possible by chance went to the isolates. As a comparison 350 passes in five-member teams which in each case contained two sociometric pairs and one rejected by both pairs, were recorded. Everyone had the chance to get 70 passes. Thirty-four passes or 48.6 per cent of those statistically possible by chance went to the respective rejected players.

Finally, let us investigate whether there are game conditions in which the same team combinations, i.e., a group with a constant affect structure uses different communication paths. We assume that communication paths alter with the difficulty of the given task and thus with the increased performance demand.

Hypothesis: *The stronger the opponent, the less distribution of passes is determined by sociometric choices.*

As a test of the above hypothesis, passes were evaluated in different games; in fact, 400 passes for each category of Table 7. Those data acquired in the training situation are assigned the value of 1 as the expected values.

Table 7 Difficulty of the opponent and distribution of passes

	Training	TS weak	MS opponent	TS strong	MS opponent	TS far superior opponent	extremely important MS
1.0	1.0						
0.9		0.91	0.89				
0.8				0.79	0.78		
0.7						0.70	
0.6							0.68

TS: Training game.   MS: Championship game.

Those passes given to the sociometrically chosen one are those for games against different opponents divided by the expected values. The closer the point value lies to 1.0 the more passes that are given to the sociometrically chosen ones as appeared in training.

Thus, deviations from sociometric preferences do not seem to depend upon the formal importance of the game—also in the training game the goal remains as the victory—but rather upon the strength of the opponent. An exception is the extremely important championship game, which, however, is played only against strong opponents. Victories over strong teams increase the attractiveness of the group certainly more than victories over weak opponents. Summarizing, one can say:

1. "Round about" relationships depending upon the sociometric structure interfere with quick and direct communication flow and thus success.
2. Sociometrically rejected group members who also are chosen by others are more likely to be included in the communication flow than sociometric isolates.
3. High achievement stress on the group weakens those communication paths which are subjectively conditioned in contrast with those objectively conditioned ones.

SUMMARY

In the present study relations were investigated between group variables and the performance of basketball teams in the form of applied social research. The research was based upon published results from small group research. It was possible to determine a positive relationship between achievement and average achievement motivation, heterogeneity of achievement motivation, status consensus, and cohesion of the group. The sociometric structure of the team has an immediate influence upon the communication pathways during the game situation and consequently an indirect influence upon success.

It can be assumed that for each basketball team an optimal five-member combination can be determined. But in addition there is a need for study of the relevant variables with more variable and differentiated groups.

Coacting teams are characterized by individual performances that, when summed, add up to a team performance. Many of their characteristics are opposite to those of interacting teams. Coordination of effort and role specialization are much less evident here. Nor does any member of a coacting team have to modify his high need for achievement, desire to excel, and competitive nature in order to be a valuable team member.

There is much support in the literature for the hypothesis that interacting groups facilitate cohesiveness and performance. Klein and Christiansen (1969), as well as Martens and Peterson (1971), report findings that substantiate this relationship. Although Fiedler's (1954) study appears to be in opposition to this finding, Landers and Lüschen

(1974) questioned the use of assumed similarity measures as the index of cohesiveness. From the earlier discussion of the assessment of cohesiveness, the multidimensionality of the construct is evident and there is more to cohesiveness than assumed similarity of group members.

No such support exists for the hypothesis that coacting groups facilitate cohesiveness and performance.

The research dealing with sport groups by McGrath (1962), Myers (1962), and finally by Hans Lenk, in article 1.6, reveals no evidence of cohesiveness as a factor in performance. Lenk even found that open hostility among crew members did not seem to hamper performance. At first glance this seems to contradict the preceding argument but Lenk provides a rationale for such a position. If teams continue to exist despite conflicts, then there is no reason to automatically expect a lower level of performance. Several examples of high-level crews make this point very clear.

1.6 Top performance despite internal conflict: an antithesis to a functionalistic proposition*

HANS LENK
Karlsruhe-Bergwald, West Germany

As the subtitle suggests, the purpose of this paper is to refute the strict general validity of a thesis that seems to have been taken for granted in micro-sociology and which is also held to be valid in various forms by other sociologists, namely, the proposition: Only small groups, which are low in conflict, or highly integrated can produce especially high performances. It is asserted that a cohesive group is more productive (Hare, 1962). "With generally increasing performances there would be a corresponding increase in orientation to one's partner or fellow group members."

From *Sport, Culture and Society: A Reader on the Sociology of Sport.* Edited by J. W. Loy and G. S. Kenyon, New York: Macmillan, 1969. Reprinted by permission of Macmillan Publishing Co., Inc. Copyright © 1969 by Macmillan Publishing Co., Inc.

*Translated by Dr. D. Elisabeth Kenyon from Hans Lenk, "Maximale Leistung trotz innerer Konflikte," in *Kleingruppenforschung und Gruppe im Sport, Kölner Zeitschrift für Soziologie und Sozialpsychologie,* 10 (1966), 168–172.

"For group achievement, internal competition" would be "inhibitory." "The stronger the intra-group relationships" and group integration, "the greater would be the performance and vice versa" (Lüschen, 1964). "An organization"—hence also the cooperative characteristic arrangement of a small group—would be "the more successful, the more the informal structure echoes the formal" (Konig, 1961), therefore, the stronger the officially planned cohesiveness manifests itself in the informal structure of relationship.

The antithesis to be advanced here may be surprising, and thus shall be brought out for discussion. The argument is as follows: even violent internal social conflicts in high performing teams of a certain kind need not noticeably weaken their performance capacity, if the team continues to exist despite the conflicts. Indeed, as the conflict develops and becomes more pronounced, even an improved performance can result.

A discussion of the antithesis seems to be especially important. However, in a previous publication with a different title, the precise sociometric data and the matrix and vector analyses have appeared; thus the technical details can be dispensed with here (Lenk, 1962; 1965).

An unconditional axiom which is characterized by "only" or "all," "every," "always," "imperative," like the thesis to be refuted here, can be denied through the presentation of only one contrary instance. Its negation, a logically equivalent proposition, can already be proved through one single example. The referred to antithesis can be derived easily. If there would be a team that performs at its best despite the deepest of internal conflicts, or whose performance, despite the development of conflict, improves as far as possible, then the antithesis would be proven and, therefore, the original thesis would be clearly refuted, as they are incompatible with each other. The initial sociometrically and participant observed team, the German Olympic Rowing Eight of 1960, showed sharp subgroup conflicts and leadership conflicts which were even commented upon in the press. This was a racing team consisting of athletes from two clubs, four from each.

However, this team came together originally purely out of comradeship, without the cooperation of any official club representative. At that time all the rowers considered the team as a compatible extra unit, between the two clubs. Conflicts did not occur. During the two years in which the team existed, the managing committees of the clubs x and y increasingly introduced club-centered motives into the team. The members of the combined team subsequently split into club cliques, through which conflicts emerged more distinctly. The vast majority of the questionnaire answers traced the division into the two contrary cliques back to the club-centered influence and almost unanimously now considered the joint team a mere service one. Several times conflict almost led to the destruction of the team. By means of sport, within this eight, no performance detriment as a result of the tensions within the group was noticeable. But there should have occurred a performance decrement in comparison with the initial situation (the compatibility and conflictlessness among members from different clubs), as the training regimen and the technical control of the work-outs remained on the same level. At best there could have been only a small performance increase. Actually, the performance did increase and paralleled the sharpness of the conflict during the two years in which the eight existed. Performance was systematically measured using their very frequent training sessions over eight by 560 meters in racing tempo. The team became unbeaten Olympic champions. A sport team, therefore, is able to achieve, in spite of strong internal conflicts, the highest of performances. The conflicts did not noticeably cause any performance decrease.

The second example team, the world champion eight of 1962, was not a combined racing team, but rather a club team. However, there developed within it a complete clique of four rowers in which each man was chosen by each other, thus setting themselves apart from the other rowers. The latter, however, chose members of the clique also. Performance envy or position jealousy did not determine their choice. They did not form an anti-clique.

As the emotional unity of a partial group of a social system always creates strong social tensions, indeed, even rejections and animosities from those which are excluded, it can positively be concluded here: the extremely strong formation of the clique could not have occurred as a result of personality evaluations and sympathies. As a matter of fact, the clique consisted of, according to the judgment of the trainer and others, precisely the strongest rowers of the eight. The image of performance capacity of the single rower as judged by the others formed the priority criterion in the top rated team.

A significant curiosity is revealed by the sociogram of the captain's election: a completely symmetrical structure with regard to the two most mentioned rowers. Both were chosen by two others and chose themselves; due to the equally strong leadership polarity the team had a latent leadership conflict. Disagreements—concerning technical questions—would arise if the team's independent decisions would differ from the suggestions of the leading rowers. Like the first one, this second eight also was not able to develop independently and to guide itself. Here, too, only an external authority (such as the coach) could lead the team and keep it together as a unit.

Because of the distinctive leadership dualism and the extremely strong tendency of the clique to separate from the others, one had to predict in 1962 (Lenk, 1963), that the team would split into two opposing groups. The aversions would have to be intensified emotionally especially among the leadership polarities, and the team would be exposed to strong leadership fights.

The eight was interviewed a year later (1963) still consisting of the same members. For the non-members of the clique, now disengaged noticeably from it, based upon both the sociometric data and their behavior—twice as emphatic as in 1962—especially in terms of roommate selection, the aversion was five times as great. The non-members of the clique now developed greater unity, the antipathy among themselves had now disappeared in comparison to 1962. They were only one vote short of forming a complete clique.

For instructional-theoretical-mathematical reasons the emotional rejection no doubt stood out at this point as especially clear. The diagram of the rejections forms a subunit-subgroup. Actually in comparison to 1962, two cliques faced each other emotionally now, as it had been predicted on grounds of the sociometric structure and the leadership duality (Lenk, 1963). These leadership fights, which now had erupted vehemently, resulted in a considerably more distinct rejection of the two leading persons than in 1962. The team had lost confidence in the 1962 leaders after the conflicts had openly erupted. As the leadership sociogram shows, the team had no internal leadership any longer. It was hierarchically disorganized and was only held together by the outside authority of the coach. Nevertheless, the eight won the European championship during the year of the interview—once more against the strongest opponents of the World Championships of the preceding year. The eight had even become somewhat better in performance measured in terms of training times. The level of performance thus had not suffered from status conflicts and tension between the leadership dualities. As the amount of training and the technical control of the boat had remained the same and only an insignificant increase in muscular strength due to winter training had been achieved, the level performance could, at best, improve insignificantly. This occurred despite the conflicts.

During the following year (1964) a qualifying competition in the single sculls was held for membership in the eight-man crew, resulting in an inner contest being openly generated. Based upon these qualifying tests, two rowers were replaced by two others. The competition in no way inhibited performance; indeed the individual performance of five of the remaining rowers (as measured by their singles time) increased, because they trained even harder before the qualifying test. During that year the team proved to be slightly stronger than the year previous and won the Olympic Silver Medal. Thus internal competition within rowing teams by no means necessarily has an inhibiting effect upon performance as in part the initial thesis suggests.

In comparison to other teams studied, the two teams discussed above, i.e., the eights with the strongest tensions threatening the unity of team, showed retrospectively in four years (that is 1960, 1962, 1963, and 1964) the highest performances in the world.

This, and the fact that the development of conflict went parallel with an optimal improvement of performance, which was the highest attainable, show that the antithesis is correct: even vehement social internal conflicts within top performing rowing teams need not noticeably weaken the strength of the performance at all, when the team continues to exist in spite of conflict (everyone of the ambitious members was personally interested in the continuation of the team and the strength of its performance). With the development or intensification of an internal conflict even an increase in performance can occur.

The thesis, namely, that only low conflict groups can achieve high levels of performance, is not generally valid. Its strict general validity proves to be a prejudice (Fiedler, 1958).

These findings support the premises of the coacting group structure. Coacting group members perform in relative independence of others and can successfully meet their goals without affiliating with others to any great degree.

Group size   Group member satisfaction and cohesiveness should decline as the group size increases, for several reasons. Larger groups have communication problems by virtue of their sheer size, and often the quality of the communication suffers from depersonalization. Group members become highly specialized (for example, a person who just punts the ball and another who only kicks field goals) and similarity among members decreases. The larger the membership of the group, the greater the heterogeneity, with the resultant problem of coordinating dissimilar people. Group members will probably gravitate to those who are attractive, and cliques may form. The likelihood of organized counterforces is then increased and cohesiveness declines further.

Larger groups could, on the other hand, be more satisfying to individual group members, since they provide a greater chance of encountering attractive companions (Davis, 1969). The result might well be that increased group satisfaction would spur increased performance.

Few research studies have used only the size of the group as the independent variable in looking at cohesiveness, and this is wise. Size is not so important in itself; the interaction of size with other group properties (communication, similarity, goals) is what is significant. If the larger group is more attractive, then cohesiveness is enhanced. However, if the increased size hinders member satisfaction, group cohesiveness is reduced.

Group constancy   It is commonly believed by coaches that there is some benefit to be gained by fielding a constant line-up. This would seem especially true with interacting sports because one individual's movement is coordinated with, or in response to, the movement of others. Ice hockey teams, for example, seldom vary the pairing of defensemen and forward lines, unless some "shake-up" is deemed necessary to alter the atmosphere of the game.

Essing (1970) investigated the impact constancy or variability that the team line-up had on the success or failure of 18 soccer teams. The following correlation coefficients were reported: Between team line-up and team efficiency: .62; between average constant participation of players and team success: .47; and between the non-use of newly acquired players and success: .58. Essing concluded that there was an important interdependence between team line-up and team performance, and that constancy seemed to be an important determinant for the success of a soccer team. The reader should be cautioned that correlation does not necessarily connote causality. Nevertheless, one could conservatively state that there was a definite functional relationship between constancy of the team line-up and team success. It would be a mistake to conclude that team line-up was the only reason for success; much of the common variance remains unaccounted for.

The logic behind increased cohesiveness as a function of a constant team line-up is that interaction among certain group members is greater when they have been together longer. Increased interaction results in increased attraction, and cohesiveness is a function of interpersonal attraction.

Summary

Cohesiveness is a complex construct, and it is not likely that anyone could ever adequately define the many and varied forces acting on any group. Although the attractiveness can be assessed, the reasons for the attraction are likely to remain unknown (Gross and Martin, 1952). Whether these forces are additive or are integrated in some multiplicative way is still a mystery. The concept does seem too multidimensional, however, to fit an additive model. Cohesiveness is now seen to consist of interpersonal attraction of members, attractiveness of the group as a whole, the sense of belonging to the group, and the desire to remain in the group. All of these are important, since no single index of cohesiveness is adequate to represent the total construct.

Motivation

&

sport

2

Motivation
&
sport

2 Motivation and sport performance are collateral terms. No discussion of sport is complete without some reference to an athlete's motivational disposition, and at least some of the following questions will probably be asked, either directly or indirectly: Why does an individual participate in sport?

Do some individuals have needs that must be satisfied and expressed in sport participation?

Why do some athletes choose to participate exclusively in individual, competitive, and high risk sports?

Why does an Evel Knievel risk injury and even death in the pursuit of sport?

Why does an athlete willingly give up so much that the average person finds desirable, and accept the potentially damaging aspects of sport instead?

Why does an athlete subject himself to the stringent discipline so often required by sport participation?

Why will a team athlete practice self-denial or self-sacrifice for the sake of others?

Although sport provides opportunities to achieve success, why does an athlete risk failure?

Why are athletes willing to expose their inadequacies?

Why do some athletes perform so intensely, while others appear to be more relaxed?

What drives an athlete to be "Number One"? What forces differentiate between winners and losers? In article 2.1, this author examines the cultural and psychological underpinnings of the "Number One" feeling and sees its role in sport as an expression of the American culture as a whole.

2.1

"We're Number One"

A. CRAIG FISHER
Ithaca College, New York

Why are sport participants, both active and passive, so fond of claiming Number One status?

HISTORICAL PERSPECTIVE

The "Number One" concept seems to be a trademark of Western civilization with probably the most pronounced cases found in the United States. This does not mean to say that other cultures or countries feel that they are less than Number One in certain respects, but such claims are heard less often.

Individualism and the striving for supremacy were strong in America as early as the Pilgrim landing at Plymouth Rock. Amidst the rigors of the new continent, the only way to maintain life was to rise above oneself and execute tasks never dreamed of—braving the bitter cold winters, living on less than adequate food, watching one's family and friends starve and die, and the like.

It was inevitable from the early beginnings of American society that the work ethic was going to play an important part. For a long time there was a widespread belief (now dispelled) that any man *could* rise to the Presidency as a result of hard work and dedication. Abraham Lincoln, from the backwoods of Illinois, reinforced that belief.

Since the United States is a capitalistic country, one expects certain individuals to reach the top in their chosen field. In the early 1900s, certain men rose through the ranks of companies to the upper levels of management. Almost everyone has heard the tale of the mythical man who delivered papers as a boy and after learning the business from the ground up became the general manager of the newspaper.

From *The Physical Educator* 28(1971):183–186. Reprinted by permission.

THE GREAT SOCIETY

The heart of the preceding is that the idea of reaching the pinnacle of success and being Number One has been, in part, culturally derived. Americans worship at the altar of greatness. Consider one catchword of the 1960s—the Great Society. Implicit in this catchword is the assumption that bigger is better and that to be better is essential. What incidences of this attitude do we see in our society today? In the business world some instances in advertising come to mind. Avis states that they are not Number One in automobile rentals, therefore they pledge to try harder in order to achieve the supreme rating. Allied declares itself America's Number One mover. The Seven-Up Company compares its product to the best selling soft drink and indicates what inroads it is making toward replacing their chief competitor on the best-seller list.

The business world certainly carries no monopoly on the idea of being Number One. As an individual in school, one strives for As. Those who achieve this ideal are recognized on the honor roll. In the late 1950s and early 1960s, the key word in education was curriculum reform. The Russians launched Sputnik and a panic set in that the Communist power was further advanced scientifically than the United States. Educators and would-be educators (and who has not got at least one suggestion to improve education) placed much of the blame on education and pushed for curriculum reform, especially in science and mathematics.

In the space program, NASA officials strive for firsts in space achievements. Often it has seemed as if the scheduling of moon shots and the like, were dependent upon the estimated plans of the Russians.

SPORT IS NOT IMMUNE

A great many Americans are involved in sport, in one way or another. It would only be reasonable and logical to assume that the attitude of supremacy would infiltrate the sport subculture. In athletics there is a constant striving to dethrone the champion, to shatter the long-standing record, and to achieve gold medal or blue ribbon ranking, not just in the Olympic Games, professional sports, collegiate sports and scholastic sports, but at all levels of participation.

Vince Lombardi epitomized the zeal for success in sports. He took on heroic qualities because he openly expressed what so many Americans felt—the idea that one must strive for the top rung in whatever he does. What better way to reiterate this point than with the quotation that supported his philosophy: "Winning is not everything, it is the only thing." There was a certain charismatic quality to Lombardi possibly because he was the vehement advocate of the American tradition—the search for ultimate and unyielding success. As Friedenberg (1959) so aptly and expertly stated—in the American ethos victory is not to be trifled with. In all things give the champion preeminence!

TEMPORAL PLACEMENT

In addition to attributing the Number One concept to America, I believe that it could be temporally placed as being born in the late 1950s and early 1960s. All newborns, whether they be people, attitudes, or ideas, undergo a period of growth from conception to birth. Therefore, I do not believe that the phrase "We're Number One" arose overnight, even though its *apparent* rise to common usage has been meteoric. There must have been some precipitating factors in the American culture that promulgated its presence at this time in history. The previously discussed cultural perspective with the supremacy overtones is not a complete or satisfactory enough explanation for the emergence of the phrase.

ADOLESCENT SUBCULTURE

A major factor that accounts for the coast-to-coast shouts "We're Number One" is the fact that America is a youth-oriented society. In the United States there are some 24 million people in the 13-to-19 age range, the largest 7-year segment of the population. These individuals are a product of the post-World War II baby boom. Such a large number of people must be an influence on the society in which they live, especially when the only way they can gain esteem is through the way they dress and behave. For example, the fashions and fads that originally were the property of the adolescent age group have now permeated much of the American society. In the early 1960s, long-haired males and mini-skirted females were in fashion mainly among the youth of this country. One does not have to be very perceptive to see how this has spread from the adolescent to the adult world.

In the adolescent stage of development, Erikson states that the key task is the seeking of identity. Often in their search for identity, one of the characteristics manifest by youth is their narcissism. In this developmental stage, one is often "coerced" into feeling that he as an individual is truly Number One. Friedenberg claims that

> it takes a kind of shabby arrogance to survive in our time, and a fairly romantic nature to want to. These are scarce resources, but more abundant among adolescents than elsewhere, at least to begin with.

The narcissistic and egoistical attitudes and behavior are essential in their quest for identity. Hess and Goldblatt (1960) speak of the

> protective bravado and air of competency which the adolescent assumes to protect himself, both from arousing parental anxieties and from his own feelings of inadequacy.

Erikson (1968) also speaks of a new set of identification processes that have significant purposes and ideological forces. Adolescents search for something or someone to be true to by pursuing a variety of activities that are more or less sanctioned by society. There is some community solidarity among similar-aged youth since they are probably adopting very similar agents of identification. Erikson says that the adolescent's pursuits are

> often hidden in a bewildering combination of shifting devotion and sudden perversity, sometimes more devotedly perverse, sometimes more perversely devoted.

Sport is definitely one of these pursuits that the youth culture attacks with an intense devotion. For the most part, involvement in organized sport is part of the adolescent subculture. Arnold Beisser (1967), a psychiatrist, maintains that those who play the games well enough are privileged to drink from the fountain of youth and to continue playing for a longer period of time. Since sport, with all its pomp and ceremony, is definitely one of the most esteemed elements of the American culture, there is a great desire for people to ally themselves with sport. A Canadian psychiatrist, Daniel Cappon, speaks of this new search for eternal youth and well-being, calling it the cult of youth. The factor limiting active participation in the sport subculture is not chronological age, as many would think, but rather biological age.

GEORGE BLANDA SYNDROME

Many times in sport the youthful performer (chronologically) is expected to produce the significant events and often such is the case. Consider what happens when an older performer is the one who is responsible for the heroics. George Blanda, the oldest player in the National Football League, was directly responsible for winning several games in the 1970 season. Many of his performances took on heroic qualities since they were enacted in the face of possible defeat. What did it mean to the middle-aged spectator that the outstanding feats were performed by the oldest man in the league? There was an identification with Blanda, since in essence he was indicating by his performance that he belonged to the youth culture. This, in turn, made those who identified with him feel more youthful and enabled them to walk a little taller. Blanda was proving that a person 43 years of age could still gain success in youthful endeavors which is important in the American culture.

Part and parcel of youthful games are youthful ideas—one of which is the desire for Number One status. At this point, the reader may well be saying that many generations have had a similar historical and cultural perspective, but how does that account for the prevalence *today* of the "We're Number One" claims? The mere fact that there are greater numbers of adolescents in our society today and that they comprise a large segment of our population is not a satisfactory explanation.

LIBERALISM EMERGES

During the late 1950s and early 1960s, liberalism in our society altered its gait from a walk to a sprint and feelings, once hidden, were and are now openly expressed. Two of the well-worn phrases of recent years are: "Tell it like it is" and "Let it all hang out." The adolescent's narcissistic feelings (whether intentionally fostered or socially determined) and his drive for ego identity no longer need to be shrouded by the cloak of false modesty. Athletes and their adoring followers are flaunting their index fingers for all to see. It is as if they are saying "We're the best and we're going to make damm sure everybody knows it."

ACCENTUATED DEPENDENCE

In the United States, the period of adolescence is more marked and conspicuous than ever before. The generation of youth finds it more difficult to achieve independence for several reasons. Adolescents of the 1960s have been reared in a milieu that emphasized the importance of a college education. Therefore, instead of the adolescent becoming independent at the age of 18 or so, his dependence upon his parents lasts for several more years.

Stone and Church (1968) address themselves to the economic plight of the adolescent. There are several complications that stand in the way of youth earning their own money and therefore gaining some measure of self-sufficiency. An employer must pay a higher insurance premium for employees under 25 years of age. As a result of automation, the unskilled laborer is not needed as much as in the past. To become skilled, one needs experience but the child labor laws exclude the young adolescent from gaining this experience. With today's unionized labor and reduced working week, there is not a great opportunity for the adolescent to involve himself in a part-time job. Many of the part-time jobs that are available are not appealing to today's adolescent. All of these points together are significant in preventing the adolescent from gaining some measure of economic independence.

UNCERTAIN ADULT ROLES

Another complicating factor is the uncertainty of adult roles in society today. The adolescent has grown up with the preachings of parents who extolled the values of an education, but in our society today it is evident that hundreds of Ph.D's cannot find a job. Many male adolescents have had to be concerned about their draft status since it played such an important part in their future. With these conditions impinging upon youth, one should easily be able to see Erikson's point that many adolescents are extremely concerned with faddish attempts at establishing an adolescent subculture. One of the rallying cries emitted from the nomadic youth is "We're Number One." One would not find this to be a universal trend among adolescents because many other cultures do not retard an individual's independence to such an extent as here in the United States. In addition, there is perhaps not such a discontinuity inflicted upon youth of some other nations.

SPORT GOES BIG BUSINESS

Sport took on a different dimension in the late 1950s and early 1960s—a dimension that was to accentuate the Number One concept. This was a period in professional sport characterized by the "bonus babies." Outstanding athletes were paid astronomical sums of money to sign professional contracts. These large sums of money were made available because of the increased revenues from television. As *Sports Illustrated* (Johnson, 1969) states:

> In the past ten years sport in America has come to be the stepchild of television and . . . in the very time of its ascendancy—in the affluent and chaotic decade of the 60's that launched it toward a new Golden Age— sport finds its greatest benefactor is electronic technology.

What impact do *you* imagine this increased TV coverage and high salaries for athletes had on the youth subculture that placed a good deal of emphasis on organized sport prior to this "Gilded Age?"

CONCLUSIONS

In essence, the point I have tried to make is that the Number One feeling has both cultural and psychological causes. The statement "We're Number One" arose from the adolescent subculture of which sport is an integral

85

part. Society sanctioned the overt responses of sport participants when they claimed superiority over their opponents. It would be folly indeed to state that the exclamations of superiority were conceived wholly by sport. Instead it would be more logical to surmise that *through* sport the expression arose to its phenomenal heights and from these beginnings permeated the American culture.

Certainly television, which as Beisser stated "appears to have usurped from the pulpit the job of setting ideals and standards," has played no small part in making people aware of the Number One strivings. Newspapers and magazines accentuated the Number One idea by their prognostications and polls. Viewers and readers of mass media are led to believe that the only position worth attaining is the top one. But in reality these media only reveal the feelings that are already present in the American culture.

The "Number One" idea locates sport motivation in a broader context. We shall now try to move closer to answers to our earlier questions by trying to clarify the meaning of motivation and describing its operation in the lives of athletes.

THE NATURE OF MOTIVATION

Motivation contains or comprises physiological processes, social determinants of behavior, psychological needs, motives, and incentives, and emotional influences. The complexity of the term should be evident from its various aspects. The human organism exhibits preferences within its environment by accepting some objects and situations and rejecting others. The acceptance–rejection process in which decisions are made and acted upon acts continuously to sort out well-defined behavioral objectives. It also comprises three aspects of behavior called the *activating, directing,* and *sustaining* aspects.

The *activating,* or dynamic characteristic of motivation is described by words such as arousal, activation, stress, and tension. Although this definition was once considered to comprise the entire concept of motivation, it is incomplete in terms of present-day knowledge.

The *directing* and *sustaining* functions of motivation are characterized by *drives, needs, incentives,* and *motives.* A *drive* causes an individual to behave in a manner that satisfies an organic need (Woodworth and Schlosberg, 1954). Satisfying the need reduces the drive to behave in that particular manner. *Needs* are organic states of deficiency or excess (Woodworth and Schlosberg, 1954). *Incentives* become associated with all behaviors through learning experiences. They affect the meaning of a certain behavior for an individual and the strength of the action he chooses in order to pursue a goal. Some incentives are positive and some are negative. For most people, winning in sport is a positive incentive to participate; losing is a negative incentive that might prevent an individual from competing. Many concomitants of sport participation constitute positive or negative incentives. *Motives* determine an individual's tendency to pursue a certain course of behavior. These tendencies are relatively stable characteristics of an individual. Motives interact with the other parts of the motivation mechanism to elicit a certain behavior. Readiness to aggress or to seek power are examples of motives. Drives initiate action to satisfy needs, but incentives and motives determine the specific behavior that results.

Activation and perception

Situations contain no inherent activating potential. The degree to which a situation is able to arouse stress in an individual depends upon his *perception* of that situation, on his past experiences, and on his ability to use adaptive (stress-reducing) measures. Faulty perception may prevent a potentially activating situation from having its expected effect.

Berkun et al. (1962) report on a combat training program in which live ammunition was used to simulate actual combat conditions on the theory that the increased stress placed on the soldiers would promote a better adaptation to real combat situations. The researchers were surprised to find that the training situations elicited low levels of stress in the trainees. Because they thought that the Army would not permit such a dangerous exercise, the trainees did not believe that the bullets whizzing around were real and that the situation was precarious. Their low stress levels were therefore due to faulty perception of the situation.

An anecdote reported by Tuckman (1972) relates another case of faulty perception of a situation. Two experimenters were studying the effects of near-drowning on human subjects. One of their subjects was fastened to the side of an empty swimming pool, which was then allowed to fill. The researchers, who had left the pool area, forgot that an experiment was in progress. They remembered in time to return hurriedly to the swimming pool just before their subject would have drowned. They were frightened to the point of shock by the experience, and they quickly untied the subject and pulled him out of the water. When the experimenters asked, "Weren't you frightened?" the subject calmly replied, "Oh no, it was only an experiment." The researchers had a perception of the situation different from the subject's perception, which furthermore turned out to be opposite to the researchers' expectations.

Both the Berkun and Tuckman studies illustrate that the degree of stress caused by a situation depends upon how an individual perceives that situation.

Cognition also plays a part in the degree of stress an individual experiences in a given situation. (Cognition is learning, whereas perception is more a matter of moment-by-moment organization and interpretation of sensory inputs.) Schachter (1964) introduced a cognitive element to what had previously been a physiological concept. He suggested that cognitive factors may be the major determinants of emotional states. Cognitions arising from the immediate situation, as interpreted by past experience, would therefore provide a framework from which to label the emotions. The interpretation of a situation as stress-inducing could then be responsible for altering the individual's internal physiological systems. Cognition determines whether stress will be conceived of as pleasant or unpleasant, and it explains why similar situations can have different outcomes and activating potential.

Activation and emotion

Sport and emotion are contiguous terms—one cannot exist without the other. Whether sport is pursued from a participant's or from a spectator's point of view, it is filled with a multiplicity of emotional ups and downs. Nearly everyone has experienced the exhilaration of the last-second victory or the winning championship game, as well as the depth of despair that often accompanies defeat.

Although there is a strong postperformance relationship between sport and emotion, it is well known that feelings are heightened even before a contest begins. Perhaps the reader can recall incidents when his or her precompetitive behavior was characterized by one or more of the following conditions: pounding heart rate, increased muscular tension, hollow feeling in the pit of the stomach, dryness of the mouth and throat, and a frequent desire to urinate. Sometimes these sensations are so intense that they interfere with the upcoming performance. These physiological effects of human emotion can distort behavior, inhibit finely coordinated and complex sport skills, and hamper performance.

Success or failure in sport performance is frequently attributed to the level of readiness to perform. Newspaper sport pages are replete with accounts of athletic-contest losses after which the coach states that his team was not "up" for the contest. The implication of such a statement is that there is some mystical point along a continuum of psychological preparedness that is optimal for efficient athletic performance. This upward movement of the athletes' activation levels is commonly called "psych up."

The history of the activation concept

The modern study of emotion began with William James's article "What is Emotion?" published in 1884. He stated that physical changes ensue from perception, and it is the awareness of these changes that constitutes emotion. Cannon (1929) criticized this approach to emotion on several grounds, one of which was that internal changes occur too slowly to cause emotional feeling. He extended the concept of emotion to include emergency stress situations and developed his emergency theory of emotion—that is, the "fight-or-flight" response. Stressful situations that require behavioral adjustments cause a reflexive response that prepares the individual for running or fighting. This integrated *physiological* response is characterized by increased oxygen consumption, blood pressure, heart rate, respiration, and vascular supply. The control center is located in the hypothalamus and is influenced by hormones secreted by the adrenal glands.

In article 2.2, Elizabeth Duffy discusses the many ideas about the aspects of activation that she had been generating since the early 1930s. She continually makes the point that arousal (used synonymously with activation) can be viewed as a continuum from deep sleep to extreme effort or great excitement. The specificity–generality question of arousal measures has been raised and Duffy concludes that it is reasonable to speak of a *general* concept of arousal or energy mobilization. She cautions the reader not to confuse activation or excitability with vitality; she asserts that repeated activation leads to fatigue and a consequent reduction of vitality. This is an interesting point, because much of the conceptual sport literature states or implies that athletes should be "psyched up" for competition. When contests are lost, it is speculated that team members were not activated enough.

Duffy also discusses the relationship of activation to motivation, giving special attention to some confounding variables that mediate the arousal–performance relationship. Of special interest are her comments on overmotivation.

The more recent writings of Lacey (1967) provide evidence that arousal contains electrocortical, autonomic, and behavioral components, indicating that arousal is even more multidimensional than Duffy would have us believe.

2.2 The psychological significance of the concept of "arousal" or "activation"

ELIZABETH DUFFY
University of North Carolina, Greensboro

The concept of "arousal," "activation," or "energy mobilization," as developed by the writer over a period of many years (1932a, 1934, 1941a, 1941b, 1951) and employed by others in various contexts (Freeman, 1948; Hebb, 1955; Lindsley, 1952; Woodworth and Schlosberg, 1954), has wide applicability in psychology.[1] A fuller discussion of the topic will be presented elsewhere. Pending its appearance, however, it may be of interest to point out some of the areas which this concept should serve to illuminate.

It has been argued in previous papers (1941b, 1949) that all variations in behavior may be described as variations in either the direction[2] of behavior or the intensity of behavior. Only one part of this argument is essential for the present purpose. Whatever may be the reaction to the attempt to reduce the descriptive categories of psychology to two basic types of concept, we can proceed without dispute provided only it is agreed that intensity is a characteristic of behavior which can be abstracted and studied separately. It is the intensity aspect of behavior which has been variously referred to as the degree of excitation, arousal, activation, or energy mobilization.

I have argued that such abstraction from the totality of behavior is a necessary procedure if the psychologist is to be enabled to manipulate variables in a way likely to provide solutions to some of his problems. Confusion of the direction of behavior with the intensity of behavior, resulting in their fortuitous combination in certain psychological concepts (1941b)

From *Psychological Review* 64(1957):265–275. Copyright 1957 by the American Psychological Association. Reprinted by permission.

[1]The terms "activation" and "arousal," as used here, do not refer specifically to the activation pattern in the EEG (electroencephalogram). On the contrary, they refer to variations in the arousal or excitation of the individual as a whole, as indicated roughly by any one of a number of physiological measures (*e.g.*, skin resistance, muscle tension, EEG, cardiovascular measures, and others). The degree of arousal appears to be best indicated by a combination of measures.

[2]"Direction" in behavior refers merely to the fact that the individual does "this" rather than "that," or responds positively to certain cues and negatively to others.

and in the "trait" names used to describe personality (1949), was suggested as a possible basis for some of the unrewarding findings in many psychological investigations. Since the intensity of response can vary independently of the direction of response, it was proposed that it should be measured independently and its correlates investigated.

Perhaps a parallel may be seen in the analysis of sensory function.[3] Before progress could be made in the study of sensation and its physical correlates, it was necessary to separate the dimension of intensity from that of other sensory characteristics. In audition, for example, loudness was distinguished from pitch, and was related to a different type of variation in the physical stimulus. In vision, brightness was separated from hue, and each of these aspects of vision was related to the appropriate type of variation in the stimulus. Little progress in the understanding of sensation could have been made until suitable abstractions from the total sensory experience had been achieved, and these identifiable aspects of the totality had been investigated separately.

Measurement of the intensity of response (i.e., the degree of excitation, arousal, activation, or energy mobilization), it has been pointed out, may be achieved, at least in rough fashion, through various means (Duffy 1934; 1941b; 1951; Freeman, 1949). Among the physiological measures which may be employed are skin conductance, muscle tension, the electroencephalogram (EEG), pulse rate, respiration, and others. These measures show intercorrelations, although the correlation coefficients are not always high since there is patterning in the excitation of the individual, the nature of which appears to depend upon the specific stimulus situation and upon organic factors within the individual.[4] Nevertheless, there is evidence also of "generality" of the excitation. Hence a concept of arousal, or energy mobilization, appears to be justified.

It should be noted that the physiological measures which serve as indicants of arousal, and which correlate at least to some degree with each other, include measures of autonomic functions, of skeletal-muscle functioning, and of the functioning of the higher nerve centers. It is clear that it is the *organism*, and not a single system, or a single aspect of response, which shows arousal or activation.

---

[3]For this suggestion of a parallel, I am indebted to Dr. R. B. Malmo, who, in the fall of 1955, was kind enough to read the major portion of my manuscript for a forthcoming book, and to discuss it with his staff.

[4]The patterning of excitation is discussed more fully in the manuscript referred to in Footnote 3. It is believed that a more adequate concept of excitation, or activation, is thereby developed.

The historical roots of the concept of activation lie in Cannon's concept of "energy mobilization" during "emotion" (1915; 1929). Unlike Cannon's concept, however, the present concept of activation or arousal is designed to describe the intensity aspect of *all* behavior (Duffy, 1941b; 1949). Referred to as the "degree of excitation," it was, in 1934, defined as "the extent to which the organism as a whole is activated or aroused". Both its definition and its proposed mode of measurement have in more recent publications followed the line suggested at that time (Duffy, 1941b; 1951). When, however, studies of the electroencephalogram provided data on the behavioral correlates of changes in the EEG, it was suggested that this measure also provided an indication of the degree of arousal (Duffy, 1951).

To those unfamiliar with the concept of activation, confusion frequently arises between the degree of internal arousal (referred to by the concept) and the vigor and extent of overt responses. While the degree of internal arousal usually correlates fairly closely with the intensity of overt response, a discrepancy between the two may be introduced by the intervention of inhibitory processes, a phenomenon which has not received the degree of attention to which it is entitled. An additional source of confusion is the tendency on the part of some to confuse activation or excitability with vitality. Actually, it is suggested that these two characteristics are more likely to be negatively related than to be positively related. The tendency to be frequently and intensely aroused leads no doubt to fatigue and to a consequent reduction in vitality.

The chief point in regard to arousal, which I have repeatedly made (1941a, 1941b, 1949, 1951), is that arousal occurs in a *continuum*, from a low point during deep sleep to a high point during extreme effort or great excitement, with no distinguishable break for such conditions as sleep or "emotion." Evidence supporting this contention has been presented specifically for skin conductance, muscle tension, and the EEG (Duffy, 1951). Recently Lindsley (1952) has elaborated upon the conception as it applies to the EEG, although earlier, in his "activation theory of emotion" (1951), he had been of the opinion that "emotion" and sleep were conditions which were correlated with certain changes in the EEG, while conditions intermediate between the two were held to be as yet unexplained.

The factors which produce variations in the degree of arousal are various. They include, apparently, drugs, hormones, variations in physical exertion, and variations in what is commonly referred to as the degree of motivation. It appears that differences in the degree of arousal in different individuals may have a genetic or an environmental basis, or both. This conclusion is suggested from animal studies and from the relatively few studies of human beings in which the problem has been considered.

One of the potential contributions to psychology of the concept of arousal is that of breaking down the distinction between "drives" or "motives" and "emotion" (Duffy 1941a; 1941b). The same kinds of physiological changes may be observed to occur in these variously designated conditions, and, depending upon the degree of arousal, to produce the same sorts of effect upon behavior. It has been contended that "emotion" is in no sense a unique condition, and that our investigations should not be directed toward the study of "emotion" as such (Duffy, 1934).

In the study of "motivation," the concept of arousal is of distinct service. By means of the physiological measures which serve as indicants of arousal, we may secure a direct measure of the degree (intensity) of "motivation."[5] Any other measure must of necessity be less direct. When all factors affecting the level of arousal except the degree of incentive value or threat value are held constant, measurement of the degree of arousal affords a measure of the "motivating" value of a given situation. It also affords, incidentally, an objective measure of what is called the "stress' imposed by a situation.

Physiological measurements made in a wide variety of situations have shown the expected correspondence between the degree of arousal and the apparent degree of significance of the situation—i.e., its incentive value or its threat value (Duffy, 1951). For example, men undergoing flight training were found to show more tension of the muscles during the solo stage of training than during other stages, and during the maneuvers of takeoff and landing than during other maneuvers (Williams et al., 1946). Galvanic skin responses (GSR) obtained during replies to questions about provocative social problems were found to be smaller if the replies were in harmony with group opinion than if they were not, and "Yes" responses were found in general to be associated with smaller galvanic reactions than "No" responses (Murray, 1938).

The concept of activation holds further significance for psychology by virtue of the fact that variations in the degree of activation are, on the average, accompanied by certain variations in overt response.[6] The degree

[5]The concept of "motivation," as currently employed, is a "compound" concept which incorporates a description of both the "drive level," or arousal aspect, of behavior and also the direction taken by behavior, i.e., the selectivity of response. These two aspects of behavior may vary independently, though both are characteristically affected by a certain stimulus-condition such as hunger.

[6]These studies are reviewed in the manuscript referred to in Footnote 3.

of activation appears to affect the speed, the intensity, and the coordination of responses. In general, the optimal degree of activation appears to be a moderate one, the curve which expresses the relationship between activation and quality of performance taking the form of an inverted U. This conclusion, as it relates to muscular tension and performance, was suggested by me in 1932(b), by Freeman (1940) in several papers published around that time, and later by Courts (1942). That it holds also for other indicators of the degree of activation is suggested by Freeman's (1940) finding that skin resistance and reaction time, measured simultaneously on a single subject for 105 trials over a number of days, gave an inverted U-shaped curve when plotted on a graph. More recently the EEG has been found to show the same sort of relationship to reaction time (Lansing et al., 1956).

The effect of any given degree of activation upon performance appears to vary, however, with a number of factors, including the nature of the task to be performed and certain characteristics of the individual—such as, perhaps, the ability to inhibit and coordinate responses under a high degree of excitation (Duffy, 1932b). Organismic interaction is the basic explanatory principle suggested to account for the particular effects upon performance of various degrees of activation. Such organismic interaction may also, it appears, have some effect upon sensory thresholds. Again the possibility presents itself that the relationship may take the form of an inverted U-shaped curve.

When performance has been observed to vary under certain conditions, such as those of drowsiness, of fatigue, or of "emotion," it is suggested that the variation may be due, at least in part, to the effect of varying degrees of arousal. The disorganization of responses frequently reported during "over-motivation" or "emotion," for example, may be conceived of as resulting in part from too high a degree of arousal. Such a condition would be represented at one end of the U-shaped curve. A similar disorganization of responses, found sometimes during drowsiness or fatigue, would be represented at the other end of the curve showing the relationship between arousal and performance. In any case, it seems clear that prediction of overt response to a given set of stimulating conditions can be increased in accuracy when there is knowledge of the degree of internal arousal.

It appears also that, under similar stimulation, individuals differ in the degree of their arousal and in the speed with which they return to their former level of functioning. Moreover, there is evidence of consistency in this individual variation. Apparently the individual who responds with intensity in one situation will, on the average, respond with intensity in other situations also, as compared with other individuals. While the degree of arousal varies with the situation, the rank in arousal tends to be preserved. Different individuals appear to vary around different central tendencies—i.e., to differ in responsiveness. The easily aroused, or more responsive, individual has been found to show this responsiveness in many different forms, some of which will be described below.

For instance, subjects who showed a large number of galvanic skin responses when there was no observable stimulation also showed less adaptation of the galvanic skin response (GSR) to repeated stimulation (Mundy-Castle and McKiever, 1953).

Similarly, the frequency of the alpha rhythm in normal adults has been reported to show a significant relationship to ratings on the behavioral continuum called "primary-secondary function" (Mundy-Castle, 1953). Individuals in whom the alpha rhythm was more rapid tended to show more "primary functioning," or to be "quick, impulsive, variable, and highly stimulable." Those with relatively low frequencies of the alpha rhythm tended to show more "secondary functioning," or to be "slow, cautious, steady, with an even mood and psychic tempo. . . ." Mundy-Castle hypothetically ascribed these behavioral differences to differences in excitability within the central nervous system, the "primary functioning" individuals showing the greater excitability. A difference in neural excitability was also suggested as the explanation of his finding that there was a significant difference in the EEG activity evoked by rhythmic photic stimulation between subjects with a mean alpha frequency above 10.3 cycles per second and those with a mean alpha frequency below that rate.[7] He offered the same explanation of the greater incidence of "following"[8] in the beta range by those subjects showing little alpha rhythm, even when the eyes were closed, as compared with those subjects showing persistent alpha rhythms (1953).

Gastaut and his collaborators (1951) have also reported individual differences in cortical excitability. While their major purpose was not the investigation of individual differences, they made the incidental observation that calm individuals had a slow, high-voltage alpha rhythm (8-10 c./s.), with little "driving" of occipital rhythms by photic stimulation. Neurons showed a long recuperation time, synchrony of response was said to be noticeable, and recruitment poor. "Nervous" individuals, on the other hand,

[7]It is believed, he says, that "electrical rhythms in the brain can be initiated or augmented by a process similar to resonance; in other words, if an area of the brain is subjected to rhythmic impulses corresponding to its own latent or actual frequency, it may itself oscillate for as long as stimulation is maintained" (Mundy-Castle and McKiever, 1953). It is thought that the area may also be activated by stimulation harmonically related to its own.

[8]"Following" refers to electrical responses in the cortex occurring at the stimulus frequency.

95

were said to have a high-frequency, low-voltage alpha rhythm (10–13 c./s.), which at times was not perceptible. They were described as having a short neuronal recuperation time, little synchrony of response, good recruitment, and considerable driving by photic stimulation. In other words, "calm" as compared with "nervous" individuals showed less cortical excitability.

Differences in the EEG's of different individuals under similar stimulating conditions appear to be correlated also with differences in another form of responsiveness—i.e., differences in the threshold of deep reflexes. It has been reported that normal subjects with deep reflexes which are difficult to elicit showed a high percentage of alpha activity and little or no fast activity, while those with deep reflexes which were hyperactive had little alpha activity and a high percentage of fast activity (Kennard and Willner, 1943). However, while groups at the two extremes of reflex responsiveness differed significantly in the percentage of alpha activity, there was wide variation in the extent of such activity within any one of the groups formed on the basis of reflex status. Amplitude of rhythm was observed to be greatest in EEG records showing pronounced alpha activity.

Proneness to develop anxiety under stress, which may perhaps be regarded as a form of hyperresponsiveness, has been found, in both normal subjects and psychiatric patients, to be associated with a significantly smaller percentage of resting brain-wave activity in the alpha region when this activity is determined by automatic frequency analysis (Ulett et al., 1953). The anxiety-prone groups showed more fast activity (16–24 c./s.), or more slow activity (3–7 c./s.), below the alpha range. The significance of the slow activity is not as clear as that of the fast activity. Fast activity may be presumed to be indicative of a high level of excitation. It has been observed, for example, at the beginning of EEG recording in normal subjects who are unusually apprehensive about the procedure, and it has been found to disappear with reassurance and the attainment of relaxation (Lindsley, 1951). It appears at least possible that the slow activity may be due to fatigue from previous states of intense arousal.

In an investigation employing prison farm inmates, schizophrenics, and control subjects, to whom a group of psychological tests were given, it was reported that EEG activity above 16–20 c./s. appeared in significant amounts only in the records of those who, as rated by the psychological tests, showed anxiety to a marked degree (Kennard et al., 1955). Slow activity was said not to be very prevalent, but when it did occur, to be found most often among the patients.

These and other studies suggest that anxiety-proneness may be conceived of as a form of overarousal or hyperresponsiveness. The EEG's of the anxiety-prone seem very similar in most instances to the EEG's of other subjects whose exceptional responsiveness to the environment is indicated by active reflexes or by ratings on "primary function."

Degree of tension of the skeletal muscles is another indicator of responsiveness, or ease and extent of arousal, in which differences between individuals have been found. In almost every investigation in which tension of the skeletal musculature has been measured, wide differences between individuals in the degree of tension have been noted.[9] In the same stimulus situation, one individual would respond with a relatively low degree of tension, another with a moderate degree, and a third with a high degree of tension. Moreover, when observed in a *different* stimulus situation, the subjects, while varying in their absolute level of tension, would tend to preserve their ranks with respect to tension of the muscles. It was thus shown that different individuals vary around different central tendencies, so that one individual might be characterized as being in general tense, and another as being in general relaxed.

In early studies of muscular tension, the writer (1930, 1932a) found, in two separate investigations, that nursery school children showed marked individual differences in grip pressure while engaged in various tasks, and that there was a significant correlation between the grip pressure on one occasion and that on another, and during one task and during another. Grip pressure scores were found to be independent of the strength of grip as indicated by dynamometer scores, but to be related to ratings on excitability and on adjustment to the nursery school, the tense children being rated as more excitable and, on the average, less well adjusted.

Arnold (1942) also found that individuals tended to preserve their rank in the group with respect to pressure from the hand during repetition of the same task and during the performance of different tasks.

A study of airplane pilots in training revealed that some showed excessive muscle tension (pressure on stick and on rudder pedal) in both take-offs and landings, while others showed little tension on either maneuver (Williams et al., 1946). No individuals were found who in general tended to be tense during take-offs alone or during landing alone.

Further evidence that individuals who are more highly activated than others in one stimulus situation, as indicated by tension of the skeletal muscles, are more responsive to a wide variety of stimuli, is presented in studies by Lundervold (1952). "Tense" subjects, as compared with "relaxed" sub-

---

[9]Differences in muscle tension will, for the purposes of this discussion, refer to differences in pressure exerted by some group of muscles or to differences in electric potentials from muscles.

jects, were found to show more activity in the muscles when external conditions were changed, as by an increase in noise, the lowering of the room temperature, or the introduction of certain stimuli which caused irritation or anger. In these persons, there was not only more activity in the single muscle, but also electrical activity in more muscles, including muscles which did not participate directly in the movement. At the end of thirty minutes of noise, fifty per cent of the tense subjects, as compared with none of the relaxed subjects, showed more action potentials than they had shown before the noise began.

A similar relationship between muscular tension and another form of responsiveness was earlier shown by Freeman and Katzoff (1932), who found a significant correlation between grip-pressure scores and scores on the Cason Common Annoyance Test. Subjects with higher pressure scores tended to be more frequently or intensely annoyed—i.e., to show greater responsiveness of the sort referred to as "irritability."

It appears that, on the whole, skeletal-muscle tension in one part of the body tends to be positively related to that in other parts of the body, though the relationship between the tension in any two areas may not be very close. Parts of the body more remote from each other, or more widely differentiated in function, yield tension measures which are less closely related than those which are closer together or functionally more similar. When tension measures taken from different parts of the body, recorded during different tasks, or made at widely separated intervals of time, nevertheless show a significant positive correlation with each other, it must, however, be concluded that there is at least some degree of "generality" in skeletal-muscle tension. Moreover, from measuring the responsiveness of the skeletal-muscle system, we may apparently predict to some extent the response of highly integrated systems of reaction described as "personality traits." Indeed, in a study in which no direct measure of muscular tension was employed, but in which ratings on muscular tension and measures of sixteen physiological variables were intercorrelated and submitted to factor analysis, a factor defined as muscular tension showed correlation with certain personality characteristics (Wenger, 1943).

Since conditions of high activation may perhaps increase the likelihood of disorganization of motor responses, it is not surprising that measures of tremor and other forms of motor disorganization have been found to be related to the severity of conflicts (Morgan and Ojemann, 1942) and to neuroticism (Albino, 1948; Jost, 1941; Lee, 1931; Malmo et al., 1951a, 1951b, and 1955). Measures of irregularity in pressure appear to be among the measures which discriminate best between a normal and a psychiatric population, a finding which might be expected if, as suggested by the writer (1932b) and by Luria (1932), irregular pressure tracings are indicative of poor coordination or lack of control of responses.

Other indicants of arousal have also been shown to be related to more complex forms of response. For example, it has been said that a reasonably accurate prediction of a person's respiratory rate at a given time during a flight could be made on the basis of knowledge of his "normal" respiratory rate and the name of the maneuver to be performed (Williams et al., 1946).

Similarly, when an "autonomic factor" was obtained from twenty physiological measures related to the functioning of the autonomic nervous system, it was found that individuals differed greatly in scores on this factor, but that the correlation coefficient between early and later factor scores did not drop below .64 over a two-year period (Wenger and Ellington, 1943). Children at one extreme of the autonomic-factor scores were reported to differ significantly from those at the other extreme in certain personality traits (Wenger, 1947).

Individuals differ, not only in the degree of excitation produced by stimulation, but also in the speed with which the processes affected return to their prior level of functioning. Moreover, differences in recovery time cannot be accounted for solely by differences in the degree of arousal, for they are found when recovery is measured *in relation to the degree of arousal.* Darrow and Heath (1932), who first made use of this measure, computed a "recovery-reaction quotient" by dividing the extent of recovery in skin resistance by the extent of decrease in resistance which had occurred as a result of stimulation. The recovery-reaction quotient was reported to be related to many different measures of "'neurotic' and emotionally unstable tendencies." The investigators concluded that it was one of their best indicators of the absence of neurotic trend, but that the coefficients of correlation were not high enough to justify the use of the measure for prediction in individual cases. It would appear that the speed of recovery from arousal is an extremely significant aspect of response, and one which deserves further investigation.

Individuals who are exceptionally responsive to the environment may show their responsivity in behavior which, from a directional point of view, may be described in diverse ways. A tendency toward a high degree of arousal does not determine which aspects of the environment an individual will approach or will have a tendency to approach (i.e., have a favorable attitude toward); nor does it determine which aspects of the environment he will withdraw from or have a tendency to withdraw from (i.e., have an unfavorable attitude toward). On the contrary, the orientation of the individual in his environment is determined largely by other factors. These are, of course, the factors, both genetic and environmental, which have given to various aspects of his environment the nature of their significance, or their "cue-function." There are, nevertheless, differences in the way in which approach or withdrawal occurs which may conceivably be derived from differences in the level of activation. Among these appear to be differences in such aspects of behavior as alertness, impulsiveness, irritability, distractibility, and the degree of organization of responses. Moreover, greater responsiveness may, it is suggested, facilitate the development of aggression or withdrawal, enthusiasm, or anxiety. The more responsive individual in a certain kind of environment is no doubt more susceptible to the effects of that environment. Presumably he may become, depending upon circumstances, more anxiety-prone, more conscientious, more sympathetic, more devoted, or more irascible than a less responsive person would become under similar circumstances. We should therefore expect to find some association between a high degree of activation and easily aroused or intense responses of various kinds (e.g., anxieties, resentments, enthusiasms, or attachments). From knowledge of the individual's tendencies with respect to activation we should not, however, be able to predict the direction which his behavior would take. A more dependable association might be expected between individual differences in excitability and differences in the "dynamic" characteristics of behavior such as those mentioned above.

The effect of a high degree of arousal upon overt behavior varies, no doubt, with variations in the degree of inhibitory ability (Duffy, 1934), or, as Luria (1932) has described it, with variations in the strength of the "functional barrier" between excitation and response.[10] Depending upon this factor, a high degree of activation may, I suggest, lead to impulsive, disorganized behavior or to sensitive, alert, vigorous, and coordinated responses to the environment. Evidence in support of these statements is at present so meager, however, as to leave them in the category of speculations. It is to be hoped that further investigation will provide the basis for a more confident statement of the relationship between "personality" characteristics and individual differences in the level of activation.

[10]Luria reports that children show weakness of the functional barrier between excitation and motor response, as indicated by poor performance on a test requiring that a key be pressed down as slowly as possible. The writer (1932b) noted that, during a discrimination performance, younger nursery school children, with irregular grip-pressure tracings, had a higher proportion of their errors in the category of "impulsive" errors, or errors of overreaction.

SUMMARY

The concept of arousal or activation appears to be a significant one for the ordering of psychological data. Differences in activation, as shown in a wide variety of physiological measures, appear to be associated with many other differences in response.

In different stimulus situations, the same individual differs in the degree of arousal. Measurement of the physiological indicants of arousal affords, when other factors are constant, a direct measure of the "motivating" or "emotional" value of the situation to the individual. The concept serves to break down the distinction between the arousal aspect of "drives" or "motives" and that of "emotion," and to suggest instead a continuum in the degree of activation of the individual.

Differences in activation in the same individual are, it is suggested, accompanied by differences in the quality of performance; the relationship may be graphically represented by an inverted U-shaped curve. Further data are needed, however, to establish the validity of this hypothesis.

In the same stimulus situation there are differences between individuals in the degree of arousal. These differences tend to persist, and thus to characterize the individual. Moreover, the easily aroused, or responsive, person shows this responsiveness in many forms. It has been observed in the ease with which deep reflexes are elicited; and in the extent, frequency, and duration of reactions to stimulation, both of the skeletal musculature and of various functions controlled by the autonomic nervous system. It has been shown also in differences in cortical potentials, which are presumably indicative of differences in the excitability of higher nerve centers. These various forms of responsiveness show, in general, positive intercorrelations, though the coefficients of correlation are apparently not high enough for a measure of any one mode of responsiveness to serve as an adequate measure of the general responsivity of the individual. They appear, however, to give justification to the conception of a responsive or an unresponsive *individual,* not merely responsive or unresponsive skeletal musculature, skin resistance, or cortical potentials.

Differences in arousal are shown also in responses of greater inclusiveness and of higher integration—i.e., in responses frequently classified as personality traits. Combining with one or another directional aspect of behavior, a persistent high degree of arousal may, it appears, be observed in many complex characteristics, such as anxiety-proneness or aggressiveness.

Facts such as those presented above suggest that the concept of activation may prove useful in many different areas of psychology.

The physiology of activation

The definition of activation as *the degree of neural activity present in an individual* takes the terms *activation* and *arousal* out of the psychological realm and locates them in the neuropsychological category. A basic understanding of the physiological perspective of activation is essential to a comprehension of the constructs we shall encounter in this textbook. If the reader wants a more detailed description and explanation of arousal mechanisms than the account that follows, he or she may consult Butter (1968) and Sage (1971).

Motivational control systems operate through a combination of neural and chemical mechanisms that monitor overall performance. The intensity of the motivational state is related to the arousal function of the reticular activating system of the brain. Behavior is therefore partially a function of the stimulation and activation of the brain. Olds and Milner's (1954) study of the effect of electrically stimulating rats' brains on reinforcing certain behaviors is one of many findings in the literature that show behavior to be a function of neural activation.

Four major structures comprise the activation mechanism: (a) reticular formation, (b) hypothalamus, (c) limbic system, and (d) adrenal medulla.

The *reticular formation* is a strip of nervous tissue that extends from the *medulla* region of the brain stem to the lower *thalamus,* from which it branches into the *posterior hypothalamus* and *thalamus* regions. A vast network of nerve fibers diffuses from the thalamus region into the *cerebral cortex* (Figure 1). Input from the collateral *sensory receptors* fibers feeds impulses into the reticular formation and causes it to activate, thus forming the *reticular activating system (RAS)*.

The network of fibers that extends from the brain stem upward into the thalamus and hypothalamus and activates the *subcortical* and *cortical* areas is called the *ascending reticular activating system (ARAS;* see Figure 1). The ARAS has two distinct parts: (1) the brain stem reticular formation, which directly innervates the cortex and is responsible for long-lasting periods of activation, and (2) the diffusely projecting *thalamic nuclei,* which provide the most transitory periods of activation. Another network of fibers, called the *descending reticular activating system (DRAS)*, extends downward from the brain stem into the spinal cord and controls motor activity.

The reticular formation–cerebral cortex relationship is not one-way, because some cortical nerve fibers extend from the cerebral cortex into the reticular formation. The recticulo–cortical *feedback loop* thus formed

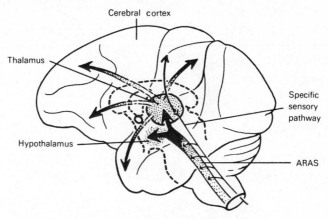

Cerebral cortex

Thalamus

Hypothalamus

Specific
sensory
pathway

ARAS

Figure 1 The ascending reticular activating system (ARAS) showing its inputs from collaterals of sensory tracts in the brain stem and its projections to the posterior hypothalamus and unspecific nuclei of the thalamus, which, in turn, diffusely project to the cerebral cortex. (Adapted from Butter, 1968).

allows the cortex to exert selective control over the arousal conditions of the lower brain by activating or suppressing the RAS. Another feedback loop is formed between the reticular activating center and the spinal cord when the descending reticular formation activates muscles by stimulating their sensory nerve terminals (*proprioceptors*), and messages are sent back to the reticular center.

Unless an individual perceives a situation as arousing, it will not activate his reticular activating system, which appears to govern the arousal continuum (Lykken, 1968). Cognition therefore exercises control over arousal and serves to adjust activation levels (Hebb, 1955).

The *hypothalamus* comprises a series of nuclei that are interwoven with the cortex, thalamus, and lower brain centers in a complex network. The *posterior* segment of the hypothalamus affects the *autonomic nervous system,* which controls the "automatic" functions of the body—breathing, swallowing, heartbeat, and so forth. The relationship between the hypothalamus and the autonomic nervous system (ANS) is shown in Figure 2. Stimulation of the posterior hypothalamus accelerates the functions of the internal organs—heartbeat rate and blood pressure are increased, digestion is speeded up, sweating becomes more profuse, and so forth. The resulting stimulation of the adrenal gland causes the release of the adrenal hormone *epinephrine,* which further stimulates

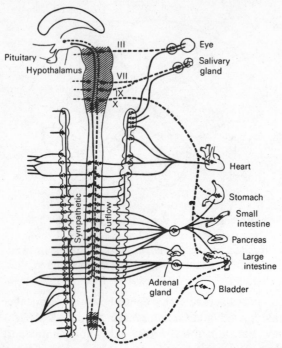

Figure 2 The autonomic nervous system (ANS), showing sympathetic outflow through the spinal cord (solid lines), and parasympathetic outflow (shaded area and broken lines) through cranial nerves and through the lowest division of the spinal cord. Some of the organs innervated by the ANS are also shown. (From Butter, 1968).

the autonomic nervous system. Epinephrine also disturbs biochemical equilibrium in the body, causing a state of *biochemical arousal.*

The *anterior* portion of the hypothalamus functions to counteract the effects of the posterior segment. Stimulation of the anterior hypothalamus decreases heartbeat rate, blood pressure, muscle tension, respiration rate, and so forth. The anterior hypothalamus affects activation by controlling the *pituitary,* or master gland of the body; it modifies biochemical arousal by controlling the secretion of the endocrine glands.

The autonomic nervous system, under the influence of the hypothalamus, imparts homeostatic balance to body functions and controls body processes. Because of the relationship between this gland and the autonomic nervous system, some psychologists call the hypothalamus ''the center of emotions'' (Sage, 1974).

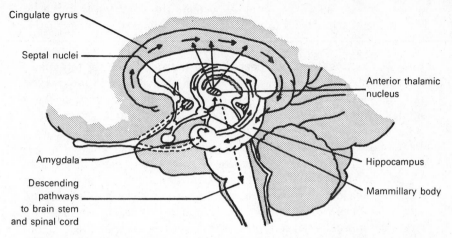

Figure 3 The limbic system. Nerve impulse flow is shown by arrows. (Adapted from Sage, 1971).

The *limbic system* lies in the inner core of the brain, surrounded by the *hemispheres.* Several component parts comprise this shell-shaped system (Figure 3), but its exact composition has not been defined. The limbic system has interconnections with the cerebal cortex and the thalami. Although its functions are not so well understood as those of other areas of the brain, it appears to contain an anatomical substrate of emotion (Hess, 1954). It has been demonstrated in animal studies that each part of the system is related to emotional behavior in some way. Animal research shows that the *amygdala* is related to the dominance–submission roles and that the *hippocampus* is related to aggressive behavior.

The limbic system functions in conjunction with the hypothalamus and plays a special role in regulating motivational and emotional responses to environmental events. It seems to provide the evaluation aspect of emotion, similar to that described earlier for the cortex.

The *adrenal medulla* is excited by autonomic nervous system activity under the control of the hypothalamus. *Epinephrine* is secreted from the adrenal medulla directly into the blood stream, where it affects the functions of the glands, the heart, and the smooth muscles of the intestine, bladder, lung, and so forth. Because the cells of the RAS are particularly sensitive to epinephrine, the adrenal medulla exerts some influence on the subcortical arousal system. The feedback loop that is formed thereby functions to prolong the activation state once it is initiated.

Activation response   It has been shown that the recticular formation, hypothalamus, limbic system, and adrenal medulla are all interrelated and that arousal or activation is a function of the integration of these entities. When the whole system is stimulated by something or someone in the environment (remember that perception determines what is, or is not, stimulating), an electrophysiological response occurs, and the system is alerted. Physiological reactions occur a relatively long time before the individual feels the ensuing emotion, and these reactions do not occur at the same rate. According to Davis, Buchwald, and Frankmann (1955), inactive subjects respond to a loud, brief noise in the following sequence: muscular tension, pulse rate, blood pressure, and respiration.

It is possible that the intensity of the body's response to a stimulus is determined by the number of feedback loops activated by that stimulus. Although several feedback loops were identified in this section, others probably exist because of the close integration of the four major components of the activation mechanism.

The assessment of activation

Because arousal effects are diffuse throughout the human organism, several different techniques are used to measure activation levels. The assessment techniques can be divided into three categories: *biochemical indicators, physiological indicators,* and *behavioral indicators and subjective reports.*

Biochemical indicators   The hormonal changes that accompany emotional arousal can be detected in the blood sugar and urine. The hormones *epinephrine* and *norepinephrine* are closely related to heightened arousal. Elmadjian, Hope, and Lamson (1957) measured urine epinephrine and norepinephrine levels in a group of professional ice hockey players before and after competition. Norepinephrine levels in the postperformance condition were five times higher than those in the preperformance condition; epinephrine levels were two to three times higher. These and other findings (Lykken, 1968) indicate that a high incidence of interpersonal aggressiveness tends to be associated with high levels of norepinephrine and epinephrine in the urine.

Physiological indicators   Heartbeat rate   The rate at which the heart beats can be measured by an *electrocardiogram (EKG)* or a *cardiotach-*

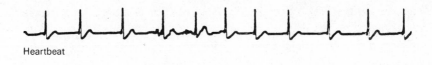

Heartbeat

Pulse rate

Figure 4 Simultaneous recording of heartbeat and pulse rate

ometer. An EKG, which is used primarily to detect heartbeat abnormalities, of the heart's electrical activity, which is picked up by electrodes and translated into impulses that are then recorded on a strip of moving chart paper (Figure 4). The heartbeat rate is one of the most dubious indicators of activation because it does not vary directly with the degree of arousal or emotional excitement (Lykken, 1968). It cannot therefore be reliably used as a measure of activation except in conjunction with other measurements.

Blood pressure   Arterial blood pressure is measured with a *sphygmomanometer.*

Muscle tension   The electrical potentials of muscles can be measured with an *electromyograph* (EMG). Tonic muscle tension is picked up from surface electrodes and produces a "spiky" record that may be evaluated from the characteristics of the spike pattern (Figure 5). Muscle tension (*tonus*) levels are roughly equivalent to levels of activation (Woodworth and Schlosberg, 1954).

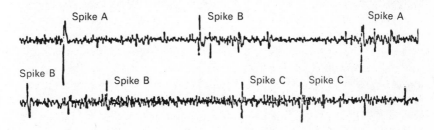

Figure 5 Characteristic EMG tracings

Cortical activity An *electroencephalogram* (*EEG*) records the brain's electrical impulses put out between two scalp electrodes. The recording shown in Figure 6 indices where cortical activity lies along the arousal continuum. The EEG tracings can therefore be used to assess the degree of cortical stimulation provided by the reticular activating system.

Three types of brain waves are shown in Figure 7. They can be identified by the characteristic frequency and amplitude of the patterns they form. The tracings are not simultaneous but are taken during various excitatory states. Each state produces waves of a different frequency and a different amplitude. High amounts of *alpha* indicate an awake state of rest and relaxation unaccompanied by attention and concentration. As arousal increases, alpha waves are replaced by *beta* waves, which represent excitement and activation. *Theta* waves indicate the sleep end of the arousal continuum.

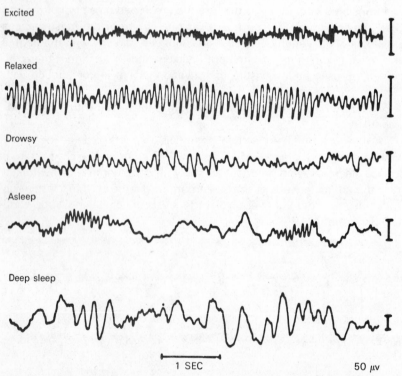

Figure 6 Characteristic EEG tracings from a normal human subject during various excitatory states from sleep to wakefulness

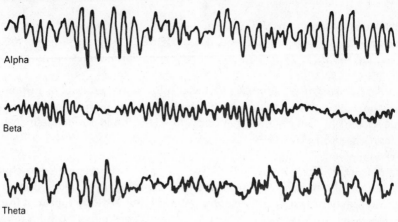

Alpha

Beta

Theta

Figure 7 Characteristic brain waves identified by frequency and amplitude

Skin resistance The resistance to passage of electrical currents across the skin is a measure of arousal. The more aroused or alert the individual, the less resistance is afforded by the skin and the more freely the current flows (reduced skin resistance equals increased skin conductance). A *galvanometer* measures the amount of skin resistance and records the *galvanic skin response (GSR)* on a graph. Figure 8 shows the GSR paired with the heartbeat rate of two subjects.

Skin conductance is lowest during relaxation and highest during excitement. There is considerable evidence to support the hypothesis

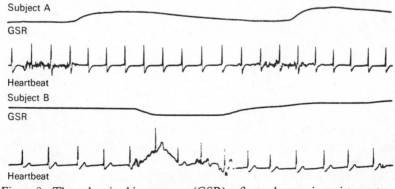

Subject A

GSR

Heartbeat

Subject B

GSR

Heartbeat

Figure 8 The galvanic skin response (GSR) reflects changes in resistance to the body's own electricity as it passes through the skin. Heartbeat and GSR often duplicate each other's responses, but GSR is much more reliable.

that the plantar and palmar (sole of foot and palm of hand) skin surfaces change as a result of arousal (Lykken, 1968). Galvanic skin response may be the most important psychophysiological measure in assessing levels of activation.

Palmar sweating   Increased arousal causes a higher level of sweating in the palms. A technique for measuring sweat gland secretion was developed by Sutarman and Thompson (1952) and further refined by Johnson and Dabbs (1967).

Behavioral indicators and subjective reports   Many reactions are characteristic of emotional behavior and heightened arousal states. Some of these are identified in the responses that Shaffer (1947) collected from pilots when they were asked to report their "sensations" during aerial combat. The following list shows the percentage of cases in which each reaction was felt:

Reactions	%
Palpitations of the heart	86
Muscular tension	83
Irritability	80
Dryness of mouth & throat	80
Cold sweat	79
Stomach contractions	76
Feeling of unreality	69
Frequent desire to urinate	65
Trembling	64
Sense of confusion	53
Feeling of weakness	41
Forgetting details after mission	39
Feeling sick	38
Inability to concentrate	35

The reader should be able to identify physiological assessment techniques applicable to most of these reactions. Many of the reactions listed could be assessed by a keen observer or by self-report measures (asking the individual).

At this juncture a point made by John Harmon and Warren Johnson, in article (2.3), dealing with the emotional responses of football players and wrestlers, is salient to Shaffer's study. They reported that two of their wrestling subjects were war veterans who "stated that their pre-contest anxiety was sometimes as great if not greater than their pre-invasion or pre-air combat anxiety had been during the war." From this, one might safely speculate that Shaffer's reported sensations would be equivalent to those of athletes in stressful situations. Many of the conditions seem to fit the athletic environment, at least from a phenomenological standpoint.

2.3 The emotional reactions of college athletes

JOHN M. HARMON
Boston University, Massachusetts

WARREN R. JOHNSON
University of Maryland, College Park

This research was preceded by exploratory efforts by the first writer in 1929 at Evansville College and by the second writer in 1947 at the University of Denver (Johnson, 1949). The two years (1948–1947) of investigation involved in the present research at Boston University required a type of co-operation on the part of coaches which was a tribute to their open-mindedness and demonstrated their recognition of the need for improved coaching through the aid of systematic research.

Psychologists have traditionally found the study of emotion an exasperating, though fascinating, subject. As a rule, experimental research upon emotion has been carried out in college laboratories where the circumstances ordinarily cannot simulate normal life conditions. The present research was carried out "on the firing line" of high pressure college football competition.

STATEMENT OF THE PROBLEM

To explore the emotional aspects of athletic sports contests, to the end that this competitive phase of modern school life may be more fully understood as an educational experience.

From *Research Quarterly* 23(1952):391–398. Reprinted by permission of the American Alliance for Health, Physical Education, and Recreation.

It was hoped that some light might be thrown upon:

(a) Certain physiological concomitants of emotion in a series of genuine emotionally charged situations.

(b) The extent to which men are emotionally disturbed in relation to the anticipated importance of contests.

(c) Laying a further basis for comparing the emotional "charge" characteristically associated with various athletic sports contests.

(d) The implications of emotional upset for various aspects of the athletic conditioning program.

(c) Which physiological indicator of the test battery would, when used alone, best represent the battery.

RESEARCH TOOLS

Four tests of emotional reactivity were selected for this study: pulse rate, systolic blood pressure, diastolic blood pressure and galvanic skin response (G.S.R.). All four indices have been used by earlier investigators of human emotion and a limited validity has been established for each (Batcher, 1943; Beebe-Center, 1950; Boas and Goldschmidt, 1932; Darrow, 1929; Dunbar, 1947; Hunt, 1941; Kuno, 1930).

A special G.S.R. apparatus no larger than a camera was designed and constructed for this research (Ruckmick, 1936). The one-quarter inch electrodes were embedded one inch apart at one end of a plastic bar, the dimensions of which were 12 inches by 2 inches by $\frac{1}{2}$ inch. Subjects being tested merely supported the bar by placing the electrodes on two fingers of one hand (palm up) and elevating the bar to approximately 30 degrees. This technique insured a constant pressure on the finger surfaces (Lund, 1942; Richter et al., 1943; Ruckmick, 1936). The subjects always used the same two fingers (index and middle fingers of right hand) when tested. Approximately 5 seconds were required for the administration of the G.S.R.

A reliability study of the four indices employed in this study and of the investigator was conducted with 48 college seniors. The battery was administered to the subjects once and then readministered to them approximately five minutes later. The resulting correlation coefficients were above .94 in each instance. Significance ratios indicated that the observed differences in means from Test 1 to Test 2 could not be accepted as true differences.

The research tools were employed in a second preliminary study involving nineteen varsity track men as subjects. Records were kept on these men throughout the 1949 spring season. Important administrative details were worked out in relation to establishing "normal" levels of reactivity for individuals and devising means of testing just prior to scheduled meets. In addition to providing interesting information on the reactions of track men, this study established the research pattern which was to be employed in the major project. . . .

RESEARCH PROCEDURE

The major project was the testing of the Boston University football team just prior to each of its games of the 1949 season. (The investigator was unable to accompany the team for one game of the season.)

1. Subjects

42 football players served as subjects throughout the season. It should be noted that most of the team members were World War II veterans and were somewhat older and more experienced competitors (average age 22 years and average experience 7 years) than the usual college athlete. It is consequently entirely possible that in terms of emotional reactivity these subjects did not constitute a representative group of college athletes.

2. "Normal" reactions (category 1)

A "normal" G.S.R., pulse rate and blood pressure were established for each subject. This value was the median of five measures taken with each instrument under the following conditions:

(a) The subjects had not exercised vigorously either on the day tested or on the day before that.

(b) The subjects had not eaten within two hours of being tested.

(c) A scheduled game was not to be held for at least two days.

(d) The subjects were under no known emotional stress at the time of testing. It seemed reasonable that in spite of extraneous emotion factors, an average of these five sets could be taken as approximating the true normal of each subject.

This "normal" value on each instrument was the criterion for all subsequent changes in reactivity prior to games.

3. Pre-game reactions (Category 2)

(a) The subjects were tested in the dressing rooms while they made preparations for play. Test period: about 20 minutes. Testing was completed approximately 25 minutes before game time. Three carefully trained graduate students assisted in the obtaining of the pulse rates and blood pressures.

(b) Each subject sat quietly for one minute before being tested. This limited rest period was necessitated by the circumstances of the pre-game testing.

(c) Prior to being tested, the subjects: (1) had not exercised vigorously (had, indeed, been resting in nearby quarters); (2) had not eaten within two hours; (3) were under no known emotional stress due to causes other than the game situation; (4) had not as yet been subjected to any form of "pep talk."

MAJOR FINDINGS

Figure 1 shows the relative excitation of the team for each game as compared with the established "normal," in terms of galvanic skin response. Graphic representation of systolic blood pressure was found to be quite similar in form to the G.S.R. Pulse rate, too, followed a similar, though not as variable a pattern.

Of interest in Figure 1 is the fact that it seems to bear a suggestive relationship to the following circumstances. The Boston University team began the season with aspirations of becoming one of the country's top teams. Early in the season the football coaching staff ranked each coming game in terms of its probable "importance" to Boston University's progress. The coaches ranked the games independently as follows: 1, 2, 6, 5, 7, 4, 3. After the third game (number 2 on the chart) there were three games with teams which, as the season developed, were known to be comparatively weak. Game 6, on the other hand, was a bowl game test which, after a considerable build-up, was lost by Boston by one point. The seventh game was plainly anticlimatic; many players considered the season over and took little interest in this contest. The result was a surprise loss for Boston University. The extremely low mean G.S.R. for this seventh contest suggested before game time that the team was extraordinarily "down" for the game. . . .

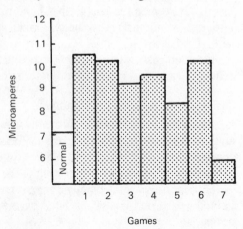

Figure 1 Mean Reactivity of the Team Under "Normal" Conditions (Not Excited or Emotionally Upset) and from Game to Game, As Measured by Galvanic Skin Response. (Games 1, 2, 6 & 5 (in that order) were rated "most important" by the coaches before the season. Before game 7, the team was plainly apathetic; quality of play was low.)

SUMMARY AND CONCLUSIONS

The pre-contest emotional reactions of the Boston University track and football teams were measured throughout the respective 1949 seasons by means of four physiological indicators: galvanic skin response, systolic blood pressure, diastolic blood pressure, and pulse rate. A team "normal" or "non-emotional" value was derived to serve as the basis for determining extent of emotional upset before each contest. Before the football season began, the coaching staff estimated the probable importance of each scheduled game; this estimate was eventually compared with the extent of excitation measured before the various games.

1. Emotional disturbance just preceding contests is evidently of sufficient intensity to be measured via three of the four physiological indicators selected: G.S.R., pulse rate and systolic blood pressure.

2. The battery could distinguish category 1 ("normal") from category 2 (pre-contest).

3. A close relationship was found to exist between the coaches' preseason estimate of the importance of the games and the measured team reactions. In light of this relationship, the hypothesis is suggested that emotional reactivity goes with "upness" for football competition. In this research, the team was measurably "up" or "down" before every contest.

4. Galvanic skin response closely approximated the composite criterion and was the best single indicator. G.S.R. had the further advantage that it could be administered within a few seconds. Pulse rate and systolic blood pressure were approximately equal in relation to the criterion while the diastolic blood pressure showed no significant differences between the "normal" and the "disturbed." From the point of view of simplicity, however, pulse rate, which is demonstrably responsive to emotional excitation, may well be the most practical coaching tool.

5. Analysis of the data on individual performers indicated that team reactions reflected most nearly the reactions of the individuals who played in the games regularly. With the exception of the one player who was rated by the coaches as "great" (actually All-American candidate), the individual performers were markedly variable in their physiological reactions from game to game.

6. Future studies in which measures of pre-game emotional reactions are correlated with evaluations of "quality of performance" in subsequent competition may provide a valuable coaching tool for ascertaining psychological "readiness" to compete. Such studies will necessarily take into account the probable differences in emotional reactivity of high school, college, and professional performers.

Martens (1974) included a number of subjective reports of behavioral arousal in his review of arousal and motor performance. The following questionnaires assess either perceived stress or state anxiety: Zuckerman's (1960) Affect Adjective Check List; Kern and Bialek's Subjective Stress Scale (Berkun, Bialek, Kern, and Yagi, 1962); the State–Trait Anxiety Inventory (Spielberger, Gorusch, and Lushene, 1970); the Somatic Perception Questionnaire (Landy and Stern, 1971); the Activation–Deactivation Adjective Check List (Thayer, 1967); and the Word Association Test.

Summary

Many indicants of arousal can be measured. Assessment of arousal states is not all that simple, however, and the reader must be aware of two confounding issues. First, is the arousal concept unidimensional or multidimensional? The answer to this question is crucial to determining whether or not there is one index of arousal. Evidence leans toward arousal being a many-sided construct. Typically low intercorrelation coefficients are found among arousal measures. Ax (1953) reported an average correlation of .12 between heart rate, blood pressure, galvanic skin resistance, respiration, and skin temperature. Interestingly enough this correlation is similar to that reported by Boon, Fisher and Mumford (1974) between heart rate and the palmar sweat data collected in a sport setting.

The second issue is whether or not some responses are more likely than others to appear in an individual. Are there individual patterns of response? Lacey (1950) established that individual patterns of response exist and that each pattern is stable over a period of time. Moreover, individual patterns of identical reactions occur in different situations. Apparently everyone has his own way of reacting to environmental stimuli and how the individual perceives those stimuli is what colors his emotional response.

ACTIVATION AND PERFORMANCE

Facts about the relation between performance and activation can be derived from the neurophysiological underpinnings of arousal. It was stated earlier that when the activation mechanism—especially the recticular formation—is stimulated the system produces an alerting kind of response. When this occurs, arousal increases. This increased arousal has the potential for facilitating performance on some tasks while at the same time inhibiting performance on other tasks.

Sage (1971) stated that a certain amount of cortical arousal is necessary or specific sensory messages die at the cortex. During a period of near-sleep, certain stimuli do not promote activity, or if they do, the movement is often not well coordinated. Anyone who has been awakened from a deep sleep by the ringing of a telephone can attest to the stumbling behavior that ensues. Coordinated movements are not associated with sleep states of activation. Though stimuli are present, they are not easily translated into appropriate motor responses. In such cases, sensory flow does not equal motor flow. More precisely, we can say that

> Moderate arousal has an organizing effect on behavior because it enhances neural transmission.

> Low arousal inhibits the transmission of impulses because sensory input is not fully processed at the cortex. (This can be related to reduced amounts of chemical transmitters that are responsible for the transference of electrical impulses across the synapses.)

> High arousal so activates and disrupts the system that there is an inability to integrate and coordinate the sensory input with the motor output.

Sage (1971) also reports that this high level of activation results in a *narrowing of the behavioral repertoire*. In this situation, the responses somehow become limited and are not necessarily connected with the appropriate stimuli. Furthermore, even though they are found to be incorrect, they appear again and again without any alteration. An example that relates to this point is that of a basketball player who makes an error in practice and is activated (incensed?) by the coach to approach the situation in a more intelligent manner. Awareness of the error with increased activation to perform well does not always alter the behavior. The error is made again and again and the higher the activation, the less the chance for successful performance.

A sport cliché comes to mind that might be interpreted according to this concept of narrowing behavior. It is often said in sport that when the going gets tough (meaning the siutation becomes stressful) the athlete will return to the "well" (his well-learned behavior). This behavior may not be absolutely appropriate in the situation—for example, if time is running out in a basketball game, stress can cause a player to shoot when he has an open shot even though his team is ahead and needs possession more than points. It is as if cognition did not play a large part in this decision.

Additionally, high arousal results in a *restriction of perceptual selectivity*. The individual is super-alert in this condition and is thus being bombarded with stimuli. Central stimuli are attended to, but those on the periphery are not. In sports that demand a high level of response orientation (constant change of movement in response to another's movement), failing to perceive movement on the visual periphery hurts performance. This post hoc interpretation might be applied to the 1964 Ali vs. Liston boxing match, in which Liston pursued Ali in an enraged state. Failure to see an opponent's subtle weight shifts and limb movements is not conducive to a successful boxing performance, nor to success in some other sports.

Moderate arousal is a good prelude to most task performances and provides a "set" or readiness to perform. This level of attention maximizes perception of new stimuli. However, the evoked potential of one sense modality is blocked when attention is distracted to another (Lykken, 1968). The reason is that cerebral processing of sensory inputs is apparently a single-channel mechanism and will not allow two functions to be performed with absolute simultaneity if they both require conscious attention. High activation still further reduces this processing capacity, and in sport, even during a contest, there are variations of stress (hence of activation). Basketball illustrates this point well in terms of perceptual distraction. Picture a dribbler trying to bring the ball up-court against a double-teaming pressure defense. He must advance the ball across the mid-court line in 10 seconds. He must attend to many visual stimuli in order to maneuver to the open spots and avoid losing the ball. The dribbler has his back to his team-mates, and one of them yells for the ball. What happens? Either he attends to his dribbling or he attends to the yelling. In my experience, too often the ball is thrown to the team-mate and he is not open to receive the pass. The result is another turnover.

All too often the yell for the ball cannot be dismissed because one of the tenets of the game is to find the open man. The coach should teach players not to yell for the ball, except under special conditions. In stress situations, only a certain amount of information can be processed.

Two ideas have been put forward in the attempt to explain the relationship between arousal and performance. They will be referred to as theories, but the reader is cautioned not to take the word "theory" too literally. The two ideas are (1) *drive theory* and (2) *inverted-U theory*.

Drive theory

It is postulated that as drive increases, the dominant response is increasingly emitted whether correct or not. Thus increased arousal sometimes facilitates performance and sometimes impairs performance. The reader will notice that arousal has been interchanged with drive in the last sentence. No subterfuge was intended; a close relationship exists between reticular activation and the psychological concept of drive. Drive and arousal are synonymous and interchangeable, or at least drive is a source of arousal (Duffy, 1957; Malmo, 1959). The facilitation–distraction idea can be rephrased to provide a slightly different perspective—increased drive impairs performance early in the learning while it facilitates already well-learned responses. This can again be restated in a slightly different form—drive facilitates performance but hampers learning.

Martens (1971) undertook a comprehensive review of the literature testing the drive hypothesis and its relevance to motor performance. It is always difficult to compare the findings of a great number of studies because of the different methodologies used. The one great problem, however, is that the drive theory cannot be tested unless it can be determined when a task is well learned. At what point does any motor task become well learned? If task performance does not improve under increased drive, then one can speculate that the task is not well learned.

The implied continuum of learning here is properly termed *habit hierarchy.* Since the habit hierarchies for the motor responses on motor tasks are far from being established, Martens (1974) had to conclude that "drive theory remains operationally non-functional for complex motor behavior."

Inverted-U theory

In the early 1900s, two researchers working in the Harvard Psychological Laboratory (Robert Yerkes and John Dodson) had become interested in the relation of strength of stimulus to rate of learning. They selected one of Yerkes's favorite subjects, the dancing mouse, and set out to discover what strength of stimulus (weak, medium, or strong) was most favorable to the acquisition of a discrimination habit. Both strength of stimulus and task difficulty were manipulated experimentally.

Their findings were unequivocal. Clearly the medium stimulus was much more favorable to the habit acquisition (learning or performance). All subjects who trained under the weak or strong stimulus learned more slowly than those trained under the medium strength stimulus. These findings led to the phrasing of what we know now as the Yerkes–Dodson Law: ''. . . an easily acquired habit, that is one which does not demand difficult sense discriminations or complex associations, may readily be formed under strong stimulation, whereas a difficult habit may be acquired readily only under relatively weak stimulation'' (Yerkes and Dodson, 1908).

Figure 9 represents the results of their research. In each of the three curves, fewer trials were needed for learning under the medium-strength-of-stimulus condition. There is an optimum amount of motivation for each of the three task difficulties, and it should be noted that this optimum depends on the difficulty of the task. The optimum is reached with weak motivation when the task is difficult, but strong motivation is required to produce the optimum level on the easy task.

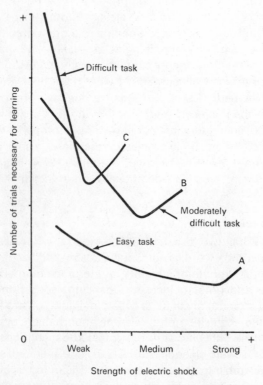

Figure 9 Schematic diagram illustrating the Yerkes-Dodson law

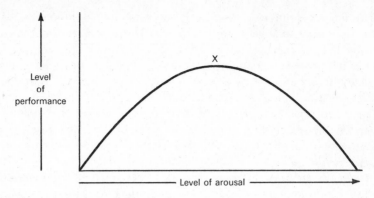

Figure 10 Inverted-U performance-arousal curve

Notice that nowhere has there been any mention of emotion or arousal in the discussion of the Yerkes–Dodson study. Along these lines, the most significant experiment was conducted by Freeman (1940). He conducted three experiments relative to the relationship between performance levels and activation levels. The most significant feature was the inverted-U relationship between reaction time and activity levels. Figure 10 represents this finding diagrammatically, and the curvilinear relationship between arousal and performance is quite evident. Plotting performance scores against levels of arousal results in an inverted-U curve.

The physiological explanation of this finding was discussed earlier, and the reader may recall that performance was hindered at low arousal levels by inadequate attention, and disrupted at high arousal levels by the narrowed perception that resulted from excessive attention.

Although research examining the veracity of the inverted-U hypothesis has its problems and equivocal findings, much research, especially animal studies, supports the hypothesis. One early study with human subjects is worth reporting, even if only for its sensationalism. Patrick (1934) shut a subject in a cabin with four doors, and the subject's task was to escape through one of the doors (one was always left unlocked). Naturally, the experimenter confounded the situation by varying the escape door. Patrick found that the subject very quickly began to adopt a fairly rational strategy. However, when the motivation to escape was increased by shooting nails at the subject or giving light shocks through the floor, the subject's responses became less rational, more stereotyped, and definitely more inefficient.

This finding is not at all difficult to understand. When too much is at stake, performance is likely to deteriorate. The coach realizes this only too well. His charges perform well in practice and look unstoppable, but the reality of game competition has led him to be quite pessimistic about expecting too much. For two weeks prior to the Super Bowl IX game in 1975, sports columnists and commentators were asking the question, "How much does experience count?" The implication was related to activation: if the game meant too much (because one team had never experienced competition for such high stakes), performance might be disrupted. All the same, the experienced team lost.

Rainer Martens and Daniel Landers (1970) tested the inverted-U theory, using motor peformance data, and obtained typically U-shaped performance curves. Subjects were grouped according to their anxiety levels and tested under varying degrees of manipulated stress.

Studies of the relation between arousal and performance sometimes do not actually assess arousal levels. This is true especially in field studies, where existing situations are often operationalized as being arousing. Two such studies, independent of each other, assessed basketball free-throw shooting performance during various game situations. Giambrone (1973) collected data during the 1969 Big Ten basketball season relating free-throw shooting to various situations. He reported no significant relationship between performance and any of those situations.

However, Ahart (1973) reported some indication that free-throw shooting performance was related to score differential at the time the shots were taken. Shooting percentages relative to score were as follows:

Score differential

Points behind			Points ahead		
9+	5–8	1–4	1–4	5–8	9+
53%	69%	50%	53%	72%	55%

Shooting percentages were greater when the score differential was moderate, and less when the score was close or when the differential was great. Results could be interpreted from the perspective of the inverted-U. Moderate activation (score differential: 5–8) increases the shooter's attention to the task and results in good performance. High activation (score differential: 1–4) disrupts the performance of the finely coordinated task because success seems to mean more when the game is close. Low activation (score differential: 9+) results in low task attention and poorer performance. At the individual level, not all athletes were more successful at the moderate score differential; some shot best when the game was close and some shot best when the score differential was high. I took preliminary steps to replicate this study on a national level through the NABC (National Association of Basketball Coaches) during the 1975–76 year. If the earlier findings are repeated, several implications for coaching decisions will be evident. Perhaps the player who shoots the technical fouls could be selected in relation to his known probability at that score differential. When the game is nearing conclusion and ''it's anybody's ballgame,'' the player who shoots well in low-score-differential situations ought to have the ball in case he is fouled. Does the coach just have to accept that, for many athletes, the free-throw shooting percentages will be lower during close contests and when the spread is large? He might consider some accommodation training in his practice sessions in order to modify this behavior.

The reader is reminded that the results of the foregoing research project are speculative and the score differentials are operationally described as producing different activation levels. This is a good example of one of the drawbacks of arousal research in the field—namely, no direct assessment of arousal levels, only inferred levels. Martens (1974) has addressed himself to this and other drawbacks of arousal research.

The inverted-U theory appears to provide a reasonably good explanation of some sport performances, notwithstanding Morgan's (1973) comment that it is a nice simplistic concept based on rats running down T-mazes. Up to this point, the discussion of the inverted-U has been simplistic, and additional considerations are mandatory. Several factors must be considered before any wholesale acceptance of the inverted-U concept can occur.

Task demands and *situational characteristics* modify the arousal–performance relationship. Sport skills could be analyzed from many perspectives in order to comprehend the difficulty of learning and performing them. It is certainly useless to speak of the optimum arousal level without specifying the task, since this level is contingent upon the ease with which the task can be mastered.

Joseph Oxendine, in article (2.4), reformulates the Yerkes–Dodson Law to make it more applicable to sport. He has established a table of selected sport skills and matched each of them with a numerical optimum arousal level. For the most part the discussion is academic, since the tabled values have little or no practical use. On the other hand, however, this article has been directly responsible for promoting arousal research relative to sport performance.

2.4   Emotional arousal and motor performance

JOSEPH B. OXENDINE
Temple University, Philadelphia, Pennsylvania

One of the most widely accepted principles of human behavior is that people perform best when "motivated." This principle is validated when keenly interested children exhibit greater enthusiasm and performance on school tasks than less interested children. Highly excited individuals performing unexpected feats or attaining unusual levels of performance is further evidence. However, empirical evidence seems to indicate that high levels of excitement interfere with efficiency in certain activities. In one stiuation, therefore, a high level of motivation may place the individual at a distinct advantage, whereas, at another time a person so stimulated would be hindered. The relationship between arousal and performance is a complex one and does not appear to follow a straight line. This paper will investigate several aspects of this phenomenon.

WHAT IS EMOTION?

One difficult problem in analyzing the arousal–performance question is that of defining and categorizing human emotion. The terms "motivation," "excitement," or "arousal," though often used interchangeably may imply different things to different individuals. When one speaks of emotional arousal he may be referring to one or a combination of the following "negative" conditions: fear, anger, anxiety, jealousy, embarrassment, disgust, boredom, or rage. "Positive" states may include: joy, elation, ecstasy, interest, happiness, and love. The list is limited only by one's vocabulary and point of view. Although the emotional states result from different situations,

From *Quest* 13(1970):23–30. Reprinted by permission.

the physiological response of the individual is often similar. Certainly, there is a high degree of overlap in both physical and psychological reactions to many of the indicated conditions.

Since it is not yet possible to establish distinct lines of demarcation between the various terms describing emotion, perhaps the most useful approach is to describe emotion on the basis of level of arousal or activation. In this way the emotional state may be placed on a continuum from high to low activation as follows: excited, alert and attentive, relaxed, drowsy, light sleep, deep sleep, coma, and death. Different levels are reflected in physiological changes which are controlled by the autonomic nervous system. Extensive investigation of the physiological response was carried out by Cannon in 1929, and more recently by Hanson (1967), Husman *et al.* (1968), Johnson (1949), and Skubic (1955). Woodworth and Schlosberg (1963) present a thorough description of the known responses. Heart rate, blood pressure, muscle tension, respiration, galvanic skin response, and many other bodily functions have been identified as being sensitive to changes in emotional arousal.

In this discussion, emotional arousal will refer to those conditions in which one's "normal" physiological functions have been intensified.

AROUSAL AND MOTOR PERFORMANCE

Any effort to develop generalizations regarding the role of emotional arousal and motor performance must consider several factors. According to Cratty (1968), Husman (1969), and Oxendine (1968) the optimum level of arousal varies with the particular motor task, i.e., different levels of arousal for most effective performance. In addition, the optimum arousal state varies from person to person. For example, high anxiety versus low anxiety, extraversion versus introversion, and experience versus nonexperience are some of the individual variables making it difficult to establish definitive guidelines for all persons. Furthermore, even for the same person the optimum level would be expected to vary somewhat from day to day. This principle is supported by Lewin's "Life-Space" concept which indicates that individuals respond to situations according to both internal and external stimuli.

Despite the limitations presented by the task and the individual variables, an effort will be made to generalize on the basis of research and literature available. The Yerkes–Dodson Law, now more than a half century old, can be used as a point of reference. According to this Law, complex tasks are performed better when one's drive is low while simple tasks are performed better when drive is high. Therefore, drive which is either too great or too low for a particular task may result in impaired performance. It is assumed here that "drive" is somewhat related to motivation or arousal. There is abundant empirical research evidence to support this widely accepted generalization, and, in addition, several plausible explanations have been offered. Nevertheless, the Law fails to answer many questions for the teacher or athletic coach interested in gaining more specific guidelines for the conduct of his activities. For example, when the Yerkes–Dodson Law is used, there is a question of which tasks are "complex" and which are "simple." Furthermore, what is "high drive" and "low drive"? With the uncertainty and latitude inherent in the Law, the researcher or the practitioner can explain any results on the basis of the task being either complex or simple or the level of drive being either high or low, whichever seems to support the results in a given situation. Such reflective explanations, however, are of little value in predicting performance. Though offering a rough guide as an explanation of emotional arousal and performance, the Yerkes–Dodson Law is inadequate in terms of today's needs.

On the basis of research evidence, scientific literature, and empirical observation the following generalizations are offered on the arousal-performance topic:

1. A high level of arousal is essential for optimal performance in gross motor activities involving strength, endurance, and speed.
2. A high level of arousal interferes with performances involving complex skills, fine muscle movements, coordination, steadiness, and general concentration.
3. A slightly-above-average level of arousal is preferable to a normal or subnormal arousal state for all motor tasks.

Arousal effects on strength, endurance and speed. As an example of the positive relationship between arousal and physical *strength*, the following incident is cited by Oxendine (1968):

> The following case was described in a newspaper a few years ago. A man, after having jacked up his station wagon to change a tire in his driveway, was called into his house. Moments later, one of his children, who had been observing the proceedings ran into the house to tell his father and mother that the car had fallen off the jack and on another child. Both parents ran outside, and the quick-thinking father immediately began resetting the jack in order to lift the car off the child. The mother, seeking more immediate results, took hold of the car and manually lifted it so the child could crawl out from under! So great was the strain that, in the process, a bone was broken in her back. Certainly, this feat was outside the expected performance possibilities of the woman, who was described as average in size.

Most persons can recall unusual feats of strength when persons have been confronted with emergency situations. These incidents run the gamut from "superhuman" actions by men during war to little old ladies carrying refrigerators downstairs and outside a burning house.

B. L. Johnson (1965) reported that subjects with induced motivational techniques made significant gains in strength, whereas, a nonmotivated group did not. One technique which simulated the competitive aspects of an athletic contest increased strength scores to a greater degree than other motivational techniques. Johnson further reported that subjects with below average strength and subjects with above average strength made similar improvements under conditions of motivation. Gerdes (1958) found that motivated subjects increased performance in pull-ups and push-ups.

On the basis of research and observation, there is every reason to believe that a very high arousal state will result in most extraordinary strength performances. Therefore, the gymnast performing an "iron cross," the weight lifter pressing a heavy weight, or the student doing a leg lift with a dynamometer—each would do his best if greatly aroused.

As an example of the relationship between arousal and *endurance,* I am reminded of the following personal incident which occurred approximately three years ago. I was nearing the completion of a three mile run which ended with a long uphill climb through a wooded area and the customary painful level of fatigue had become very evident. Suddenly, out of the bush sprang two large Weimaraner dogs, noticeably unhappy, and, in fact, exhibiting a high level of unwarranted hostility. After about 15 seconds of stressful uncertainty, I was rescued by the owner. As I resumed jogging I realized that not only had my pace increased but there was a total absence of any sensation of fatigue. I could not attribute the sudden burst of energy to the 15 second "rest."

Cannon (1929) cites the case of John Colter who along with a companion was seized by a group of Indians in Montana in 1808:

Colter was stripped naked; his companion, who resisted, was killed and hacked in pieces. The Chief then made signs to Colter to go away across the prairie. When he had gone a short distance he saw the younger men casting aside everything but their weapons and making ready for a chase. Now he knew their object. He was to run a race, of which the prize was to be his own life and scalp. Off he started with the speed of the wind. The war whoop immediately arose; and looking back, he saw a large number of young warriors, with spears, in rapid pursuit. He ran with all the speed that nature, excited to the utmost, could give; fear and hope lent a supernatural vigor to his limbs, and the rapidity of his flight astonished himself. After nearly three miles his strength began to wane. He stopped and looked back. Only one of his pursuers was near. The Indian rushed toward him, attempting to cast his spear and fell headlong. Colter seized the spear, killed his enemy and again set out, with renewed strength, feeling, as he said to me, as if he had not run a mile.

Fatigue results in an increase in the threshold of a muscle and, thus, motor responses become slower. During fatigue, muscle thresholds increase from 100 percent to 200 percent and occasionally much higher in situations involving extreme amounts of work. Muscles usually return to their normal condition in 15 minutes to two hours of rest. Cannon (1929) reported research in which fatigued animals were injected with adrenalin immediately after the cessation of long work periods. He reported that animals with threshold increases of 150 percent had this decrement cut in half within five minutes as a result of the adrenalin. Rested animals did not increase their muscle response time with the injection of adrenalin. He concluded, therefore, that the injection of adrenalin had a counter action on the effects of fatigue.

While it is unlikely that Indians, Weimaraners, or injections of adrenalin will be used as a regular means of increasing endurance in sports participants, it does seem clear that situations eliciting strong emotional arousal will result in significant endurance gains.

Incidents seeming to show a positive relationship between fright, anger, or other forms of arousal and *speed* are within the experiences of most persons. Unfortunately, in these situations accurate measures of speed are not usually made. Whereas, feats of strength are usually verifiable, it is rare that anyone is available to clock frightened people over a measured course. Nevertheless, the belief remains that a child being chased by either a bully or a ghost will run faster than when told by the teacher to "run as fast as you can." In experimental situations, a relationship between movement speed and motivation has been shown by Gerdes (1958), Miller (1960), Henry (1961), and Strong (1963). Thus, there is ample reason to assume that sprinters will run faster and swimmers will swim faster if highly aroused.

AROUSAL EFFECTS ON COMPLEX AND FINE CONTROLLED MOVEMENTS

Numerous situations can be cited from sports in which highly motivated or aroused individuals performed less well on complex tasks. The typical young baseball pitcher who becomes highly excited in a tense game situation is less likely to throw strikes than in practice or a routine game situation. Similarly, erratic or subpar performance in a high pressure situation may be expected from the basketball player shooting a free throw, a gymnast in a balancing routine, or a diver attempting a fancy drive. Frequent interference in activities requiring complex and controlled movements appears to support the Yerkes–Dodson Law.

The interference effects of high emotional arousal appear to have greater detrimental effects on tense or highly anxious persons than on those less anxious. Carron (1965) reported that a shock stresser (electric shock from a constant current electronic simulator) had a detrimental effect on high anxious male college students in a *balancing* task, whereas low anxious subjects were unaffected. Late in the learning period, however, the detrimental effect of the stresser on high anxious subjects was lessened. In reviewing several research studies in this area, Carron concluded that in tasks of low difficulty, high anxious subjects were found to be superior to low anxious subjects. However, in *tasks of high difficulty*, low anxious subjects proved superior. Stress seemed to be particularly detrimental when persons were largely unacquainted with a particular activity. However, experience in the activity tended to reduce the adverse effects of stress. Bergstrom (1967) reported that experienced airplane pilots performed less well on a *complex motor task* during stressful conditions. The stressful situation used was distracting flashing lights and the performance of a secondary task along with the main task. Bergstrom reported that the human pilot can perform extremely difficult and complex tasks in a calm laboratory situation or a simulated cockpit. When the system is airborne, however, the pilot's performance seriously deteriorates as a result of the stress. Pinneo (1961) reported that as tension increased so did the errors in a complex tracking task.

In a study of *steadiness*, Eysenck and Gillen (1965) reported that high drive subjects performed at an inferior level to low drive subjects in a hand steadiness test. Basomity *et al.* (1955) found a decrement in performance in hand steadiness following the administration of adrenalin, and Haugy (1954) reported an increase in fine tremor after the administration of a stimulant drug. Several authors report that muscle tension and tremor is a normal characteristic of increased tension. Such tension may easily result in the inability of the pass receiver in football to catch the ball. The same may be true for the basketball player attempting to catch the ball or retrieve a rebound, or the field hockey player unable to exercise the typical "give" with the stick when receiving the ball.

Husman (1969) states that as emotion goes up, functioning *intelligence* goes down. Of course, effective intelligence is an important factor in athletic contests, not to mention I.Q. tests and performance in general daily routine. However, rising emotion and declining intellectual functioning is probably not a straight line relationship. That is, there is no evidence to indicate that an emotional state slightly above normal is less effective than a "normal" or even below average level. Nevertheless, there is little question about the distracting effects of extreme levels of emotion on any type of performance involving reasoning powers. Such interference may be particularly harmful when the performer is in an activity requiring quick thinking or fast decision making. Extreme examples of this interference occur when the individual "freezes" or "goes blank."

EMOTIONAL AROUSAL AND PERFORMANCE IN SPORTS

Research dealing with the role of emotional arousal in ordinary sports activities is sparse. Some studies have attempted to determine the level of arousal associated with participants in different sports without determining the relationship between that level and subsequent performance. Other studies specifically designed to relate arousal to performance level usually consider the team as a whole to make a generalization about a particular sport. One of the few studies in this specific area was conducted by Harmon and Johnson (1952) who found that a major college football team played its best game of the season when aroused to the highest level. On the other hand, the team performed poorest when the arousal level was at the lowest state. However, to generalize that a football player performs best when he is most highly motivated is a rather crude generalization. The game of football is so varied and complex that optimum emotional arousal for the different skills may vary from near the norm line to extreme high levels. For example, the offensive guard or tackle required to block the individual straight across the line will probably exhibit speed and power most effectively if he is motivated to the highest possible degree. On the other hand, the open field runner is required to exhibit agility, balance, and judgment in direction as well as good running speed. Therefore, a moderate level of arousal may be most helpful. Finally, the quarterback when throwing a pass, and the field goal kicker would probably perform best at a low level of arousal so that they relax and focus their attention on the task at hand and, thus, make the accurate and rather delicate responses necessary for success. For the performance of individual tasks in football, therefore, it appears that different levels of arousal would be ideal for players at different positions.

Without adequate research relating emotional arousal to specific sports skills, suggestions as to the most appropriate level for different sports activities are speculative. Nevertheless, Table I includes a summary of sugges-

Table I Optimum arousal level from some typical sports skills

Level of arousal	Sports skills
#5 (extremely excited)	football blocking and tackling performance on the Rogers' PFI test running (220 yards to 440 yards) sit up, push up, or bent arm hang test weight lifting
#4	running long jump running very short and long races shot put swimming races wrestling and judo
#3	basketball skills boxing high jumping most gymnastic skills soccer skills
#2	baseball pitchers and batters fancy dives fencing football quarterback tennis
#1 (slight arousal)	archery and bowling basketball free throw field goal kicking golf putting and short irons skating figure 8's
0 (normal state)	

tions regarding the optimal arousal level for the typical participant in a variety of sports activities. These are based on some reflections on the research and opinions which relate to the components necessary for performance in the activities listed.

In Table I, the #5 level refers to extremely high levels of excitement approaching "blind rage" while the #1 level suggests a condition only slightly more intense than a normal relaxed state. Skills are placed on the scale at a point seeming to reflect the needed ingredients for excellent performance. That is, those activities high on speed, strength, or endurance needs but low on complexity, fine muscle control, and judgment are placed nearer to #5. Those activities placing high priority on fine muscle control and coordinated movements but low on strength and speed are placed nearer to #1. Of course, many skills require a combination of these several factors and, thus, fall somewhere in between #1 and #5. For example, the boxer, though needing the strength, speed, and endurance afforded by high emotion must devote attention to analyzing his opponent's moves and figuring out a way of maximizing his own strengths while exploiting his opponent's weaknesses. In addition, he must protect himself. Consequently, the boxer who becomes unduly angry or "loses his head" is an easier target for the more composed boxer. Similarly, the sprinter in a short race is likely to lose some efficiency at the start of the race and during the first few steps if a state of extreme tension exists at the starting blocks. However, in a slightly longer race, i.e., 200 yards, the negative effects of extreme tension would be minimized while the benefits (speed and endurance) would be maximized. For longer races such as a mile or greater, there is a tendency for the highly aroused runner to throw caution to the winds, fail to pace himself, and tire badly near the end of the race.

For an activity such as golf putting, an extreme level of arousal is often devastating. The golfer is likely to putt the ball much too strongly because of his general muscular tension or, on the other hand, much too easily, because of his fear of overputting. The same holds true for other skills emphasizing accuracy and precision. I have never known a basketball coach to say to a young player who has just missed an important free throw, "You did not try hard enough." Rather, most problems arise when individuals try too hard.

ESTABLISHING THE DESIRED AROUSAL LEVEL

Understanding the optimal level of arousal for each activity is only part of the information needed to make effective use of emotions in motor skills. Also needed is a means of determining the arousal level of an individual or group at a particular time, and further, the ability to alter it. Each of these topics is appropriate for a major investigation. Only a brief overview will be presented here.

Since emotional arousal as considered in this discussion is reflected in physiological responses, the only accurate means of determining one's condition is by the measurement of these responses. Usually this requires the use of some equipment of varying degrees of sophistication. Several experimental psychology books including the one by Woodworth and Schlosberg, *Experimental Psychology* (1963), describe procedures used in the measurement of most responses related to emotional arousal. However, experienced athletic coaches and physical education teachers have developed ways of making empirical judgments as to whether an individual is "up" for an impending event. In 1929, Cannon described a highly aroused football player as "sitting grimly on a bench, his fists clenched, his jaws tight, and his face the grayish color of clay." Today's football coaches recognize these and other behaviors as being characteristic of the highly aroused player.

Changing arousal state in the desired direction requires an understanding of some basic principles of psychology and skill in using certain techniques. Most texts relating to the psychology of behavior or teaching devote large portions to these processes. The following techniques have been used in practical and experimental situations to raise the level of arousal for participation in motor activities: competition (challenges), praise and reproof, rewards and punishment, "pep" talks, music, and hypnosis. Ironically, most of these have been used both to heighten and to lower the level of arousal. For example, in one situation music with a stirring, rhythmic beat and with increasing intensity may be used to raise one's general level of excitement. In another situation, soft or soothing music may be used to calm overly excited participants prior to competition. A great deal of research is essential before refinement can be made in the use of these or other techniques for promoting the desired arousal level of athletic participants.

Certainly it is important to know task characteristics before attempting to understand the arousal–performance relationship, but it is also important to know the conditions under which the task is to be performed. The situation supplies information to the subject; D. O. Hebb (1955) refers to this as "cue function." Situations are bound to be perceived differently by different individuals. What arouses one individual to the upper end of the continuum is perceived by another as a commonplace occurrence. Therefore no one situation will activate all exposed individuals in the same way. This is why we shall argue later for the discontinuance of group activating techniques, especially the "pep talk." Some athletes are bound to be at less than optimum arousal level and others are bound to be past the optimum point. Activation and deactivation, if utilized, must be applied with some discrimination.

The other category of factors relates to *person characteristics,* of which skill level and personality will be discussed. As the individual advances on the learning curve, the level of optimum arousal required for maximum performance naturally increases. The responses are becoming well learned, and increased arousal (up to a point) will enhance performance. Several studies have assessed arousal relative to skill ability.

Sullivan (1964) compared the approach–avoidance feelings expressed by college wrestlers prior to competition and reported differences between the inexperienced and veteran athletes. The veteran wrestlers reported low approach feelings the night before the match and these feelings escalated and peaked at the time of the handshake to begin the competition. However, the inexperienced wrestlers reported their highest approach feelings the night before (giving the coach a false sense of readiness to compete) but as the meet approached, these feelings declined until they were low at competition time.

A similar finding has been reported by Epstein and Fenz (1965) with experienced and inexperienced sport parachutists. Acute sensitization, followed by gradual adaptation to the stress, is characteristic of these individuals. The veteran jumpers report their highest fear the morning of the jump and this declines so that it is at the lowest point at the moment of free-fall. They are then activated in anticipation of the landing. On the other hand, the novices are most fearful when told that it is time to jump. From that point on, their self-report fear measures decline. The parachutists in Epstein's and Fenz's study and the wrestlers in Sullivan's study reveal an adaptation relative to their experience and skill in the task.

Naturally the personality characteristic that appears most related to arousal and performance is anxiety. Anxiety is the uneasy feeling derived from some stressor and can influence behavior. It can be viewed as a stable personality characteristic (trait anxiety) or as a transitory mood (state anxiety). Situations are perceived differentially by individuals differing in trait anxiety, but it appears that the ranking of response intensity remains quite similar for all individuals (Duffy, 1957). If traits are stable aspects of personality, then perhaps little modification relative to the activation response can be expected. The adaptation is likely to occur at the state level. This somewhat parallels Kane's (1971) suggestion of the possibility of two functionally related arousal mechanisms—a tonic arousal system and an arousal modulating system. The former maintains one's gross level of arousal and the latter controls the level at which the tonic arousal system functions.

Duffy (1957) expands on this process of adaptation and refers to the ability of the individual to inhibit and coordinate responses. The expected relationship between arousal and performance is confused by this ability.

This point was made earlier in discussing the role of the cortex in modulating the intensity of activation experienced in the reticular system. Because of this ability to adapt, it is not always evident that high degrees of arousal will inhibit performance. As Duffy states, ''a high degree of activation may, I suggest, lead to impulsive, disorganized behavior or to sensitive, alert, vigorous, and coordinated responses to the environment.''

For any given value of performance except the optimum, there are two possible arousal values—for example x_1 and x_2 on Figure 11. Corcoran (1965) suggests that the appropriate level can be assessed by increasing or decreasing arousal and noting the change in performance. If performance decreases when arousal is increased, then the original performance was already past optimum.

The crucial point here is that if maximum performance is desired and the concept of optimum arousal accurately reflects reality, then the adjustment of activation states is necessary to achieve this goal. It is to this question that the next section is addressed.

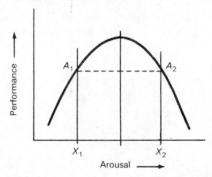

Figure 11 Low arousal (X_1) results in performance A_1 and high arousal (X_2) results in performance A_2. Performance A_1 and A_2 are equal but result from dramatically different arousal levels.

Adjusting activation levels

Since sport performance often occurs under widely stressful conditions and is itself a complex integration of movement patterns, maximum performance is made more difficult by activating athletes. The claim made here is that stress must be *controlled* and not increased as is the common practice of coaches. This author addresses himself to the issue of ''psyching up'' athletes in article 2.5, finding that for many individuals and in certain sports too much arousal can interfere with performance.

135

2.5

Psych up, psych down, psych out: relationship of arousal to sport performance

A. CRAIG FISHER
Ithaca College, New York

If you have ever watched television on any Saturday afternoon in the fall, you undoubtedly have noticed some rather large, apparently uninhibited uniformed individuals jumping up and down and beating each other on the shoulders and about the head. This is college football, and you are witnessing a display of heightened arousal. This exuberant emotional state is somehow supposed to be related to the upcoming football performance. It is easy to see that individuals are "psyched up" and therefore the teams are ready to perform collectively at a high level of performance. Or are they?

Athletic coaches commonly believe that athletic performance improves in a direct relationship to increased arousal. As the athlete gets more "psyched," his or her chances of performing optimally increase. This belief is the partial embodiment of the psychological principle referred to as *drive theory.* The coach who interprets poor performance as the result of athletes not being "up" or ready for the contest is supporting drive theory. An extension of this is the belief that the level of arousal is open-ended and there is no limit to how "super-psyched" one can become. Bo Schembechler's statement prior to the highly publicized 1974 Ohio State–Michigan football game typifies such a feeling. The Michigan head coach stated in a press interview: "No team can ever get too high." He was saying, then, that there are no limits to how much teams can be aroused and that the higher the arousal level, the greater the expected performance.

One of my purposes here is to discredit such statements and in so doing attempt to show that drive theory is not a reasonable concept.

Several variables stand in the way of wholesale acceptance of the drive concept as it relates to sport performance. Can you picture Jack Nicklaus or Johnny Miller on the eighteenth green needing an eight-foot putt to win $30,000 first place money in the same arousal state as Saturday's college football player? As the golfer's arousal level increases, what happens to his chances for a successful putting performance? Are they increasing or de-

---

Paper presented at New York State Association for Health, Physical Education, and Recreation convention, Kiamesha Lake, January 1974. Reprinted by permission.

creasing? Olga Korbut thrilled sport viewers all over the world with her uneven-parallel-bar routine in the 1972 Olympic games. Would her performance have been facilitated on her back flip if she had been super-aroused just before going into that difficult maneuver? Does increased arousal facilitate the Little Leaguer's hitting performance when the tying and winning runs are on second and third base and his team is down to two outs?

One of the concomitants of heightened arousal is increased muscle tension, and in sporting activities requiring steadiness and balance this resultant tension is likely to be devastating. The point I am making is that the *nature of the task* must be considered before one can even attempt to understand the relationship of arousal to sport performance. Undoubtedly some sport skills allow for extremely high levels of arousal, namely large-muscle movements such as running, football line blocking, and weight lifting. Other tasks, however, require fine, coordinated movements; extreme arousal levels are therefore bound to lower the performance of these tasks. Apparently there are optimum levels of arousal for each sport skill—too little does not activate the performer to his or her best performance level and too much interferes with movement patterns. The optimum point is specific to the task. A certain arousal level is necessary for the most efficient transfer of sensory input to motor output; beyond that point of optimum arousal, performance is damaged. inverted U-theory

✗ Drive theory is over-simplistic and fails to consider the achieved *skill level* of the athlete. A specified level of arousal—and this level can be assessed by various techniques both simple and complex—could interfere with performance today and that same level might enhance performance a month from now.

Basically, high arousal levels are not conducive to initial learning and performance, and it is unfortunate that we have been programmed to introduce those relay contests so early in the learning curve. We are not facilitating learning or performance by introducing the stressor of competition in the beginning stages of learning; in fact we are probably interfering with learning and performance by having the performers focus their attention on success and not on the performance.

All aspects of human behavior must be understood in light of the concept of individual differences. The conditions that facilitate optimum performance in one individual are detractors in another individual. Once we accept this idea, it is difficult to place any faith in psychological gimmicks that are supposed to arouse a *group* of individuals. Knowledge of individual differences certainly prompts us to question the value of team motivation and pep talks to the entire squad.

137

It is entirely possible and highly probable that coaches do more "psyching out" than "psyching up." Perhaps the "psych up" routines are in fact performed for the coach's own benefit. By the application of his many psychic tricks, the coach can more closely imitate the behavior of the super-coaches Knute Rockne or Vince Lombardi, who supposedly could squeeze out the legendary 110 percent effort (Kroll, 1972). Who has not heard of the fiery pep talks of Knute Rockne or seen Pat O'Brien playing them on the screen. I emphasize "supposedly" because of the following direct statement made by Rockne in correspondence with Coleman Griffith at Illinois: "I do not make any effort to key them up, except on rare, exceptional conditions. I keyed them up for the Nebraska game this year, which was a mistake, as we had a reaction the following Saturday against Northwestern. I try to make our boys take the game less seriously than, I presume, some others do" (Kroll and Lewis, 1970). Is this the Knute Rockne we all *know?* Is it possible that his legendary pep talks, those exhortations that caused three touchdown deficits to disappear early in the third quarter, were just that—*legends?* Sport history is filled with such legends, and they are difficult to dispel.

We are quick to attribute unsuccessful athletic performance to the athlete's not being emotionally ready or "up" for the game, but too successful a motivational talk and too much induced stress during preparation for the contest can be just as devastating. My thesis is that they are even *more* detrimental to performance. The emphasis placed on competition and winning is an extremely strong stressor in itself without adding a verbal assault.

Some athletes cannot easily handle the stress and tension of athletic competition. Glenn Hall, a perennial all-star goaltender with the Chicago Black Hawks, never learned to tolerate that stress in all his years as a professional hockey player. He reportedly "lost his lunch" before every contest he ever played and sometimes even before practice. Would additional arousal preparation have facilitated his performance? Hall's body was telling him that the stress was disruptive—certainly no additional "psyching up" would have aided his performance.

Wayne Walker, retired linebacker with the Detroit Lions, was interviewed before the 1974 Super Bowl and made what I feel is an accurate comment about arousal. He said that the biggest enemy to optimum athletic performance was being "up" too high. Without realizing it, he was acknowledging the concept of an optimum arousal level.

What is rather disturbing is that these facts are available and known but the practice of "psyching up" without limits continues. Cal Stoll, Head Football Coach at the University of Minnesota, reported in a presentation at the 1973 AAHPER National Convention, that after one of his theatrical motivation performances the athletes played like zombies for the first quarter. Yet it is doubtful that he will discontinue his arousing techniques. "Psyching up" for athletic performance is too much ingrained into football coaching lore. There are some hopeful signs, however. The newest "super coach" on the horizon is Don Shula of the Miami Dolphins. One of the Miami players, Larry Csonka, was quoted in an Associated Press release as saying about Shula, "He's a realist. He doesn't try to fire you up with phony emotion. He only asks that you want to win." Other coaches might do well to emulate *that* kind of behavior.

In an interesting research article on football players, Langer (1966b) pointed out some useful ideas. High-anxiety players (Glenn Hall might be a good example) need to be calmed down rather than aroused; they are anxious enough without additional stressors. Langer also revealed that the better football players (at Utah State University) tended not to be responsive to stress-inducing comments made by coaches before games, but that the poorer players tended to react to the coach's comments with a debilitating level of anxiety. The "psych up" does little for the proficient athlete, but it translates into poorer performance for the less-skilled athlete. It is unfortunate for the highly anxious individual if the coach interprets the resulting poor performance as a lack of emotional readiness. The coach then subjects that individual to increased stressors so that he *will* be "up" for the next contest. The cycle is apparent—poorer performance begets increased stressors and increased stressors beget poorer performance.

Are there any remedies for these athletes who are activated to such high emotional states? I think the first step toward helping them is to realize that arousal can be both facilitative and detrimental and that the sport situation has natural arousing tendencies for the great majority of performers. Just being aware that competition is imminent is likely enough to activate many athletes. Perhaps those mental images of the contest that flash across the mind are so scary that they interfere with physiological functions.

Physiological reactions to psychological events can be controlled in several ways. The techniques are varied and could be classified under the following headings: Medical, Therapeutic, Psychological, Muscular, Physiological, and Mystical. Regardless of the technique, the aim is to regulate the activation level either with the help of a trained clinician or by some learned self-imposed method. All of the techniques I will mention can eventually be brought under the athlete's control.

In the 1930s an American physician named Jacobson (1938) wrote a book about what he called Progressive Relaxation, in which he outlined a method of relaxation training for controlling residual muscle tension. To control tension one must first be able to recognize it. This is done by tightening and relaxing various muscle groups at varying intensities of contraction—maximum, moderate, slight, and so forth. Once nearly imperceptible levels of tension can be felt, these can be modulated and reduced even lower. The basic premise of Progressive Relaxation, or relaxation training, or tension control, is that there is a direct line from the muscular system to the emotional states. If you control the muscular systems and reduce tension, you are able to gain self-control of the emotions. Jacobson himself has mastered the technique so well that he can even turn off sense receptors. He reportedly can relax with his eyes open and prevent images that appear on the retina from being translated into pictures in the brain.

This method is undergoing a period of new growth today under the formulation of the American Association for the Advancement of Tension Control. The Association has been organized to acquire and disseminate knowledge about tension reduction. It will appeal to various people in its six divisions: Dentistry, Medicine, Physical Therapy, Psychology, General, and Education. Consider the practical application of controlling anxiety in your situation—before an examination, before the principal or department chairman supervises one's teaching, and, of course, prior to athletic competition.

Eastern European sport psychologists have long realized that athletic performance is as much a function of psychological preparation as physical preparation (Vanek and Cratty, 1970). Schultz, in Germany, devised Autogenic Training. It has many of the characteristics of Progressive Relaxation but also uses the power of suggestion, somewhat like hypnosis, to adjust activation levels. It can be used with athletes whose pre-contest activation is either too high or too low, and can also be used to minimize tension levels in post-game situations.

Most coaches who feel that arousal is related to athletic performance usually concern themselves only with pre-game arousal and lose track of the importance of this emotional state after the contest is over. In my way of thinking, if you are going to manipulate athletes' emotions toward heightened arousal states before a contest, then you have an ethical obligation to reduce that level once the contest is over. For every "upper" there should be a "downer." This is emotionally healthy for the athlete and allows him to start at a relatively low level in preparation for the next contest instead of starting from a heightened level. In tournament play, I would think that this would be essential, since teams might play two or three games within a very short period of time. This technique has received reasonable attention in European countries and is practiced by athletes on their national teams. Not only are the various muscular and physiological processes modified *during* the participation phase in the training, but the effects continue for a period of time *after* the sessions are over—some as long as 24 hours after.

In recent years many Americans have been "turned on" to the practices of a guru named Maharishi Mahesh Yogi. More than 100,000 people in this country have received instruction in Transcendental Meditation. This technique does not require intense concentration; it is easily learned and after short periods of training one becomes an "expert." Contrary to what you might already believe, you do not have to change your life-style or contort your body into weird positions. The time commitment per day is approximately one half-hour, two sessions of 15 minutes each. The practitioner sits in a comfortable position with eyes closed. By a systematic method he has been taught, he perceives a suitable sound or thought. Because his mind is allowed to experience this stimulus freely, certain bodily functions are modulated. Evidence is available to show that meditators are able to control many of their physiological responses, some of them which are linked to emotional states, especially anxiety.

Undoubtedly you have noticed the number of biofeedback instruments that are advertised in the journals you read. Their only purpose is to give the practitioner of meditation or relaxation some information about whether he is indeed controlling the biological actions he is attempting to control.

The last methods of arousal control I will mention could be placed under the heading of Psychological Coaching Practices (Cratty, 1973).

1. *Model training.* You are probably already using this method. It consists of an attempt by the coach to hold practice for the sport skills under game-like conditions. Competition and heightened anxiety must be present in your practices if you expect your athletes to be able to perform under those conditions. Athletes then learn to deal with these emotional states.

2. *Withdrawal from the psychological field.* Coaches have never liked to see happy, smiling, noisy athletes dressing for a contest and waiting for the beginning of a game. They ought to be thinking about the job they have to perform (as if they could possibly forget). The idea of playing cards or little games or piping in music seems like a good idea to set a relaxed mood and allow some concentrations on aspects other than the upcoming competition. You and I have our withdrawal mechanisms in use all the time and as long as they are not used to excess, they assist in maintaining mental health.

3. *Social isolation.* Arousal is contagious and some athletes are highly susceptible to behavior modification in an activation sense. In addition, some tasks are so fine and complex that any arousal much past base-line

level would probably be detrimental. Y. A. Tittle, retired quarterback of the New York Giants, used to come to the dressing room two hours before the arrival of the remainder of the team, dress, remove himself from the later discussions of the upcoming contest, and basically avoid interaction with his team-mates. This was a technique he felt was necessary in order to facilitate his performance or not deter from his performance.

4. *Selective association.* Certain athletes can be therapeutic for other athletes. Highly anxious individuals should affect low anxious individuals in a way that raises the anxiety of the low individual. There also are reversal effects of the low-anxiety individual on the high-anxiety individual. This refers more to state anxiety (transitory mood) than to trait anxiety (stable personality).

— I am not advocating the abolition of motivational gimmicks that tend to arouse or "psych up" athletes as long as one is aware of the variables that relate to this condition. I do caution you against any *unorganized* attack on your athletes' senses for the purpose of activation because their performances will probably suffer and your results will be in opposition to both your wishes and their desires; instead of "psyched up" athletes, you will have "psyched out" athletes.

Because so much emphasis is placed on winning, it is not reasonable to expect to see many athletes in a lethargic state in the face of athletic competition. Instead of giving much consideration to "psych up" gimmicks, I suggest considering some desensitization or "psych down" maneuvers. This means possibly having to run counter to common practices, but the coach who does this is truly attempting to understand the psychological consequences of athletic competition.

It seems only reasonable that those in charge of sport (coaches) should be concerned with allowing the athlete to achieve the best performance his or her talent will allow. The "110 percent effort" and "playing over one's head" are both fictitious ideas and do not seem to serve any worthwhile purpose. The important point is that "talent will out" if conditions are right. No one can, or should, expect more from an athlete than his abilities allow. That is why it is so important to question this overwhelming belief that the next highest level of activation is necessary for increased athletic performance.

Previous discussion has centered on a variety of behavioral problems emanating from heightened arousal states, and only the very skeptical reader could fail to accept or appreciate the fact that too much activation can be harmful to the performance or learning (or both) of certain sport skills or patterns of skills. Fortunately, many athletes have the ability to adapt to certain stress situations and adjust their levels of activation accordingly. It is also probably more than speculation that this propensity is associated with successful athletic performance. Vanek and Cratty (1970) reported such a finding derived from the German and Russian sport psychology literature. The better athletes are able to adjust their activation level up *or* down when needed and can also maintain a level for as long as needed.

But what of the athlete who is not yet proficient and does not seem to be able to handle the emotional aspect of sport competition? We all agree that the athlete's physical ailments should be cared for, but our practices do not reflect a similar concern about the athlete's emotional problems. Morgan (1973) said it well when he stated that the athlete's emotional first aid is as important as his physical first aid, perhaps even more important.

Sage (1971) is certainly correct in his statement, "The fact that over-arousal may disrupt performance does not seem to be known or appreciated by most physical educators and coaches." At least that statement holds true generally in this country. However, trainers and coaches in some other parts of the world realize the importance of adjusting levels of the athlete's activation in order to achieve maximum performance. Vanek and Cratty (1970) document this point. A few athletes in this country are actively involved in personal programs of stress adaptation or emotional control, but these are exceptions. These methods are not weird or occult; they make a certain amount of sense.

Apparently there is some movement away from the overemphasis on the "pep talk" as a way of preparing athletes for competition. Morgan (1973) provides a concise treatise on the wisdom of using this motivational gimmick. If one believes that the concept of individual differences applies to athletes, then how can one expect a group activation technique to be beneficial to all? On any team the arousal continuum is likely to extend all the way from phlegmatic to frenetic. How can a single presentation with emotional overtones bring everyone to a level of optimum performance? Furthermore, if all coaches use such a technique, what is gained? If the athletes have merely all been moved along the arousal continuum (assuming that indeed the "pep talk" has an effect on behavior), has anything really been changed? Morgan dismisses the pep talk quickly and labels it a subterfuge. Another point that deserves to be made about any sensitizing device is that participation in the strenuous activity may well "wash out" the effects. Morgan indicates that the results from four research studies support this contention.

We have two additional concerns about "psyching up" athletes. The first is that tension states may be quite stable precompetitively, at least for those athletes who are proficient (Langer, 1966). If such is the case, much time might be wasted that could be used more advantageously. The second concern is a humanistic one: does the coach have the right to heighten the athlete's arousal and manipulate his emotional outlook, especially if at the conclusion of the contest he feels no obligation to return the athlete to "normal"? A vivid case of a coach "playing" with the emotions of his athletes is afforded by Cal Stoll (1973), head football coach at the University of Minnesota. Stroll describes one of his spectacular pregame motivational gimmicks (in this case it was Anita Bryant singing "The Battle Hymn of the Republic") which had reduced every athlete to tears. In his earlier stage-setting for his coaches, he predicted the point at which the athletes would "break."

Some stress is inevitable and certainly desirable for proficient athletic performance; the issue here is to control the dysfunctional effect and enhance the functional one. Here a further reference to the concern that European trainers, coaches, and sport psychologists have about activation is warranted. Vanek and Cratty (1970) describe curves of activation along the time continuum—*long term tension* (weeks and months prior to competition), *prestart tension* (days before competition), *start tension* (just before performance), and *post tension.* During this entire period a variety of concerns are emphasized in each of the periods—for example, (1) be careful not to peak too soon and (2) be wary of growing activation in the prestart period; (3) avoid emotional contagion from one athlete to another in the start period; and (4) be aware of the emotional state of the athlete upon completion of the contest because this level bears a relationship to the upcoming contest.

A more detailed description of the scope of precompetitive activation is offered by Filip Genov of Bulgaria, in article 2.6. Genov refers to activation as "general mobilization readiness" and comments on many related variables that are studied by European sport psychologists. He reminds the reader that only the athlete can mobilize energies for competition and that coaches must be wary of incorrect and untimely intervention in the readiness cycle. A great many factors related to mobilization readiness are discussed briefly.

2.6

The nature of the mobilization readiness of the sportsman and the influence of different factors upon its formation

FILIP GENOV
Union Bulgare de Culture Physique et des Sports,
Sofia, Bulgaria

Long ago it was established that, at the execution of a certain activity, one is already in a special state of readiness to execute that action. Marx (1937), when comparing the work of a bee with the work of a man, remarked that: ". . . the worst architect differs from the best bee only in this, that before making the cell of wax he has already constructed it in his "head" (pp. 197–198).

Other authors investigating this state of readiness noticed that before executing a particular action man first creates a definite aim which has been called "readiness for the execution of a certain action" (Uznadze, 1961), "way of action" (Beritov, 1961), "acceptor of the action" (Anokhin, 1965), and "motive task" (Bernstein, 1963).

In sport psychology and physiology this state of the sportsman before the onset of action is studied as both start and prestart states (Chernikova, 1937; Puni, 1949; Krestovnikov and Vasileva, 1955; Genova, 1957; etc.). Levitov (1964) defined the state of man before the execution of a certain action as a psychic state and called it "start readiness." In the last few years many authors have directed their attention to the investigation of the immediate preparation of the sportsman before the execution of separate actions. They have pointed out the timely parameters of this immediate preparatory state. Concerned with this topic are the works of Gheron (1953), Dychkov (1955), Genov (1961), Genova (1961), Puni (1961), Parvanov and Popov (1963), Dimitrova (1963), Petrovich (1966), etc. In addition, the question of the immediate preparation of the sportsman for successful participation in competition has been studied by Rudik (1964), Gagaeva (1962), Genov (1961), and others; the intensity and stability of attention of the sportsman in a state of readiness for the execution of a certain action during competition by Genov (1965); the speed of reaction by Krestovnikov and Vasileva

(1955); the consciousness, purpose, and speed of verbal reactions by Genova (1957, 1959), Genov (1966d, 1967), and Radchenko (1966); and the state of mobilization readiness of the sportsman by Genov (1966a, 1966b, 1966c).

During the past ten years we have been studying the peculiarities of the state of immediate readiness of the sportsman before the execution of separate actions and activities. The investigations were made on competitors in different kinds of sport: weightlifters, track athletes, wrestlers, gymnasts (of both sport and artistic gymnastics), rowers, basketballers, footballers, etc. We carried out the investigations during high level competitions—the Olympic Games in Mexico City, 1968, World, European, and National Championships, and international tournaments and training sessions. Among the sportsmen examined 102 are bearers of gold, silver and bronze medals from international competition and also have held 58 world records. On the whole more than 2,000 sportsmen have been examined.

In this state of mobilization readiness of the sportsman, the following variables have been studied: the intensity and stability of attention, the timely characteristics of concentration, the direction of attention of the sportsman during concentration, the productivity of mental activity, speed of motor reactions, the motor tempo, the subjective assessment of the degree of muscle effort, frequency of pulse, muscle tone, etc. Those factors have been studied and classified which tend to impede the sportsman from mobilizing and completing successfully a given action. The numerous data we have collected concerning changes in the psychological and physiological functions of the sportsman in a state of mobilized readiness allow us to adequately characterize this state. In this paper we shall dwell only on some general conclusions derived from the investigations we have made.

Before the execution of a certain sport action begins, a corresponding state of immediate readiness for the execution of that action develops. This can be seen particularly when the sportsman has to carry out some difficult action of great social importance for him. In this case he must mobilize and put into action all the forces at his command.

In order to demonstrate the influence of immediate preparation upon the outcome of an action, we made the following study. A group of juniors had to press with maximum strength a dynamometer, to execute a standing long jump, to make five penalty shots in basketball, and then to run 15 meters at maximum speed. First, they executed the task without any preliminary immediate preparation and then performed it after a preliminary immediate preparation. The results indicated that the investigated sportsmen had increased their performance by 13.01 percent on the dynamometer, 8.77 percent in the long jump, 27.62 percent in the penalty shots and 13.62 percent in the 15 meter run. In the control group no such improvement was noticed. Thus immediate preparation is a necessary condition for the successful execution of a given activity. Besides that, it is obvious that the more difficult the action the more necessary is the preliminary immediate preparation. The time given by sportsmen to the execution of special exercises before a given action helps them to develop a higher level of readiness for that action, which enables them to achieve greater success.

This state of immediate readiness before the execution of a given activity or action we have called *mobilization readiness*, since it involves a real mobilization of the sportsman's available forces for the execution of that activity.

The process of preparing for a sport involves different stages. There are three basic aspects of this preparation process: psychic, biological and motor. During the course of preparing for a sport many psychic functions and processes undergo a development that is specific to a given sport. The same also occurs for some physiological functions. But at the same time the level of these functions, on the one part psychic and on the other physiologic, during the execution of a certain action are always in a certain system. They always manifest themselves in connection with the execution of some actions. One puts namely this preparedness in the state of mobilization preparation (readiness) because in the daily life of the sportsman this preparedness is usually in a slumbering state. Therefore, in the execution of a sport activity for which a sportsman has been prepared, especially when it is necessary to achieve maximum results, a real mobilization of the available forces takes place. In this period of mobilization the psychic and physiological processes and functions necessary for the execution of a certain action are activated. As a result of this activation, the sportsman is placed in a state of "mobilization readiness" which enables him from the very beginning to execute an action with that intensity of muscle effort and precision of coordinated movements which are necessary for the successful execution of the action. This state in which the sportsman puts himself before the start should not be considered independent of his former preparation. The preparedness developed during the process of training provides the basis for the mobilization of the forces of the sportsman. In a word, the sportsman cannot mobilize that which is not available. Before a certain action he puts into a state of mobilization readiness his previous preparedness for the execution of that very action.

The state of mobilization readiness should be considered as involving psychic and physiological processes and functions of the sportsman which are the best for the beginning and execution of a certain action. The onset of these processes and functions takes place on the basis of a system conditioned by the character of the action to be done.

In the state of mobilized readiness, prior to the execution of an activity consisting of different actions, we distinguished a *general* readiness, and prior to the execution of separate actions a *concrete* mobilization readiness. As a confirmation we shall present the results from the investigation of our diploma candidate, Romanov. He investigated the efficiency of penalty shots in basketball as a function of different degrees of mobilization readiness. He found that before warming up and prior to mobilization readiness sportsmen achieved 43.6 percent precision but after immediate preparation 59.6 percent. After warming up, but without immediate preparation before the execution of the penalty shots, they achieved 50 percent precision and after the immediate preparation 62 percent. During the execution of the penalty shots at the time of rest without an immediate preparation, they reached a precision of 60 percent and with immediate preparation 72 percent.

Therefore, we see that when general mobilization readiness was present performance in the execution of penalty shots increased and that even in the presence of a general state of mobilization readiness the formation of concrete mobilization readiness before a given action always had a positive influence upon the results. Not only the coaches, but also the sportsmen should keep this in mind.

Putting the sportsman in a state of mobilization readiness is a fully conscious and purposeful process. In this case the coach plays a very important role, if he can find the right tone and words for help. Each incorrect intervention of the coach or of any other official can lead only to negative results and consequences. Therefore, one should not forget that no one but the sportsman himself is able to mobilize his forces for a certain activity.

When investigating the different levels of mobilization readiness we found two basic varieties: the *adequate* and the *inadequate*. There is an adequate readiness when it ensures successful results of the executed action. Inadequate mobilization readiness is present when there is no basis for successful execution of impending action or for attainment of a definite result. Mobilization readiness may be inadequate not only because it is insufficient, but also because it is excessively high. The insufficient mobilization of forces hampers successful execution of action, while the excessive one is dysfunctional only in those cases where it is necessary to keep a certain coordination of movements and efforts at the execution of an action.

We shall present an example. At the 1966 World Weightlifting Championships in Berlin, the world champion and record holder in the heavyweight category, Zhabotinski, began the snatch of 160 kilograms. This weight was relatively light for his capabilities, but because he underestimated it, he was unable to lift the bar sufficiently. As a result, the snatch failed. On his second attempt he pulled the bar too strongly, and it fell behind him. Only on the third attempt did he snatch the weight and fix it over himself. This example shows inadequate mobilization readiness on the first two attempts, insufficient on the first and excessive on the second. Only on the third attempt was mobilization readiness sufficient, *i.e.*, adequate for lifting the weight.

The state of mobilized readiness of man before the execution of any action is considered by psychologists as primarily a psychic state. Our investigations and those in the physiological literature show that before the execution of an action, and especially before competitions, not only does a mobilization of psychic activity occur but also mobilization of many physiological functions—increased pulse rate, greater frequency and depth of breathing, and increased muscle tone. At the same time changes occur in the capacity of the sportsman to execute some actions requiring a precision of execution. For example, strength, speed, flexibility, and other qualities grow.

All this permits us to consider the state of mobilization readiness as not only a psychic state, but also as a total state before the execution of an action. In this total state we distinguish three basic components: *psychic, biological, and motor.* These three components are reciprocally bound and conditioned, *i.e.*, the good state of one reflects positively upon the others and *vice versa.*

It is necessary to note that in the state of mobilized readiness we can observe not only a rise in the level of certain psychic and physiological functions, but also a system formed by these functions or as Levitov (1964) says, "something similar to a syndrome." In the state of mobilization readiness of the sportsman we see just this syndrome with its components consisting of psychic and physiological functions. In addition, one should note that the mobilization of the sportsman is always functional for the execution of a specific action, and, for this reason, the structure of this action determines also the structure of his mobilization readiness.

From the point of view of psychology the state of mobilization readiness includes all three components of the psychic activity of man: cognitive, emotional and volitional. These three components are in different structural

149

relations in accordance with the impending action of activity, but they always manifest themselves together.

Our investigations have established that mobilization readiness is determined by many factors. The knowledge of these factors can help the sportsman learn how to quickly and precisely form the appropriate state of mobilization readiness. These factors are:

1. *The structure of the state of mobilization readiness is determined by the structure of the impending action.* The structure of mobilization readiness is a model for the execution of an impending action on the highest level. For instance, in one and the same sport prior to different actions the muscle feeling resulting from the muscle efforts involved is different in one and the same sportsman. It is more precise and sharper in the weightlifters before the snatch than before the jerk and press, and in the gymnasts more precise for the horizontal bar than for floor gymnastics. Before lifting a weight the weightlifter readies himself to lift just that weight and if, immediately before going on the platform, the weightlifter is asked to diminish the weight by 5 kilograms and to lift the bar in the same movement, the weightlifter usually in this case is unable to lift the bar. This happens because he has not prepared himself to lift the new weight. And for the formation of this "purpose" he needs some time. For this reason the state of mobilization readiness is determined by the structure of the impending action, not only by its form but also by the degree of effort which is necessary for its execution.

2. *Degree of preparation for action.* The sportsman can be mobilized for the execution only of such actions for which he has been prepared through training. If the structure of the impending action is not well mastered this can affect his mobilization readiness.

3. *The surroundings and conditions of execution influence mobilization readiness.* They are: the stadium, sport hall, swimming pool, climatic conditions, tools, opponent, public, referees, coaches, etc. On the basis of received and processed information concerning these conditions, a plan is made for the execution of the impending action. The sportsman needs full and exact information about the conditions in which he is going to compete: But we should not forget that excessively detailed information can also hamper, especially such things as the formation of confidence in the sportsman.

4. *Personal and social importance for the sportsman of attaining this or that result in an action.* The relation of the sportsman to the action is built upon this basis. If the actions are of great social importance for the sportsman, they help him to better and more completely mobilize his forces and *vice versa.*

5. *Self-assessment of the sportsman concerning his preparation and determination to achieve the aim and tasks in the competition.* This self-assessment often differs from the assessment of the task provided by trainers and officials to sportsmen. Only that task has a directing force which the sportsman chooses for himself. On the basis of the self-assessment of the adequacy of his preparation, confidence (or uncertainty) is formed concerning the attainment of a certain result. On this basis arises one or another emotion.

6. *The degree of difficulty of the tasks to be executed by the sportsman in a certain action.* More difficult tasks require a higher level of mobilized readiness and vice versa. For example, weightlifters give less time for the formation of mobilization readiness when facing smaller weights than when they are confronted by record weights. In the last case the psychic and physiological processes proceed on a higher level.

7. *The personal experience of the sportsman in the formation of a similar state of mobilization readiness.* New and unexperienced sportsmen give less time to the mobilization of their forces than do the more experienced and qualified. There arise smaller changes in their psychic functions as compared with those of the better qualified. Their ability to achieve mobilization readiness is created and educated in the process of training and taking part in competition.

8. *The state of health of the sportsman.* The presence or absence of sickness, traumas, fatigue, etc., affect the level of mobilization readiness. Sport activity requires great tension in the sportsman's muscle-motive apparatus as well as in his vegetative system. If there are some breaches, or if the sportsman gets some signals that he is unable to endure these tensions, his mobilization readiness is affected. By a conscious volitional effort sportsmen can execute, risking very often their health, certain actions.

9. *Preceding state of the sportsman.* High or low spirits, for instance, influence the formation of mobilization readiness. It is necessary that before the competition, the sportsman get rid of different thoughts connected with failures in his family or similar things, because they can become dominant in his consciousness and provoke negative emotional states. The creation of good spirits and dispositions by means of humor, songs, music, etc., is a good basis for the formation of an adequate state of mobilization readiness in the sportsman.

10. *Presence or lack of necessary time for the formation of adequate mobilization readiness.* The more difficult the task the more time one needs for the mobilization of necessary forces. So for instance, at the platform the

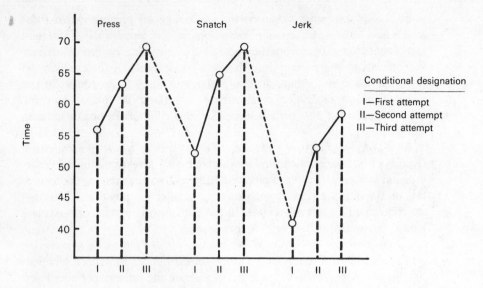

Figure 1 Dynamics of the duration of time of concentration of L. Zhabotinski (USSR) at the World Championships in Teheran (1965)

weightlifters, and at the start the high jumpers, need a longer time in the last stage of the formation of mobilization readiness when they stand before a greater weight or a higher height than when they stand before smaller weights or lower heights.

In Figure 1 we show the data of concentration of Zhabotinski at the World Championships in Teheran (1965). It is evident that with the increase of the weight of the bar in each of the three movements (press, snatch and jerk) the time for concentration increases also, *i.e.*, there is an increase of the time necessary for the formation of mobilization readiness. On the basis of our investigations concerning the length of concentration time of the best weightlifters in the world, we established the optimal limits of concentration time, *e.g.*, for finishing the formation of mobilization readiness when the weight of the bar is increased in the second and third attempts in the separate movements.

11. *Individual peculiarities of the sportsman.* The psychic processes and phenomena of sportsmen when in mobilization readiness differ on such factors as speed of reaction, intensity and stability of attention, length of concentration, pulse, muscle tone, etc. For every sportsman, before the

execution of a certain action there is an optimal level of proceeding for the separate psychic processes and phenomena in the formation of mobilization readiness. Therefore, together with the establishment of the general characteristic of a certain state of mobilization readiness, before the execution of an action, one should bear in mind that there is also a specific level and dynamic for every sportsman.

12. *Ability of the sportsman to regulate the level of mobilization readiness.* It was established that it is of great importance for the sportsman to be skillful in regulating the level of mobilization readiness. It is sufficient, if he says to himself that this task is not difficult for him, that he will easily cope with it, for him to decrease the level of his mobilization readiness at once. Immediately, this reflects upon the level of many psychic functions; for example, the intensity and concentration of the attention decreases too. Figure 2 shows the intensity of attention of the master in weightlifting, Dimitrov, at the National Championships in 1965. We see in this picture that before the snatch he has shown the lowest productivity on the correction test (7 combinations). The first time he does not jerk the weight. Why? Dimitrov himself answered this question: "Such a weight I always snatch. For me it is sufficient to clean it, and then I always jerk it very easily. After such a clean I jerk much heavier weights. For me it is important that I clean and put it on the breast. I thought it was not such a big weight and that I could cope with it easily. I managed to clean it but I was unable to jerk it from the breast. This happens to me for the first time." It was namely this preliminary underestimation of the weight that had affected the degree of his mobilization readiness and this, in turn, affected the intensity of his attention. But we have observed opposite cases too. So for instance, at the same Championships, Strashimirov had his highest productivity in the correction test before the jerk (see Figure 2). After he finished both movements —press and snatch—it became clear that he would be able to rank third if he could jerk the weight put on the bar. For this reason he developed the idea that he had to jerk that weight. This he managed to fulfill by way of self-determination. He jerked the weight and reached his goal. The increased state of mobilization of his forces reflected in the intensity of his attention when he worked on the correction test.

These two examples show the great importance of the role of the sportsman himself in the regulation of the degree of his mobilization readiness. This level is dynamic and sometimes wavers within the limits of a minute or even of some seconds, and, therefore, it is not possible when measuring the level of some functions of the sportsman always to have objective indices

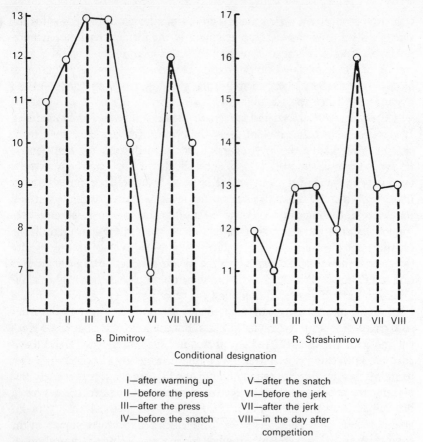

B. Dimitrov R. Strashimirov

Conditional designation

I—after warming up   V—after the snatch
II—before the press   VI—before the jerk
III—after the press   VII—after the jerk
IV—before the snatch VIII—in the day after
                      competition

Figure 2 Dynamics of the working productivity of heavy athletes during competitions (with the corrective figure test)

for the level of his mobilization readiness. The factors we mentioned determine mobilization readiness and for this reason we must take them into consideration, especially concerning the formation of this state of the sportsman.

In summary, it was established that from some functions in the state of mobilization readiness of sportsmen, we can get objective indices showing the degree of mobilization readiness. By the application of some methods we have been able to establish objective indices on the degree of mobilization readiness of sportsmen in different kinds of sport. There is no doubt that the results are of great importance for the immediate preparation of sportsmen, especially before the execution of difficult and responsible actions connected with great risks or having great social or personal importance for them.

Desensitization techniques   The desensitizing techniques that follow are protective mechanisms against overstress and could be called "psych down" maneuvers. They are meant to reduce the negative effects of a heightened arousal state, which can disrupt performance.

Specific techniques to be discussed in light of their methodologies, purposes, effectiveness, and specific relevance to sport are (1) progressive relaxation, (2) programmed deep muscle relaxation, (3) autogenic training, (4) hypnosis, (5) transcendental meditation, (6) yoga, (7) a simple relaxation response method, (8) biofeedback, and (9) "just relax!" Table 1 summarizes selected research findings relative to the physiological parameters modulated by some of techniques. Many of the data were gathered by Benson, Beary, and Carol (1974). The table is not claimed to be complete.

Progressive relaxation   In 1908 at Harvard University, Edmund Jacobson began his long years of devotion to relaxation and its benefits on the human body. In 1929, he published his book entitled *Progressive Relaxation,* presently in its fourth edition. Progressive relaxation seeks to control emotions by controlling the skeletal muscles. Jacobson believes there is a direct relationship between the two systems—control of one implies control of the other.

The body has only so much energy and cannot afford to waste any on expenditures due to neuromuscular tension in muscles not requiring it. Jacobson (1938) refers to such an energy waste as an "effort error." The first step in combatting the residual tension is recognizing it and sensing when it is not there. The technique is very simple—lying in a resting position, the individual alternately contracts and relaxes a muscle with decreasing intensity until the contraction is nearly imperceptible. This procedure is followed in various sequences with a variety of body parts. Jacobson explicitly declares that this program of nervous reeducation is bound to take several weeks or months to complete. Eventually the technique can be extended to the whole body. No instructor is needed, and all the information needed for relaxing either in a resting state or while active, can be found in Jacobson's book.

Cratty (1973) considers the assumption that peripheral muscular tension adjustment directly affects emotional and physiological states a

Table 1 Physiologic parameters supporting the existence of the relaxation response during the practice of various mental techniques*

Parameter	Programmed Relaxation	Autogenic Training	Hypnosis**	Transcendental Meditation	Zen and Hatha Yoga	Relaxation Response Technique
Oxygen consumption	N.M.	N.M.	↓(7)	↓(13,14)	↓(12)	↓(4)
Respiratory rate	N.M.	↓(10)	↓(3)	↓(1,14)	↓(2,12)	↓(4)
Heart rate	N.M.	↓(10)	↓(3)	↓(13,14)	↓(2,12)	N.M.
Alpha waves	N.M.	↑(10)	N.M.	↑(13,14)	↑(12)	N.M.
Skin resistance	N.M.	↑(10)	↑(6,8)	↑(13,14)	↑(2)	N.M.
Blood pressure	N.M.	?(10)	?(5)	0(14)	0(2,12)	N.M.
Muscle tension	↓(9)	↓(10)	N.M.	N.M.	N.M.	N.M.
Reaction time	N.M.	N.M.	N.M.	↑(11)	N.M.	N.M.

N.M. = not measured
? = inconclusive results
0 = no change

1. Allison (1970)
2. Bagchi and Wenger (1957)
3. Barber (1971)
4. Beary, Benson, and Klemchuk (1974)
5. Crasilneck and Hall (1959)
6. Davis and Kantor (1935)
7. Dudley, et al. (1963)
8. Estabrooks (1930)
9. Jacobson (1938)
10. Luthe (1969)
11. Shaw and Kolb (in press)
12. Sugi and Akutsu (1968)
13. Wallace (1970)
14. Wallace, Benson, and Wilson (1971)

*Adapted from Benson, Beary, and Carol (1974)
**Suggested deep relaxation.

tenuous one. However, it has previously been noted that reduced proprioception (sensation or feeling) in the skeletal muscles would indeed lead to reduced stimulation of the reticular activating system. Jacobson's assumption therefore seems plausible.

In addition to Jacobson's own findings of reduced muscular tension (Table 1), there is support for the use of programmed relaxation. Consider Steinhaus's (1964) statement:

> Complete relaxation means relaxing all muscles of the body as completely as possible. It is useful to induce sleep and to gain the maximal values of relaxation for the organs that are governed by the autonomic or involuntary nervous system. Differential relaxation means differentiating between muscles that are necessary for an activity and those that are not. It also means differentiating between strong and weak contractions of the active muscles and relaxing them as much as is consistent with doing the job in hand, effectively. Thus differential relaxation should be practiced continually in connection with every activity.

This leaves no doubt of the importance attributed by Steinhaus to progressive relaxation. Morgan (1973) has made reference again and again to the value of programmed relaxation in mediating anxiety produced in sport situations.

Robert Nideffer and William Deckner, in article 2.7, report a case study of a shot putter who improved his performance following the use of progressive relaxation. The reader is cautioned to take special notice of the authors' assertion that alternative explanations are possible, especially in view of the fact that their conclusions were drawn from the study of only one subject.

2.7

A case study of improved athletic performance following use of relaxation procedures

ROBERT M. NIDEFFER
University of Rochester, New York

C. WILLIAM DECKNER
Nashville, Tennessee

Summary.—In addition to its usefulness in areas of abnormal psychology, progressive relaxation is suggested to be of use to persons undergoing the temporary stress of athletic competition. A case study of improved performance in shot-putting is reported, and it is suggested that tension adjustment techniques may become a useful part of preparation for various athletic endeavors.

The detrimental effects of extremely high levels of tension prior to and during performance of athletic activities which emphasize endurance, e.g., long distance running, is generally recognized within athletic circles. However, with regard to activities which require the ability to exert intense effort for brief periods of time, e.g., weight lifting, the importance of relatively low levels of muscular tension is not widely accepted and, in fact, is apparently contrary to the prevailing conception that an athlete must be "worked up" in order to put forth maximum effort. It is suggested here that the optimal levels of muscular tension are often exceeded under the stress of competition for the latter type of activity as well and that tension reduction techniques can be beneficially used as part of preparation for these activities. The present case study of a shot-putter who had apparently reached a plateau in his performance is relevant to these suggestions.

S was a 20-yr.-old student who participated in intercollegiate shot-putting. He was 6 ft. 2 in. tall and weighed 210 lb. When first seen, he held the conference record in the shot: 52 ft., 3 in. While he was highly motivated

From *Perceptual and Motor Skills* 30(1970):821–822. Reprinted by permission of the author and the publisher.

to improve his performance, it was the opinion of his coaches that he had reached the limits of his physical potential. He practiced diligently and there was very little to improve in his form; his coaches felt he was simply too small to put the shot a greater distance. (Many shot-putters weigh more than 250 lb.) He had set the record of 52 ft., 3 in. the previous year; and, after many practice sessions and competitive meets, he had only been able to equal this distance four times. At the time he was seen, there were only 4 weeks remaining in the track season.

Procedure. S was seen only once. He was told that the tension he, and probably all athletes, felt during a track meet could result in a tightening of his arm, shoulder, and other muscles which are involved in shot-putting. It was suggested that this could prevent him from propelling the shot with maximal force. After this brief explanation, he was instructed in a progressive relaxation procedure. [Relaxation procedures are described in detail by Paul (1966), Schultz and Luthe (1959), and Wolpe (1958).] He was asked to practice the procedures twice a day, for 10 min. at a time, and also immediately prior to competition. He was given a written outline of the relaxation exercises and the interview was concluded. No attempt was made to desensitize *S* to scenes of competitive events.

Results. Two weeks after the initiation of the relaxation exercises, one of the authors received a long distance call from *S*. He had put the shot 52 ft. 7 in., setting a new conference record. In the remaining 2 weeks of the track season he began regularly putting the shot still farther in practice. In the final meet of the season he put the shot 53 feet, again setting a conference record.

There are, of course, possible explanations for these results other than the relaxation procedures. Regular practice and maturation cannot be ruled out as contributing to this athlete's improved performance. That a measurable and rather consistent improvement occurred within 4 weeks following introduction of the relaxation procedures, after a long period of no improvement, is suggestive of the important role of the procedures; but the same caution which must be exercised in drawing conclusions from any case study is necessary here.

It should be noted that *S* was not seen because he experienced unusual or in any sense abnormal tension and anxiety. The interview was accepted by *S* at the suggestion of one of the authors. In interview and in everyday interpersonal interaction, *S* was a poised and confident person. Moreover, prior to and during competition he was very likely no more anxious than other athletes. Accustomed to competition in various sports, he had been shot-putting for 6 years with considerable success.

In conclusion, a question for controlled research is the way in which tension level interacts with the different requirements of various types of athletic activities to impair or enhance performance. For the short-term intensive effort activities and endurance activities already mentioned, it may be found that tension levels under competitive stress are simply too high for maximal performance. For other activities, high levels of tension *per se* may not impair performance, but performance may be impaired when an athlete practices at one (relatively low) level of tension and performs in competition at a different (probably considerably higher) level of tension. Differential tension in practice and competition seems likely to be deterimental in activities which require precise timing and coordination, e.g., shooting a basketball. While doubtless there are individual differences in the ability to reduce the tension elicited by competitive events, explicit procedures by which to approach lower levels systematically may be of value to many athletes.

In 1968 a Czechoslovakian sport psychologist named Vanek tried progressive relaxation in an attempt to relax a very tense boxer at the Mexico City Olympic Games (Morgan, 1973). The attempt was successful to the extent that it mediated much of the boxer's anxiety and left him extremely relaxed—he came out of his corner smiling and carrying his arms at his side. Presumably he was still smiling when he was KO'd in one minute and thirty seconds of the first round. Perhaps this athlete needed the feeling of anxiety to perform, or maybe the progressive relaxation was so effective that it moved him too far down the arousal continuum. Some care must apparently be taken in adjusting arousal states.

Programmed deep muscle relaxation For individuals unwilling to make up their own program of relaxation, several programmed methods are available. For ten dollars, a tape of instructions and a booklet describing the method can be purchased. The method of one of the tapes (Marquis) is very similar to Jacobson's. Several graduate students have attested to its effectiveness in reducing their anxiety.

Autogenic training This method was developed in Germany in the 1920s through the observations of Oskar Vogt and was reformulated in the 1950s by J. H. Schultz, a German neurologist and psychiatrist.

Autogenic training is based on six psychophysiologic exercises devised by Schultz in 1956. These "standard exercises" are practiced in a quiet environment, in a horizontal position, with eyes closed.

Exercise 1 focuses on a feeling of heaviness in the limbs.

Exercise 2 focuses on a cultivation of a sensation of heaviness in the limbs.

Exercise 3 deals with cardiac regulation.

Exercise 4 consists of passive concentration on breathing

Exercise 5 cultivates a sensation of warmth in the upper abdomen.

Exercise 6 cultivates a feeling of coolness in the forehead.

The participant must be passive and not pursue the training with any intensity or compulsion—"just let it happen." A trained clinician is required until the individual has learned to shift into the relaxation response on his own.

Cratty (1973), from his earlier association with Vanek, reported the widespread use of autogenic training by European athletes, particularly in Czechoslovakia and the Soviet Union. It is of particular value in the competitive period just prior to performance. From Table 1 (p. 156), it can be seen that Luthe (1969) has reported typical relaxation response parameters—reduced circulatory, respiratory, and muscular tension conditions with increased generation of alpha brain waves and increased skin resistance.

Hypnosis Hypnosis is less useful in sport than some of the other techniques, because it requires properly trained personnel. Morgan (1973) states that hypnosis is highly effective for controlling anxiety but its usefulness in producing better performance is questionable. He reports an incident of a golfer whose success was closely tied to his performance on the first hole. A good hole meant a successful round, but a bad hole meant a frustrating round. Hypnosis was used successfully to change these feelings; however, like Vanek's boxer, he smiled but performed badly.

In article 2.8 Warren Johnson reviews the literature on hypnosis and motor performance and answers questions about the use of hypnosis in sport. Results are not as dramatic as popularly believed and are sometimes the opposite of what is expected.

2.8 Hypnosis and muscular performance*

WARREN R. JOHNSON
University of Maryland, College Park

In this paper I shall (1) review the experimental literature on hypnosis in relation to gross muscular performance, (2) illustrate some ways in which hypnosis has been useful to athletes, (3) suggest some uses of hypnosis as an experimental tool, and (4) endeavor to answer several questions concerning the use of hypnosis in sports competition.

Although in popular opinion hypnosis bestows superhuman powers and although some subjects do, indeed, display marked increments in performance under certain hypnotic conditions, the fact remains that the controlled studies conducted to date do not present clear-cut or consistent evidence of heightened performance in the hypnotic or posthypnotic states. Reviews by Hull (1933), Gorton (1949) and Crasilneck and Hall (1959) dealing with the physiology of hypnosis include brief discussions concerning muscular performance. The conclusions reached by these reviewers were necessarily based upon experiments which involved small muscle and usually mild work, and few subjects. In those studies criteria of depth of trance were usually not clearly specified; the exact suggestions given were usually not reported; and it is often not possible to determine just what role hypnosis actually played in the experiments. A single short review concerned with hypnosis as it might relate to performance in sports is available (Cofer and Johnson, 1960).

Studies which have included measures of large muscle work, rigorous controls and reasonably large numbers of subjects have produced evidence decidedly favorable to the hypnotic state. Roush (1951), whose study is unique with respect to its large number of subjects—twenty—and very severe criteria of trance depth, reported statistically significant advantages to the hypnotic state in all her tests—grip strength, elbow flexion strength and a hanging by hands test of endurance. Similarly, Hottinger (1958) found that the performance of his six subjects improved significantly in the hyp-

From *Journal of Sports Medicine and Physical Fitness* 1(1961):71–79. Reprinted by permission of Edizioni Minerva Medica.

*Appreciation is expressed to Milton Erickson, M.D., of Phoenix, Arizona, for his critical reading of this paper.

notic state in tests of back and leg strength and appreciably in the Sargent jump. However, their grip strength did not improve. In a third study involving seven students, Ikai and Steinhaus (1961) reported results highly favorable to performance following hypnosis, but hypnotic controls were not specified in detail.

On the other hand, Orne (1959) found that if sufficiently well motivated, all of his nine subjects were able to hold a kilogram weight at arm's length longer in the nonhypnotic state even though his hypnotic suggestions were calculated to elicit maximum performance. (Incidentally, Orne's paper, "The Nature of Hypnosis: Artifact and Essence" should be studied by anyone seriously interested in the range of methodological problems and pressing questions confronting research workers in hypnosis.) Our own studies of strength, endurance, and power in the nonhypnotic, hypnotic and posthypnotic states have also resulted in generally negative findings; however, there were indications that endurance performance (supine press of a 47 pound barbell to exhaustion) improved when hypnosis was introduced. Our only consistently positive findings have occurred when negative suggestions were given. That is, we have always been successful when we have given suggestions designed to make performance worse than usual.

Our experimental studies of the effects of hypnotic suggestions upon physical performance may be summarized as follows.

In our first experiment entitled "The Effects of Post-Hypnotic Suggestions on All-Out Effort of Short Duration" (Johnson et al., 1960), the particular suggestions did not improve the performance of the subjects in an all-out dash of 100 revolutions on the bicycle ergometer set for 26.8 pounds resistance, (average time about 40 seconds). It is interesting to note, however, that these subjects invariably reported feeling better after the ride when the posthypnotic suggestions were given even though they had no recollection at nonhypnotic levels that suggestions had been given to them at all. Interestingly, this is apparently the only reported experimental study of hypnosis which has included severe respiratory and circulatory as well as gross muscle responses.

In a second study (Johnson and Kramer, 1961), stereotyped hypnotic and posthypnotic suggestions designed to contain both cognitive and affective elements and presented at both deep and light trance levels as well as in the nonhypnotic state did not result in statistically significant improvements in the performance of twelve subjects. The physical tests were grip strength, Sargent jump and supine press to exhaustion of a forty-seven-pound barbell. However, although the group performance was not significantly different in the various conditions of the study, the performance of one subject in the supine press test was quite remarkable and his scores had to be excluded from the statistical analysis.

This subject was a professional football player and habitual weight trainer weighing about 235 pounds and having a mesomorphic body type of perhaps 5-7-1 by the Sheldon system. Like the rest of the subjects he had practiced the supine press in advance of the study so as to plateau his scores and to insure against muscular soreness during the study. In his first testing session, the suggestions were given but hypnosis was not utilized; his score was about as usual, 130. Hypnosis was then introduced and in the next three testings his scores were 180 (when he was stopped by the investigator), 230 and 333 respectively. In contrast, the next strongest athlete began the study at fifty-seven presses and reached a maximum of seventy-five.

To determine whether this individual was dependent upon hypnosis to perform in this way, he was later retested without hypnosis and was stopped by the investigator at 350 presses. Prior to this testing he spoke of having an entirely new idea of his potentialities and was absolutely certain that he could surpass his old record. It is noted that he recovered quickly after each exercise bout and reported a complete freedom from muscle soreness.

Some months later it was possible to employ the technique of age regression to ascertain possible reasons for the sudden tapping of performance resources. (In hypnotic age regression the subject does not *remember* in the ordinary sense, but presumably relives events of his past. Penfield has elicited what appears to be similar behavior by means of electrical stimulation of the temporal lobes.) When led to relive and verbalize his first trance state test this subject gave a distinct impression of having accepted the suggestions as vivid reality and apparently his performance became, literally, a matter of life and death to him. In the age regression to that first performance in hypnosis he confirmed what he had said after his posthypnotic performance. That is, he would give up in complete fatigue and then watch in amazement as his arms continued to raise the weight, seemingly by themselves.

— A common explanation of heightened performance in the hypnotic state is that suggestibility is increased, inhibitions are removed and there may be selective anesthesia for pain and fatigue. However, this case led to the speculation that Gellhorn's explanation of exceptional muscular performance under conditions of emotional excitement might also have application to exceptional performance in the hypnotic state. That is, it may be "due not only to the action of the adrenal medullary secretions on the striated muscles but also to the intensification of discharges from the motor cortex resulting from impulses which reach the motor cortex from the hypothalamus (Gellhorn, 1960)."

In a third experiment, when different types of hypnotic and posthypnotic suggestions were compared as to their effectiveness in altering performance in a test of endurance—the supine press to exhaustion of a forty-seven-pound barbell—it was found that although moderate *pep talk* type suggestions seemed to get better results with most subjects than more quietly reasoned suggestions or suggestions intended to take effect posthypnotically in response to a signal while the subjects exercised, this advantage was not at statistically significant levels. However, posthypnotic suggestions designed to deteriorate performance were invariably successful. This was true in spite of the fact that the subjects had no posthypnotic recall that such suggestions had been given to them, and they were completely mystified that their most desperate efforts failed to bring their performance up to customary levels.

So much for our very modest list of experimental studies. I will now briefly describe two case studies which illustrate quite different ways in which hypnosis may be used to affect gross motor performance. I would like to emphasize that although a number of subjects are not involved, I attach great importance to case studies which may reveal potentialities of the human nervous system.

In the first of these which was published with the title, "Body Movement Awareness in the Non-Hypnotic and Hypnotic States" (Johnson, 1961a), exceptional ability to verbalize complex bodily movement in the hypnotic state was demonstrated. A very successful baseball player requested assistance in getting out of a protracted batting slump. Before being hypnotized, he was asked to describe in detail just what had gone wrong with his batting; but he was unable to do this in spite of much effort to describe and demonstrate physically the several movements. Subsequently in the deep trance state and with instructions to verbalize spontaneously at a signal, the subject—to his own complete surprise—was able to make a meticulous analysis of his movements while batting and to pinpoint a number of errors of foot work, pelvic rotation, grip on the bat, timing of swing and use of his eyes. Moreover, when given a choice as to whether to recall this analysis posthypnotically or to have it more gradually *come to him* as he played, he elected the latter more gradual and less self-conscious choice.

This man's batting—which this investigator has at no time observed—immediately improved and he finished the season with a .400 average. Of psychological interest is the fact that when he returned to report on his season he attributed the entire analysis to the investigator and was quite sure that he remembered receiving direct and specific suggestions to correct his movements. To repeat, however, he alone was responsible for his corrective analysis. One must wonder at the extent to which vague or uncertain bodily states might be verbalized under hypnotic conditions such as these.

The second case study was published under the title "Hypnotic Analysis of a Case of Aggression Blockage in Baseball Pitching" (Johnson, 1961b). A professional baseball pitcher requested hypnotic suggestions which would make him more aggressive when he played because he could perform at his best only when he was unreasonably angry. Since psychiatric evaluation of this man did not contraindicate approaching the problem at hypnotic levels, he was trained to enter a deep trance and, in due course, to experience age regression.

When regressed to childhood he revealed that he had severely injured his younger brother and that the experience was especially painful to him because he had escaped punishment. This event seemed to provide the model of the cycle of rage, attack, guilt reaction and aggression avoidance which was later to manifest in the sport situation. That is, the rage which accompanied successful pitching was followed by a severe but unconscious guilt reaction from which the subject protected himself in subsequent games by *easy going* and *lackadaisical* play until, finally, his hostile feelings would build up and spill over in another highly successful rage.

This subject was soon able to realize that aggressive behavior need not be antisocial or unsportsmanlike and need not be followed by feelings of guilt. He was then able to pitch consistently well throughout the season with no further recurrence of rage–guilt reaction cycle.

Before turning to the question and answer portion of my paper, I would like to describe a use of hypnosis as an experimental tool which I believe has a place in, for example, certain fatigue and nutrition studies. The phenomenon of posthypnotic amnesia makes possible the obliteration from conscious recall of what occurs in the trance state. In a recently published study of warm-up (Massey, Johnson, and Kramer, 1960), when the subjects were tested on the bicycle ergometer, it was always posthypnotically such that they were unaware they had warmed up or not; and, indeed, they remained in ignorance, at nonhypnotic levels at least, as to the nature of the study. Similarly, in food deprivation studies it would be possible to keep subjects in ignorance of whether or not they had eaten or how much or what; and it would be possible to give suggestions which would increase or reduce feelings of hunger regardless of whether or not food were eaten.

It is presumed—and I stress this emphatically—that any such research would be under strict medical supervision.

Let us turn now to several questions which my students have helped me to identify as being of special interest.

(1) *Question* How might the discrepancies in the published reports concerning the effects of hypnosis on muscular performance be explained?

Answer There are a number of possibilities. The most obvious are those related to experimental controls. For example, how about the trance depth? It is perhaps significant that Roush imposed the most rigid criteria of deep trance hypnosis that I am aware of in a study—and her findings were uniformly favorable to the hypnotic state. (In this regard it is important to realize that there are many degrees of trance depth ranging from the very light—in which the subject is well aware of his surroundings—to the very deep stuporous condition of the profound trance.) How about the suggestions given and their mode of presentation? The most dramatic improvement in performance that we have observed was in response to stereotyped suggestions, calmly stated and designed to persuade the subjects to do their best; but I am under the impression that efforts to *whip up* subjects with even very moderate *pep talk* type suggestions such as we used are more likely to be effective with most subjects. How about the possibility that a subject is faking hypnosis? Orne has shown that experienced hypnotists can be fooled by subjects who know relatively little about hypnosis (Orne, 1959). How about the physical fitness level of the subjects? Although this consideration has not been tested experimentally and no study that I am aware of mentions the physical fitness level of the subjects, my experience has led me to suspect that hypnotic suggestions are more likely to improve the strength performance of nonathletes than of athletes; and conversely, that hypnotic suggestions are more likely to improve the endurance performance of athletes than nonathletes. If these observations are correct, it is probably because by training, athletes already know how to require something approaching maximum contraction from their striated muscles; and in regard to endurance, the athletes can stay with a task long enough to become bored and/or uncomfortable with it and are likely to be helped by suggestions which minimize discomfort and divert attention from the unpleasant side effects of the task. At any rate, nearly all of the subjects in our studies have been athletes and I gather that most of those involved in the other published studies have been nonathletes.

(2) *Question* To what extent is hypnosis used by athletes today?

Answer One can only speculate. Some psychologists, psychiatrists, and professional hypnotists have told me that over the years they have, on occasion, helped athletes in various ways. The recent publicity given to hypnosis, coupled with the popular impression that hypnosis bestows something like magical powers, has doubtless led many athletes to seek out this kind of assistance. Of course a few such instances have been publicized but most have not.

(3) *Question*   Has hypnosis actually helped athletes to perform better?

Answer   Yes, in a variety of ways, some of which have nothing to do with increasing strength or endurance. And, of course, it has also failed to do so. There is no question in my mind that the baseball players referred to earlier in this paper were helped by their respective analyses at hypnotic levels. Many other examples of what appear to be improved performance due to hypnosis could be given; but I will mention only a few.

A renowned medical hypnotist told me recently of his having done such things as increase the aggressiveness and confidence of some athletes, improve the steadiness of marksmen and the performance of a shot-putter. An Australian psychiatrist and former champion swimmer has described to me the work with hypnosis of a physiologist-swimming coach in Australia; and he was quite confident that his man had helped his swimmers gain the self-assurance and self-discipline needed for high level performance in competition. This psychiatrist, by the way, was unequivocal in his belief that the Australian coach had used hypnosis quite legitimately, for it had merely helped the athletes achieve something like their full potential. Gale (1960), a medical hypnotist, has described uses of hypnosis in sports along lines of relaxing athletes and helping them learn skills. Other hypnotists have reported having helped athletes adjust more adequately to the rigors of training, sleep better, gain weight and so on. As far as I know no one has claimed to have elevated a mediocre talent to champion level performance by hypnosis.

When an athlete performs well after having received hypnotic suggestions it is always possible to raise the question: Might he not have done just as well on that occasion if hypnosis had not been employed? This question is unanswerable. Sports like track and swimming would provide an excellent testing ground for studying the entire question experimentally; but sports in which one is working directly against an opponent—sports like wrestling, boxing, and football—would be useless in this regard because they lack controllable conditions.

(4) *Question*   Is it actually possible to increase the aggressiveness of athletes by hypnosis; and if so is it safe to do so?

Answer   Two men who deserve to be called authorities on hypnosis, one a psychiatrist and the other a psychologist, have told me of having done so successfully. Both were quite confident that no harm was done to the athletes psychologically. Indeed, the medical hypnotist explained that the only ill effect that he had observed in such cases was that the athletes were subsequently somewhat more difficult to hypnotize.

Now these men were professionally qualified to make judgments regarding the basic mental health of their subjects and the advisability of using hypnosis in this way. But generally speaking I am under the impression that students of mental health would recommend extreme caution when considering the matter of manipulating aggressiveness, for this is certainly one of man's fundamental conflicts and is often a major consideration in the behavior disorders. I personally have never been willing to use hypnosis in this way without psychiatric participation. However, I have asked quite a few subjects in deep trance states how suggestions designed to make them more aggressive in sports would make them feel. All were happy with the idea and wanted suggestions which would encourage them to be more aggressive in a sportsmanlike way. On the other hand, all but one felt threatened by the idea of receiving suggestions which might encourage unsportsmanlike aggressiveness; and typically they would begin to emerge spontaneously from the trance unless reassured that no such suggestions were intended. I have encountered only one athlete who did not care whether suggestions given to him would make him more aggressive in antisocial as well as social ways. The meaner the better was his motto. At any rate, it seems noteworthy that suggestions designed to heighten sportsmanlike aggressiveness were invariably acceptable and desired.

This question of the effects of hypnotic suggestions upon aggressive behavior can be studied experimentally with built-in safeguards to protect the welfare of the subjects.

(5) *Question* When changes in behavior are brought about by means of hypnosis, do these changes last or are they transitory?

Answer When hypnosis is used in therapy, its effects are sometimes lasting and sometimes not; and I suspect that the same is true of its use in relation to physical performance. If a change is for the better and is rewarding to the subject, then one might expect the behavior to be self-perpetuating. The professional football player referred to earlier who performed so remarkably in the endurance test when given hypnotic suggestions told of acquiring a new concept of his capabilities when he saw what he could do. Rightly or wrongly, he felt too that this new self concept was related to his subsequent achieving of first string all-star standing.

Be that as it may, experienced people with whom I have talked about this matter are inclined to think of hypnotic effects lasting for appreciable periods, especially if the suggestions are reinforced occasionally. Still, there are many cases in which nonreinforced, hypnotically induced changes have lasted for years.

(6) Question Assuming that improvement in some muscular performance is accomplished by hypnosis, could not some other technique such as a pep talk, greater discipline or a drug have done just as well?

Answer This is another unanswerable question; but it is like asking: Although penicillin stopped this infection, might not some other treatment have worked just as well? Penicillin is no less valuable because other means may also get results.

(7) Question Does improving performance by hypnosis bring about dependency on it?

Answer This has not been my experience nor that of other experienced persons with whom I have talked concerning the reactions of normal people. However, many people feel exceptionally good and relaxed after having been *hypnotized* and enjoy repeating the experience because it is gratifying to them.

(8) Question Is it safe to hypnotize athletes?

Answer The present state of uncertainty on this question is suggested by the fact that a recent article in a medical publication argued both that (1) hypnosis is dangerous because it may make athletes go beyond their limits and damage themselves and (2) hypnosis is useless because all it can do is help athletes attain their potential.

My feeling is that it is not possible to give a yes or no answer to this question without knowing the circumstances in specific cases. One would have to know *how* hypnosis was used. None of the several psychiatrists—including the one who worked with me—who know of my previously mentioned work with the baseball players seemed to see anything hazardous in those hypnotic analyses; and neither young man seems to have suffered from the experience. Quite the contrary. These appear to be examples of cases in which hypnosis was definitely instrumental in improving performance in competition. Moreover, the sports-minded psychologists and psychiatrists with whom I have discussed this matter have all felt that the cases which they have participated in or observed were not hazardous to the athletes.

On the other hand, it is exceedingly important to emphasize that there may be very serious dangers associated with hypnosis even though the subjects are *known* to be in good mental health. For this reason I believe that it would be extremely unfortunate if coaches generally were to feel free to begin hypnotizing their athletes in the hope of improving their performance.

Nothing that I have said in this paper should be interpreted to mean that I would encourage such a development. Following are some of my reasons for feeling this way.

Although there is far from universal agreement as to the nature or effects of hypnosis, I suspect that most experienced hypnotists would agree that generally speaking it is easier to make people sick than it is to make them well. That is, a healthy person can be made to feel very bad in a variety of ways by means of hypnotic suggestions, but one cannot be at all sure in advance that hypnotic suggestions will cure any given ill person. Moreover, it may be recalled that in a controlled experiment, our suggestions designed to damage physical performance were always successful—which was certainly not the case with our suggestions intended to improve performance. Considerations like these have led me to conclude that people tend to respond better to suggestions that will have a negative effect on them than to those intended to have a positive effect. I have wondered whether this situation might be due to our traditional methods of child rearing in which the young are led (or programmed) to believe that they have been or are chronically on the verge of being *bad*, in danger or sick.

At any rate, if one is to claim that hypnosis can increase muscular performance, improve self-confidence, reduce nervousness, and so on, he must also take into account the other side of the coin which warns that hypnosis can be used with greater probability of success to make such things worse.

Monroe (1960), who has written on the possible dangers of hypnosis in medicine, has said: "It seems to the author axiomatic that any medicine or medical procedure that can be good for the patient might also be bad. Anyone who has observed the hypnotic trance is aware of the intense suggestibility and increased cooperation of the subject . . . such increased cooperation might under certain circumstances be exploited by the unethical." I would add to this the thought that this increased cooperation might also be exploited by the well-intentioned but ignorant, insensitive or careless. Thus, to cite one of many possible examples of the misuse of hypnosis, a woman physician recently told me that she attempted, by direct hypnotic suggestions, to *dispose of* a patient's nightmares—and of course profoundly upset the patient. Similar problems could and undoubtedly would arise in sports if coaches were to feel free to begin using hypnosis without intensive training and clear understanding as to its appropriate and inappropriate uses.

Another very important factor bearing upon whether or not hypnosis is safe is the hypnotist himself. What kind of personality should he have? The enormously respected behavior scientist Hilgard, who is now conducting intensive research on hypnosis at Stanford, commented in a personal communication: "Any investigation that intrudes as much as hypnosis does into the life of an individual must be conducted by mature and sensitive people. Under these circumstances I see no danger in it." Obviously, these qualities—which of course are not guaranteed by academic or professional degrees—must be coupled with suitable training in hypnotic technique and study of personality functioning.

CONCLUSIONS

The basic purpose of this paper is to encourage a variety of research projects which will shed light upon the nature and potentialities of hypnosis with reference to physical performance.

It is popularly believed that to *hypnotize* an athlete is to attempt to super-charge him by direct suggestions in something of the manner of a stimulating drug. This paper is intended to point out that direct suggestions designed to improve muscular strength and/or endurance cannot be counted upon to be effective—although under certain conditions they may be; and it is intended to emphasize that hypnotic or posthypnotic suggestions designed to reduce physical performance are much more likely to be effective. A further intent of this paper is to illustrate a number of uses of hypnosis in relation to physical performance and research which have nothing whatever to do with stimulating individuals to greater effort. These uses may have to do with investigating certain neuromuscular and psychological problems which may profoundly affect and perhaps limit physical performance, or they may have to do with controlling the psychological variable in certain types of experiments.

Finally, although this paper is intended to expand the general understanding of hypnosis and its applications in the study of human performance, it is not intended to encourage its use by individuals lacking training not only in hypnotic technique but in psychodynamics as well.

Table 1 on page 156 shows that when deep relaxation was suggested to individuals in a hypnotic state, certain physiological parameters were altered in the direction of relaxation. The effects of hypnosis are varied, however, and no one has found a unique physiological index that adequately defines the hypnotic state (Barber, 1971).

Transcendental meditation This is alleged to be an easily learned technique that appears to elicit the relaxation response effectively (Table 1). It requires little time per day (40 minutes) and has no mystical overtones except perhaps the repetition of the "mantra" (the stimulus, usually a Sanskrit or Tibetan phrase, that elicits the relaxation). Meditation with an awareness of the mantra is the key to restful wakefulness. Transcendental meditation can make one more alert mentally while less aroused emotionally and subcortically (Brown, 1974). Is this not what we are looking for in sport—readiness to perform alertly without the disruptive concomitants of heightened arousal? Whether this state can indeed occur and enhance the performance of athletes in high-stress situations remains to be seen.

In the meantime, transcendental meditation is gaining respectability from scientists and a number of athletes are becoming involved. It is rumored that Joe Namath and Bill Walton have undergone meditation training. Alert TV watchers noticed Arthur Ashe doing TM during breaks at Wimbledon. Steve Hrubosky, St. Louis Cardinal pitcher, also uses TM. G. Jacobson (1973) reported that Craig Lincoln, Olympic medal winner and diving coach, extols the virtues of the technique. Lincoln made the following comments: "The whole idea behind meditation is that it is a means of resting for dynamic activity." The physiological benefits include greater stamina and faster reaction time; the psychological benefits are heightened perception and clarity of mind.

Chris Kanellakos, in article 2.9, offers an expanded description of transcendental meditation as it relates to both scientific scrutiny and applicability to use by athletes.

2.9 Transcendental meditation . . . what's it all about?

CHRIS KANELLAKOS
Menlo Park, California

If Transcendental Meditation improved Craig Lincoln's diving enough to win him a medal in Munich, as he believes it did, or if notables like astronaut Russell L. Schweickart, Alfred L. Jenkins of the State Department, and others, plus 250,000 Americans claim that this restful exercise offers perfect preparation for activity, isn't it logical to assume that TM, as it is often called, might also benefit the athlete?

Bill Walton and UCLA teammates, several members of the N.Y. Jets, and many other athletes are already giving it a try.

Precisely what is TM?

It is an effortless mental technique, practiced each morning and evening for 15 to 20 minutes, as one sits comfortably with his eyes closed.

The person begins by *thinking* of a sound (or mantra) chosen for him by a TM instructor. That sound eventually disappears, the mind experiences subtler levels of thought, and, finally, by transcending, arrives at "the source of the thought."

This process expands the conscious mind by bringing it into contact with the field of creative intelligence, while the body is still in deep rest. At the end of the 20-minute period, all the body's tension has been released, and the meditator emerges fresh and vigorous, ready for action.

Careful research into TM's physical and psychological effects leaves no doubt that it does benefit the athlete's performance. Once considered a fad, this ancient mental technique is now keeping scientists and researchers busy with projects that measure the effects of TM on the practicing individual. It was introduced to this country in the early 1960s by Maharishi Mahesh Yogi (1968), an Indian monk, and spread from the campuses to "middle" America, bridging even the famous generation gap. Since its practice takes only about 20 minutes twice a day and requires no special belief, age, or education, anyone can take it up.

"Anyone who *believes* in it!" I remarked once, skeptically, to my husband,

From *Scholastic Coach* 43(March 1974):48ff. Reprinted by permission of the author and the publisher.

Demetri Kanellakos, an electrical engineer in radio-physics and a meditator who spends his lunch hours running around the track at Stanford's Angel field.

"No, you don't have to believe in it. Just do it!" he emphasized. "Remember, I was skeptical myself when I started TM four years ago, and only three weeks later I noticed that during meditation my breathing rate decreased, my pulse slowed down, and I came out of it with a feeling of complete rejuvenation, ready to tackle the most difficult project, or breeze around the track in sizzling temperatures."

Three months later he wrote a memo to the Physiology Department of Stanford Research Institute, where he works, proposing a study of the physiological changes on meditators.

"Psychobiologists," he explained, "already know the three states of consciousness: that of wakefulness, during which we have thoughts, experiences, and self-awareness; that of deep sleep, during which we have neither experiences nor awareness; and that of dreaming, during which thoughts emerge but no self-awareness.

"During TM we enter a *fourth* state of consciousness, the Transcendental state, during which we have no thoughts at all, and yet we are fully aware. There is a lot to learn about that state."

His proposal was carefully studied, and tabled. Several weeks later, he walked in and laid a booklet on the table.

"That's Keith Wallace's Ph.D. thesis!" he announced. "Keith is a physiologist at UCLA. His work shows that during TM the cardiac output decreases and the lactic acid is carried away three times faster than during ordinary rest; and it stays down longer. I bet that's why I feel much lighter when I jog."

A few months later, Keith Wallace, Herbert Benson, a cardiologist at Harvard Medical School, and Dr. Archie Wilson of the U.C. Irvine Medical School reported in the *American Journal of Physiology,* (Sept. '71), and later in *Scientific American* (Feb. '72), the results of a detailed study of 36 meditators.

They noticed that during TM the metabolic rate was noticeably reduced and the oxygen consumption fell sharply to an average of 18%, as compared to a mere 9% drop only after several hours of sleep.

Measurements of the blood lactate, the substance associated with high blood pressure, neurosis, and anxiety attacks, proved that the concentration "declined precipitously . . . nearly three times faster than the rate of decrease of people normally resting . . ." More surprising was the fact that at the end of the post-meditative period, the lactate level was still down.

Another interesting finding was that the galvanic skin resistance to an electric current increased 2.5 times during meditation. This indicated that although the subjects were deeply relaxed, they were in a thoroughly wakeful state—a fact also confirmed by brain wave tests.

Which brings us to the paradoxical, two-word description of the Transcendental state: restful alertness. Proponents of TM claim that the deep rest reached through TM rejuvenates the nervous system, and enables the meditator to tap that reservoir of energy and intelligence of which about 90%, psychologists tell us, is left untapped.

Other researchers, such as Robert Shaw and David Kolb at the University of Texas, had also proved that TM speeds up reaction time, indicating increased perception and alertness, and better coordination of mind and body.

And in the U. of Sussex, John Graham (1971) found increased auditory ability and refinement following TM. Breath rate decrease was also reported by Dr. John Allison in *The Lancet* (April, 1970), a British medical journal.

Physiologically, then, the mental state of meditation is a shift from very high to very low, a change in the restituting mechanism of the human organism, for a recuperation prior to returning to a more dynamic activity. That state of "underactivity" is considered important by Dr. Ernst Gellhorn, professor Emeritus of the U. of Minnesota Medical School, and Dr. William Kiely of USC, who wrote in *The Journal of Nervous and Mental Disease* that the clinical effects of certain behavior therapies which employ skeletal muscular relaxation as a technique for modifying central nervous system arousal, were beneficial and that EEG (electroencephalograph) patterns in states of meditation proved that conditions reflective of very low dominance were compatible with full awareness.

Just as enough rest and sleep are vital to the athlete, TM is considered a must by meditator athletes, who claim that it is the only way to feel completely reinvigorated.

Eddie Bell told the *New York Post* that he was amazed at the results. "After 20 minutes of it," he explained, "I felt refreshed, like I'd slept seven or eight hours. I felt like I had my whole day ahead of me. It was like I'd been in a much deeper form of relaxation."

"The whole metabolic rate is reduced during meditation," Demetri Kanellakos explained. "As the breathing rate and oxygen intake increase, they allow the respiratory mechanisms to slow down. Upon return to the normal wakeful state and full activity, there is a harmonious cooperation between the metabolic rate mechanisms and the cardio-respiratory system; the athlete is more fit, energetic, and more confident.

"In other words, TM does to you what a tune-up does to your car engine."

In examining the psychological effects of TM, Dr. David Orme-Johnson (1973) of the U. of Texas, El Paso, measured the galvanic skin resistance of meditators and non-meditators, while subjecting both groups to repeated loud noises. It took the non-meditators about 26 repetitions to get accustomed to the noise and stop producing changes in the GSR amplitude. The meditators adjusted after 12 such trials.

This quick adjustment to the environment is correlated with better functioning of the autonomic nervous system. To the researcher, the results mean better resistance to environmental stress and, therefore, less chance of psychosomatic disease and behavioral instability.

Dr. Theo Fehr (1974), a psychologist at the U. of Cologne, West Germany, and his colleagues studied the effects of TM on 49 TM teachers, through a comprehensive paper-and-pencil personality test.

He divided the subjects into two groups; one consisting of those meditating up to four years, and the other of those meditating from four to 11 years. Each group was compared to a separate control group of non-meditators.

The results showed that the first group scored lower than the control group in the irritability and inconsideration level. The second group of the more experienced meditators also scored lower in nervousness, depression, tension, and neuroticism, and scored higher in sociability and calmness.

What does all this mean to an athlete? It means that freedom from depression, tension, and psychosomatic disease can make him a happier person and therefore a better athlete than the individual who gets irritable and loses his cool. Through TM, he can gradually acquire the qualities that are characteristic of self-actualized people.

A major breakthrough occurred during hearings before the Committee on Crime in the summer of 1971, when Drs. Benson and Wallace reported their findings on a study concerning drug abuse among meditators. In a letter to Congressman Claude D. Pepper, Dr. Benson wrote:

. . . Our recently completed study entitled "Decreased drug abuse with transcendental meditation: A Study of 1,862 Subjects," indicated that individuals who regularly practiced transcendental meditation: (a) decreased or stopped abusing drugs, (b) decreased or stopped engaging in drug selling activity, and (c) changed their attitudes in the direction of discouraging others from abusing drugs. No data were collected concerning hard-core addiction, but 16.9% claimed use of narcotics such as heroin, opium, morphine, and cocaine before starting the practice of . . . meditation. After 22-23 months of meditation, only 1.2% claimed continued use of these drugs.

Dr. Benson warned that no data on the socioeconomic background of the subjects had been available and suggested that further investigation into the effects of TM was necessary.

As research gained momentum, Dr. Leon Otis, director of the Dept. of Psychobiology and Physiology at Stanford Research Institute, agreed to supervise the pilot study Demetri Kanellakos had proposed before.

Dr. Otis himself did some preliminary work in August 1971, at the California State U. at Humbolt, where a TM teacher's course was under way. He learned that 84% of 396 drug users reported that they had given up drugs after starting meditation. This included 42 of the 49 opiate users.

A random sampling of TM practitioners on the mailing list of Students' International Meditation Society (SIMS), Los Angeles, showed less impressive but still significant results. Of 199 practitioners, 109 claimed to have completely given up drugs. Seven of 10 opiate users made the same claim.

Dr. Otis explained at the beginning of the SRI pilot study:

> There have been reports that TM has been helpful in reducing drug abuse. Therefore, we believe that it is in the public interest to conduct a helpful investigation under controlled conditions to find out what effects, if any, this technique has on changing behavioral patterns and possible abnormal physiological function.

He also stated that this study was not an endorsement of the technique, but only an investigation into the professed benefits. At a later date he reported that some data collected at SRI suggested the effectiveness of TM in producing subjectively-felt beneficial effects, which might be summarized as increased self-regard and decreased anxiety.

Whether it is the decreased anxiety or the complete lack of tension, most meditators have lost interest in all the socially accepted stimulants and depressants. In the four years that we have entertained TM advocates in our livingroom, I can recall having served only one cup of tea and one glass of wine. The standard drink always has been pineapple juice on the rocks!

An athlete's cup of coffee or scotch and soda can become addictive enough to cause him tenseness and irritability or an unsuspected tolerance which can interfere with his health and performance. I asked one TM advocate what he would say to the man who would like to begin TM, but who liked his morning coffee and pre-lunch martini.

"He doesn't have to give them up," he assured me. "You see, you don't have to change your life-style just because you begin to meditate. It's just that, chances are liquor won't appeal to you after a while."

While studies are continuing, the application of TM to students is being seriously considered by educators. The National Institute of Mental Health has awarded the International Meditation Society a $22,000 grant to train 100 high school teachers to teach meditation.

Paul J. Andrews, the project director of Drug Education in Massachusetts, in a letter to SIMS wrote, in February 1972:

> . . . Without question, I would highly endorse the efforts of the Students' International Meditation Society in providing a non-chemical alternative to drugs . . . for young people.

TM has also been offered for credit under the title, Science of Creative Intelligence, at such universities as Yale, Stanford, California state universities at Chico and Sacramento, and others. TM centers have sprung up all over the country, under the initials SIMS.

"Give it a fair chance," a proponent of TM recommends. "It only takes four sessions to learn, about two hours each, on four consecutive days. The rest is do-it-yourself. Simple, practical, rejuvenating.

"What have you got to lose?"

Yoga Many meditation practices and physical techniques are associated with Yoga. Hatha Yoga emphasizes physical methods of altering consciousness. Table 1 shows that the practice of Yoga is associated with deep relaxation of part of the autonomic nervous system without accompanying drowsiness or sleep.

Simple relaxation response techniques H. Benson and his colleagues have studied the physiological changes associated with transcendental meditation. They then tried to find the answer to the question "Were the results specific to transcendental meditation or would they be associated with other techniques?" Various components of Zen, Yoga, and relaxation methods were then combined to establish the simple relaxation response technique. The essential components of this technique are as follows (Benson, 1974).*

---

*The reader can obtain more information about this technique by reading the entire article published in *Harvard Business Review* (July–August 1974).

a) *A mental device.* There should be a constant stimulus e.g., a sound, word, or phrase repeated silently or audibly; fixed gazing at an object is also suitable. The apparent purpose of these procedures is to minimize one's attention to other stimuli.

b) *A passive attitude.* If distracting thoughts occur during the repetition or gazing, they should be disregarded and one's attention should be redirected to the technique. One should not worry about how well he is performing the technique.

c) *Decreased muscle tonus.* The subject should be in a comfortable posture so that minimal muscular work is required.

d) *Quiet environment.* A quiet environment with decreased environmental stimuli should be used. Most techniques instruct the practitioner to close his eyes (Beary, Benson, and Klemchuk, 1974).

The mechanics of performing this simple relaxation technique can be taught in a very short period of time (one hour) and one needs no trained instructor. It is suggested that the following instructions be given to individuals for the purpose of learning the technique.

—Sit in a comfortable position.

—Close your eyes.

—Deeply relax all your muscles, beginning at your feet and progressing up to your face—feet, calves, thighs, lower torso, chest, shoulders, neck, head. Allow them to remain deeply relaxed.

—Breathe through your nose. Become aware of your breathing. As you breathe out, say the word 'one' silently to yourself. Thus: breathe in . . . breathe out, with 'one.' In . . . out, with 'one' . . . .

—Continue this practice for 20 minutes. You may open your eyes to check the time, but do not use an alarm. When you finish, sit quietly for several minutes, at first with your eyes closed and later with your eyes open.

—Remember not to worry about whether you are successful in achieving a deep level of relaxation—maintain a passive attitude and permit relaxation to occur at its own pace. When distracting thoughts occur, ignore them and continue to repeat 'one' as you breathe. The technique should be practiced once or twice daily, and not within two hours after any meal, since the digestive processes seem to interfere with the elicitation of the expected changes.

Some preliminary research has established that this simple relaxation technique evokes a relaxation response (Table 1) in a fashion similar to progressive relaxation, autogenic training, and transcendental meditation. The great value of such a technique is its simplicity and ease of acquisition. Such a technique could be easily taught to athletes who suffer from too much emotional upset prior to competition. Nearly every coach can probably recall athletes whose performance seemed adversely affected by their inability to adapt to the stress of competition. For those athletes some kind of emotional first aid is certainly needed.

Biofeedback   Biofeedback is not a relaxation technique so much as it is a way of *learning* to relax. The learner uses a biofeedback machine to continuously monitor one of his or her own physiological processes—for example, brain waves or muscular tension. By feeling one's physiological states and observing the machine's display at the same time, one learns to recognize the relaxation state and to produce it again and again by conscious choice. After one or two sessions the machine is no longer needed.

"Just relax!"   In a close basketball game a foul is called and your player has a chance to make two shots to put your team ahead with only one second remaining. Victory rides on his shoulders. You, as the coach, get off the bench and exhort the athlete to "just relax!" Is this effective in reducing stress? We don't know the answer to this question at present, but more than speculation supports the suspicion that muscles become more tense if the individual is instructed to relax. Future research may provide a more conclusive answer.

Summary

The relaxation response is characterized by decreased circulatory and respiratory responses, decreased muscular tension, and several other physiological adaptations. Basically, this response is a protective mechanism against overstress. Various desensitization techniques have been shown effective in eliciting a relaxation response. The individual's belief in the technique may be an important factor in eliciting the response. Maybe future research will establish the most efficient method for a given individual. Many techniques may lead to relaxation—so may prayer, a day at the beach, or a day off.

It is also worth asking if relaxation is the optimum arousal state for *all* kinds of endeavors and *all* individuals. The concept of optimum arousal was discussed earlier and it was pointed out that too little or too much arousal can lead to inferior performance. The utility of the technique depends on whether the athlete's level of arousal is above or below his or her optimum level. Some athletes may need tension and anxiety to perform well (perhaps the boxer described by Vanek was such an individual); if this is taken away, performance may suffer.

The ultimate goal is to have the athlete adapt in a way that will give optimum performance and greater pleasure from the sport experience.

DIRECTION AND SUSTAINMENT

At the outset of this section the point was made that motivation has three components—activation, direction, and sustainment. It is to these two latter aspects of motivation that the remainder of our comments and readings in this section will be addressed.

One of motivation's great attractions for a coach is the application of specific techniques to improving performance. Can motivation be manipulated? Too often, in my estimation, discussions of motivation in sport situations have "gimmickry" as their prime focus: What technique was used with athlete A or team B to get improved performance? Certainly gimmicks do work on occasion, or at least performance appears to be affected by their application. However, for each such successful application there are probably many unsuccessful ones. Gimmicks are situation-specific and their influence is transitory. A firm foundation in personality and motivational theory is certainly a requisite to any prescription or use of a motivational gimmick. Logically, is it likely to have any effect? Are the possible effects guaranteed to improve and not hinder performance? Is it likely to effect athletes in a differential manner?

William Hammer, in article 2.10, provides a brief look at the need-reduction approach to motivation. He lists several needs that apparently are related to sport and then discusses three motivational schemas— incentive motivation (reinforcement), fear motivation, and attitude motivation. The schemas or motivational stances are then the basis of the coach–athlete interaction. This very practically oriented article may be somewhat simplistic, but it should give the reader some insights into motivational techniques applied to coaching. The section on fear motivation is especially interesting.

2.10 A brief look at motivation in coaching

BILL HAMMER
University of California, Santa Barbara

Motivation theories of many well-known experimental psychologists conflict and in some cases actually lead to amotivational and irrational acts by coaches. We shall examine here some motivational strategies that *are* useful in coaching, as well as supplying some hints on how they may be used in appropriate ways.

Broadly speaking, the study of motivation is a seeking for the causes of behavior—why do people behave as they do? One approach to motivation is the study of needs, and in a coaching context an appropriate method would be to determine the psychological needs of athletes and try to satisfy those needs.

PSYCHOLOGICAL NEEDS OF ATHLETES

Needs occur in a sequence or hierarchy. The more basic needs have to be satisfied before the other needs can be dealt with. The physical environment, the cultural environment, and heredity all play a part in determining this hierarchy. Individual differences probably play a part too; one person's needs may not have the same priorities as another's. A random list of needs that are especially relevant to athletes might contain the following:

Recognition (identification)
Approval
Self-esteem
Achievement
Challenge (for example, adventure and decision-making)
Expression

Every coach could probably make his own list, expanding or condensing this one or substituting other needs.

MOTIVATIONAL METHODS

Relevant and effective methods need to be developed for motivating the so-called "new breed" of athletes. This means that the coach must be sensi-

From *North American Society for the Psychology of Sport and Physical Activity Bulletin* (March 1971):16–23. Revised version reprinted by permission of the author.

tive to the athlete's needs and must have a clear understanding of his own perception of the coaching function. The modern coach is usually orderly, well-organized, and selective. He has high ego strength and works at the sport he knows best. His duties are to teach the athlete certain skills and to assist him in his personal and physical development, with the goal of helping him do his best. Often the athlete has no idea of what his best might be; he is likely to need a great deal of unlearning before he can make real progress.

The coach may apply any of the motivational approaches described below, either singly or in combination. He must be aware, however, that he is not the one who is going to perform. Therefore his effectiveness will depend largely on his ability to transmit to the athlete some of his own ego strength.

Incentive motivation

Incentive motivation attempts to reinforce good performance with tangible rewards. Immediate reward may be the most effective way to drive the learning curve down (shorten the learning process), though it probably does not produce the most long-lasting results.

When incentive motivation is used, the athlete is made aware of the level of performance necessary to show improvement at each stage of his training. As long as he continues to perform at the prescribed levels, he continues to receive the rewards.

As effective as it is in shortcutting the learning process, incentive motivation has a serious drawback when used as the only method: athletes continually rewarded tend to "get fat" and become less likely to respond to rewards. This "fat cat" syndrome often overtakes professional teams that win year after year, as it did eventually even in the case of the Yankees in baseball. Another drawback is that the practice of relying on rewards for performance creates an unreal situation. In actual competition athletes may do their best and still lose. In such instances even the coach's verbal reinforcement may not compensate for the absence of the expected external reward.

Nevertheless, incentive motivation can work. Even losing can be taken in stride if the athlete is aware that it does not cancel out the growth in his ability. But if the athlete has been conditioned too heavily to work for the external reward, one mediocre performance may lead to a leveling-off of his development. It is then difficult for him to recover his momentum. If incentive motivation is being used, at least one of the coaches must present an overriding success image that the athlete can identify with. Without a success image incentive motivation is difficult.

Fear motivation

Fear may be one of the strongest motivating forces affecting the performance development of an athlete. Critics of fear motivation have complained that it stimulates the basest of human feelings, but their argument is overridden by one simple fact about fear motivation: it works.

Fear motivation exploits primarily the athlete's fear of authority. This is a potent force. It has been said that the athlete needs and wants authority; it spells out a set of rules to him and it gives him a sense of security. Knowing what is expected of him, what the goals are, and what steps he must take to achieve those goals relieves him of a great deal of anxiety that might otherwise slow his progress. Needless to say, if fear motivation is used, there must be a unity of authority within the coaching staff.

Fear motivation operates on three fears: the fear of being caught, the fear of punishment, and the fear of being humiliated by a bad performance in competition.

Fear of being caught

Athletes are usually expected to follow a set of training rules. To be caught violating those rules is embarrassing.

Fear of punishment

Athletes cannot perform well in contact sports without undergoing long hours of physically hard work. When an athlete is not performing at the expected level, extra work may be used as a punishment. Fear of being burdened with this extra work stimulates the athlete to persist and endure, as well as to maintain a high level of concentration and alertness.

Verbal criticism is another form of punishment. The fear of criticism is most often exploited when fatigue and pain are introduced into the athletes' practice.

Fear of separation

One of the strongest fears of team athletes is the fear of separation (from the team). The more the athlete's identification with the team has been nurtured, the more he wants to belong, and the more his ego is involved in the team's achievements, the more he will fear separation from the team and the more effectively he can be motivated to perform. This fear can be best exploited if the team has a tradition of success or is having a winning season. There are also some drawbacks: If you keep threatening to separate athletes from the team but don't do it, you lose credibility and the threat becomes ineffective. If you do separate an athlete, you have lost him anyway.

Attitude motivation

Attitude motivation consists of establishing or changing an athlete's attitude toward success, that is, applying a method, setting attainable goals, and coaching the athlete to believe he can reach those goals. To the degree that a person's beliefs about his abilities become self-fulfilling prophesies, nurturing positive expectations can improve performance.

Attitude motivation attempts to change three essential determinants: attitude, consistency, and control. Skill acquisition and challenge are constantly programmed to reinforce the athlete's growing belief in his ability to achieve. Realistic goal setting and a success mentality combine to give the athlete's development greater momentum.

Two conditions that favor the satisfaction of the athlete's motivational needs are (1) a continual pattern of aspiration and (2) knowledge of results (feedback). There must always be movement toward a goal that is both satisfying and attainable. The goals must be chosen and perceived in such a way that the athlete can sense continued movement toward those goals even in the face of a losing performance.

The combination of positive verbal programming and instruction produces a success mentality. Specific objectives for the coach include the following:

1. Crystallize the athlete's thinking. Set a certain level of accomplishment and develop orderliness and self-confidence.
2. Set specific objectives in terms of attitude development and set deadlines for achieving those objectives. Feed back to the athlete continuing information on results so he can visualize his progress. When you achieve a goal, set a new and higher goal.
3. Develop the athlete's desire to satisfy a need-oriented goal in relation to a logical sequence of events necessary to achieve it.
4. Focus the athlete's attention on his strengths and avoid reinforcing his tendency toward self-criticism or toward focusing on his weakness.
5. Encourage in the athlete a mental set that ignores obstacles, criticism, and failure. Foster the belief that if these three elements are missing, something is wrong.

6. Develop the athlete's awareness of internal cues that tell him what his own body is perceiving, so that he can redirect his energies in moments of stress or distress.
7. Introduce novelty, distraction, and play so that the athlete can respond to anxiety as a perfectly normal occurrence.

To use attitude motivation the coach and his staff must be believers. They must themselves have a positive attitude, since any negativism will undermine their efforts.

The athlete's motivation can be sustained at a high level only if his progress is a continuing process of opening and then closing loops. Each goal achieved (closing a loop) builds confidence, which should be immediately applied to the challenge of a new goal (opening a loop). The loops should form a pattern of continuing development, and this is the task of the coaching staff—the loops must be large enough to sustain aspiration and small enough to sustain confidence. Success is most likely if the coach accomplishes the following:

1. Develops a blocking-out or rejection of attitudes that defeat the team or the person.
2. Communicates a sense of security by his choice of words, his tone of voice, and his personal warmth.
3. Provides a pleasant stable environment for training.
4. Provides avenues of escape when threats or failures occur.

There is probably no one best motivational model or technique in coaching. The coach's own creativity, adaptability, and concern for the athlete will usually dictate his approach.

Motivation is too complex to be adequately understood in a simplistic way. Therefore it is necessary to consider—in greater depth—some of the points that Hammer has raised.

Motivational viewpoints

A complete review of even the major motivational theories is outside the scope of this textbook. However, Madsen's (1968) book, *Theories of Motivation,* will provide the serious student with a springboard into several interesting theories of motivation. We shall deal here only briefly with selected theories.

Need-reduction theory   Hull (1943) postulated that behavior arises and is modified according to the individual's needs—organisms *must* act to reduce needs. Motivation was the multiplicative resultant of habit and drive. Habit is learning by the individual of a particular response associated with a particular stimulus. A felt need generates a drive to energize an organism, and habit directs an action to satisfy the need and thereby reduce the drive. In his later writings, Hull accepted incentive as a supporting drive in the energizing process.

Maslow (1954, 1968) proposed a theory of need gratification to account for behavior. His hierarchy of needs (physiological, safety, affiliative, esteem, self-actualization, cognitive, and esthetic) is well known. Needs are gratified in the order stated and only when a lower need's deficiency is eradicated will higher needs be attended to. In such a schema, if the athlete is worried about injury his behavior will be directed to reduce that deficiency and will not be addressed to other aspects of his behavior—decision-making, for instance.

The need-reductionist position suffers somewhat from the fact that sometimes motivation increases as the goal nears, rather than decreasing as the goal (need) is becoming satisfied. As one is provoked by frustration to aggress against another individual, does the act of aggression dissipate the need to aggress? Discussions in the Aggression and Sport section of this book would indicate that such is probably not the case. Since Maslow's need-reduction theory does not depend on the concept of drive as much as Hull's theory does, it partially escapes the following sharp criticism. Cofer and Appley (1964) dismiss drive as being a useless concept, even a liability. Their claims are particularly damaging because their work on motivation is so highly accepted and widely cited. Drive was always a confusing term because it referred sometimes to the intensity aspect of motivation, and at other times to the directing force of behavior.

Achievement motivation theory   McClelland, Atkinson, et al., (1953) posited a very popular motivational theory that is presently receiving a great deal of attention. In a specific and limited concept, achievement motivation attempts to account for the direction, intensity, and sustainment of behavior. It must be emphasized at the onset of discussion that this schema is only applicable in an achievement-based situation—that is, one in which the individual intends to perform at optimum behavioral strength. In an achievement situation, two kinds of variables are operative: (a) achievement-oriented motives, and (b) situational variables.

Achievement motivation is a function of the strength of two motives—motive to succeed (M_s) and motive to avoid failure (M_{af}), in conjunction with the situational variables—incentives for success and failure (I_s, I_f) and probabilities of success and failure (P_s, P_f).

These additional conditions must be met before achievement motivation is a possible interpreter of behavior in achievement situations: (1) Individuals must be *willing to accept the outcomes* of their actions and must not attribute the resultant effects to others. (2) The situation must not be so ambiguous that the individual could possibly perceive a maladaptive performance as adaptive. (3) *Knowledge of results* is essential for correct interpretations of actions. (4) The situation must possess a certain *degree of uncertainty,* with neither success nor failure being a foregone conclusion.

Whether or not sport situations meet these requirements can be debated. Do athletes usually perform with the intention to do their best? Are sport roles so clear that the individual knows what is expected of him in all situations? Is it likely that the majority of athletes expect to win or lose solely on the basis of their own performances? Is "copping out" on oneself less prevalent in sport than in other situations? A treatise could be written on the application or misapplication of achievement motivation to sport performance.

The chief obstacle to relating achievement motivation to sport is that not all athletes participate in sport with the intent to maximize their capabilities. Various reasons for participating in sport are discussed in the section dealing with Incentive Motivation.

What is success? Is success to be expressed in absolute terms (winning) or in relative terms (comparison to previous performances)? This certainly would be nice for the coach to know, and would appear to be essential before applying the achievement motivation concept to the sport setting.

McClelland, Atkinson, *et al.* consider M_s and M_{af} to be learned dispositions characterized by stability and permanence. The stability of the fear of failure motive (M_{af}) has been suggested by Heckhausen (1968) in a review of studies dealing with physiological parameters (blood pressure, muscle tension, and uric acid concentration in blood) relative to success and fear motives.

Reinforcement theory   For the behaviorist, in the strictest sense of the word, motivation is not in the vocabulary. From the Skinnerian point of view, behavior is not a function of inner qualities such as needs, drives, or motives but is under the control of reinforcers. Behavior is strengthened or weakened according to the consequences of the action—that is, according to whether the response leads to a positive or negative outcome. Rushall and Siedentop (1972) have written an interesting book in which they relate operant conditioning (manipulating behavior by reward or punishment) to the sport setting.

In article 2.11, William Straub gives the reader an assortment of views on motivation from well-known people in physical education and sport. He explains how behaviorism differs in its approach to motivation and speaks favorably toward applied behavioral analysis. The Skinnerian outlook is quite relevant today in education and so its introduction into sport was inevitable.

2.11 Motivation of the individual athlete and team

WILLIAM F. STRAUB
Ithaca College, New York

MOTIVATION DEFINED

Before examining some of the motivational literature we should define the term motivation as we plan to utilize it. To do this I consulted a number of different sources both in physical education and in psychology. First of all, let us examine what some of the leading sports psychologists have to say about this topic.

Bryant Cratty (1973) makes a good distinction when he classifies motivation into primary subdivisions. For study purposes, Cratty separates "why people choose one activity and not another" from "why individuals perform with varying degrees of intensity." Our concern here will be with the intensity question. Cratty (1973) goes on to say that motivation for him denotes "the factors and processes that impel people to action or inaction in various situations."

Bob Singer (1972) approaches the study of motivation by repeating an old cliche: "You can take an athlete to the game, but you can't make him

---

Revised version of a paper presented at the New York State Association for Health, Physical Education, and Recreation convention, Kiamesha Lake, January 1974. Reprinted by permission.

play." Singer goes on to say that physical attributes, skills, and abilities have a strong effect on outstanding performance but the "ideal" level of motivation for the given task must be present if the athlete is to demonstrate superior skill. Later in his coverage of motivation, Singer cites Atkinson's definition of the term. Atkinson (1964) says that motivation deals with variables that incite or direct a person toward activity, and ultimately toward a specific goal. Dorothy Harris (1973) talks about motivation as an abstract concept; since we cannot observe it directly, but can only observe the behavior resulting from it. Ogilvie and Tutko (1963), after acknowledging the fact that the motivating forces in athletics are exceedingly complex, report that needs for love, social approval, status, security, and achievement are some of the reasons for participation in sport.

Frost (1971) says that "motivation has to do with the various factors which incite and control behavior." After interviewing many college and professional athletes who were participating in a number of different sports, Frost concluded that personal pride was the primary factor that drove athletes to high levels of competition.

In their application of Skinnerian psychology to sport and physical education, Rushall and Siedentop provide a completely different explanation of the concept of motivation. Following Skinner, they say "Motivational explanations of behavior are of limited usefulness," (Rushall & Siedentop, 1972). Instead they place emphasis on shaping the environment to bring about the desired response. We shall have more to say about this S-R concept later.

Turning to psychological definitions of motivation, Charles Cofer (1972), a leading authority, says "motivation signifies the causes or the 'why' of action." Cofer postulates a significant relationship between motivation and emotion. Skinner, the psychologist who many believe has had the greatest influence during the twentieth century, has not defined motivation. Being a cultural determinist, Skinner does not think that it is important. Perhaps Skinner's cultural determinism is best expressed in his statement: "People are extraordinarily different in different places, and possibly just because of the places." (Skinner, 1971).

For our purposes I should like to operationally define motivation in the behavioristic sense as the discovery of R-S relationships, those between behavior and the external events that determine it.

MOTIVATION—A REVIEW OF THE LITERATURE

When one considers the time and effort psychology has devoted to the study of motivation it is surprising that even today psychologists know so little about it. Of course, it is true that psychologists have spent what seems to be an inordinate professional amount of time studying animal behavior. For example, they talk about big "D" (drive), energizing properties of frustration, and Skinner's operant conditioning paradigms. One soon learns, as a student of the behavioral sciences, that psychology is not an exact science. And, I am certain that this announcement will come as a disappointment to coaches who are looking for definitive answers to practical questions.

APPROACHES TO ATHLETIC MOTIVATION

Before discussing the application of Skinner's behaviorism or what is commonly called operant conditioning to the motivation of the individual athlete and team, I should like to mention some of the bizarre attempts that have been made to motivate athletes. A couple of years ago, a young college football coach reportedly threw a chair through a locker room window in order to motivate his team. Apparently it worked, because they defeated one of the best teams in their conference. At the 1973 AAHPER Convention in Minneapolis last April I heard a lecture by Coach Cal Stoll, Head Football Coach at the University of Minnesota, in which he stressed the inspirational value of the pep talk. Stoll said that he appeals to the emotions of his players by utilizing sound, lighting, and nationalism. His pre-game staging of the Battle Hymn of the Republic sung by Anita Bryant while the lights are dimmed and a spotlight is focused on Old Glory is a real tear jerker. Stoll concluded by stressing the importance of novelty. If you use a motivational technique too often, according to Stoll, it will lose its value.

One of the most far-out approaches to motivation was reported by Knute Rockne in his book *Coaching*. Rockne describes a 1925 incident in which a track coach at a midwestern university trained his runners by sprinting them against dogs. The coach reasoned that a runner would run faster because he was in competition with a faster animal. This same coach, according to Rockne, tied his long-distance runners by a rope to a Ford car, and they broke world records.

Today, we are far more sophisticated. We race our runners against mechanical rabbits that travel around the inside curb of our all-weather tracks.

Let us now turn to Skinner.

Applied behavior analysis

Few sports psychologists have attempted to apply Skinnerian psychology to sport. Brent Rushall and Daryl Siedentop are the first scholars to do so.

Rushall elaborated on what he called Applied Behavior Analysis at the First Canadian Congress for the Multi-Disciplinary Study of Sport and Physical Activity in Montreal in 1973. According to Rushall, Applied Behavior Analysis is a behavior technology that has its origins in operant (Skinnerian) psychology (Rushall, 1972).

The basic premise of Applied Behavior Analysis is that behavior is controlled by its consequences. Students of psychology will recognize that ABA, Applied Behavior Analysis, is an outgrowth of Edward Thorndike's Law of Effect. In Skinnerian fashion, proponents of ABA like Rushall attempt to control and modify behavior by manipulation of the environment. Perhaps some concrete examples of the use of Applied Behavior Analysis in sport will help to clarify the concept. The examples which are cited grew out of three Master's theses, directed by Rushall, which were completed at Dalhousie University in Nova Scotia.

Problem 1
A swimming coach was having trouble with the attendance of his athletes. The attendance of the swimmers was described as poor and irregular, punctuality was poor, and some athletes often left practice early. Attempts to control these problems had failed.

Proposed solution
The obvious solution was to devise some method of consequential control for attending, tardy, and leaving-early behaviors. This was achieved by establishing contingencies for publicly marking an "attendance board."

Experiment
A multi-baseline experimental design was used to show that the contingency of behaving appropriately and self-recording on the attendance board was an effective control procedure. The three dependent variables were number of absentees, latecomers, and early leavers for the group.

Results
Absenteeism was reduced by 45 percent; late arrivals by 63 percent, and early leaving behaviors were completely suppressed. Post checks indicated that the effort was persistent.

Rushall, in his address, related other incidents in which Applied Behavior Analysis was used to solve coaching problems. For example, another swimming coach was dissatisfied with the intensity of his practice sessions. It seems that some swimmers were not completing the distances that would allow them to perform well in high-school-level competition. Again, ABA was used to solve this problem. A "lap board" was developed and each swimmer recorded the number of laps that he swam on the board. As indicated above, some of the solutions are very simple, and to me they confirm the time-worn slogan "you get what you emphasize."

As expected, Rushall—following these and other experiments—believes that the application of Applied Behavior Analysis has a bright future in our field. Rushall hypothesizes that because of the increasing pressures of accountability, teachers and coaches will seek avenues for changing behavior. The mark of a good coach or a good teacher, in Skinnerian terms, is that you have changed the behavior of your pupils or athletes. In other words, when you began the class or season, students were measured in terms of skills, attitudes, and knowledge appropriate to the sport you are teaching; at the end of the unit or sports season the pupils are measured again in terms of the performance objectives that were established. If the pupils improved, you are—according to Skinner—a good teacher. A central question that arises in the application of the concept of accountability is "Who should establish the objectives?" Should it be the pupils, parents, principal, the teacher, or members of the board of education? As expected, this question has not been definitively answered. Personally, I believe that the concept of accountability, as stated above, is far better than the present method of evaluating coaches. The win–loss record is not, in my opinion, a valid indicator of coaching success. And, the practice of firing coaches who have poor win–loss records is indicative of the lack of sophistication in educational administration. This practice may also tell us something about the nature of sport in capitalistic societies such as ours. If sport is a microcosm of society, as John Loy and Gerald Kenyon indicate, then we need to change, in some instances, societal values.

Let us sum up the Skinnerian approach to motivation of the individual athlete and team. Applied Behavior Analysis comes under the domain of Skinner's operant conditioning. That is to say, ABA is a form of contingency management or behavioral control. And, as we have indicated above, contingency refers to the relationship between a behavior and a consequence. In sports terminology, the relationship may be between attending practice (behavior) and receiving the praise of the coach and one's team-mates. As shown, contingency management refers to changing behavior by controlling and altering stimulus-response relationships. Lloyd Homme (1970) has called contingency management "motivation management." Token systems, point systems, and contract systems are other forms of contingency management.

There are other ways to motivate the individual athlete and team. There are also critics of Skinner's operant conditioning approach to motivation.

One of the frequently mentioned objections is that his procedures are dehumanizing. That is to say, there is little concern for the individual, the person. Humanistic psychologists such as Carl Rogers would certainly insert an "O" into Skinner's S–R paradigm. The "O" in S–O–R refers to the organism and indicates, in a humanistic sense, that the person is always to be considered in the application of contingency management procedures.

Other approaches

Although practitioners of operant psychology seldom mention motivation, other psychologists have spent their entire life trying to understand and control it. After all, the goals of science are understanding, prediction, and control of natural phenomena (Kerlinger, 1973).

At a far more practical level, the personality of the coach plays an important role in the motivation of the individual athlete and team. Frequently, a team personality develops as a result of the interaction of the personalities of players and coach. If the coach is outgoing, a hard worker, and student of the sport, his players frequently model his behavior. On the other hand, if the coach is withdrawn, lacks confidence and watches the clock, players will probably also display such behavior. The thought is advanced by the writer that personality of coach may be sports-specific. That is, some coaches may be better suited to coach some sports than others. For example, the "hard-nosed," authoritarian coach may be more suited to football coaching than to individual sports like tennis and golf. Perhaps the "nice-guy" coach is more suited to coaching the lifetime sports. It is difficult to determine where the "intense and driven" coach fits in. His lack of composure frequently gets him into trouble with game officials and school administrators.

The "easy-going" coach is usually not found in the contact sports like football and ice hockey. Although he appears to suffer no pressure, frequently he is full of ulcers by the ripe old age of 30. The "business-like" coach is noted for his organizational expertise. Practices are planned to the minute and they usually are conducted efficiently and without interruptions.

All of the above personality types may be recognized on the sports scene. Changing personality is a difficult job. Finding the sport that best fits one's personality appears to be a far better approach to athletic motivation than attempting to mold personality to fit a sport. Most psychologists agree that changing the underlying structure of personality is a long and arduous task.

MOTIVATION OF THE INDIVIDUAL ATHLETE

Motivation of the individual athlete is critical to team success. When individual players are motivated, the team usually performs well too. Much of the time of the sports psychologist is spent in discovering the best reinforcers for each athlete. The coach's praise may be all that is needed for some players, yet it may be ineffective as a motivator for others.

Much has been said and written about the type and schedule of reinforcement in psychology. Usually positive reinforcement (praise) is thought to be better than negative reinforcement (blame). Both types of reinforcement change behavior of players, but positive reinforcement is thought to produce the best results over time.

This is not to say that constructive criticism should not be utilized. However, a steady diet of criticism usually results in withdrawal by the athlete. According to psychologist, Thomas Tutko, "The important thing for the coach to remember is that criticism tends to destroy rather than build desirable traits in a person."

In shaping behavior early in the learning process it is best, according to S-R theorists like Skinner, to reinforce any activity that is in the correct direction.

FINAL STATEMENT

The scientific study of athletic motivation is just beginning. At present sports psychologists do not have a body of knowledge to adequately answer most of the practical questions asked by coaches. Far more research is needed.

What appears to be the most fruitful approach to the motivation of the individual athlete and team is Applied Behavioral Analysis, a form of behavioral control. Through the application of Skinner's operant conditioning procedures the athletic environment is shaped to bring about the desired response. This approach to athletic motivation is best explained by Rushall and Seidentop in their book: *The Development and Control of Behavior in Sport and Physical Education.* Perhaps the best attempt to use contingencies of reinforcement in sport is the application of stars on helmets for specific types of behavior. From all the information I can gather on this topic, it is working well. That is, in a Skinnerian sense, it is producing the desired response.

Behaviorists have found, in experiments with pigeons and rats, that conditioning is more effective when it is intermittent, that is, when the desired behavior is reinforced most of the time but not all of the time. The implication of this in sports is that coaches can expect better performance if they occasionally withhold the reward—praise, gold stars, or whatever—even though the athlete has given a superior performance.

The use of negative, or aversive, reinforcement (punishment) is controversial even among behaviorists. Skinner believes that negative reinforcement is unreliable and often ineffective, and that it can even be detrimental, either by confusing or disorienting or angering the subject, or by reinforcing the unwanted behavior. Other behaviorists use aversive conditioning and consider it effective.

Not all reinforcement is dispensed by a controlling person, such as coach, teacher, or parent; some of it comes from the task itself. A task can be pleasant or unpleasant, challenging or boring, meaningful or meaningless. It follows, therefore, that an athlete's motivation can sag when repeated success at a repetitive task leads to boredom and satiation.

John Vogel, in article 2.12, reports the results of his study of the effects of repeated successful completion of a simple task. Those results appear to support the idea that there is an optimal level of stimulation needed to sustain motivation.

Would Vogel's results hold for motor tasks? Even when the task was difficult, success seemed to quickly reduce the task's motivational value. This suggests that increasing task complexity is necessary to maintain motivation at a high level. It should be fairly evident what this means to the coach. Practice sessions become boring because the tasks are reasonably well learned (at least in the athletes' eyes) but must be performed again and again. To increase the complexity of the task or to add novelty to the situation is the remedy for satiation.

2.12

Satiation of the success experience[1]

JOHN L. VOGEL

Baldwin-Wallace College, Berea, Ohio

Concepts of optimal stimulation and stimulus satiation have received increasing attention in recent literature. Common observations suggest that even the successful completion of a task may become a satiation experience, and that the organism appears motivated to seek new tension or challenge. The present study involved a repetitious task and a recording of subjects' reaction to the task following each trial, both prior to successful completion of the task, and continuing with repeated success experiences. On both measured dimensions subjects show a rapid and statistically significant decrease in their evaluation of the task experience. The findings are interpreted as supportive of motivation theory expressed in terms of optimal tension or activation level. The findings are related to observed human behavior in its pursuit of new activities and goals.

Discussion of concepts such as curiosity, optimal tension, and sensation-seeking appears in the literature frequently. Observation of behavior, our own and others, makes it increasingly apparent that tension elimination and drive reduction are inadequate as explanatory constructs. Harlow (1953) and Hebb (1955) raise some of the key issues in their own provocative style. Fiske and Maddi (1961) present a theoretical structure based on the maintenance of the organism's level of activation or arousal. Fowler (1965) integrates the sizeable literature on "curiosity and exploratory behavior." The concept of an optimal level of stimulation has recently been quantified in a Sensation-Seeking Scale (Zuckerman, Kolin, Prince, and Zoob, 1964).

It is a common observation that man does indeed seek new experiences and does appear to work at maintaining an optimal level of tension. The research literature in the area is already extensive, but is limited largely to

---

From *Journal of Experimental Research in Personality* 2(1967):208–211. Reprinted by permission of the author and Academic Press, Inc.

[1]Material costs for this study were supported by Faculty Research and Publications, Baldwin-Wallace College. The author wishes to express appreciation to S. Lee Whiteman for extensive encouragement and suggestions. He was the vital catalyst for much of what is reported here.

animals, demonstrating curiosity behavior or the reinforcement value of variation in stimuli. Although man also regularly displays such behavior, he is something less than a favorite research organism in this area.

One observes the climber who seeks ever higher mountains, the tennis player seeking a tougher opponent, and the professional person who changes jobs (and even careers). One sees people pursuing thrill sports and looking for new and challenging parlor games. All of these seem to be manifestations of a real human tendency to be motivated by the process of accomplishing rather than accomplishment and rest at the goal. The research reported here is an attempt to reproduce such commonly observed behaviors in the laboratory.

The behaviors observed appear to have in common a loss or waning of interest or attraction at or soon after the point of perceived successful achievement. The research problem was to develop a task challenging enough to produce success and the predicted satiation and loss of interest within a reasonable number of trials. As a measure of motivational level, it seemed reasonable to simply ask the subjects how they felt about the task. When a person seeks a change in vocation or avocation he knows and can express how he feels about his present situation. It was recognized that all subjects would not reach the success point simultaneously on any series of task trials, but the assumption was made that the success experience would have subjective equivalence for subjects if there was no opportunity to compare performance with others. In this exploratory study, it was hypothesized that the subjects would find the task decreasingly pleasant and meaningful once they mastered it. As success on the task became routine, it was hypothesized that subjects would rate the task as significantly more unpleasant and meaningless.

METHOD

Subjects

Thirty-three college students volunteered for the experiment. There were 14 males and 19 females in the group. Mean age for the group was 20.2 years. There were eight sophomores, 18 juniors, and seven seniors. Only one subject was eliminated; he completed the task successfully on the first trial and failed on the second trial, thus generating no data relevant to this study.

Task

A diamond-shaped paper and pencil maze was developed for this study. Pilot work on this maze indicated that most subjects could complete the maze in a minute or two. To produce repetition or a sequence of experiences, the subjects were allowed 30 seconds/trial. The same maze would then be presented for the second and subsequent trials. Under these conditions nearly all subjects would reach a solution after the first trial and before the tenth trial. In the present study a series of 15 trials were used.

Rating forms

Measurement of subjective response to the task was taken after each 30-second trial. Although a large number of dimensions would have been desirable, the scale was deliberately kept small to prevent loss of continuity in the series of trials. In the present form two scales were used:

Dislike/Unpleasant .... Like/Pleasant
Meaningless/Boring .... Meaningful/Challenging

Subjects were instructed to circle one number on each scale to indicate their immediate reaction to the task trial just completed. In the series of trials the polar labels were rotated to prevent response set.

A 12-point scale form was developed for rating after the whole series of trials had been completed. Eleven items were drawn from the first three factors isolated by research with the Semantic Differential (Osgood, Suci, and Tannenbaum, 1961). A final item on the Challenging–Boring dimension was thought to be particularly relevant to a college population and was added. These items were rated on a seven-point scale similar to that proposed for the Semantic Differential instrument.

Finally, the Sensation-Seeking Scale (SSS) (Zuckerman, Kolin, Prince, and Zoob, 1964) was utilized.

Procedure

Experience in pilot studies had indicated the probable interference of experimenter variables in attempting to measure something so volatile as momentary response to task experience. In this study all instructions were tape-recorded by an assistant. He spoke firmly but softly, in a manner thought to depersonalize the experimenter without destroying confidence in the situation.

All the material for the experiment (except the SSS) was formed into a booklet secured by plastic ring binders. Introductory pages contained a sample maze of simple design, a copy of the two-item rating scale, and a sheet on which the subjects supplied their age, sex, and class standing. Each trial consisted of the diamond-shaped maze and a second sheet containing the two-rating items. The trials were separated by a stiffer sheet to prevent pressing through from one trial to the next.

Subjects were asked to follow each detail of the instructions, to start, to stop, to turn the page, and so on, only as instructed. When the introductory pages had been observed and completed, the subjects were instructed to begin on trial one of the mazes. After 30 seconds they were stopped, instructed to turn the page, and told to complete the ratings. After a five-second interval, the subjects were told to turn the page, turn the cover sheet, and begin the second maze. The process was completed through fifteen trials.

After the last trial the subjects were directed (by the recording) to turn to the larger rating form which contained full printed instructions. When this was completed, the experimenter (who generally left the room while the recording was on) distributed the SSS, which was then completed by all subjects.

Analysis of data

Ratings by trial were tabulated by standardizing trials around the first success (S) trial for each subject. All trials for that subject were numbered in reference to his success point. Mean ratings are computed across comparable trials. The number of cases in the different trials are variable, since subjects reach success at different points. Three subjects reached success on an early trial, repeated their successful trips for several trials, then failed on an isolated later trial. For these subjects, data was retained only through the series of successes, with the isolated failure and subsequent trials eliminated. Mean ratings on the two scales were computed for each trial, from S-minus-six, through S, to S-plus-thirteen.

RESULTS

Mean scores on trials preceding success, at the success point, and on trials succeeding and repeating the success experience are shown in Fig. 1. The curvilinear relationship on the dimension from unpleasant to pleasant is apparent in the figure. In contrast, ratings on the dimension from meaningful to meaningless show a linear relationship. Compared to the success trial, mean ratings on both dimensions decrease to a statistically significant difference (.05 level, Mean sign, Chi square) as early as the S-plus-3 trial. Obviously, subsequent trials increase the difference and levels of significance of the differences.

In the examination of individual records it was apparent that while most subjects rated the task very positively at or around the point of success, the ratings of some decreased more rapidly than others. It was thought that those whose ratings decreased least, i.e., who tended to maintain a high

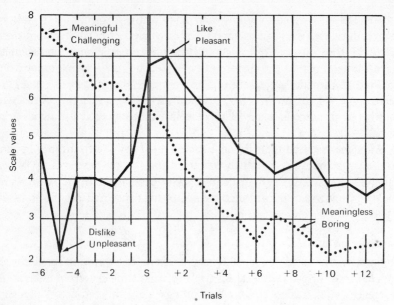

Figure 1 Mean ratings on task trials before, at, and after success experience

evaluation of the task after completing it successfully many times, would be those with least need for sensation-seeking. Conversely, those whose ratings decreased rapidly might be expected to have a high need for new sensation and experience. The difference between the sum of three ratings at and around the success trial and the sum of the last three ratings for that subject was interpreted as a Decrement Index. A high decrease was interpreted as a high loss of morale under repetitious stimulation, while a low score was taken to indicate the retention of such morale. Eleven subjects in each group, the upper and lower third were compared on the three Semantic Differential factors in the final rating. Comparisons were also made on the added dimension of challenging–boring and scores on the SSS instrument. Those who show high decrement (high loss of morale) did finally judge the whole task to be less pleasurable, to have less potency, and to be less in the direction of oriented activity, but none of the differences was statistically significant. On the dimension from boring to challenging, subjects with the larger decrement did rate the task to be more boring (difference significant at 0.1 level, Mean sign, Chi square). This finding merely confirms what the subject had been telling us in his sequential ratings of the trial series. On the SSS instrument the two groups showed essentially identical mean scores.

DISCUSSION

Under the experience of a repeated task long after the task has been mastered, subjects show a statistically significant loss of interest and morale. Some subjects show this loss more than others, but the two groups are not distinguishable on the SSS, providing no support for the validity of the instrument. Approach to the success experience appears to show increment or decrement of subjective evaluation, depending on which dimension of the experience is rated. The subjects find the challenge of a new task highly meaningful but also relatively unpleasant in the experience of task failure. The first dimension may be conceptualized in terms of stimulus or task satiation. The second dimension may then be described in terms of hedonism and some kind of personal or ego gratification. Whether or not a subject, given the opportunity, would abandon the task many trials before the success point would probably be a function of the relative impact of pleasure and/or meaningfulness for that subject. Approaching and achieving success maximizes the pleasure experience, but already the stimulus repetition or satiation has reduced the meaningfulness of the task. After the success point, the task becomes increasingly less pleasant and less meaningful. The successful completion of a fairly difficult task seems to lose motivational value rather quickly. Apparently all subjects would have a tendency to abandon the task as they developed satiation of the success experience.

It is tempting to draw parallels from these findings to real life situations such as marriage or personnel turnover in industry. Such inferences are intriguing but must be drawn with caution. The scale dimensions used here are complex variables in themselves, not clearly unidimensional, and in any case, apt to have idiosyncratic meaning for each task as well as subject. Further, it would be hazardous to draw parallels between the 45-second task intervals in this study to hours, days, months, or years in a real life situation. It may also be that the subjective experience of time intervals is not the same before, during immediate, and during repetition of the success experience.

It is recognized that a subject's affective evaluation of an experience does not lead directly to a theory of motivation, need, or drive. It is evident, however, that if tension-reduction and drive-reduction are adequate motivational concepts, the successful completion of a task should remain pleasant and meaningful. The rapid deterioration of such affects suggests a need in the organism for new tasks and challenge. It indicates that the organism is at least uncomfortable in the newly acquired and now routine gratification of an earlier need.

How much reinforcement is enough, and how much should be positive and how much negative? In responding to our question about the ratio of positive to negative reinforcement, Rushall has stated that an 80:20 ratio (positive being the greater) has worked well in his crew coaching.

We have only touched on reinforcement theory in this section; the reader interested in knowing more about it is referred to *The Development and Control of Behavior in Sport and Physical Education* (Rushall and Siedentop, 1972).

Incentive motivation   Birch and Veroff's (1966) approach to motivation is behavioristic to the extent that they do not look for determinants of action in physiological mechanisms. One cannot help seeing the close relationship between the questions they ask and those that individuals interested in sport ask:

Why does an individual select one activity rather than another?

Why is the activity carried on with such vigor?

Why does the activity persist in the face of competition from other activities?

The Birch and Veroff motivational schema is activity-oriented, and behavior is seen as a function of the strongest set of tendencies competing at the moment. This is called the *principle of action.* Birch and Veroff introduce the concepts of *availability, expectancy, incentive,* and *motive,* which they say are the factors determining the strength of tendencies underlying activities.

Richard Alderman, in article 2.13, explores the theoretical and practical implications of incentive motivation. In particular, he views motivation from the Birch and Veroff perspective; after elaborating on the principle of action, he describes the major incentive systems that account for most of one's behavior. It is easily seen how relevant the incentive systems are to the discussion of why one initially participates in sport and additionally why the participation is so intense.

2.13 Incentive motivation in sport: an interpretive speculation of research opportunities

RICHARD B. ALDERMAN
University of Alberta, Edmonton

The purpose of this paper is to explore the theoretical and the practical implications of the concept of incentive motivation as it applies to behavior in competitive sport and physical activity. This exploration—one might call it a speculation—will revolve around one central question that constantly surfaces in sports motivation: namely, what is it about the sport or activity itself that helps to determine whether or not the person actually engages in it? What is it about a sport that either attracts or repels an individual participant, and what is it that causes him to continue or terminate his participation? It is the thesis of this paper that one of the major processes underlying the answers to these questions is incentive motivation.

INCENTIVE MOTIVATION: HULL AND SPENCE[1]

The term incentive motivation, in its current connotations, first started to receive direct attention in psychology as an expansion of Clarke L. Hull's idea in the 1930s that *rg* (the organism's anticipatory goal reaction) could be considered an effective determinant of action. Though anticipation was not included in Hull's elaborate 1943 theory $[_sE_R = F(D) \times f(_sH_R)]$, subsequent criticisms by Tolman (1932) of its inadequacy in explaining *latent learning* and the immediate effect on performance of a shift in the amount of reward or incentive caused Hull (1952), and later Spence (1956), to revise and elaborate the theory to include anticipation or expectancy of the goal as one of the fundamental determinants of molar action. Though Hull still maintained that the frequency and delay of reinforcement influenced the growth of habit, he had now introduced amount of incentive (or *K*) into his equation. This revision was prompted by the results of two general lines of research popular during this period.

From *The Status of Psychomotor Learning and Sport Psychology Research.* Edited by B. S. Rushall. Dartmouth, Nova Scotia: Sport Science Associates, 1974. Reprinted by permission.

[1]For an excellent discussion of incentive motivation the reader is referred to Atkinson (1964).

The first were studies dealing with "latent" learning, which indicated relatively sudden and substantial changes in performance when food was introduced into the goal box of a maze for the first time after several trials in which animals had run the maze while hungry without a food reward.

The second group of findings were the comparable large and sudden shifts in performance observed in studies by Tolman and co-workers when the reward was changed from a "more attractive" (large) one to a "less attractive" (small) one, and vice-versa. Spence (1956) interpreted these findings largely in the sense that, though Hull had explained the "direction" of these changes in his growth of habit strength, the theory as it stood at that time did not explain the *abruptness* of these performance shifts. According to Hull's habit theory, such changes should have been gradual over time, the result of small increments in habit strength. The upshot of all this was Hull's revision of the theory in 1952. This change was consistent with Spence's position that the relative excitatory strengths of competing responses are a function of the relative strengths of the two fractional anticipatory goal responses, and the latter are dependent on which drive is present and which is absent (Spence et al., 1950). That is, in an animal in which one drive is more salient than another (for example, he's hungrier than he is thirsty), the proprioceptive cues for that drive are stronger and give the response of seeking food greater excitatory strength. Thus when the animal is hungry, proprioceptive cues from anticipatory eating responses are stronger than those from anticipatory drinking. (We will see shortly that this is, in essence, what happens with competing responses in sport selection in youngsters.) Spence and others felt strongly at this time that such anticipatory goal reactions might become conditioned to environmental stimuli and proprioceptive stimuli in addition to the drive stimulus Hull had originally emphasized. Though the discussion thus far has been restricted to conceptualizations based mainly on animal studies, Spence's idea that a generalized anticipatory goal reaction (that is, incentive motivation) functions to excite locomotor habits that are evoked by the complex of stimuli that are immediately present leads us in a somewhat roundabout way to Atkinson's and McClelland's treatment of incentive value in human achievement motivation.

INCENTIVE VALUE: ATKINSON AND McCLELLAND

I will not dwell on the Atkinson–McClelland paradigm of achievement motivation, except for the way it interprets the functioning of incentive value in achievement settings. McClelland has continuously emphasized Tolman's concept that two important situational variables operate in typical achievement settings: first, the extent to which the individual *expects* that his performance will be successful, and second, how attractive that success appears to him, that is, how much *incentive* it presents to him. It is assumed that a person's past experience in similar situations will influence his expectancy of success in the current situation. This has been represented in the paradigm as the "probability of success" that the person subjectively estimates. Personal expectancies thus become a powerful factor in assessing the motivational drive of a person in any achievement setting. The matter of incentive value operates in much the same way. In sizing up a particular task that confronts him, the individual anticipates a certain pride of accomplishment if he is successful. And in successfully achieving some goals there will undoubtedly be more sense of accomplishment than in completing others. So what occurs is simply that the person assesses the value of certain accomplishments in terms of his past experiences in which his success has been acclaimed and he has experienced a sense of pride. One would naturally anticipate greater satisfaction from winning an Olympic medal than from winning a local gift voucher at his home club. This suggests that the incentive value of success becomes an important determinant of strength of motivation to achieve at a particular task.

Probably one of the most interesting facets of the interrelationships between expectancy and incentive is the realization that they are, in fact, interdependent. This was developed initially by Atkinson (1964) when he stated that one of the simple assumptions of this paradigm is that the incentive value of success at a task is probably equal to the apparent difficulty of the task. The easier the task, the less the incentive value of success at it, and vice-versa. Such an assumption is partially modified by the functioning of people's levels of aspiration and their personalities in that—according to a substantial amount of the need achievement research—tasks of intermediate levels of difficulty were more attractive to people with high achievement motives.

Such a finding makes incentive a less clear-cut concept as it relates to expectancy. This is subsequently brought out by Atkinson (1964) when he talks about the differential effects success and failure have on different people, particularly in terms of their personalities and the difficulty level of the tasks they are engaged in. That is, as we know intuitively, *sometimes* success strengthens the subsequent probability of the same response and sometimes it doesn't. *Sometimes* failure reduces the subsequent probability of the same response and sometimes it doesn't. Thus the assumptions pertaining to incentive and expectancy (namely, $Is = 1 - Ps$) only *describe* the conditions that exist in instances of achievement-oriented behavior.

They do not explain *why* the incentive values of success and failure are related to an individual's expectations. They merely acknowledge that the incentive values of anticipated consequences, in achievement-oriented actions, are *related* to the strength of expectancy. This is so simply because the value of a so-called *rewarding* event is *not* dependent on the past frequency of attaining it, and both are determinants of the strength of a subsequent tendency to perform the same activity.

Though this whole relationship is much more complex than what we have described here, it does have one clear message for us in sport and physical activity. That is, the consequences of an individual participation in sport will have varying degrees of incentive value to him and will influence not only his subsequent activity in that sport, but also the intensity with which he participates. This, to a large extent, will be a function of how successful he expects to be. It is such an observation that now leads us directly to David Birch's and Joseph Veroff's (1966) treatment of incentive systems in human motivation.

INCENTIVE SYSTEMS: BIRCH AND VEROFF

The Birch and Veroff treatment of incentive in their paradigm of human motivation is entirely consistent with what has been described here. That is, they take the position that four major sources of effects determine goal-directed or instrumental action in human behavior. These determinants are called *availability, expectancy, incentive,* and *motive* and are seen by the authors as being a function both of the characteristics of the person himself and of the person's environment. Each determinant is seen as contributing independently to the strength of a person's goal-directed tendencies, the decisions he makes regarding alternative choices, and the subsequent courses of action he actually pursues.

Briefly, the four determinants are described as follows:

1. Availability

This refers to the extent to which a particular stimulus situation (or environment) makes available particular courses of action. Aggressive actions are more likely to occur, for example, in contact sports such as football and hockey than in sports such as gymnastics or tennis. That is, situations give rise to, and permit, certain specifiable courses of action. Thus, to understand an individual's motivated actions in a typical sports situation requires of the observer a knowledge of what responses are actually available to the participant. Such responses are naturally a function of the present situation and of the person's past history. Situational characteristics, such as the type of game being played or the specific physical environment where the game is in progress are straightforward. Historical factors, however, are more interesting and revolve around two factors. First, are the *habits* a person has incorporated in past situations similar to the one that now confronts him. We know that particular courses of action (such as aggressiveness) are more likely to occur when there is a past history of such action in that situation. Thus the availability of a course of action is dependent on the habits of the person, which in turn are related to previous similar actions of that person in the past. Secondly, certain situations *suggest* relevant goals to the individual. A person, for example, who is disposed to anticipate achievement as an outcome of some action is more likely to think of courses of action which will yield achievement than one who is not so disposed. Such a person, because of his past history, will anticipate achievement outcomes and will think of responses instrumental to achievement.

2. Expectancy

This attributes anticipation to the individual and thus permits the *outcomes* or *consequences* of particular courses of action to, in fact, determine those actions. If a child has enjoyed success in a particular sport, the suggestion of further participation in that sport generates in him an expectancy of more attractive participation outcomes. Even though expectancies may occur as a result of direct or immediate perceptions of a relationship, they are generally, like availability, a function of past associations. Expectancy, though just another way of saying "the expectancy that engaging in a course of action will lead to a particular goal," serves the important function of linking a possible course of action to its probable outcome or consequences.

3. Incentive

This refers to the incentive values that are attached to the consequences or outcomes of these particular courses of action. If people consistently approach situations possessing certain kinds of consequences, then those consequences are said to have *positive* incentive value for those people. If they avoid certain situations, then the situations are seen as having *negative* incentive values for them. Thus the incentive value of an expected outcome (and its strength) becomes an important determinant of the courses of action a person chooses to pursue. Though absolute measures of incentive value are hard to come by, we know intuitively that some outcomes have more powerful incentive value than others; for example, winning a championship game has more positive incentive value to the players than winning an exhibition game.

4. Motive

This refers to the basic personality disposition a person has to various *general* classes of incentives. The strength of such an attraction to a general class of consequences can be seen as referring to a motive for that class. For example, people are said to have a high achievement motive if they generally are attracted to situations mainly involving achievement incentives, that is, they generally are attracted to situations in which there are good possibilities that they will be evaluated. Motives, in this sense, thus become modifiers of incentives. That is, the incentive value of a particular consequence becomes even stronger or more powerful if the individual also has a strong motive for that class of incentives. The incentive value attached to winning in sport, for example, will be even higher for people with strong achievement or power motives.

With such a descriptive analysis of the main determinants of motivation in mind, Birch and Veroff (1966) now proceeded to expand it into a paradigm consisting of what they feel are the major incentive systems that account for man's significant recurrent instrumental behaviors, that is, the major goal-directed behavior all people engage in. And it is here that we can now begin to see the implications the paradigm has for understanding motivation in physical activity and competitive sport settings. They postulate that a motive, the incentive itself, and related goal activities form a network of motivational variables that can be called an *incentive system*. And they feel that seven major incentive systems can account for most of our motivated behavior. These seven systems are termed the sensory, curiosity, affiliative, aggressive, achievement, power, and independence incentive systems, and though some amalgamate with each other in day-to-day behavior, it is best to view them independently and in isolation at this point. The authors justify their stance on the basis that each system has been manipulated in research studies and each system figures in the common developmental problems each person faces during growth and development. That is, there is general agreement among psychologists that people are typically confronted by developmental problems revolving around the following:

1. Regulating their bodily experiences (sensory incentive system)
2. Reacting to new stimuli (curiosity incentive system)
3. Depending on social contact with others (affiliative incentive system)
4. Reacting to frustration by others (aggressive incentive system)
5. Evaluating their own performance (achievement incentive system)
6. Withstanding the influence of others (power incentive system)
7. Operating on their own (independence incentive system)

In discussing each system, and attempting to relate the discussion to motivation in physical activity and sport, we might keep in mind the following questions

1. What is the actual goal-attainment in each system? What goal is the person striving for and under what conditions does this struggle take place?
2. What motives underlie the system and how do they help explain a shift from one activity to another?
3. How does the enjoyment of a particular goal work against itself to reduce that enjoyment?
4. What are the environmental conditions? Are incentives actually available to the person?

SENSORY INCENTIVES

Sensory incentives depend on the stimulation of sensory or bodily experiences: tasting, hearing, smelling, seeing, and feeling. Pain, for example, is a negative sensory incentive. Sensory incentives are quite naturally a part of physical activity and sport. The good feelings one gets from various forms of vigorous exercise, from bodily contact, or from the smooth execution of a complex physical skill can all be explained in terms of sensory incentive value.

Many psychologists also feel that sensory incentives underlie the striving for release from tension, accumulated from too much or too little stimulation. The businessman who releases his tensions on the squash court might be a case in point. The good feelings he has after the game have sensory incentive value for him.

The negative sensory incentive of physical pain is one most of us have experienced and as we all know, different people have different pain thresholds—some can handle it or ignore it more effectively than others. Nevertheless, negative incentives cause avoidance rather than approach and it is in this sense that we can understand why some kids refuse to play in some sports or participate in some kinds of activities. If these activities or sports have unpleasant or noxious outcomes, such as pain or injury, children will anticipate those outcomes and avoid them by not participating.

In terms of sensory *motive*, we have good reason to believe that definite individual differences exist in people's levels of activation or the levels of stimulation they are attracted to. This has been constantly demonstrated in the literature on anxiety, arousal, and drive levels. People differ in their customary levels of arousal. Some are high anxious individuals, some low, and some are hyperactive, while some are only slightly active. Part of the explanation for such a phenomenon could be the different types of sensory motives people have. If a person comes from a background of frequent and intense stimulation, and this stimulation is constantly connected to bodily sensations, a strong sensory motive is gradually incorporated into his or her psychological make-up. For such a person, any experience having strong sensory incentives attached to it will be attractive. Physical contact sports or physically demanding activities such as rowing or long-distance running or swimming all have this attraction for these people. And though many other motives—particularly the social ones like achievement—may also be operating, it would seem that such sports could not be attractive to people with lower needs for sensory stimulation. I have recently explored tension seeking in sport as a function of each individual's customary level of acti-vation, that is, those who have normally high levels of activation actively seek exciting and tension-filled experiences. I have little doubt that, again, such a phenomenon has as its basis, strong sensory motives.

Intense bodily stimulation, such as violent or sustained vigorous phys-ical exercise has within it a built-in reduction mechanism of its own. That is, and particularly in this sense, the harder one goes at his exercise, the more quickly he will drain himself of the desire for that activity. When the consummatory value of activity is reduced to its lowest optimal point, that activity ceases and the person shifts to some other behavior. It is the activity that has reduced itself. Eating a large steak is an excellent example. It also applies in exercising and is probably one of the major reasons for staleness in athletes or slumps and losing streaks in sport. The satisfaction, particularly in sensory terms, in an activity decreases as one experiences it. We obviously know and accept this when we switch bored athletes to other activities to keep their interest up.

With reference to the availability of sensory responses in our environ-ments, it is obvious that physical activity and sports participation have them in abundance. Almost any movement activity provides numerous sensory opportunities and, depending on the person's past experiences and habit structures, virtually automatic releasing properties for sensory needs. The boy or girl knows that an afternoon at the swimming pool is going to be exhausting but great, and can't wait to get there. If we do anything in our sports program, we should make sure that pleasant sensory experiences are available to children.

CURIOSITY INCENTIVES

One of the reasons children choose to participate in sport is the incentive value they attach to trying something new or different. There is little doubt that such curiosity incentives operate strongly in the pure play of little children, and there is good reason to believe that similar incentives retain their significance into ages in which sports participation starts to occur. The desire to optimize stimulus complexity is a major factor in this basic attraction. The inherent complexities of games like baseball, football, hockey, and basketball provide the child with constantly changing new stimuli and the need to optimize such complexities motivates them to participate in such sports. This general effect on the child is focused by him in terms of his perceiving changes in stimulation. Such changes elicit the curiosity motive incentive system and all that is required for the system to operate is a recognition by the person of some change in the pattern of stimulation impinging upon him or her. Sports do this for children, especially sports we could describe as highly variable. All of us have conflicting needs for both predictability and variability in our lives, and the latter need relates to curiosity incentives. Children often participate initially just to see what the sport is like, or because their friends are doing it, or because their parents did it, and they want to find out for themselves.

A strong curiosity motive is probably related to the general human disposition toward complexity. From very young babies to adults there seem to be actual individual differences in the way people tend to make discriminations. Some children are taught to make many constant discriminations, while others are not. The former contributes to strong curiosity motives, the latter does not. Children who participate in a wide variety of activities probably have significantly strong curiosity motives and are doing so because of the attraction of stimulus changes. This is further reinforced by considering boredom as having strong negative curiosity incentives attached to it.

In reference to sports motives, the curiosity motive and its related incentives probably do not last long. Undoubtedly other motives take over and become salient. That is, once you've discovered something and your curiosity is satisfied, the sport will have to have other major attractions.

ACHIEVEMENT INCENTIVES

Much has been made in recent years about achievement motivation in sport and physical activity, so I will not dwell on it at any length here. Certainly in our culture this is probably the *master* incentive system working in sport as we know it. Here the incentives are interpreted by the person as successful competition with standards of excellence applied to one's performance. If a child does better than he did the last time, or better than another person, or better than some external standard, then he or she is said to have successfully competed with a standard of excellence. In each of the performances, strong achievement incentives were operating and the more difficult the task is (up to a point), and the more public evaluation of these performances there is, the stronger the incentive value will be.

It must be realized at this point that both absolute and relative standards of excellence are used by sports participants. And that they are linked closely to individual differences in level of aspiration. People, and children in particular, tend to lean heavily on absolute or external standards when they are *unaware* of their own actual capabilities (a type of social comparison). However, when a person has some idea of how capable he is, then he will judge his own performances by his own capacities—that is, a relative standard of excellence. This, of course, is the motive pattern we should encourage in children's sport—have them judge the excellence of their performances by their own standards. Unfortunately, we refuse to let them do this by forcing external, absolute standards on them, like winning all the time, or getting their name in the paper.

The achievement motive is naturally generated in children who have been instilled with the values of success in life. This disposition to achieve thus becomes a strong personality pattern, particularly in children and adults involved in a competitive sports program. There is, in fact, a strong possibility that people low in achievement motive do not long stay in sport. Such people probably are overly concerned with failure and withdraw from competitive situations to avoid unpleasantness. The negative achievement incentive value attached to failure in sport is undoubtedly a reason for people dropping out of sport, especially when the culture overemphasizes the importance of success.

It is also fairly clear that when excellence is fully attained in sport, the person usually shifts to some other activity. Thus, it is not the enjoyment of success that is the strong incentive but rather the striving *toward* success. There are indications that public recognition that a task is complete is not necessarily important for a person to feel that he is through with the task. It seems to be more important for *him* to feel psychologically that he is finished with the task. There is little doubt that this is the feeling that keeps great athletes going in times of self-doubt or non-recognition by the public.

From the literature there are indications that three main response systems dominate the achievement environment of people. The first of these is *competence,* and the main question here is how important is it for a child to have skill in order for him to respond to achievement incentives in sport? If children were never judged by absolute standards of excellence in sport, were only judged according to their own capacities, then they all would have high achievement motives and in competitive sport would choose achievement behaviors.

This never happens. Comparisons are always being made and usually achievement standards are highly ambiguous. Everyone has his own idea of what a good hockey player is, or what is necessary to be a great gymnast. Because of this, children experience both success *and* failure and their achievement motivation is directly affected. To breed success in young athletes requires a precise assessment of exactly what kinds and levels of competence are required in the activity. This is true simply because competence and the motive to achieve are highly related.

The second major response system, *a sense of effectiveness,* exists because not all competent people feel competent. The old belief that one has only to try in order to succeed is often the only response available to one in achievement settings such as sport. Such an attitude is inculcated into our children at very tender ages. Most children in our sports program are conditioned toward sensing the potential for their own effectiveness. This leads directly to high achievement motives and the importance of successful performance.

The third response system revolves around the critical importance of a *masculine identity* for successful achievement. In our culture, achievement is linked to a masculine sexual identity and women in sport have suffered from it for many decades. Achievement behaviors, or even dispositions, are readily available to boys in sport but not to girls. Attitudes and value systems that load heavily on what a girl will do with her life are often incompatible with achievement motivation. To retain a feminine identity then, most girls in our culture modulate their efforts to achieve. The converse is also true—boys successfully generate a masculine identity in order to achieve.

AFFILIATION INCENTIVES

Many children elect to participate in sport because of the affiliation incentives attached to that participation. This is the attraction to other people in order to feel reassured from these other people that one's self is acceptable. Such incentives are particularly important for little children in sport when they are anxious over their own self-evaluation or self-worth. A feeling of acceptance can come about through exchanging feelings or attitudes with them, or through contact with children associated with previously attained incentives. Affiliation needs are most easily satisfied by people perceived as similar to one's self. This is a strong reason for kids wanting to "make the team."

215

The two most powerful affiliation incentives are both negative incentives: fear of social isolation and fear of rejection. Anxiety generated by being socially isolated drives children to seek affiliation with groups of their own kind, particularly elite groups such as sports teams. Fear of rejection generates much the same kind of anxiety. Children seek affiliation because of strong drives toward self-evaluation. Also, in order to achieve evaluation in the absence of external, absolute criteria, they seek membership in groups for purposes of *social comparison.* Such comparison provides them with information about how worthwhile they are and exactly how valuable their capacities are. Once such anxiety is allayed, children can easily forego friendship. This is why childhood friendships tend to be relatively transient. As children mature, their reasons for friendship become more diffuse and, as a result, more stable. Thus such strong affiliation incentives can be seen as major determinants of children's *initial* participations in competitive sports programs. The desire for affiliation with attractive social and elite groups such as sports teams or clubs, though possibly *generated* by feelings of anxiety, can be satisfied simply by belonging to a group in which one's teammates are similar in age, ability, and sex. One can also speculate that as children grow older and develop self-confidence in their team membership, affiliation incentives become less salient or are replaced by stronger, more relevant incentives such as those connected to achievement.

If a person's affiliation incentive entails obtaining acceptance from another person, then it follows that his most effective available response is to perform activities that are attractive to other people. Sport in particular provides such opportunities in two ways. First, there is the natural importance of playing or performing well on one's team or in one's group. Such performance engenders admiration, support, and social approval and has strong affiliative incentive value for the individual. Second, there is the potential of sports membership for inducing love for oneself from other people on the team. This is done by establishing close social and emotional bonds with one's teammates and with one's coach. Liking or loving others inspires them to like or love you. It is one of our human paradoxes that those of us who are unable to love or truly like other people are those who seek the incentive the most, while those who are well-liked or loved by other people do *not* depend on the incentive that much. It thus becomes extremely important for coaches to recognize those players or athletes who are seeking affiliation incentives in this manner, because to reject such attempts would seriously undermine that person's self-worth. It is also interesting that people seeking affiliative goals often try to do things to please other people that in fact are things that serve to irritate those people.

This irritation leads to rejection, and such rejection simply causes the rejected person to seek the affiliation incentive even more strongly.

AGGRESSION INCENTIVES

The purest aggression incentive is the wish to do intentional harm or injury to another person, and the greater the injury, the greater the incentive value to the aggressor. Though such an interpretation might be distasteful to most of us, the fact nevertheless remains that an aggression incentive is said to be present when the intentional destruction or injury of another person occurs or is sought. Intuitively we can accept this in a sport such as boxing, where the best prizefighters tend to be those who truly enjoy hurting or injuring their opponents. Such an interpretation revolves around the concept of "reactive" or "goal" aggression, aggressive behavior that is engaged in, for and of itself, with no other goals or objectives. Injuring or harming the other person is the only goal. Such a context, of course, is relatively rare in sport, where most of the aggressive behavior is what we call "instrumental" aggression—aggressive behavior directed toward attaining goals unconnected to the aggression. One is aggressive, for example, in basketball, in order to capture many rebounds in a game. It is the number of rebounds that is the goal, not the aggressive behavior itself.

Although the idea has been advanced that the greater the frustration experienced by the person, the greater the aggression incentive, we must nevertheless remember that frustration is not the *only* antecedent to aggression. This is so even when the interference causing the frustration is "aggressive" interference. It is easy to accept, particularly in competitive sport situations, that when the agent of frustration (for example, an opposing player) is perceived as *intentionally* interfering with one's goals (for example, catching a pass in football), then the aggression incentive becomes even more salient or immediate. Most aggression behavior in sport, it could be speculated, probably does revolve around frustrating circumstances, but it is important to remember that the pure frustration–aggression hypothesis of Miller, Dollard, and associates has not, in fact, been verified. Frustrating situations such as these generated through keen competition in sport seem to be situations in which aggression incentives naturally appear. Regardless, then, of whether or not a pure linkage generally exists between aggression and frustration, the question remains, "In what manner do the particular consequences of aggressive action have incentive value to an individual participating in competitive sport?" And, going one step further, "Does such incentive value determine the choices a person makes in his sports participation and the intensity with which such participation is pursued?"

Two ideas have been explored that could answer such questions. The first is the idea of constitutional differences as having a bearing on the development of the aggression motive in individuals. Some infants, from birth, are extremely reactive and seem to experience sudden pain or discomfort constantly. Tantrums, for example, are thought to be response reactions to pain such as teething. (Other babies can be quite phlegmatic.) One can consider that aggressive dispositions are gradually developed in children for whom such pain stimuli are severe and constant. The second idea revolves around the family conditions that a child is constantly exposed to and that he incorporates into his psychological structure. Here, as we know, parents, siblings, or even the micro-world of the child can be constant and severe sources of pain to the child. Such experiences set the stage for the development of strong aggressive motives and it is these motive-states that we normally label "resentment." That is, children are so often thwarted or blocked in their desires by other members of the family (particularly their parents) that a reservoir of resentment remains with them sometimes for a lifetime. Children socialized in such a background seek aggression incentives quite naturally when confronted with opportunities such as competitive sport. We can often see such resentment spilling out on the hockey rinks and football fields across the country.

Thus if we have a person with a strong *motive* state for aggression, based either on constitutional differences or on a reservoir of resentment, or both, and we provide him with opportunities in which aggression incentives are available and highly important (as in competitive sports), then we will see extremely aggressive behavior. Add to this the fact that physically aggressive behaviors are *also learned* from the imitation of hyper-aggressive parents, and we have a partial explanation of the salience and power of aggression incentives in sport.

INDEPENDENCE INCENTIVES

By independence, we mean accomplishing an activity without help. Independence incentives thus become salient when attached to courses of action the individual chooses and engages in without the direct aid of other people. In fact, we could say that the independence incentive is operating particularly for people who *resist* other people assisting them. Such a desire can connote negative-affiliation incentives, and this kind of incentive has been described as "counterdependency"; that is, some people see independence as a means of preventing affiliative dependence. And such reactiveness may be either historical or situational in nature. Sports participation obviously can be a function of either. We can sense that some athletes are participating in an individual sport simply because they have an emotional investment in being independent; being "on their own" is important to them in and of itself. Such athletes are the ones who *enjoy* training by themselves, succeeding by themselves, and failing, if necessary, by themselves. Counterdependency, is slightly different. Here we probably have the athlete who chooses individual sports as a negative reaction to membership in team sports, simply because he doesn't want to be dependent on someone else. Townsend (1958) assumes here that a person who is reactively interested in independence has also a strong incentive to be dependent. The conflict between the two produces counterdependency strivings. Coaches would be well advised to make themselves aware of the crucial distinctions between these two kinds of independence motivation in some of their athletes.

Again, the disposition toward independence is incorporated at early ages and in particular kinds of parental and family environments. During the time when children are attempting to master their own environment, there are greater or lesser pressures against their sense of autonomy. Pressure to accomplish things on one's own would naturally contribute to establishing the independence motive in the child's personality. Sports participation for the young is often used as a vehicle for such development. Many children, in fact, quickly recognize in sport opportunities to be independent of their parents or siblings. It is in this sense that independence motivation becomes an integral part of sports participation. It is here also that independence attains an interesting juxtaposition with competence. That is, in order to be independent from other people, one must be competent. If one is not, then one has to depend on help from other, more qualified people. Thus people who achieve independence are usually those who are competent. For children and adults participating in sport, a conflict between independence and achievement incentives often quite naturally occurs—that is, sometimes, to remain independent, the individual has to forego the solution of a problem, or the further improvement of a particular skill. Some athletes, we know, are like this—they will not allow anyone to assist them, even when such assistance promotes their accomplishment. For such people, continued independence in the face of failure is a highly probable action sequence and it is the responsibility of the coach or instructor to recognize the behavior for what it is and deal with it accordingly.

Three situations, however, exist in which other incentive systems become dominant over independence incentives, and these occur regularly in sport. The first is the need for social evaluation. Independent athletes will in fact interrupt their concentration on independence incentives when some sort of outside evaluation of their ability or performance becomes salient. Such behavior can be seen when an athlete will agree to be part of a formal competition in which achievement incentives are dominant. The second is the replacement of independence incentives by curiosity incentives. When a person becomes interested in another sport, the continued independent activity in the original sport will cease. Here we can see why some boys and girls shift from one sport to another. The third is rise to dominance of achievement incentives as a person unsuccessfully persists in an independent activity. Highly independent athletes, if faced with continued failure, will turn to others for advice, help, or instruction.

POWER INCENTIVES

Last but not least are those incentives attached to the controlling of other people's attitudes, opinions, and decisions. The power incentive is thus characterized as the condition of obtaining the means of influencing other people's decisions. The coach is power-motivated, then, when for him the important incentives attached to coaching are related to having control over his players. This is the so-called "ego-tripping" that we hear so much about. And although the term is quite incorrect (in Freudian terms especially), the behavior is prevalent enough today in competitive sport to justify an analysis.

Power incentives involve not only attempts at having power over other people, but also indirect attempts to establish one's self in a power position. Though any social situation can be interpreted as the influence one has over others, it is probably more productive in this context to restrict our discussion to the influences that cause another person to *change* his attitude about someone or something. A teacher, or a coach, for example, satisfies a power incentive when one of his students or athletes learns something from him. We all know such an outcome as being extremely gratifying and worthwhile, particularly when the world at large delivers social approval. When Lombardi turned the Green Bay Packers from the laughing stock of the NFL into champions, he satisfied particularly strong power incentives. When a player, or an athlete, is able to switch spectator opinion of him from derision to approval, then he has in a sense satisfied a strong power incentive. Coaches tread this line constantly. The success of their teams is of direct personal concern to them because of the massive outside social evaluations they are exposed to. The higher the level of competition, the more powerful become the various incentives attached to success or failure, so much so, in fact, that in many cases power incentives become dominant over others simply because the coach reads such situations as basically power struggle situations. If he gets his players to do things his way, everyone will be successful. This is why some situations such as winning in sport may appear to involve achievement incentives, but in actuality could involve power incentives.

Intermeshed in these struggles for control is the desire of some individuals not only to influence other people, but also to *resist* any influence from them. Thus power incentives are also attached to successfully withstanding another person's influence. And it is here that we have the classic example of personality conflicts between coaches and their athletes. Each is resisting the other's influence while at the same time trying to gain control over the other.

However, let's return briefly to the earlier question, "Are power incentives determining factors in why or how some children participate in competitive sport?" Undoubtedly they are. Some children can easily see that by participating in sport they will change the opinions certain people have toward them. The little boy knows that if he scores a goal in a peewee hockey game, his father, his coach, his teammates, and spectators will automatically hold higher opinions of him than if he doesn't. If such incentives are salient for him, then he is engaged in basic power motivation. An older boy or girl knows that through successful sports participation, he or she can gain recognition, status, and prestige from peer groups, and for many young sports participants, at any time these are in fact the major incentives.

Though "influence behavior" is abhorrent to most people, it is nevertheless a fact of life. As some psychologists have stated (particularly Berlyne), all people have a unidirectional drive upward to improve themselves, and when such a drive becomes dependent on social evaluation, power motivation is operating.

SUMMARY

It is reasonable to contend that in order to explore the motivational determinants underlying sports participation, we must be clearly aware of the following:

1. Incentives operate differently for different people in different situations.
2. The expectancies they have are a function of the incentive values they attach to perceived outcomes.
3. Some incentives work with or against other incentives.
4. A determination of exactly which incentive systems are most salient for a person at any given moment is necessary if we are to understand his behavior at that time.

Although the seven incentive systems have been treated here as being somewhat distinct and isolated, human behavior is, of course, the outcome of many combinations of incentives, all interacting at the same time. It was even mentioned that conflicts might arise between the incentive systems and the individual would be caught between a positive and a negative incentive. Such is the case, for example, when the individual wishes to pursue some independent action but he feels constrained by affiliative ties to others.

MOTIVATION AND PERFORMANCE

Motivation is usually viewed as perhaps second only to skill ability as a factor in sport success, and I imagine there are many individuals who might give motivation the gold star ranking. Motivation is considered the intangible that makes the difference between winning and losing. Talent is important but when competitors are equal in ability, motivation can provide the margin of victory. This kind of talk is common among players and coaches, and it is supported by experimental psychologists. Young (1936) reported a striking difference between performance levels of subjects of similar aptitude but dissimilar motivation. Woodworth and Schlosberg (1954) spoke of ability and motivation relative to performance in the following manner: ''Both ability and motivation are factors in performance, and if either of them is entirely lacking, the performance does not occur. Ability is like a machine which cannot do its work unless power is applied.''

Level of aspiration

An individual's aspirations are much related to the achievement motive discussed earlier in Birch and Veroff's incentive motivation schema. ''Level of aspiration'' can be an ambiguous term, since a person's aspirations have many levels. The Little Leaguer aspires to a career in professional baseball—in this case, aspiration is a hope that is quite remote in reality but perhaps very real to the aspirant. The National Football League athlete aspires to All-Pro status, since his past performances have been outstanding—here, aspiration is more of an expectation, since there is enough positive feedback to make this a realistic possibility. Aspiration, then, can be a ''hoped-for'' condition, but it can also connote expectancy. It might be wise to operationalize aspiration as aspiration *and* expectation. Level of aspiration would then refer to motivation to achieve ideal goals, and level of expectation would refer to the pursuit of realistic goals.

Level of aspiration is part of the goal-directed aspect of motivation. Generally, level of aspiration rises after success and drops after failure. Initial study on this subject was undertaken by Hoppe (1930) and served as a stimulus to future research. Out of 165 cases, Hoppe reported a 32 percent increase in level of aspiration after success and a 27 percent decrease after failure. Later studies verified the direction of these findings and revealed even greater increases and decreases in aspiration after success and failure, respectively.

It is commonly believed that one can have too much of a good thing. Gilinsky and Stewart (1949) reported that expectation of failure developed more quickly when failure followed uninterrupted success than when it followed intermittent success and failure. Is this not the point Rushall made when he spoke of reinforcing his athletes at an 80:20 positive–negative ratio? Constant success soon loses its effectiveness and athletes fall into the "fat cat" syndrome. Vogel's article (2.12), dealing with satiation of the success experience, is relevant to this point.

Another point was raised by Hoppe—success and failure cannot be conceived in objective terms. It is necessary to take into account the performer's aspiration or expectation or both. The following two equations will explain this more clearly:

Level of aspiration − performance = goal discrepancy
Level of expectation − performance = attainment discrepancy

How much discrepancy will the individual tolerate? Success and failure are contingent upon the answer to this question. If the level of expectation is realistic and honest (none of the often recommended "shooting for the stars") and the ensuing performance falls short of the projected value, then failure is the result. On the other hand, if the performer has allowed some leeway, the same performance might be deemed successful. Success and failure must be defined in terms of the individual.

How do individuals judge their levels of attainment so as to determine whether their performance was successful or not? Relative and absolute standards of judging excellence were discussed earlier but need to be brought to bear on the present discussion. Birch and Veroff summarized their discussion on this point by stating:

> Both external and absolute standards of excellence are especially important in determining the levels of aspiration in ambiguous achievement settings, and internal and relative standards of excellence are most easily applied to performance situations when it is clear what performance is required and how well a person can do it.

Additionally, the consequences of any action (a loss, for instance) must be attributed to one's performance and not to chance before the performance can be classified as success or failure. If the individual is able to rationalize the situation, he might be able to convince (really deceive) himself that the loss was not the result of his faulty performance. It would seem that the sport situation, with its myriad of statistics, ought to provide excellent opportunities to allow the individual to see himself as he really is. Although this might seem harsh when one considers the athlete who has little talent, it is still better to correctly perceive than to be deceived.

This view might be an idealistic one, since success is sometimes, maybe even often, contingent on the "bounce of the ball," the "rub of the green," and the "luck of the draw." This detracts from the individual's acceptance of his own power to succeed or fail and allows an "out" that in some cases is a true explanation. Another related phenomenon also masks the concept that skill is the sole determinant of success. Superstition is rampant in sport, and it gives rise to a host of ritualistic behaviors that are viewed as important antecedents to successful performance. Nearly every imaginable gimmick has been used in one situation or another, and I am sure the reader who is interested in superstition and sport will even find out about some unimaginable ones in the following sources: Beisser (1967), Gmelch (1972), Gregory and Petrie (1972, 1973). Malinowski (1948) claimed that magic (rituals, taboos, and fetishes) is prevalent in all situations of chance and uncertainty. If that is correct, then the athlete is perhaps less likely than persons in other situations to see a clear relationship between his performance and successful outcomes. Sport might then have to be classified as one of these chance-ridden and uncertain settings.

Level of aspiration is also related to the difficulty of the task and the accompanying chance to succeed. If the task is too difficult and the chance of succeeding is only 10 percent, then no performance is likely to be seen as unsuccessful. Atkinson (1958) theorized that when there is a 50:50 chance of succeeding, the individual will raise his level of expectation and will work harder to achieve the goal. Intermediate probabilities of success promote enhanced expectation, whereas extreme probabilities (10:90 or 90:10) decrease levels of expectation. Research relating Atkinson's hypothesis to expectation and other variables has generally supported the premise (see Martens and White, 1975).

One could interpret upsets in sport contests according to the preceding discussion. When the odds for success are strongly in one team's favor (4:1 for example), that team's motivation to succeed is not at the optimum level. The resultant performance will, therefore, be less than maximum. If the opponents do not share the pre-game view that they will probably lose, or if sloppy play by the odds-on favorite in the early stages of the contest, leads them to re-evaluate their chances for winning, conditions are ripe for an upset. Coaches never like their teams to be picked as "sure" winners and perhaps are being honest when they claim that "on any given day any team in this league can defeat any other."

Thus far the discussion has centered around the individual and level of aspiration as if no one else were involved in goal setting. However, others are definitely involved in this process—coaches, parents, and peers. From a coaching standpoint, the concept of expectancy should perhaps replace aspiration. This would hopefully lead to choosing realistic rather than ideal goals. Presumably every coach would like to know just what goals each athlete perceives as important and worth pursuing. Such knowledge might in fact lead to widespread discouragement in the coaching profession. I suspect the athletes would not match the coaches' motives to achieve and would profess less lofty goals.

The findings from a research study by Brehm and Cohen (1962) suggest that goals ought to be professed in public, either orally or in writing. In their words, a pronounced commitment leads to a higher motive to achieve (perhaps more correctly a higher incentive). The individual realizes that failure will threaten self-esteem, especially since "all his cards are on the table," and will, therefore, be likely to increase his motivation to avoid the discrepancy between expectation and attainment.

Zander (1974) has extended the concepts of achievement motivation to groups, and has speculated that groups with high motives to succeed will choose moderately challenging goals while those high in motives to avoid failure will choose extreme goals. Goal setting is a compromise between these two motives, for groups just as it is for individuals. One sure way for a group (team) to develop strong fears of failure is to have failed often in the past. This is one of many good reasons for defining success in ways other than winning. To have performed as well as one can should in no way be construed as failure. Zander explains the vicious cycle that results from repeated failing. Group members begin to feel that their performance is inadequate and as they begin to feel unimportant in the group, membership becomes less significant. As membership declines in motivational value, so does performance, and the cycle is

225

complete. If the group reduced its goals, it would have a greater chance to succeed. Often this cannot be done, however, because the members' goals were set for them, or they were coerced into setting overly high goals. In an authoritarian sport setting, would athletes aspire to less than the league championship?

Results from industrial studies (and industrial psychology is somewhat akin to sport psychology) show that when managers set unrealistically high goals, they may be forcing failure on the group—including setting in motion the vicious cycle described above. Even if, as is likely, the group members decide to set their own level of expectation, they still must *perform* against a much higher level. Attainment of less than the manager-set goals will be construed by management as unsuccessful performance. The reader could substitute the word "coach" for "manager" and "team" for "group" without altering the meaning of these statements.

The remedy is only too clear. Include athletes in the goal-setting process; structure the situation so they will not feel too threatened to state their honest expectations; and take their expectation levels into account in determining future coach–athlete interactions. This does not mean that attempts should not be made to adjust their expectations, but it does negate the imposition of the coach's goals on the athletes. Conflicts are inevitable if the difference between expectancy levels is great. This is a good example of the power struggle between coach and athlete referred to earlier.

If athletes do not possess motives to avoid success and do not experience *both* fear of success and fear of failure, then much of the foregoing could be labeled academic. However, such is not the case. Beisser (1967), in his fascinating book *The Madness in Sports,* describes a case study of a tennis player who did all he could to fail even though he was highly talented. In his role as a psychiatrist, Beisser discovered that the athlete had a high motive to avoid success. Ogilvie (1968c) elaborated on this condition, labeling it success phobia (fear of success).

Consider the following remarks made by a hockey player: "I was more worried about making too many mistakes than to even think about scoring two goals." What is the overriding performance motive? The athlete does not approach the game with an intent to succeed but rather with a fear of performing badly. The author of these words was not a Little Leaguer but Syl Apps, Most Valuable Player of the 1975 National Hockey League All-Star Game. Similar comments appeared on questionnaires completed by several National Hockey League goaltenders (Fisher and Schoen, 1972). It may be that in competitive sports, the motive to avoid failure is at least as strong as the achievement motive. Hope for an outstanding performance may be overshadowed by fear of an inferior one. An average performance is therefore a satisfying one.

Level of aspiration is clearly intertwined with the individual's concept of success. Darrell Mudra (1971), a head football coach, offers some suggestions on improving the perception of success from both the coach's and the athlete's perspective: "What is it from your point of view? Try not to interfere with the players' right to do this also. We need to acquire habits of success. What may be habits of success for one person can be habits of failure for another. Try to avoid getting caught in the trap of accepting the success stereotypes." By success stereotypes, Mudra means the elitist statement, "Winning is the only thing."

In speaking about the attachment of success to sport performance, Alderman (1974b) asserted that setting *reasonably* high goals can serve as an incentive in itself. If successful performance (in the athlete's own terms) becomes an end in itself, then losing and the consequent fear of failing to meet some absolute standard are robbed of some of their devastating effects. The pressure to win can be removed if the athlete aspires to and expects high-level performance. There certainly is no intent here to diminish the intensity of participation; overly ambitious goals often promote a reduction in goal-directed behavior and results opposite to what is intended.

Aspiration and even intention do not always succeed in producing desired behavior to reach goals for several reasons: (a) social prohibition of certain actions—for example, aggression; (b) physical impairment; (c) lack of the necessary ability; and (d) approach–avoidance. It is to this last point that the next section is addressed.

Conflict model of sport involvement

With any potential course of action there are bound to be conflicts, and this is true in sport settings. The decision whether or not to act, and with what intensity, has to be made before any action ensues. The confounding issue is that there are positive aspects of the goal that produce approach feelings, while at the same time there are negative aspects that produce avoidance feelings. Action might be viewed as the resultant of the arithmetic difference between approach and avoidance.

Picture a swimmer who runs into an icy lake but on entering quickly comes to a halt. He takes a few steps forward and a few back, repeating this process several times. The "swimmer" is vacillating between the anticipated pleasure of swimming (approach) and the unpleasant sensation of freezing (avoidance). What is the final action going to be? In simplistic terms, if the approach feelings are greater than the avoidance feelings, the individual will eventually take the plunge. However, if the water is just too cold, the individual may be satisfied to return to the beach to pursue more pleasant endeavors. This latter decision may not be final, and several renewed attempts may be made to enter the water.

Conflicts can take many forms, including approach–avoidance, approach–approach, and avoidance–avoidance. An example has already been given for the approach–avoidance situation. In the approach–approach conflict, two goals are vying for the individual's attention. Suppose an individual has a good part-time job after school and is encouraged to try out for the basketball team. If he makes the team, he will give up his job and the money he would get from it; if he keeps his job and does not even try out for the team, he feels he is not using his athletic ability—he is not actualizing that part of himself. It is also true that either decision will result in some positive gains.

The avoidance–avoidance situation does not offer a similar opportunity. Consider the football player who does not enjoy the rough contact aspect of the game but whose community places such a high value on football participation that he joins the team. He particularly dislikes the daily blocking and tackling drills. He is caught in a double-bind situation because when he avoids the contact the coach heaps ridicule upon him. The situation leaves no out; he must choose the less threatening of two unpleasant alternatives.

A double approach–avoidance conflict is also possible and is represented diagrammatically in Figure 12. From the possible benefits to be derived from sport participation, the individual anticipates success and

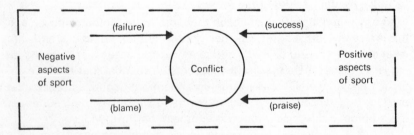

Figure 12 Double approach-avoidance conflict

the accompanying praise that success usually engenders. The individual's achievement and affiliation incentive systems are both involved in his approach feelings. On the negative side, however, the chance of failing is quite apparent and with it chances for negative responses from peers, parents, and coach.

The line enclosing the conflict situation represents a barrier that prevents the individual from easily escaping and avoiding the situation. Many of the choices an athlete has to make are not open-ended choices. This is a significant point, because it provides some insight into the dilemma an athlete faces when the coach responds to a complaint by saying, "If you don't like it, then get out!" The athlete's decision is not that simple and the coach knows it. Why can't the athlete just quit? He is trapped by the potential need gratifications he sees in sport—that is, affiliation, achievement, and so forth. The external pressures placed on him to be a football player (see Beisser, 1967) might be so immense that the consequences of quitting would seem intolerable. Trapped in this situation (both by himself and by others), the athlete cannot "get out." For this individual and for thousands of others, sport participation is a command involvement.

Knowledge of performance results

Knowledge of the result of one's performance allows one to match attainment with aspiration (expectation), and if the situation is one controlled by the individual (as opposed to one in which an external force dictates the performance level), then one can make adjustments. Bringing attainment and aspiration more in line sustains motivation. (The results of a large differential between actual and expected performance were discussed earlier.)

The connection between knowledge of results (feedback) and increased performance was demonstrated in two different studies utilizing weight-lifting as the measure of performance (Wright, 1906; Crawley; 1926). The task involved lifting a 15-pound weight every two seconds while keeping in time with a metronome. A visual record was made of the exertions. On day one, the subjects were not allowed to see the visual record but said that their performance was maximum. The next day the subjects watched the recording being made and saw their previous day's score. They surpassed the previous results by up to 13 percent. The interpretation was that the knowledge of results provided an increased incentive (level of aspiration). Even though the subjects insisted that the previous results had been maximum, their performance increased.

Woodworth and Schlosberg (1954) reported performance increments on reaction time, accuracy of perception and judgment, and target accuracy. They also reviewed some studies which point out that feedback need not be pleasant to be effective. Even a strong electric shock accompanying a correct performance maintains task motivation.

The implications are quite evident. Immediate and exact knowledge of results enhances task motivation. Therefore the coach would be well advised to assess the athlete's performance correctly and provide the performance analysis as soon as possible. This writer has developed a basketball player effectiveness scoring sheet that allocates point values (both positive and negative) for ten or twelve different acts—for example, forcing a jump ball (+); being the cause of a jump ball (−); stealing the ball (+); giving the ball up by interception or rule violation (−); and so forth. By the morning following a contest, the "ledger" would show the player's effectiveness. It is not uncommon for the high scorer to be ranked as only moderately effective and for another less proficient scorer to be ranked as highly effective. The scoring sheet allows each athlete to maximize his own strengths—scoring, rebounding, assisting, or whatever—and be awarded point values.

Morgan (1973) reported on a "sleight-of-hand" feedback technique that also improved performance. The athlete's reported performance is downgraded slightly. For example, an athlete lifting 60 pounds in a prescribed weight exercise is told that he is lifting 55 pounds. When the weight is increased to 65 pounds, the athlete is told he is lifting 60 pounds (his maximum for the prescribed exercise), and he is equal to the challenge. This subterfuge seems to increase motivation, though the extent to which it can be applied is unknown.

Intrinsic and extrinsic motivation

Motivation is intrinsic when the activity itself supplies the reward, extrinsic when the activity is a means to an end. For example, if one eats spinach because it tastes good, the motivation is *in*trinsic. If one eats spinach because otherwise one will not be given any ice cream, the motivation is *ex*trinsic. From a management (industrial or sport) viewpoint, motivation is often seen solely in extrinsic terms. This is where chicanery and gimmickry enter the picture, and where situations begin to be manipulated to produce performance increments. This is not to imply that extrinsic motivation is inherently bad, but only to point out that its use is not entirely free of problems.

Generally, rewards applied to certain behaviors tend to strengthen them whereas punishment tends to extinguish them. Wallace Kennedy and Herman Willcutt, in article 2.14, review fifty years of research literature on praise and blame as incentives. Although they support the general premise that praise is often a superior incentive, they also note certain confounding issues. This article is a synthesis of the literature dealing with positive and negative reinforcement on various behavior, none of it sport-specific, however.

2.14 Praise and blame as incentives[1]

WALLACE A. KENNEDY
Florida State University, Tallahassee

HERMAN C. WILLCUTT
Florida State University, Tallahassee

33 articles spanning 50 years of research on the effects of praise and blame on the performance of school children are reviewed. Praise generally acts as a facilitator to performance, though often it is indistinguishable from practice effect. The single exception in recent years is the decrement in performance from praised underachievers. Exceptions to the generally decremental effect of blame on the performance of children are underachieving children, very bright adolescents, and Negro children working under Negro examiners. The problem of subject-reinforcement history is presented as a major contributor to the confusion in the literature, and the use of functional designs is suggested as a solution.

Experimental studies using various incentives for motivating discrimination, learning, and performance in human and animal subjects compose the greater part of the literature of psychology. The history of child psychology is spanned by studies seeking to evaluate the effectiveness of praise and blame as incentives for school children. The present review is confined to empirical studies considering the effects of the verbal incentives, praise and blame, on discrimination, learning, and motor tasks in school-age children below the college level. Philosophical and theoretical papers will be considered only when they are derived directly from empirical data.

From *Psychological Bulletin* 62(1964):323–332. Reprinted by permission of the authors and the American Psychological Association.

[1]The research reported herein was supported through the cooperative research program of the Office of Education; United States Department of Health, Education, and Welfare; Cooperative Research Project No. 1929.

Eight years prior to Binet's monumental work on intelligence, Binet and Vaschide (1897), measuring the effects of verbal encouragement on the physical output of children, found that all 43 subjects improved their scores. In a later effort Kirby (1913) gave verbal encouragement, knowledge of results, a practice period, and then a retest to 1,350 third and fourth graders working arithmetic problems. Although all of the subjects achieved a gain, it is impossible to say whether the improvement was due to praise, knowledge of results, or the period of practice.

Although college students were utilized by Gilchrist (1916) and Gates and Rissland (1923), their work, which is therefore not pertinent to this review, must be mentioned because it provided the methodology for the later Hurlock studies which formed the beginning of the great surge of interest in the literature on the effectiveness of praise and blame as incentives for school children. Hurlock (1924) first studied the effects of verbal incentives on school children by dividing 408 third-, fifth-, and eighth-grade children into groups by age, sex, race, and intelligence, administering an intelligence test in a test–retest design, a 1-week span between testings, and using praise, reproof, and control groups. Her overall conclusion was that neither praise or reproof was superior to the other as an incentive and that both tended to result in a greater improvement than did practice alone.

Further analysis of the different groups suggested that older children responded more to both praise and reproof than did the younger ones; that girls improved more from practice than did boys and were less influenced by either praise or reproof than were the boys; that Negro children reacted more favorably to praise, white children more to reproof. (This latter difference, however, was only slight, and, according to Hurlock, showed that the two races were more alike than different in respect to their reactions to these incentives.) Hurlock (1924) felt that some incentive was more essential for superior children, if their work was to be kept up to the maximum of their ability, than for inferior ones. Both praise and reproof seemed to serve this purpose. Reproof had its greatest effect on the children rated by their teachers as superior in school work; praise was of greater value for children rated as average and inferior.

Concerning the then current controversy over the constancy of the IQ, the next year Hurlock (1925a) followed up her work on intelligence test performance and again found no difference between the effects of praise and blame, both incentives raising the IQ significantly more than did practice alone.

Hurlock's (1925b) most distinguished work on praise and blame was an attempt to study these variables over a longer period of time.

> In a classroom, do the children who constantly receive praise for their work show more improvement from day to day than do the children who are reproved or who are completely ignored?

She used five modifications of the Courtis Research Test in Arithmetic over a period of 5 days, 106 children from Grades 4–6, the incentives administered in groups before the other members of the class, except for the isolated control group. Increased accuracy was found only in subjects who were praised or reproved, the greatest improvement being made by the praised group.

> These results as a whole point conclusively to the fact that regardless of the factors of age, sex, initial ability, or accuracy, praise is decidedly the most effective. . . . Reproof, when first used, seemed to be about equal in value to praise, but with continued use its effectiveness showed a decided decline.

Two years later less difference was found between the groups, but the same trends were apparent when Cohen (1927) replicated the Hurlock (1925b) study.

A clinical interpretation was given by Bird (1927) to an analysis of factors influencing learning on a reading readiness test based on 100 children from 4 to 6 years old. Eight of the children were excessively dependent upon praise, four were more satisfied by admonition than indifference.

In the first major review of the literature in this area, Hurlock (1931) made no attempt to criticize or comment upon the past performance of researchers, or to point out new directions for later research to explore. In looking over the studies prior to 1930, confusion of results from research studying the effects of verbal incentives on children already is apparent. In the two earlier studies, verbal encouragement was found to improve the scores of all participating children on both the motor task of Binet and Vaschide (1897) and the regular classroom task of Kirby (1913). Neither study employed a control group or attempted to compare effects of praise versus reproof.

A very careful researcher, Hurlock, in two studies using an intelligence test as the task, one more or less a duplication of the other, found neither praise nor reproof to be superior, although both were more effective than practice alone. In a third study using a regular classroom task she found praise to be decidedly more effective than reproof, although both were still superior to practice alone. This latter finding was substantiated by Cohen's duplicate study. On a reading readiness test Bird found withheld praise caused delayed learning in some children, and reproof was necessary to encourage the best efforts of others.

None of these studies with differing results used the same age levels: Kirby used third and fourth graders; Hurlock's two earlier studies used Grades 3, 5, and 8, while her later study, and that of Cohen, used Grades 4 and 6; Bird used nursery and kindergarten children. Yet in the studies using multiple grades, no age differences were found. Could differences in methodology be responsible for such clashing differences in results?

1930 TO 1940

Beginning the work of the next decade, Warden and Cohen (1931) studied the effectiveness of schoolroom incentives on 38 fourth graders working arithmetic problems. They concluded that the commonly-used incentives of verbal praise and reproof were not as effective as might be supposed, that any change in the regular classroom routine worked as an incentive.

From their review of the literature, Davis and Ballard (1932) concluded that praise is better than reproof; that boys are more influenced by reproof, girls by praise; that, generally speaking, positive incentives are better than negative incentives for all ages, grades, and levels of intelligence.

Studying the relative effectiveness upon comparable groups of children of a number of different types of external incentives, Chase (1932) concluded that some motivation, whether positive or negative, is more effective than none. In a retest of 102 of Chase's original 213 children, Anderson and Smith (1933) concluded, in agreement with Chase, that some motivation is more effective than control motivation. There were differences between the two studies, however, in reference to the effectiveness of failure on the performance of the subjects, differences which might possibly be explained by the difference in age distribution between the two samples, since all of the original subjects could not be utilized in the follow-up study, and those used were older than they had been previously. Necessarily there were no younger subjects in the follow-up study, and older subjects were added.

The review by Brenner (1934) led him to conclude that the obvious conflict of results was bound to occur due to the varying experimental conditions and general inadequacies of the studies, but also "in a large measure to the faulty formulation of the problem." He felt that all the studies in the literature to date erred in assuming an absolute level of difference between incentives, which "act in specific situations, depending upon all the factors of the situation as a whole . . . and derive their attributes, so to speak, from the situation in which they are active." Brenner (1934) stated that no general conclusions could be drawn regarding the effectiveness of praise and blame, but that their interaction with many other conditions needed to be considered.

> Proper application of the incentive in a given situation depends upon the insight of the teacher. The effectiveness or worth of a teacher depends upon his ability to make adequate use of motivation.

Brenner himself investigated the effects of immediate versus delayed praise and blame and found no significant differences between the two.

Nor did Benton (1936), studying the influence of incentives on intelligence test scores, find any difference between praise, reproof, or control motivation.

The first study which attempted to take into account personality differences was conducted by Forlano and Axelrod (1937) at the fifth-grade level. They concluded blame to be more effective than praise, but speculated as to whether more trials would have brought about significance for the praise groups.

The chief concern of Murphy, Murphy, and Newcomb (1937), who list and digest in a series of tables a large number of studies concerning incentives, is the problem of:

> The relationship between the individual personality and the situation. . . .
> All of the experimental work attempting to analyze the effects of praise and reproof . . . was until recently carried out without any references to the values or means of the situation to the individual child and its relation to his own personality.

They call attention to the inconsistencies in the literature and attribute this confusion to a failure to consider the individual in relation to the cultural background and his own peculiar personality makeup.

Schmidt's (1941) concern is expressed at the conclusion of his excellent review of the literature:

> This review of the literature leaves no definite conclusions to be drawn as to the effectiveness of praise and blame as incentives to learning. This has been brought about, it is felt, through there being no clear-cut conception of the basic principles involved, or through a non-realization or non-differentiation of what was being sought and what was actually being done. It is true that performance has been mentioned frequently in the literature cited, but this has been done casually and interchangeably with learning.

On one point all of the studies during the decade 1930 to 1940 agree: the experimental incentives were administered regardless of the actual performance of the children. This in itself is a somewhat artificial approach, since classroom teachers would supposedly be using the incentives to fit the occasion. But whether or not the answers were correct or incorrect, or the performance satisfactory or unsatisfactory, during this decade, as for previous pertinent research, subjects were administered the incentives at random.

Warden and Cohen (1931) not only found praise and reproof groups to be not significantly different from each other or the control group, but also to be inferior to promise of a game in motivating fourth graders on a regular classroom task. Brenner (1934) also found no differences between praise, blame, and control groups, even when divided into delayed and immediate praise and blame. Nor did Benton (1936) find any differences between praise and control: he did not make use of a reproved group.

Yet Chase (1932), using a motor task, found both praise and reproof to be better than control, and failure to be better even than praise. However, this latter finding was contaminated by previous incentive condition and method of administering the task. Anderson and Smith (1933), in a follow-up study, agreed with Chase's finding and definitely concluded blame to be more effective than praise. And Forlano and Axelrod (1937), endeavoring to take into consideration the personality of the subjects, found a significant difference only in the introverted subjects, where blame was more effective than praise or control. There were no differences in effectiveness of incentives for the extraverts.

None of these later studies agreed with Hurlock (1925b) that praise is more effective than reproof. The tendency for this period of research leans either toward no differences between praise and reproof, or toward reproof as being more effective. There is still no generally accepted conclusion from most researchers in the field of effectiveness of verbal incentives for schoolchildren. It is no wonder that researchers are beginning to end their reports with statements to the effect that praise and blame must be used wisely and with understanding for the specific pupil at the specific time.

1940 TO 1950

In an effort to study the effects of reproof, Potter (1943) concluded that at higher ages reproof had little effect on performance, while at lower age levels the effect varied.

Klugman (1944), making use of the equivalent forms provided by the

1937 revision of the Stanford–Binet, concluded that there was no significant reliability difference between praise and money as reward conditions; that there was a substantial superiority of the scores of Negro children tested with the money incentive over those tested with the praise incentive; and practically no difference between Negro and white children when money was the incentive; that white children showed a substantial superiority over Negro children when praise was the incentive. He (Klugman, 1944) accounted for the lack of significant difference between the incentives on the basis that the task was "so challenging that the use of one incentive rather than the other made little or no significant difference [p. 268]." When evaluating his results it must be taken into account that he did not make use of a control group.

Like Forlano and Axelrod (1937) earlier, Thompson and Hunnicutt (1944) were interested in the effects of praise and blame on the work achievement of introverts and extraverts. The methods of the two studies were similar with the latter studying its subjects over a longer period of time: six repeated measures under the reward conditions as opposed to three trials in the earlier study. Both the total praise and blame groups were significantly superior to the total control group, causing the authors to conclude that the effectiveness of verbal incentives in motivating pupils was more noticeable when introverts and extraverts were not differentiated. But there was no significant difference between the praise and blame groups.

Unlike Forlano and Axelrod, who found introvert blame to be significantly superior to introvert control and introvert praise, Thompson and Hunnicutt, for the first three trials, found no significant difference between these groups. On the final three trials, repeated praise increased the performance of the introvert-praise group until it was superior to introvert blame and extravert praise, answering in the affirmative Forlano and Axelrod's question as to whether repeated trials would raise the effects of praise to significance. Repeated blame increased the performance of the extravert blame group until it was superior to extravert praise and introvert blame. On none of the tests did the extravert praise or introvert blame groups differ significantly.

Thus, for this study of fifth graders divided into introverted and extraverted groups, application of praise and blame, when repeated often enough, had differential effects: introverts achieved a higher level of performance when praised, extraverts when blamed. Reminiscent of Brenner (1934), the authors (Thompson & Hunnicutt, 1944) commented upon this conclusion by stating:

The results of this study indicate that praise, as well as blame, can be used unwisely by the elementary schoolteacher if he does not fully appreciate and understand the different personalities present in his classroom. Praise and blame should not be judged on an either-or basis, but should be used to fit the case.

Whether it was the effect of World War II, a shift in interest by investigators in the field, or high standards for the next step set by Schmidt (1941), the decade 1940–1950 added only three studies to the investigation of the effects of praise and blame on the performance of school children. Only one of these, Thompson and Hunnicutt, endeavored to compare the effects of both praise and blame on student subjects.

Potter (1943), studying the effect of reproof on the performance of children at different age levels, found that it decreased performance of third graders, increased that of sixth graders, and had little effect on ninth and twelfth graders. In the first study not to employ a control group since that of Bird (1927), Klugman (1944), trying to establish a relationship between praise and money as incentives, found no differences in performance on the Stanford-Binet.

1950 TO 1960

In the 1950–1960 decade there began to appear in the literature a parallel line of investigations using knowledge of results as reinforcement, rather than praise and blame. There is, of course, a certain amount of overlap, but for reasons of clarity, simplicity, and emphasis, this series of studies will not be discussed.

To test whether praise was more effective when used in massed or spaced distributions, Mech, Kapos, Hurst, and Auble (1954) studied 240 fourth graders divided into massed versus spaced-reinforcement groups, further divided by 0%, 50%, and 100% verbal reinforcement. The massed-trained group performing significantly better, it was concluded that the intertrial interval is a factor determining the effectiveness of praise. It is unfortunate that in this study reward condition is confounded with percentage of reinforcement. Also there is the question of a fatigue factor. One group finished in approximately an hour, the other in 3 hours.

In his study to determine if the motivational needs of blind children are similar to those of sighted children, Kent (1957) hypothesized, from results of the Thompson and Hunnicutt (1944) study, that introverts would respond more readily to praise, extraverts to reproof, but found that either incentive was better than none for all groups except the public-school blind, where

239

there was no difference between incentives and control. Praise was found to be more effective regardless of personality type or visual status.

Studying the effect of verbal incentives on reading improvement, Silverman (1957) concluded that teacher use of praise and reproof cannot predict the reading growth of pupils, but can predict total verbal output. A methodological disadvantage of this study, along with those of Potter and Brenner, was the use of intact classrooms and thus the inability to assign subjects randomly.

Terrell and Kennedy (1957), using a variety of reward conditions, rewarded and reproved their subjects according to their performance, and concluded that the candy-reward group had learned the task and had transposed this learning significantly more quickly than the other groups. Neither praise nor reproof was significantly more effective than the control group.

Verbal encouragement and praise were concluded to have a definite facilitating effect upon the psychomotor performance of mental defectives by Ellis and Distephano (1959).

Studying the effect of praise and blame on a localization problem, Sandstrom and Weinz (1958) concluded that due to the conflict between encouragement and an unattainable reward the praised group's performance was inferior to that of the reproved group.

The decade 1950–1960 doubled the number of studies of the previous decade and introduced interesting variations to the research theme. Blind children and mental defectives were studied; experimental incentives were administered according to the performance of the subjects; massed versus spaced praise was studied; and teacher use of praise and reproof in the classroom was recorded in an effort to evaluate its effect on reading improvement.

Results were just as varied, but almost predictable: Massed praise was found to be more effective than spaced praise; even for blind children praise and blame were more effective than control motivation, except for public-school blind where there was no difference between groups and where performance itself was significantly inferior to that of residential-school blind and public-school sighted children; teacher use of praise and reproof in a classroom cannot predict reading growth in pupils; candy is a significantly more effective reward than praise or reproof, neither of which is better than a knowledge-of-results control group; praise is significantly more effective for mental defectives than no incentive; reproof is better than praise if the reward offered is unattainable, although both are better than no information on results of performance.

Although Sandstrom and Weinz (1958) found reproof to be more effective, the conclusion was qualified by conditions in the praised group. No really radical findings are noted for this decade. Possibly its importance lies in the varied forms that the research was taking, in an evergrowing effort to try to reach some valid decision as to the effects of praise and reproof on the performance of school children.

1960 TO DATE

No significant differences were found between praise and control groups in the Dollins, Angelino, and Mech (1960) study on the effects of teacher praise upon 75 elementary school children scored below the thirtieth percentile on the California Test of Personality.

Stevenson and Snyder (1960), studying the use of praise and reproof with mentally-retarded children, established clear evidence that the effect of a particular incentive condition is influenced significantly by the preceding incentive condition: praise as the original incentive maintained higher performance even when followed by blame or no incentive, while with more praise performance was increased; blame followed by praise led to increased performance, but a decrement in performance was apparent for blame followed by no incentive. The authors concluded that when the examiner's statements led subjects to assume that a particular level of performance is expected or that his performance is less satisfactory than that of other subjects, failure increases motivation; but when the the examiner's statements only comment upon subject's performance, failure lowers motivation.

Studying the relationship between concrete and abstract reinforcement on the sharing of preschool children, Fischer (1961–62), in a finding consistent with that of Terrell and Kennedy, concluded bubblegum as a reward was more effective than praise.

Metz (1961–62), studying the effects of stress and praise on creativity, concluded that stress facilitated performance of low scholastic-aptitude subjects, inhibited that of high scholastic-aptitude subjects, while praise facilitated the performance of all subjects.

Analyzing the effects of praise and blame as a function of intelligence, Kennedy, Turner, and Lindner (1962) studied two groups of adolescents with IQs from 124 to 150 and from 95 to 116. For the superior group no differences in performance were found between the three incentive groups, while for the average group blame caused a significant decrement in performance.

To test the Kennedy, Turner, and Lindner findings on adolescents, Willcutt and Kennedy (1963) used the same procedure on fourth graders. At this grade level there was no significant relationship between intelligence and effectiveness of verbal incentive. There was a significant difference at this age, however, between incentives, praise being superior to either reproof or no incentive. One point to consider, however, in comparing these two studies, is that there were no students in the fourth-grade group with IQs comparable to the superior adolescents in the earlier study, the superior fourth graders being in the IQ range 111–130.

Changing the task from a discrimination problem to performance on an intelligence test, the grade level to second and third, and controlling for class and caste social groups rather than levels of intelligence, Tiber and Kennedy (1964), studying the effects of incentives on the intelligence test performance of different social groups, contrary to expectations, found no difference in effectiveness of incentives for any of the social groups, yet, as in previous research, found a significant difference in IQ scores between these social groups. The authors suggest that explanations of IQ differences between cultural groups must be based on causes other than lack of intrinsic motivation provided by the intelligence test itself.

Studying the effects of praise and blame on the paired-associate learning of 90 boys retarded and nonretarded academically (IQ means 107.2 and 108.8, respectively), Van De Riet (1963) found that blame was significantly more effective for the educationally retarded group, praise more effective for the noneducationally retarded group. She defended her hypothesis, that praise produced anxiety in the academically retarded group, with clinical observations.

Bluhm (1964), using the same discrimination task as Kennedy, Turner, and Lindner and Willcutt and Kennedy, studied the effect of anxiety upon the reaction to praise and blame of 472 fourth, seventh, and tenth graders divided by means of the discomfort relief quotient method described by Mowrer (1953), and found that reward condition does not interact significantly with anxiety level. Thus the main effect of the reward condition does not seem to be related to the level of anxiety.

Kennedy and Willcutt (1963) undertook a factorial study broad in scope and design. Their investigation of the effects of praise and blame on a discrimination task under the variables of grade, intelligence, sex, race, social class, school, and examiner concluded that, although the study came about due to evidence in the literature that the effects of praise and blame on subject peformance was highly variable, for this study, using a discrimination task with speed as the criterion, the effects of praise, blame, and control were quite consistent regardless of subject differences: reproof had a debilitating effect upon performance, while praise resulted "in a somewhat higher increase than that coming from practice alone."

Using the same discrimination task, Vega (1964), following up the Kennedy and Willcutt (1963) study to test the effect of the race of the examiner on the reaction to praise and blame of 324 Negro second, sixth, and tenth graders, found that for the three white examiners the results were the same as in the original study. For the three Negro examiners, however, there was a significant difference, with all three incentive conditions, praise, blame, and control, resulting in improvement in scores. The significant difference between the white and Negro examiners is based squarely on the subjects' reaction to blame. For the white examiners in both studies, blame caused a decrement in performance, even for the white subjects of the original study. However, for Negro subjects with Negro examiners, blame, as well as praise and no incentive, resulted in an increment in performance.

What have the 11 studies in the early part of this decade demonstrated about the effectiveness of praise and blame with school children? Anxiety seems to be unrelated to the effectiveness of verbal incentives, with the possible exception of the minority group of academically retarded children. Socioeconomic, school, and examiner variables seem not to be significantly related to the effectiveness of verbal incentives, with the exception of Negro subjects' reactions to blame under Negro examiners. Blame has been found generally to have a debilitating effect on the performance of school children. Praise has been found generally to have a facilitating effect on the performance of school children.

It now appears, then, that when one corrects for practice, as with the use of a control group, praise is a reasonably stable incentive, from study to study contributing an incremental effect upon the performance and learning of school children. An exception is the reaction of severe underachievers whom praise inhibits. Van De Riet (1963), in her explanation of these conflicting results, has suggested what is apparently the largest weakness of studies in this area, that thus far there has been very little control of the reinforcement history of the subjects, and that here a factorial design does not seem to be effective.

Blame, on the other hand, has fairly consistently exhibited an inhibiting effect upon the performance of school children. Exceptions to this general debilitating effect of blame are underachievers, Negro subjects performing under Negro examiners, and very bright adolescents.

Further clarification in this area would seem to await a functional design which in some way controls the reinforcement history of the subject. Using human subjects with such a complex phenomena as the effect of verbal praise and blame, control of the reinforcement history over a long span of time seems impossible, and there is some question as to the sufficiency of short-term control. Cross-cultural control of reinforcement history seems to raise more problems than it solves and would not appear to be any answer at all.

If an activity is inherently interesting and people are involved, is there any purpose in additionally reinforcing it? Greene and Lepper (1972) are concerned that extrinsic motivators may turn play into work. If we reward every behavior, we are in danger of undermining intrinsic motivation and making every activity the means to an end rather than an end in itself. Winning is nice (remember there are other kinds of success), but the values derived from sport result from the participation, not from the outcome of the contest. When a coach views motivation solely from the extrinsic viewpoint and constantly seeks new and more powerful gimmicks, he runs the risk of making motivation manipulative, materialistic, and repressive (Biehler, 1974). The athlete becomes conditioned to these constant nuances and develops a consumer mentality (Maccoby, 1972). Everything then has a price, and the coach too is faced with the question, "What will I get out of it?" A vicious cycle has begun. The coach stimulates the athletes constantly, they become conditioned to it and expect it, and the coach has to invent one new technique after another. How many gimmicks are there? What is there new to activate the athlete who constantly expects new excitement—no payoff, no action. How can sport participation possibly be *play* under such circumstances?

Greene and Lepper derived their "overjustification" hypothesis from research they conducted. Their concerns about excess extrinsic motivation being potentially damaging to intrinsic motivation are derived from self-perception theory. If individuals are induced to participate in an interesting activity by rewards, the rewards can become the motive for participation: "A person's intrinsic interest in an activity may be decreased by inducing him to engage in that activity as an explicit means to some extrinsic goal." Participation, then, begins to be chosen because of an ulterior motive. Mosher and Orlick (1974) extended the "overjustification" hypothesis to laboratory tasks involving motor performance (treadmill running and stabilometer). Their findings were not wholly in support of the overjustification hypothesis and they seriously questioned whether their tasks continued to be intrinsically motivating once the novelty wore off. They are now looking at the fitness award system in Canada in light of the overjustification hypothesis. Are not most sport activities inherently interesting? Children certainly give one the impression that they enjoy "their" games during free-play periods. If excessive rewards *de*motivate sport participants, then the use of extrinsic motivation in sport situations ought to be seriously questioned. (It is only the practice of *viewing* motivation as extrinsic that is questioned here, because certain rewards do enhance sport performance.)

Mudra (1971) reported some empirical findings on improving athletic performance. Addressing himself to both intrinsic and extrinsic motivation, he said, "Coaches and players need to be constantly evaluating the football activity itself to improve their own perceptions of its value. To be highly motivated a player must believe in the values of participation."

This says that the athlete must see an intrinsic value in sport if it is to have meaning to him. As for extrinsic motivation, Mudra stated that "external motivators such as stars on helmets should only be used to help focus on important low level skills." This ties in with our assertion that most sport activities are inherently interesting. The continual practice of the fundamentals could easily be interpreted as the least exciting aspect of sport. Mudra is urging us to use extrinsic motivation when appropriate—that is, when a necessary activity is dull and repetitive—but to encourage participation for its own sake if the activity can sustain interest.

The final caution to be exercised relates to team performance. Zander (1974) asserted that the motivation to achieve team goals is reduced by the overapplication of extrinsic rewards to individuals. By singling out individuals and heaping rewards on them, a coach risks undermining team effectiveness. In short, unless extrinsic motivators are used sparingly and cautiously, they may do more harm than good.

Task versus affiliation motivation

Hollander (1967) has asserted that motivation to participate in groups can be divided into two motivational clusters. Some individuals choose a group activity in order to be with others like themselves; others are motivated by the task demands of the activity. For most people both of these motives are involved in varying degrees, and an individual's motives are likely to vary from time to time between the two poles of achievement and affiliation (even though the motive is suspected to be predominantly stable).

The usual assumption about affiliation and achievement in sport settings is that closely knit teams are successful and win more games than less cohesive ones. In this light, consider Martens's (1970) conclusion based on data derived from 144 college intramural basketball teams: "Teams high in task motivation win more games and are more satisfied with the season's participation than are teams lower in task motivation. Teams high in affiliation motivation, on the other hand, are not as successful but are more satisfied than teams lower in affiliation motivation." The discussion of the relationship between cohesiveness and sport performance will continue in more depth in the Affiliation and Sport section.

SUMMARY

An attempt has been made here to explain the many-sided concept of motivation—intensity, direction, and sustainment. Sport participation was placed within Birch and Veroff's incentive systems and the fit seems good. Sport performance was viewed from various directions—level of aspiration; conflict model of involvement; intrinsic and extrinsic motivation; and task and affiliation motivation.

The athlete's own definition of success is crucial to the understanding of motivation. Hubbard (1968) spoke of an apparent competitive paradox—some successful athletes quit while they are champions, whereas some unsuccessful athletes keep coming back for more. The confusion clears up when we stop equating success with winning. The time has come to re-evaluate our concept of success and failure.

After over 800 pages of their exhaustive look at motivation, Cofer and Appley (1964) leave us with the following conclusion: "It is clear that a comprehensive, definitive psychology of motivation does not yet exist. Nor, for that matter, would it be reasonable to expect that one should." They think that motivation has been expected to explain too much, since not all behavior is motivated. The directional component of behavior is determined by innate and habit factors as well as situational stimuli. In other words (Shakespeare's), "Some are born great, some achieve greatness, and some have greatness thrust upon them." One might do well to keep this in mind when considering sport performance in the context of motivation.

Aggression

& sport

3

Aggression
&
sport

3 Aggression, violence, and hostility are timely issues that are disturbing to all members of society. The news media bombard us with descriptions of out-bursts of violence until we wonder how long we can survive. No component part of society is immune to these reported hostile acts, but few social institutions openly condone and cater to aggressive behavior as does sport. Consider the following statements derived from unpublished interviews with National Football League players:

> Football is . . . a violent game and you have to ready yourself and almost change your personality because you have to break down some of the things that are wrong—or some of the things that are not accepted in our society. One thing is violence. It's a violent game. You're physically attacking another person. (Howard Mudd, San Francisco 49er's)

> I've never been beaten yet that I didn't immediately try to retaliate. (Forrest Gregg, Green Bay Packers)

> . . . it's just a satisfaction just to see a man laying on the ground that you put there. (John Niland, Dallas Cowboys)

When asked if he works up a sense of hostility against his opponent, Mudd replied:

> You have to say you have to be hostile. But there's a difference between being hostile and uncontrollably violent and being aggressively violent or controlled violence or controlled hostility. You say to yourself, "Well, I have to be hostile, I have to be aggressive because I have to go out and smack the man in the nose."

The aggression and violence expressed in these statements are sometimes reflected in spectator behavior. Incidents of rioting during soccer matches in England, Turkey, and Latin America (Sheed, 1969) and of audience brawling during high-school football games here in the United States are examples of this phenomenon.

The prevalence of sport-related aggression throughout the world raises two important questions:

1. Does sport (active participation by the athlete and less active participation by the spectator) serve as a positive outlet for aggression?
2. Does sport teach and offer opportunities for approved aggressive behavior, thereby encouraging further aggressive responses outside the sport situation? \

If the answer to the first question is "yes," then continued claims can be made for the value of sport to society. If, however, the second question comprises a true statement, then a very serious look must be taken at the ramifications of sport involvement.

Before these two vital questions can be answered, the nature of aggression and the relationship between sport and aggression must be carefully studied. Aggression has been described as an instinct, a drive, a basic energy source, an emotion, an intention to do harm, and a class of behaviors (Tedeschi, Smith, and Brown, 1974). Although there are problems in clarifying psychological constructs such as aggression, a definition of the construct can usually be operationalized so that discussion can start from a common base. Aggression, however, is difficult to define. Social scientists define aggression as harm-doing behaviors initiated by the intent to do harm. However, because the degree of intent to do harm varies, and may even be absent, not all aggressive-appearing acts should be similarly classified. This apparent confusion about the role of intent has resulted in definitions of aggression being drawn from two different perspectives. The term *reactive aggression* implies that initiated or retaliatory intent to harm another is present. Anger is usually involved, and injury to the opponent is the anticipated outcome. The term *instrumental aggression* differs from the social scientists' definition of aggression in that "striving to attain a goal" has been substituted for "intent to do harm." This type of aggression is therefore only a tool used to gain something important, such as a victory. Most human violence is instrumental in nature and is prompted not by anger but by social goals, which provide reinforcement through the availability of significant payoffs for being aggressive.

The violence and aggression expressed in the statements of the professional football players quoted previously was probably of the instrumental type. In a sport such as football, contact with others is a requisite for success, and the athlete's actions on the field might easily be misconstrued and his motives misunderstood by the naive observer. Because each player is required to *assert* himself and *dominate* another (both are personality characteristics), his act of aggressing does not necessarily contain the element of intent to do harm. The reader should be aware of the distinction between aggressive behavior (reactive) and aggressive-appearing behavior (instrumental), and should also bear in mind that the terms aggression, hostility, and violence will be used interchangeably throughout this section.

Although aggression in sports is usually directed toward others (extrapunitive), it is not unusual for athletes to inflict harm upon themselves (intropunitive). Television allows us to see many examples of intropunitive aggression—for example, a tennis player hitting the racket against his leg, or a defensive halfback in football verbally castigating himself for having performed below his expectations.

Aggression is intertwined in an individual's physiology–genetics–psychology make-up in an extensive variety of social circumstances. We shall next examine several of the theoretical viewpoints concerning this phenomenon.

THEORIES OF AGGRESSION

Frustration–aggression theory

The hypothesis of the frustration–aggression theory is that aggression is provoked by a blockage of the individual's usual response. The frustration resulting from this blockage forms the intent to injure the organism or object that is interfering with the desired response. Energy is built up by the frustrating circumstances, but if the aggressive feelings are expressed, the accumulated energy can drain off. This purging is called *catharsis.* If the catharsis hypothesis is true, and if aggressive energy can be released into substitute activities such as athletics, then man's inhumanity to man might be lessened (Tedeschi, Smith, and Brown, 1974).

When Mike Ditka of the Chicago Bears was asked if he thought football is an outlet for aggression, he replied:

There's no question about it. I feel a lot of football players build up a
lot of anxieties in the off-season because they have no outlets for them.

. . . I'm an overactive person anyway and if I don't get rid of this energy, it just builds up in me and then I blow it off in some other way which is not really the proper way.

However, because much of the aggression in sport is instrumental and involves conscious, goal-directed intent accompanied by some degree of heightened arousal, aggression expressed for the purpose of winning may not result in a purging of aggressive feelings. The lower activation level to which the athlete returns after the contest may or may not constitute catharsis. In reactive aggression, however, catharsis may be produced, possibly accompanying a release of anger. In either case, the fact remains that three and one-half decades of aggression research have not provided much empirical support for the catharsis hypothesis.

Konrad Lorenz (1974), a strong supporter of the ventilationist approach to aggression, recently stated that he doubts that watching aggressive behavior in sport has any cathartic value for the spectator. Similar doubts have been expressed by other authorities concerning the cathartic effect of participation in aggressive sports. Leonard Berkowitz, in article 3.1, reports on several experimental investigations of the catharsis hypothesis. Although catharsis appears to be a likely outcome of hostile or aggressive actions, this hypothesis has not been satisfactorily verified. Berkowitz reinterprets the literature that was formerly considered to support the idea of catharsis, and concludes that aggression is likely to beget more aggression. Despite the dearth of evidence to support the validity of the catharsis concept, the idea is an intriguing one that is not likely to vanish easily.

3.1 Experimental investigations of hostility catharsis[1]

LEONARD BERKOWITZ
University of Wisconsin, Madison

Discussions of hostility catharsis often maintain that the instigation to aggression is lowered by aggressive actions, whether directed against animate or inanimate objects, and may even be reduced by a variety of other behaviors such as competition and fantasy. The energy model of motivation on which this reasoning generally rests is coming under increasing attack, while there is growing support for standard, experimentally based analyses. Tests of the catharsis hypothesis indicate that observers do not lower their aggressive tendencies by watching other persons fight. Witnessed aggression provides stimuli that can elicit aggressive responses in these observers who are ready to attack someone, and even one's own aggressive responses may produce stimuli evoking further aggression, although several processes may contribute to this self-stimulation effect. Evidence presumably indicative of hostility catharsis is reinterpreted. It is proposed that the sight of people being injured aggressively (to an appropriate degree) is a reinforcement for those observers who are angry or who have been frequently rewarded for aggression. As a reinforcement, this stimulus might be gratifying, but it is also capable of eliciting further aggression. The catharsis hypothesis blinds us to the important social principle that aggression is all too likely to lead to still more aggression.

Several years ago the movie *The Tenth Victim* proposed a straightforward and dramatic method for controlling violence and lessening wars: The most aggressive people in society should try to kill each other

---

From *Journal of Consulting and Clinical Psychology* 35(1970)1–7. Reprinted by permission of the author and the American Psychological Association.

[1]Various versions of this paper have been presented at the Divisional Meeting, American Psychiatric Association, Chicago, November 1968; Psychology Colloquium, Michigan State University, East Lansing, December 1968; Philadelphia Psychiatric Society, Philadelphia, March 1969; Psychology Colloquium, Kansas State University, May 1969; and the Donald G. Paterson Memorial Lecture at the University of Minnesota, April 1969. The author's research reported here was supported by grants from the National Science Foundation.

in a socially sanctioned hunt, with the winner gaining a fortune. The hunters would drain their pent-up aggressive urges by killing or trying to kill others —or by dying. Onlookers, participating vicariously in the hunt, would also discharge their hostile energy as they watched the goings-on. With all of this energy drainage taking place in the hunt, there would not be any aggression left for extracurricular violence or for wars.

Essentially similar proposals based on theoretically comparable analyses have been advanced by other writers. In his book, *On Aggression,* Konrad Lorenz (1966) tells us that members of socially isolated groups must inevitably experience a build-up of aggressive drive; outsiders are not available to be attacked and thus provide an outlet for the accumulating aggressive energy. The wise person in these circumstances, Lorenz says, would smash a vase with as loud and resounding a crash as possible. We do not have to destroy other people in order to lessen our aggressive urges; it is enough merely to destroy inanimate objects.

Of course, it may be expensive to go around breaking vases, and some people have argued for a much cheaper solution to the problem of violence. All that need be done is to show lots of aggression on the TV and movie screens. If this violates our aesthetic sensibilities, or if we grow tired of Westerns and war movies, there is always competitive sports, or maybe canal digging. And what about the race to the moon? Cannot these competitive and hazardous activities provide a "moral equivalent to war"—socially acceptable and even constructive ways of reducing aggressive drive?

In one form or another, these ideas date back at least as far as Aristotle, although many contemporary discussions along these lines have been influenced by early psychoanalytic theorizing. While Freud later discarded his original belief that the display or experience of emotion could, by itself, bring about therapeutic improvement, this catharsis doctrine—maintaining that pent-up emotions can be "purged" or "discharged" by expressing one's feelings—is still inherent in such psychoanalytic concepts as displacement and sublimation.

With classical psychoanalysis and Lorenzian ethology, proponents of the energy-discharge formulation often maintain that the human body is constantly generating some mysterious substance or excitation which automatically goads man to aggression. This unmeasured and unidentified chemical or force presumably must be released in action or else the accumulating drive will burst outward, causing an impulsive explosion of violence. While many laymen seem to believe this line of thought has a sound scientific basis—largely because they mistakenly regard Lorenz's popular writings as representative of the general field of animal behavior—technically qualified authorities have severely criticized this analysis on both logical and empirical grounds (cf. Berkowitz, 1969; Montagu, 1968). Other advocates of the catharsis doctrine assume that the trials and tribulations of life result in a build-up of anger which ordinarily does not subside unless the emotion can be discharged in aggressive action, or displaced, sublimated, or transformed. Here, too, evidence is lacking.

Nevertheless, the widespread popularity of the idea of hostility catharsis is easily understood. The energy model of motivation on which this doctrine is based is a familiar one and seems to make sense. This kind of motivational analysis is probably accepted more because of its readily grasped, metaphorical nature, however, than because of its essential validity. Although those people who confine their reading to the traditional psychoanalytic literature and to the popular writings of Konrad Lorenz might not know this, the energy model of motivation is falling into increasing disrepute among experimental biologists and psychologists. The model is much too simple and even hinders the search for important behavioral determinants.[2] In the case of aggression, the energy model usually maintains that a wide variety of activities (including fantasy, competitive sports, and indirect as well as direct aggression), involving many different types of people, can lower the person's inclination to attack others. However, a rapidly growing body of carefully controlled research raises serious questions about this overly simple formulation and even casts considerable doubt on its validity. Rather than producing a lowered probability of further violence, aggression in the absence of guilt or anxiety is all too likely to stimulate still more aggression. If policymakers were to follow the classic catharsis doctrine or accept the similar ideas of Konrad Lorenz as a guide for social actions, the results could well be unfortunate indeed.

There are alternatives to the energy analyses: explanatory schemes based on ideas of stimulus–response relationships and learning. I will argue here that these alternative conceptions are better able, by far, to account for the available evidence.

But first, what is this evidence? Let me summarize some of these studies briefly.

EFFECTS OF OBSERVING AGGRESSIVE ACTIONS BY OTHERS

A decade of laboratory research has virtually demolished the contention that people will lessen their aggressive tendencies by watching other persons

[2]See Hinde (1959) for a discussion of various energy conceptions of motivation, such as that found in Lorenz's and psychoanalytic theories. Hinde argued that these concepts have impeded the development of a more adequate motivational formulation.

beat each other up. Experiments with young children, high school and college students, and even older adults, have shown again and again that under certain circumstances, witnessed aggression can[3] heighten the chances that the observer will act aggressively himself (cf. Bandura, 1965; Berkowitz, 1965b; Geen and Berkowitz, 1967; Walters and Thomas, 1963). Several different processes seem to contribute to this increased probability of aggression (cf. Bandura and Walters, 1963); (a) the observer learns something —he can acquire new aggressive action patterns imitatively through seeing how the aggressor behaves on the screen; (b) the film violence may lower restraints against aggression in audience members, either by showing that aggression pays off or by seeming to legitimize violence. Several experiments conducted in my own laboratory illustrate this legitimizing phenomenon (Berkowitz, 1965a; Berkowitz, Corwin, and Heironimus, 1963; Berkowitz and Geen, 1967; Berkowitz and Rawlings, 1963). Deliberately provoked college students saw a filmed prize fight in which the protagonist, played by Kirk Douglas, received a bad beating. In some cases, the film introduction led the audience to regard the beating as "bad" and ethically unjustified; Kirk Douglas was said to be a "good guy." By contrast, for other Ss, (subjects) Kirk Douglas was portrayed in a much less sympathetic manner so that his beating was viewed as proper and justified. Later, when all of the men were given an opportunity to attack the person who had angered them, the Ss shown the "justified" film violence generally exhibited the strongest aggression. It is as if the justified aggression on the screen made their own aggression seem morally proper, thereby temporarily lessening their inhibitions against aggression. (There is also the other side of the coin, I might add. Film violence that is regarded as "bad," unjustified, or horrible serves to restrain the observers' later aggression.[4])

But also note that the "legitimate" movie violence did not lead to a fantasy catharsis. There was no purge of anger or discharge of hostile impulses through watching the screen villain getting the beating he deserved. A re-

[3]I use the word "can" instead of "will" advisedly, since a good many situational and personal factors influence the relationship between witnessed violence and the likelihood of aggressive actions by observers, including the observers' attitudes toward the violent event, the extent to which they are set to act aggressively, the strength of their aggressiveness habits, etc. People concerned with the effects of movie and TV violence should ask not what are the consequences of media violence, but under what conditions do particular effects arise?

[4]Richard Goranson (1969) found that angry college men restrained their attacks on their tormentor after learning that the loser in the filmed prize fight had died later because of the beating he had received in the fight. Interestingly, he also found that the reporting of a death unrelated to the witnessed fight (the character played by Kirk Douglas supposedly died in an auto accident) also served to inhibit Ss' later aggression.

cently completed experiment (Turner and Berkowitz[5]) adds further corroboration to this point. All of the Ss were angered by E's (experimenter's) confederate, and again, all saw the fight scene. This time, however, before the movie went on, one-third of the men were asked to imagine themselves as one of the film characters (the person who would beat up Kirk Douglas), while another group was instructed to take the role of a watching judge, and a control group did not do any role taking. The people told to imagine themselves as the fight winner subsequently made stronger attacks on E's accomplice than did either of the other groups. The make-believe as the winning aggressor led to more, not less, open aggression following the film.

ELICITATION OF AGGRESSIVE RESPONSES

At least one other process may also be at work in witnessed violence in addition to imitative learning and the lowering of restraints: The aggressive movie can stimulate transient aggressive ideas and feelings and even overt aggressive responses. There is nothing mysterious about this principle; it can be regarded as a special case of a much more general stimulus–response relationship. Simply put, stimuli that have frequently been associated with a certain type of action are capable of evoking that response on later occasions. If a certain stimulus has been repeatedly connected with aggressive behavior, it will be able to elicit aggressive responses from people who are ready to act aggressively.

One such stimulus, obviously, is a weapon, and several experiments have demonstrated that the mere presence of guns can heighten aggressive behavior. In at least two studies involving children playing with toy weapons (Feshbach, 1956; Mallick and McCandless, 1966), the aggressive gun play led to an increase in aggressive encounters with other youngsters. Many of these encounters were much more aggressive than just a continuation of make-believe shooting at each other. Here too, then, fantasy aggression did not increase peacefulness. An experiment with college men also shows how weapons can stimulate aggressive reactions merely by being present (Berkowitz and LePage, 1967). Although nonangered Ss were not affected to any detectable extent, insulted men gave more electric shocks to their tormentor if weapons were nearby than if neutral objects or no other objects were present with the shock machine. The weapons had evidently served as aggressive stimuli, eliciting stronger attacks from those Ss who, because they were angry, were ready to act aggressively.

Aggressive behavior, even aggressive words, can also furnish aggression-evoking stimuli. The sight of people fighting, and perhaps especially seeing

[5]C. Turner and L. Berkowitz. Unpublished manuscript, 1970.

someone receive deserved or proper injury, can also provide these stimuli. Several experiments indicate that emotion arousal facilitates the occurrence of aggressive responses to the stimulus of a witnessed fight. While most of these studies were carried out in my own laboratory, two interesting investigations were conducted elsewhere. In one of these, Geen and O'Neal (1969) recently found that men who heard a loud but not painful sound after seeing the prize fight attacked their partner more strongly than did other Ss who had not watched the fight or who had not heard the sound. The excitation resulting from the loud sound had strengthened the aggressive reactions stimulated by the aggressive movie. As this experiment suggests, anger is not the only arousal state that can facilitate aggressive stimuli. Similarly, when Tannenbaum and Zillman[6] showed a brief sex film to one group of men who had just been provoked by a partner, these sexually aroused Ss then gave him stronger electric shock punishment than did similarly angered but nonsexually aroused men in the control group. The sexual arousal had evidently strengthened the aggressive responses elicited by the provocation and the opportunity to attack the partner. In a later variation on this study, these investigators obtained results consistent with the previously cited Berkowitz and LePage (1967) experiment. The strongest electric attacks on the peer tormentor were given by men who watched the sex film, and at the same time heard a tape recording of the woman character's thoughts about killing her lover. In this case, the sex arousal apparently also "energized" the aggressive responses elicited by the aggressive tape recording. This kind of phenomenon, in which sexual arousal functions like other arousal sources to facilitate aggressive responses to aggressive stimuli, could contribute to the apparent connection between sexual and aggressive motivation postulated by some writers.

Sometimes the aggressive stimuli can come from our own behavior. Under some conditions at least, an attack on an available target person leads to still stronger aggression, as if the first attack had introduced additional aggression-evoking stimuli. Some such process may be involved in the finding typically obtained with the Buss "aggression-machine" procedure; the electric shocks inflicted by experimentally provoked or thwarted men generally increase in intensity over the series of opportunities given them to punish their partner (e.g., Buss, 1963; Geen, 1968). Rather than producing a purge of all hostile inclinations, the first shocks seem to stimulate still stronger aggressive reactions. Hostile words might also have an aggression-eliciting effect. According to an experiment by Loew (1967),

[6]P. H. Tannenbaum and Z. Zillman. Unpublished study, 1969.

college students trained to speak aggressive words aloud in a learning task subsequently administered stronger electric shocks to a peer whenever he made a mistake than did a control group of Ss trained to speak only non-aggressive words. The Ss' aggressive language could have stimulated aggressive responses in them which then strengthened their electric attacks on the other person.

More obviously has to be learned about the conditions governing this kind of effect and the mechanisms producing it. Sometimes the result can be understood in terms of response generalization; thus, in the Loew (1967) study, the reinforcement given the aggressive words generalized to intensify the physical attacks. In other instances, self-justification, or dissonance reduction, may be at work; people who voluntarily attack or derogate someone else often seek to justify their initial hostility by expressing further criticism of their victim, presumably when the initial hostility is inconsistent with the values they hold for themselves and they cannot compensate the victim (cf. Brock and Pallak, 1969). Whatever the processes involved in this apparent self-stimulation to further aggression, it is clear that aggressive behavior at times leads to more, not less, aggression by the attacker. We are often told that people should express their hostile ideas and feelings; telling someone we hate him supposedly will purge pent-up aggressive inclinations and will "clear the air"—whatever this last cliché means. Quite frequently, however, when we tell someone off, we stimulate ourselves to continued or even stronger aggression.

REINTERPRETING SUPPOSED EVIDENCE FOR HOSTILITY CATHARSIS

I probably should stop now and address myself to a common criticism of the argument I have been spelling out. The objection might take this form: The traditional catharsis doctrine surely would not have gained such wide popularity if it did not have some basis in reality. Why do so many persons enjoy watching aggressive events or say that they feel better after seeing an aggressive game or movie? And further, How do I account for the pleasure that people often feel after telling someone off or hurting him?

These are important questions, clearly, and deserve careful answers. While space limitations do not permit me to give these matters as much attention as they deserve, I will say something about these problems and will try to show that there are several different mechanisms at work rather than a single energy discharge.

There is little doubt that many people find pleasure in watching others fight. What I do doubt is that this pleasure necessarily signifies a long-term

259

reduction in some aggressive drive. Sometimes the pleasure stems from the ebb and flow of excitement; the game or match is simply an exciting event which is pleasant through the build-up and decline of internal tension. Angry people, or persons with a history of aggressive behavior, are apparently particularly inclined to seek out such aggressive scenes (Eron, 1963). But again, this seems to be due to the reinforcing quality of such scenes for them rather than being due to a discharge of aggressive energy. Suggesting this, Hartmann (1969) found that deliberately provoked juvenile delinquents exhibited a greater volume of aggression toward a peer (in the form of electric shocks) after watching a movie showing a boy receiving a painful beating in a fight than after seeing a film focusing on the aggressor's actions. The sight of the movie victim's suffering was presumably gratifying in some way, but enhanced their subsequent attacks on their own tormentor. Let me point out another reason why people say that they feel better after watching aggressive events: they were so carried away by the interesting scene before them that they forgot their troubles; at least momentarily, and stopped brooding or stirring themselves up.

SIGHT OF HURT AS
REINFORCEMENT FOR AGGRESSION

Now let me return to this matter of seeing someone injured. I have suggested here, on the basis of several different experiments, that the sight of someone being hurt is a reinforcement for angry people. As a reinforcement, this perception can lead to increased aggression, but may also produce a pleasant tension reduction, especially if the injured person is the frustrater.

A series of experiments by Hokanson and his students provides pertinent physiological evidence (Hokanson and Burgess, 1962; Hokanson, Burgess, and Cohen, 1963; Hokanson and Edelman, 1966). The college students in these investigations displayed a marked increase in systolic blood pressure after being insulted by E, and then showed a quick reduction in systolic pressure after they had an opportunity to give their tormentor electric shocks. The researcher found that there was a much slower decline in physiological tension (i.e., in systolic pressure) when the angered S attacked someone other than his frustrater. According to this research, displacing hostility is no more effective than no aggression at all in reducing physiological tension. The Hokanson studies also demonstrated that physical activity, in and of itself, does not lead to the rapid decline in systolic pressure, even when the motor responses are the same as those involved in the attacks on the frustrater. The Ss had to believe that they had attacked, and presumably hurt, their tormentor if the rapid decline in systolic pressure was to occur. More recent experiments in this program (cf. Stone and Hokanson, 1969) suggest the cause of the decline in vascular response. Rather than being indicative of an energy discharge, the physiological tension reduction stems from prior rewarding experiences. That is, the rapid drop in blood pressure following aggression comes about to the extent that the person had previously learned that injuring his frustraters is rewarding or gratifying. Thus, when one group of Ss was rewarded for reacting *non*-aggressively to attacks made on them, they later displayed the "cathartic-like," quick decrease in vascular response only after behaving in a friendly, rather than hostile, fashion.

Whatever the explanation, we evidently feel better when we see that the person who had angered us has been hurt. (Of course, the extent of the injury probably must be in keeping with our level of anger toward that person and our judgment of what he deserves.) We do not have to hurt the frustrater ourselves in order to experience this pleasure. In one of our Wisconsin studies (Berkowitz, Green, and Macaulay, 1962), for example, angered Ss reported feeling better after hearing that their insulter had performed poorly on an assigned task. Similarly, in another study (Bramel, Taub, and Blum, 1968) deliberately provoked college students were relatively more interested in listening to a tape recording in which their tormentor said he was suffering than in hearing him say that he was happy—even though the Ss were told that the tape recording had been made six to nine months earlier. In comparison to a nonangered group, the recording of the frustrater's earlier suffering also led to a greater expressed liking for that person than did a control recording in which the obnoxious person said he was in a neutral mood. If we are angry with someone, the knowledge that he has been hurt or has suffered is evidently gratifying.[7]

This information, to repeat myself, is a reinforcement and, as such, can influence the probability of further aggression. We may stop or refrain from attacking our frustrater when we learn that he has been injured sufficiently, and we may feel much better than before. Retribution has been achieved. But this could well be only a temporary effect. Our aggressiveness habit has also been reinforced, so that, consequently, over the long run there actually is a greater likelihood that we will attack someone again in the future. There is empirical as well as theoretical support for this possibility. One research team (Patterson, Littman, and Bricker, 1967) observed the encounters among nursery school children over a nine-month period, taking particular

[7]Very much in the same vein, Feshbach, Stiles, and Bitter (1967) have demonstrated that the sight of an anger instigator being hurt (not seriously) facilitates learning by Ss this person had provoked.

note of aggressive and assertive actions. According to their data, the frequency of aggression by any one child after he had fought with another youngster was influenced by the victim's reactions to the initial attack. If the victim had reinforced the aggressor's behavior by showing defeat and submission, and perhaps some injury as well, there was an increased chance that the aggressor would again attack someone, particularly the first victim, later on.

CONCLUSION

The traditional energy model of aggression is clearly inadequate to account for many of the findings I have reported here. Not only is this conventional analysis much too simple, but it has also impeded recognition of the important role played by environmental stimuli and learning in aggressive behavior. Above all, this energy model and the associated catharsis doctrine have helped to justify the expression of aggression and have delayed our recognition of an important social principle: Aggression is all too likely to lead us to still more aggression.

Social learning theory

Social learning theory hypothesizes that aggressive behavior is learned. The refutation of the catharsis theory and Berkowitz's conclusion that aggression tends to beget aggression are consistent with the social learning perspective. Aggression research indicates that aggression is a contagious aspect of behavior, both intraindividually and interindividually, and that aggression and violence, once seen or perpetrated, tend to be reinforced in a *circular effect.*

In sport, if we place great value on toughness and pugnacity, if the norm for successful sport behavior is violence and intimidation, and if the successful sport role models are visibly aggressive, then an environment for learning aggression is created. The behavior models just described will reinforce aggression in observers, who see the aggressive acts; and because of the circular effect, reinforcement of themselves and of others will take place with increased frequency and intensity. Several of the recent attacks made by athletes and exathletes on the game of football testify to the circularity of violent and aggressive behavior.

Further reinforcement of learned aggression is provided by the incentives that contact sports place on aggressive behavior (consider the ''big hit'' award for the player making the most forceful block or tackle).

It is reasonable to expect that in sports where aggressive behavior is called for, the strength of the aggression habit will be increased. At the very least, the contact sport situation seems to provide an inherent program of disinhibition training, wherein no attempt is made to reduce the amount of aggressive and violent behavior exhibited by the athletes.

A more detailed explanation of social learning theory will be found in the section on Personality and Sport.

Biological instinct theory

Based upon their research studies of animal behavior, ethologists Konrad Lorenz, Robert Ardrey, and Anthony Storr conclude that aggression is instinctive, or genetically determined. Despite the questionable validity of generalizing research evidence from one species to another, data derived from these animal studies may have interesting implications for man. If the ethologists' position that man has the inborn predisposition to aggress is true, then control of this genetically determined behavior poses problems. Lorenz (1974) reveals his unmistakable concern with this possibility when he says that ''man must know that the horse he is riding may be wild and should be bridled.''

Another important concept of the ethologists is that man is a territorial animal who will fight to defend his own territory. This idea appeals quite naturally to those persons interested in sport behavior because the concept of territory is utilized in several sports, the purpose of which is to encroach on another's territory while protecting one's own. Perhaps a football team gives ground more grudgingly near its goal line because its members become more aggressive as a result of the greater threat to their territory. However, a more logical interpretation of this phenomenon might be that fewer offensive options are available.

Although the biological, or instinct, theory of aggression is an interesting one that drew widespread coverage in the 1960s when Lorenz, Ardrey, and Storr first published their books, there is little reason to believe that the results of their animal studies can be directly applied to man's behavior. Although biological factors may well determine specific animal behaviors, social factors are likely to supersede biological factors in the formation of human behaviors. How much can be understood about man from the behavior of animals may be implicit in Boulding's (1968) statement:

> The critical question is how much we could learn about the jet plane
> from studying the wheelbarrow or even from studying the automobile; if
> the jet plane is man, the automobile perhaps is the mammal, the
> wheelbarrow the fish, in terms of relative complexity of system.

In an essay review (article 3.2), Leonard Berkowitz provides an informative critique of the writings of Lorenz, Ardrey, and Storr and of the simplistic genetic-determinism view of aggression they propound. Berkowitz also discusses the role of learning in aggression, and he further reviews the catharsis hypothesis that participation in sport provides a release of aggressive emotions.

3.2 Simple views of aggression: an essay review

LEONARD BERKOWITZ
University of Wisconsin, Madison

The theme of this essay will be drawn from a dust jacket. On the back of the book *Human Aggression* by the British psychiatrist Anthony Storr (1968), we find the following comment by Konrad Lorenz, widely renowned as the "father of ethology": "An ancient proverb says that simplicity is the sign of truth—and of fallacy . . . However, if the simple explanation is in full agreement with a wealth of data, and quite particularly, if it dovetails with data collected in altogether different fields of knowledge, simplicity certainly is indicative of truth." Four of the books reviewed here offer essentially simplistic messages. With the writers represented in the fifth work, I shall argue that the conceptual simplicity advocated by these volumes is definitely *not* "indicative of the truth." All of the books deal with man's capacity for violence, a problem deserving—no, demanding—careful and sophisticated consideration. The four volumes I shall concentrate on, those by Lorenz [*On Aggression*] (1966), Ardrey [*The Territorial Imperative*] (1966), Storr [*Human Aggression*] (1968), and Morris [*The Naked Ape*] (1968)—and especially the first three—provide only easy formulas readily grasped by a wide audience rather than the necessary close analysis. Being easily understood, their explanation of human aggression helps relieve the anxiety born of the public's concern with war, social unrest, race riots, and student protests, but is an inadequate, and perhaps even dangerous, basis for social policy.

From *American Scientist* 57(1969):372–383. Reprinted by permission.

All four voice essentially the same message: Much of human behavior generally, and human aggression in particular, must be traced in large part to man's animal nature. Aggression often arises for innately determined reasons, they say. The authors differ somewhat, however, in how they believe this nature leads to aggression. For Lorenz, Ardrey, and Storr (whom I shall refer to as the Lorenzians), a spontaneously engendered drive impels us to aggression, even to the destruction of other persons. Morris, on the other hand, views many of our aggressive acts as genetically governed responses to certain environmental conditions and to signals sent to us by other people. Nonetheless, over and above their similarities and differences, all four volumes present a highly simplified conception of the causes of and possible remedies for human aggression, and I think it would be well for us to look at a number of these misleading oversimplifications.

THE ROLE OF LEARNING IN HUMAN AGGRESSION

Facing the writers at their own level, one misconception I shall not deal with here is their relative neglect of the role of learning in human aggression. Our behavior is influenced by our experiences *and* our inherited biological characteristics. I have argued elsewhere that innate determinants do enter into man's attacks on others, primarily in connection with impulsive reactions to noxious events and frustrations. These constitutionally governed impulsive responses can be modified by learning, however. The Lorenzians do not appear to recognize this kind of modification in these volumes. They draw a very sharp distinction between learned and innately determined responses, thus ignoring what is now known of the complex interplay between nature and nurture. Lorenz has admitted this on occasion, and the journalist, Joseph Alsop, has recently reported him as saying, "We ethologists were mistaken in the past when we made a sharp distinction between 'innate' and 'learned.'" Of course, there is also an experience-is-all imperialism at the opposite extreme. In sharp contrast to many ethologists and zoologists, social scientists typically have long ignored and even denied the role of built-in, biological determinants. Ashley Montagu's (1968) critical discussion of Lorenz in his introduction to *Man and Aggression* is illustrative. "The notable thing about human behavior," he says, "is that it is learned. Everything a human being does as such he has had to learn from other human beings."

Some book reviewers for the popular press, aware of these opposing stances, have approached the present volumes in terms of this kind of polarization. *If* human aggressiveness is learned, Lorenz *et al.* are obviously incorrect, but on the other hand, innate determinants to aggression presumbably must operate as described by Ardrey, Lorenz, Morris, and Storr. Ardrey, Lorenz, and Storr pose the issue in these simple terms. Critics dispute their views, they maintain, primarily because of a misguided "American optimism"; American social scientists, psychologists and psychiatrists, having a liberal belief in the perfectability of man, want to attribute social ills—including violence—to environmental flaws which might be remedied rather than to intractable human nature. The critics certainly would recognize the existence of man's innate aggressive drive if they could only shed their honorable but mistaken vision of Utopia.

There are other alternatives, however. Some of human aggressiveness might derive from man's biological properties, characteristics which he shares to some degree with the other animals. He might even be innately "programmed" to respond violently to particular kinds of stimulation, much as other animals do. But his animal characteristics do not have to function the way Lorenz and his associates say they do. The Lorenzian analysis of aggression can be criticized on a logical and empirical basis independently of any general assumptions about the nature of man.

The volume *Man and Aggression,* edited by Montagu, serves as a counterpoise to the Lorenzian books. A number of journalist-reviewers have assumed that Lorenz's views are shared by virtually all students of animal behavior. The Montagu volume clearly shows that there is not the unanimity of support that the laymen believe exists. Many eminent zoologists, as well as comparative psychologists, have taken Lorenz's analysis of aggression seriously to task. *Man and Aggression* is a compilation of generally damning criticisms of the Lorenz and Ardrey books by such authorities as S. A. Barnett, J. H. Crook, T. C. Schneirla, and Sir Solly Zuckerman, as well as Lorenz's old opponent, J. P. Scott. For those people who have read only the Lorenzian analyses, Lorenz may speak for all ethologists; Lorenz is equated with all of ethology in the Storr book, *Human Aggression.* Yet he is not all of the science of animal behavior, and there are many good reasons in the animal as well as human research literature to question the over-all thrust of Dr. Lorenz's argument on grounds besides the "overbold and loose" nature of the Lorenzian contentions generally recognized by many readers.

We need not here review the many objections to the Lorenz and Ardrey volumes that are summarized by the critics included in *Man and Aggression.* However, some of the oversimplifications and errors of reasoning and fact that are characteristic of these two books are also prevalent in the Storr and Morris works, and I think it is important to point out several of these common weaknesses in the extension of popular biology to human aggression.

THE USE OF ANALOGIES

As nearly every critic of these Lorenzian books has pointed out, the writers are excessively free-wheeling in their use of analogies. They frequently attempt to explain various human actions by drawing gross analogies between these behaviors and supposedly similar response patterns exhibited by other animal species. Attaching the same label to these human and animal behaviors, the writers then maintain that they have explained the actions. For Lorenz, man is remarkably similar to the Greylag Goose. The resemblances (that occur to Lorenz but not necessarily to other observers) are supposedly far from superficial ones, and he believes that they can only be explained by the operation of the same mechanisms in man and goose. ". . . highly complex norms of behavior such as falling in love, strife for ranking order, jealousy, grieving, etc. are not only similar but down to the most absurd details the same . . ." and therefore, all of these actions must be governed by instincts.

The analogy emphasized by Ardrey, of course, is based on animal territoriality. Man's genetic endowment supposedly drives him to gain and defend property, much as other animals do, presumably because this territorial behavior provides identity, stimulation, and security. Basing part of his argument on a study of the lemurs of Madagascar, Ardrey contends that there are two types of societies, noyaux (societies said to be held together by the inward antagonism of the members) and nations (societies in which joint defense of territory has given rise to ingroup leadership and cooperation). The examples of noyaux listed by Ardrey include, in addition to the Madagascar lemurs, herring gull colonies, certain groups of gibbons, and Italy and France.

Morris's analogy, needless to say, is between humans and apes. His theme is that "*Homo sapiens* has remained a naked ape . . . in acquiring lofty new motives, he has lost none of the earthy old ones." We cannot understand the nature of our aggressive urges, he says, along with Ardrey, Lorenz, and Storr, unless we consider "the background of our animal origins." Unlike the Lorenzians, however, he doubts the existence of an innate, spontaneous aggressive drive, and emphasizes, to the exclusion of such a drive, the genetically determined signals he believes both apes and people send to their fellows. All four authors make much of the control of aggression by supposedly innate appeasement gestures, although Morris seems to have greater confidence in their efficacy than do the others. He even tells us how we should respond to an angry traffic policeman on the basis of this analogy between human and animal behaviors: The policeman's aggression can (theoretically) be turned off automatically by showing abject submission in our words, body postures, and facial expressions. Moreover, it is essential to "get quickly out of the car and move away from it towards the policeman." This prevents the policeman from invading our territory (our car) and weakens feelings of territorial rivalry. The looks people give each other are very important signals. Morris maintains in accord with a rapidly growing body of experimental-social psychological research, but, in contrast to these investigators, he oversimplifies greatly. Morris contends that prolonged looking at another is an aggressive act. In reality, persistent eye-contact can also be a very intimate, even sexual, encounter, or may arise from a search for information or social support.

This type of crude analogizing is *at best* an incomplete analysis of the behavior the writers seek to explain. Important data are neglected and vital differences are denied. J. H. Crook's excellent paper in *Man and Aggression* (which should be read by every person who has written a favorable review of the Lorenz and Ardrey books) notes the many important considerations omitted by the Lorenzians in general and Ardrey's treatment of territoriality in particular. Where Ardrey, following Lorenz, maintains that territorial behavior is a highly fixed, species-specific action pattern produced by energy accumulating in certain centers in the nervous system, the truth cannot be packaged as easily as this. Many different conditions enter into animal territoriality. The outcome is a complex interaction of ecological and social conditions with internal states so that territorial behavior is far from inevitable as a species characteristic. Territorial maintenance, furthermore, involves different components, such as attack and escape. Those components are probably governed by somewhat different, although often interrelated, mechanisms, and appear to be susceptible to different environmental and internal conditions. Given these complexities and the multiplicity of factors involved in the territoriality displayed by birds, we cannot make simple statements about the functions and causes of territoriality even in these species, and it is highly unlikely that human concern with property is controlled by the same processes. Crook's conclusion is certainly reasonable: "The likelihood that the motivation control of territorial behavior is at a different level from that of fishes and birds suggests that human resemblances to the lower animals might be largely through analogy rather than homology." Sixteen years ago, Daniel Lehrman (1953) remarked, in an outstanding critique of Lorenzian theory, "it is not very judicious, and actually is rash . . . to assume that the mechanisms underlying two similar response characteristics are in any way identical, homologous, or even similar," merely because the actions of different species or entities seem to resemble each other (in the eyes of the writer, we might add).

THE MOTION OF RITUALIZATION

The same comment can be made about the analogizing involved in Lorenz's and Storr's use of the notion of ritualization. Theorizing that there are evolutionary changes in behavior as well as structure, and that particular action patterns, such as appeasement gestures, have evolved from other behaviors, Lorenz argues that responses originally serving one function can undergo alteration in the course of evolution so that they come to have a different function as well. The drive or energy motivating the original action presumably still powers this altered behavior. According to Lorenz, the appeasement or greetings ceremonies performed by humans and animals alike have become ritualized in this manner through evolutionary developments but still make use of transformed aggressive motivation. Lorenz thinks that the smile of greeting, as an example, might have "evolved by ritualization of redirected threatening." Storr, adopting Lorenz's reasoning, also speaks of "ritualizing the aggressive drive in such a way that it serves the function of uniting" people. For both of these writers, diverted aggressive energy powers the social bonds which tie individuals together in affection and even love. Now, we must ask, is there really good reason to contend, as Lorenz does so authoritatively, that the human smile, the appeasement gesture of the macaques (baring the teeth), and the triumph ceremony of the geese must have evolved in the same way from some original aggressive display? The supposed similarity between the human, monkey, and goose behavior does not mean, as Lehrman pointed out, that the processes underlying these actions are "identical, homologous, or even similar." Elaborating further, in his essay in *Man and Aggression,* Barnett says there is no justification for the "confident, dogmatic assertions" Lorenz and his followers have made about the hypothetical process, "ritualization." Harlow's observations regarding monkey development are also troublesome for the Lorenzian analysis of the genesis of social bonds. Affectional patterns generally emerge *before* aggressive ones in these animals, making it unlikely that the earlier, affectional–social acts are "driven" by aggressive motivation.

The dangers of unwarranted analogizing can also be illustrated by referring to another example of "ritualization" mentioned by Storr. It appears that the Kurelu, a primitive people in the heart of New Guinea, engage in frequent intertribal warfare. But instead of killing one another, the warriors shoot arrows at each other from a distance just beyond arrow range and rarely hit each other. Although this type of warfare seems to resemble the threat ceremonies exhibited by a number of animal species, we certainly cannot argue that the Kurelu behavior and animal threats have evolved in exactly the same manner or are based on similar biological mechanisms.

Furthermore, both action patterns may ultimately lead to a cessation of attacks—but probably for very different reasons. It is also improper to insist, as the Lorenzians do, that competitive sports are the same type of ritual as the Kurelu warfare and animal threats merely because some writers have applied the same label to all three sets of phenomena; the surface resemblances do not guarantee that all have the same evolutionary causes and that all operate in the same or even in a similar way.

When we come right down to it, there seems to be a kind of "word magic" in this analogizing. The writers appear to believe that they have provided an adequate explanation of the phenomenon at issue by attaching a label to it: a person's smile is an *appeasement gesture;* athletic events are *rituals* comparable to certain animal displays, etc. Storr shows just this kind of thinking in the "proof" he offers for the notion of a general aggressive drive. Aggression is not all bad, Storr insists (in agreement with Lorenz); aggression is necessary to the optimal development of man. It is "the basis of intellectual achievement, of the attainment of independence, and even of that proper pride which enables a man to hold his head high amongst his fellows." The evidence he cites for this statement is word usage: ". . . the words we use to describe intellectual effort are aggressive words. We *attack* problems, or *get our teeth* into them. We *master* a subject when we have *struggled with* and *overcome* its difficulties. We *sharpen* our wits. . . ." (Italics in the original.) Waving his words over the particular behavior (in this case, striving for independence and achievement), he has thus supposedly accounted for these actions—and has also swept aside the many studies of achievement motivation by McClelland and his associates suggesting that there is very little similarity between the instigation to aggression and achievement motivation.

Popular discussions of the role of evolution in behavior can also be criticized on this basis. Even if it can be shown that a given behavior pattern has "evolved," such a demonstration does not explain the performance of that action by a particular individual in a specific setting. The application of the word "evolution" does not really help us to understand what mechanisms govern the behavior in this individual or what stimulus conditions affect these mechanisms.

INSTINCTIVE HUMAN ACTIONS

The Lorenzians (and Morris as well) also display this same word magic in the ease with which they refer to human actions as instinctive. Without taking the trouble to specify the criteria they employ in making their designations, they go scattering the label "instinct" around with great relish. As an illustration, in his book *On Aggression*, Lorenz talks about people having an "instinctive need to be a member of a closely knit group fighting for common ideals," and insists that "there cannot be the slightest doubt that militant enthusiasm is instinctive and evolved out of a communal defense response." Doubts must exist, however. The Lorenzians offer neither a precise definition of what they mean by "instinct" nor any substantial evidence that the behavior in question, whether human aggression or militant enthusiasm, is innate even in their vague usage of this term. Several of the writers in *Man and Aggression* (e.g., Barnett and Schneirla), as well as other scientists such as Lehrman, criticize Lorenz severely for his excessively casual employment of the instinct concept. Lorenz elsewhere has acknowledged this imprecision in his popular utterances (see, for example, the previously mentioned article by Alsop), saying that he has used the word only in a shorthand sense.

Nevertheless, the over-simplification regarding "instincts" so prevalent in the Lorenz–Ardrey–Storr writings is difficult to excuse as only shorthand. To say this is not to deny the role of innate processes in human behavior; such determinants apparently exist. Psychologists, together with other students of behavior, have shown, as an example, that human babies have a built-in preference for certain visual stimuli, and do not start with blank neural pages, so to speak, in learning to see and organize complex visual stimulation. The difficulty is that ideas such as Lorenz's "instinctive need to be a member of a closely knit group fighting for common ideals" are, in actuality, extremely drastic departures from the more precise instinct concept found in technical ethological discussions. When they write for an audience of their peers, ethologists generally describe instincts, or better still, instinctive movements, as behavioral sequences culminating in "fixed action patterns." These patterns, which are at the core of the instinct concept, are thought of as rigid and stereotyped species-specific *consummatory* responses generally serving to end a chain of ongoing behavior. Can this definition be applied to "militant enthusiasm"? What is the rigid and stereotyped action that unerringly unfolds to consummate the hypothetical enthusiasm pattern?

SPORTS AS OUTLETS FOR AGGRESSION

We now come to the most important part of the Lorenzian instinct conception, and the feature that has the gravest social implications: the supposed spontaneity of the behavior. The stereotyped instinctive action is said to be impelled by a specific energy that has accumulated in that part of the central nervous system responsible for the coordination of the behavior. The energy presumably builds up spontaneously and is discharged when the response is performed. If the instinctive activity is not carried out for a considerable period of time, the accumulated energy may cause the response to "pop off" *in vacuo*. Aggression, according to Lorenz, Ardrey, and Storr—but not Morris—follows this formula. "It is the spontaneity of the (aggressive) instinct," Lorenz tells us, "that makes it so dangerous." The behavior "can 'explode' without demonstrable external stimulation" merely because the internal accumulating energy has not been discharged by aggressive actions or has not been diverted into other response channels as, for example, in the case of such "ritualized" activities as sports. If violence is to be lessened, suitable outlets must be provided. Lorenz believes that "present-day civilized man suffers from insufficient discharge of his aggressive drive," and together with Ardrey and Storr, calls for more athletic competitions—bigger and better Olympic games. (Denying the Lorenzian formulation, Morris maintains that we do not have an inborn urge to destroy our opponents—only to dominate them—and argues that the only solution is "massive de-population" rather than "boisterous international football.")

This conception can be discussed at various levels. Neurologically, for one thing, Lorenz bases his assertions on observations regarding cardiac and respiratory activities and simple motor coordinations. With such critics as Lehrman and Moltz we must question whether or not these findings can be extended to more complex neural organizations, to say nothing of human aggression. (The Lorenzian interpretation of these observations can also be disputed, as Moltz has shown in the 1965 *Psychological Review*.)

There are empirical difficulties as well as this problem of the long inductive leap. Basing their arguments on a number of studies, Hinde (1960) and Ziegler (the latter in an important 1964 *Psychological Bulletin* paper) have proposed that many apparent demonstrations of internally-driven spontaneity can be traced to external stimuli and the operation of associative factors. The responses evidently are evoked by environmental stimuli rather than being driven out by spontaneously accumulating internal excitation. Moltz has also summarized evidence disputing the Lorenzian notion that response performance is necessary if there is to be a reduction in the elicitability of the instinctive action pattern. As Hinde has suggested in several papers, stimulus satiation rather than a response-produced discharge of instinctive action-specific energy may cause a lessening in response elicitability.

COMPLEX ASPECTS OF ANIMAL AND HUMAN AGGRESSION

Going from the simple motor coordinations of the lower animals to the more complex aspects of animal and human aggression, the available data are even less kind to the Lorenzian formulation. Of course Lorenz maintains that his ideas are supported by a substantial body of observations. They are upheld, he says, by the failures of "an American method of education" to produce less aggressive children, even though the youngsters have been supposedly "spared all disappointments and indulged in every way." However, as I have pointed out elsewhere in discussing this argument, excessively indulged children probably expect to be gratified most of the time, so that the inevitable occasional frustrations they encounter are actually relatively strong thwartings for them. There is little doubt that these frustrations can produce aggressive reactions, and Lorenz's criticism of the frustration-aggression hypothesis is a very weak one. Belief in this hypothesis, by the way, does not necessarily mean advocating a completely frustration-free environment for children. Child specialists increasingly recognize that youngsters must learn to cope with and adapt to life's inescapable thwartings, and thus must experience at least some frustrations in the course of growing up. Nor do most contemporary psychologists believe that frustration is the only source of aggression. Violence can have its roots in pain as well as in obstacles to goal attainment, and can also be learned as other actions are learned.

Aggression, in other words, has a number of different causes, although the Lorenzians seem to recognize (or at least discuss) only one source. Here is yet another erroneous oversimplification: their notion of a unitary drive that is supposedly capable of powering a wide variety of behaviors from ritualized smiling to strivings for independence or dominance. This general drive conception is very similar to the motivational thinking in classical psychoanalysis, but is running into more and more difficulty under the careful scrutiny of biologists and psychologists. Indeed, contrary to Storr's previously cited argument, there is no single instigation to aggression even in the lower animals. Moyer recently has suggested (in the 1968 *Communications in Behavioral Biology*), on the basis of many findings, that there are several kinds of aggression, each of which has a particular neural and endocrine basis.

THE FLOW OF AGGRESSIVE ENERGY

Also like the traditional psychoanalysts, the Lorenzians speak loosely of aggressive energy flowing from one channel of behavior to another. This hypothetical process, mentioned earlier in conjunction with "ritualization,"

273

must be differentiated from the more precisely defined response-generalization concept developed by experimental psychologists. Reinforcements provided to one kind of reaction may strengthen other, similar responses. Rewarding a child for making aggressive remarks can increase the likelihood of other kinds of aggressive reactions as well. The reinforcement influence generalizes from one kind of response to another because the actions have something in common. (The actor might regard both types of responses as *hurting* someone.) It is theoretically unparsimonious and even inadvisable to interpret this effect as an energy transfer from one response channel to another. The Lorenz-Storr discussion of ritualization, and the related psychoanalytic concept of sublimation as well, employs just this kind of energy-diversion idea. We cannot here go into the conceptual pitfalls of this analytical model. (The interested reader might wish to read Hinde's article on energy models of motivation in the 1960 *Symposia of the Society for Experimental Biology.*) But there is a fairly obvious flaw in the Lorenzian statement that pent-up aggressive energy can be discharged in competitive sports. Rather than lessening violence, athletic events have sometimes excited supporters of one or both of the competing teams into attacking other persons. This has happened in many countries: in England, as Crook points out and as Storr should have recognized, in this country at times when white and Negro high school basketball teams have competed against each other, and most dramatically, [1969] in Czechoslovakia when the Czechs defeated the Russians in hockey. In these cases, the team supporters were so aroused, even when their team won, that they were extremely responsive to aggressive stimuli in the environment.

Experimental tests of the hostility catharsis hypothesis also argue against the energy-diversion idea inherent in both Lorenzian and psychoanalytic theorizing. This well-worn notion maintains, of course, that the display of aggressive behavior in fantasy, play, or real life, will reduce the aggressive urge. Although there is no explicit reference to a catharsis process in Storr's book, his belief that aggressive energy can be sublimated certainly is consistent with the catharsis doctrine. Lorenz comes much closer to a frank acceptance of this idea in his contention that "civilized man suffers from insufficient discharge of his aggressive drive," and in a bit of advice he offers to people on expeditions to the remote corners of the world. Members of socially isolated groups, he says in *On Aggression,* must inevitably experience a build-up of aggressive drive; outsiders aren't available to be attacked and thus provide an outlet for the accumulating aggressive energy. If a person in such an isolated group wishes to prevent the intra-group conflict that otherwise must develop (Lorenz insists), he should smash a vase with as loud and resounding a crash as possible. We do not have to attack other people in order to experience a cathartic reduction in our aggressive urge; it's enough merely to destroy inanimate objects.

SUMMARY

Summarizing (and simplifying) a great many studies, research results suggest that angry people often do (a) feel better, and (b) perhaps even experience a temporarily reduced inclination to attack their tormentors, upon learning that these persons have been hurt. This phenomenon seems to be quite specific, however; the provoked individual is gratified when he finds that the intended target of his aggression has been injured, and does not appear to get the same satisfaction from attacks on innocent bystanders. Besides this, the apparent reduction in the instigation to aggression following an attack is probably often due to guilt- or anxiety-induced restraints evoked by the attack and/or the arousal of other, nonaggressive motives, and is not really the result of an energy discharge. Standard experimental-psychological analysis can do a far better job than the energy-discharge model in explaining the available data. Recent experiments indicate, for example, that the lessening of physiological tension produced by injuring the anger instigator comes about when the aggressor has learned that aggression is frequently rewarded. This tension reduction, or gratification, is evidently akin to a reinforcement effect, and is not indicative of any long-lasting decline in the likelihood of aggression; people who find aggression rewarding are more, not less, likely to attack someone again in the future. The reinforcement process can also account for the appetitive behavior Lorenz and Storr seem to regard as prime evidence for the existence of a spontaneous aggressive drive. Provoked animals will go out of their way to obtain suitable targets to attack, while youngsters who are frequently aggressive toward their peers generally prefer violent TV programs to more peaceful ones. But this search for an appropriate target or for aggressive scenes probably arises from the reinforcing nature of these stimuli rather than from some spontaneous drive, and again, does not mean that there has been an energy discharge when these stimuli are encountered. Quite the contrary. There is some reason to believe that the presence of such aggression-reinforcing stimuli as other people fighting can evoke aggressive responses from those who are ready to act aggressively—much as the sight of food (which is a reinforcement for eating) can elicit eating responses from those who are set to make such responses.

In the end, the Lorenzian analyses must be questioned because of their policy implications as well as because of their scientific inadequacies. Their reliance on casual ancedotes instead of carefully controlled, systematic data, their use of ill-defined terms and gross analogies, and their disregard of hundreds of relevant studies in the interest of an oversimplified theory warrant the disapproval generally accorded them by technical journals. But more than this, the Lorenz-Ardrey-Storr books can also have unfortunate social as well as scientific consequences by impeding recognition of the important roles played by environmental stimuli and learning in aggressive behavior, and by blocking awareness of an important social principle: Aggression is all too likely to lead to still more aggression.

Physiological theory

The basic concept of the physiological theory of aggression is that inborn neural mechanisms located in the hypothalamus of the brain mediate aggressive responses when they are activated by particular stimuli. Aggression is therefore neither solely biological nor solely environmental; the key to its understanding lies in the interaction between the nervous system of an individual and his environment.

In article 3.3, Kenneth Moyer places the catharsis and circular effect theories in perspective and pronounces each of them inadequate to explain aggressive behavior. He discusses violence in sport, as well as the pervasive attitude that sport is an outlet for aggression. Moyer's treatment of the subject of aggression and violence adds another dimension to our study of the nature of aggression.

3.3   The physiology of violence

K. E. MOYER
Carnegie-Mellon University, Pittsburgh, Pennsylvania

Six hundred years before the birth of Christ the prophet Ezekiel wrote, "the land is full of bloody crimes, and the city is full of violence." In 1969 the National Commission on the Causes and Prevention of Violence reported violence "is disfiguring our society—making fortresses of portions of our cities and dividing our people into armed camps." In each

From *Psychology Today* 7(July, 1973):35–38. Copyright © Communications / Research / Machines, Inc., Ziff-Davis Publishing Company.

of the 2,569 years in between we can find more evidence of man's inhumanity to man—and his failure to do much about it.

Violence is the bitter fruit of human aggression. Before we can control violence, we must understand the roots of aggressive behavior. At present we have two major theories that attempt to dig them out.

The first, in its broadest outlines, proposes that aggression is a biological phenomenon built into the gene structure. Man has a certain amount of aggressive "energy," the theory runs, and our only hope for controlling it is to provide culturally acceptable outlets. The second theory proposes that man has no inborn impulses to violence, but that he learns it. According to this position, we can ignore biology and develop a system of aggression control based on reinforcement and modeling theories.

Neither theory, as far as I can see, takes into account the growing body of literature on the physiological bases of behavior. Recent findings in this area require modifications in both theories, and point the way to a physiological model of human aggression. My basic premise for such a model is that the brain contains inborn neural systems that, when active *in the presence of particular stimuli,* result in aggressive behavior toward those stimuli.

There is abundant evidence that these neural systems exist. Many investigators have induced aggression in cats and rats by using electric current to stimulate particular areas of the animals' brains. My colleague, Richard Bandler, has elicited aggression from rats by chemical stimulation of certain parts of the hypothalamus.

We know that the same sorts of neural systems exist in man. Experimenters have induced both verbal and physical aggression in human beings by stimulating the brain with electricity. After their displays of aggressive behavior, subjects reported that they felt the emotions that normally accompany such aggression. Vernon Mark and Frank Ervin (1970) offer many examples in their book, *Violence and the Brain.* As long ago as 1961, H. E. King (1969) described a mild-mannered female patient who became aggressive when the part of her brain called the amygdala was electrically stimulated. She was verbally hostile and threatened to strike the experimenter. Researchers could turn her hostile feelings and aggressive behavior on and off with the flick of a switch. Violence can also be produced by the pressure of tumors in the same region of the brain. Charles Whitman, who climbed to the top of the clock tower at the University of Texas and shot and killed 14 people and wounded 31 others, had a rapidly growing tumor near the amygdala.

We must now find out what turns the brain's neural systems on and off in a normal person outside the laboratory.

GOOD DAYS AND BAD DAYS

In common-sense terms, a person's aggressiveness depends upon his mood. In physiological terms, his aggressiveness depends upon the state of his nervous system, which in turn determines his mood. When a person is happy, only a small number of different things can make him angry. When he is irritable, a great many things can throw him into a rage. But even on an irritable day, it takes a specific stimulus to make a person act aggressively. Fighting does not take place in a vacuum.

However, the appropriate stimuli are not the only factors that determine whether a person will behave aggressively. The appearance of aggressive behavior is also dependent upon the state of the neural systems that govern this behavior. When these systems are active *and* the appropriate stimuli are present, the person will act aggressively.

This interaction between a person's environment and his nervous system is the key to my model of human aggression. Suppose that in the nervous system there are three possible threshold states (that blend into a continuum) for any aggressive system. With the highest threshold the system is insensitive, meaning that the usual stimuli that provoke destructive behavior will not fire the neural systems that control aggression. Because it lacks the usual sex hormones, a male mouse castrated before puberty will not, as is customary, attack a second male mouse. The castrated mouse is insensitive to stimuli that ordinarily would provoke attack.

The second threshold level of the aggression system is the normal one— the level at which we operate most of the time. The cells of the neural system that control aggression are not firing, and only stimuli within a narrow range can activate them.

The third threshold level is the spontaneously active one. Here the cells already are firing, and the organism is restless. But the organism will *act* aggressively only when an appropriate stimulus appears. Human beings in this state feel hostile. They may have many aggressive fantasies, and any of numerous stimuli will trigger their aggressive thoughts and behavior.

The aggression system floats between the three threshold levels (or more accurately, up and down the continuum). Many factors can affect it, which accounts for the fluctuating level of aggression in a single person and for varied normal aggression levels among human beings.

FOMENTING AGGRESSION

The first factor influencing the sensitivity of the aggressive system is heredity. Kirsti Lagerspetz (1964) in Finland has been able to breed a highly aggressive strain of mice. Jerome Woolpy has developed a strain of rabbits that will attack the experimenter. Although we have no comparable data on man, I believe that just as we inherit a tendency toward epilepsy, we inherit our aggressive tendencies.

The second factor is input from other neural systems in the brain. Stimulation of these areas will not initiate aggression, but it can intensify or inhibit ongoing aggression.

For example, experimenters can increase the intensity of aggressive behavior by stimulating the brain's arousal system (midbrain reticular formation). Michael Sheard and John Flynn (1967) demonstrated the relationship between arousal and aggression in cats. First they stimulated a cat's lateral hypothalamus and it attacked a mouse. Then they stimulated the cat's midbrain reticular formation. Although the cat showed a mild arousal response, it did not attack. But stimulating both the midbrain and the lateral hypothalamus increased the intensity of cat attack on the mouse.

Other experimenters have inhibited aggressive behavior and hostile language in psychotic patients by stimulating the septal regions of their brains. According to Robert G. Heath (1963), the patients change at once from disorganized rage to happiness and mild euphoria. The patients feel good; they smile and their muscles relax. This reaction indicates that activation of the brain's septal region is incompatible with activity in the aggressive system that produces attack behavior.

Changes in the blood chemistry also influence the sensitivity of the aggression system. These changes are due primarily to shifts in the steroid hormone levels. A number of studies have shown that hostility and irritability are components of premenstrual tension. Crimes of violence committed by women, for instance, appear to be tied to the menstrual cycle. J. H. Morton and his associates surveyed 249 female prisoners and found that 62 percent of the crimes of violence were committed during the premenstrual week, and that only two percent of the violent crimes were committed at the end of the period. I believe that hormonal changes resulting from stress may also influence the sensitivity of the neural systems controlling irritable aggression.

LEARNING AGGRESSSION

The last factor that affects the threshold for aggressive behavior is the most complicated: learning. Experience influences aggressive behavior just as it influences other basic behaviors. By using rewards and punishments, we can teach an animal to overeat or to starve. In the same manner we can teach animals and man to show aggressive behavior or to inhibit it.

The laws of learning apply equally well to responses we label destructive and to those we label constructive. These learned responses interact with, and at times override, hereditary and endocrine influences on aggression. Habit patterns can nullify blood chemistry. If we punish an animal in the presence of food, we will inhibit its eating response, no matter how actively its neural systems that control hunger are firing. The same principle holds true for aggression.

Man, of course, learns better and faster than any other animal. This means that his hereditary and endocrine influences on aggression are more open to modification by experience than are those of other animals. It means that we will find considerable diversity among human beings in the stimuli that will elicit or inhibit aggressive behavior. It means that man has less stereotyped and more varied outlets for expressing his anger and hostility than other animals.

After reviewing the factors that influence an individual's threshold for aggression, we end with a picture of man that conforms to neither major theory of human aggression. It is not enough to say that man's aggressiveness is biologically programmed. It is not enough to say that man's aggressiveness is learned. According to our physiological model, we must say that man's aggressiveness depends upon a number of fluctuating factors. Consider some specific instances:

The person who inherits a low threshold for hostility will find many targets for his aggression if he lives in a deprived, frustrating and stressful environment. However if he is surrounded by love, and exposed to little provocation, his aggressive behavior will be sharply limited.

A hypoglycemic patient may feel intense, irrational and mounting hostility as his blood sugar level drops. A candy bar will decrease that feeling of hostility, and if the patient gets a candy bar before an appropriate target for his hostility appears, he will not act aggressively.

EXPLAINING AGGRESSION

During puberty, a boy's tendency to fight gradually increases over several years as the testosterone level in his blood increases. Harold Persky and his colleagues (1971) studied 18 young men and 15 older men and showed that the production rate of testosterone correlated closely with several psychological measures of aggression and hostility in the younger men.

A girl may become irritable just before her menstrual period, or she may become irritable because of a cutting remark made by her teacher. In either case, the chances of her making an aggressive response to an appropriate stimulus skyrocket. Whether her lowered threshold for aggression actually results in aggressive behavior will depend, in part, on her previous experience with any targets that appear. If she has been negatively reinforced for expressing hostility toward her parents, the chances are slight that she will become aggressive with them. But if she stumbles over her dog, she may kick it.

If the girl's neural system has been activated by a teacher's sarcasm, the traditional psychoanalytic formulation would consider the kick as displaced aggression, i.e., the aggressive "energy" is transferred from one object to another. Physiologically, however, the two instances are not essentially different except in the manner in which the neural system was initially sensitized. In both instances the tendency to respond aggressively may be of the same intensity and in both cases, the particular object responded to depends on the past learning of the individual.

In none of the above cases can we summarize aggression in the way that psychologists like Lagerspetz, psychoanalysts like Anthony Storr (1968) and ethologists like Konrad Lorenz (1966) do—as a biological drive. Nor can we summarize it as a learned response, as John Paul Scott (1958), Ashley Montagu (1963) or Albert Bandura (1963) would do. We would be misguided to try to control aggression with a scheme derived solely from either group's premises.

Lorenz tells us in *On Aggression* that there is an absolute link between hostility and affiliation. He suggests that there is no love without aggression, and warns that the elimination of aggressive tendencies would be disastrous.

He cites convincing evidence that, in the course of human evolution, tendencies to intraspecific aggression and social bonding developed together. But it is an unwarranted extrapolation to claim that social bonding necessarily depends on a viable system for hostility. There is no physiological support for such a model.

The evidence, in fact, points in the opposite direction. Destruction of the neural system for aggression may release social tendencies which have been inhibited. The vicious monkeys raised by Heinrich Klüver and Paul Bucy (1937) not only lost their excessive hostility when their temporal lobes were removed, but they soon became friendly and tried to play with the experimenters.

Surgery on the neural systems that control aggression has recently cured a significant number of pathologically hostile human patients. In general, these persons show increased capacities for positive affiliative tendencies after their operations. One of R. F. Heimburger's (1966) patients laughed for the first time in his life after his surgery.

In Human Aggression Storr says, "The idea that we can get rid of aggression seems to me to be nonsense . . . it is no use supposing that we can change human nature into something pacific and gentle." Storr suggests that we should participate in some form of physically aggressive competition either directly or vicariously as observers. But a physiological model of aggression leads to the opposite solution.

VIOLENCE IN SPORT

Aside from man's learned destructive responses, his hostile behavior depends upon the sensitivity of the neural systems that control aggression. If those systems do not fire, he has no "aggressive energy" to drain off. Physically competitive sports are likely to activate those neural systems. Competition causes stress and generates a high level of arousal. Unless the persons involved have strong inhibitory tendencies, the result frequently *is* violence. For instance, a referee's decision during a soccer match in Lima, Peru, nine years ago touched off a riot that resulted in the deaths of a number of spectators.

Jeffrey Goldstein and Robert Arms (1971) compared the hostility of spectators before and after the 1969 Army–Navy football game. They measured indirect hostility, resentment and irritability, using the Buss-Durkee inventory, in 97 subjects before the game and 53 subjects after the game. Then they measured the hostility of spectators at an Army–Temple gymnastics meet in the same way—interviewing 49 subjects before the meet and 32 subjects after the meet. Result: the football spectators scored significantly higher on the scales after the game was over; the gymnastics spectators, who had watched a physically unaggressive event, did not.

Physically competitive sports have many values, but their use as an outlet for aggressive behavior is not one of them. Instead of developing physically competitive programs to control aggression, we should learn which stimuli fire the neural systems that inhibit feelings of hostility.

Although I do not believe that aggression is simply a learned response, learning certainly plays an important role in aggression control. Rewarding nonaggressive responses to stimuli that normally evoke aggression, or punishing expressed aggression will curtail hostile behavior. Much of man's destructive, aggressive behavior has nothing to do with the neural systems that control aggression, and is not accompanied by feelings of anger or hostility. The trigger man for Murder Inc. or the bombardier on a mission over a hostile country may feel no animosity toward his victims. He kills not because he is angry, but because he is rewarded for killing. Society must deal with this "instrumental" aggression in the same way that it deals with any other learned response.

In the search for effective ways to reduce the violence in our lives, a physiological model of aggression opens up one method of control that is foreign to both major theories of aggression: physiological manipulation. This idea is controversial and it has a great potential for abuse. But it follows naturally from the notion that a person's tendency to feel and behave aggressively partially depends upon the activity of particular neural systems within his brain.

There are three basic ways to shut off the neural bases for aggression. We can resort to surgery. It is easy to turn the wild cat *Lynx rufus rufus* into a tractable and friendly animal by removing a very small portion of its amygdala. Heimburger has shown that placing small lesions in the same area of the human brain will reduce aggressive behavior in as many as 80 percent of pathologically hostile patients.

We can also desensitize the neural systems that control aggression by manipulating certain endocrine mechanisms. Experimenters have used the hormone progesterone to control the irritability that accompanies premenstrual tension. A synthetic sex hormone, Stilbestrol, will control hypersexuality and irritable aggression in males. We have at our disposal a number of other pharmacological agents that tend to reduce hostility, for example, the tranquilizers Librium and Valium.

We can control aggression by electrical stimulation of the neural systems that inhibit hostility and anger. Implanting electrodes in a person's brain and hooking him up to a radio receiver is not science fiction. We now have miniaturized radio receivers that can be implanted beneath a person's scalp. The patient shows no signs of being under external control, but can receive hostility-reducing currents of electricity.

Each of these techniques is unquestionably effective, and each is valuable to the patient and to society. However, the concept of physiological manipulation raises serious ethical issues, which will have to be resolved before we can develop the techniques past the experimental stage.

Aggressive behavior is man's greatest problem. Our vision of how to control aggression is limited by the blinders of our inadequate theories. Unless we find ways to put adequate theory into practice, the advanced technology of destruction will solve our problems for us.

Where does sport fit into the physiological perspective? In the stimulus–response view of aggression, the sport situation that calls for retaliation, physical contact with others, and the intense pursuit of victory at all costs might activate the neural mechanisms to an unusually high degree. If these mechanisms are activated frequently and for long periods of time, they might conceivably become easier to activate. Such easy activation might then cause the individuals involved to become sufficiently inured to aggression that they would make fewer conscious attempts to interpret nonsport situational determinants rationally. The question raised by this speculation is that behavior triggered in a sport situation may carry over into behavior exhibited in nonsport situations. If this is the case, then highly aggressive sports must have a very negative effect, and if such sports are to be retained, some degree of control should be placed on both the participants and the factors that provoke violent behavior.

Although some of the evidence presented by Moyer to establish the credibility of the physiological theory is disquieting, the following statement of Tedeschi, Smith, and Brown (1974) provides a hopeful viewpoint:

> the only clear conclusion that is warranted by the available evidence
> is that there is no biologically generated energy that must be manifested
> in aggressive behaviors. Environmental factors initiate such activities,
> though internal factors may intensify the responses that are elicited.

ASSESSMENT OF AGGRESSION

The assessment of aggression is an important but difficult task that suffers from several rather large problems, one of which is *person perception.* We know that aggression must be intended in order for an observed behavior to be accurately classified as reactive aggression. More often than not, however, the assessment of intent depends upon the value judgment of the observer rather than upon the disposition of the observed, and if person perception is faulty, the mere observation of behavior frequently results in a confused aggression assessment. Although sport psychologists and physical educators use paper-and-pencil inventories in addition to direct observation as tools for the assessment of aggression, these inventories have limited validity and reliability. This difficulty, when coupled with the problems inherent in direct observation, results in typically low interrater reliability, even when aggression has been given a narrow operational definition in order to facilitate data collection.

Another problem that confuses the assessment of any personal construct involves the presence of several levels of functioning of that characteristic. Holtzman (1964) has identified four levels of functioning for the hostility construct. The first level is called "hostility in fantasy and imagination." Tools such as the Rorschach and the Holtzman Inkblot Techniques, the Thematic Apperception Test, and the Rosenzweig Picture-Frustration Test are used to assess this *projective* level of aggression. The second, or "inferred conscious self" level, can be assessed using various personality inventories and the Buss–Durkee Hostility Scale. Within certain limits, direct quotations are supposed to elicit a true picture of the subject's *conscious awareness* level of aggression. The third level, called "objective observed self," is assessed by peer ratings; it suffers from person perception because intent, being an aggressor characteristic, is not easily identified by the observer. The fourth level of functioning is the "intervening psychophysiological process or processes" level, which includes activation adjustment and hormonal changes. Although the assessment of this level is more complex than that of the other three levels, it contains the greatest validity and objectivity. All four levels are not usually assessed at the same time. It is of the utmost importance to remember that arbitrary choices must be made during nearly all methods for assessing aggressive behavior.

Psychologists have utilized the "shock box" paradigm in order to avoid the problems inherent in the usual techniques for the assessment of aggression and to enable themselves to collect data on a variety of subtopics related to aggression. "Shock box" research is based on the work of Buss (1964), who defined and measured aggression in terms of the amount of electric shock one person is willing to deliver to another person. Buss's scheme not only gives the subject the opportunity to shock another person, but allows that person to shock the subject back. If the subject is given an intense shock by an opponent who intends to hurt him, he is, by definition, being attacked physically. From this premise, experimental psychologists can design a variety of testing situations, record the results, and from careful statistical analysis of their data, make some interesting assessments of aggression. The psychological literature is replete with various deceptions used to keep the subjects naive and in varying degrees of shock—some of which makes one wonder about the investigator's own aggression level.

deniably true that much violence surrounds the sport scene. vvny is aggression and violence so prevalent in sport? Is it inevitable that aggression be part of sport? Smith (1971a) studied these questions and proposed three possible answers. First, Smith suggested that violence is an inevitable by-product of some sports, because their emphasis is on collision. Football is popularly called a collision sport rather than a contact sport, because intentional contact is part of the game and success depends upon the magnitude of the collisions. Even the game of basketball, formerly a noncontact sport, has been reclassified at the professional level as a contact sport. Other sports are played at such high speeds that unplanned contact is an eventuality. Contact, whether planned or unplanned, often leads to violent retaliation. Although cross-cultural evidence indicates that aggression is not an *inherent* aspect of athletic competition, it seems to have become a natural part of some sports.

Smith's second answer raised the possibility that athletes and non-athletes may vary in the degree of inherent aggression they possess. Sport, by natural selection, attracts individuals who are best able to meet the psychological and physical demands of the task. In contact and collision sports, highly aggressive individuals with talent should theoretically become proficient performers. However research evidence does not provide convincing support for this speculation, although athletes are sometimes reported to be more aggressive than nonathletes.

Smith's third answer provided the most interesting explanation. He stated that athletes display aggression because it is expected, even when they have no desire to do so. An ice hockey player is expected to retaliate when the gauntlet is dropped. This behavior is socialized in novices very early in their careers, despite the fact that fouls constitute illegal aggression. Rules and penalties could provide negative sanctions, but if aggression and toughness continue to be equated with success and applauded by peers and coaches, aggressive behavior will continue in spite of the penalties levied upon it.

Athletes sometimes use aggression to intimidate their opponents in order to inhibit the opponent's performance. The following portion of an interview with Dick ''Night Train'' Lane (Detroit Lions), a renowned defensive football player, is an example of this ''scare'' tactic.

> You know when I'd meet Jim Brown this week I'd try to take a lot out
> of him the first time I tackled him. I tried to let him know that I'm

there. . . . I'm not trying to hurt him or anything. I'm trying to put a fear into him so when he, so if he happens to get through that line and he don't want to break my way, he wants to break away from me, see! Jim Taylor will tell you we've played many, many duels. He's come around there and Thurston has come around there and he's thrown his block and I still come up to tackle sometimes, you know. The other times I catch him up in a pile or something and I'll lower the boom on him, let him know that he's gonna get hit.

Volkamer (1971) studied more than 1800 soccer matches in an attempt to identify the specific sport situations that are related to aggressive responses. He found that losers committed more fouls than winners; that visitors committed more fouls than the home teams; that low-score games produced more fouls than high-score games; that games in which the score differential was very low or very high produced fewer fouls; and that team ranking (high–medium–low) affected the number of fouls. Volkamer's study suffered from a common in-the-field research problem—that of a great many uncontrolled variables. One of these variables affects the interpretation of intent when fouls are operationalized to represent aggression. Fouls can occur without the intent to harm, and the intent to harm can be present without a foul being committed. Although trained observers would add reliability and objectivity to the data of such a study, the problem of person perception would still exist.

Jeffrey Goldstein and Robert Arms conducted an in-the-field study of the effects of watching a football game or a gymnastic meet on spectator aggression (article 3.4). The major concern of their study was to determine whether observing a contact sport such as football would reduce aggressive responses (catharsis hypothesis) or would heighten them (circular effect theory). The failure of this study to find evidence to support the catharsis hypothesis is consistent with other aggression research.

Goldstein and Arms also found that hostility increased among spectators after observing the football game, but no such increase was found in spectators of a gymnastic meet. This finding seems to lend credence to the concern that certain sports may have serious consequences in conditioning aggressive behavior.

3.4

Effects of observing athletic contests on hostility*

JEFFREY H. GOLDSTEIN
Temple University, Philadelphia, Pennsylvania

ROBERT L. ARMS
Temple University, Philadelphia, Pennsylvania

Hostility was assessed among male spectators before or after a football game to determine the effects of witnessing a competitive and aggressive sport on observers' tendencies to aggress. As a control, male spectators were also interviewed before or after a competitive, though nonaggressive, sport (a gymnastics meet). The results indicate that hostility increased significantly after observing the football game, and this increase in hostility did not interact with subjects' preferred outcome of the game. No such increase in hostility was found for those observing a gymnastics meet. The findings are discussed in terms of various theoretical approaches to aggression.

In May, 1964, a riot, precipitated by a referee's decision, erupted at a soccer match in Lima, Peru, killing a number of spectators; the war between El Salvador and Honduras has been traced to a soccer match between those two countries (Lever, 1969), and additional outbreaks of violence have occurred at soccer matches in Great Britain and at boxing matches in New York's Madison Square Garden.

Of course, where large numbers of people gather for public events, many of the preconditions for collective behavior exist (cf. Milgram and Toch, 1969; Turner and Killian, 1957; Zimbardo, 1969). Nevertheless, the nature of such competitive and aggressive sports may, in itself, increase spectators' predispositions to engage in violent behavior. The present study examines the arousal of hostility among spectators at athletic contests.

From *Sociometry* 34(1971):83–90. Reprinted by permission of the authors and the American Sociological Association.

*This study was supported by a grant to the first author from the Bolton Research Fund, Temple University. We thank the Department of Recreation, Philadelphia, for their cooperation. The assistance of Jerry Suls and the comments of Robert Lana, Thomas Ostrom, and Ralph Rosnow on an earlier draft of this paper are greatly appreciated.

Although a number of laboratory studies have examined hostility and aggression as a function of observing violence (e.g., Bandura, Ross, and Ross, 1963; Berkowitz, Corwin, and Hieronimus, 1963; Feshbach, 1961; Geen and O'Neal, 1969), the natural setting contains many characteristics not present in such situations. Spectators at a sports event are likely to be more involved than laboratory subjects since school ties and ego identity increase their stake in the outcome of the event. Observers are apt to be more committed in the field setting since they must pay a price for admission. The observed event in the natural setting differs from that typically used in laboratory studies; a sports event, such as a football or soccer game, is a sanctioned and carefully regulated form of interaction in which penalties are imposed for the violation of rules and in which some kinds of violence are condoned. In laboratory experiments the observed aggression is usually a film of an overt aggressive act which cannot usually be interpreted as justifiable. Given these several differences between the laboratory and field settings, a priori predictions concerning changes in hostility among observers at athletic contests are not possible. However, an examination of theoretical interpretations of aggression leads to several mutually exclusive hypotheses.

Recently a number of books have appeared which suggest that the observation of competitive aggressive sports will serve to reduce hostility among spectators (Ardrey, 1966; Lorenz, 1966; Storr, 1968). This type of vicarious hostility catharsis has been reported in only a few laboratory experiments (cf. Bramel, 1969; Feshbach, 1955, 1956, 1961). If the observation of aggressive sports does result in a hostility catharsis, then spectators' post-game hostility should be less than pre-game.

Most laboratory experiments on the observation of aggression report that observers are likely to be more aggressive after viewing violence than before. Frustration–aggression theories (Dollard, Doob, Miller, Mowrer, and Sears, 1939; Berkowitz, 1969) suggest that aggression is most likely to occur in observers who are angry, frustrated, or whose goal-directed behavior has been thwarted. If watching one's preferred team lose a game can be regarded as frustrating, then observers whose preferred team loses should be more aggressive than those whose preferred team wins and than those who have no team preference.

Other approaches to aggression are not dependent upon a prior state of frustration and suggest that witnessing violence may reduce the strength of inhibitions against aggressive behavior (Bandura and Walters, 1963). Thus, all spectators at an aggressive athletic contest, regardless of their team preferences, should show an increase in hostility.

To determine the relative merits of these theoretical positions, a field study was conducted in which spectators at a football game were interviewed before or after the game. As a control condition, spectators were also interviewed at a competitive, though nonaggressive sport. The interview was designed to assess hostility, team preference, and additional demographic data.

METHOD

Interviews were conducted at the 1969 Army-Navy football game and also at an Army-Temple gymnastics meet held during the same month. The Army-Navy football game was chosen for study because it is played on "neutral" territory (Kennedy Stadium, Philadelphia), thus assuring a relatively even split among observers' team preferences. The Army-Navy game is more than just a "game" to most spectators; it is a traditional rivalry and emotional involvement in its outcome is quite high.

Interviewers (*I*s) were 13 paid undergraduate students who, several weeks prior to the game, received detailed instructions concerning interview procedures. Each *I* memorized a prepared introductory speech to be presented to each subject. The speech explained the study as a survey of spectators' attitudes at various intercollegiate athletic contests conducted by Temple University. Pairs of *I*s were randomly assigned to entrances of the Kennedy Stadium and were to conduct interviews only with subjects about to enter their assigned gates. The subjects consisted exclusively of adult males.

Immediately after arrival at the assigned entrance, *I* was to interview the first adult male approaching that gate. After completing an interview, *I* was to approach the very next eligible subject. This procedure was employed to eliminate any systematic factors which may have biased subject selection. The *I*s also recorded the number of people who refused to be interviewed.

The interview began with the introductory speech. All subjects were assured that the interviews would be anonymous. A number of demographic questions were then asked. These items served two purposes: to check on the equivalence of the various groups in the study and to engage the subject's involvement in the interview. The questions concerned distance traveled to the game, frequency of attendance at football games, cost of tickets, and number of other people accompanying the subject. Subjects were also asked to indicate their preferred team, if any, and in the former case, how upset they would be if their preferred team lost the game.

Following these items were three scales taken from the Buss-Durkee inventory, designed to measure hostility (Buss & Durkee, 1957). Hostility was used as the dependent variable in the study because it was felt to be sensitive to influence by situational factors. Hostility is used here as one index of overt aggression. Each hostility scale consists of a number of statements to be answered "true" or "false" by the subject. The scales employed were the indirect hostility (9 items), resentment (8 items), and irritability (11 items) scales, each of which was found to have satisfactory reliability in a number of independent investigations reported by Buss (1961). Included among these 28 hostility items were eight filler questions concerning football, placed at random intervals throughout the hostility portion of the interview schedule. These items were designed to minimize suspicion about the true nature of the study.

Following completion of the hostility items, subjects were asked to state their reactions to the study and to indicate what they felt the study was about. Subjects were then thanked for their cooperation and dismissed. The total time required for each interview was approximately 10 minutes. the post-game interview was identical to the pre-game interview, except that the tense was changed in a few items where that was appropriate.

In the control condition, five *I*s were employed at the Army–Temple gym meet. They were to interview only male spectators and the interview schedule was nearly identical to that employed at the Army–Navy football game. The only difference between the two interviews was that gymnastics items were inserted for football items on the appropriate questions.

RESULTS

Comparability of groups

Football game data
Before the game, 59 eligible subjects refused to be interviewed from a total of 156 subjects approached (37.8%). There were 44 post-game refusals of the 97 approached (45.5%). . . . A total of 150 subjects completed the interview, 97 pre- and 53 post-game.[1]

A 2 × 3 analysis of variance was computed for each dependent measure, the factors being Time of Interview (pre- or post-game) and Preferred Team (Army, Navy, or no preference). . . . Analysis of demographic data revealed no significant differences among any of the six groups, for distance

---

[1]This difference reflects the greater variance in arrival time than in departure time. Subjects began arriving for the game as much as two hours prior to its scheduled starting time. Nearly all subjects left the stadium within 30 minutes of the termination of the game.

traveled, frequency of attendance at football games, cost of tickets, or number of companions. Thus, the six experimental samples were considered to come from the same population. The subjects' comments about the interview indicated no suspicion of the true purpose of the study.

Gymnastics meet data

Because the gymnastics meet was not held on "neutral" territory as the football game was, over 90% of the subjects favored the home team (Temple). Because of the small number of subjects who had no team preference or who preferred Army, these groups were combined and only before-after comparisons were made.

A total of 49 pre- and 32 post-game interviews were completed. Only 4% of the subjects approached refused to be interviewed, and there were no differences in refusal rate for the before and after groups. The higher refusal rate at the football game may have been due to the difficulty encountered in getting into and out of the stadium, which placed a greater premium on time at that event.

There were no differences between the before and after gym meet groups on distance traveled, age of subjects, or number of companions with subjects. However, pre-meet subjects attended gym meets significantly more often than post-meet subjects. . . . This may reflect the fact that the less involved (those who attend meets less frequently) left the gym meet earlier and were, therefore, overrepresented in the post-meet sample. On the whole, the pre- and post-meet groups are considered to be equivalent.

Comparability of football and gym meet groups

The before and after subjects at the football game and the gymnastics meet were compared on distance traveled to attend the event, frequency of attendance at such events, age, and number of companions with the subject, in a 2×2 unweighted means analysis of variance. These results indicate no differences among any of the four groups on distance traveled or number of companions. Subjects attending the football game, however, were significantly older than those at the gymnastics meet . . . and they attended football games significantly more often. . . . The only interaction obtained was for frequency of attendance, in which post-gym meet subjects attended meets less than pre-meet subjects, and this finding has been discussed above. Taken as a whole, the pre-post football and pre-post gym meet subjects are considered equivalent.

Hostility data

Football game

Group means for each of the three hostility subscales from the Buss–Durkee inventory were highly intercorrelated, and separate analyses for each subscale lead to similar findings. Therefore, a single score, the sum of the three subscales, was computed for each subject. The possible range of hostility scores was from 0 to 28, with the higher figure representing maximum hostility.

The mean hostility scores by group are presented in Table 1. Analysis of these data indicate that, regardless of subjects' preferred team, post-game hostility was greater than pre-game. . . . Neither the main effect for Preferred team . . . nor the interaction effect . . . was significant.

Gymnastics meet

As with the football game hostility data, the three Buss–Durkee subscales were combined into a single hostility score. The pre-meet hostility mean (12.00) was not significantly different from the post-meet hostility mean (12.71). . . . Thus, hostility did not significantly increase as a result of observing the gymnastics meet.

Table 1 Mean football game hostility scores by condition

| | Preferred | | | |
	Army (winning team)	Navy (losing team)	No preference	Total
Pre-game	n = 38 10.42[a]	n = 47 11.72	n = 12 11.67	11.20
Post-game	n = 18 13.33	n = 30 13.17	n = 5 15.00	13.40

[a]The higher the score, the greater the hostility.

DISCUSSION

Hostility data collected at the football game indicates that, regardless of team preference and the outcome of the game, subjects were significantly more hostile after observing the game than before. A number of alternative explanations for this finding may be eliminated on the basis of data obtained at the gymnastics meet. The gym meet includes many similarities to the football game: subjects are seated for two to three hours in a large and compact crowd where outbursts of cheering and applause occur. Therefore, the relative increase in hostility found at the football game, but not at the gym meet, cannot be attributed to any of these factors, although it should be borne in mind that the spectators at the football game were slightly older and attended football games more often than their counterparts at the gym meet. In addition, there was a slight, though nonsignificant, increase in hostility among the gymnastics spectators. There are a number of differences between the two events, however, which cannot be eliminated as possible explanations for the present findings: the absolute number as well as the density of others was greater at the football game; norms for expressive behavior at a football game differ from those at a gym meet, where the crowd is usually less vociferous, and where the general activity level is lower owing to the absence of vendors, bands, and cheerleaders. It seems, however, that one major difference between the nature of the two events is that a football game involves multiple players in direct physical contact with one another, while a gym meet involves individual performances in which no contact can occur. It seems likely, therefore, that the increase in hostility is due to the nature of the observed event; watching an aggressive sport leads to an increase in hostility among spectators.

One methodological difficulty in the present study is the possibility of a subject selection bias: it may be that more hostile observers are attracted to a football game than to a gymnastics meet. This may be indicated by the higher refusal rate at the football game. However, it might be reasonably assumed that subjects who refuse to be interviewed are more hostile than those who are cooperative, and thus the differential refusal rate would lead one to expect fewer hostile responses at the football game among the cooperative subjects.

No support for a catharsis effect is obtained in the present study, contrary to the many popular notions (Ardrey, 1966; Lorenz, 1966; Storr, 1968) that such an effect would occur. Elicitation of hostility catharsis, if it does occur, may require more intense or more direct aggression than that present in a football game.

The failure to find an interaction of preferred team and game outcome seems to support a general disinhibition notion. That is, the act of observing an aggressive sport may reduce subjects' inhibitions against aggression and result in increased hostility. Whether disinhibition is a result of an increase in aggressive drive or is due to the heightened salience of hostility cannot be determined from the present data.

CONTROL OF AGGRESSION IN SPORT

Does the amount of aggression expressed in sport really constitute a problem, or does it just appear to? Isn't sport the same today as it has always been? The concerns expressed in these questions are reflected in the following words of Jerry Izenberg, a syndicated sports columnist, who implies that sport should be re-examined by those in control of it:

> The breeding of violence during athletic events is nothing new. The acceptance of it is. There has been a tendency among both educators and those who run the professional sports to underplay the enormous problems which America's emotions have been producing for the past decades on the playing fields. . . . The violence in our gymnasiums and on our playing fields is a very real thing if you are thinking in terms of something which has its genesis in the grandstands and bleachers.

Spectator violence is no more condoned or accepted today than it ever was, but the increasing acceptance of on-the-field violence has become a concern of prime importance.

Dick "Night Train" Lane's interview, in which he spoke of behaving superaggressively in the presence of the most proficient running backs in professional football, describes a system of counterattack based upon the theory that one of the most effective ways to reduce the opponent's aggressiveness tendency is to escalate one's own attack level until it supersedes the opponent's level by a significant amount. The expected result of this maneuver is that the opponent will realize who holds the upper hand and will adjust his behavior accordingly. Knott and Drost (1972) tested this hypothesis in a nonsport situation. They found that attack-escalating behavior is self-defeating because instead of the expected effect on the opponent, aggression in him is increased. Circular reaction operates to aggravate the interpersonal conflict even more.

While some people express concern about the magnitude of aggression expressed in sport, others extol the virtues of competitive sport as an agent for learning discipline and self-control. The following statement taken from an interview with Vince Lombardi illustrates the latter viewpoint:

> I don't know of any other place where you can find a discipline that takes for man to control himself, you see, that it takes on a football field. In other words, he's going to go in there and knock somebody's block off, and at the same time he's got to control it to some extent.

Zillmann, Johnson, and Day (1974) studied the effect of athletic participation in contact and noncontact sports on aggressive behavior. Their results fail to support Lombardi's hypothesis that participation in contact sports such as football breeds the control of aggression. They conclude that regular participation in noncontact sports, however, does help people to cope with provocation and to control aggression. Zillmann, Johnson, and Day's study supports the premise that in contact sports, the athlete is constantly undergoing disinhibition training and is acquiring the habit of expressing his aggression. Such a learning pattern cannot become established in noncontact sports, however, because even though an athlete may be severely provoked, he tends not to express his aggressive feelings.

Although it is difficult to see how aggression control can be attained if the situation fosters the expression of hostile behavior, John Paul Scott supports Lombardi's belief that sport can ameliorate aggressive behavior. In article 3.5, Scott discusses the role of sport in controlling both participant and spectator aggression and violence. Scott's article centers around methods of social control and the recent breakdown of social control in society. His contention that sport plays a major role in developing peaceful behavior is not without its detractors, whose points of view are delineated in the other articles in this section. However, Scott does make a serious case for sport as a controlling agent for social aggression, and he enumerates several plausible methods by which to accomplish this goal.

3.5 Sport and aggression

J. P. SCOTT
Bowling Green State University, Ohio

The control of undesirable violence is one of the major problems of our time. Such destructive behavior may occur on many levels of organization: between individuals, in conflicts between groups within a society (such as gang wars or riots), or in conflicts among societies on a

From *Contemporary Psychology of Sport.* Edited by G. Kenyon. Chicago: Athletic Institute, 1970. Reprinted by permission. Copyright 1970 by Athletic Institute.

global basis. In the following paper I shall examine the role of sports as a means of controlling violence. As you will see, sports have a major role to play in developing peaceful behavior and one which is too often forgotten.

I may add that I am speaking from personal experience as well as on the basis of objective scientific studies. As a boy and young man, I took part in many sports, particularly in track and football, and I can say from a subjective viewpoint that I have never felt more peaceful and relaxed than after a good hard game of football.

GENERAL THEORETICAL BASES

Factors influencing aggression

As I have shown in my book some ten years ago (Scott, 1958), fighting is affected by factors operating on all levels of organization. There are genetic or hereditary factors, physiological factors, organismic factors (including learning), social factors, and finally ecological or general environmental factors. Furthermore, each species has behind it an evolutionary history of the development of fighting, and each individual has his own personal developmental history of behavior which may or may not include fighting. In short, there is no one cause of fighting, but rather multiple causes. It follows that there is no one perfect, simple method for the control of fighting. Each of the above general types of factors may be used to either enhance or decrease the incidence of fighting between individuals. In the paragraphs below I shall summarize the major findings from each of these areas and later discuss their applicability with respect to participation in sports.

The origin of social fighting

Only the highest forms of animal life show true social fighting, or agonistic behavior, but almost all animals show some sort of defensive behavior against injury by a predator: usually to turn and threaten or attack it. Social fighting probably evolved from such behavior, and it is easy to see how reflexive defensive reactions could result in agonistic behavior in individual development as well as in evolutionary history. If we put two mice together, one may start to groom the other, and if the first gets a little rough, the second may turn around and bite. The first mouse bites back, and the fight is on. If the two cannot escape from each other, the interaction becomes a circular one, each animal stimulating the other to more and more violent behavior, until serious injury results.

The same sort of behavior can be seen in nursery school children. One child accidentally pushes another, who pushes back a little harder, the first one retaliates, and so on, until both are crying. The problem is how to keep this tendency toward circular interaction and ever-mounting violence under control so that it does not become destructive.

The physiology of fighting

As can be seen from its evolutionary history, fighting is basically an emergency reaction. Accompanying and following the outward behavior there are tremendous physiological changes, all having the effect of preparing the body for violent effort. Notice that these changes all *follow* fighting or the stimulation to fight, rather than preceding it. There is no evidence of any physiological mechanism that would produce a cumulative need for fighting apart from that aroused by emergency situations. However, as so often happens in civilized life, we may be subjected to a long series of emergency situations but have our fighting behavior totally suppressed by training. The resulting prolonged upset physiological condition accompanied by feelings of strong emotion can be both physiologically and psychologically harmful. We must conclude that suppressive training by itself is not a completely satisfactory method for the control of aggression.

General methods of social control

Fighting has now been studied in many different species of nonhuman animals, both in the laboratory and under natural conditions. As we examine these animal societies, it is obvious that there are several general methods of the social control of fighting which apply not only to them but also appear to be important in human societies.

In accordance with the general principle of adaptation, social fighting tends to evolve in forms of behavior which are socially useful and minimally harmful. If we watch two goats fighting, we see that they do this in a very formal fashion, always in individual combat with adequate warning signals given in advance, after which the two goats rise on their hind feet and clash their horns together, with little harm done to either. In short, the form of fighting is genetically *ritualized,* just as some forms of human sport such as boxing are culturally ritualized forms of fighting.

In addition, most fighting is reduced to threats and avoidance by the formation of a dominance order. For example, in a litter of young puppies there is a long period in early development in which no fighting occurs. Then the young puppies begin to playfully fight with each other, mouthing and pawing each other's bodies. Occasionally the play becomes rough, one animal or the other gets hurt, and the two animals then struggle with each other for several minutes in a more serious fashion, until one gives up and goes away. The next time the pair gets into conflict the loser quits as soon as the victor threatens, and this soon becomes a firm habit. These conflicts occur before the teeth of the young pups are well-developed, and they never do each other serious harm. The end result is a dominance relationship developed in early life and maintained into adulthood.

Another interesting animal example is that of the baboon troops studied by Washburn and DeVore (1961) in South Africa. These troops are normally composed of adult males, adult females, and large numbers of growing young of various ages all living together. Among the males there is a definite dominance order, with one large male being dominant over the rest. The young animals do not get into the dominance order until they begin to play with each other. This play consists of running, chasing, and grappling with each other. Occasionally it gets so rough that one small baboon will give a cry of pain. At this point one of the older males comes over and threatens all of the play group, who immediately stop their activity. The result is that the young animals learn to avoid getting too rough, and, like the puppies, learn to develop their own dominance order without doing each other actual harm. In both cases, the young animals have learned to *control harmful aggression through play.*

Dominance organization appears to be very important in all of the primate societies that have so far been studied. We can conclude that the same phenomenon should be important in human societies and raise the question of whether human play behavior brings harmful aggression under control.

The phenomenon of social dominance also illustrates the enormous importance of training in the control of aggression. When an animal is dominant, it will invariably attack or threaten the subordinate if given provocation. The same animal in a subordinate relationship with another will never attack or retaliate. The general principle is that *individuals fight in the situations in which they have been trained to fight, and are peaceful in those in which they have been trained to be peaceful.*

Training for peaceful behavior is also accomplished by another major mechanism which begins to operate far earlier in life than dominance. In any highly social species of mammals or birds, there is an early period in development when the young animal easily forms social bonds with other individuals, usually members of the same species and also other animals that may happen to be in close contact for long periods. This normally results in the formation of close attachments to particular individuals at a time when the young organism ordinarily does not fight or is physically incapable of so doing. This brings into play a control mechanism which has very great importance with respect to fighting behavior, that of *passive inhibition*. To give an example, young mice reared together in the same litter grow up peacefully as young animals, and when the time comes when they are able to fight other individuals, they continue to live peacefully together. This is explained by the principle of passive inhibition, which simply means that an animal can form habits of not fighting as well as of fighting. Perhaps an even better example is that seen in a goat flock. When two kids are born as twins and nurse from the same mother, they live peacefully together and usually maintain this habit as adults, whereas the same kids may get into conflicts with other kids of the same age and certainly with older goats and thus become part of a dominance order. There is every reason to believe that passive inhibition is very important in human beings, that young children form habits of not fighting during the time when as infants they are incapable of fighting, and that these habits persist into adult life.

Finally, one important method of social control is found only in human societies. This is the teaching and enforcement of a verbal code or codes of behavior relating to fighting. Depending on the society or the situation, the verbal code may range from one which completely forbids any form of overt violence, or even of thinking about violence, to the opposite extreme where violence and warfare are glorified by the code. These extremes of verbal models of behavior can both produce undesirable effects. If fighting is completely suppressed, abnormal behavior may result. On the other hand, the overemphasis of fighting and destructive behavior may lead to the eventual destruction of the human society involved.

These general methods of social control are so effective in any well-organized human or animal society that very little overt fighting is ever seen by the casual observer. However, social control does occasionally break down, and with the resulting social disorganization there may be a strong increase in destructive fighting.

BREAKDOWN OF SOCIAL CONTROL: SOCIAL DISORGANIZATION

Direct interpersonal or interindividual social control is based on social relationships. It is axiomatic that a crowd of strangers who have not had time or opportunity to develop social relationships with each other, form a disorganized group compared with individuals who have either grown up with each other from birth or who have had long previous associations. Gottier (1968) recently tested the theory that social disorganization produced in this way should result in an increase in fighting. Cichlid fishes of the species known as Jack Dempseys normally fight with each other when they first meet. As a result they form a dominance order in which each fish threatens those fish which rank below him in the dominance order, and avoids those fish who stand above. Gottier compared the amount of fighting in a well-organized dominance hierarchy compared with that in which a new individual was introduced daily and found that the amount of fighting and threatening went up by 200 or 300 percent.

When we examine (Scott, 1962) the incidence of destructive violence and fighting in our society, we find that it is associated with social disorganization of various sorts. The slum areas of our large cities—no matter which nationality or race they include—often include many immigrants who are complete strangers to each other, and there are many instances of broken and disorganized families. The skidrows of our big cities are inhabited by homeless wanderers without families. Even in the affluent areas of middle class suburbia, the extreme mobility associated with industrialized life, with families moving from house to house and even from city to city every two or three years, may result in a weakened form of social organization and a loss of control which may be expressed in forms ranging from drug-taking to outright violence and vandalism.

Finally, there is a built-in period of social disorganization which normally occurs in our society. The young person, and particularly the young male, breaks away from his parental family at about the age of 18 or so, and normally does not form a new family for several years later. It is this age period between 18 and 25 in which the highest numbers of crimes and violence occur, and it is also the time when there is the highest incidence of automobile accidents. Social control frequently breaks down in men of this age, which is also the age when sport is of greatest importance in our society and when it might play a great deal more important role than it does with respect to the control of aggression.

THE FUNCTION OF SPORTS IN THE CONTROL OF AGGRESSION

Organized sports and games, whatever their nature, are a form of social organization; hence, they exert some degree of social control, both over the participants and over the spectators. It follows that sports by their very nature must counteract the factor of social disorganization as a cause of destruction and violence.

I have no wish to join the controversy concerning the definition of sport (Loy, 1968). Rather than precisely defining its boundaries, it is more important to try to subdivide what everyone considers to be sports and games into meaningful categories. One of the concepts that emerges from the work of Sutton-Smith (1968) is that games in our society belong to two cultures:

one child-dominated and the other adult-dominated. In the games that children play when out of sight and control of adults, the rules are either made up by the children as they go along or are handed down from older children. Consequently, these activities are somewhat independent from adult-dominated sports and games in which the rules are written and only changed with difficulty by the adult associations which have assumed control of them.

Both these cultures have the function of preparing individuals for participation in adult life and particularly in providing ways for the control of undesirable aggression and violence. If you watch a group of very young children trying to play a game, you observe that most of their time is spent arguing about what the rules are and whether the players have conformed to them. This provides training in the practice of organized cooperative living according to rules and eventually of living according to laws. In many cases, the rules and concepts of childhood games are closely related to general concepts in our society. For example, the idea of "fairness" is very close to that of equal treatment under the law. Again, in adult-dominated contact sports, such as football and ice hockey, there are rules which define the limits of physical violence, and there are persons assigned to see that these rules are obeyed and to proscribe penalties for their violation. In short, games and sports are training grounds for the control of aggression.

THE CONTROL OF AGGRESSION THROUGH TRAINING

How important is training in the control of fighting? Can sports really have an important effect on the expression of violent behavior? First, let us see what training can do to a nonhuman animal. The common house mouse is a species which normally lives mostly upon the food which man has accumulated and within the shelters which man has designed for himself. If a wild mouse colony grows up under free conditions with plenty of food and shelter, its numbers increase very rapidly as litter after litter is born and grows up to maturity. These mice which have grown up with each other are very tolerant and show little if any fighting. Consequently, under favorable conditions, as in an old-fashioned rick or granary, mice can live together in enormous numbers in a relatively peaceful fashion. On the other hand, the same mice will attack strangers who try to move into the favorable area, and they usually drive them out. There is almost never any severe injury or death resulting from such activity because under free conditions, the mouse which is beaten is allowed to escape and can easily do so.

Using these fundamental facts about the species, we can take mice into the laboratory and, using suitable training methods, can cause them to become either entirely peaceful or to become efficient and merciless killers. Analyzing the reasons why mice that grow up together do not fight, we see that early in their development before they are able to fight they have formed habits of being peaceful through the mechanism of passive inhibition. Experimentally, we can introduce strange mice to each other and prevent their fighting during the first few meetings. The longer they have not fought, the stronger the habit of not fighting, and we can in this way produce an entirely peaceful pair of mice.

On the other hand, we can take another naive mouse and train him to be a very efficient fighter. This is done by simulating an attack, by dangling a helpless mouse against the fighter, and then allowing him to apparently win. After a mouse has experienced a series of such easy victories, we can match him up with an inexperienced fighter. He attacks vigorously, soon wins because of his superior experience and initiative; and from this point on he becomes a very difficult mouse to defeat in any kind of combat. Mice trained in this way will not only attack other males on sight, but can also be trained to attack females or even the harmless young, which they normally never do.

Thus, we can demonstrate that mice have the capacity either to live peacefully together or to become blood-thirsty killers, depending on the kind of training and experience which they have received. In a normal and well-organized mouse society living under natural conditions, the mice become peaceful with respect to familiar individuals and aggressive with respect to unfamiliar ones, but do not ordinarily show either extreme of behavior which can be achieved by artificial training.

There is every reason to believe that training is equally important among human beings. We cannot make comparable experiments, for obvious reasons, but social psychologists who have experimented extensively with the expression of aggressive acts in milder situations find similar major effects of training (Berkowitz and Buck, 1967). Furthermore, we have evidence from cultural anthropology in the form of natural experiments. For instance, the Hopi and Zuni Indians were trained not only to restrain aggressive behavior completely but also taught that any kind of hostile thoughts were bad and should be repressed. At an opposite extreme, the Zulus of South Africa were trained to be efficient warriors and told that the only proper occupation of a man was to be a professional killer of people. A similar code of behavior was followed by many of our own cultural ancestors in Europe in the Middle Ages, for whom fighting, rape, and pillage were a normal way of life. One can argue that different cultures like the Hopi and Zulu were the product of different heredity as well as different training, but this argument falls down when we compare the behavior of the ancient Vikings with their modern descendants, the Scandinavians, who are among the world's most civilized, cultured and nonviolent peoples.

Therefore, if games and sports give training in the control of aggression, it should be effective. Perhaps the most important kind of training involves passive inhibition. Bringing groups of people together in peaceful and enjoyable activities automatically forms habits of being peaceful, and while people are engaged in these activities they cannot commit destructive acts. The games technique is particularly useful for introducing strangers, as it insures that they will begin formation of peaceful habits with respect to each other.

Furthermore, many games and sports have the effect of inducing situations which can easily lead to aggression, such as painful contact or intense competition, but training the participants to restrain themselves from violence in these situations. One of the first principles of competitive sports is that the person who loses his temper is likely to lose the game, either because he loses his judgment, or through violation of the rules.

Thus, sports and games provide powerful methods, both positive and negative, for training individuals to live together in a peaceful fashion.

THE CONTROL OF AGGRESSION IN SPECTATORS

There is a good deal of objective evidence to show that people who watch sports involving scenes of violence become emotionally aroused and consequently show more tendency to become actively aggressive thereafter. Leonard Berkowitz and his students (Geen and Berkowitz, 1966) have used an experimental situation in which college students watch one of two films, one involving a brutal boxing match and the other a film of an exciting track race. After this they have the opportunity (as they think) to deliver electric shocks to another person, and those who have watched the boxing match deal out more intensive shocks. However, the amount of punishment or pain that they try to inflict depends very much on previous training. For example, both men and women will refuse to give heavy shocks to a girl, but will go ahead and punish a man severely (Taylor and Epstein, 1967).

It follows that spectators of sports involving some degree of violence will become excited to express violence themselves, but that this will ordinarily be expressed or restrained according to the training which they have previously received.

Thus, the spectator sports, and especially those involving violent contacts or intense competition, create rather than solve a problem in the control of aggression. Unless the persons who compose the crowds have been thoroughly trained in the principles of sportsmanship, violent behavior is likely to break out afterwards. It is noteworthy that most cases of this sort have involved high school night games. There seem to be two factors involved. One of these is that the students and other spectators mostly fall into an age group in which the greatest amount of violent behavior is found in our society because of developmental disorganization, and the other is that under cover of night it is less easy to detect violators of the rules. It would probably also be found that those individuals who commit violence of this sort (and many do not) have had less training in the nature of sportsman-like behavior.

THE PHYSIOLOGY OF AGGRESSION IN RELATION TO SPORTS

It has been argued in the past (usually by writers having little actual experience participating in sports) that taking part in the violent contact sports provides an outlet for the indirect expression or sublimation of feelings of anger or hostility. It has also been argued that such feelings arise spontaneously, and hence, some sort of socially approved outlet is necessary.

There is no doubt that feelings of anger and hostility do arise, whatever their cause. While the practice of using sports as an outlet for these feelings has some merit, it also has some limitations, principally that sublimation in applying violence against some inanimate object, as for example a punching bag, is never really as satisfactory as retaliating against the object or individual who was the cause of the anger in the first place. If such feelings of anger and hostility are allowed direct expression against another individual, the chief result is simply to form a strong habit of performing this kind of violent behavior, whatever it is. In the past, one solution has been to culturally ritualize such conflicts in forms which are relatively non-harmful, such as boxing matches. There is no doubt that this is a relatively effective way of settling a quarrel, but it is never an emotionally satisfactory one for the loser of the combat.

The hypothesis of catharsis

On the hypothesis that there is some sort of cumulative drive toward aggressive behavior, it would follow that persons who express violence should in that way get rid of their feelings and be more peaceful for a considerable time thereafter. The experiments that have been done along these lines do not bear out this hypothesis (Berkowitz, 1964). Children who become angry and are allowed to express it in some way do not become more peaceful but actually learn to be aggressive. Every time aggression is expressed, it helps to form a stronger habit, and the emotional content behind it becomes less and less necessary. Far from being a good way to control aggressive behavior, this practice actually leads to its increase.

While certain kinds of sports and athletics can be used as a controlled and non-harmful outlet for hostile feelings, this needs to be done with a good deal of care in order to be sure that harmful violence does not result. It certainly should not be considered a major use for sports. As pointed out above, most games are designed to control feelings of hostility rather than to release them. What sports can do effectively is to restore physiological behavior through violent effort, and this in turn will help to alleviate emotional disturbances.

Restoration of physiological balance upset by strong emotion

Beginning with the work of Walter B. Cannon (1929), it has been shown that emotion of anger is very largely a phenomenon of the central nervous system, probably located in the hypothalamus. The more peripheral symptoms of anger, such as high blood pressure, have relatively little effect on behavior. The whole array of symptoms produced by anger are designed to put the body into an emergency condition ready for some sort of violent activity. If the activity is repressed as it usually is as the result of previous training, the physiological state aroused by anger may be maintained for hours. In some recent experiments with mice (Bronson and Eleftheriou, 1969), these animals remained physiologically upset for at least twenty-four hours after fighting, and such effects could be produced merely by the sight of a fighter, without any conflict taking place. This suggests that the principal physiological function of sports which include violent activity is not to sublimate the emotion of anger, but simply to provide the kind of activity which will restore the body to normal homeostatic balance.

Anyone who has competed in major sport events knows that the commonest emotion, and particularly before a contest, is that of fear or anxiety. And he can likewise remember the marvelous feeling of relief once the contest actually begins. It is probable that this kind of emotion (*i.e.*, anxiety) is far more common under conditions of civilized living than is anger. In short, violent exercise is nature's tranquilizer.

While the hypothesis of catharsis will give an explanation for the calming effect of violent exercise, a safer and more general way to look at this phenomenon is that of restoration of physiological balance following any sort of emergency emotions.

HEREDITY, AGGRESSION, AND SPORTS

With very few exceptions, male mammals are more aggressive than their female species mates. Correlated with this, males are likely to be bigger, stronger, and better equipped with offensive weapons such as horns. Among man's closest animal relatives, the primates, the condition varies from the baboons in which the males are two or three times as large as females, to gibbons in which males and females are almost equal in size. One can only guess as to what the original condition of the human species may have been, but it would appear that man falls into an intermediate group with moderate physical differences between the sexes. On the average, males are bigger and stronger than females, and more likely to indulge in overt violence, but there is a good deal of overlap between the two sexes (Scott, 1958).

In addition to these differences between the sexes, there is every indication that there is an enormous amount of variation between individuals with respect to both physical strength and aggressive tendencies, the two of which may not necessarily be correlated. In nonhuman animals such genetic differences are easily demonstrated. In dogs we have the terrier breeds which have been selected for their ability to start and win fights, and, at the other extreme, the hound breeds which have been selected for their ability to get along with strangers. Similar extreme differences in aggressiveness have been produced among the different chicken breeds.

Because of the strong effects of training, it is difficult to collect scientific data on genetic differences between human families and individuals, but there is every reason to believe that there are large genetic differences between individuals with respect to such characteristics as irritability, which may lead the individual to start fights, and physical strength which may enable him to win them.

From this evidence it follows that the need to express violent physical activity will vary a great deal from individual to individual, and that, while there are major average differences between men and women, there will be some women who have more need for violent activity than some men. It also follows that if sports are going to be a major factor in the control of aggression, we must develop both a wider variety of sports suitable to different kinds of individuals and a social or educational system which permits a much wider degree of participation in sports.

THE DEVELOPMENT OF PEACEFUL LIVING

As I have indicated above, heredity may under certain conditions cause major differences between the behavior of two individuals with respect to fighting or destructive violence. This does not mean that aggression is inherited directly, but rather that the individual has inherited certain genes which can modify his capacity to express aggressive behavior, either in an upward or downward direction. The final result comes from the interaction of these hereditary factors with various viable environmental influences including the very powerful ones of negative and positive training. As I have said above, we can use sports to develop in people habits of peaceful and enjoyable activity which automatically prevent their indulging in destructive and violent behavior and also teach them some of the rules of living in a group.

However, one cannot suddenly take an individual at the age of 15 or so when he may first begin to show possibilities of exhibiting destructive behavior and make a sportsman of him overnight. Developing a sportsman (I prefer this concept over that of developing an athlete) must start reasonably early, and here we have two psychological principles which are extremely important. One of these is the success principle. An individual who is successful in a given activity becomes motivated to perform it again, and the final peak of his motivation is the result of the number of times which he has been successful. This is, of course, derived directly from reinforcement theory. If we are going to motivate young people to take part in sports we must put them in situations in which they can be successful.

Success, in turn, is in part the result of developmental age. The second important principle is that the best age in which to start learning a particular kind of physical activity is the age at which the child can first perform it reasonably successfully. There is an optimal period for learning each kind of physical skill for each individual child. In general, one can say that most children do not achieve general physical skill and good motor control until the age of 7 or 8, when the nervous system first becomes mature. Of course, there are many exceptions, both with respect to particular sorts of skills, and resulting from variation between individuals.

SUMMARY AND CONCLUSIONS

The current role of games and sports

Games and sports can act as a powerful force for the control of destructive violence and have actually been used in this way in the past, either consciously or unconsciously. However, our society is undergoing rapid changes, many of which weaken these traditional controls.

One of the characteristics of our modern American society is geographical mobility, and this is having the effect of weakening the child-dominated games culture. For the child from a middle-income family, whose parents move every three to five years, there is less and less opportunity either to receive or to pass along the traditional games culture of children, and this function is being taken over by the parents when it persists at all. Groups of children playing by themselves are replaced by parent-dominated groups such as the Cub Scouts.

In lower-income families, mobility has similar effects, and where this is accompanied by family disorganization as well, there are essentially no controls left except those provided by the gang organizations of teenagers and young adults, which are often organized for destructive purposes. In either case, the traditional balance and connection between child and adult cultures has been upset, with a consequent weakening of games as a means for the control of aggression.

Among adult-dominated sports there is an increasing tendency to emphasize excellence at the expense of participation as these sports become professionalized and institutionalized. Baseball provides an excellent example. There are periodic attempts to change this sport, which requires a great deal of skill and is essentially a public spectacle, into a form with large numbers of participants. Softball was a game in which almost anyone could hit or catch the ball and hence could attract a large number of players. Yet, the ball was soon made harder and harder, with the result that it now takes almost as much skill to play softball as regular baseball. Little League ball was another attempt to broaden the base of participation, but it too seems to be going the way of emphasis on excellence of a few skilled players.

Why should this tendency exist? One obvious reason lies in the reactions of spectators. Watching the unskillful efforts of amateurs is unexciting, and spectator pressure demands that things be more exciting. One way to increase excitement is to get more skillful players. Another is for the promoter to deliberately increase the amount of violence in the sport, as has been done with professional wrestling. Carry this a little farther, and you have gladiatorial combats. From this point of view, professional wrestling is a decadent sport. (The same sort of result has arisen in television, where we have unusually strong competition for spectators. After hours of watching, the spectators get bored, and only scenes of slaughter and sudden death will arouse them.)

Here we have a circular situation. The more successful a sport is in attracting spectators, the more pressure toward increasing excellence and decreasing participation, with even more spectators. While watching sports provides some control over the expression of violence, it is a much weaker method than participation. Also, spectator pressure toward introducing violence into sports results in arousing increasing motivation toward disorderly and violent behavior among spectators.

Sports: an effective method of controlling violence

While the current situation in our society is far from encouraging, the fact remains that games and sports provide effective methods for the control of undesirable aggression.

First, games and sports are one way of organizing life along peaceful and non-harmful lines. This in itself combats one major cause of aggression —social disorganization.

Second, games and sports in childhood provide training in living according to rules; an essential technique for successful adult social life.

Third, rules learned in this way, plus habits of participation in sports, are particularly valuable for the control of violent behavior in the young adult age group, which represents a built-in developmental period of social disorganization in our society. (Persons working with this age group have long known that sports participation is an effective technique, but we are now beginning to appreciate the theoretical reasons *why* it works, and hence to know its limitations as well as its advantages.)

Fourth, apart from their effect in combating social disorganization, games and sports work psychologically in two different ways. One of these is through passive inhibition: the mere fact of not fighting forms a habit of not fighting in a particular situation. The other is through exposing individuals to situations that normally elicit fighting, such as intense competition or pain, and teaching them to restrain themselves.

Finally, games and sports have the physiological effect of restoring normal physiological balance through violent exercise, when this balance has been upset by strong emotions such as fear and anger. Many sports actually provoke such emotions and then relieve them, which gives the player practice in dealing with such emotions.

Thus we have a situation in which games and sports provide powerful techniques for the control of violence, but a set of general social conditions which have the effect of weakening these methods.

Positive recommendations

What can be done to increase the effectiveness of games and sports? The answer is that we must in some way reverse the trend toward excellence at the expense of participation. If we really want to work toward a peaceful and nonviolent society we must change our goals toward encouraging every boy and girl to participate in some or many games and sports. Because of individual differences caused by heredity and experience, this means developing a variety of activities and games. We also need such activities for older people as well as young ones.

It also means developing activities with lower standards of performance; which essentially means non-spectator sports. We now have a few sports that can be both, such as swimming and skiing. The point about these sports is that competition is a non-essential part of the activity; that either swimming or skiing is an enjoyable activity in itself (or, in psychological terms, a self-reinforcing one). If ski resort operators are wise, they will continue to provide instruction, a variety of slopes, and even cross-country skiing to encourage wider participation. Fortunately, this sport is not one which lends itself to large crowds of spectators, with the resulting pressure toward increasing excellence and decreasing participation.

I have no recommendations as to how we can bring about this change in goals. Perhaps the current public awareness of the dangers of the continued trend toward increasing violence may help. And certainly the persons in our society who most clearly occupy key positions of power with respect to the future of games and sports are those educators and scientists who work with them.

SUMMARY

Although Scott asserts that sport teaches appropriate behavior by imposing rules of acceptable conduct, the repeated incidents of violence associated with sport cause some consternation among even the most avid supporters of Scott's position. It does not seem likely that aggression and violence are inevitable outcomes of sport participation, but when winning is emphasized above all other concerns, undesirable forms of behavior, including hostile acts, become a natural result. Approval and rewards reinforce aggressive behavior in sport participants, and the possibility exists that such behavior may spill over into nonsport situations.

The influence of sport in our lives has been made pervasive by the media. All sports have their role models—individuals who possess the charisma, flair, and talent to make them stand out. Because behavior is copied either consciously or unconsciously from these models, we should be very much concerned about the vast amount of publicity the aggressive models receive.

The catharsis theory that participation in sport provides a positive outlet for aggressive behavior is no longer universally accepted. Experimental evidence has caused a reassessment of this once-popular belief, as the preponderance of scientific data indicates that the expression of aggression results in the production of more aggression rather than in its release.

Control of sport-generated aggression may begin with sport itself. Because sport is a form of social organization, it comprises the power to legislate against inordinately aggressive behavior. Sanctions should be increased, and very strict penalties—perhaps even criminal proceedings,[1] if such a measure would be warranted by a comparable nonsport situation—should follow extremely aggressive acts. Something drastic must be done to reduce the ambivalence of the sanctions—on the one hand, aggressive behavior is penalized; but on the other hand, it is applauded by coaches, peers, and spectators. Fighting in ice hockey is treated in this ambivalent manner.

Sport needs to be reoriented away from the "winning at all costs" philosophy, with the associated violation of ethics and the frustrations, anxieties, and traumas of losing. The use of war symbols—"trenches" for the line of scrimmage, "bomb" for a long pass, "sack" for tackle—should be reduced. Aggression in sport can be de-emphasized by accentuating the positive values of sport participation. When aggression in sport has been brought under control, a return to the enjoyment of sport as games of skill will be possible.

---

[1]After this apparently prophetic paragraph was written, a related incident in a National Hockey League game resulted in an indictment being brought by a grand jury against Dave Forbes of the Boston Bruins on a felony charge of aggravated assault. The alleged aggressive act occurred when the butt end of Forbes's stick hit Henry Boucha of the Minnesota North Stars just above the eye as both were leaving their respective penalty boxes after completing penalties for fighting. Boucha subsequently required thirty stitches around his right eye, and after he reported vision problems, underwent surgery to correct a fracture near the eye. Conviction on an aggravated assault charge can carry a prison term of up to ten years. The Associated Press (January 4, 1975) reported Boucha's sentiments about the situation: "They [the courts] are going to put across their point even if they don't convict him [Forbes]. It will make people aware of what's going on in the NHL."

Personality

& sport

4

Personality & sport

4 People have long believed that certain psychological characteristics are related to success in athletic endeavors. No intelligent individual would ever make light of physical skills or talent, but what is the margin of success when athletes have equal talent? In certain situations—the start of the Olympic 100-meter dash, for instance—it is believable that any one of several athletes *could* win the gold medal. How much each of them wants to win is often supposed to decide the outcome.

In recent years, psychologists have collected personality data in the hope of clarifying the association between personality and athletic success. Researchers have sought answers to several specific questions:

Is there a specific personality profile that characterizes a certain sport athlete; that is, is there a "football type" or a "field hockey type"?

Do successful athletes and teams fit a specific personality profile?

Does athletic participation influence the personality of the athlete?

Do individual sport athletes have one kind of personality and team sport athletes another?

Does sport participation alter sex role orientation in males and females; that is, does it enhance or detract from the male athlete's sense of being masculine or the female athlete's sense of being feminine?

Certain objectives underlie the attempt to assess the athletic personality. If there is such a thing as a "football type," then the football coach could select individuals who have the qualities needed for successful performance. This becomes increasingly important if we find that certain personality profiles predispose to success. Still another, perhaps more humanistic, course of action might be to promote within the individual the characteristics that allow for increased self-actualization and therefore increased performance.

If it could be shown that mere participation in sport actually influences the personality of the participant, then perhaps various claims could be made for participation—enhancing cooperation, building leaders, reducing aggressive tendencies, and the like. Such claims have long been made, of course, but without seriously considering the evidence.

There is little consensus in the area of personality from the psychologist's point of view. Even definitions of personality vary according to theoretical viewpoints, perhaps necessarily so. We shall look briefly at a sampling of these definitions.

"Personality is a flowing continuum of organism–environment events (Murphy, 1947)."

"Personality may be defined as that which tells what a man will do when placed in a given situation (Cattell, 1965)."

Personality is ". . . basically phenomenological in character and relies heavily upon the concept of self as an explanatory concept (Rogers, 1951)."

Personality is the ". . . dynamic organization within the individual of these psycho-social systems [mental activities and attitudes as they have social connotations] that determine his unique adjustment to his environment (Allport, 1937)."

"Personality is a stable set of characteristics and tendencies that determine those commonalities and differences in the psychological behavior (thoughts, feelings, and actions) of people that have continuity in time and that may or may not be easily understood in terms of the social and biological pressures of the immediate situation alone (Maddi, 1970)."

Personality can be defined from a biophysical viewpoint, from a social learning viewpoint, or from any position between the two. It has been seen as static, as dynamic, and as something between static and dynamic. We could safely say that a theory exists for any way of perceiving personality. This makes understanding of the term difficult.

The common path is to define it operationally, a convenient path as long as the definition is reasonable. Perhaps there is no right or wrong definition; perhaps personality, being the metaphysical construct that it is, denies the answer to the question. If the theory is useful in predicting behavior, or allows for a clearer understanding of behavior, then it has passed the test of utility.

Physical educators seldom have a sound theoretical framework behind the questions they ask, and this is especially true in personality assessment of athletes. The result is often a rather self-contradictory position—for example, assessing personality change as a function of athletic participation by methods based on assuming that personality is static and rather unchanging after early childhood.

To provide some possible theoretical frameworks from which to view personality, we have chosen three positions: constitutional theory, factor theory, and social learning theory.

CONSTITUTIONAL THEORY

Individuals are often judged by their appearances as if there were some relationship between their physical make-up and expected behavior. The coach who approaches the sturdily built student and asks why he is not trying out for the football team is a case in point. Since the student fulfills the physical prerequisites, he is expected to be able to satisfy the psychological demands of the sport. The basic tenet of the constitutional approach to personality is that human behavior can be explained from a biological perspective. In other words, physique is the key to understanding personality.

Although this is hardly a novel idea (stereotypes of extreme physiques have existed for centuries), William H. Sheldon provided much exacting information about the behavior–physique relationship. However, since the whole theory smacks of genetic determinism, it is unacceptable to many social scientists. It is particularly unacceptable to those who feel that behavior is shaped by external stimuli. Nevertheless, some behavioral consistencies do seem to be associated with specific body types. Since one's physical appearance can hardly be divorced from personality (recall the concept of mind–body unity), the constitutional theory deserves some recognition and inquiry.

Sheldon developed biophysical categories to explain human behavior and his typing system naturally involved two components—physique and temperament. From his work he derived a basic taxonomy of human beings on the basis of each person's physical and psychological constitution. Sheldon secured 4000 photographs of college males in standardized poses. From photographic analysis and actual diameter measurements, he isolated three core components for the assessment of physical structure: *endomorphy* (roundness and fattiness), *mesomorphy* (muscularity), and *ectomorphy* (linearity). These three components are rated on a seven-point scale to produce the somatotype. The individual the coach approached in our example might have been typed as 2–6–1, indicating a very heavily muscled person with low fatty and linear components.

Psychological assessment was derived from a factor-analytic approach of 50 traits to locate clusters having positively correlated dimensions. Eventually, Sheldon was able to select 20 traits for each of the three previously mentioned somatotypes. He called these three temperament components viscerotonia (being relaxed and social), somatotonia (being assertive and motoric), and cerebrotonia (being tense and socially restrained). These components are also rated on a seven-point scale.

The so-called proof for constitutional theory lies in the relationships between the somatotype and temperament categories. Sheldon reported high positive correlations between physique and temperament components: endomorphy / viscerotonia (.79), mesomorphy / somatotonia (.82), and ectomorphy / cerebrotonia (.83). Such correlations formed the basis for Sheldon's constitutional theory of behavior. We have to be cautious about assigning causal roles, since a high correlation does not establish one component as a *cause.* Nevertheless, personality seems to be somehow functionally related to somatotype.

Sport psychologists are especially interested in the relationship between mesomorphy and somatotonia. The behavioral tendencies of the muscular individual make him a prime candidate for many sports. He craves vigorous action and rough and dynamic play. His number one reason for playing is to exercise his motional element (need to be physically active) and superiority drives. Besides craving physical action, he has the bodily coordination needed to participate in sport at a high level of skill. Are these not the characteristics the football coach expected of the student he was trying to recruit in our example?

At the elementary school level, behavior–physique correlates are evident to anyone watching interactive situations. Especially in play activities, leadership is granted to those individuals who can back up their dictates with action. Thus, it is the children who are larger and more muscular than average who control the games and who have the greatest ability in this area. This is to be expected, since the necessary constitutional qualities—speed, agility, and strength—are all present in this body type.

In everyday social relationships, people often judge character on the basis of first impressions. This practice has some degree of scientific support; that is, the percentage of first impressions that prove accurate is too high to be explainable on the basis of chance alone. However, there are two possible ways to explain this fact.

According to the first theory, people's reactions have a physical basis. Their physical make-up therefore partly determines their behavior, and that physical make-up is part of their appearance. The second theory is that people tend to behave as they are expected to, that the expectations of others tend to become self-fulfilling prophesies.

Both are convincing theories. It seems entirely reasonable to assume that one perceives the environment in light of his own physical capacities and behaves according to those perceptions. It is also likely that people modify their reactions to a person according to the way they perceive his physical make-up. Does the social environment determine personality, or is the social environment determined in part by physique? This is a complex question related to another complex question: Is behavior inner-directed or outer-directed?

The constitutional approach to personality has intrigued a number of researchers, possibly because of its neat and compact nature. However, attributing independent variable status to physique is probably too simplistic when so many other factors appear to influence behavior. Sheldon conceded that, and his view on the limitations of his theory is clear: "To try to explain a personality from the constitutional pattern alone is as futile as to attempt such an explanation solely from the life history of the individual" (Sheldon and Stevens, 1942).

No other study has ever yielded the high correlations between physique and temperament reported by Sheldon. Correlation coefficients of replicative studies are typically in the .10 to .30 range and these certainly are not impressive. Several individuals have criticized Sheldon's methodology and statistical interpretations.

Many questions surround Sheldon's work. Is it useful? Is it better than another system? Is it a theory or a hypothesis? Are the correlation coefficients reliable? One could go on and on. What cannot be ignored is something much more important than the answers to such questions. Sheldon made the scientific community consider biological factors when it was nearly blind to them. His research stimulated study and provoked re-evaluation of current theories. At the time he established his "theory," the area of personality was mired in a sea of drive theories, mind–body dichotomies, Freudian psychosexual determinants, and social learning. No consideration was being given to the individual as a *biological organism* with a unique constitution.

Doubtless the whole answer to personality does not lie in the constitutional approach. Sheldon recognized and openly acknowledged this, but remained firm in his conviction that organismic factors have an important place in personality theory. Whatever one chooses to label them—genetic factors, constitutional factors, biological factors, chemical functions, or physiological phenomena—there are more factors in personality than the environmentally produced reactions. The organism by virtue of its unique existence within its own set of experiences is the personality. Even after all the weaknesses of Sheldon's constitutional theory have been spelled out, what does one say in the long run about a 35-year-old theory that will not perish?

FACTOR THEORY

Most of the sport personality literature in North America has been based on factor theory. Personality has been assessed as a combination of traits—the internal behavioral patterns that distinguish one individual from another. According to this perspective, behavior is expected to be quite consistent and predictable, and the specific situation in which behavior occurs is not very important. From Cattell's definition of personality (p. 316), it can readily be seen that prediction of future behavior is an important purpose of personality research. Certainly the prediction of athletes' behavior is a highly intriguing idea and one in which coaches and sport psychologists alike are interested.

Although Cattell is certainly not the only factor theorist, it is his approach to personality that we shall describe in detail. In establishing his well-known Sixteen Personality Factor Questionnaire (16 PF), Cattell used the questionnaire approach, in conjunction with life records and objective tests, to collect data. Through factor analysis he was able to identify 171 source traits that could be clustered to comprise 16 surface traits. The 16 surface traits, which became known as factors, were discrete items, since they had low intercorrelation coefficients. Since there were similar dimensions that eventually comprised the surface trait, Cattell was at first somewhat reluctant to name each factor by one description lest he be misunderstood. After years of testing, however, the factors have been named and it has become customary to speak of a given trait in terms of a single word (for example, intelligence) or in terms of a continuum (for example, introversion–extraversion). By using the terms *source traits* and *surface traits,* Cattell indicated that there are different levels of behavior. Overt behavior is reflected in the surface trait, while behavior is caused by the source trait.

Traits were earlier defined as the enduring and persistent behavioral patterns that are characteristic of a given individual. Cattell suggests that some traits are common to those sharing similar experiences; some are unique in a specific combination or strength only to one individual; and some fit in the gray area between common and unique. This view of man is described clearly by Kluckhohn and Murray:

Every man is in some respects (1) like all other men, (2) like no other man, and (3) like some other men.

In this mathematically derived theory of personality, certain factors have been isolated from the total personality. Anyone using the 16 PF as an instrument of personality assessment must therefore accept this basic premise—personality *can* be factored into discrete dimensions and the separate characteristics can be isolated and discussed. If this is contrary to one's belief, then the 16 PF will not be seen as a viable instrument.

Behavioral consistency is a basic tenet of factor theory. It might be expected that in any discussion of behavioral consistency the genetic determinants are being discussed. Nevertheless, both hereditary and environmental influences are recognized and integrated into the theory. In Cattellian terms, behavior is a function of biologically based drives (ergs) and acquired attitudes (sentiments). Such aspects as self-assertion, affiliation, exploration, and anxiety are classified as ergs, whereas the interests an individual exhibits toward a given object are called sentiments. Because Cattell was greatly concerned about the lack of hereditary components in other personality theories, he developed a technique to assess the magnitude of the genetic influence on behavior. From his research (preliminary though it was), he found that intelligence was heavily influenced by heredity, whereas surgency (according to Cattell, the quality of being happy-go-lucky, impulsively lively) and tough-mindedness were dominated by the environmental role. If we are looking for behavioral changes as an outcome of athletic participation, it would certainly seem wise to look at the factors that are apparently most susceptible to change. It would seem ridiculous to look for changes in intelligence as a result of being an athlete for a period of time.

Cattell included the term *prediction* in his definition of personality and was particularly concerned with two problems: (1) what an individual will *do* in a given situation, and (2) what an individual of given endowments will *become* in a given environment. There is no mistaking the interactive aspect of heredity and environment. As far as sport is concerned, the question of what an individual will *do* has received most of the attention directed at prediction. One of the objectives constantly stated in the sport personality literature is to predict future performance from an assessment of traits. This objective relates to success, which is important to all sport participants and many nonparticipants. Personality assessment is intriguing to coaches as long as the knowledge derived can be used to increase performance. Of necessity, the question of what an individual will become can only be answered by longitudinal studies; as yet sport personality inquiry is almost devoid of this approach.

As far as prediction is concerned, if one does not believe that personality has a reasonable degree of consistency across situations, then he will not find the trait approach a useful approach to assessment. The 16PF questionnaire is not composed of sport-related questions, and therefore the relevance of the athlete's self-report behavioral measure might be questioned.

Factor theory also differentiates between trait and state behavior. Traits are presumed to be fairly stable across many situations, but it is realized that individuals change their facial expressions and body language as their mood changes. This transitory aspect is referred to as the state. A good example is Spielberger's concept of trait and state anxiety —some people are observed to be anxious most of the time, whereas others are sometimes calm and sometimes anxious. In a sport situation in which aggressive behavior is observed, that behavior may be caused by a trait (the athlete is an aggressive athlete) or by a state (the athlete is in an aggressive mood).

Although there are individual and even daily variations in the ways in which people react in similar situations, there is a *reasonable* degree of consistency in their behavioral patterns. Thus it is useful to construct a system that will explain what has been observed or will predict what will be observed. The trait approach to personality is built on certain observed patterns of action resulting from needs and motivations interpreted in the context of the situation. Therefore traits are inferred from behavior and do not really reside within the individual as is commonly believed.

The great limitation of sport personality literature is that the context for observing traits is not the sporting environment; in fact the context is usually not even sport-related. Most researchers make the assumption that the traits derived from a classroom-administered paper-and-pencil inventory that asks no sport-situation questions will be relevant to actual sport performance.

Another serious drawback is that the gap between the self-report measures and actual behaviors is undoubtedly wide. Sport predictions derived from trait assessment have not been successful. Typically, personality traits account for less than 10 percent of behavioral variance in any given situation. That means that 90 percent remains unaccounted for. Such findings certainly breed little confidence in any explanation of future behavior based on the level of the personality trait. Nevertheless, trait assessment of athletes is likely to be as correct as a coach's subjective evaluations.

SOCIAL LEARNING THEORY

Sport is supposed to be a powerful force in today's society. Many human characteristics are supposedly developed by sport participation. It is argued that sport enhances cooperation among individuals, allows opportunities for the enhancement of leadership qualities, and generally improves the human lot. This viewpoint fits social learning theory, whose basic premise is that environment is the most important agent of personality formation. The individual interacts with the environment in an adaptive way, and this includes interactions with significant others— individuals who make an impact on the individual and therefore possibly affect his behavior. Personality is learned, and ensuing behavior can be understood only with the full appreciation of the cultural context within which behavior occurs.

In the view of the social learning theorists, however, trait psychologists confound the understanding of personality by searching for answers inside the organism; that is, they seek traits from which they can predict behavior. Social learning theorists say that behavior can only be explained as a function of (1) the variables significant enough to affect future actions and of (2) the individual's past experiences, which naturally color his perceptions. Behavior varies as situations vary; hence the social learning theorists subscribe to the concept of *situation-specificity*. Personality responses are not independent of stimuli, and consistency in several different situations is not expected.

Can personality traits be as specific as motor abilities? Doubtful as this may seem, we should bear in mind that trans-situational generality is not impossible in approximate situations. We can reasonably expect most children to be excited in anticipation of Christmas, and athletic competition can be expected to produce excitation in athletes. Without some consistency in behavior, trying to understand personality would be ridiculous. If an individual responded differently every time to the same situation, there would be little to understand, explain, or predict. One should not interpret behavior-specificity as being antithetical to behavioral consistency. Rather, we can say that behavior is always affected by context.

Social learning theorists address themselves to two key questions:

How does experience change an individual?
By what process does one adapt to the environment?

The first question deals with the malleability of personality, and the second with the mechanics of personality change (and personality change is quite compatible with this theoretical position). Although other personality theories hold that personality is formed early in life, social learning theorists assert that the social milieu continues to play a significant role in the formation of personality throughout one's life. Those who want to study the effects of sport participation on various human characteristics might be wise to adopt a social learning position rather than a position that declares personality to be static and unchanging after early childhood, since in the latter case one's research ideas and personality beliefs might be antithetical.

Instead of perceiving personality as traits, some social learning theorists describe personality as habits, or modes of response. Habit structure therefore depends upon the *unique* events to which the individual has been exposed. It should be easily seen from this explanation of behavior that personality cannot be viewed apart from the situations that have shaped it. If one takes this idea of personality to the extreme, behavior can be simplistically reduced to a stimulus–response bond. This is reminiscent of Pavlov's dogs salivating in response to the sound of a tuning fork. However, it seems a little more humanistic (and *realistic*) to replace the S–R bond with S–O–R, in which the organism has something to say about his response. In certain sport situations, the athlete must suppress retaliatory aggressive responses to remain in the game or at least to avoid a penalty. Certainly not all behavior is conditioned without modification during special circumstances, some of them being unique. Actions then are regulated to a large extent by anticipated consequences. Reinforcement (or lack of reinforcement) can strengthen responses.

Social learning theorists describe the effects of others on personality in terms of modeling and imitative behavior. Individuals who see an unusual set of responses by others tend to exhibit these same responses when placed in the situation themselves. Perhaps this fact might account for the sport practices that continue to be manifested year after year—one coaches as he was coached. At least on the surface, coaches and athletes seem to have the capacity to be models and to have their behaviors emulated. Although the day of viewing the athlete as a demi-god is gradually drawing to a close, many individuals continue to seek out these heroes and imitate their actions. Personality changes and develops by example.

The social learning theory of personality is in conflict with trait theory. Advocates of the former find untenable the idea that generalized and stable traits can determine behavior in a variety of situations. Everyday behavior is much too flexible to be predicted from a few general traits. Trait psychology looks for consistencies in behavior and in so doing omits a great deal of individual variation by disregarding situational variations. Apparent consistency in behavior is a function of situational similarities, not of personality.

Any area of psychological research is fraught with theoretical and methodological dilemmas, to be sure, but personality assessment contains more than its share. Wayne Holtzman, in article 4.1, raises two key questions for the reader to consider: (1) what can be expected of personality information relative to predicting behavior? and (2) how much information is necessary in order to comprehend an individuals's behavior?

Holtzman explains the enduring criticism that has been directed toward the atomistic approaches to personality assessment. Single-minded adherence to either factor theory or social learning theory promotes such an atomistic view. Factor theory attributes behavior to personal traits; social learning theory attributes it to situations. A more realistic approach to personality assessment would be the interactive one (traits $\times$ situations = behavior).

Holtzman considers the question of choosing a method that is idiographic (looking at the person as an individual) or nomothetic (looking at individuals from a normative or comparative viewpoint) and argues that any combination of these approaches can be used.

He also discusses the ethical implications of personality assessment. This is particularly useful to those interested in sport personality assessment since several "mail-order" personality assessment services are now available to the coach. Some writers have expressed concern over how this information will be utilized by the coach—will it be used to assist the athlete in his sport performance or will it be used to achieve some negative end?

4.1 Recurring dilemmas in personality assessment[1]

WAYNE H. HOLTZMAN
University of Texas, Austin

Summary: Six unresolved issues related to recurring dilemmas in personality assessment are (1) the meaning of personality assessment, (2) how many things must be known about an individual to understand his personality, (3) how personality variance can be separated from method variance, (4) whether we are building a culture-bound theory and technique of assessment, (5) whether we can ever develop a systematic, comprehensive personality theory closely linked with empirical data, and (6) the moral dilemmas created by personality assessment.

It is highly fitting that this symposium has been organized to commemorate the 25th anniversary of the classical publication, "Explorations in Personality," by Henry Murray and his associates at the Harvard Psychological Clinic. Murray's emphasis upon the intensive study of normal individuals, his use of a diagnostic council for weaving together into a coherent whole the rich and often contradictory bits of information about an individual, and his ingenious, tailor-made techniques of assessment still stand today as methods to be emulated by others. Much of what I see as recurring dilemmas in personality assessment was recognized by Murray although their manifestations take a different form today than 25 years ago.

To attempt to cover in any systematic manner all the dilemmas still current in the field of personality assessment would indeed be presumptuous of any one person, particularly within the few minutes available to a symposium speaker. It's bad enough to look squarely at one or two dilemmas. Being confronted by all of them at once is sufficiently overwhelming to

From *Journal of Projective Technique and Personality Assessment* 28(1964):144–150. Reprinted by permission of the author and the publisher.

[1]Presented at the annual meeting of the American Psychological Association in Philadelphia, August 31, 1963. This paper was written while the author was a Fellow at the Center for Advanced Study in the Behavioral Sciences, Stanford.

drive out of the field all but the stouthearted or foolhardy. Being both fool-hardy and stouthearted, I shall present what I see as six major, unresolved issues that continue to plague us in our attempts to develop the theory and technique of assessment.

1. *What do we mean by personality assessment?* Whether one prefers to emphasize the social stimulus value of the individual, the way in which he adjusts to his environment, the manner in which his behavior is organized, or the subjective aspects of the phenomenal self depends largely upon the theory of personality employed. In a similar manner, what a given psychologist means by personality assessment is determined mainly by the particular techniques he chooses to employ and the assumptions implicit in them. We all tend to use the same words though rarely the same music. The resulting cacophony is confusing indeed, even to the untrained ear. Thus one person will insist on *his* set of personality traits as defined by *his* techniques, while another uses the same trait names with entirely different operations. Most of us are guilty of such egocentrism in the name of operationism. Certainly it's a free world where everyone can choose his terms and techniques as long as he states at least some of his conditions, but it frequently leads to rather silly statements, misunderstanding, and even public rejection.

Until recently within the field of individual differences, the domain of personality assessment was largely reserved for what was left over after covering human ability, interests, and attitudes. In the usual textbook survey of techniques, the various tests were neatly classified according to the domain covered, leaving personality as the residual and lulling the student into a false sense of security that he had a firm grip on things. Today, however, the world of individual differences is again in ferment. Some claim the whole of the field as the rightful domain for personality assessment; others prefer to abandon any classification system for different domains, concerning themselves with assessment in general. The fad among personality psychologists is to look closely at cognition, perception, and learning, while the expert on abilities worries about motivation, response sets, and other non-cognitive aspects of test behavior. In all probability such a diffusion of ideas will lead to a more satisfactory theory of assessment than previous piecemeal efforts. In the meantime, however, it is likely to become even more difficult to specify clearly what we mean by personality, a dilemma of definition and conception to which I see no good answer in the immediate future.

2. *How many things about an individual must we really know to understand his personality?* The strong criticism of atomistic approaches in personality

assessment that was so characteristic of much debate during the past thirty years has had its effect. The battleground has shifted but the basic issue is the same. To understand an individual's personality, must one take into account all aspects of the individual and his situation as they interact to produce manifestations of the personality? Or, is it possible that sufficient understanding for effective differential prediction of behavior can be achieved by increasingly complex, multivariate approaches to assessment? The current issue concerns how holistic must one be, not atomism versus holism.

If indeed it is true that a huge amount of past and present information about an individual must be properly digested, together with detailed knowledge of the future circumstances likely to prevail, then it is highly unlikely we will ever reach a very satisfactory level of understanding in the sense of prediction from personality assessment. While I'm inclined to think we can still achieve efficient differential prediction of important things about a person by improving our techniques of assessment, I must admit that this belief is based largely on faith rather than hard evidence.

Nevertheless, we have moved a long way in our conception of how to deal with complex information about an individual obtained simultaneously from different levels of his functioning and at different points in time. Even the old arguments about idiographic versus nomothetic assessment of personality are rapidly breaking down in the face of multivariate models which can account for both kinds of information at the same time. The general model suggested years ago by Cattell (1946) is a useful one from which to proceed since it allows for any amount or kind of assessment on one axis, any number and type of persons on a second axis, and any number of repeated measures on different occasions or situations on a third axis. These three broad, orthogonal dimensions—traits, persons, and occasions—yield the general case for almost any conceivable way in which the individual is approached, requiring only the assumption that individual differences exist and are measurable, an assumption that underlies all empirical approaches to personality assessment. What one stresses within this general model and how he goes about measuring and analyzing it can vary greatly, of course, and accounts for the wide variety of theory and technique prevalent today.

The general case itself, when taken seriously, is exceedingly difficult to achieve since it requires repeated measures on the same individuals using the same techniques of assessment. Most of our methods of personality assessment have questionable validity when applied on more than one occasion, let alone many, unless a rather long time period intervenes. One good example of the possibilities for Cattell's general model is the ambitious investigation undertaken by Mefferd, Moran, and Kimble where a small number of schizophrenic patients is assessed daily for a large number of days under different courses of treatment. In one preliminary report (Mefferd et al., 1960), they describe the first results obtained in the analysis of about 100 measures repeated for 245 successive days on a single patient. Among the techniques employed are included ward behavior ratings, brief mental tests, indices of physiological arousal, constituents of blood and urine, and such exogenous variables as air temperature, drug treatment, and ward environment. The overwhelming rate at which information accumulates in such a study would make analysis impossible if it weren't for some automatic coding, high speed computers, and multivariate statistical processing. The appropriate statistical model is multiple time series analysis. Elsewhere (Holtzman, 1963a), I have outlined some of the problems in such analysis, with illustrations drawn from the data collected by Mefferd and his colleagues.

Whatever method of analysis is employed, Cattell's P-technique model for the single case is thoroughly idiographic in nature. It is in the choice of a particular method of analysis that one encounters serious controversy similar to the nomothetic one of actuarial versus clinical prediction. The important point is that one no longer needs to think simply in terms of idiographic versus nomothetic or of statistical versus clinical. The general model for personality assessment allows for any combination of these approaches. It is largely a matter of purpose, personal preference, or feasibility with existing techniques rather than theoretical considerations as such, although one's theory is relevant to this choice.

But the fundamental issues still remain as to choice of which persons to study under what conditions and with what techniques of assessment. And even if one develops a complex, multivariate model for prediction purposes, there is little empirical evidence as yet that it will work that much better than the relatively simple, isolated methods of the past, as far as prediction is concerned. The concept of hostility provides as good an example as any of the problems that will be encountered. One can speak of hostility as a generalized state, a predisposition to become hostile, or as a specific state which is linked to particular situational and internal conditions. The generalized trait of hostility requires trait stability over different occasions, while the specific state of hostility only demands valid measurement of hostility under specific conditions. The former requires a nomothetic approach across different individuals while the latter is best studied by repeated testing of single individuals. Only rarely are the two approaches combined. And yet, without some such combination, important, unevaluated interactions between the steady and fluctuating trait systems may completely obscure the meaning of the results.

Quite aside from the problem of coping with both generalized and specific manifestations of the same process is the difficulty encountered in choosing assessment techniques and scores or signs for the techniques which are appropriate to the personality construct in question. At least four systems or levels of functioning have been studied with regard to hostility though rarely at one time: (a) hostility in *fantasy* and imaginal processes as revealed by such devices as the Thematic Apperception Test, the Holtzman Inkblot Technique, or story completion tests; (b) the *inferred conscious self* as revealed by various self-report inventories; (c) the *objective observed self* as indicated by peer ratings; and (d) the intervening *psychophysiological processes* as reflected by Lacey-type indices of autonomic reactivity or hormonal balance from analysis of biochemical constituents. It is easy to see why serious attempts to take into account various levels of functioning while also dealing with the problems of interaction between steady and fluctuating traits are almost non-existent, even when attention is focused on a single general concept such as hostility or anxiety.

A major dilemma is that in any practical situation one must continually make rather arbitrary choices and exclude all but a small portion of the general model for personality assessment. One is repeatedly haunted by the question, Can we ever really understand a personality?

3. *How can one separate personality variance from method variance?* A third fundamental dilemma of great concern to many psychologists is the inevitable confounding of personality traits with the particular method for assessing them. In recent years, special attention has been given to the difficulties arising from such response sets as Tendency to Acquiesce or Social Desirability which often overshadow the substantive meaning of items in personality inventories. The interaction between examiner and subject in such projective techniques as the Rorschach or TAT poses a similar dilemma that has led many clinicians to insist that the examiner himself is part of the instrument, that he must listen with his "third ear" and sharpen his intuitive acumen to a high degree or he will surely fail.

Campbell and Fiske (1959) have suggested that for most personality constructs it should be possible to design experiments employing a multi-trait multi-method matrix for teasing out the relative contributions of content and method. Given two or more traits and two or more methods for assessing the traits, the resulting scores can be intercorrelated and the results arranged in a rectangular matrix for close inspection and possible further analysis. Placing one's data in such a matrix is a sobering experience that usually serves to dramatize how much the measurement of a given personality trait is really a function of the method used rather than the theoretical construct.

4. *Are we building a theory and technique of assessment which is culture-bound within western, industrialized society?* As the psychologist in the United States and Western Europe reaches out to other societies he is becoming acutely aware of the restricted bounds within which his work applies. Many react by quickly closing the curtain and renewing their efforts to develop a theory based on college sophomores or hospitalized schizophrenics who are at least somewhat malleable and readily available. Others are struggling to establish cross-cultural comparative studies or replication in foreign cultures to test the limits of their systems. The most difficult problems of translation to maintain equivalence arise with respect to questionnaries, inventories, and other verbally loaded instruments. Even with the best of literal translations across different western societies one can hardly be sure of the semantic properties of the words used. The recent study by Peck and Diaz-Guerrero (10) of the meaning of the term, "respect," in Mexico and the United States revealed marked differences in the connotations of the work, both cross-culturally and among subcultures of both countries.

As Lindzey (1961) has pointed out in his survey of projective techniques and cross-cultural research, the relationships between the subject and examiner, problems of communication, and the confounding of culture and personality create serious dilemmas in any attempt to extend personality assessment to other cultures, especially primitive ones. Even in the case of nonverbal, "meaningless" stimuli such as inkblots, serious difficulties of interpretation arise.

An anthropologist, Edwin Cook, recently returned from a two-year visit to a most inaccessible part of New Guinea where he and his wife have been conducting studies of culture change with increasing western contact. He reduced the problems of communication and his relationship to the tribesmen to a negligible minimum by living within the community and meeting the inhabitants strictly on their own terms many months before beginning any personality assessment. The fact that culture and personality are confounded in his study is irrelevant to his particular problem of culture change. The stimuli and methods of administration for the Holtzman Inkblot Technique are about as culture-free as it is possible to get (Holtzman, 1961). While most of the variables with which he is working appear to be satisfactory for his purposes, the problems of interpretation from a personality rather than cultural point of view still loom large. Let me illustrate more specifically by citing a particular response that he obtained and the rich local meaning associated with it.[2]

The response, "kotsamba", was given to Card 7A, an inkblot which is mostly black and white with little red spots often suggestive of blood. Kotsamba is a small, greenleafed, purple flowering plant which seems devoid of particular significance until viewed in the light of additional ethnographic information. According to Cook, the flowered plant is important in at least two contexts. After a person is buried, a few of these plants are uprooted and thrown on top of his grave. Ancestor worship and the local animistic beliefs suggest more than mere decorative value for the plant. A second association of considerably deeper meaning to kotsamba is indicated by the following text. At the conclusion of a ceremonial pig festival which may last for 15 months, the majority of pigs are killed as sacrifices to the ancestors. Kotsamba is dipped in the pig blood by men, brushed over a woman, and stuck under the thong of her rear net covering to insure that her pigs will grow big and fat. Since Card 7A has only red color suggestive of blood, rather than purple or green color like the flowering plant, the response of "kotsamba" must refer to the ceremonial plant covered with pig's blood, an association charged with emotion and superstition. Given the difficulty of grasping the nuances of a strange vocabulary and the problem of understanding a sharply divergent world view, even a skilled anthropologist intimately acquainted with the culture has difficulty of interpretation while a psychologist would be completely lost.

5. *Can we ever develop a personality theory that is systematic, comprehensive, and closely linked with empirical data?* Closely related to the first four dilemmas posed is our recurrent failure to develop a satisfactory theory of personality. In their comprehensive review of personality theories, Hall and Lindzey (1957) were notably impressed by the diversities, disagreements, lack of formal clarity, and lack of demonstrated empirical utility characteristic of personality theories. About the best that can be said of most theories is that they stir the imagination, strike a respondent cord here and there, and have a heuristic value in stimulating research. Certainly there is no single widely accepted theoretical position today, nor does it seem likely that one will emerge in the near future. Man is simply too complex an animal to capture so easily.

[2]Personal communication from Edwin A. Cook to the writer.

Implicitly or explicitly, we all have some kind of theoretical position that we employ as a point of departure in personality assessment. As often as not, however, we are hard-pressed to rationalize our personality theory with our assessment techniques. Perhaps it is expecting too much to ask that our practice be in accord with our theory. Perhaps we should be content with theory that is sufficiently vague and general to allow maximum freedom for what we want to do.

A rather interesting and fresh approach to this dilemma has been opened up by high speed computers and the possibility of constructing models that can be tested by computer simulation of personality. If one does not require that a theory account for all personality phenomena but only for a limited segment of human behavior, then it is possible to conceive of a small system of formal constructs and properties which can be spelled out in a logic diagram and incorporated in a computer program. Loehlin (1963) has recently achieved some success in the simulation of a rather primitive personality he calls Aldous. Three subsystems provide Aldous with a means of mediating his response to his environment—recognition, emotional reaction, and action preparation. Aldous has both immediate and permanent memory, with a learning subsystem that modifies the latter. Aldous can introspect in a superficial way by responding to questions in a verbal report that is printed out by the computer. The press of his environment can be manipulated along several dimensions to study its impact upon his personality development and, with additional programming, several Aldouses can be constructed to form a small social system.

As I have indicated elsewhere (Holtzman, 1963b), Loehlin's simulated personality model is actually static and fairly simple in design. It should not be difficult, however, to build into Aldous additional properties, including the attribute of self-modification which is essential to any realistic personality model. The use of a higher capacity computer would make it possible to introduce more dynamic features that would lift Aldous above his present primitive level to a degree that would make computer simulation of personality a highly useful approach to model construction and the testing of theory. It should be kept constantly in mind, however, that the psychology of machines is only a pseudopsychology unless a reasonable goodness of fit is assured between the machine model and real organisms, at least with respect to the limited system of traits and relationships being simulated.

6. *Moral dilemmas created by personality assessment*   Most of us are so concerned with the substantive and theoretical problems of personality assess-

ment that we often overlook the ethical and social implications of our work. It comes as a rather rude shock to find the general public crying out in righteous indignation about our techniques and the way in which we use them. While there has always been a small group of extremists who want to censor the work of psychologists and who demand an end to personality assessment, the reactionary movement has developed sufficient force recently to push numerous legislative bills aimed at banning personality testing in schools and other public agencies. Although the fears of some people that we have powerful, secret techniques for uncovering private information about an individual or controlling his personality are obviously unjustified at present, there is strong evidence to suggest that such methods will indeed be developed in the near future.

Several principles in the current version of the APA Code of Ethics are of particular interest since they embody unresolved moral dilemmas which face us. Corollaries of Principles 6, 7, and 16 deal with confidentiality of information and invasion of privacy, the welfare of individuals who submit to personality assessment, and the problem of harmful after-effects where stressful situations are involved in assessment. The basic moral dilemma in each instance arises from a conflict of two values: (a) the individual human being has a right to maintain his privacy and personality without threat of intrusion; and (b) a better understanding of human behavior, which can only be achieved in its fullest sense by experimentation and probing investigation of the human personality, is of benefit to mankind. The current ethical code reduces the dilemma to specific issues that confront us every day in personality assessment, issues that in the last analysis can only be settled by repeated juridical review rather than by simple pronouncement.

These six dilemmas, five substantive and one moral, hardly cover all that can be said about recurring dilemmas in personality assessment. Much can also be said about the really significant progress that has been made in the past 25 years. Perhaps some of these issues will simply fade away with time. But if past experience is any indication of the future, we can expect most of them to be with us for a long time to come.

Before 1960 very little research dealing with sport groups had been conducted. Two clinical psychologists, Bruce Ogilvie and Thomas Tutko, were pioneers in assessing athletes' personalities. In article 4.2, Ogilvie summarizes a massive review of sport personality literature (up to 1968) and arranges the material according to the assessment instrument used.

The reader should realize that most of the sport personality literature is trait-oriented and that all conclusions must suffer the inadequacies of that approach. Unlike most sport personality researchers, Ogilvie reports several consistent findings in the personality structure of high-level competitors. He provides partial support for the concept of sport ''types'' when he concludes that certain personality characteristics are associated with certain sports (for example, the ''footballer type'').

In recent years, Ogilvie and his colleagues have devised their own sport personality assessment device (*Athletic Motivation Inventory*). The personalities of thousands of athletes have reportedly been assessed by this device in the last few years. On the basis of these data (which are not published), Ogilvie has continued to advocate views similar to those given in his article.

4.2 Psychological consistencies within the personality of high-level competitors

BRUCE C. OGILVIE
San Jose State University, California

This review of the literature relating to the personality structure of high-level competitors will be limited to the general findings of studies that measure similar or identical traits. Since there is no literature to be found that is based on longitudinal studies of the potential effect of high-level competition on the character formation of youthful competitors, some of the most recent data for age-group swimmers will be reviewed in cross-sectional form. I feel that some of the trends were so consistent for both boys and girls from age 10 to age 14 that it becomes possible to speculate more intelligently about the effects of competition on personality. These data will have to be interpreted with caution because of the highly select sample they represent.

Original version of an article published in the *Journal of the American Medical Association* 205(1968):156–162. Reprinted by permission of the author and publisher. Copyright 1968, American Medical Association.

BASES FOR INVESTIGATION

Research interest in athletic personality, motivation, and the possible effect of competition on character formation developed from extensive clinical experience with problem athletes. During a period of several years, athletes from every sport representing every level of athletics, from high-school age-group competition through professional sports, have been referred for psychological reasons. The range of psychological problems and the nature of the psychological conflicts associated with competition has covered the entire spectrum of conflicts. The variety of somatic complaints and the severity of the emotional reactions to the stress of high-level competition contributed to serious doubts about the value of athletic competition. As a psychological consultant to competitors who responded with such a wide range of negative reactions to the stress of college, professional, or Olympic participation, I was forced to look more critically at athletics. Three examples should suffice to make my point.

The first example is the long-jumper who performed at near the national standard during practice but failed to gain a single point during actual competition. In an attempt to understand his unconscious need to hang one spike over the take-off board and therefore be consistently disqualified, we taped an interview during the period of his greatest stress. Relatively free association brought forth the following repetitious statements: "Watch me, Mom," "This is it, Mom," "Now's the time, Mom," which continued until he disappeared down the runway.

The second example is the young man who found it impossible to compete if any of his competitors showed a personal interest in him.

The last example is the pro football player who developed a neurotic depression because he failed on one particular play; he concluded that he was totally unworthy because he lost the game and destroyed the season for his teammates.

Multiply these cases fortyfold, adding others that vary in behavioral reactions and intensity, and you will see the seeds of doubt that gave birth to the past five years of investigation.

This review, with but a few exceptions, will deal with investigations published since 1960. The two most comprehensive reviews prior to 1960 have been published by Scott (1960) and by Cofer and Johnson (1960). John Kane has co-authored a chapter with F. W. Warburton entitled, "Personality related to sport and physical ability," which is one of the most comprehensive reviews available to date (Kane, 1966).

Sociometric and psychometric studies have been designed to answer many practical and academic questions. A significant number of investigators have directed their attention to determining the contribution that games, recreation, and competition have made to the socialization process. Other investigators have directed their energies toward determining the contribution of athletic participation to personality and character formation (Cratty, 1968). More recently there has been considerable emphasis on the identification of the personality variables that can be found to relate significantly to athletic achievement. The selection of criterion groups of athletes such as those who have sufficient talent to participate in professional sports or to represent their country in the Olympic Games does permit reliable statements about the personality of the successful athlete. The comparison of athlete to non-athlete at the various levels of competition has provided a limited understanding of the character structure of those who retain continuing interest in athletics.

The variety of objective personality questionnaires used to investigate athletic personality includes the instruments that have been used most frequently for selection of personnel in business or industry. Included in this review will be The Minnesota Multiphasic Personality Inventory (MMPI) (Hathaway and McKinley, 1951), The California Psychological Inventory (CPI) (Gough, 1957), The Edwards Personal Preference Schedule (EPPS) (Edwards, 1954), The Maudsley Psychological Inventory (MPI) (Eysenck, 1959), and The Cattell 16PF IPAT (16PF) (Cattell and Eber, 1957).

INSTRUMENTS USED

The Minnesota Multiphasic Personality Inventory

Booth (1958) used the MMPI scales to investigate the differences between college athletes and non-athletes. He found varsity athletes significantly lower in anxiety than freshman athletes, non-athlete freshmen, and upper-class non-athletes. The trait called dominance distinguished the varsity athletes and upper-class non-athletes from freshmen athletes and non-athletes. Athletes who were categorized as "individual" athletes scored significantly higher in depression than those who were team members. He found twenty-two items that discriminated between relatively good competitors and poor competitors. These findings substantiate to some degree the study by LaPlace (1954), in which he found major-league baseball players significantly more self-disciplined, having higher initiative and being better able to get along with others than minor-league players. Slusher (1964) investigated the differences between high school athletes and non-athletes and found significant differences for the variables femininity, intelligence, and hypochondriasis. Athletes were significantly lower for femininity and intelligence, but higher for hypochondriasis, which suggests a much greater concern for bodily health. Sports-specific personality patterns began to receive some empirical support. Basketball players as a group showed the greatest overconcern with physical symptoms and tended to be higher in depression. Football players had the greatest tendency to exhibit psychopathic deviations under stress. Swimmers possessed the greatest emotional stability. Baseball players scored highest on hypomania which suggests that they turn their tension and anxiety into some form of behavioral expression. Wrestlers were most like football players, having scored significantly higher for abnormal fears and worries.

Freshmen and varsity football and track athletes were compared using three institutions: Air Force Cadets, a university sample, and a state college sample. No differences were significant within or between these six samples. Each team compared with a San Jose State control sample selected at random from a sample of 2000. All team profiles for the MMPI were almost identical to that of the controls, which in turn was identical to that established by the new Wisconsin study norms. These studies, completed in 1964, are highly consistent with the data for thousands of athletes representing all major sports and support the conclusion that athletes attending a four-year college or university cannot be differentiated by the variables contained in the MMPI. The dimensions related to emotional stability covered a range from average in a small number of teams to high average for the majority, with a number averaging in the superior range. This instrument has proved of special value in designing behavior modification programs for problem athletes (Ogilvie and Tutko, 1966). Significant deviations on certain scales have provided reliable data for determining the most ideal approach to coaching.

There are limited data for female athletes. Black (1961) studied differences between women judged "most athletic" and selected groups of other college women. In terms of MMPI, they were significantly higher on masculinity, were more confident, had higher energy, and were freer from fears about health and less self-conscious.

California Personality Inventory

The investigations using the California Personality Inventory are relevant here because a number of the dimensions are similar to those in the MMPI. Recent investigations by Schendel (1965) using the CPI support the hypothesis that differences exist between athletes and non-athletes. He found that eight scales significantly discriminated at the junior high level, four at the high school level, nine at the college level. The high-school athletes were significantly more poised, ascendant, and self-assured than their peers. College athletes were significantly lower than their peers for achievement, potential, and intellectual ability.

The Edwards Personal Preference Schedule

The EPPS was found to discriminate significantly between nationally licensed sports car racing drivers and novice drivers entering driver training school (Johnsgard and Ogilvie, 1967). The licensed drivers were significantly higher in intraception, succorance, and nurturance. The data suggest that the competitive selection process favors drivers who are well integrated, dominant, and independent with extreme achievement needs. This difference has particular meaning when we realize that we are comparing a sample of human beings who measure at the 86th percentile for achievement (on the basis of national college norms) with trainees who average at the 81st percentile. This dimension exceeds slightly the standard they set for another personality dimension—endurance—the trainees reaching the 75th percentile while the licensed drivers attained the 77th percentile. When the licensed drivers were separated into the top achievers and bottom achievers, on the basis of the previous year's performance ratings, three EPPS differences were significant. Success was significant related to the needs of dominance, autonomy, and aggression. These were the same traits that distinguished the drivers from professional basketball players. The basketball players were found to be significantly more intraceptive, nurturant, and succorant. Subsequent data collected for driver trainees offer empirical support for the generalization that men who seek to drive fast cars in competition share a highly predictable personality structure.

Analysis of the comparisons between select university athletes, Air Force Cadet athletes, and State College athletes leads to increased caution in interpreting the general findings (Ogilvie and Tutko, 1967). EPPS profile similarity is highly correlated across various levels of academic qualification, but personality differences of considerable significance have been found. College athletes tend to have significantly higher need for aggression and self-abasement, while Cadets and university teams are higher in need for achievement, intraception, and dominance. College athletes were significantly more succorant, nurturant, and deferential. The college athletes were significantly higher than the controls for achievement, abasement, change, exhibition, but lower in nurturance. Olympic swimmers were distinguished by their extreme need for achievement, autonomy, and aggression. For both team and individual sportsmen, EPPS profiles tend to move toward increased deference, achievement, endurance, and dominance as one moves from amateur to professional levels of participation. Recent data (Ogilvie and Tutko, 1970) collected for samples of high-school coaches offers substantial support for the concept of a "coaching personality." Three regional samples and one national sample composed of university and professional coaches have produced psychological profiles for the EPPS that are remarkably similar. It has been possible to combine these profiles into a single sample for the traits of achievement, endurance, deference, order, abasement, dominance, and aggression. Men in this profession are distinguishable from the national college norms in that the presence in their profiles of the foregoing personality variables is highly predictable. It can also be predicted that they will have low needs for exhibition, affiliation, succorance, nurturance, and change. The "coaching personality" also presents some interesting insights into these needs, because these combined samples represent measurement of the personality five to fifteen years after active participation in athletic competition. It is possible to state reliably that the former athlete who remains associated with competitive athletics will be a hard-driving, ambitious, highly organized individual. He will seek leadership roles, have a great psychological endurance, and tend to be quick to accept blame. These men find it easy to express aggression without excessive guilt. They characteristically have a very low need to express interest in the problems of others, nor do they expect others to show them special concern or interest. They are less inclined than most to study the motivation of others and would be quite slow to change their life style.

Thorpe (1958) reported that women physical educators categorized as undergraduates, graduates, and teachers shared similar personality patterns for the EPPS. When compared with national norms for women they were high in their need for deference, order, dominance, and endurance. These women were low in their need for autonomy, succorance, nurturance, and aggression. Neal (1963) studied United States women athletes competing in the 1959 Pan-Am Games and a control group of non-athlete females. The female competitors were significantly higher than the control group in need for achievement, autonomy, affiliation, and nurturance.

Since at least two national studies are now in process using the EPPS to investigate the personality structure of women physical educators, it seems appropriate to share the limited data we have collected in this area. Female physical educators average at the 79th percentile for achievement, 82nd percentile for autonomy, 67th for dominance, and 79th for aggression. They fall slightly below the national norms for the needs of deference, intraception, succorance, abasement, and nurturance. The Neal study contained the most representative sample of high-level female competitors;

they appear to have psychological profiles that overlap outstanding male competitors only for the traits achievement and autonomy. Male and female physical educators, on the other hand, seem to share many more personality variables in common: High goals, leadership needs, endurance, orderliness, and deference describe both males and females. Both are low in autonomy, succorance, change, and nurturance. The personality need identified as aggression does not show enough consistency to allow a confident prediction. Consistent data for successful women physical educators strongly supports the concept of a "female coaching personality."

The Maudsley Psychological Inventory

The MPI, which measures two important aspects of personality—neuroticism and extraversion—has received limited application in the study of sport personalities. Eysenck (1959) defined neuroticism as a general emotional extraversion and a tendency to general emotional breakdown under high or prolonged stress. Extraversion is defined as the tendency to be outgoing and uninhibited in social behavior, as contrasted with being reserved and cool and tending to avoid others. Rasch and Mozee (1963) used the MPI to investigate competitive weight lifters and body-builders and failed to find significant differences from a control group of non-athletic college students. Rasch reported that college wrestlers could not be distinguished from controls in these two personality dimensions. Knapp (1965) found that the high-ability British lawn tennis players were high on extraversion and low on neuroticism, but not significantly different from British non-athletes. One of the most thought-provoking studies using the MPI and the Junior MPI was directed by Whiting, at Leeds, England (Whiting and Stembridge, 1965). In studying people who showed a persistent inability to learn to swim both at the pubescent and at the college level he found the non-swimmers significantly more neurotic and introverted than the swimmers. The implications of this study are of great significance in terms of child training or rearing practices. The potential lasting effect of early athletic failure due to insensitive coaching or teaching demands that we design studies to replicate these findings. It becomes increasingly more important that we develop and increase the reliability with which we can identify the individual differences of those we seek to teach. The potential destructiveness of early failure experiences in the life of the child who tends toward introversion justifies a much greater research emphasis.

The Cattell 16PF Personality Inventory

The Cattell 16PF Personality Inventory has been used more broadly in the investigation of physical educators, coaches, and athletes (both male and female), hence this instrument will receive special emphasis here. Cross-cultural comparison plus data on age-group competitors greatly increases the reliability of the statements that can be made about the personalities of athletes.

Cofer and Johnson (1960) found in their extensive review of the literature that slightly less than 20 studies have made a contribution to our understanding of the personality structure of high-level competitors. In an effort to structure a psychological model of the inner qualities that complement standard setting performances, they searched for studies that were similar enough to permit general statements. Cofer and Johnson concluded that there was adequate evidence to support the generalization that "the exceptional athlete could be described as a special breed." Kane (1960, 1966b) in his summary of the literature for English-speaking subjects tested with the Cattell 16PF Personality Inventory, concluded "that there was little doubt that at least a footballer type exists." Recent investigations offer statistical evidence that although outstanding athletes in general share many personality traits in common, nevertheless both sport-specific patterns and team versus individual differences are to be predicted. The most reliable statements about personality and sport-specificity are derived from the investigations of racing car drivers. We have 16PF data based on representative samples of drivers spanning a range from entering novice trainees through the most successful licensed drivers in the world. As stated by Johnsgard, "preliminary analysis of the personalities of sports racing drivers indicated that some common personality traits are characteristic of men throughout the broad spectrum of driving performance." The correlation of the psychological profiles for four separate samples of trainees and licensed drivers based upon the 16PF offers one of the strongest proofs of the existence of a "sports car racing driver personality." Heusner (1952) pioneered the use of the 16PF when he compared British and American Olympic athletes against the national norms. He found that these 41 champions were significantly more emotionally stable, dominant, venturesome, and bold, uninhibited, placid, self-confident, and self-assured.

The 16PF has reliably discriminated between successful and losing football teams. Kroll and Peterson (1965a) compared five winning and five losing teams and were able to find significant differences favoring the winning teams. Winning teams were described as more venturesome and bold, more self-assured, more self-confident and placid, more self-controlled and having more abstract mental ability. Nelson and Langer (1963) and Langer (1966a) investigated the relationship underlying athletic performance and some psychological variables using both the 16PF and reliable inventories that measure anxiety. The first investigation established that the major psychological variable related to successful performance was basic anxiety. Resting level of anxiety, pre-game anxiety and the coach's game-by-game rating of individual performance were found to be significantly related to success. Football players who were rated high on performance had lower resting levels of anxiety with a rise in pre-game anxiety that was never beyond control. Players rated poorer in performance had significantly higher resting levels of anxiety or allowed pre-game anxiety to get out of control. Basic anxiety as measured by the 16PF was significantly related to season rating of success. Factor analysis of team profiles enables the authors to describe the successsful football player as having higher ego strength, being more venturesome and bold, being more self-disciplined, being below average in fluctuations of anxiety, and having better control from game to game. They concluded that their data support the general statement that the successful athlete has internal mechanisms for preparing for competition.

Kane (1964) investigated the personality structure of 100 young professional football players by factor-analyzing their 16PF profiles. Two major psychological factors were found to be significant in terms of contributing to the personality structure of these professionals, who were rated as the most talented in England. Factor I strongly supported a high capacity for emotional control, high capacity to retain integration and high personal persistence. Factor II, Kane felt, was support for the relationship between athletic excellence and extraversion. These young men could best be described as enthusiastic, happy-go-lucky, surgent personalities. Factor III described them as tough-minded, no-nonsense persons who were especially free to express realistic aggression. This factor also included self-sufficiency and a tendency to be reserved and cool. Factor IV was labeled radicalism with high loading for free-thinking and experimental outlook, He found that these talented men took a very direct, practical approach to life. Factor V was general abstract ability, which was related to learning or comprehending. Factor VI was labeled ruthlessness with high loadings on shrewdness. Kane felt that the psychological meaning of this factor was that these athletes possessed persistent, energetic efficiency.

When cadets selected for admission to one of our national academies on the basis of high or moderate athletic ability were compared with those appointed more on the basis of academic ability, significant differences in several traits were found in favor of those appointed for academic ability. More important for this review is the finding that 16PF profiles were extremely consistent for the important traits high abstract ability, emotional stability, high ego strength, tough-mindedness, placidity, self-assuredness, high self-control and low level of resting tension. These 149 cadets shared a personality structure that was similar to Kane's football professionals of comparable age. When service cadets are compared with highly select university athletes who must meet similar academic standards, their psychological profiles appeared to be highly consistent (Ogilvie, 1968b). The cadets were significantly more emotionally stable, more self-assured, more self-disciplined, and less anxious. University track athletes were almost identical to cadets, differing significantly only for the traits happy-go-lucky tendency, toughmindedness, and radicalism. The university athletes tended to be freer thinkers. The cadet sample provided an opportunity to present evidence with respect to personality structure of subjects who were much more representative of a national sample.

Kane (1962) has expressed a particular interest in the relationship of higher athletic ability and extraversive tendencies. He reported that care must be taken in generalizing about this trait because there was a tendency for team versus individual sport differences to appear. The relationship of these differences to introversion has been shown to change with sport, age of competitors, and level of competition. Kane tested samples of 13- to 16-year-old males using the Cattell HSPQ, which measures 14 of the 16 traits contained in the adult 16PF. Motor ability and emotional stability were found to be significantly related, as was extraversion. Hardman (1962) reported consistently high relationships between motor skills and such personality dimensions as enthusiastic, happy-go-lucky, extraverted tendencies. Physical ability as measured by motor skills was also found to be significantly related to tough-mindedness, dominance, and grown-up-mindedness. Hardman concluded "that competitive skills are in some way an extension of a surgent, tough-minded, self-reliant personality." His sociometric ratings also correlated with dominance, self-assertion, aggression, surgency, and group-mindedness. Popularity, extraversion, excitability, and generalized anxiety were all found to be significantly related, a finding well documented by past sociometric research (Cowell, 1960; Kane, 1965). There is high predictability that athletic skills and high motor ability are significantly related to peer acceptance at the onset of adolescence.

The evidence from the studies of the highly select group of swimmers at the nationally famous Santa Clara Swim Club confirms the need for caution in discussing the relationship between high motor ability and extraversion. The criterion for acceptance as a member, as determined by Coach George Haines, seems to this investigator to be the most stringent that has been observed anywhere in the Western World. When the entire team is separated by sex and age grouping, the cross-sectional analysis suggests that when common personality traits are examined, the relationship between personality and competition becomes hazy. When we control for sex differences and level of competition, we find that boys and girls become much more alike (sex differences diminished) between the ages of 10 and 14 years of age (Ogilvie, 1967). The 10-year-old boys were on the cool, reserved, introverted end of the scale, while those swimmers who remained in an extremely competitive training program until the age of 14 measured more warm-hearted, outgoing, and extraverted. There was a shift toward greater emotional stability and higher conscience development from ages 10 to 14 years. (This has some theoretical interest in view of the study of the United States 1964 Olympic swimming team. Emotional stability tended to distinguish the medalist from the non-medalist Olympic competitors.) The populations of boys showed an extreme increase for the personality dimensions self-assertion, independence, and aggression. The most significant shift with age occurred for the personality dimension sober-serious versus happy-go-lucky surgency. Since surgency–soberness correlates most significantly with the dimension extraversion–introversion, one is forced to respect the possible contribution of this trait to continued competition. These young men moved toward increased emotional stability with increased age. This finding has considerable significance in light of the most recent finding for the relationship between anxiety control and emotional stability. The highest correlation found within an entire university basketball league for any of the personality traits included in the 16PF was between anxiety and emotional stability. Criticism can, of course, be leveled at the cross-sectional comparison method of analysis because attenuation factors cannot be separated from personality changes as a reflection of trait conditioning during competition training.

These data support the generalization that increased control of anxiety, self-control, self-assertiveness, toughmindedness, and extraversion all increase with age. These highly select young male competitors appear to possess the personality traits that have been demonstrated to be most descriptive of world class athletic competitors. The data for the young females, mean ages 10 and 14 years, lend considerable support for the foregoing conclusion. They move toward a more outgoing warmhearted selection of women with increased age, but do not reach the level of young males for this trait. Relative to national norms there was a tendency for the girls to be more intelligent and more emotionally stable, to have higher conscience development, and to become more tough-minded, more individualistic, more self-disciplined, and slightly less anxious and tense.

In the absence of longitudinal data, profile comparisons have been made with those of Rushall (1967), who published the only study reporting findings for Indiana age-group swimmers. It is not possible to estimate the level of selectivity of these youthful competitors in relation to the Santa Clara Swim Club, but the fact that they represent an area so close to the nationally known James Counsilman does suggest that they would be a highly select group. The Indiana girls ($N = 43$) tended to be more outgoing, more individualistic, and more self-sufficient. The SCSC girls ($N = 53$) tended to be more intelligent, more emotionally stable, less excitable, more self-assertive, more venturesome–bold, more individualistic, slightly more self-assured, and slightly more tough-minded. These two groups of swimmers were very similar for the personality traits phlegmatic versus excitable, happy-go-lucky versus sober, venturesome versus shy, group dependent versus self-sufficient, and undisciplined versus self-controlled. Reviewing the same dimensions for boys, the differences in profiles indicated that SCSC (N = 47) were more emotionally stable, more venturesome, more controlled-self-disciplined, more relaxed, and less tense. Indiana boys ($N = 27$) were more excitable, more toughminded, and more happy-go-lucky. Slight differences favored SCSC boys for the traits intelligence, self-sufficiency, and outgoing–warm-hearted. Although we lack adequate control data based on samples of youngsters who are not as highly select as these swimmers, these comparisons do evidently support the notion that those who remain in highly competitive programs share many personality traits in common. There will be differences in the degree to which these traits are found within groups who are matched for age, but no critical statement can be made until some effort is made to control for the degree of selectivity of youthful competitors. Aside from all the possible qualifications, these data suggest a movement toward extraversion with age for males and a lesser movement for females.

Cross-cultural data as reported by Kane for British female subjects decrease the probability of the general statements that can be made about the female who attains a high level of athletic achievement. In his published studies of two small samples of British Olympic sportswomen, including swimmers and athletes, he reported a similarity coefficient of 10.85. These women were remarkably similar in personality structure. They were outgoing–warmhearted, happy-go-lucky, and high in the trait of extraversion. They were low on emotional stability and conscience development, and high in anxiety with higher than average resting levels of anxiety. Kane compared these Olympic females with a sample of British women physical educators, many of whom had been outstanding sportswomen. The two samples were found to be quite similar. The PE women were happy-go-lucky, were low on self-assertion, were low in emotional stability, tended to be apprehensive-worried, tended toward high resting levels of anxiety, and were significantly extraverted.

There seems to be considerable support from 16PF data for the assertion that cross-cultural differences exist for certain personality traits and that they are particularly evident for female comparisons. Cultural differences do prevail for males but seem to be much more a manifestation of sport-specific differences such as comparisons of track with basketball or other team sports (Ogilvie and Tutko, 1967). A profile comparison of Rushall's highly successful university swimming team and the highly successful San Jose State women's swimming team supports the conclusion that United States competitors share many more personality traits in common independent of sex. These two teams with exceptional records were quite similar in terms of mean profiles. The Indiana males were slightly brighter and slightly more outgoing. The college women were much more venturesome-bold, more experimental, lower in resting level of anxiety, and less tense. Both samples would be described as outgoing, bright, emotionally stable, self-assertive, happy-go-lucky, high in conscience development, and tending toward tough-mindedness and self-sufficiency. They were also similar in that they were slightly distrustful of others, tended to be wrapped up in inner urgencies, and tended to follow their own urges. These two samples, which are matched for age, level of competition, and educational level, offer support for trait similarity. The cultural differences between United States and British females received further support when British women in team sports were compared with American female competitors (Kane and Warburton, 1966). In general, British Olympic swimmers and team athletes were more outgoing–warmhearted and tended to be more extraverted. United States females tended to be more reserved–cool; slightly more self-assertive, venturesome, tough-minded, and self-sufficient; and much less anxious and tense. These women share many common traits of personality, but the differences in emotional stability, conscience development, and resting level of anxiety would probably prove significant for a sample of this size.

The reliability of our statements about the personality structure of successful athletes has been greatly reduced by our failure to control for such factors as culture, educational level, age, and sex. Of particular significance to this review has been the failure to control for team versus individual sport. There is a growing body of evidence that sport-specificity with regard to certain traits of personality can be predicted. Peterson, Ukler, and Trousdale (1967) compared the personality structure of women's team versus women's individual sports. They tested 156 AAU and U.S. Olympic women using the 16PF. The sample of 38 individual sports women represented swimming, diving, riding, fencing, canoeing, gymnastics, and track. The 59 team women represented the 1964 Olympic volleyball team and 10 AAU basketball women. Women individual competitors were found to be significantly more dominant, aggressive, venturesome, self-suficient, and experimental. Team sport-women were significantly more tough-minded and shrewd-worldly wise. When SJS women swimmers were compared with these two high-level competitors, they were found to lie between the team and individual sportswomen or to achieve a profile that was identical to individual sportswomen. They differed most from the team sportswomen on the traits self-assertion, venturesomeness, inner-urgencies, forthrightness, experimentation, self-sufficiency, and resting tension. Had these women been combined into a single sample without regard to team versus individual sport distinctions, the most reliable description would be as follows: These 97 women are cool-reserved, bright, emotionally stable, self-opinionated, venturesome, and tough-minded. They appear to be similar to the general population for the traits sober versus happy-go-lucky, confidence development, placid versus apprehensive, and casual versus controlled. It does seem that United States sportswomen share many more traits in common with those found for both British and U.S. sportsmen. These women tend to be no-nonsense types of persons who are emotionally stable, assertive, and socially bold, and who possess reasonable self-control. They are independent and possess the qualities that incline them toward leadership roles. As reported previously, the similarity of psychological profile greatly increased for sportswomen, even for the British, when they were separated on the basis of international achievement (Ogilvie, 1965). Even though these were very limited samples, the fact that the personality profiles were almost identical with that for the U.S. women does offer further support for the relationship between certain traits and athletic achievement.

When the most restrictive standards are applied in order to establish the highest order of criteria for athletic success, the significance of specific personality traits does receive considerable empirical support. A number of investigations can be used to substantiate the relevance of these traits in terms of how they may actually contribute to the attainment level of athletic success. When nationally licensed sports-car racing drivers were compared with novice drivers participating in the Sports Car Club of America Race Drivers School, significant differences emerged. The licensed drivers were higher in abstract ability, more emotionally stable, had more highly developed consciences, were more venturesome-bold, were more self-assured, were more tough-minded, had lower resting levels of anxiety, were more resistant to emotional stress, were more creative, and had higher leadership potential. These differences are all the more remarkable because the novice driver trainees had an almost identical profile but differed only in terms of degree on each of the traits. Based upon the second-order traits derived from the 10 primary traits, the licensed drivers were significantly lower in neuroticism and anxiety, and higher for tough poise (Johnsgard and Ogilvie, 1967).

The 1964 Olympic male swimmers were divided into gold medalists and non-gold medalists in order to establish the highest possible criteria for excellence in swimming. Important trends appeared, none of which achieved statistical significance. The medalists tended to separate themselves for the traits emotional stability, self-sufficiency, self-assurance, self-control, self-discipline, and liberality of thinking. In terms of second-order factors they tended to be lower in anxiety, lower in neuroticism, more independent, and slightly better able to handle emotional stress. When Kane separated his world-class tennis women from tournament-level women, he found them to be more emotionally stable and to have higher ego strength, higher self-confidence, and lower resting levels of anxiety. Returning to the data for age group swimmers, the observed changes of personality structure from age 10 to age 14 seems to offer some empirical support for the predictions that could be made about personality and athletic success. The changes observed cannot be attributed to character formation, as conditioned by competition, but must be accepted as the interaction of a number of variables that can only be identified at the termination of the longitudinal study. The shifts that are consistent both for boys and girls are that both became more outgoing-warmhearted and more emotionally stable, had increased conscience development, and increased tough-mindedness, became more forthright, had increased self-control, and moved from high resting tension to low levels of tension.

Two further investigations worthy of review deal with the personalities of national and regional coaches. The most significant traits found in the profiles of men coaching at the highest national competitive level were emotional stability, conscience development, trusting nature, tough-mindedness, self-control, and low resting levels of tension (Ogilvie, 1965). These findings were highly consistent for 132 high school coaches representing every major sport (Ogilvie and Tutko, 1970). With a single exception the entire national sample of coaches had been active members of one or more professional teams. Every member of the high school coaching samples had participated on college or university major athletic teams. It may be assumed therefore, that we have been collecting data on individuals who have been active participants at various levels of competition some 5 to 15 years after the termination of their active athletic lives.

REVIEW OF MOST SIGNIFICANT PERSONALITY TRAITS

An examination of the limited data made available when a common measure of personality such as the IPAT 16PF is used does permit a more rational speculation about the relationship between the athletic achievement and personality. Admittedly, we do not have sufficient empirical data to support the generally held philosophy that competitive sports, in some way, make a positive contribution to character formation. There is considerable evidence from the data now being analyzed, based on large samples of members of the coaching fraternity, that athletic competition may limit personal growth in other areas. The probability is very high that we have only succeeded in collecting data for those individuals whose character formation was such that they could endure the stress and strain necessary for high-level achievement in athletics.

The traits reviewed and found significant in the various studies do not assume a clear hierarchical order. It seems reasonable, therefore, that parental and educational emphasis be placed on the following traits if our concern is with the development of physical excellence—emotional stability, tough-mindedness, conscientiousness, controlled self-discipline, self-assurance, ability to relax–low tension level, trust–freedom from jealousy, and—for males—increased extraversion.

In terms of logical expectations, the studies reviewed consistently support the significant contribution of emotional stability to athletic success as well as coaching success. It would be unusual had this not been the case, since these factors have consistently been found to be positively related for every other area of investigation in which human achievement has been the focus. The exception was in relation to cross-cultural differences for women competitors. The generalization holds true only when we apply rigid standards of excellence, a rating such as international-class athlete. Emotional stability may be characterized as facing reality calmly, avoidance of emotional upset, learning to control feelings, avoiding feelings that might interefere with problem-solving, and refusing to retreat to childish, less mature solutions for conflicts. There are few areas of human commitment that have the potentiality for reinforcing life's realities found in high-level competitive athletics. The very nature of sport demands that one place his ability before the public eye, which results in an awareness of one's failings in a way that is inescapable. Unconscious denial of failure or unconscious fear of placing one's talent on the line can rarely be used as defense against reality. The "moment of truth" is axiomatic in the life of the great competitor. Therefore, it was to be expected that those who remain and excel would have a higher than average potential for coming to grips with reality. To be a winner it is essential that failure to achieve or failure to realize the coach's goals be accepted as a personal responsibility, which, of course, demands emotional strength. Successful athletes are achievement-oriented people who derive personal satisfaction for their striving. High achievement needs are based upon personal attitudes about the probability of success or failure associated with each investment of self. Such people are at their best when the odds are slightly against them. Ambitious people take little joy in having their ability go uncontested. The great athletes I have interviewed don't dwell on their losses, but concentrate on the part of their performance that limited their excellence.

The trait tough–tender-minded, as defined by Cattell (1965), contains a number of tendencies that become polarized within the personality structure of the individual. At the tender end of the continuum would be the person who is demanding, impatient, dependent, gentle, sentimental, imaginative, and easily anxious, and who likes to be with people. At the tough-minded end of the continuum would be the person who is emotionally mature and independent-minded and has a hard realistic outlook. This person overrides his feelings, is not fanciful, does not show anxiety, and is self-sufficient. Cattell reports that this trait is culturally determined; therefore it seems essential that we examine the behavioral expectancies with the tendencies of an individual to fall at one or the other of the extremes of this trait. Cattell described the tender-minded person as being basically involved in "imaginative escapism or even an undisciplined mind," while the tough-minded person makes a cold, realistic appraisal of the facts and does not allow himself to become involved in sentimental overreaction. On the positive side, tender-mindedness is related to creativity, but it has also been shown to be strongly associated with neuroticism. We have collected data on over 10,000 athletes ranging from high school through the most select professional athletes such as those found in sports-car racing. The licensed race driver sets the standard for tough-mindedness, followed very closely by three separate samples of driver trainees tested in 1966, 1967, and 1968. One might expect that the individual who is accelerating from zero to 180 miles per hour in a pack of cars, with each driver trying to enter a turn only wide enough to accomodate a single car, must have a high degree of hard-headed realism. This trait is also one of the most pronounced in the personality of professional coaches. The need to endure the stress associated with press, fan, and owner reactions to their administration, while retaining the capacity to make hard-headed decisions essential for achieving their goals, would seem to make this trait a prerequisite for tenure.

The consistency with which one can predict the increased probability of tough-mindedness as being significantly related to athletic ability and athletic achievement received support from even the more limited data available for sportswomen. The relationship between this trait and athletic achievement received support from factor-analytic studies of national-level competitors and was also related to team success. Some reservations might arise as to the virtue of offering social rewards for the reinforcement of the behaviors that would eventually contribute to tough-mindedness. The balance provided by the presence of other positive traits seems at this level of investigation to be an important control over the exaggeration of any single personality trait.

The trait conscientiousness is of particular significance as a control or suppressor of tough-mindedness. Conscientiousness is also relevant in terms of the other seven traits that have been selected for emphasis. Cattell (1965) described the person at the negative end of the pole as being a quitter, fickle, frivolous, immature, relaxed, indolent, neglectful of social chores, and changeable. The positive end of the pole would be the person who is conscientious, persevering, staid, and rule-bound, Cattell uses this trait as being synonymous with superego formation. To quote him, "it has much to do with persistence in super-personal goals and ideals, and with attempts to exercise powerful self-control." This trait is low in sociopaths but high in face-to-face leaders. The polls show that fair-mindedness in a leader is one of the primary demands of followers. Neither the investigations reviewed nor the strong support within our numerous studies would permit a general statement relating to cause and effect. Conscientiousness has received more social comment than any other athletic trait in that every appeal to youth, every address at an awards banquet, and every philosophy of physical education holds this trait out as a primary goal. Longitudinal studies are now in progress, but it will be five or six years before reliable statements can be made about the relationship between athletic participation and conscience development. The only evidence was the magnitude of the change in this trait for swimmers 10 to 14 years of age. Should this finding receive confirmation, it would indicate that conscience development is the primary character trait in determining the probability of a youngster remaining in competitive swimming. It is not possible from cross-sectional analysis to attribute significance to the possibility that children with shallow superego structures gradually eliminate themselves from the stress of competition, or to the possibility that some positive reinforcement of character formation does occur. At present, we must consider that an interaction of both these factors has accounted for the observed improved sense of responsibility on the part of the children. The relative contribution of other traits of personality, such as persistence and emotional stability, to this dimension must contribute in some way to the attenuation of this sample of swimmers (attrition that occurred from age 10 to age 14). We cannot state unequivocally that high-level athletic competition contributes to a refined conscience, but the evidence strongly supports the tendency for those with sensitive consciences to remain in highly competitive programs.

The trait self-control contains a number of interrelated personality variables; the person at the negative end of the continuum would be characterized as one who is casual, is careless of protocol, is untidy, follows his own urges, disregards orderliness, and has difficulty following through with a routine. At the positive and of the continuum is the person who is controlled, socially precise, self-disciplined, and in the extreme perhaps even compulsive. This person shows the socially approved behavior and foresight characteristic of chosen leaders. Cattell used the synonym "will power" as the most general descriptive label for this trait. This old-fashioned term seems, to this investigator, to retain the meaning in terms of behavioral expectancies. That we found so much empirical support by the use of psychometric devices seems to emphasize once again the necessary personal integrational forces that are essential in order that one may remain with the highest level of athletic competition. This was such a distinctive feature that it became predictive of both individual and team success. Hundreds of hours of interviews with some of the world's most outstanding athletes, both amateur and professional, resulted in one consistently repeated spontaneous statement with reference to pride and achievement. In terms of psychological measurement, self-control is one of the most significant contributors to the complex statement "he has pride," which is used so universally by great athletes to characterize other greats.

The trait relaxed versus tense has been shown to be significantly related to athletic achievement. The athlete at the positive end of the continuum is described as relaxed, tranquil, torpid, and unfrustrated. At the negative end of the scale, the athlete would be tense, driven, overwrought, and fretful. There is a growing body of evidence that self-control and low levels of tension interact positively to contribute to successful athlete performance. The relationship between low anxiety and team and individual success is consistent both for sportsmen and for sportswomen. The licensed sports car racing drivers set the standard for absence of tension, followed by the samples of driver trainees. The measurement of this trait for youthful competitors indicated that only the 14-year-old SCSC girls failed to improve over the 10-year-olds. The Indiana 14-year-old boys and girls appeared to be low average for the tense–relaxed dimension. The behavioral expectancies associated with the tense individual are a negative view of group unity, existing leadership, and orderliness. They tend to admit more common frailties, disagree more, are more susceptible to annoyance, have less confident assumptions of skill in untried performances, and tend more toward hard-headed cynicism.

During a number of years as a consultant I have found that this trait has provided the most reliable indication that the psychological threshold for stress has been exceeded (Ogilvie, 1964). The physical signs associated with this form of emotional tension and anxiety covered the broad spectrum encountered in clinical work with psychosomatic disorders of every description. The body of the competitor often spoke the language of fear with greater eloquence than could be verbalized by the individual. Performance and coordination, even of the motorically gifted, suffers dramatically when physiologic and psychologic boundaries intersect. Present research supports a growing concern with teaching techniques of tension reduction that will enable each performer to master exaggerated forms of pre-event anxiety.

If verified by future investigations, these initial findings have serious implications for teachers and coaches. Factor-analytic studies offer strong support that anxiety is a unitary trait that has a distinctive hereditary base. Particular emphasis must be placed on the significance of success and failure for those youthful competitors who rate high in resting levels of anxiety. There is empirical support for the hypothesis that a curvilinear relationship is obtained for anxiety rising from age $8\frac{1}{2}$ to $15\frac{1}{2}$ and then dropping steadily to age 35, followed by a slow rise to age 65 (Cattell, 1965). An important goal would be providing the best emotional climate for the child as a learner, but greater emphasis must be placed on individual differences with respect to this personality trait. The highly anxious must receive greater reinforcement during early phases of training for competition. It is my experience that the coach can be taught to condition his athletes in the most wholesome techniques for containing anxiety.

The trait self-assured versus apprehensive, worried, received much empirical support at every level of competition for both males and females.

The limited data for age-group swimmers offered more support for SCSC boys and girls, although Indiana boys and girls appeared at least average for this trait. The positive end of the continuum described the athlete as confident, adequate, cheerful, and serene. At the negative end would be the depressed, excessively guilt-prone, easily upset, and even phobic athlete. The behavioral expectancies for the individual measuring high in apprehension appear clinically as some form of depression. This form of self-punishment can assume the character of a "free-floating anxiety reaction." These individuals respond to unbearable stress by expressing serious doubts about their ability and utilizing some self-punishing form of defense in order to displace the real tension. The very nature of competition acts as such a reality reinforcer that the rationalization of failure becomes increasingly more difficult. The highly consistent relationship between self-assurance and attained level of athletic competition seems almost too obvious. The challenge in how to use athletics as a creative positive force in the lives of youth is great. Unfortunately, serious investigation of the means of producing such ends has received little attention.

The trait trusting versus suspicious may seem to be one of the most unexpected findings contained in this review. Past research using other psychometric devices has contributed to a personality dimension that we have labeled "coachability" (Ogilvie and Tutko, 1966). This is the tendency to be open to teachers and authorities and to have a basic respect for the instruction of others. Cattell (1965) defines the positive end of this trait as a tendency to be trusting, adaptable, free of jealousy, and easily able to get along with others. The negative extreme would be the person who is suspicious, self-opinionated, and hard to fool. The behavioral expectancies at the negative end would be slowness in making friends, a tendency to feel superior to others as a defense, and an extreme tendency to brood and to be irritable. The finding that successful coaches move athletes toward the trusting end of the scale is consistent with the coaches' proclivity for making quick adjustments. This also supports emotional stability with respect to their increased capacity for accepting personal responsibility for their achievement. The tendency to project negative feelings or attitudes onto others would certainly reduce one's capacity to learn. The athlete with a paranoid attitude toward life presents a special challenge to both the coach and the team. During the past 15 years we have experimented with recommended handling programs for athletes who fall at the extreme suspicious end of the scale. The delicate balance that must be established between the athlete and coach has been a particular problem, but individual cases of success have offered us much encouragement that open communication can be achieved.

The final trait, outgoing versus reserved, seems to be much more predictive of highly successful male competitors and British females. The literature does suggest a movement from introversion toward increased extraversion but to the same degree that is found for males. At one end of the scale we have people who are outgoing, warmhearted, good-natured, cooperative, attentive to people, soft-hearted, and adaptable. The other pole would be the person who is critical, grasping, obstructive, cool, aloof, hard, precise, and rigid. Behaviorally one moves toward others and social participation or conversely, away from others with a desire to be alone. In the extreme the cool, reserved person may even resent encroachment upon his space.

With the exception of race drivers and such individual-sport athletes as distance runners, the studies reviewed support a tendency for successful male athletes to be on the warmhearted end of the scale. This was consistent for national-level British women athletes, who measured as extremely outgoing and warmhearted, but was inconsistent with our studies and those in the literature for U.S. sportswomen. There is perfect consistency in measures showing that high-level female competitors who represent the U.S. tend to be cool, reserved, and less sociable. The movement for girls in age-group swimming away from the introversion end of the scale to decreased introversion by the time they are 14 years of age has a number of possible interpretations. In light of the cross-cultural consistencies in data showing that for males extraversion was related to continuation in athletics, two major questions evolve. First, cultural differences are quite apparent for women with the extraversive traits contributing more to continuation for British women than for U.S. women. The data do suggest that extremely introverted U.S. females have a higher attenuation rate than extraverted females. There is evidence that introverted children swimmers have a greater tendency to retain fears associated with past traumas centering around water and swimming experiences. There is much evidence that reward-and-punishment conditioning effects are not independent of one's temperamental predisposition toward introversion or extraversion.

Cattell (1965) reports that the trait sociable versus reserved was the most readily verified trait found in his voluminous research. He attributes to heredity the major contribution to this trait and holds the environment only slightly accountable for variation of it. It may be assumed therefore, that attempts to condition young athletes toward extraversion would be both unwise and unnatural. It would be far more realistic to accept a wide range of individual differences for this trait and adjust our teaching to the form that is most compatible with the personality structure of the young competitor.

SUMMARY

The literature has been reviewed with respect to the relationship between personality structure and athletic achievement. The various approaches have included the comparison of athletes and non-athletes, physical educators with non-physical education teachers, professional athletes with amateurs, and national champions with the norms of people in general. Studies were included in which the same psychological instrument has been used with sufficient frequency that sample comparison could be reasonably attempted. The psychological tests that have been included are the Minnesota Multiphasic Personality Inventory, The California Personality Inventory, The Edwards Personal Preference Schedule, The Maudsley Psychological Inventory, and (with special emphasis) the Cattell 16PF IPAT. The 16PF permitted a review across the various age ranges and offered evidence about female competitors. This instrument also provided our first opportunity for cross-cultural evidence. The presentation of the evidence based on cross-sectional analysis of highly select youthful competitors has been offered in order to improve our speculation about the nature of selection process.

Even making all the possible reservations, we find sufficient evidence to support the hypothesis that general sport personalities do exist. The examples of "footballer personality," both male and female, "coaching personality," and "race-driver personality" have received considerable verification. The concept of team versus individual sportsman also received empirical verification.

The studies reviewed strongly support the tendency for certain personality traits to receive greater reinforcement within the competitive world of athletics. There is insufficient evidence to conclude that high-level competition makes a positive contribution to personality. We can state with some certitude that those who retain their motivation for competition will have most of the following personality traits: ambition, organization, deference, dominance, endurance, and aggression. There will be fewer introverted types in adult-level competition. Emotional maturity will span a range from average to high average and be complemented by self-control, self-confidence, tough-mindedness, trustfulness, intelligence, high conscience development, and low levels of tension. Such traits as autonomy, exhibitionism, and affiliation prove to be less general traits. The traits of succorance, nurturance, and need for change proved to be underdeveloped in the various athletic and coaching samples. The implications of specific trends in the personalities of coaches and certain personality trends such as introversion for the teacher and coach were emphasized.

Does participation in athletics alter personality? Alfred Werner and Edward Gottheil, in article 4.3, tested in a longitudinal study the premise that athletic participation affects personality structure. They used the Cattell Sixteen Personality Factor Questionnaire (16PF), the most popular device for assessing sport personality. Their results raise doubts about the credibility of the sport participation / personality development relationship.

In this study, participation in athletics was required of all the subjects because they were enrolled in a military academy. Since athletic participation was not voluntary, one might speculate that those who entered the academy as non-athletes might not pursue sport with a great deal of intensity. Would changes in personality be expected even if the commitment to athletic participation was at a low level? This might be a possible explanation for Werner's and Gottheil's findings, as well as the more obvious conclusion that sport participation does not significantly alter one's personality.

4.3 Personality development and participation in college athletics

ALFRED C. WERNER
United States Military Academy, West Point, New York
EDWARD GOTTHEIL
United States Military Academy, West Point, New York

On the basis of their past histories of athletic participation, a group of 340 cadets entering the United States Military Academy were designated as athletes, and another group of 116 were designated as athletic nonparticipants. The Cattell Sixteen Personality Factor test was administered shortly after entrance and again shortly prior to graduation.

Entering cadet athletes were significantly different from nonparticipants on seven of the 16PF scales. The proportion of athletes who graduated from the academy was significantly greater than the proportion of nonparticipants who graduated.

If participation in athletics in college has an effect on personality structure, the effect would be expected to be greater on individuals with little previous athletic participation than on accomplished athletes. However, despite four years of regular athletic participation, the designated nonparticipant group was not found to change in personality structure as measured by the 16PF Test: (a) to a greater extent than the athletes; (b) in a different pattern than did the athletes; (c) nor so as to become more like the athletes.

Thus, no evidence was found to support the view that college athletics significantly influence personality structure. Further research is warranted with different tests, different groups, and at lower age levels.

The development of certain personality characteristics has long been considered an important objective of athletic participation. The view that participation in competitive sports contributes to the development of desirable personality characteristics is widespread. Active sports participation by all students has become a goal of school athletic programs.

From *Research Quarterly* 37(1966):126–131. Reprinted by permission of the American Alliance for Health, Physical Education, and Recreation.

At the United States Military Academy, athletics for all became a reality in 1919 when General of the Army Douglas MacArthur was superintendent. Since that time every cadet, throughout his four years at the Academy, has participated in sports and has played on some varsity or intramural team in addition to the regular and extensive courses in physical education and physical training.

PURPOSE OF THE STUDY

New cadets entering the Academy differ in the extent of their prior participation in secondary school athletics. In a survey extending over a 10-year period, it was found that 65 percent of the entering new cadets had received secondary-school sports letter awards (prior athletes), 15 percent had participated in athletics but received no letter award (prior nonathletes), and 20 percent had not participated in sports to the extent of remaining on any athletic squad for at least two months (prior nonparticipants).

Since cadets entering the Academy differ in the extent of their prior participation in sports and since all cadets after entering the Academy participate regularly in an intensive athletic program, the following questions concerning the effect of athletic participation on personality structure may be investigated:

1. Do entering cadet athletes differ from prior nonparticipants in personality structure?
2. During their stay at the Academy, and consequent athletic participation, will the prior nonparticipants change more than the athletes in personality structure?
3. Will the pattern of personality change in the nonparticipants differ from that of the athletes?
4. As a result of these changes, will the personality profiles of the nonparticipants and athletes become more similar?

METHODOLOGY

There were 752 new cadets who entered the class under study. Of these, 454 had previously won sports letter awards and for the purpose of this study were classified as the athlete group. The nonparticipant group was made up of 191 cadets who had not remained on any athletic squad for at least two months prior to entering the Academy. The remaining 107 cadets had participated in athletics but had received no letter award (prior nonathletes). This middle group, in terms of athletic participation, was not included in the analysis so that the more diverse groups could be compared.

Table 1 Cattell's interpretation of the sixteen personality factors

Low score description	Personality factors	High score description
Aloof, cold (Schizothymia)	A	Warm, sociable (Cyclothymia)
Dull, low capacity (Low "g")	B	Bright, intelligent (High "g")
Emotional, unstable (Low ego strength)	C	Mature, calm (High ego strength)
Submissive, mild (Submissiveness)	E	Dominant, aggressive (Dominance)
Glum, silent (Desurgency)	F	Enthusiastic, talkative (Surgency)
Casual, undependable (Low superego strength)	G	Conscientious, persistent (High superego strength)
Timid, shy (Threctia)	H	Adventurous, "thick-skinned" (Parmia)
Tough, realistic (Harria)	I	Sensitive, effeminate (Premsia)
Trustful, adaptable (Inner relaxation)	L	Suspecting, jealous (Protension)
Conventional, practical (Praxernia)	M	Bohemian, unconcerned (Alaxia)
Simple, awkward (Naïveté)	N	Sophisticated, polished (Shrewdness)
Confident, unshakable (Confidence)	O	Insecure, anxious (Timidity)
Conservative, accepting (Conservatism)	Q_1	Experimenting, critical (Radicalism)
Dependent, imitative (Group dependence)	Q_2	Self-sufficient, resourceful (Self-sufficiency)
Lax, unsure (Low integration)	Q_3	Controlled, exact (Self sentiment control)
Phlegmatic, composed (Low ergic tension)	Q_4	Tense, excitable (High ergic tension)

The Sixteen Personality Factor test (Cattell, Saunders, and Stice, 1950) developed by Cattell was administered to this class of cadets shortly after entering the Academy and again shortly prior to graduation. The 16 scales are described in Table 1.

Table 2 Comparison of the mean personality factor scores of athletes and nonparticipants

16P-F scales	Athletes N = 340 Entrance	Graduation	Mean difference	Nonparticipants N = 116 Entrance	Graduation	Mean difference
A	17.1	18.2	(+) 1.1	14.5	16.9	(+) 2.4
B	19.7	19.8	(+) 0.1	19.8	20.1	(+) 0.3
C	38.3	36.2	(−) 2.1	38.8	37.1	(−) 1.7
E	26.5	30.0	(+) 3.5	25.4	28.7	(+) 3.3
F	29.5	32.1	(+) 2.6	27.7	29.8	(+) 2.1
G	27.9	25.9	(−) 2.0	27.9	26.1	(−) 1.8
H	37.5	36.9	(−) 0.6	35.2	35.8	(+) 0.6
I	13.1	14.6	(+) 1.5	13.4	14.6	(+) 1.2
L	16.1	18.3	(+) 2.2	15.2	17.7	(+) 2.5
M	15.3	18.8	(+) 3.5	14.5	17.7	(+) 3.2
N	24.5	25.7	(+) 1.2	23.9	25.6	(+) 1.7
O	9.0	13.0	(+) 4.0	7.9	12.6	(+) 4.7
Q_1	18.1	20.1	(+) 2.0	19.7	21.6	(+) 1.9
Q_2	17.1	20.8	(+) 3.7	19.4	22.8	(+) 3.4
Q_3	27.4	23.8	(−) 3.6	28.7	25.1	(−) 3.6
Q_4	11.5	16.1	(+) 4.6	9.6	14.7	(+) 5.1

The mean scores on the Sixteen Personality Factor test, at entrance and at graduation, for the 340 athletes and the 116 nonparticipants who remained to graduate from the Academy, are presented in Table 2. Only the graduating subjects were selected for study so that comparison could be made between the same groups of individuals at entrance and at graduation. The proportion of graduates was significantly greater among the athletes than among the nonparticipants. . . .

A PREVIOUS STUDY

Werner (1960) investigated the first question. He compared the 16PF Test personality profiles of the entering new cadet athletes and the nonparticipants and found the secondary-school letter award winners to be significantly more sociable, dominant, enthusiastic, adventurous, tough, group dependent, sophisticated, and conservative than the cadets with little or no prior participation in sports. The two groups were thus found to be diverse in terms of these personality scores when they entered the Academy. However, these differences could be explained either by the fact that athletic participation influences personality structure or that individuals with certain personality structures elect to participate in athletics.

THE PRESENT STUDY

In order to evaluate whether the prior nonparticipant group changed in personality structure, as measured by the 16PF Test, more than did the athlete group, the difference between the mean score at entrance and the mean score at graduation on each of the 16 factors was calculated for the athlete group ($N = 340$) and for the nonparticipant group ($N = 116$). The absolute sum of these differences was 38.3 for the athletes and 39.5 for the nonparticipants (Table 2). This was found to be not statistically significant ($t = .38$). While no significant difference was demonstrated between the groups in the total amount of change, there might still be important differences in the pattern of change from entrance to graduation. Thus, for example, on a factor such as sociability, both groups could demonstrate a change in mean score of two points, but in one group this would mean greater sociability and in the other group less sociability. Therefore, the athlete and nonparticipant groups were compared with regard to the direction of change in mean score from entrance to graduate on each of the factors. The direction of change was similar on 15 of the 16 factors (Table 2). When the athletes scored higher on a given scale at graduation than they had at entrance, so did the nonparticipants, and if the athletes scored lower, the nonparticipants did likewise. There was one exception and this could be expected on the basis of chance alone. Thus, the pattern of change in the two groups was not found to be dissimilar.

The next question was whether cadets who had participated very little in athletics prior to entering the Academy would change as a consequence of athletic participation so as to become more like athletes in personality structure. If this occurred the personality factor profiles of the athletes and nonparticipants would be more similar at graduation than at entrance.

The athletes were found to be significantly different from the nonparticipants on seven of the personality factors at entrance (A, F, H, Q_1, Q_2, Q_3, Q_4). With seven of 16 variables showing a significant difference between the groups, a significant change (c .05) toward more similarity on retest would require that the groups remain significantly different on no more than two variables (based on the test of significant differences between proportions). At graduation, however, significant differences were again found in the same direction on five of the variables (A, F, Q_1, Q_2, Q_3). In addition, one significant difference was found on factor E that had not been demonstrated at entrance. The mean scores of the athletes and of the nonparticipants on the 16 factors, at entrance, were correlated so as to evaluate the similarity in the shape of the personality profiles. The product-moment coefficient of correlation between these scores was found to be 0.987 ($N = 16$ factors). At graduation, a similarly calculated coefficient of correlation was found to be 0.983. Thus, the personality profiles of the two groups are strikingly similar both at entrance and at graduation, but they were, in fact, more similar at entrance than they were at graduation.

DISCUSSION

If participation in college athletics has an effect on personality structure, it seems reasonable to believe that the effect would be greater on individuals who had not previously participated in athletics than on experienced athletes. Since cadets entering the United States Military Academy differ in the extent of their prior participation in sports and since they all participate regularly in an intensive program of athletics after admission, it was possible to test several hypotheses concerning the effect of athletic participation on personality structure at the college level.

On the basis of their past histories of athletic participation, a group of entering cadet athletes and a group of athletic nonparticipants were designated. The groups were, of course, somewhat heterogeneous. The nonparticipants were not all total nonparticipants and the athletes were not all of equal ability and experience in the same sports. Nevertheless, the two groups differed in the extent of their prior participation in athletics and at entrance to the Academy they differed significantly in their test scores on seven of the 16 Personality Factor variables. This difference could be explained by assuming that prior athletic participation had influenced personality structure, but could also be explained by the assumption that individuals with certain personality structures elected to participate in athletics.

Despite regular participation in athletics over a four-year period at the Academy, the nonparticipants were found to not have changed in personality structure, as measured by the Cattell 16PF Test, to a greater extent than the athletes. Their pattern of personality structure change did not differ from the athletes, nor did they become more like the athletes.

While no evidence was found in this study to support the assumption that college athletics significantly influence personality structure, it is certainly recognized that this is but a preliminary study in this broad field of investigation. It is suggested that further research in this area is highly warranted with different tests and different groups, and most certainly with lower age groups.

In an earlier article, Ogilvie was explicit in his assertion that distinct sport personalities exist. George Sage, in article 4.4, tests the postulate of sport-specific personalities using personality data collected over a ten-year period and encompassing eight sport groups. Whereas Ogilvie reported consistent findings, Sage's preliminary review left him so confused that he avoided any hypothesis statement.

Personality is a multidimensional construct that demands complex statistical analysis. Sage used a multivariate technique that combines all personality characteristics into a single structure or profile. This can be contrasted with Werner's and Gottheil's approach in which all the personality characteristics were analyzed separately. The reader should have little problem in seeing the logic behind multivariate analysis of personality data: personality exists as a totality rather than as separate characteristics.

The result of Sage's study cast doubts on the existence of sport types, since no differences existed across the eight sport groups. These results contradict those that Ogilvie reported earlier, and the reader must now reassess the premise of sport personality types.

In addition to the results discussed by Sage, there is another interesting finding that ought to be mentioned. The eight sport teams were divided on a time dimension to see whether team personality remained the same over the 10-year period. The 1967–71 football teams were higher in need for achievement, dominance, and aggression, and lower in nurturance than the 1962–66 football teams. These findings certainly do not support the contention that today's athletes have less desire to win and a greater need to be pampered than those of earlier years.

4.4

An assessment of personality profiles between and within intercollegiate athletes from eight different sports

GEORGE H. SAGE
University of North Colorado, Greeley

INTRODUCTION

In recent years psychologists and physical educators have become increasingly interested in assessing the personality of sports performers. There has been a general premise that athletes in a given sport possess unique and definable personality attributes which are different than athletes in other sports. Indeed, part of the folklore of the athletic world is that these personality differences exist—thus American football players are frequently characterized as being hyperaggressive and highly masculine. Athletes in other sports are stereotyped with other personality traits. If there are indeed personality traits capable of differentiating athletes in one sport from athletes in another sport, this information could be useful for diagnostic and prognostic purposes by coaches.

As one phase of a larger project investigating socialization and sport, the present study was concerned with personality profiles of university athletes who participated on eight different sports teams over a ten year period. The purpose of this study was to assess the profiles of college athletes from eight sports at the University of Northern Colorado to determine if there were significant differences in team personality profiles between the various sports. A second purpose was to ascertain whether there were personality differences within sports when the sports team was divided into two groups on a time dimension.

REVIEW OF LITERATURE

Past research has produced equivocal results with regard to sport-specific personality traits. Several investigators have found personality differences between various sports groups. Slusher (1964) reported differences between the various high school sport groups which he tested. Kroll and Crenshaw (1968) found that wrestlers and football players possessed similar personality profiles while gymnasts and karate performers differed from each other. On the other hand, some investigators have found no differences between sports groups. Lakie (1962) found similar personality structures for intercollegiate athletes in football, wrestling, basketball, golf, tennis, and track, while Singer (1969) reported no significant differences in personality profiles between collegiate tennis and baseball athletes. Rushall (1970) investigated personality variables of sports performers with different levels of achievement in baseball, basketball, swimming, and football and reported no systematic trends in personality difference for any of the groups studied. Darden (1972) assessed personality profiles of competitive body builders and weight lifters and reported no significant differences between the groups.

A few investigators have studied personality differences of athletes in a single sport who possess different levels of demonstrated achievement. Kroll (1967) studied the personality profiles of wrestlers classified into three levels of achievement and reported that there were no differences between wrestlers in the three groups. Berger and Littlefield (1969) found no significant differences between outstanding college football athletes and nonoutstanding football athletes on any of the 18 items of the California Psychological Inventory, nor on a composite score. However, Straub (1971) reported personality differences between Big Ten Conference intercollegiate football players and players from each of the other three conferences which he studied. Other studies could be cited to show the conflict in findings in this area of research.

Several possible reasons for the conflicting findings of the various researchers might be advanced, such as differences in assessment instruments, limitations on the number of subjects, variability in age and achievement level of the competitors, and the variety of analysis techniques.

Past research is so conflicting that it did not suggest the identification of any specific hypotheses for this study. Thus this investigation must be considered exploratory in nature. However, from a broad inquiry into athletes' personalities, such as this study, subsequent investigators may be able to derive important hypotheses about personality and sports performers.

PROCEDURE

Intercollegiate lettermen athletes at the University of Northern Colorado between 1962 and 1971 in eight sports (football, basketball, baseball, wrestling, gymnastics, swimming, track, and tennis) constituted the population (N = 646) for this study. Athletes who had lettered in more than one sport were classified with the sport in which they earned the most letter awards. The Edwards Personal Preference Schedule (EPPS) was used to assess the personality of the athletes. The EPPS has been administered at the University of Northern Colorado since 1960 and EPPS scores were available for over 80 per cent (N = 532) of the lettermen athletes. The EPPS consists of 225 pairs of statements and the subject is forced to make a choice response to one of two statements which is most characteristic of himself. This instrument measures 15 relatively independent normal personality variables. . . .

RESULTS

Multiple discriminant analysis comparisons were made between the athletes in the eight sports groups. Discriminant function analysis reduces multiple measurements to a single variable. Thus, in this case the 15 personality traits provided a profile score for each individual in each group, and group profiles were analyzed for significant differences. . . . The multivariate generalized hypothesis that no differences existed in personality profiles between groups was regarded as tenable. . . .

To determine whether there were personality differences within sports when a sports team was divided into two groups on a time dimension, each sports team was divided into a group of lettermen from 1962 to 1966 and a group of lettermen from 1967 to 1971. Group profiles were analyzed by discriminant function for significant differences. . . . The multivariate generalized null hypothesis that no differences existed in personality profiles of football lettermen from 1961 to 1966 and lettermen from 1967 to 1971 and wrestling lettermen divided in the same manner was rejected. . . . For lettermen in the other sports divided in the same yearly blocks, the null hypothesis that no differences existed in the personality profiles was regarded as tenable.

Univariate F tests were applied to the football and wrestling groups to ascertain the individual trait differences. . . . Football lettermen from 1967 to 1971 were significantly (.05 level) higher in need for achievement, dominance, and aggression and significantly lower in need for nurturance than the 1961 to 1966 football athletes. Wrestlers from 1967 to 1971 were significantly lower in need for affiliation and abasement than the 1961 to 1966 wrestlers.

DISCUSSION

The generalized, multivariate, null hypothesis that intercollegiate athletes in eight different sports had similar personality profiles can be regarded as tenable, when using the .05 level of confidence. This finding is in accord with Singer's (1969) data, as he did not find differences between collegiate baseball and tennis players. It is also in accord with Rushall's (1970) study with various collegiate athletic categories with different levels of achievement, and it is in line with Kroll and Crenshaw's (1968) finding that college football players and wrestlers exhibited similar personality profiles. On the other hand, the present finding is at variance with research reported by Ogilvie (1968a, 1968b) and Kane (1966a).

The finding of this study that no significant personality differences exist for athletes in eight different sports suggests that attempts to generalize sport specific personality types from limited data, as some recent investigators have done, should be done with great caution. Although the University of Northern Colorado athletes in this study were not, as a total group, national or international level in achievement, they must certainly be ranked as very highly skilled in their sport, so they may be viewed as representing an athletic elite. If indeed various sports either attract or develop sport specific personalities, these differences should have shown up in this study because all of the subjects have competed in their sport for at least four years and some have competed as many as ten years; all have attained a considerable measure of success in their sport.

It is suggested that claims such as those of Ogilvie (1968b) and Ogilvie and Tutko (1966) that there are personality dimensions which are essential to sport success and which differentiate athletes in various sports must be viewed with suspicion. There is no attempt here to deny that these investigators and others may have found differences between athletes representing different sport groups which they studied, but it is suggested that the power of their findings for diagnostic and predictive purposes is weak.

The generalized multivariate, null hypothesis that intercollegiate athletes within different sports divided on a time dimension had similar personality profiles can be regarded as tenable for five of the sports (tennis was not included in this analysis). For two of the sports, football and wrestling, there were significant differences in the personality profiles within these sports. Thus, over a ten year span there were no significant changes in personality profiles within most of the sports studied.

The findings with regard to football and wrestling do not lend themselves to easy interpretation. In the case of football, the fortunes of the teams have differed considerably during the two time periods studied. In the years from 1962 to 1966 the teams won 19 games and lost 26 and did not win any championships whereas from 1967 to 1971 the teams won 36 games and lost 8, winning three conference championships while playing about the same schedules as during the 1962-1966 period. That the 1967-71 teams were higher in need for achievement, dominance, and aggression and lower in nurturance, might be suggestive of differences in football performance, however a conclusion of this kind would be highly tenuous, particularly since Kroll (1967) with wrestlers, Kroll and Carlson (1967) with karate participants, Parsons (1963) with swimmers, Singer (1969) with baseball players, Berger and Littlefield (1969) with football athletes, and Rushall (1970) with several sports groups reported no significant differences between higher- and lesser-skilled athletes in personality profiles. However, Kroll and Peterson (1965a) did find significant differences between losing and winning football teams.

UNC wrestling teams have been Rocky Mountain Conference champions 29 of the past 30 years, and the skill level of the participants does not seem to have changed much in the past 10 years. The fact that the wrestlers from 1967 to 1971 possess lower needs for affiliation and abasement provides little meaningful data to add to the already substantial body of literature on the personality of wrestlers.

In the sport personality literature various groupings of athletes have been contrasted—team versus individual, combative versus non-combative, and males versus females, to name only a few. Additionally, in recent years, researchers have tried to correlate personality characteristics of athletes with all kinds of physical abilities—even shoulder flexion. It is as if every human quality were related to personality; this can approach nonsensical levels. Walter Kroll, in article 4.5, itemizes various controversies of general personality assessment and sport personality assessment, and also describes several possible theoretical models that could be tested. He claims that the general personality literature is both extensive and confusing, whereas the sport literature is only confusing. Since Kroll wrote his article, the sport personality literature has retained its confusion but has now unfortunately added extensiveness to its qualities.

Particular attention should be paid to the point of view typified by Hunt concerning the sources of behavioral variation. Research along this line has repeatedly demonstrated that knowledge of either the person trait or the situation accounts for only a small amount of behavioral variance. Kroll makes the point well when he asks that researchers pay more attention to the unaccounted-for variance. In most sport personality research studies, as in personality research in general, neither traits nor situations adequately account for a significant amount of variation. For a more detailed look at this aspect of personality research, the reader is directed to the research by Endler, Hunt, and Rosenstein (1962, 1965, 1966, 1968, 1969, 1973).

Kroll closes his article with the oft-heard plea that what is needed to advance sport personality research is to ask the questions that are especially pertinent to sport. This is in opposition to most of the research, which has used a general approach to answer a specific question. Is it any wonder that confusion reigns?

4.5 Current strategies and problems in personality assessment of athletes

WALTER KROLL
University of Massachusetts, Amherst

The profession of physical education has long been aware of the importance of personality variables in its conduct of educational physical activity programs. Ever since the beginning of the twentieth century when the New Physical Education was espoused by leaders like Thomas D. Wood and Clark Hetherington, aims of the profession have universally included at least one specific objective dealing with desirable personality development. Whether called emotional-impulsive (Nash), development of instinct mechanisms (Hetherington), or personal-social attitudes (Cowell and Schwenn), physical education has continuously held itself obligated to the structuring of satisfactory learning experiences in an educational environment for inculcation of suitable personality traits and attitudes. In no small way, social and moral aspects of personality dynamics have often tended to overshadow the importance and emphasis given to physical or neuromuscular objectives in physical education. Even when the nation was in an uproar over the physical unfitness of American youths, for example, a well-received article in the Association's journal appeared with the revealing title, "Is Physical Fitness Our Most Important Objective?" (Weiss, 1964).

From *Psychology of Motor Learning*. Edited by L. E. Smith. Chicago: Athletic Institute, 1970. Reprinted by permission. Copyright 1970 by Athletic Institute.

Belief in the principle of mind–body unity extends beyond the domain of professional physical education in an educational setting. The role of physical activity has been explored concerning its therapeutic potential in social adjustment, mental health, juvenile delinquency, and as an aid in the diagnosis and treatment of maladjustment (Layman, 1960a). As a result of such inquiries, physical activity is accepted in many quarters as an adjunctive therapy in socio-medical settings (Layman, 1960b; Davis, 1952). Release of aggressive feelings, reduction of anxiety, social mobility, and enhanced sociometric status have also been linked to physical activity. Currently, preliminary reports on perceptual–motor relationships are capturing the profession's imagination as evidence suggesting that physical activity may actually contribute to cognitive development in a direct and causal manner rather than via some indirect route.

Although physical activity and personality are recognized as interacting components of some consequence to professional physical education in an educational setting and to adjunctive therapies in a socio-medical environment, it is in athletics where personality is accorded its most notable position as a factor of accentuated importance. Based upon considerably less objective evidence than exists for the role of personality variables and physical activity in educational or therapeutic endeavors, personality is rather universally proclaimed an important and essential prerequisite for successful athletic performance. Few coaches or athletes would deny that personality is a factor of crucial significance in achieving athletic success (winning). Some experienced observers even go so far as to suggest that certain personality traits are the only real differentiators between success and failure in athletics. Support of such a position is based upon the thesis that concerted efforts to equalize physical athletic talent at any particular quality level of competitive sports have been highly successful.

This brief introduction could be greatly amplified but I believe it is sufficient to suggest that personality has been widely acknowledged as an important aspect of physical activity. Research concerning personality and physical activity has, of course, been conducted from each of the reference frames mentioned, i.e., educational physical education, therapeutics, and athletics. Although the primary emphasis in this paper is upon personality in athletics and current strategies (and problems) in assessment and research, such a focus does not exclude the domains of therapeutics and professional physical education from consideration. If personality factors are operative in physical activity then studying extreme or classical samples as typified by athletes has implications for all levels of physical activity. Such a posture implies acceptance of a dimensional rather than a categorical system for personality and is in accord with Eysenck's (1964) doctrine of continuity in which personality is assumed to be "due to a combination of quantitative variations along some designated continua." In Eysenck's model, of course, the major continua are represented by introversion–extraversion and stable–unstable.

By studying personality in athletics we accept the notion that elements of the same description are likely to apply at lower intensity levels of physical activity, i.e., in intramural sports, physical education classes, voluntary participation, etc. Research findings at either end of a continuum may contribute to a knowledge structure applicable at the other end as well as at any points along the continuum. Studying non-athletes, for example, may contribute as much (or more) as studying champion athletes just as studying psychotics may produce knowledge about normals. This is not to say that descriptions or assessment techniques developed at either end of the continuum would be completely—or even partially—satisfactory at the other end without some modification. Need for such moderation in extrapolation is reflected in Holtzman's (1965) contention that ". . . the MMPI is not a satisfactory instrument for determining personality dimensions since it was constructed for an entirely different purpose." Even though it was designed to provide "clinical scales for the diagnosis of psychiatric populations (Holtzman, 1965)" the MMPI has produced research data of interest to other levels of personality research.

My purpose is, then, to review with you some of the problems in athletic personality research. The comments made are bound to elicit debate since many are contrived to make implicit assumptions explicit. . . .

GOALS AND OBJECTIVES OF PERSONALITY RESEARCH IN ATHLETICS

A basic premise of almost quasi-mystical potency for personality research in athletics is that athletes possess unique and definable personality attributes different from nonathletes. It is also commonly held, moreover, that in addition to differentiation from nonathletes, athletes in one sport can be distinguished from athletes in another sport. The basis for such sweeping assumptions is partly generated by widespread acceptance of classification schemes for athletic and physical activities. One of the most frequently cited classification systems, for example, dichotomizes athletic activities into team sports versus individual sports. Other categorical plans suggest combative versus noncombative, indoor versus outdoor, or use of a missile and/or implement versus nonuse of a missile and/or implement in the activity. A variety of classification plans exist including some with more categories such as that provided by the Committee on Curriculum Research of the National College Physical Education for Men (LaPorte, 1955): aquatics, dancing, team sports (court and diamond games plus field sports), gymnastics, and individual and dual sports.

Such classification schemes have been popularized chiefly by physical education curriculum experts in order to provide some framework for establishing an ideal educational program. Individual activities are typically evaluated for potential contribution to achievement of stated educational objectives. Thus, weight training is rated as contributing to a physical fitness objective but making a smaller contribution to a social objective. Golf, on the other hand, is typically rated as a good contributor to the social objective and a poor developer of physical fitness. With such assessments of activity potential for contribution to achievement of educational ends, a curriculum is designed which hopefully balances learning experiences for optimum results.

Implicit in the curriculum decision-making process is the belief that: (a) different physical activities make unequal contributions to individual objectives in a heterogeneous set; and (b) different physical activities make distinctive kinds of contributions to the same objective. Some activities are excellent for development of physical fitness while others make their major contribution to a social objective. But even when several activities are mutually linked to the same objective their contributions may be distinctively different. Thus, while both contact and non-contact sports may contribute to a social objective they do so in different ways: contact sports are assumed to be developers of aggressiveness and masculinity while a non-contact sport such as golf is judged good for development of social and cultural refinement. Although such curriculum decisions and judgments must be made, the factual basis for much of the accepted policy guiding classification systems and evaluative curriculum decision-making remains obscure.

If personality attributes of athletes could be found which are capable of differentiating athletes from nonathletes and athletes in one sport from another, certain advantages would result. First, there would be promise for development of personality techniques for screening of potential athletic talent eventually leading to a procedure by which aspiring candidates for athletics could be matched with a sport (or sports) for which they were best suited and in which they would be most likely to experience success. Coupled with the knowledge already available and quickly being accumulated on motor characteristics necessary for success, a practical system of athletic counseling could be realized. Secondly, if success prerequisites in terms of personality attributes were established for an athletic sport then the manner in which participants were trained could be modified so as to promote optimum cultivation of the personality success attributes. In a similar manner, knowledge of the effects and demands of particular athletic activities could permit therapeutic uses of physical activity and curriculum rather than subjective insight and an opinion consensus.

Research strategy and research problems

The amount of research data concerning personality and athletics is not very extensive but it is admittedly confusing. The amount of research data concerning personality in general is, of course, both extensive and confusing. Thus, we are only behind in one phase of our work. Several excellent reviews of the literature have recently appeared (Layman, 1960a; Kane, 1964; and Husman, 1969) describing the present status of knowledge concerning personality factors in athletics. Universal acknowledgement was made of the problem of valid and reliable assessment techniques in these reviews and lack of suitable measurement instruments continues to plague definitive research undertakings. In addition to lack of acceptable measurement tools, a superabundance of theoretical models for personality structure, personality dynamics and development results in an entangling web of conflicting results.

Since the personality researcher in athletics makes use of the theories and research tools developed by personality research in general, he inherits both the good and the bad in his attempts at defining a personality model for athletics. At best, then, research dealing with personality in athletics will find itself beset with many irritating problems of considerable potency. Some of the general problems in personality are needlessly compounded in athletic personality work, however, because of inadequately conceived paradigms and less than adequate attention to matters of experimental design and statistical analysis. Other specific problems stem from nonrecognition of the fact that problems in general personality work carry over into athletic personality research. A few of the more important of these research problems will be considered as they relate to relatively specific issues in athletic personality work.

Measurement problems. In the opening sentence dealing with personality in the 1969 *Annual Review of Psychology,* Adelson said: "The field of personality these days is marked by abundance, diffusiveness, and diversity." Shortly thereafter Adelson cited Sanford's (1968) description of personality research as a "disconcerting sprawl" and suggested that personality research is characterized by a conglomerate of loosely related topics "each of which more or less goes its own way." Fiske's (1963) chapter on Problems in Measuring Personality likewise acknowledged the "critical weakness in the scientific study of personality" due in some part to the "relative lack of adequate measurement operations." He cited inadequacy of common personality definitions as leading to damaging specificity of personality measurement instruments. Thus, personality inventories purporting to measure the same or highly similar components seldom show intercorrelations above .50. When assessment of the same component is attempted by different methods—e.g., inventories versus projective techniques—the intercorrelations are even lower.

Such abundance, diffusiveness, and diversity is not peculiar to studies of personality structure alone for Adelson also points out that there is no general agreement as to the composition of anxiety even though hundreds of studies have been conducted. Cofer and Appley (1964) concur with such a description for motivation as they note: "It is clear that a comprehensive, definitive psychology of motivation does not yet exist." The goal of synthesis and integration for personality structure and personality dynamics, both singly and together, seems less achievable today than it was before in that "we appear to be in an era of such extreme methodological and conceptual specialization that communication between investigators, never satisfactory to begin with, threatens to break down" (Wiggins, 1968).

Compounding such acknowledged dilemmas in personality structure and personality dynamics has been the relatively recent "Crisis in Methodology" (Adelson, 1969) generated by the disturbing findings concerning response sets. Studies delineating the effects of social desirability (SD) and acquiescence (Acq) have suggested that such response sets can have equivocal and pervasive effects upon the derived scores from many personality inventories. This issue, according to Christie and Lindauer (1963), entails more than internal psychometric argument involving preferences in methodological measurement strategy, and, instead, lays open the question of the validity of a good deal of completed and on going personality research. Thus, the question has been raised of whether response sets are more important in self-report inventories than the substantive content of items in such inventories themselves.

Several reports have shown, for example, that the effect of response sets is of considerable importance in an inventory such as the widely used MMPI. Edwards (1966) disregarded substantive content and constructed an artificial MMPI by matching his own personality statements with MMPI items simply on the basis of known endorsement frequency (EF) and social desirability scale values (SDSV). The first two factors on the EF and SDSV constructed MMPI correlated .98 and .67 respectively with actual MMPI factor loadings. Similarly, Jackson and Messick (1961, 1962) divided MMPI scales into true and false-keyed subscales. Factor analytic results showing a factor comprised of almost all the true subscales and another factor containing almost all the false subscales led to the conclusion that direction of item-keying was an important "determinant of the factorial structure of the MMPI." The amount of concern with such contamination of test validity by response sets is reflected in the fact that approximately 25 per cent of the articles between 1964 and 1967 reviewed by Wiggins (1968) dealt with this problem.

As overwhelming as these and other measurement problems are in personality research, they do not—in my opinion—constitute the greatest source of difficulty for the athletic personality researcher. Indeed, even if the measurement deficiencies currently being debated were to be cleared up to the satisfaction of personality experts I doubt the muddled picture seen in athletic personality research would be much affected. Such an attention getting and easily criticized position is based upon two major arguments each of which has some merit even if outweighed by deficiency.

Psychiatric versus normal. First of all, much of the theoretical frame-of-reference in personality research is heavily imbued with clinical identification of psychiatric or quasipsychiatric populations. As Garfield (1963) has pointed out, the clinician's view of personality emphasizes pathology and usual appraisals of normal personality are likely to be couched in terms of susceptibility to maladjustment or the presence of latent pathological features. Tests devised for compatibility with mental health or psychiatric goals, no matter how well constructed, rather than assessment of normal personality would seem to promise less help in athletic personality work than is needed.

As Crites (1964) has argued, dissatisfaction with the abnormal personality orientation has led counseling psychologists to the practice of adapting personality instruments for the assessment of normal personality. Outside of the California Psychological Inventory (CPI, Gough, 1957) and, to a lesser extent, the Cattell Sixteen Personality Factor Questionnaire (16PF, Cattell, and Eber 1957), there hardly exists a satisfactory inventory capable of assessing normal personality with adequately established internal and external validity. An inventory such as the MMPI, for example, was developed for identification of psychiatric populations and its empirically constructed clinical scales are poorly suited to dimensional analysis of personality structure in normals (Holtzman, 1965). Studies employing the MMPI on athletes typically result in conclusions dealing with psychopathic deviation (Pd), paranoia (Pa), depression (D), hysteria (hy), or other psychiatric features rather than a discussion of normal or "successful" personality (see, for example, Slusher, 1964). Although identification of psychiatric obstacles is of acknowledged importance, athletic personality research would seem better suited to a different reference frame.

Major pre-occupation with psychiatric deficiencies and clinical-therapeutic approaches to athletic personality seems to fix attention at one end of the personality continuum. Although capable of making important contributions, it tends to emphasize weaknesses and neglects consideration of the personality strengths necessary for successful athletic performance. In many respects there seems to be some correspondence between clinical-therapeutic approaches in athletic personality work and the prevention and treatment of athletic injuries. As any team physician or coach can attest, the absence of physical injury does not insure the physical condition necessary for success. In the same way, then, the absence of psychiatric deficiency does not insure the presence of personality attributes necessary for success. It would seem that personality attributes necessary for success are of at least equal importance to personality attributes of a psychiatric nature preventing success. Research effort in athletic personality should be encouraged, therefore, in a manner paralleling work in athletic conditioning as opposed to athletic injury management.

There are currently two good examples of the kind of contributions made by a clinical-therapeutic approach to athletic personality work. One of these is a book by a practicing psychiatrist, *The Madness in Sports* (Beisser, 1967) in which an intriguing set of case studies is used to exemplify the psychodynamics of psychiatric disturbances in athletes. The other is a book by a pair of widely published clinical psychologists titled *Problem Athletes and How to Handle Them* (Ogilvie and Tutko, 1966). In both of these books there is the usual absence of cited scientific references for support of clinical observations and conclusions other than Recommended Reading or Bibliography. Although one book noted that "psychological investigations must provide the reliable data that will enhance and complement coaching skill, the authors did not choose to "present the more scholarly experimental documentation of our research findings in the area of athletic motivation."

Too often, as reflected in these examples, the bulk of clinical-therapeutic efforts is presented in a form resistant to affirmation or cross-validation by reasonably objective techniques. Since affirmation is made difficult, denial of findings is almost impossible except by judgment. Although definitive work is provided full of strong assertions and packed with practical suggestions for immediate application, such work demands complete reliance upon the author's capability to translate and apply general theory to the behavioral situation being examined. One must recognize the genuine contributions that insight and personal analysis of psychodynamics can make when applied to athletic personality work, but one must also weigh Meehl's (1954) study showing how poor clinical diagnoses are when compared to even weak objective tests. Thus, many choose to follow Cattell's recommendation (Cattell and Butcher, 1968) concerning clinically derived insights: ". . . it is necessary to distinguish insight from fantasy by rigorous empirical methods."

My point is that the psychiatric and mental health overtones which influence a good share of personality work are likely to hold center stage for quite some time. If one's goal is to define the personality deficiencies preventing successful athletic performance then the wealth of clinical-therapeutic research will be of inestimable value. If, however, one's goal is closer to the one described earlier for athletic personality then such clinical-therapeutic research will be of value in a narrower and quite limited dimension. Acceptance of a dimensional system for personality (Eysenck, 1964) does not automatically obligate the athletic personality researcher to complete reliance upon the methodology and set of operations pertinent to the study of personality deficiencies. Just as we recognize that health is more than the absence of disease, we must recognize that athletic personality is more than the absence of psychiatric deficiencies. Even further, we must recognize that the instruments and techniques suitable in one area may not be completely satisfactory in the other.

Normal versus super-normal. Even if we can hope that personality instruments will be developed which are adequate for the assessment of normal rather than deficient personality, the probability of achieving implicit research goals in athletic personality work will only be minimally increased. I base this contention partly on the results of studies dealing with the prediction of academic achievement, job placement and personnel classification, and guidance counseling in which personality instruments have been of minor value, far overshadowed by more specific ability tests. Involved also is the innocent idea that competitive sports are a special kind of a behavioral situation resembling the unique and exceptional more than they do the average and general; i.e., competitive sports represent a super-normal rather than a normal system.

The belief that personality attributes are important to academic achievement is probably as widespread as the belief that personality is important in athletics. Although various personality attributes have been linked to academic achievement, however, few studies have been able to show any dramatic rise in prediction over and above that produced by traditional ability measures. Certainly personality has not been shown to correlate with academic achievement to the extent that popular belief would predict. The point to be emphasized here is that personality measures must add to the predictive efficiency obtainable through standardized ability tests. Attempts to improve prediction by use of personality and other non-intellectual components have, in the words of Middleton and Guthrie (1959), "yielded quite discouraging results." Some individuals, on the other hand, would become excited over the finding reported by Cattell and Butcher (1968) that addition of the fourteen factors of the High School Personality Questionnaire improved prediction of the total score on the Stanford Achievement Test over and above the predictive capability of ability scores alone. Others would note that this significant increase was actually a rise from .72 to .79 and agree with Cattell and Butcher's observation that the "effects reported are not spectacular."

Research done in conjunction with the National Merit Scholarship Corporation has shown that academic achievement in college can be predicted from several personality inventories. The California Psychological Inventory was reported to be the most successful instrument with several scales predicting college grades in the high .10's and .20's, hardly an overwhelming result (Astin, 1964). Astin also noted, moreover, that simple self-ratings on such traits as scholarship, persistence, or drive to achieve actually predicted grade point average better than the personality inventories. Astin concluded that it was economically unwise to use elaborate personality inventories in attempts to improve prediction of academic achievement when simple self-ratings were generally superior. Parallel evidence suggests that the CPI can hardly be called a valid predictor of college grade point average (Holland, 1959; Johnson and Pacine, 1961) nor does it predict college major very well (Hase and Goldberg, 1967). Indeed, in the study by Hase and Goldberg college major was simply a dichotomy between liberal arts versus non-liberal arts and 11 CPI empirical scales gave a cross validated multiple R of .30.

Such studies are representative of many which could be cited in defense of the argument that personality inventories alone have not been shown to be adequate instruments for prediction of academic success or for choice of college major. Similar evidence is available to show that personality inventories are not adequate for job placement or vocational guidance. In place of personality instruments we find employment of specifically designed assessment techniques. The inherent demand characteristics of the task, be it academic achievement or an occupation, are analyzed and specific, relevant assessment measures devised which emphasize empirical rather than rational validity.

A model for personality in athletics

Throughout our previous discussion we have assumed that athletic personality research had a definite and universally accepted purpose. Let us turn our attention away from problems and strategies in measurement which supposedly prevent achievement of our expressed goals to an even more important issue, that of the conceptualized role of personality in athletics. Needless to say, the scientific goal of personality research in athletics calls for development of a comprehensive knowledge structure in the form of an accepted theory or predictive model. It is not unfair to say that studies done so far on athletes seem guided by the single objective of demonstrating personality differences between athletes and nonathletes (or between athletes in one sport from another) in order to identify personality traits characteristic of athletes in a specific sport. When significant differences are shown the inference is often made that such traits are desirable prerequisites for entry into a particular sport and that either by inherent possession or environmental development these traits should exist in high concentration for successful performance in the sport.

Personality attributes which have been demonstrated as significant differentiators between athletes and nonathletes or between athletes in different sports are certainly personality features somehow linked to athletics. Contending that such traits are essential characteristics for success in a sport, however, is quite a different matter. Not only must a personality attribute differentiate athletes from nonathletes but it must be shown to differ on logical dimensions between known levels of ability in the same sport and/or that participation enhances the magnitude of the trait before any confidence can be attached to the claim that it is related to successful performance. Even then the trait might still represent a necessary but not a sufficient personality characteristic for success in the sport. If another research uncovers successful athletes who do not possess the trait in established dimensions then the whole argument for the trait representing a personality success prerequisite fails.

Now achievement of such a personality model in athletics—i.e., one which identifies unique characteristics essential to success—may be highly desirable, but there is no guarantee that such a state of affairs actually exists and such a model is still only a hope rather than a fact. There are, in fact, other possibilities and a short time ago several hypothetical models were suggested for personality research in athletics (Kroll, 1967). These alternative reference frames appeared as part of an article dealing with experimental data and do not seem to have received much attention. At this early stage of development, it may be a good idea to keep as many plausible options open as possible for athletic personality research. Hence, these models will again be presented in modified form along with some brief arguments as to their suitability. Several of these models are less appealing than others to goal-oriented fields such as education and adjunctive therapy which understandably prefer more teleologically acceptable theories. Nature, however, often has ideas of its own in such matters and the well-intentioned researcher may have difficulty imposing his own will upon reality. My argument is not for acceptance of these models but rather that there is a need to acknowledge the options and not to pursue a pre-conceived and limited objective regardless of how wholesome and advantageous that goal may be in certain professional applications.

First, there may be a set of personality factors which prompt individuals to elect participation in a particular sport. Those individuals who possess the most fortunate combination of these features are then seen as continuing on and experiencing success in the sport. Any individual lacking these traits would fail to survive very long even if he elected to begin participation. In this hypothetical model both those individuals entering the sport as well as successful veterans in the sport would exhibit similar personality profiles possibly differing only in intensity. A second alternative is that no pattern exists which is associated with initial entry into a sport, but either by modification of existing and alterable personality characteristics or attrition of inappropriate patterns only those individuals possessing suitable or alterable patterns will persist and experience success. In this case, early participants may exhibit heterogeneous patterns but successful veterans would possess homogeneous personality patterns. Both of these two cases would hold promise for identification of personality features characteristic of an athlete which are essential for successful performance and allow practical applications in educational and therapeutic settings.

Most athletic personality researchers seem to express overwhelming preference for these two potential models but there are other alternatives. A third possibility is that both neophytes and successful veterans possess dissimilar and nondiscriminant patterns: i.e., unique personality factors appear to be non-existent and unrelated to athletic performance. Fourth, a similar pattern may exist at entry but participation and attrition results in a dissimilar and nondiscriminant pattern among successful veterans. These latter two models postulate the absence of identifying success characteristics for talented performers and seem professionally if not scientifically less attractive than the first two cases. Thus, whenever results compatible with options three or four occur there appears an expression of apologetic embarrassment and the researcher often reveals his disappointment by second guessing his study blaming lack of precision, poor subject cooperation, faulty measurement instruments, sample composition, and the like for nonsignificant findings.

A fifth model alternative can be added in which opposite discriminatory patterns may be demonstrated in untried novices and successful veterans. Under this scheme the presence of certain traits in novice participants could indicate that just the opposite traits were required for success and characteristic of veteran performers. Some support for such a model was presented in a study on amateur collegiate level wrestlers (Kroll, 1967) when it compared its results with a study done by Slusher (1964) involving high school athletes. Slusher concluded that wrestlers and football players displayed the most neurotic MMPI profile of the five athletic groups and norm sample studied. Results from the collegiate level sample, however, suggested just the opposite was true since the wrestlers demonstrated a low factor I score on the Cattell 16PF Test. It was speculated that participation in the sport of wrestling might conceivably be responsible for amelioration of a "dominate neurotic profile" and development of a tough, masculine, and aggressive profile.

Although support for each of these five models is scarce, evidence from a parallel search for physical success prerequisites and distinguishing characteristics suggests that model possibilities other than the more attractive ones (models one and two) merit careful consideration. We know, for example, that successful dash men are seldom developed from a non-descript set of physical capabilities. The chances of developing middle and long distance runners, however, are much better. As far as physical characteristics, then, one might say dash men conform to model one and distance runners to model two. Disallowing extremes of ecto-and endomorphy in somatotypes, there is good evidence to assume that amateur wrestlers in the United States requires no specific somatotype prerequisite for success (Rasch, 1958; Kroll, 1954). Thus, beginning and successful wrestlers would each exhibit dissimilar and nondiscriminating somatotype profiles and generally conform to model three predictions.

Model four, meanwhile, calls for discriminating characteristics among beginners but not among successful veterans. Several studies have demonstrated support for the idea that strength is more important for beginning wrestlers than for advanced wrestlers (Gross, Griesel, and Stull, 1956;

Kroll, 1954, 1958; and Rasch and Kroll, 1964). Among beginning wrestlers in college physical activity classes Gross, Griesel, and Stull reported a correlation of .498 between McCloy's General Strength Quotient and the ability to learn wrestling. The other studies showed that the importance of strength declined as the skill level of wrestling went up. To some degree, at least, these data suggest conformity to the postulates of model four. Thus, in the same sport we see need for model three to understand somatotypes and model four to incorporate strength findings. Work done by Fleishman (1963) and others (Jones, 1962) also support the idea that the importance of various component abilities is modified with changes in criterion skill performance.

Model five proposes that an opposite set of discriminating characteristics may be present in untried novices and successful veterans. Such a model would appear to be most attractive for use in educational and therapeutic environments since it infers acceptance of the premise that the demand characteristics of an activity can be achieved through the developmental effect of participation itself. Such an outlook also prescribes acceptance of a kind of deficiency-compensation principle whereby individuals seek to overcome some deficiency by participation in an activity which is perceived as necessitating just the opposite of the deficiency for success. Thune's (1949) finding of an inferiority complex among weight trainers, for example, has been widely interpreted as conforming to this deficiency-compensation principle. Individuals dissatisfied with their physique and muscular strength would thus elect participation in weight training while competitive weight lifters would be characterized by diametrically opposite characteristics.

Whether or not any of these models will ever be shown to be valid remains to be seen but they can at least be used to moderate our interpretation of unsettled personality research in athletics. Bland acceptance of *any* preconceived and poorly verified paradigm can be disruptive to productive research efforts. A noted researcher in this area (Husman, 1969), for example, reviewed the vast array of conflicting results and implied a sort of predilection to models one or two by his statement that "such conflicting evidence . . . is undoubtedly due to instrumentation and methodological inaccuracies." Reacting to Husman's paper at the same conference, Singer (1969) also generally implied acceptance of a model one or two reference frame as he expressed the hope for future "application of such information to the sports' scene." In common with Husman, Singer also saw promise that "with better measuring devices and techniques . . . there will occur greater agreement between experimental results." Contrasted against these two homogeneous positions is one forwarded by Rushall (1970) who, after a comprehensive study of athletic personality, concluded that "personality is not a significant factor in sport performance."

My point is this: we know from much more extensive evidence concerning exercise physiology that physical characteristics and physiological success prerequisites are related to athletic performance in a multiplicity of ways. Because of the amount of accumulated reliable knowledge, we are not surprised when a study shows dash men do not possess excellent levels of cardiovascular endurance or that weight training regimes fail to improve maximal oxygen uptake. We are not disturbed by such findings because we more fully understand the role of aerobic and anaerobic energy sources and recognize that sprints and weight lifting require anaerobic energy and should not be expected to develop or require aerobic fitness characteristics. Thus, even though we classify cardiovascular endurance as an important component of physical fitness we accept the fact that all competitive sports do not make equal demands upon fitness components.

We also know that some activities make very little demand for *any* physical fitness factors but instead require high levels of skill for success. Bowling is an example of such a low fitness and high skill activity. Other sports, such as distance running, necessitate superb levels of physical fitness for competitive success and make much smaller demands upon skill. Thus, we see a physical trait such as cardiovascular fitness varying from nil to high importance as far as an essential characteristic in successful athletic performance. In light of such evidence it would seem unwise to conclude that skill is unimportant in athletics because cardiovascular fitness rather than skill is the chief success prerequisite for distance running nor is it prudent to judge fitness unimportant because skill is the major differentiator between good and bad bowlers. Why, then, is it unreasonable to hold open the possibility that personality attributes may represent an important success factor in some sports but not in others, or at some quality levels but not at others? When viewed from model one alone, such personality data would indeed appear confusing. Viewed from other models—which are already accepted in the physical realm—the results would not seem conflicting at all.

Thus, when personality studies fail to show distinguishing characteristics between athletes and nonathletes we must be ready to consider the findings as evidence for a model three or four and not quickly and resolutely classify the results as conflicting or question the research procedures employed. To be sure, measurement in personality is far less than adequate. But we cannot proclaim its inadequacy for non-significant or conflicting results and implicitly accept its adequacy when findings more to our liking are realized. In a similar manner, we cannot allow a review of confusing data to prompt a conclusion that there is no order for personality factors in athletics. We have far too little acceptable research dealing with athletic personality to venture definitive conclusions at the present time.

We have also learned through physiological studies, by the way, that many (if not most) competitive sports do not supply sufficient development of demand characteristics by mere participation. Thus, physiological preparedness necessary for the mile run is not achieved by running one mile a day nor is the physical condition demanded by football developed by game-like scrimmages alone. Complicated training programs are instead devised to attain the necessary physiological characteristics demanded by the activity. Whether called supplemental, off-season, or pre-season conditioning, such training programs are considered essential for successful athletic performance. The same is true for skill as exemplified by the numerous specific drills that are utilized in athletic training. If the physical analogy holds, there may be need to examine the potential models for athletic personality from the same reference frame. There may very well be need for personality training regimes as well as special physical conditioning programs in athletics.

Janus' outlook

Any honest appraisal of the work in athletic personality must conclude that the picture is unsettled. Only clinical interpretations have been able to come up with anything approaching a definite conclusion while studies with objective measurements of personality continue to offer conflicting results. Part of the acknowledged confusion, however, is due to the fact that we have naively expected too much of personality inventories and other general assessment techniques. Because of an abundance of encapsulated personality philosophies and unrelated measurement instruments, structural personality factors cannot always be expected to discriminate in the kinds of operations and situation in which we have hoped for significant differences. Disregarding methodological measurement problems, personality inventories postulate a number of static traits each of which is poorly defined as to composition and thus poorly represented in the item pool. Such a catholic lens for personality may not have the proper focal length for identification of the elusive characteristics important in athletic personality research. We have, in effect, gone fishing for minnows with a nomological net designed for whales and have no right to complain about the poor catch.

A similar observation would seem to hold for efforts in the area of personality dynamics. We have little knowledge, for example, of the potency of various situations in athletics to elicit activity of personality features and allow prediction of behavior. Even if motivation for success were a general and consistent factor in individuals and even if the demand characteristics of athletic tasks were specified, the individual incentive for success in particular tasks could vary sufficiently to disallow predictable and discriminating behavior. One of the outstanding authorities in the field of motivation, moreover, cautions against acceptance of a generalized achievement motivation rather than a situation locked and specific multidimensional structure. In fact, Heckhausen (1967) suggests that an achievement motivation in "practically every situational relationship" is observed in "certain apparently neurotic cases." Anxiety, likewise, can be situation locked to particular conditions, is modified by experience, and lacks a common agreed upon definition.

In this connection Hunt (1965) discussed the problem of whether static personality traits constituted the major source of behavioral variance, or, as social psychology argues, that variations in particular situations mediate behavior. The conclusion reached was that interactions between the two determined behavior. The recommendation given by Hunt was to seek instruments capable of predicting behavior of individuals in various kinds of situations rather than clinging to the belief in "static dimensional traits." Thus, the depicting of stable and permanent personality traits (structure) or the description of behavior in specific, monetary situations (dynamics) alone is not sufficient.

It is embarrassing to suggest that Lewin's equation of $B = f(P, E)$ requires acknowledgement in athletic personality research. The bulk of research in athletic personality, however, has been aimed at specific definition of personality structure through use of a variety of inventories. Much less has been done on the interaction of supposedly stable personality attributes and the demand characteristics of particular environmental situations. Almost nothing has been accomplished on developing specific and pertinent measurement tools for assessment of personality attributes in athletic situations.

This latter observation is, I believe, the major cause of discouraging results in athletic personality research, i.e., lack of effort in developing specific and unique assessment tools for athletics. Due to a traditional practice of borrowing knowledge constructs and research tools from related disciplines in an eclectic and parasitic manner, physical education research in the area of athletic personality can by typified as one continuous series of "piggy-back" rides. Progress in general personality research is awaited with the enthusiastic expectation that new strategies developed in the psychiatric ward or the college admissions office will provide the needed illumination in athletic personality work. *It may be time for athletic personality researchers to recognize that the unaccounted for variance characteristic in general personality research constitutes a more important challenge than the duplication of accounted for variance.* The methodological research strategies developed in other areas may be efficiently employed to identify discriminatory personality features in athletics. Once having netted our whale, however, we should seek to expand its meaning in both depth and breadth, and seek to refine its discriminating power in the specific and pertinent realm of athletics.

It seems very unlikely that the measurement instruments designed for the study of general personality structure and dynamics will ever offer more than guideposts for the kind of definitive work demanded by the goals of athletic personality research. What seems needed is concerted effort to develop specific assessment techniques capable of explaining behavior in situations pertinent (and perhaps unique) to athletics. Having established our own measurement operations we can back-track through to establish relationships with general personality assessment techniques. The major shift in strategy will be that low correlations between general tests and our empirically successful specific tests will be viewed as unaccounted for variance in the general standardized tests and not vice-versa.

I am not suggesting abandonment of general personality theory and measurement techniques. I am suggesting that contemporary research strategy almost totally emphasizes use of general personality theory in an attempt to reproduce or verify the presence of accounted for variance in athletic situations. Rather than being satisfied when a general instrument also accounts for some variance in our pertinent athletic situations, our attention should be directed toward the variance for which these instruments fail to account. The development of achievement tests in specific academic areas, for example, extends the accounted for variance beyond that attributable to a general intelligence measure. In the same measure, more intense effort is needed in the area of extending accounted for variance in athletic personality work beyond that provided by general personality assessment techniques. We need to transmute and not merely transfer personality theory to athletic personality research.

It would be expected of me to suggest research topics worthy of execution, and I can at least give you one good example of the kind of change in research strategy I am advocating. For several years now Kenyon at Wisconsin has been at work developing an instrument capable of assessing the multidimensional-structure of attitude toward physical activity. Based upon the idea that physical activity can be reduced to logical subsets by use of "perceived instrumentality" of various classes of physical activity, Kenyon (1968a) has defined six model dimensions of attitude toward physical activity which have survived cross validation rather well. These six dimensions are not reproducible by any metamorphosis of existing personality scales and constitute the unique and specific dimensions of attitude toward physical activity: (1) a social experience; (2) health and fitness; (3) pursuit of vertigo; (4) an aesthetic experience; (5) catharsis; and (6) an ascetic experience. Some consideration has also been given to a seventh, chance.

Kenyon (1968b) has justifiably claimed that adequate assessment of attitude(s) toward physical activity could "aid in the development of a sociopsychological theory of sport." If anything, Kenyon has been most unassuming in forwarding the importance of the implication and potential application of his work in this area. Over and above these potential applications and important returns, however, is the fact that his work represents the first major and concerted effort which has not depended upon use of "standardized" personality instruments for definition of the model domain. Instead, certain variables with established importance in explaining related social phenomena were compared against the instrument developed to assess attitude(s) toward physical activity. Thus, variance represented by the attitude toward physical activity domain has to be accounted for by other general assessment tools. Some may argue this change reflects only a transfer of confusion from one area to the other. If so, at least the amount of reliable knowledge which exists is in our special interest domain and not the other.

Before closing, I want to emphasize once again that I am not advocating abandonment of general personality theory and use of current assessment techniques. We will continue to need application of general personality theory in athletic situations in order to help identify the more promising areas for further work. At the same time, however, I have suggested that such confirmation of general theory should be coupled with equal efforts at new applications and development research. It seems doubtful to me that general personality theory will ever be successful in adequately defining the structure of the areas most pertinent to athletic psychology. The unaccounted for variance in competitive spirit, physical motivation, athletic anxiety, sportsmanship, and competitive stress warrants direct attack. Until such time as we stop the piggy-back rides and change the copy-cat strategy, the bright hope for advances in athletic personality will remain a dim prospect.

Brent Rushall has been responsible for some of the most sophisticated and high-quality research in sport personality. In article 4.6 he reports three such examples of his endeavors. He addressed himself to the questions of personality change as a function of football participation, the relationship between personality and football success, and the possibility of delineating distinct personality characteristics of the football type.

Rushall's findings paralleled those of Werner and Gottheil when he found no personality changes over three seasons of football participation. Personality was also not related to success in football performance, since the personality characteristics of the better-skilled athletes did not differ from those of the lesser-skilled athletes. Furthermore, the football athletes did not differ from the general population in any consistent personality pattern. Therefore Rushall concluded that his data did not support the sport typology concept.

Statistical significance between groups is due in large part to the size of the groups. Rushall suggested that researchers increase the power of their analysis by insisting that statistical differences have practical significance. Findings from his third study reveal the fallacy of considering statistical significance without additional interpretation. Personality information accounted for approximately 17 percent of the between-performance-levels variance and that percentage reached statistical significance. The reader should recall the point that Kroll made earlier concerning accounted-for versus unaccounted-for variance. In Rushall's study although 17 percent reached statistical significance, 83 percent of the variance remained unaccounted for by the personality data. It would be folly to accept significance in such a case but the sport personality literature is replete with such findings.

4.6

Three studies relating personality variables to football performance*

BRENT S. RUSHALL
Dalhousie University, Halifax, Nova Scotia

The purpose of these studies was to investigate the relationship of personality variables to classifications of [American] football performance. The main concerns of the investigations were (1) to locate personality variables which changed as a result of participation in football, (2) to assess their relationship to performance levels and success, and (3) to contemplate the contribution of variance sources to the relationship.

RELATED RESEARCH

Several theoretical models of personality development have postulated the effects of learning as being effected by a specific environment and causing change in personality (Bijou and Baer, 1966; Cattell, 1965). The possibility of personality change exists with consistent participation in collegiate football. Werner and Gottheil (1966) assessed changes in personality with participation in athletics at West Point. They concluded that personality changed little over a four-year period. The assertion that athletics produces change in personality is frequently made. The opinions and postulations that propose a relationship of change in personality through participation in athletics are related by Cattell (1960) and Warburton and Kane (1966). Cratty (1968) stated that certain combinations of personality traits had been shown to be predictive of superior performance in athletic activities.

It is generally contended that personality variables contribute to the discrimination of standards of performance and success in athletic activities. Since football requires physical performance, it could be expected that these assertions hold true for its participants. More specifically, Kroll and Peterson (1965a) found that a number of *Sixteen Personality Factor Questionnaire* (16PF TEST) traits discriminated successful football teams from different environments.

From *International Journal of Sport Psychology* 3(1972):12–24. Reprinted by permission.

*This study was supported by research grants Nos. 30-101-50, 32-103-55, and 30-250-50 of the Indiana University Foundation.

Several studies concerned with the relationship of personality variables to physical performance categories, pool subjects from a number of environments to produce group classifications (Kroll, 1967; Rushall, 1969; Slusher, 1964). In doing this the assumption is made that all environmental effects are equal and that revealed relationships are due only to the independent variables which define each category. Results would be contaminated by differential environmental effects if these assumptions were not true.

STUDY ONE

The purposes of this study were, (1) to assess personality changes which occurred through participation in a university football environment, (2) to relate personality variables to levels of football performance, and (3) to determine what personality variables differentiated successful and unsuccessful football teams.

Procedures

Subjects were members of the 1966, 1967, and 1968 football teams of Indiana University, Bloomington, Indiana. The 16PF TEST form A was used to assess personality at the spring practice prior to each competitive season. . . .

Repeated measures were made on certain members of the squads for two and three year periods to evaluate personality changes during the years of participation. A total of 48 F tests was made to determine the changes. This increased the probability of obtaining a significant result through chance alone. It would have been more appropriate to use a multivariate analytical procedure. However, no multivariate procedure was available at this time which was applicable to repeated measures experiments. Each squad was classified into first, second, and other string categories of performance. The successes of each squad were markedly different. A stepwise multiple discriminant analysis was used to analyze two-group comparisons. A canonical correlation analysis was performed to relate personality factors to the grouping classifications.

Results

. . . Only 50.11 percent of the total variance was accounted for by all the information contained in the 16 personality factors. . . .

No significant canonical correlation was revealed in relating personality to the nine year-level categories. This indicated that no set of personality factors was related to any subset of groups.

The two-way analysis of variance conducted on the 30 individuals participating in the 1966 and 1967 programs revealed only factor C (emotional stability) as being discriminatingly higher in the second year. Factor H (adventurousness) was significantly increased for the 42 participants in the 1967 and 1968 programs. Factor C was significant in differentiating between the years for the 16 individuals who were in the program for the three year span. A Duncan's multiple range test revealed that the 1967 scores were significantly higher than the 1968 scores.

Discussion

The results of assessing change in personality over the three time periods showed that no consistent changes occurred across groups. The members of the three-year analysis were included in each two-year analysis and should have biased results toward compatible findings with the longer period contrast. This did not occur. The changes which occurred appeared to be specific to each group and independent of the common environment. Therefore, football participation did not change personality traits in any notable way.

The 1966 team had a 1–8–1 win, loss, tie record and the 1967 team had a 9–1–0 record, was conference co-champion, and represented the Big Ten Conference at the Rose Bowl. The 1968 team had a 6–4–0 record. The stepwise multiple discriminant analysis did not reveal any personality differences between the first string teams of each year. This indicated that personality was not related to success in football. This finding did not support the conclusions of Kroll and Peterson who contrasted differentially successful teams from different environments.

The lack of consistency of inclusion of factors in significant two-group comparisons indicated that levels of performance in football were not discriminated by personality factors. This was further supported by the failure of the canonical correlation analysis to reveal any significant subset relationships.

The environment in this study was consistent across groups. Some individuals appeared in more than one group, thus introducing the problem of correlated error terms. The sensitivity for detecting significant comparisons was decreased in this analysis. However, given this limitation, the data trends were obvious. The analysis still remained the best available using presently available methods.

STUDY TWO

The purposes of this study were (1) to evaluate the existence of a football player's personality, (2) to assess the relationship between personality variables and football performances classifications, and (3) to consider the universality of this relationship.

Procedures

Five college and six high school football squads were tested with the 16PF TEST form A. A *t* test was performed on the sten scores for each classification to assess the deviation from normal on each personality factor. Normality of distributions and practical and statistical criteria were used to establish the significance of the deviations. Multiple *t* tests of this kind inflated the probability of statistical significance. The practical and distribution criteria tended to decrease the inflation. However, the frequency of occurrence of significant deviations should be contemplated with caution.

The intra-squad classifications for performance were the same as in the first study. The three performance categories were compared with each environment (one high school provided only the first and second string classifications). A stepwise multiple discriminant analysis was used to analyze the two-group comparisons in each environment. A canonical correlation analysis relating performance categories to personality variables was also performed on the data of each squad.

Results

Only five factors appeared with a frequency equal to or greater than chance when considering deviations from normal across all classifications. For the first string high school category, factors E+ (more intelligent) and Q2⁻ (group-dependent) occurred with chance frequencies. The second string high school category had only factor B+ occur with a frequency equal to chance. Factors F+ (surgency) and Q3⁻ (lack of will-power) occurred with chance frequencies in the other string college category.

No factor was evident as being a consistent discriminator between grouping classifications in the stepwise discriminant analysis. No significant canonical correlations were revealed in any analysis.

. . . No factors occurred with any notable frequency in discriminating the first and second string classifications. In discriminating the first and other string performance classifications in high schools, 12 factors occurred with a frequency greater than chance. They were A (sociability), B (intelligence), C (emotional stability), F (surgency), H (adventurousness), I (realism), L (protension), M (bohemianism), N (shrewdness), O (insecurity), Q1 (radicalism), and Q2 (self-sufficiency). Two factors, E (dominance) and F occurred with frequencies greater than chance in discriminating college first and other string classifications. In the other comparisons, no notable frequencies were evident.

In considering the between groups variance accounted for by personality over the replicated environments, the values varied greatly. These values . . . indicated a lack of consistency between environments.

Discussion

The lack of traits which were significantly deviant from normal indicated that no consistent profile of personality factors emerged for any performance classification. This result indicated that no football player's personality existed. Rather, it indicated that those who played football were drawn from a normal sampling of personality types.

In the first string-other string high school comparisons a large number of factors emerged with frequencies greater than chance in the discriminant functions which produced the significant two-group comparisons. These frequencies, although exceeding chance, were not impressive but indicated a possible trend. A similar feature occurred with two factors in the same comparison in college football environments. On further contemplation of the first string-other comparisons, it was found that the discriminant functions of the various environments were not similar in their constituent factors and the numbers of factors included in them. A strict evaluation of these data lead to the conclusion that the discriminant functions which produced the frequencies were not consistent in their make-up, the included factors varied in their loadings between environments, and the functions varied in length. Personality information did not appear to be potentially capable of predicting superior performance in football. The use of a discriminant function of personality information to differentiate levels of performance in football did not appear a feasible pursuit in the light of these data.

The failure of any personality factor to emerge as a consistent discriminator between all levels of performance indicated that personality was not an important factor in football performance. Further support for a lack of relationship was offered by the nonsignificant canonical correlations. No set of personality factors was related to any of the performance classifications indicated.

The percentage of contribution of the personality information to the total variance varied. The trend of the decrease in percentage of accountable variance with increase in sample size, and the between environment fluctuations in this variance supported the assertion of a lack of the relationship under consideration.

The lack of consistency in findings across all environments indicated that each environment was different. Thus, the pooling of subjects from various environments to produce performance categories would contaminate data with differential environmental effects.

STUDY THREE

The purpose of this study was to contemplate the influence of environmental variance and environmental-performance level interaction variance upon studies designed to assess the relationship between personality variables and physical performance categories.

Procedures

The six high schools (N = 282) and five college environments (N = 348) of the previous study and their 16PF TEST results were used in this study. To assess the contemplated influences, a variety of independent groups analyses were conducted using personality factors as dependent variables. A multiple discriminant analysis was used to contrast groups. The analyses were (1) pool environments and contrast the three performance categories, (2) pool performance categories and contrast the environments, and (3) divide the subjects into environments by performance levels categories and contrast the groups. It was possible to reduce the matrices in the discriminant analysis to a U-statistic which indicated the remaining variance after classificatory variance had been removed. This, U was a ratio where

$$U = \frac{\text{remaining within variance}}{\text{total variance}}$$

The value (1-U)100 represented the percentage of between groups variance which was accounted for by the criterion variables. It was possible to combine these indices from each analysis to form a factorial analysis of variance since the variance estimates were based upon a sum of squares analysis. The structure of such an analysis was similar to that of a normal factorial analysis of variance with the one difference being the use of multivariate information as the dependent variable. These analyses were conducted for both high school and college environments.

Results

. . . In the analyses, each method of classification and the interaction of these classifications accounted for a significant proportion of the total between subjects variance.

Discussion

In both high school and college football, personality information and a performance level classification system accounted for a significant proportion of the between subjects variance. This indicated that there was a tendency for personality types to be found in a specific performance category. This tendency was of statistical significance only as the information could account for only 16.68 percent of high school between subjects variance and 17.12 percent of college variance. The analyses indicated that levels of performance in football were differentiated to a trivial degree by personality information.

In both high school and college analyses, the environments and the environment-performance level interactions were significant sources of variance. Personality variables accounted for a greater proportion of between environments variance than between performance levels variance in both high school and college football. This indicated that the samples contained a greater proportion of variance due to environmental phenomena than performance qualities. Further, the significant interaction components in each analysis indicated that the personality tendencies for each performance level varied with each environment. Consequently, because of these findings, the procedure of pooling individuals from different environments for investigative purposes on this topic would be an erroneous procedure.

CONCLUSIONS

The first study showed that participation in football was not related to changes in the personality of football players. Personality was not evidenced as being a significant factor in football performance. Personality factors did not discriminate between performance levels or successful and unsuccessful teams when environment was held constant. The claim that athletics, in this case football, affects personality, was not supported in this study.

The second study showed that a football player personality type did not exist in either high school or college environments. Performance classifications were not consistently differentiated by personality factors. Personality information cannot be used to indicate performance ability or potential in football.

The third study conclusively demonstrated that personality variables were not related to football performance. Environmental effects have a stronger influence on personality than do performance abilities. The procedure of combining subjects from different environments when contemplating personality relationships is incorrect. In such experiments the control of environmental effects must be contemplated.

The three studies showed that personality is not related to football performance. None of the positive assertions about the relationship which exist in the literature could be supported by these data.

SUMMARY

The purpose of these three studies was to investigate the relationship of personality variables to classifications of football performance. In the first study, the football squads of a large university were assessed on the *Sixteen Personality Factor Questionnaire* for three consecutive years. Individuals were assessed as to what changes in their personality occurred with varying lengths of participation in football. The squads were differentiated into three levels of football performance. Changes in personality were not seen as being consequential to participation in the college program. Levels of performance were not differentiated by personality traits nor was success in competition reflected in personality. In the second study, a single investigation designed to evaluate the relationship between personality and football performance categories was replicated in six high schools and five college environments. The data did not support either of two hypotheses. Performance categories were not consistently differentiated by a set of personality factors. No football player's personality was evidenced. Personality information did not appear to be useful for indicating football performance. In the third study, the influence of two sources of variance was considered in relating personality to football performance. It was found that performance levels, environments, and the interaction effects of these two variables, were all significant in their contribution to the total variance.

The importance of between environments variance indicated one important consideration for investigations on this topic. The three studies supported the negation of the existence of a relationship between football performance and personality.

At the 1974 meeting of the North American Society for the Psychology of Sport and Physical Activity, Craig Fisher, Dean Ryan, and Rainer Martens (article 4.7) discussed the present and future status of sport personality research. Fisher concentrated his discussion on the fallacies of personality assessment. He raised an issue that has been mentioned many times before and that concerns the relevance of the questions being asked: "If sport behavior is the concern, then sport questions and situations ought to be the medium for data collection." The fallacy of mediation relates to the causes of behavior. One of Rushall's cautions is directly applicable to this point—be wary of attributing independent variable status to personality. There are undoubtedly many factors that are relevant to the causation of behavior; personality may be the cause, but it need not be. No matter how sophisticated the research designs and statistical analysis may be, the personality data cannot be made more objective than it was in its raw form. To believe otherwise is to fall into the trap called the fallacy of misplaced sophistication. In conclusion, Fisher paints a rather bleak picture of personality assessment unless alterations are made in the way it is pursued.

A major part of Ryan's contribution to the discussion is addressed to the ethics of personality assessment—the uses and abuses of personality data. On the basis of his conclusion that at present sport personality data can only describe groups—and not very well at that—it follows that prediction of the athlete's performance is far from possible. He reports that the literature offers the reader many personality differences among groups of athletes, but the differences are not consistent. In one situation groups may differ on extraversion, whereas in another situation assertiveness may be the discriminator. On several occasions throughout the article, Ryan makes reference to the variance within subjects as contrasted to the variance between subjects. In simplistic terms, although studies reveal variability between groups, there is often as much or more variability within groups, that is, greater variability within groups of athletes or groups of non-athletes than between athletes and non-athletes. When such a finding occurs it breeds little confidence in between-group differences.

Martens provides a synopsis of methodological problems in personality research, namely, (1) the operational definitions of variables, (2) sampling, (3) statistical analyses, and (4) theoretical bases. In his estimation the first three problems can be readily solved but the latter will require a reorientation of premise. For this reason Martens concentrates much of his discussion on the trait, situational, and interactional paradigms. It is clear that the interactional view of personality is the most logical. Fortunately for those interested in the assessment of sport personality, there are several approaches that complement the interactional paradigm. Martens briefly mentions some of these.

4.7

Current status and future direction of personality research related to motor behavior and sport: three panelists' views

4.7.1 *In search of the albatross*

A. CRAIG FISHER
Ithaca College, New York

Before writing the *Rime of the Ancient Mariner,* Coleridge searched for a unifying thread to unite his ideas, something that would provide meaning and insight to his writing endeavors. As Whalley (1969) reported, ". . . the albatross was exactly what Coleridge was looking for. It was a rare species of bird, of exceptional size, solitary, haunting a limited and strange and, for Coleridge, evocative zone, harmless yet by tradition beneficent." It was the right symbol for his purpose.

How does this relate to the subject at hand? The albatross was a good omen to sailors and it was believed to control the weather; in essence then it controlled the navigation scene. In the poem, the mariner shot the albatross and the wind stopped blowing and the sun parched everything. Like the ancient mariner who intentionally committed this dastardly deed, many psychologists have unintentionally muddied the waters of the sea of personality. Even though their intentions were honorable, they have formulated and accepted as truths or partial truths many fallacious concepts.

In search of the key to the understanding of personality, I would like to describe some of these aforementioned fallacies.

THE FALLACY OF SALIENCE

Inconsistencies naturally arise when the behaviors being contrasted and correlated are assumed to be significant and salient for the individual. Of course correlations are low when behaviors formulated in some rather in-

From a panel presentation entitled "Current Status and Future Direction of Personality Research Related to Motor Behavior and Sport" at the North American Society for the Psychology of Sport and Physical Activity convention, Anaheim, Calif., March 1974. Reprinted by permission of authors.

nocuous, uninvolving situations are contrasted with behaviors formulated in salient situations. With such strategies behavior appears to be more whimsical than congruent.

Not all behavior is conscious, cognitive, or salient. Some behavior is peripheral and some is central. Block (1968) claimed that "it is specious to contrast such peripheral behaviors [choosing which theater aisle to walk down, for example] of an individual with the way in which he copes with centrally involving situations such as friendship formation or aggression imposition. . . ."

In a similar vein, I am prepared to claim that some of the questions on the paper-and-pencil personality inventories are not tapping salient areas of the individual's behavior. When one then compares or attempts to predict future sport behavior from these inventories, what chance for success is there?

It is important to seek answers among comparable levels in the behavioral hierarchy if any consistency is sought. A possible hierarchical structure might appear as follows (Holtzman, 1965):

Level 1. Specific response of low referent generality
Level 2. Habitual-response level
Level 3. Trait
Level 4. Type of high generality

You cannot add apples and oranges easily and you will need a lot of ingenuity and magical powers to produce that silk purse out of the sow's ear—these materials are not on the same level.

THE FALLACY OF MEDIATION

Behaviors may not be mediated by the same underlying variables (Block, 1968). The assumption is often made that what you see is what they got; you can be easily fooled if that is your credo. For example, during a basketball game you watch two extremely proficient athletes demonstrate a wide variety of shots and sequences of movements that result in scores. Player No. 1 has spent years developing his repertoire and combinations of movements that you are seeing. On the other hand, player No. 2 may spontaneously exhibit or manifest similar combinations with no less accuracy assuming that he is proficient and your observations validated that precept.

These phenotypically equivalent behaviors are not mediated by similar conditions. Player No. 1's proficiency is mediated by controlled and deliberate development, whereas Player No. 2's proficiency is mediated by his kinesthetic spontaneity. In another situation, where prior practice has little effect, player No. 1's performance is now reduced. The uniqueness of a new defense, for instance, has caused a breakdown in his performance.

In personality assessment of individuals from an observational standpoint, or for that matter any standpoint, you do not always see everything. Under certain conditions even a person highly disposed to aggress will remain overtly inactive; and on the other hand meek and mild Clark Kent turns into Superman. There are extrinsic factors such as role demands and prior experiences impinging upon the individual and these factors complicate the behavioral assessment. If the mediating variables underlying behavior are not considered or analyzed (if possible), then behavior may appear paradoxical. "I want to punch back but I will wait until the official is looking the other way." If the observer only records my initial reaction (non-action) and misses my revenge (action), then he misses the "correct" observation and is befuddled because I have been diagnosed as an aggressive person.

THE FALLACY OF REIFICATION

Our initial observation of behavior is described in terms of adverbs of action—"John behaves aggressively"; and next behavior becomes adjectival—"John has an aggressive disposition." One short step away is the noun—"John has a trait of aggression." The aggressive-appearing behavior has now become reified into a stable characteristic. Reification treats personality variables as if they brought about behavior and obscures their relevance to the situation.

Persons tend to treat their evaluation of others' behaviors as though such evaluations represented real qualities rather than mere value judgments. Personality characteristics are as much a function of the observer as the observed. Jones and Nisbett (1971) summarized the problems associated with reification by delving into the distinction between primary, secondary, and value qualities. Primary qualities, such as bulk, shape, and mass, reside in the object and exist apart from the way one perceives the object. Secondary qualities, such as taste, color, and odor, have no existence apart from an interacting organism. Value qualities, such as beauty and propriety, reside in the observer. Failure to distinguish between primary, secondary, and value qualities is one of the primary reasons for the attribution of personality traits. "We never quite get over our initial belief that funniness is a property of the clown and beauty is in the object."

THE FALLACY OF MISPLACED CONCRETENESS

There is a strong tendency to explain another person's behavior in terms of personal dispositions but to explain one's own behavior in terms of situational variables. It seems rather strange how more multidimensional and complicated our behavior is than that of others. If one person is observed striking another, then he is aggressive. If you see me do it and call me aggressive, I will explain the sequence of events leading up to my overt aggression. It is important for me to provide the situational concomitants so that you will correctly interpret my actions. We realize the variability of our own behavior—our mood, the size of the other guy, who is watching, future repercussions, and the like—but we do not always consider these variables for others' behavior. Because of the lack of information on the part of the observer, faulty interpretations result.

How should one view personality? Should it be viewed in terms of traits? in terms of dispositions? in terms of situation-specificity? or phenomenologically? (Fisher & Ahart, 1973).

Endler (1966, 1969, 1973), Endler and Hunt (1968, 1969), and Endler, Hunt, and Rosenstein (1962) have done much to reveal the proportion of variance attributable to persons, situations, modes of response, persons × situations, persons × modes of response and situations × modes of response. Typically personality traits account for less than 10 percent of behavioral variance in any given situation. The situation alone does little better in accounting for behavioral variance. The question of trait or situation being the greater source of behavioral variance is a pseudo-issue. Endler (1973) said that this question is like asking whether air or blood is more essential to life. A more sensible question is "How do individual differences and situations interact in evoking behavior?"

Cattell (1973), as representative of the trait approach, leans too far along the stability-of-behavior continuum. On the other hand Mischel (1968), as representative of the situational approach, leans too far in the other direction along the same continuum. In the literature, there is only sparse support for the trait approach, but this does not automatically make the situation approach better. The person × situation approach typically accounts for more variance than either person or situation alone.

The Lewinian model of personality ought to receive high marks:

$$B = f(P \times E)$$ [Behavior (B) is a function (f) of the person (P) interacting with the environment (E)

Yinger's (1965) *Principle of Multiple Possibilities* fits very nicely here. A person has many tendencies to behave—some strong and some weak—and each requires a facilitating environment. It is not enough to have knowledge of the individual if prediction is desired, nor is it enough to know the situation. "I know persons who like to play tennis if the weather is perfect, the opponents generous, the partners handsome [or beautiful], and the after-game refreshments plentiful. Others will sweep snow off the court, skip lunch, and play with anyone hardy enough to survive such enthusiasm."

THE FALLACY OF MISPLACED SOPHISTICATION*

It is common for psychologists to apply so-called sophisticated methods of analysis to data hardly warranting such careful attention. It is as if TRUTH will be more forthcoming from manipulating data than looking for it in the real world. The favorite pets are factor analysis, complex analysis of variance designs, the concept of statistical significance, and multiple regression analysis. Dunnette (1966) classified this numerical meandering under a heading called "The Fun We Have." This game has many variants, including "My Model is Nicer than Your Model!," "Computers I Have Slept With!," or the best game of all: "A Difference Doesn't Need to Make a Difference if It's a Real Difference." Others have referred to this practice as staticulation.

What a nice game! You all have experienced the warm glow of statistical significance. How nice to be entertained by the song and dance of the null hypothesis. In reality however, the small r's, t's, and F's do not allow one to predict behavior accurately. Rushall (1971) brought our attention to the idea of practical significance in sport personality research. Does it make much sense to state that the mean difference between aggression of athletes and non-athletes reached statistical significance at the .05 level, when the mean difference is extremely low? What decisions can be made from that information? Skinner (1956) is rather unequivocal in his feelings toward staticulation and predicting performance:

> When you have the responsibility of making absolutely sure that a given organism will engage in a given sort of behavior at a given time, you quickly grow impatient with theories of learning. Principles, hypotheses, theorems, satisfactory proof at the .05 level of significance . . . . nothing could be more irrelevant. No one goes to the circus to see the average dog jump through a hoop significantly oftener than untrained dogs raised under the same circumstances, or to see an elephant demonstrate a principle of behavior.

Perhaps this digression into learning might provide us with a parallel thought for personality.

*Adapted directly from Dunnette (1966).

Edwards and Abbott (1973) speak about the pseudo-sophisticated approach sometimes used in testing a theory:

> The theory is often vague, but that is not necessarily a handicap.
> Theoretically inclined investigators are often able, with the aid of a vague
> theory, to deduce hypotheses that they believe to be relevant to the theory,
> whereas, if the theory were more precise they might not be able to do so.
> In some cases the relevance of the hypothesis to the theory may be apparent
> only to the investigator who formulated the hypothesis.

Upon his return from the jungle of factor analysis, Lykken (1971) states that the factor-analytic model does not meet the structure of nature and that it cannot be relied on to identify either the number or character of the basic personality dimensions. Application of multiple factor analysis in personality research has just not paid off. So the next time you encounter long rows and columns of summary indexes devised by Karl Pearson, remember that the variables are quite arbitrary. There is *nothing* sophisticated statistical analysis can do with arbitrary variables to allow us to draw conclusions about the real world.

THE FALLACY OF TAUTOLOGY

The key terms *personality* and *trait* have been defined in two apparently different ways: in terms of observable patterns of ongoing behavior and in terms of inferred dispositions to behave in patterned ways. Though dispositions refer to future actions and sound somehow more intrinsic to a person than do behavior patterns, the difference is only verbal. To say that a person is disposed to be punctual or that he has been observed to show up promptly time after time amounts to the same thing. A trait, therefore, is a descriptive, not an explanatory concept. The failure to grasp this point exposes us to the dangers of two fallacies—that of *tautology*, or thinking in circles, and that of *reification*. . . . To say that a person is prompt because he has the trait of punctuality is an excellent example of a tautology in which what looks like an explanation adds nothing to the original observation (Janis et al., 1969).

Appropriately we have now come full circle and we are back where we came from. Personality has undergone the explanation of salience, been mediated, reified, misplaced, oversophisticated, and subjected to circular reasoning and still no albatross appears. Where are we now?

MYSTERY OF THE MISSING PROGRESS*

Personality psychology and assessment are struggling through heavy weather. There is no generally accepted paradigm—nothing that is free of challenge and controversy. Little is accomplished, I think, in supplanting traditional paradigms of personality research with social behavior theory as Mischel would have us do. An excessive situational approach to personality leads to errors and, although it has been less obvious, research that studies only inner "traits" also leads to errors. The vital point is that behavior is always situational and personal.

Yinger (1963) postulated a scaling technique to account simultaneously for the situation and the disposition. The likelihood of any behavior occurring is predicted by the product of the value of the "predisposing" factors (located in the individual) and the "precipitating" factors (located in the situation). The point value of each scale can be anywhere from zero to ten. If the predisposal score is high, one would expect to see great behavioral consistency across situations; and if the precipitating score is high, one would expect great behavioral consistency across persons. Therefore the more similar the situation, the more likely it is that the observer will be able to record similar behaviors.

Theoretically, let's set a threshold score of 50 out of 100. This score must be surpassed for the aggressive behavior in which we are interested to be manifested. If the predisposal score were less than five, then the individual would not exhibit the behavior no matter what the situation. A predisposal score of five would indicate that under a precipitation score of 10, the aggressive behavior would be exhibited. If the predisposal score were seven or greater, the aggressive behavior would be more likely to appear. This scaling technique, though stated in simple mathematical terms, theoretically reinforces the earlier statement that behavior is always situational and personal.

There is such a thing as behavioral consistency; there are traits and dispositions. On the other hand, it is erroneous to assume that the case for consistency rests on finding the evidence for these traits. Wallach and Leggett (1972) suggested that "the place to look for consistency . . . is in behaviors and behavioral effects that provide us with inherently meaningful information about people—not in relationships . . . among 'test responses' whose claim to our attention is that they supposedly refer to some hypothetical trait or disposition." They further suggest that a leaf should be taken from the behaviorists and that is "their tendency to choose as objects

*Adapted directly from Hathaway (1972).

of study behaviors which they care about as such, instead of focusing on presumptive signs of hypothetical entities." I think this indicates a clear mandate for those of us interested in various sport behaviors to look for the *specific* aspects in which we are ultimately interested and not assess behavioral or personality dimensions that have peripheral relevance. Psychologists have suffered under the common delusion that gathering data from real people emitting real behaviors in the real world is too difficult, unwieldy, and plain unrewarding. Perhaps it is time to try a humanistic approach and cure our delusions.

We wanted personality information to predict success and non-success, but that dream has never been realized. Personality psychology is almost entirely a descriptive discipline. Why then do we continue to probe?

Kane (1973) acknowledges that our sport personality information at best allows us to describe and not predict but if "we could explain 20 percent of the variance in sports performance by virtue of personal information then I think that the effort would be well worthwhile—and as a matter of fact I think this is about the level that we can expect."

Not only do we have a personality, but also a physique, an anatomy, a physiology, a social role, and status. Why did we ever think that personality would give us a complete predictability index?

Butcher (1972), I'm afraid, provides a very bleak outlook on the whole question. He sees no foreseeable new horizons for personality assessment but neither does he advocate a wholesale evacuation of the apparently sinking ship. By examining drawbacks and limitations of instruments and assumptions (and I would like to stress assumptions), we can make progress.

For those of you who will continue to search for those answers that you deem important, let me leave you with a quotation from Sarason (1966): "An objective study of personality is not for the faint-hearted, nor for the impatient, nor for the person who is uncomfortable with uncertainty. It is much like the young child—developing rapidly, at times clumsy and frustrating, at times remarkably perceptive, fascinating, and promising."

4.7.2　The questions we ask and the decisions we make

E. DEAN RYAN
University of California, Davis

I'm on the panel, not because I'm a personologist or a psychologist who knows a great deal about personality, but rather because I'm concerned with where we, the people in sports psychology, are going in this area of personality. It sounds as if I'm going to talk about where we're going. What I'd really like to do is discuss where we are and where we've been.

There is nothing new in what I have to say—it's been said many times before. I feel strongly, however, that it should be said again. I see big contradictions between the questions we seem to be interested in and the way we're going about answering these questions, and I'm also concerned about how the research we've already done is being used. We've been doing basically the same thing in the area of personality since I started attending research meetings of this kind 10 or 15 years ago. Our basic approach has been to select a subsample that seems to differ from some norm on some dimension—any dimension it seems—then take the easiest or the most convenient personality scale available and see if we can find differences—again, any difference—usually with little or no theoretical basis for making predictions. For example, using the CPI we might compare football linemen with the backs at Cal Tech and conclude on the basis of that study that football linemen are outgoing, more adventuresome, and more extroverted than backs. Or we'll compare people with a high max $\dot{V}O_2$ with those having a low max $\dot{V}O_2$ to see what personality differences there are between the two groups. The scale we use doesn't seem to make any difference, we're just trying to see if there are differences. It isn't surprising that we occasionally find differences between these groups, but by the same reasoning it isn't surprising that on those few occasions when we attempt to replicate a study we usually fail to find the same differences as in the initial attempt.

An old study by Lakie (1962), summarizes this area fairly well. He compared athletes at four different institutions: Stanford; University of California, Berkeley; San Jose State; and Chico State. As we'd suspect, he did find personality differences between different groups of athletes at each of the schools, just as most of the other studies have. The interesting thing was, he didn't find the same differences at any school. For example, at Stanford he might find that the football players differed from the track athletes on some trait, while at Berkeley, the football players and track athletes didn't differ but the tennis players might differ from the wrestlers. Those findings are, in a sense, consistent with most of the findings in our area; that is, lots of differences, but very little pattern.

Cooper (1969), in reviewing the literature, notes that the results are contradictory and somewhat confusing. The second part of Lakie's study seems to give pattern to the whole area. When he combined *all* the football players from *all* the schools and compared them with *all* the basketball players from *all* the schools, and so on, he found no differences between any of the groups.

It would appear quite probable that in most of the studies we've done the differences that have existed are due to the specific sample rather than to some real difference between joggers, or whoever we might be interested in.

There have been a few individuals, most notably Bruce Ogilvie and Tom Tutko, of San Jose State University, who have gone beyond this. They have used a single personality scale and measured large numbers of athletes. Frankly I'm not certain what all of their results have been, but at the very least they have been able to describe what the average professional football player is like, according to the particular personality scale they are using, how the average football player differs from the average race car driver, and so on. The critical question, as far as I'm concerned, is can they do *more* than simply *describe* samples? According to a recent book entitled *The Coach* by Ralph Sabock (1973), Ogilvie and Tutko have identified certain personality traits that *create* high degrees of anxiety among athletes, traits that indicate which athlete can and should take a good scolding and those who cannot, and traits that indicate which athletes need to be left alone or praised.

While Ogilvie's and Tutko's work has been most influential in the area of personality and sport they have not been alone. Other psychologists are making claims that they too can distinguish certain groups of athletes from certain other groups on the basis of personality types. In a recent issue of *The Physician and Sports Medicine*, a Dr. Arnold J. Mandell, who is the team psychiatrist for the San Diego Chargers and Head of the Psychiatry Department, School of Medicine, University of California, San Diego, was quoted as making the following statement:

> Players at different positions show different personality traits. Linebackers are analytical, intelligent, highly controlled. They'll kill you if given permission. Defensive linemen will "kill" also, only just for the fun of it. They are usually sloppy, casual about details. Where defensive ends take pride in their antisocial behavior, defensive tackles get sadistic pleasure in the attack and maintain a satirical "humor."

In another section of this article, he describes wide receivers as

> elegant and vain, highly individualistic and isolated from others. If a wide
> receiver weren't starring on the gridiron he would be on the stage because
> showing off comes easily. Running backs are also loners, but in a more
> sullen way. They are generally withdrawn, angry, antisocial, paranoid,
> and mistrustful, yet they can be playful types (Maddox, 1974).

Doctor Mandell does not say how he measured the personality disposition, how large his sample was, or how much variability there was within
his sample, but he, or at least the author of the article, leads the reader to
believe that there are certain identifiable types that belong in certain positions.

The important question, it seems to me, is can we reliably identify individuals who, for example, are capable of accepting a good scolding on all
occasions, or can we, on the basis of certain personality measures identify
those individuals who will perform in certain predictable ways? Basically,
we are asking the question "can certain personality traits be reliably identified that will enable us to predict how that individual will behave in a wide
variety of settings?" Our behavior as researchers says we believe we can;
otherwise, we wouldn't continue to use the trait scales as we have in the
past. The behavior of the coaches and teachers suggest they also believe
they can. I have heard rumors that the selection of the 7th and 8th men on
the last U.S. Olympic volleyball team was made on the basis of certain personality measures. I know of one boy who was cut from a basketball team
in a small Northwestern college because he scored low on measures of competitiveness in a personality scale.

Again, it seems to me that our concern must be with the validity of our
measures. What does the research say about our ability to predict behavior
when we have only a personality measure? It's difficult to evaluate Ogilvie's
and Tutko's work because for the most part their data are unpublished. We
don't know about the variability within subgroups, that is, whether all people identified as having a certain personality trait behave in the same way or
whether there are some individuals in the group who behave quite differently, even though they all have the same identifiable trait. For example,
will all people identified as aggressive behave aggressively in all situations,
or will we find some people identified as aggressive who behave in a nonaggressive fashion? To the extent that we find these differences in behavior
within groups identified as having certain personality traits, we are in error
in making predictions about individual behavior on the basis of that particular trait.

While we don't know about Ogilvie's and Tutko's work we do know what other psychologists have found. Perhaps it's summarized best in an article by Hunt written in 1965. He says,

> Individual differences have been conceived typically after the fashion of static dimensions and have been called traits. Those who have attempted to measure personality traits however, have all too often found even the reliability and validity coefficients of these measures falling within a range of .2 and .5. If one takes the square of the coefficient of correlation as a rough "rule of thumb" index of the proportion of the variance attributable to persons, it would appear to be limited to somewhere between 4 and 25 percent of the total. This is incredibly small for any source which is considered to be *the* basis of behavioral variation, but we personologists have blamed our instruments rather than our belief in the importance of static dimensional traits.

Hunt's words are echoed in a book by Mischel entitled, *Personality and Assessment* (1968). Mischel says, "The results of trait-state assessments . . . taken collectively, lead to clear conclusions. With the possible exception of intelligence, highly generalized behavioral consistencies have not been demonstrated, and the concept of personality traits as broad response pre-dispositions is thus untenable." Later he says, "The initial assumptions of trait-state theory were logical, inherently plausible, and also consistent with common sense and intuitive impressions about personality. Their real limitation turned out to be empirical—they simply have not been supported adequately."

If it is true that personality traits typically contribute so little in predicting behavior, and it appears certain that this is so, we seem to have at least two major problems. One, the problem for the researcher. The basic research paradigm that we have been using for years in physical education simply is inadequate. We must recognize that personality is far more complex than we have assumed. Some psychologists, such as Mischel, imply there are few if any broad enduring traits, while even Cattell acknowledges the necessity of using individual roles, states, and settings, in addition to traits to predict behavior. We must look for new approaches. We must recognize the influence of environmental factors on performance, or possibly the interaction between environmental variables and personality measures.

I'd like to look now at the second problem I see—the possible abuse and misuse by coaches and teachers of the personality research presently available to us. If, as I mentioned before, a player is screened out of the U.S. Olympic volleyball team because he scored low on a personality test, when in fact that test will not accurately predict an individual's behavior in volley-ball, then we have done a grave injustice to that individual. When we cut a boy from a basketball team because he scores low on a scale of competitive-ness when the score will not predict how good or bad a competitor the individual will be, again we have done an injustice. In this basketball ex-ample, the boy went out for tennis, made the squad, and according to his coach (who didn't know about the personality test) the player won a number of close matches because he "tried so hard."

How can personality tests be used? Are they of any practical value? At the very best, these personality measures *may,* and I emphasize *may,* serve to screen large groups of individuals, and if we measure enough individuals we may find significant differences in performance between groups who score at either end of the scale. Within any such group, however, there is going to be great variability. A good example was presented by L. B. Hendry in a 1970 *Quest* article. He presented the personality profiles of the seven top players on the English international table tennis team, using the 16PFI. Even for this very select group the wide range of scores is apparent. If you happen to be personnel manager for Minnesota Mining, or a recruiter for the army, and want to screen out large groups of individuals who might be poor risks, and don't care if in the process you eliminate many good people, then the personality measures *might* be justified. For example, during World War II through the use of multiple regression, the Air Force developed a battery of 20 tests that were used to select men for various jobs such as pilot or bombardier. The tests repeatedly yielded predictors that correlated between .50 and .60 with passing versus failing the training course. Remem-ber, this accounts for only 25 to 35 percent of the variance. Incidentally, for a test that did reasonably well in predicting men who would complete training, it was totally unable to predict *any* of the criteria of competency under military conditions, such as number of missions completed, number of planes downed, or number of promotions or decorations received (Holt, 1971). In other words, the test was designed specifically for one task. When the task varied slightly, the test was completely unable to predict. If instead of screening large groups of people, with little concern for the large number of individuals who will be improperly classified, you're trying to pick out the *individual* who is best suited for a certain task, personality scales simply won't do it.

Through the use of our present personality results there is an even more insidious chance for abusing individuals. Many are familiar with Rosenthal's work on experimental bias. In one study (Rosenthal and Fode, 1963), the experimenters devised a person-perception task in which 20 photographs of people that had previously been judged neutral with respect to reflecting success or failure were used. The subject's task was to rate each photo along a success–failure continuum. Several experimenters were led to expect high ratings; several expected low ratings. Those experimenters expecting high ratings got significantly higher ratings than those expecting low ratings. Indeed, there was no overlap in the distribution. Even more dramatic was the widely quoted study, *Pygmalion in the Classroom* (Rosenthal and Jacobson, 1968), involving elementary school children in San Francisco. When teachers were given completely fictitious predictions that particular students would make rapid academic progress during the school year, these students did in fact achieve more than those for whom no growth spurts were predicted, even though by the end of the year the teachers had generally forgotten which students had been so classified. In a study cited by Knowles and Prewitt (1969), a computer mistracked slow students into a high-powered curriculum for bright students and fast students into a low-track curriculum for not-so-bright students. When the mistake was discovered a year later, the "slow" students were acting "smart" and the "fast" students were acting "dumb."

The implication of this for work in personality is obvious. To the extent that we or the coach or teacher accept these personality measures as valid predictors of behavior we are apt to misperceive behavior. There are several studies that clearly indicate that we perceive what we are "set" to perceive, and miss much of what else goes on around us. If we are "set" to see some person as a "poor competitor" we are apt to note each instance of his poor competitive behavior and fail to observe the many occasions when he competes very effectively. A sports article by Red Smith in the New York *Herald Tribune* in 1951 (see Hastorf et. al., 1970) points this out in a rather amusing way.

> You see, Steve Ellis is the proprietor of Chico Vejar, who is a highly desirable tract of Stamford, Connecticut, welterweight. Steve is also a radio announcer. Ordinarily, there is no conflict between Ellis the Brain and Ellis the Voice because Steve is an uncommonly substantial lump of meat who can support both halves of a split personality and give away weight on each end without missing it. This time, though, the two Ellises met head-on, with a sickening, rending crash. Steve the Manager sat at ringside in the guise of Steve the Announcer broadcasting a dispassionate, unbiased, objective report of Chico's adventures in the ring. . . . Clear as mountain water, his words came through, winning big for Chico. Winning? Hell, Steve was slaughtering poor Fiore. Watching and listening, you could see

what a valiant effort the reporter was making to remain cool and detached. At the same time you had an illustration of the old, established truth that when anybody with a preference watches a fight, he sees only what he prefers to see. That is always so. That is why, after any fight that doesn't end in a clean knockout, there always are at least a few hoots when the decision is announced. A guy from, say, Billy Graham's neighborhood goes to see Billy fight and he watches Graham all the time. He sees all the punches Billy throws, and hardly any of the punches Billy catches. So it was with Steve. "Fiore feints with a left," he would say, honestly believing that Fiore hadn't caught Chico full on the chops. "Fiore's knees buckle," he said, "and Chico backs away." Steve didn't see the hook that had driven Chico back. . . .

Where does this leave the people doing research and teaching in this area? First, as researchers we must recognize what other psychologists have recognized, that traits as measured by personality tests will by themselves simply not predict behavior in a wide variety of situations. We must change our research approach to reflect this fact. Just as important, we must make the practitioner aware of this fact, so our previous research, and the research of others, is not going to unfairly handicap individuals. Coaches and teachers are very pragmatic people who want to know how they can use our research information *now*. My feeling is, at this stage of our development in the area of personality and performance, we simply don't have the knowledge that will permit the coach or teacher to effectively predict behavior. While it's a very strong statement, I believe that to the extent we let coaches and teachers think we *can* predict behavior, we are being either naive or downright dishonest.

4.7.3 The paradigmatic crises in American sport personology[1]

RAINER MARTENS

University of Illinois, Urbana–Champaign

The non-scientific interest in personality as related to sport has been enthusiastic around the world, but the scientific advances have been disappointing. Locker-room speculations and experiential insights into the "whys" of behavior in sport and the psychic constitution of athletes are interesting and in some cases informative, but of undetermined validity. Students have shown a fascination for the topic "sport psychology," and personality is of prime interest within this area. Students enroll in sport psychology classes to hear the answers to such questions as "Why does one athlete succumb to the pressure of the big game and another athlete excel in this situation?" "Why do so many outstanding athletes act like prima donnas?" "Are weight-lifters really queer?" "Does participation in sports truly develop leadership qualities?" "Does participation in contact sports make a person more hostile? Less hostile?" "Why do "Blacks" excel in certain sports?" "Can female athletes handle the stress of high-level competition?" "Does participation in certain sports as compared to other sports develop a person's self-concept or body image differently?" "Does everyone become as anxious as I do before a big contest?" "Why do I hate to lose so much?" In other words students come to learn about their own inner motives, fantasies, and doubts, as well as their joys and excitements when involved in sports.

What do students hear about personality when they enter sport psychology classes? One of two teaching styles is likely to prevail. The instructor will engage in philosophical speculation and exchange experiential insights with the students, attempting to impart an aura of respectability to his personal observations by institutionalizing them through the educational process. Or the instructor will tell them about personality research methods and theories and about the specific studies which have been done in sport

This section of the panel presentation was published in *Sportwissenschaft* 5(1975):9–24 and is reprinted also by permission of Verlag Karl Hofmann.

[1]Personology is the theory and research in the broad area of personality—the study of individual differences. This investigation was supported in part by a research grant to the Motor and Leisure Behavior Research Laboratory via the Herman M. Adler Center by the Department of Mental Health of the State of Illinois.

personology. The first style is likely to be interesting and entertaining, but no reliable information is conveyed. The second style "turns off" the student for it does not answer his questions. Indeed many are turned off by the seeming triviality and artificiality of most of the research on sport personality. While students are curious about their motives, aspirations, fears, doubts, joys, biases, self-image, and values, they frequently hear about thematic apperception tests, novel motor tasks, anxiety-inducing electric shocks, crafty deceptions, and thousands of Pearson's r's.

The professor of sport psychology has a real dilemma when teaching sport personology. Does he attempt to answer the students' questions knowing full well the information is unreliable or speculative at best? Or does he bore them by telling them about the seemingly inconsequential research that has been done? One alternative has been to try to educate students to the fact that they are asking the wrong questions, and to become educated they must learn to appreciate the perspective of the scientist. But *is* the student asking the wrong questions? Or is it conceivable that students are asking the right questions, but the problem is that sport personologists simply have not been able to answer the questions?

We shall briefly examine the direction that scientific sport personology has taken in the United States, and what this direction has taught us. We shall present a synopsis of the methodological problems in sport personology. Finally, we shall give considerable attention to the controversy raging in American personology about situational versus dispositional approaches in the study of personality, and then suggest some implications for sport personology.

WHY SPORT PERSONOLOGY?

Before attempting to answer the question "Why sport personology?" it will be helpful to answer the question, "What is personality?" Hollander (1967) has stated that personality is "the sum total of an individual's characteristics which make him unique." Allport (1961) perceives personality to be ". . . the dynamic organization within the individual of those psychophysical systems that determine his characteristic behavior and thought." Guilford (1959) defines personality as ". . . a person's unique pattern of traits" and McClelland (1951) describes personality as ". . . the most adequate conceptualization of a person's behavior in all its detail." All these definitions share the view that personality refers to the unique characteristics of the individual. Personality is an abstraction or hypothetical construction from or about behavior. The objective of personality psychology (personology) is to obtain reliable statements about personality or individual differences in order to understand and predict behavior.

We may oversimplify by saying that sport personology functions within the larger goal of personology, but with particular emphasis on understanding and predicting behavior in sport contexts. More realistically, an examination of research in sport personology will reveal that two goals or purposes have been operative.

1. The determination of the role that sport plays in personality development or change.
2. The determination of the influence of personality on sport performance.

More specific objectives for the first goal include answering such questions as "Does athletic participation in general influence the personality of the athlete?" "Does success or failure in sport participation influence the personality?" "Are there critical periods in the person's development in which sport may play a particularly important role in personality development or change?" "Do specific competitive experiences produce changes in the personality of an individual, such as participation in sports in which aggression is likely to occur?" "What attributes of certain sports differentially influence personality development, such as team versus individual sports?"

The second major goal of sport personology research has been attempts to answer the following questions: "Do individuals with different personality characteristics prefer different sports?" "Do various personality profiles determine success in certain sports?" (Or a variation of this question is to ask "Do athletes have different personality profiles from non-athletes?") "Does changing the personality in certain ways, if this is possible, increase the likelihood of success in sport?"

Associated with this question is the attempt to answer the question "What are the unique characteristics of superior athletes?" If the unique characteristics of superior athletes can be identified, then the coach can either select athletes with these characteristics or implement programs that will change the athletes' personalities in conformance with the superior athletes' personalities, resulting in greater success.

Why have these two purposes within sport personology emerged? The first purpose—that of facilitating personality development—has considerable social value. Accomplishing this purpose gives sport an important function in society and has potential therapeutic value. For example, sport psychologists have frequently claimed that participation in sport has the capability of reducing violent behavior or of controlling juvenile delinquency. Unfortunately the evidence to substantiate these claims has not been convincing. The second purpose of sport personology—that of facilitating sport performance—has considerable practical value. Particularly in Western societies, competence, to a degree of incredible excellence, is manifested to no greater extent than in sport. Coaches and athletes alike are always interested in learning ways in which sport performance may be facilitated. If knowledge about the psychic constitution of the individual, or his personality, can improve performance in sport, then this knowledge is of value to them. It should be noted that these two purposes are not totally unrelated. For example, understanding how personality is related to performance may permit the programming of activities to maximize resocialization of juvenile delinquents.

METHODS IN PERSONOLOGY

Thus far we have directed our attention toward what we have been studying in sport personology and why. Now we shall briefly review how we have been studying personality—that is, the approaches that have been taken in studying the personality of the sport participant.

The methods personologists use to study personality are largely determined by the conceptual or theoretical perspectives taken. Personology has been rich with different theoretical frameworks for studying human personality. One long-standing typology has been the nomothetic versus idiographic approaches to the study of personality. The *nomothetic* approach places emphasis on particular personality traits studied in many persons in order to make generalizations about how such traits determine behavior in people in general. The *idiographic* approach places emphasis on the detailed examination of an individual in order that generalizations can be made about the person in a variety of life contexts. Thus the idiographic approach tries to study the whole personality and the nomothetic tries to isolate one or several properties of personality in order to establish general principles of personality functioning.

Following this typology, the measurement of personality can be conceived in two ways: (1) the measurement of individual attributes or dispositions, and (2) the measurement of the whole person with emphasis on integration of the personality. The life history, which is a chronological story of the main facts of a person's life, and the interview are two common techniques for assessing the whole personality. The psychological inventory, which comes in two forms—the objective or structured method and the projective or unstructured method—has been the common method used to assess dispositions or traits. A final method of measuring personality consists of making direct observations of behavior.

All of these methods have advantages and disadvantages. The life history and interview, and in some cases direct observations, are difficult to quantify. Thus the reliability and validity of these methods are difficult to determine. The psychological inventory is more easily quantified, giving it a higher reliability. The validity of the psychological inventory, however, is frequently suspect. It should be apparent then that among the weaknesses of personality research is the difficulty in obtaining valid measures of personality.

Another typology for the methodological approaches to personality was developed by Carlson (1971) and is based upon the observation of Kluckhohn and Murray (1949), who wrote that every man is ". . . like all other men, like some other men, and like no other men." Carlson described the three major methods used in the study of personality as (1) experimental methods ("like all other men"); (2) correlational methods ("like some other men"); and (3) clinical methods ("like no other men"). The characteristics of these three approaches are shown in Table 1.

In reviewing all the research reported in two major personality journals (the *Journal of Personality* and the *Journal of Personality and Social Psychology*) for the year 1968, Carlson found that 57 percent used the experimental method and 43 percent used the correlational method. None reported the use of the clinical method in these two journals. This does not imply, however, that the clinical method is not in use; it merely reflects the methodological bias of these two journals.

What have been the methodological preferences in American *sport* personality research? To answer this question an extensive review of the sport personality literature was made from 1950 through 1973. This literature search identified 202 references to sport and personality. Fifty-three percent of the references were in proceedings or books and 47 percent appeared in journals. The following journals were predominant publishers of this literature: *Research Quarterly, Journal of Motor Behavior, Perceptual and Motor Skills, Journal of Sports Medicine and Physical Fitness, Quest,* and *Medicine and Science in Sports.* Unpublished master's and doctoral theses were not included nor were the many studies that examined the relationship between specific personality characteristics and some aspect of motor behavior or physical fitness. If this literature were included, the number of references

Table 1 Methodological approaches in personology

Experimental (general)	Correlational (differential)	Clinical (individual)
Seeks to discover general laws of human nature	Seeks to discover the differences in psychological processes among different kinds of subjects	Seeks to discover the intricate organization of psychological processes within the unique individual
a. Disregards pre-existing subject variables and uses random assignment to treatment conditions and/or treats subjects' scores as a continuous dimension	a. Seeks to identify group differences on the basis of pre-existing subject variables	a. Extensively studies one or more individuals (case method)
b. Emphasizes situational factors as major sources of variation in human nature	b. Emphasizes intrinsic intrapersonal structures as baselines for further inquiry	b. Seeks to examine organization of psychological processes within the individual
c. De-emphasizes genetic variation and constitutional bases of individuality	c. Emphasizes both genetic variation and cultural determinism as sources of critical differences	c. Uses assessment methods for deriving the intrinsic structure and dynamics of the individual and representing this intrinsic structure
d. Experimentally manipulates independent variables as the source of S variability	d. Seeks natural occurrences of the phenomena under study	d. Identifies general psychological problems emerging from the examination of individual personality
	e. Emphasizes discontinuities	e. Provides a field for testing the formulations derived from general and differential inquiry

would easily triple. Obviously there are investigations reported in other sources that have escaped this literature search. The following summaries should not be considered as complete but more probably as representative.

Some characteristics of the 202 references are presented in Tables 2 and 3. It is interesting to observe that nearly one of every five papers on sport

Table 2 Content of the sport personology literature

	Frequency	Percent
Data-based studies	160	79
Reviews, method, or position papers	42	21
Total	202	100

Table 3 Method used in data-based studies

	Frequency	Percent
Experimental method	16	10
Correlation method	142	89
Clinical method	2	1
Total	160	100

personality is a review, position, or method paper, with most of the 42 papers in this category being review papers. It is clear from Table 3 that the predominant method is the correlation method. Only 10 percent of the data-based studies manipulated some independent variable and observed its influence on some dependent variable. Most of the studies using the experimental method investigated the influence of particular environmental manipulations on subjects differing on such personality dispositions as authoritarianism, aggressiveness, achievement motivation, anxiety, and internal–external control. Very little literature has been published using the clinical method of studying personality in sport.

WHAT IS KNOWN?

The substantive direction, the methodological strategies, and the quantity of research in sport personology have been reviewed. Here we shall examine the quality of this body of research. In other words, what reliable knowledge has been obtained from the millions of dollars spent, the thousands of hours devoted, and the thousands of subjects tested in the study of sport personality? The answer is disappointing. It is nearly impossible to find any consistent results in the literature. Few investigations report reliable evidence and those that do are of questionable validity. Unfortunately, after years of study we know very little about personality as related to sport. Other serious analyses of the sport personology literature have concluded the same thing. For example, Rushall (1972) sees the status of sport personology like this:

> After all the years of research no clear findings are available. Physical education and sports personality researchers are not yet off the ground. It is evident that the investigative process must be restored in new directions, utilizing new techniques and designs, adopting theoretically sound bases for each work, and avoiding all the errors of the past.

Because so little is known but so much research has been done, it should be informative to focus on the problems plaguing sport personality research. Why has this research yielded so little reliable information? Ryan (1968) gives us some indication when he wrote:

> The research in this area has largely been of the "shot gun" variety. By that I mean the investigators grabbed the nearest and most convenient personality test, and the closest sports group, and with little or no theoretical basis for their selection fired into the air to see what they could bring down. It isn't surprising that firing into the air at different times and at different places, and using different ammunition, should result in different findings. In fact it would be surprising if the results weren't contradictory and somewhat confusing.

Three classes of problems can be identified in the sport personality literature. They include conceptual, methodological, and interpretative problems. We shall only briefly review the methodological and interpretative problems, but then devote considerable attention to the conceptual difficulties.

Methodological problems include:

1. The inability to clearly operationalize important variables   For example, what is the distinction between an athlete and a non-athlete or an inferior and superior athlete? To what extent must a sport be organized and to what degree must a person be involved in the sport for a person to be considered an athlete? It is difficult to determine whether athletes differ on personality characteristics if an athlete cannot clearly be distinguished from a non-athlete.

2. Poor sampling procedures The most common error in this category is the sampling of many athletes from one or two teams and then generalizing across many teams. Although 50 football players may be randomly selected from three teams to study the effects of playing football on personality, it must be recognized that any conclusions are based on a sample of only three teams.

3. Inappropriate statistical analyses Two statistical errors that occur frequently are the use of multiple *t* tests when analysis of variance or discriminant function analysis should be used and the use of univariate statistical analysis when multivariate statistical procedures are appropriate.

4. Inappropriate measures of personality dispositions Most sport personality research has used objective inventories to assess personality. The selection of these tests is usually based on convenience to the investigator rather than the underlying conceptual structure of the test. Seldom is a rationale given for using a particular personality inventory. Many scales that have been used for measuring normal athletes were not developed for measuring normality, but for identifying abnormality.

Three interpretative errors are prevalent in the sport personality literature:

1. Inferring causal relationships from correlational evidence.
2. Reporting generalizations unsupported by empirical evidence. For some reason, many reviewers of the sport personality literature have chosen to overlook a particular study's limited scope or its methodological deficiencies. Instead they elect to reach rather profound conclusions that go well beyond the constraints of the data.
3. Clinically assessing personality for the prognosis of success in sport and remediation of personality deficiencies. This problem is isolated to only a few individuals, Bruce Ogilvie and Thomas Tutko being the best known. Ogilvie and Tutko (for example, 1971) have received wide public acclaim through their assertion that they have been able to identify with the Athletic Motivation Inventory unique personality profiles of very successful athletes. On the basis of that assertion they offer for a fee to assess athletes' personalities and from this information to predict success as well as suggest to the coach ways to "handle" an athlete so that the athlete may maximize his potential. This dubious enterprise is unsubstantiated by any reported data by Ogilvie

and Tutko and is clearly inconsistent with the conclusions regarding reliable knowledge reached in this paper. It is painfully obvious that at this time sport personology is not capable of rendering reliable clinical assessment of personality for the purpose of predicting characteristics. A more complete discussion of both methodological and interpretative problems may be found elsewhere (see Kroll, 1970; Martens, 1975; Rushall, 1969; Smith, 1970).

PARADIGMATIC ISSUES IN PERSONOLOGY

The position of this paper has been that the sport personality literature has not provided reliable data or useful generalizations, but this should not be construed to mean that we have not learned anything from this body of research. The first step toward progress in this area is the recognition of previous errors. In the last few years several researchers have addressed themselves to identifying these errors (for example, Rushall, 1972; Ryan, 1968). Although all three classes of errors are important, interpretative and methodological errors appear to be easier to correct. Interpretative errors can simply be eliminated by reviewers or clinicians discontinuing these practices, or by educating the public to their inadequacies. Methodological problems can be corrected by more careful use of sampling and statistical procedures and by keeping abreast of methodological developments in psychology. Perhaps the methodological problem more difficult to resolve will be the assessment of personality dispositions. This problem, however, is closely related to the theoretical or conceptual problems facing not only sport personology but indeed all of personality psychology. Thus we turn our attention in this direction.

"Conceptual problems" refers here to the controversial issues regarding the proper scientific paradigms, orientation, or models used for studying personality and the many theoretical issues that proliferate in the general personology literature. It is not too difficult to summarize what the conceptual problems of sport personology have been. Trait psychology was the first scientific paradigm that evolved for the study of personality. Early sport personologists borrowed the method used to assess personality—measuring traits—from this scientific paradigm, but did not concern themselves with the underlying assumptions of this paradigm or theories related to it. Some 30 years later the situation has not changed substantially. As may be seen by examining the sport personality literature, interest has remained consistently at the descriptive level, with apparently no interest in theoretical or paradigmatical issues. Of course, the neglect of these issues in no small way accounts for the low informational yield obtained from the sizable investment made by sport personologists. If one problem can be identified as the most important issue in sport personology, it is the need for researchers in this area to become aware of the paradigmatic issues and theoretical developments in general personality psychology. Below we shall review the paradigmatic issues in personality psychology and suggest which of these paradigms has the greatest potential for fruition in sport personology.

The term paradigm is used here as defined by Kuhn (1970) to refer to accepted scientific practices that become models from which coherent traditions of scientific research emanate. Two such paradigms have been in rivalry with each other recently in the personality literature. One paradigm is the trait or dispositional approach and the other is the situational approach.

Trait psychology is based on the assumption that personality traits, the fundamental units of personality, are relatively stable, consistent attributes that exert generalized causal effects on behavior. The trait approach considers the general source of behavioral variance to reside within the person, minimizing the role of situational or external environmental factors. Mischel (1968) summarizes the trait approach this way:

> Psychologists who accept the basic assumptions of trait theory believe that the personality is made up of certain definite attributes or traits. They also assume that particular traits, or "mental structures," are common to many people, vary in amount, and can be inferred by measuring their behavioral indicators. . . . Most important, it is widely assumed that traits are relatively stable and enduring predispositions that exert fairly generalized effects on behavior. . . . These predispositions either may be acquired through learning or may be constitutionally or genetically inherent.

A well-known trait typology is extraversion and introversion. These traits emphasize a person's general tendency to respond in an "open" manner or a "closed" manner, without considerable regard for the situation.

The trait approach has also been called the dispositional approach, but the term disposition has been used with another, quite dissimilar meaning. Dispositions have been defined by social psychologists (for example, Hollander, 1967) as a tendency to respond in certain ways dependent upon how the person perceives a particular situation. More recently personality psychologists have labeled this latter meaning of dispositions as the interactional approach to personality. We will consider this interactional paradigm as a viable alternative to the trait and situational paradigms. To avoid confusion, the following labels will identify these three paradigms:

Trait (or dispositional) paradigm   The study of personality by accounting for human behavior largely in terms of traits that exert fairly generalized effects on behavior.

Situational paradigm   The study of personality by accounting for human behavior largely in terms of the situation in which it occurs.

Interactional paradigm   The study of personality by accounting for human behavior in terms of both the person and the situation in which the behavior occurs.

Trait versus situational paradigms

Trait psychology has been pitted directly against situationism by many personality psychologists, or so it would seem. The central assumption of the trait approach is that traits exert widely generalized causal effects on behavior that results in consistencies across situations. This assumption has been attacked by Mischel (1968) and others. They have presented cogent arguments that there is little evidence that trait-determined behavior is consistent across situations, with the exception of some intellective variables. Mischel observes that response patterns even in highly similar situations often fail to be strongly related. It is primarily the inability to show behavioral consistency across situations that has led to the heavy attack on trait psychology.

As an alternative, the situational paradigm attempts to account for behavior largely in terms of the situation in which it occurs. Thus behavior is expected to change from one situation to another, and organismic factors are either ignored or given a subsidiary role. The situational paradigm is exemplified by a Skinnerian model of man and by the social behavior theories. In other words, to explain behavior it is necessary to explain the relationship between environmental stimuli and the responses to these stimuli. The situationist would say that the study of personality is essentially the study of observable behavior.

The situational paradigm has been as heavily criticized as the trait paradigm. The central assumption of situationism is that individuals behave differently across situations and that behavior across subjects in similar situations is minimally different. In a provocative review, Bowers (1973) has compiled an impressive case against the situational paradigm. He points out that considerable evidence shows that behavior is not consistent within situations across subjects. When the experimental method is used, these individual differences within a situation are typically shown as error variance in the statistical analysis. Bowers observes that every time nonsignificant results are obtained in experiments manipulating environmental variables, this is potential evidence that behavior is consistent across situations. Instead nonsignificant results are usually explained away as being due to ineffective environmental manipulations or to other procedural inadequacies. Bowers concludes:

> The fact that a great deal of environmental tinkering is often necessary before clear treatment effects emerge is often shrouded from public view by the nonpublication of negative results. More important, such tinkering, when it is unsuccessful in rejecting the null hypothesis, is seldom taken as evidence regarding the relative stability of behavior across situations. Now, if one wants to argue that behavior is situation-specific, then it must be possible to conclude that it is not situation-specific; otherwise, the assertion that behavior is situation-specific is nonfalsifiable. In other words, if [truly] changed environments can only be inferred from changed behavior, then the potential circularity of the situationist model becomes actual and vicious.

A corollary to this issue then is that the experimental method is particularly sensitive to showing behavioral change, while correlational techniques identify behavioral stability. Correlational methods in psychology have not held the status that experimental methods have. Thus because psychology has been biased toward the use of the experimental method, psychology has been biased toward situationism. Mischel (1968) has criticized trait psychology for its seemingly low correlations (the inimical .30), which account for less than 10 percent of the variance. However, when studies have directly compared the variance of situations to persons, situational factors have frequently accounted for no more than 10 percent of the variance either.

Those studies that have directly compared the percentage of variance accounted for by the situation and the person (trait) provide the strongest evidence to refute the situational paradigm. At least 15 investigations have shown that both situations and persons account for a small percent of the variance. Bowers (1973) reviewed these investigations and reported that the mean total variance accounted for by the person was 12.71 percent and that the mean total variance accounted for by situations was 10.17 percent. Actually these data suggest that neither a trait nor a situational approach is adequate to explain human behavior. Bowers' review of these data indicated that twice as much behavioral variance was explained by the interaction between the situation and the person.

In conclusion, then, both the trait and situational paradigms warrant rejection. Situationism has been an overreaction to trait psychology. Trait psychology reified internal structures to the neglect of the environment, while situationism hailed the environment as the only important source of behavioral variance. A case will be developed below for an interactional paradigm, which has long been called for by social psychologists and behavioral geneticists.

It is interesting to note that although for some reason the trait and situational paradigms have been posed as adversaries, when the positions of many contemporary personologists are examined in depth, few perceive the issue as a simple one of trait psychology versus situationism. Indeed, situationists recognize that the *person* is an important source of behavioral variance and trait psychologists recognize that the *environment* is important in explaining behavior. So what, one might ask, is the controversy? The controversy is more subtle than most of the literature reflects it to be. The trait versus situational paradigms as reviewed above present each position as black and white. Actually both positions are much nearer each other, resulting in some gray.

The difference between these paradigms is the emphasis that is placed on the *cause* of behavior. The trait theorists are inconsistent on what is the cause of behavior. A very few perceive traits to be real internal states that are genetically determined. Most trait theorists view traits as phenotypic—as a function of both genetic and environmental factors. Most trait psychologists have not intended to refute the role of situations—traits alone were not conceived as explaining all behavior. Allport (1937) has written "No single trait—nor all traits together—determine behavior all by themselves. The conditions of the moment are also decisive. . . ." While the trait theorist recognizes the environment as a determinant of behavior, emphasis is placed on the person to *explain* the behavior.

On the other hand, situationists have attempted to account for individual variation in behavior by detailed study of the idiosyncratic conditioning or reinforcement history of the organism. Thus to explain differences in a person's behavior in the same situation, situationists attribute it to "earlier objective differences" in the individual's history. Bowers (1973) sees this explanation as inadequate. He writes:

> This situationist recourse to earlier "objective conditions" is not entirely satisfactory, since at any point in an individual's development yet another appeal to still earlier "objective conditions" is necessary to account for differences he manifests vis-à-vis his peers. The invocation of ever-earlier objective conditions to explain individual differences finally runs head long into a biological or genetic point of view. . . .

This position is not dissimilar to the trait paradigm, since organismic differences are assumed to exist at the very beginning, thus "the situation must be specified in terms of the particular organism experiencing it" (Bowers, 1973). Nevertheless, the situational paradigm, though it recognizes the person as a source of behavioral variance, places emphasis on the environment to explain behavior. The important point is that both of these positions recognized the other as a source of behavioral variance, and thus both dovetail into an interactional paradigm.

Interactional paradigm

Interactionism considers situation and person variables as codeterminants of behavior without specifying either as primary or subsidiary. Instead the primacy of situation and person variables is dependent upon the sample of people studied and the particular situation they are in. The interactional paradigm suggests research designs in which the behavioral effects of environmental and individual-difference variables, and their interactions, are concurrently studied. These designs reduce error variance and help establish construct validity for personality variables. Interactionism then applies treatments not to random samples, but to subjects who differ on theoretically relevant dimensions. These types of designs have been in use to a limited extent in personality psychology, and many of these studies have reported significant Person × Situation interactions. Every study in which significant interactions are obtained between person and situation variables is evidence for the interactional paradigm and evidence against the situational and trait paradigms.

While the person often responds in different ways to certain situations, interactionism recognizes that situations are sometimes a function of the person. Wachtel (1973) has made the astute observation that much of a person's social environment is a manifestation of his own behavior. In other words, people often create environments for themselves that are consistent. Wachtel (1973) asks "how do we understand the man who seems to bring out the bitchy side of whatever women he encounters."

An interesting example of how persons create social environments is seen in the study of competition. Kelley and Stahelski (1970) observed that certain competitors have a tendency to elicit competitive behavior in persons who normally respond cooperatively. In many activities a highly competitive person may so dominate the situation that other normally cooperative persons will be forced to compete in order to survive. Hence a person may frequently display consistent behavior in particular situations, but these situations may be of his own creation. Of course, a person's tendency to do this is indeed a characteristic of his personality.

Little scientific attention has been given to how the person shapes his environment, primarily because of our predominant use of the experimental method, in which the experimenter creates the environment and responses by the subject to change it are considered as "error" or are ignored. For some facets of personality research, it is becoming painfully obvious that the experimental method is less satisfactory than correlational and interactional analyses (in reference to the method and not the paradigm) applied to naturalistic and clinical data. Adelson (1969) observed that hypothesis-testing with tight designs that limit both stimulus conditions and the range of responses is unlikely to be a successful strategy, given the quantitatively underdeveloped state of personality theory.

INTERACTIONISM AND SPORT PERSONOLOGY

The conclusion of this essay for sport personology should be obvious by now: The interactional paradigm is the direction that sport personality research, indeed all personality research, should take. But we again must ask: Have we not known for a long time that neither environment nor organismic variation alone can account for behavior? Has not the nature-nurture controversy long been resolved in psychology? Most of us would answer yes to these questions, yet the positions reviewed in this paper make it clear that nature (trait psychology) is still pitted against nurture (situationism). The differences in these positions, however, are more apparent than real when a close examination of each is made. But recognizing that nature is not opposed to nurture, that person–environment interactions occur, is not the same as coming to grips meaningfully and successfully with the problem of the interaction of organisms and environments. The interactional paradigm is an attempt to come to grips with this problem. [Mischel (1973) and Vale and Vale (1969) are two examples of strategies within the interactional paradigm that attempt to come to grips with this problem.] The sport personologist who adopts the interactional paradigm will have no difficulty in finding personality theories that are complementary to it. A few examples are Rotter's (1954) social learning theory, Heider's (1958) and Festinger's (1957) cognitive consistency and dissonance theories, Schachter's (1959) cognitive theory of emotion, Atkinson's (1957) achievement motivation theory, Kelley's (1967) attribution theory, and Zajonc's (1968) cognitive theory.

The major argument here is that although the interactional paradigm tends to prevail conceptually, much empirical research is based on the trait or situational paradigms. It was noted earlier that general personology has been predominantly situational. In sport personality literature, however, the trait paradigm pervades. The question then is "Will sport personologists follow the path of personality psychology and swing from the trait paradigm to the opposite extreme, the situational paradigm?" Some events within the broad field of sport psychology, including motor learning, may be taken as evidence of a trend toward situationism. For example, the recent publication of a text by Rushall and Siedentop (1972) titled *The Development and Control of Behavior in Sport and Physical Education* develops a Skinnerian application of situationism to sport. Also observe the neglect of individual differences in motor learning research with its total reliance on environmental variables.

Because the interactional paradigm is conceptually unchallenged and is empirically warranted, sport personologists can avoid situationism and proceed directly to the development of interactional paradigms. The determination of behavior in sport environments among different individuals must obviously consider the sport environment and the individual. Thus the first step toward improving the quality of research in sport personology is not the correction of methodological or interpretative errors, although these too must be corrected, but is the adoption of a viable experimental paradigm for studying personality.

In article 4.8, Dean Ryan explores the rather intriguing characteristic of pain tolerance as it might relate to sport involvement and performance. This question is relevant and is an example of the kinds of concerns that need to be explored to shed some light on the confusing relationship between personal characteristics and sport performance. Ryan introduced Petrie's idea that some individuals are augmenters of pain and others are reducers. Intuitively, superior contact-sport athletes might be expected to reduce the painful stimulation that various situations provide. In the latter part of the article, Ryan carries the concept of perceptual augmentation and reduction to other sport concerns.

4.8 Perceptual characteristics of vigorous people

E. DEAN RYAN
University of California, Davis

In a schoolyard a group of boys are playing baseball. A fast pitch is lined to left center field for what appears to be a sure hit. The center fielder, however, somehow anticipating where the ball is headed makes a rather routine catch for the out. In the library of the same school two girls sit quietly studying a history text. Suddenly one of the girls looks up and remarks, "Doesn't that just drive you wild?" The other girl with a look of surprise inquires, "Doesn't what drive me wild?" "That clock. The ticking is so loud that I can't concentrate." The second girl comments that she was completely unaware of any noise made by the clock. In another corner of the library two boys are discussing their impending visit to the dentist. One is quite upset over the prospects because the experience has always been so painful; the second boy is unconcerned because the drilling never bothered him.

These three isolated incidents have two very obvious, but frequently overlooked, points in common. First, perception is involved in practically everything we do. It is difficult to think of any act that doesn't involve perception of some kind. The simplest acts, such as bending over to pick up a ball, or placing a glass on a table, are really quite complex. There must be an obvious coordination between what one perceives and what one does. In the example of the boys playing ball the batter had to see the ball to hit it. The outfielder probably saw the pitcher, knew where the ball was pitched, watched as the batter stepped into the pitch, heard the ball being hit, and finally saw the ball in flight. In the example of the girls in the library it was the sound that was being perceived; in the example of the boys going to the dentist, the perception of pain was remembered.

The second point the three incidents have in common is that although we all may receive the same objective stimulus complex we don't all perceive it the same way. The outfielder, for a variety of reasons, was able to perceive where the ball was going and get to it quicker than most other players. One girl in the library was bothered by the loud ticking of the clock, the other girl was completely oblivious to the noise. To her it simply wasn't loud. The boys visiting the dentist both had the same drill used on their teeth. To one it was a very painful experience, to the other it wasn't.

In all probability each of us is living in a world that is unique to us alone. Although we may all receive the same physical stimuli, each of us perceives it in a different way. For the physical educator the crucial question is whether these differences in perception influence our choice of activities or our performance in them, and if so, how?

One approach to this general area was made by Ryan and Kovacic (1966). They felt that the ability to tolerate pain might be related to the type of activity (or lack of it) that a person engaged in. In many sports, such as football or boxing, the ability to withstand pain would appear to be essential to successful performance, while in sports such as tennis or golf, the ability to withstand pain is probably less important. An individual with a high pain threshold might be oblivious to the bumps and bruises received in a football game; the individual with a low pain threshold might avoid such contact.

To test this hypothesis three groups of male students were selected. One group who participated in contact sports (football, boxing, or wrestling) during college, a second group had participated in noncontact sports only, such as tennis or golf, and a third group had not participated in varsity athletics of any kind.

Three methods were used to deliver controlled pain. Radiant heat was used to measure the pain threshold, that is, when pain was first noticed, and two other methods were used to measure how much pain the subject was willing to endure. The first, gross pressure, was assumed to be representative of the bumps and bruises received in body contact, and the second, muscle ischemia, was assumed to be representative of the pain associated with severe muscle fatigue.

There were no differences between the groups in pain threshold. They all perceived the sensation of pain at approximately the same point. There were, however, significant differences in how much pain the three groups were willing to tolerate. For both measures of pain endurance the group composed of contact athletes tolerated the most pain, the nonathletes tolerated least, and the noncontact athletes fell between. After each subject had received the first pain trial the experimenter commented that the subject's score was quite a bit lower than the average of the group tested, and the subject was asked to take the test a second time. This was done regardless of the subject's actual score. The contact athletes made marked improvement

433

on the second attempt, the noncontact athletes improved some, but the non-athletes actually tolerated less pain than on the first attempt. These results clearly indicate that there is a relationship between differences in perception and the type of activity in which a boy chooses to participate.

The question of cause and effect—whether a boy learns to tolerate pain because he engages in contact sports, whether he engages in contact sports because he can more easily tolerate pain (either for physiological or psychological reasons), or whether the two covary with a third but unexplored source—is, of course, unanswered by these data. It has been suggested that pain threshold is associated with physiological components. If this is true, then the results of this experiment suggest that differences between activity groups are psychological in nature and probably the result of cultural or environmental influences. There are, however, a number of possible explanations for these results, some with a psychological slant, others more physiological in nature, but all capable of at least partially explaining the differences found in this study.

Zborowski (1952) has suggested that two culturally determined attitudes, pain expectancy and pain acceptance, are important to differences in pain response. Pain expectancy is the anticipation that pain is unavoidable in a given situation. Pain acceptance is characterized by a willingness to experience pain. As an example, labor pain is generally expected as part of childbirth in all cultures. In some cultures, the pain is not accepted and various means are used to alleviate it, but in others pain is accepted, and little or nothing is done to relieve it. It may be that the differences found in the study of athletic participation are due to differences in pain acceptance. The contact athletes, and to a lesser extent the noncontact athletes, have frequently been in situations where pain is unavoidable. Through parental or peer pressure it is possible that the ability to tolerate pain has been associated with "manliness" by the athlete and as such is socially valued. The nonathletes, on the other hand, have much less often been in situations where pain is unavoidable and thus have not associated the ability to tolerate pain with socially desirable traits or characteristics.

Another possibility may be that because of repeated experiences with pain, the contact athlete will be more realistic in his evaluation of the significance of pain and thus will fear pain less than the nonathlete. It has been pointed out that the significance of the pain experience is important in determining how "painful" the experience appears to be. An ache beneath the sternum, since it suggests the possibility of sudden death from heart failure can be a wholly upsetting experience, but the same intensity and duration of ache in a finger is a trivial annoyance and is easily disregarded (Beecher,

1959). It is possible that contact athletes, having had previous experience with the two types of pain used in the test, were fully aware that the pain experienced was not of a harmful nature. The nonathletes, because of little experience with this type of pain, had no way of knowing whether or not the cleat used in the experiment might break a bone or puncture the skin. The differences on the second trial can be explained the same way. The contact athlete, having experienced the initial pain, would have some reference point from previous experience and be aware that the stimulus was not going to do physical damage. The nonathlete, on the other hand, having had limited experience with painful stimulation, would be less apt to know how serious the pain actually was, and thus, due to apprehension, tolerate less on the second trial.

The most intriguing explanation, however, is that the relationship between pain and type of athletic activity might have been due to differences in a general perceptual characteristic of "augmenting" or "reducing" sensory inputs. It has been demonstrated that certain individuals appear to consistently reduce the intensity of their perceptions while others tend to consistently augment the intensity of perception (Petrie, 1960). Pain and suffering are related to these contrasted perceptual types. Those who reduce the intensity of perception tolerate pain well, those who augment tolerate pain poorly. Those individuals who tend to consistently reduce have been shown to be more extraverted than those who augment, less tolerant of sensory deprivation, more mesomorphic, and to judge time as passing more slowly than augmenters. Significantly more reducers were found in a delinquent group and significantly fewer augmenters than would be expected by chance.

All of the characteristics of the reducer, tolerance of pain, intolerance of sensory deprivation, mesomorphy, extraversion, and to an extent the characteristics of the delinquent, have frequently been associated with athletic groups. If indeed, the reducers suffer from lack of stimulation as suggested by Petrie, then they would need change, movement, speed, and possibly body contact, rather than more sedentary pursuits.

To test this hypothesis a second experiment was conducted. It was hypothesized that groups participating in contact sports would possess the perceptual pattern of the reducer and thus reduce most in their estimation of kinesthetically perceived size, have faster reaction times, faster movement times, judge time as passing more slowly, and would tolerate most pain. Groups not interested in athletics would possess the perceptual characteristics of the augmenter, and thus reduce less in their estimation of kinesthetically perceived size, have slower reaction times, slower movement times, judge time as passing faster, and tolerate less pain. Groups participating in noncontact sports would tend to fall between the other two groups on all tests.

A questionnaire was administered to a group of high school students. They were asked their likes, dislikes, hobbies, and recreational pursuits. On the basis of their answers three groups of subjects were selected. Group I was composed of boys who expressed a liking for contact athletics and were at the same time actually participating in contact sports (football or wrestling). Group II was composed of boys who expressed an interest in noncontact sports and were also participating only in noncontact sports (golf, tennis, track), and Group III was composed of boys who had expressed a dislike for athletics and were inactive as far as sports were concerned. The subjects assumed they had been randomly selected and were unaware that athletic participation was a factor.

The subjects were tested on simple reaction time, movement time, pain tolerance, time estimation, and augmentation and reduction as measured by the change in kinesthetically perceived size. The results are summarized in Table 1. There were significant differences between groups on all tests except reaction time and movement time, with the group composed of contact athletes tolerating most pain, underestimating time, and reducing subjective estimation of kinesthetically perceived size. The group of nonathletes tolerated least pain, overestimated time, and had a tendency to enlarge subjective judgment of width on the kinesthetic test. The noncontact athletes fell between the other two groups on all tests.

The study clearly supports Petrie's theory of a generalized tendency for certain individuals to consistently reduce or diminish their perception of stimulation and for others to consistently augment or enlarge perception. Further, the study indicates that the type of activity an individual chooses

Table 1 Mean scores for athletic subgroups

Task	Contact athlete	Noncontact athlete	Nonathlete
Reaction Time	0.201 sec.	0.208 sec.	0.213 sec.
Movement Time	0.117 sec	0.123 sec.	0.117 sec.
Time EST (120 sec.)	103.6 sec.	119.1 sec.	122.3 sec.
Time EST (20 sec.)	18.3 sec.	20.7 sec.	21.5 sec.
Pain Tolerance	285.75 mm/Hg	231.00 mm/Hg	207.50 mm/Hg
Change/Kinesthetic Size	−0.258 in.	−0.212 in.	−0.095 in.

to participate in is related to his perceptual type. The contact athlete displayed the characteristics of the reducer making the greatest subjective reduction of kinesthetically perceived size after stimulation, tolerating most pain, and consistently judging time as passing more slowly than did groups composed of noncontact athletes or nonathletes.

Differences in pain tolerance could be explained by simply assuming that contact athletes were more motivated to withstand pain, although it would be difficult to explain why motivation of the two athletic groups would differ. Further, time estimation and estimation of kinesthetically perceived size are less amenable to changes in motivation. No amount of conscious effort should induce a naive subject to vary time or kinesthetic sensitivity in one direction or another.

We have mentioned augmentation and reduction and the work of Petrie as it related to the study of athletic participation, but now let us examine the work of Petrie and her associates more closely. What is it that is being investigated, and what are the major findings? Finally, does the theory provide a basis for further work in areas related to physical education and athletics, and to education in general?

Petrie's original interest was in the control of pain and suffering. She observed that when patients suffering from severe pain had a prefrontal lobotomy to relieve the pain certain personality characteristics were changed. Surgery to the prefrontal areas of the brain so increased the tolerance for pain that the patient could sleep without pain and wake without moaning. The source of pain had not been dealt with, nor had the threshold for pain been altered, instead the person experiencing the pain had been altered. The patient appeared more extraverted, more tolerant of pain, and less tolerant of sensory deprivation.

Her work in this area indicates that a normal person—one without prefrontal lobotomy—who is exceptionally tolerant of pain has the personality and perceptual style of the individual after prefrontal lobotomy, whereas one who cannot tolerate pain resembles in personality a patient before prefrontal lobotomy.

On the basis of her work Petrie has identified three perceptual types. First, the reducer, who is tolerant of suffering and who tends subjectively to decrease what he perceives. Second, the augmenter who is just the opposite of the reducer. The augmenter tends to be intolerant of pain and to subjectively increase what he perceives. Finally the moderate who alters only slightly what he perceives.

Augmentation and reduction have been estimated by measuring the change in kinesthetically perceived size after stimulation. Subjects are blindfolded and feel with the thumb and forefinger of the right hand a standard wooden bar. At the same time, with the thumb and forefinger of the opposite hand they feel a long tapered wooden bar and attempt to locate an area that seems as wide as the test bar. A larger (or smaller) test block is then rubbed. Thereafter, the original test bar is again equated with the tapered bar, and the difference between the two subjective estimations is computed. At the end of the period of rubbing, the test bar is usually perceived by the extreme reducer as being about halved in size, by the extreme augmenter as about doubled. The augmenter enlarges the estimated size of the block after stimulation with both a larger and a smaller test block. The reverse is true for the reducer, who decreases in both cases.

There would seem to be accumulating evidence that what is being measured kinesthetically is one aspect of the generalized tendency for the reducer to diminish the perception of all stimulation and for the augmenter to enlarge it—two contrasting processes manifesting themselves in persons with different personality characteristics.

As mentioned, the reducers tolerate pain well, the augmenters poorly, and the moderates fall between these two extremes. This has been shown to be true of the experimental pain of heat, muscle ischemia, and pressure as well as the pain of surgery and the pain of childbirth (Petrie, 1960).

If the reducers' tolerance for pain is partially due to their tendency to diminish the intensity of stimulation they receive from the environment, then that tendency should become a handicap in a situation where there is a sparsity of stimulation. To test this hypothesis a number of subjects were placed in tank-type respirators where stimulation was at a minimum. The augmenters, as measured by kinesthetic sensitivity, tolerated starvation of sensation better than did the reducers, as measured by their willingness to remain in the tank significantly longer than the reducers (Petrie, Collins, and Soloman, 1960).

This difference is exactly the reverse of the behavior of these two types under stress of pain.

In studying a group of young delinquents (Petrie, McCulloch, and Kazdin, 1962) it was found that there were significantly more reducers among the delinquents than would be expected by chance, and significantly fewer augmenters. In addition reducers have been shown to be more mesomorphic (Wertheimer, 1965), to judge time as passing more slowly than the augmenters (Petrie, 1960), and to be more extraverted (Petrie, 1960). Further, there is some indication of a sex difference with the males leaning more toward the reducing end of the scale and the females more toward the augmenting end (Petrie, Collins, and Soloman, 1960).

Recently a list of 150 adjectives were given to a small group of high school students. They were asked to check those adjectives that they felt most closely described themselves. Thereafter, those adjectives checked by reducers in the group were compared to the adjectives checked by the augmenters. The reducers described themselves as: alert, cautious, clear-thinking, conscientious, dependable, determined, dreamy, efficient, enthusiastic, impatient, individualistic, industrious, intelligent, leisurely, modest, obliging, organized, practical, precise, quick, relaxed, self-confident, and tactful. The augmenters described themselves as: bossy, careless, imaginative, logical, loud, sensitive, and serious. The total number of adjectives checked appeared to differ between the two groups, with the reducers checking approximately 20 per cent more adjectives than the augmenters. An individual checking a great number of adjectives has been described as emotional, adventurous, wholesome, conservative, enthusiastic, frank, and helpful. He is active, apparently means well, but tends to blunder. The individual checking few adjectives tends more often to be quiet and reserved, more tentative and cautious in his approach to problems, and perhaps at times unduly taciturn and aloof. He is more apt to think originally and inventively, but is perhaps less effective in getting things done (Gough and Heilbrun, 1965). These results should be viewed with some skepticism, since the sample size was quite small. Nevertheless, the results are interesting, since the augmenters and reducers describe themselves in much the same way as would be predicted from studies cited earlier.

Although Petrie's work encompasses over 10 years of research the theory is still in the formative stages. Much of what has been covered in this discussion has been oversimplified for the purpose of explanation and clarification. Much more basic research must be done before we have a complete picture of the typical reducer and augmenter.

How is this theory related to athletics, physical education, and education in general? In spite of the fact that the concept of perceptual augmentation and reduction is incomplete, there are many fascinating avenues for the physical educator. We have already seen that the contact athlete tends to be a reducer and the nonathlete an augmenter. Where do we go from here?

Again for clarification let us oversimplify the picture. At the elementary or junior high school level the reducer would tend to be male, extraverted, loud (whether he sees himself this way or not), unable to sit in one place too long, always going to get a drink or go to the toilet, often poking the person in front or back of him, and unable to concentrate or pay attention for extended periods of time. The augmenter, on the other hand, is more apt to be female, introverted, quiet, able to concentrate and pay attention. All of us have seen these types in our work with children. These descriptions lead to a number of predictions. First, in the typical classroom the young reducer would appear to be at a decided disadvantage. Here is a person who reduces all stimulation. He is placed in a setting where stimulation is typically at a minimum. Further reduction of the already minimal stimulation would be expected to be uncomfortable. Remember, the reducer could stand less confinement than the augmenter. Thus we would predict that the reducer would need to seek additional stimulation of one kind or another. For this reason we would expect the reducer to be more of a behavior problem, at least in the younger years, and we would expect his academic achievement to be less than it should be in relation to his ability. In other words we would expect the reducer to be an underachiever. Whether this is actually so is open to question. There have been no studies in this area. We do know, however, that among both delinquents and athletes there are more reducers than you would expect by chance. Perhaps the reducers, lacking stimulation, have turned toward either athletics or delinquency for additional stimulation. The education of both the reducer and augmenter should take into consideration both their vulnerabilities and strengths. It is quite possible that the test of kinesthetic sensitivity might be an excellent screening device in the counseling and understanding of children.

This same reasoning brings us to a second point—the similarity between the delinquent and the athlete. Perhaps both groups have the same basic need. Perhaps through more varied programs of physical education activities we can head off the potential delinquent, enabling him to get the needed stimulation in a desirable way. Petrie (Petrie, McCulloch and Kazdin, 1962), in discussing the delinquent, states,

> We suggest that the education of such delinquents and predelinquents needs to make allowance for their vulnerabilities and strengths. They need change, movement, and speed, actual rather than "symbolic" instruction, bright colors, music, and company. The fact that many of these "delinquent" youngsters come from deprived homes means that their needs are even greater than the needs of a similar perceptual type, youngsters who are fortunate enough to have swimming, rowing, traveling, club activity, and the like as part of their birthright.

There is still another possible implication for physical education. Can the pattern of the reducer be temporarily changed through physical activity? It has been suggested that stimulation in one sense modality can influence performance in other sense modalities. What would the effect of physical stimulation be on the reducer and the augmenter? Would activity temporarily relieve the reducer's need for stimulation or would it make him more of a reducer? What about the augmenter? Again there is no research on this subject. There is, however, a study that may give us a clue. An experiment was conducted to determine the effect of audioanalgesia on kinesthetic augmentation and reduction (Petrie, Holland and Wolk, 1963). Audioanalgesia is a recently developed method of trying to increase tolerance for pain by exposing the patient at the time of his pain to stimulation with sound. Audioanalgesia had a marked influence on the augmenter, making him more like a reducer. There appeared to be a slight change in the reducer toward the augmentation end of the scale. The change, however, was not significant.

Another basic question that may have implications for physical education centers around the problem of exactly what is reduced. Let us look at several examples for clarification. It has been written that occasionally musicians, particularly drummers, will take narcotics because the musician says that he feels as if he were floating in air. Everything, including the individual, seems to be moving very slowly. Because everything seems to be moving so slowly apparently the person is able to react more rapidly than would be possible without the drug. Suppose the same thing happened in athletics. If a ball appeared to be coming toward home plate very slowly, would we be better able to hit it? As the ball was hit, if it appeared to move very slowly would we, as outfielders, be able to get to it faster? Could it be that some individuals actually see motion as being slower than the average person? Could this be one of the reasons why some athletes seem to consistently get the jump on the opponents? Could it be that the reducer actually reduces the speed of objects around him? If so, we would expect him to be able to react faster than the moderate or the augmenter. Still another question can be asked. Can we, through stimulation, temporarily change our perception of speed? Common sense says we can. If we look at a pitch thrown from 50 feet away for a few times, what will happen when the pitcher moves back to his regular distance? We would expect the ball to appear to move slower than it did, thus giving the hitter a better chance to hit. Will the results be the same for both augmenters and reducers?

There are a number of points that complicate our discussion of speed. Our perception of how fast an object is moving depends on the background, or the "field" that surrounds the objects. Imagine yourself standing on top of the Empire State Building. As you look down you see tiny cars moving very slowly along the street. In this example you have a very small object against a very large background or field. If you are standing on the street corner, however, the cars would seem to zip by at a very rapid rate. Here the object is very large in relation to the field or background.

At this time we don't know what the augmenter is augmenting. The same is true of the reducers. Does the reducer diminish the size of the field in relation to the object being judged? If so, reduction would seem to be a disadvantage. On the other hand, if everything is reduced, both the moving object and the background, then reduction would seem to be an advantage. If the object being judged is reduced and the background is not influenced, then again reduction would be advantageous.

Some people have commented that when Petrie describes the augmenter and the reducer she is simply describing the introvert and the extravert. To an extent this is true. Petrie's contribution, however, is in suggesting *why* people behave as they do. The reason the individual tolerates pain or is intolerant of sensory deprivation is, Petrie suggests, because of his perceptual characteristics. He is either increasing or decreasing the intensity of stimulation. With this knowledge we are in a position to better understand and predict behavior.

Much of the discussion, including the reasons for and possible consequences of augmenting and reducing stimulation, is pure speculation based on little more than wild guesses. There has been, as yet, too little basic research in the area to allow us to say with reasonable certainty just what we can actually expect. With the little evidence that is available, however, the concept of augmentation and reduction as a general perceptual characteristic does appear to have implications for physical education and athletics.

While the emphasis in this chapter has been on perceptual augmentation and reduction it should be understood that this is only one small aspect of perception. There are unlimited opportunities for research in the area.

Recently Ryan and Lakie, in an unpublished study, investigated the reaction times and movement times of baseball players as contrasted to people who had not played baseball. The statement had been made that the reason some ball players "get the jump" on a ball hit in their direction was because they had faster reactions. For a number of reasons this didn't appear to be the answer to the investigators. Two groups of subjects were selected, one group composed of subjects who had played baseball in high school or college, the second group composed of subjects who reported that they did not play baseball. Their reaction times and movement times were tested under three different conditions. A timer was constructed that could be activated by either light or sound. In the first testing situation, when a red light, located on the left of a display panel, was lighted, the subject would strike a red button located on the left of a switch panel. When a green light, located in the middle of the display panel, was lighted, the subject would strike a green button located in the middle of the switch panel, and when a yellow light, located on the right of the display panel, was lighted, the subjects would strike a yellow button on the right of the switch panel. When the lights came on two clocks were activated. One would measure how long it took the subject to start after the light signal (reaction time) and the second clock would measure how long it took the subject to move to the switch once he had reacted (movement time). In this condition, sometimes called a test of disjunctive reaction time, there was no difference between the two groups of subjects in reaction time or movement.

In the second condition a gun was constructed to fire a plastic missile. When the missile was fired to the subject's left he would strike the red button on the left of the switch panel. When the missile was fired directly at the subject he would strike the green button in the middle of the switch panel, and when the missile was fired to his right he would strike the yellow button on the right of the panel. The noise of the missile being fired activated the timers, and as before, the clocks were stopped when the appropriate button was touched. In this second condition again there was no difference between the two groups on reaction time or movement time.

In the third condition a rubber batting tee was placed in the middle of a large gym. A batter would hit a tennis ball off the tee to the left of the subject, to his right, or directly at him. As before the subject would respond by striking the appropriate button. The sound of the bat activated the clocks which were stopped as the subject hit the appropriate switch. The batter was instructed to stand flat footed (not to step into the ball) and do all he could to prevent subjects from guessing where the ball would be hit. There was a significant difference between the two groups in reaction time, with the baseball players reacting faster than the non-baseball-players. In fact some of the baseball players were reacting in 70 to 80 milliseconds. For simple reaction time to sound, that is, reaction time when no choice of movement has to be made, the average time for an adult to react is approximately 140 milliseconds. For a choice situation we would expect that time to increase considerably. Thus, the reaction time of 70 to 80 milliseconds indicates that subjects were actually starting to react before the ball was hit. When questioned after the experiment none of the subjects were aware of clues that would permit them to react before the ball was hit. They reported that they were unable to guess where the ball was going before it was hit. In spite of the fact that they could report no clues, it is obvious from their reaction times that they were picking up information. Unfortunately, the study sheds no light on the question of what the baseball players were seeing that the nonbaseballers weren't. It seems clear, however, that it is a perceptual process of some kind that accounts for the increased speed rather than the baseball players simply being inherently faster.

Would it be possible to train people to "see" faster? During World War II tachistoscopic training was used to improve observers' ability to identify aircraft. Pictures of airplanes or ships were flashed on a screen at 0.01 second. Frequently, the people were unable to see anything on the first exposure. After training, however, observers could tell how many aircraft were in a flight, and what type of plane was pictured. After the war this same technique was used to improve reading skill. Words or groups of words were flashed on the screen, and the reader was forced to read larger blocks of material. Could tachistoscope training be used to increase the perceptual ability of a hitter, or a fielder, or a tennis player at the net? An experiment to determine the value of such a process would be very easy to design and conduct, and if the results were positive the technique would prove most valuable in a practical sense.

Tachistoscopic training has already been used in an effort to improve the perceptual ability of football players (Damron, 1955). Although the results of the study were inconclusive because there was no control group, it would appear that the ability to recognize fundamental football defenses quickly is improved through the tachistoscopic training. The same technique might be used to train passers to spot receivers downfield.

Another question seems appropriate. Is peripheral vision related to perception of speed? In our earlier discussion of speed we stated that it seems reasonable to assume that perceived speed depends on the relationship between the moving object and the background that it is moving across. If the background is large in relation to the size of the moving object, speed would seem relatively slow, while the reverse would be true if the moving object were large in relation to the background. The individual with a wide field of vision would be expected to perceive speed differently from an individual with "tunnel vision." Are individual differences in peripheral vision related to perception of speed? If so, are these differences great enough to be of practical value in athletics? If so, can we increase peripheral vision?

Many of the suggestions in this chapter are rather superficial. Even if we knew the answers performances might not be influenced a great deal. Some of the suggestions and questions raised, however, are important from both a theoretical and a practical standpoint. Of one thing we can be certain. Perception plays an extremely important part in behavior, and an understanding of its influence on man in action is essential.

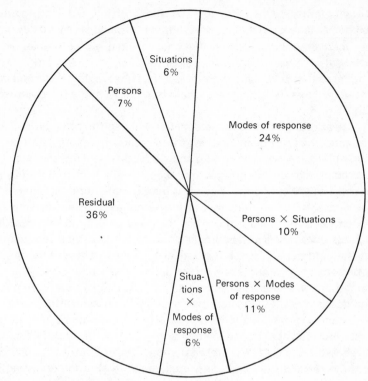

Figure 1 Partition of total behavioral variance*

*Adapted from Endler, N.S.S., and J. McV. Hunt. "Sources of Behavioral Variance as Measured by the S–R Inventory of Anxiousness," *Psychological Bulletin*, 65:336–346, 1966.

Most sport personality investigations have used the trait approach and unfortunately this trend continues, even in light of very damaging evidence. Too few individuals have seriously internalized Holtzman's question about how much information we need about another to adequately assess his behavior. Several of the articles in this section mention the issue of accounted-for versus unaccounted-for variance. Figure 1 should help clarify this question as well as provide a comparative glimpse of the trait, situational, and interactional approaches to personality assessment.

It is readily seen that person and situational variance account for little of the total behavioral variance. The remaining unaccounted-for variance is large (87 percent). Combinations of interactions provide a larger percentage of variance than either the person or situation variance. One cannot help noticing the largest single source of variation—the residual, which is interpreted as error variance. This paradigm is most damaging to trait psychology, and it is hoped that more people will consider the facts before setting future research courses that are doomed to failure.

The relationship between personality and sport participation and performance has not been what was anticipated by many researchers. Many of the premises concerning the possibility that personality data could differentiate sport groups and success within a group have not been consistently supported. I suspect the ultimate hope for personality assessment lies in the prediction of future behavior. This certainly has not been realized; indeed, there are those who contend that research endeavors thus far have failed even to describe behavior adequately.

It is time to depart from the practice of using all-encompassing general personality inventories to make inferences about individuals in athletic situations. There certainly is a large enough gap between paper-and-pencil inventories and real personalities without confounding the issue by altering the situational perspective. The atomistic view of personality must be abandoned. In addition, only sport-relevant characteristics should be assessed. Surely intuition tells us that it is fruitless to attempt to relate such a factor as intelligence to sporting achievement when there are so many reasons for sport success. There is little doubt that a new approach is needed in assessing sport personality.

Glossary

Adrenocortical   Pertaining to the interaction of the adrenal glands and cerebral cortex.

Analysis of variance   A statistical test of difference among two or more means simultaneously. The sum of squares is partitioned into known components of variation.

Assertive   Forceful or bold.

Attenuation   The unreliability of the correlation between variables.

Canonical correlation   The maximum correlation between a set of predictor variables and a set of criterion variables.

Cognition   The mental process by which knowledge is acquired.

Correlation   A measure of the degree of relationship between two sets of measures. The relationship can be in either a positive or a negative direction.

Criterion   In psychological testing, an external standard to which test results can be compared to determine a test's validity (its ability to measure what it is supposed to measure).

Dependent variable   The factor that has been affected by some other factor(s). This is the factor that the experimenter measures.

Desensitization   A technique that reduces one's susceptibility to a sensitizing or activating agent.

Determinants   Influencing or determining factors.

Dichotomy   Division into two presumably opposing components, poles, or forces, as in "mind/body dichotomy."

Discrete   Distinct or consisting of separate parts.

Displacement   A defense mechanism consisting of turning one's aggression toward a safe target when the real object of that aggression is too threatening.

Energy mobilization   Gathering of bodily energy in preparation for action.

Ethology   The study of an animal's behavior in its natural environment.

Factor analysis   Statistical method of deriving common factors from a number of measures. Individual measures that are highly intercorrelated are then clustered. Factor analysis is particularly useful in testing hypotheses concerning the nature of human abilities.

Factor theory   Theoretical position based on factor analysis in which factors are derived mathematically.

Genetic determinism   A model of human nature in which behavior is seen as caused primarily by hereditary factors.

Hypochondriasis   Persistent conviction that one is ill when illness is neither present nor likely.

Hypomania   Emotional excitement with overactivity and flights of ideas; sociable, impulsive, self-centered, unreliable, energetic behavior.

Independent variable   The factor that is the causal agent of change. This is the factor that the experimenter manipulates so he can measure observed changes.

Inner-directed behavior   Behavior guided by one's own inner values and sensitivities.

Intercorrelation coefficient   The relationship between two items.

Intraception   Understanding of how others feel.

Longitudinal study   A study conducted over a long period of time. This is seldom seen in the literature because of the time required.

Mediation   The underlying causation of overt behavior.

Model   Mental picture or construct of reality or of some aspect of reality.

Motional element   Predisposition to be physically active.

Motoric   Physically active.

Multiple regression   The weighting of the independent variables in order to predict some outcome.

Multivariate Involving simultaneous consideration of several variables, as multiple discriminant function analysis.

Null hypothesis The negative or "no differences" form of a statement that is subjected to statistical analysis.

Nurturance The trait of treating others with kindness and sympathy.

Operant conditioning Learning obtained with reward-and-punishment training procedures.

Operational definition A definition based on the observable characteristics of that which is being defined; for example, aggressiveness is defined as being pushy and forceful.

Outer-directed behavior Behavior guided by a wish to satisfy others, gain others' approval, or conform to external codes and models.

Paradigm Model or hypothetical design.

Peer A person of equal standing, as a classmate.

Perception The organization and interpretation of sensory experiences.

Photophobic Intolerant of light to an abnormal degree.

Psychopathic Characterized by aggressively anti-social behavior.

Replication The collection of more than one observation under identical conditions.

Response set Behavior predetermined and not open to change, and in which cognition does not play a part.

Self-abasement Low self-esteem; feeling of inferiority to others.

Somatic Of or pertaining to the body; physical.

Somatotype Physique or morphological type of a human body.

Sublimation Channeling prohibited impulses into socially acceptable activities; for example, diverting sexual energy into artistic creation.

Succorance Leaning on others to provide help and affection.

Surgency Cheerfulness and a happy-go-lucky attitude.

Taxonomy A categorization or classification.

Trait conditioning Consolidation of a personality characteristic.

Variance A measure of the spread or dispersion of scores derived from the standard deviation.

Ventilationist A model of aggression in which a basic assumption is that hurtful aggression can be made less likely by releasing ("ventilating") the aggressive impulses in harmless ways. In contrast, the social learning model sees aggression as contagious and each act of aggression as stimulating further acts of aggression.

Vicarious Experienced through imagined participation instead of actual participation, specifically by identifying or empathizing with the person actually having the experience.

References

Adelson, J. "Personality." *Annual Review of Psychology* 20(1969):217–252.

Ader, R., and Tatum, R. "Free-operant Avoidance Conditioning in Individual and Paired Human Subjects." *Journal of the Experimental Analysis of Behavior* 6(1963): 357–359.

Ahart, F. C. "The Effect of Score Differential on Basketball Free Throw Shooting Efficiency." Master's project, Ithaca College, New York, 1973.

Albert, R. S. "Comments on the Scientific Function of the Concept of Cohesiveness." *American Journal of Sociology* 59(1953):231–234.

Albino, R. D. "The Stable and Labile Personality Types of Luria in Clinically Normal Individuals." *British Journal of Psychology* 39(1948):54–60.

Alderman, R. B. "Incentive Motivation in Sport: An Interpretive Speculation of Research Opportunities." Paper presented at the Sixth Canadian Symposium for Psychomotor Learning and Sport Psychology, October 1974, at Halifax, Nova Scotia. (a)

Alderman, R. B. *Psychological Behavior in Sport.* Philadelphia: Saunders, 1974. (b)

Alker, H. A. "Is Personality Situationally-specific or Intrapsychically-consistent?" *Journal of Personality* 40(1972):1–16.

Allee, W. C., and Masure, R. H. "A Comparison of Maze Behavior in Paired and Isolated Shell Parakeets." *Journal of Comparative Psychology* 22(1936):131–155.

Allison, J. "Respiratory Changes During The Practice of the Technique of Transcendental Meditation." *Lancet* 1(1970):833–834.

Alpert, R., and Haber, R. N. "Anxiety in Academic Achievement Situations." *Journal of Abnormal and Social Psychology* 61(1960):207–215.

Allport, F. H. "The Influence of the Group Upon Association and Thought." *Journal of Experimental Psychology* 3(1920):159–182.

Allport, F. H. *Social Psychology.* Boston: Houghton Mifflin, 1924.

Allport, F. H. "A Structuronomic Conception of Behavior: Individual and Collective: I. Structural Theory and the Mastery Problem of Social Psychology." *Journal of Abnormal and Social Psychology* 64(1962):3–30.

Allport, G. W. *Personality: A Psychological Interpretation.* New York: Holt, Rinehart and Winston, 1937.

451

Allport, G. W. *Pattern and Growth in Personality.* New York: Holt, Rinehart and Winston, 1961.

Allport, G. W. "Traits Revisited." *American Psychologist* 21(1966):1–10.

Anderson, H. H., and Smith, R. S. "Motivation of Young Children: The Constancy of Certain Behavior Patterns." *Journal of Experimental Education* 2(1933):138–160.

Anokhin, P. K. "New Studies in the Work of the Brain: Science and Humanity." *Knowledge.* Moscow, 1965.

Ardrey, R. *The Territorial Imperative.* New York: Dell, 1966.

Arnold, M. B. "A Study of Tension in Relation to Breakdown." *Journal of General Psychology* 26(1942):315–346.

Arnold, M. B. "Physiological Differentiation of Emotional States." *Psychological Review* 52(1945):35–48.

Asch, S. E. *Social Psychology.* Englewood Cliffs, N.J.:Prentice Hall, 1952.

Astin, A. W. "The Use of Tests in Research on Students of High Ability." *Journal of Counseling Psychology* 11(1964):400–404.

Atkinson, J. W. "Motivational Determinants of Risk-Taking Behavior." *Psychological Review* 64(1957):359–372.

Atkinson, J. W. *Motives in Fantasy, Action, and Society.* Princeton: Van Nostrand, 1958.

Atkinson, J. W. *An Introduction to Motivation.* Princeton: Van Nostrand, 1964.

Atkinson, J. W. *Motives in Fantasy, Action and Society.* Princeton: Van Nostrand, 1968.

Atkinson, J. W., and Feather, N. T. *A Theory of Achievement Motivation.* New York: Wiley, 1966.

Atkinson, J. W., and Litwin, C. J. "Achievement Motive and Test Anxiety Conceived as Motive to Approach Success and Motive to Avoid Failure." *Journal of Abnormal and Social Psychology* 60(1960):52–63.

Averill, J. R. "The Dis-position of Psychological Dispositions." *Journal of Experimental Research in Personality* 6(1973):275–282.

Ax, A. F. "The Physiological Differentiation Between Fear and Anger in Humans." *Psychosomatic Medicine* 15(1953):433–442.

Ax, A. F., and Wenger, M. A. "Comments." *Polygraph Newsletter* 1(1955):5.

Back, K. "Influence Through Social Communication." *Journal of Abnormal and Social Psychology* 46(1951):9–23.

Bagchi, B. K., and Wenger, M. A. "Electrophysiological Correlates of Some Yoga Exercises." *Electroencephalography and Clinical Neurophysiology Supplement* 7(1957):132–149.

Bandura, A. "Vicarious Processes: A Case of No-trial Learning." In *Advances in Experimental Social Psychology.* Vol. 2. Edited by L. Berkowitz. New York: Academic Press, 1965.

Bandura, A. *Principles of Behavior Modification.* Toronto: Holt, Rinehart and Winston, 1969.

Bandura, A.; Ross, D.; and Ross, S. "Imitation of Film-mediated Aggressive Models." *Journal of Abnormal and Social Psychology* 66(1963):3–11.

Bandura, A., and Walters, R. H. *Social Learning and Personality Development.* New York: Holt, Rinehart and Winston, 1963.

Barber, T. X. "Physiologic Effects of Hypnosis and Suggestion." In *Biofeedback and Self Control 1970: An Aldine Reader on the Regulation of Bodily Processes and Consciousness.* Edited by T. X. Barber et al. New York: Aldine-Atherton, 1971.

Bardwick, J. *Psychology of Women.* New York: Harper and Row, 1971.

Basomity, H.; Karchin, S. J.; and Otken, D., "The Evocation of Anxiety and Performance Changes Under Minimal Doses of Adrenalin." *American Psychologist* 10(1955):388. Abstract.

Basowitz, H. *Anxiety and Stress.* New York: McGraw-Hill, 1955.

Bass, B. M. *The Orientation Inventory.* Palo Alto: Consulting Psychologists Press, 1962.

Batcher, R. R. "Electronic Aids in the Biological Sciences." *Electronic Industries* 2(1943):86–88.

Bayer, E. "Bietrage zur Zweikomponenten Theorie des Hungers." *Zeitschrift für Psychologie* 112(1929):1–54.

Beary, J. F.; Benson, H.; and Klemchuk, H. P. "A Simple Psychophysiologic Technique Which Elicits the Hypometabolic Changes of the Relaxation Response." *Psychosomatic Medicine* 36(1974):115–120.

Beebe-Center, J. G. "Feeling and Emotion." In *Theoretical Foundations of Psychology.* Edited by M. Nelson. New York: Van Nostrand, 1951.

Beecher, H. K. *Measurement of Subjective Responses: Quantitative Effects of Drugs.* New York: Oxford University Press, 1959.

Beisser, A. *The Madness in Sports.* New York: Appleton-Century-Crofts, 1967.

Bem, D. J. "Constructing Cross-situational Consistencies in Behavior: Some Thoughts on Alker's Critique of Mischel." *Journal of Personality* 40(1972):17–26.

Bendig, A. W. "The Effect of Repeated Testing on Anxiety Scale Scores." *Journal of Consulting Psychology* 26(1962):392.

Benson, H. "Your Innate Asset for Combating Stress." *Harvard Business Review* 52(July–August, 1974):49–60.

Benson, H.; Beary, J. F.; and Carol, M. P. "The Relaxation Response." *Psychiatry* 37(1974):37–46.

Benson, H., and Wallace, R. K. *Drug Abuse: Proceedings of the International Conference.* Philadelphia: Lea and Febiger, 1972.

Benton, A. L. "Influence of Incentives Upon Intelligence Test Scores of School Children." *Journal of Genetic Psychology* 49(1936):494–497.

Berelson, B., and Steiner, G. A. *Human Behavior: An Inventory of Scientific Findings.* New York: Harcourt, Brace and World, 1964.

Berger, R. A. and Littlefield, D. H. "Comparison Between Football Athletes and Nonathletes on Personality." *Research Quarterly* 40(1968): 663–665.

Bergstrom, B. "Complex Psycho Motor Performance During Different Levels of Experimentally Induced Stress in Pilots." In *Emotional Stress.* Edited by L. Levy. New York: American Elsevier, 1967.

Bergum, B. O., and Lehr, D. J. "Effects of Authoritarianism on Vigilance Performance." *Journal of Applied Psychology* 47(1963):75–77.

Beritov, I. S. *Nervous Mechanisms in the Behavior of the Higher Spinal Animals.* Moscow, 1961.

Berkowitz, L. "Group Standards, Cohesiveness, and Productivity." *Human Relations* 7(1954):509–519.

Berkowitz, L. *Aggression: A Social Psychological Analysis.* New York: McGraw-Hill, 1962.

Berkowitz, L. "Aggressive Cues in Aggressive Behavior and Hostility Catharsis." *Psychological Review* 71(1964):104–122.

Berkowitz, L. "Some Aspects of Observed Aggression." *Journal of Personality and Social Psychology* 2(1965):359–369. (a)

Berkowitz, L. "The Concept of Aggressive Drive: Some Additional Considerations." In *Advances in Experimental Social Psychology.* Vol. 2. Edited by L. Berkowitz. New York: Academic Press, 1965. (b)

Berkowitz, L. "The Frustration–Aggression Hypothesis Revisited." In *Roots of Aggression.* Edited by L. Berkowitz. New York: Atherton Press, 1969.

Berkowitz, L. "Frustrations, Conflicts, and Other Sources of Emotional Arousal as Contributors to Social Unrest." *Journal of Social Issues* 28(1972):77–86.

Berkowitz, L. "Sports, Competition and Aggression." *The Physical Educator* 30(1973): 59–61.

Berkowitz, L., and Buck, R. W. "Impulsive Aggression: Reactivity to Aggressive Cues Under Emotional Arousal." *Journal of Personality* 35(1967):415–424.

Berkowitz, L.; Corwin, R.; and Heironimus, M. "Film Violence and Subsequent Aggressive Tendencies." *Public Opinion Quarterly* 27(1963):217–219.

Berkowitz, L., and Geen, R. G. "Stimulus Qualities of the Target of Aggression: A Further Study." *Journal of Personality and Social Psychology* 5(1967):364–368.

Berkowitz, L.; Green, J. A.; and Macaulay, J. R. "Hostility Catharsis as the Reduction of Emotional Tension." *Psychiatry* 25(1962):23–31.

Berkowitz, L., and LePage, A. "Weapons as Aggressive-eliciting Stimuli." *Journal of Personality and Social Psychology* 7(1967):202–207.

Berkowitz, L., and Rawlings, E. "Effects of Film Violence on Inhibitions Against Subsequent Aggression." *Journal of Abnormal and Social Psychology* 66(1963):405–412.

Berkun, M.; Bialek, H.; Kern, R.; and Yagi, K. "Experimental Studies of Psychological Stress in Man." *Psychological Monographs General and Applied* 76(1962):1–39.

Berlin, P. "A Theoretical Explanation of the Motives of Collegiate Women Athletes: An Explanatory Study." Unpublished paper, University of North Carolina, Greensboro, 1972.

Bernstein, N. A. "New Lines of Development in Physiology and Their Correlation with Cybernetics." In *Philosophical Questions of the Physiology of the Higher Nervous Activity and Psychology,* 1961.

Berridge, H. I. "An Experiment in the Psychology of Competition." *Research Quarterly Supplement* 6(1935):37–42.

Bethe, D. R. "Success in Beginning Handball as a Function of the Theory of Achievement Motivation." Ph.D. dissertation, Ohio State University, 1968.

Biehler, R. F. *Psychology Applied to Teaching.* 2d ed. Boston: Houghton Mifflin, 1974.

Bijou, S. W., and Baer, D. M. "Operant Methods in Child Behavior and Development." In *Operant Behavior: Areas of Research and Application.* Edited by W. H. Honig. New York: Appleton-Century-Crofts, 1966.

Bindra, D. *Motivation: A Systematic Reinterpretation.* New York: Ronald Press, 1959.

Binet, A., and Vaschide, E. "Experiences des Forces Musculaire et du Fond chez les Jeune Garcons." *Année Psychologie* 4(1897):15–63.

Birch, D., and Veroff, J. *Motivation: A Study of Action.* Belmont, Calif.: Brooks/Cole, 1966.

Bird, G. E. "Personality Factors in Learning." *Personnel Journal* 6(1927):56–59.

Birney, R. C.; Burdick, H.; and Teevan, R. C. "Analysis of TAT Stories for Hostile Press Thema." Paper presented at the Eastern Psychological Association, April 1961.

Black, J. D. "MMPI (Minnesota Multiphasis Personality Inventory) Results of Female College Students." In *Basic Reading on the MMPI in Psychology and Medicine.* Minneapolis: University of Minnesota Press, 1956. Reported by G. Lambertini. "Morphological and Psychological Traits Related to the Activity of the Athlete." In *Health and Fitness in the Modern World.* Edited by L. A. Larson. Chicago: Athletic Institute, 1961.

Bliss, E. L.; Sandberg, A. A.; Nelson, D. H.; and Eik-Nes, K. "The Normal Levels of 17-Hydroxy-corticosteroids in the Peripheral Blood of Man." *Journal of Clinical Investigation* 32(1953):818–823.

Block, J. "Some Reasons for the Apparent Inconsistency of Personality." *Psychological Bulletin* 70(1968):210–212.

Bluhm, P. M. "Discrimination Reaction Time as a Function of Incentive-related DRQ Anxiety and Task Difficulty." Ph.D. dissertation, Florida State University, 1964.

Board, F.; Persky, H.; and Hamburg, D. A. "Blood Levels of Adrenocortical and Thyroid Hormones in Acutely Disturbed Patients." *Psychosomatic Medicine* 18(1956): 324–333.

Bolles, R. C. *Theory of Motivation.* New York: Harper and Row, 1967.

Boon, M. L.; Fisher, A. C.; and Mumford, N. L. "Prediction of Gymnastic Performance from Arousal and Anxiety Measures." Unpublished research, 1974.

Booth, E. G. "Personality Traits of Athletes Measured by the MMPI." *Research Quarterly* 29(1958):127–138.

Boulding, K. E. "Am I Man or Mouse—or both?" In *Man and Aggression,* edited by M. F. A. Montagu. New York: Oxford University Press, 1968.

Bovard, E. W. "The Effects of Social Stimuli on the Response to Stress." *Psychological Review* 66(1959):267–277.

Bowers, K. S. "Situationism in Psychology: An Analysis and a Critique." *Psychological Review* 80(1973):307–336.

Bramel, D. "The Attraction and Reduction of Hostility." In *Experimental Social Psychology.* Edited by J. Mills. New York: Macmillan, 1969.

Bramel, D.; Taub, B.; and Blum, B. "An Observer's Reaction to the Suffering of His Enemy." *Journal of Personality and Social Psychology* 8(1968):384–392.

Breen, J. L. "Anxiety Factors Related to Physical Fitness Variables." Ph.D. dissertation, University of Illinois, 1959.

Brehm, J. W., and Cohen, A. R. *Explorations in Cognitive Dissonance.* New York: Wiley, 1962.

Brenner, B. "Effect of Immediate and Delayed Praise and Blame Upon Learning and Recall." *Teachers College Contributions to Education,* No. 620, 1934.

Brill, A. A. "The Way of the Fan." *North American Review* 226(1929):400–434.

Brock, T. C., and Pallak, M. S. "The Consequences of Choosing to be Aggressive." In *The Cognitive Control of Motivation.* Edited by P. G. Zimbardo. Glenview, Ill.: Scott, Foresman, 1969.

Broen, W. E., Jr., and Storms, L. H. A. "A Reaction Potential Ceiling and Response Decrements in Complex Situations." *Psychological Review* 68(1961):405–415.

Bronson, F. H., and Eleftheriou, B. E. "Chronic Physiological Effects of Fighting Mice." *General and Comparative Endocrinology* 4(1964):9–14.

Brown, B. B. *New Mind, New Body: Biofeedback: New Directions for the Mind.* New York: Harper and Row, 1974. Excerpted in *Psychology Today,* August 1974.

Brown, J. S. "Pleasure-seeking Behavior and the Drive-reduction Hypothesis." *Psychological Review* 62(1955):169–179.

Brown, B. R., and Garland, H. "The Effects of Incompetency, Audience Acquaintanceship, and Anticipated Evaluative Feedback on Face-saving Behaviour." *Journal of Experimental Social Psychology* 7(1971):490–502.

Burgess, M., and Hokanson, T. E. "Effects of Increased Heart Rate on Intellectual Performance." *Journal of Abnormal Psychology* 68(1964):85–91.

Burnham, W. H. "The Group as a Stimulus to Mental Activity." *Science* 31(1960): 761–767.

Bush, J. "Anxiety and Performance at Three Levels of Competition in Female Intercollegiate Gymnastics." D.P.E. dissertation, Springfield College, 1970.

Buss, A. H. *The Psychology of Aggression.* New York: Wiley, 1961.

Buss, A. H. "Physical Aggressionism in Relation to Different Frustrations." *Journal of Abnormal and Social Psychology* 67(1963):1–7.

Buss, A. H., and Durkee, A. "An Inventory for Assessing Different Kinds of Hostility." *Journal of Consulting Psychology* 21(1957):343–348.

Butcher, J. N. "Personality Assessment: Problems and Perspectives." In *Objective Personality Assessment: Changing Perspectives.* Edited by J. N. Butcher. New York: Academic Press, 1972.

Butter, C. M. *Neuropsychology: The Study of Brain and Behavior.* Belmont, Calif.: Brooks/Cole, 1968.

Cammalleri, J. A.; Hendrick, H. W., Pittman, W. C., Jr.; Bloch, H. D.; and Prather, D. C. "Effects of Different Leadership Styles on Group Accuracy." *Journal of Applied Psychology* 57(1973):32–37.

Campbell, D. T., and Fiske, D. W. "Convergent and Discriminant Validation by the Multi-trait–multimethod Matrix." *Psychological Bulletin* 56(1959):81–105.

Cannon, W. B. *Bodily Changes in Pain, Hunger, Fear and Rage.* New York: Appleton-Century-Crofts, 1929.

Cannon, W. B. *The Way of an Investigator.* New York: Norton, 1945.

Cannon, W. B. *Bodily Changes in Pain, Hunger, Fear and Rage.* 2d. ed. Boston: Branford, 1953.

Caplow, T. "A Theory of Coalitions in the Triad." *American Sociological Review* 21(1956):489-493.

Carlson, R. "Where is the Person in Personality Research?" *Psychological Review* 75(1971):203–219.

Carron, A. V. "Complex Motor Skill Performance Under Conditions of Externally Induced Stress." Master's thesis, University of Alberta, 1965.

Cartwright, D. "The Nature of Group Cohesiveness." In *Group Dynamics: Research and Theory.* 3d. ed. Edited by D. Cartwright and A. Zander. New York: Harper and Row, 1968.

Cartwright, D., and Zander, A., eds. *Group Dynamics: Research and Theory.* 3d ed.. New York: Harper and Row, 1968.

Castaneda, A. "Effects of Stress on Complex Learning and Performance." *Journal of Experimental Psychology* 52(1956):9–12.

Castaneda, A.; McCandless, B. R.; and Palermo, D. S. "The Children's Form of the Manifest Anxiety Scale." *Child Development* 27(1956):317–327.

Cattell, R. B. "Personality Structure and Measurement: I. The Operational Determination of Trait Unities." *British Journal of Psychology* 36(1946):88–103.

Cattell, R. B. "Validation and Intensification of the Sixteen Personality Factor Questionnaire." *Journal of Clinical Psychology* 12(1956):205–214.

Cattell, R. B. "Some Psychological Correlates of Physical Fitness and Physique." In *Exercise and Fitness.* Edited by S. C. Staley. Chicago: Athletic Institute, 1960.

Cattell, R. B. *The Scientific Analysis of Personality.* Baltimore: Penguin, 1965.

Cattell, R. B. *Abilities: Their Structure, Growth, and Action.* Boston: Houghton Mifflin, 1971.

Cattell, R. B. *A New Morality from Science: Beyondism.* London: Pergamon, 1973.

Cattell, R. B. "Personality Pinned Down." *Psychology Today* 7(July 1973):40–46. (b)

Cattell, R. B.; Beloff, H.; and Coan, R. W. *Handbook for the High School Personality Questionnaire.* Urbana, Ill.: Institute for Personality and Ability Testing, 1958.

Cattell, R. B., and Butcher, H. J. *The Prediction of Achievement and Creativity.* New York: Bobbs-Merrill, 1968.

Cattell, R. B., and Eber, H. W. *Handbook for the Sixteen Personality Factor Questionnaire.* Urbana, Ill.: The Institute for Personality and Ability Testing, 1957.

Cattell, R. B., and Eber, H. W. *The Sixteen Personality Factor Questionnaire.* Champaign, Ill.: Institute for Personality and Ability Testing, 1964.

Cattell, R. B.; Kawash, G.; and DeYoung, G. "Validity of Objective Measures of Ergic Tension: Response ot the Sex Erg to Visual Stimulation." *Journal of Experimental Research in Personality* 6(1972):76–82.

Cattell, R. B., and Nesselroade, J. R. "Likeness and Completeness Theories Examined by Sixteen Personality Factor Measures on Stably and Unstably Married Couples." *Journal of Personality and Social Psychology* 7(1967):351–361.

457

Cattell, R. B.; Saunders, D. R.; and Stice, G. F. *Sixteen Personality Factor Questionnaire.* Champaign, Ill.: Institute for Personality and Ability Testing, 1950.

Chapman, L. J., and Campbell, D. T. "An Attempt to Predict the Performance of Three-man Teams from Attitude Measurements." *Journal of Social Psychology* 46(1957): 277–286.

Chase, L. E. "Motivation of Young Children: An Experimental Study of the Influence of Certain Types of External Incentives Upon the Performance of a Task." *University of Iowa Studies of Child Welfare* 5(1932):No. 3.

Chen, S. C. "Social Modification of the Activity of Ants in Nest-Building." *Physiological Zoology* 10(1937):420–436.

Chernikova, O. "Starting Fever." In *Theory and Practice of Physical Culture.* 3d ed., 1937.

Child, I. L., and Whiting, J. W. M. "Determinants of Level of Aspiration: Evidence from Everyday Life." *Journal of Abnormal and Social Psychology* 44(1949):303–314.

Christine, R. and Lindauer, F. "Personality Structure." *Annual Review of Psychology* 14 (1963):201–230.

Church, R. M. "The Effects of Competition on Reaction Time and Palmar Skin Conductance." *Journal of Abnormal and Social Psychology* 65(1962):32–40.

Claridge, G. *Personality and Arousal.* London: Pergamon, 1967.

Cofer, C. N. "Motivation." *Annual Review of Psychology* 10(1959):173–202.

Cofer, C. N. *Motivation and Emotion.* Glenview, Ill.: Scott, Foresman, 1972.

Cofer, C. N., and Appley, M. H. *Motivation: Theory and Research.* New York: Wiley, 1964.

Cofer, C. N., and Johnson, W. R. "Personality Dynamics in Relation to Exercise and Sports." In *Science and Medicine of Exercise and Sport.* Edited by W. R. Johnson. New York: Harper and Row, 1960.

Cohen, A. "A Study of Incentives Under Schoolroom Conditions." Master's thesis, Columbia University, 1927.

Coleman, J. S. *The Adolescent Society.* New York: Glencoe Free Press, 1961.

Cooley, W. W., and Lohnes, P. R. *Multivariate Procedures for the Behavioral Sciences.* New York: Wiley, 1962.

Cooper, L. "Athletics, Activity, and Personality: A Review of the Literature." *Research Quarterly* 40(1969):17–22.

Corcoran, D. "Personality and the Inverted-U Relation." *British Journal of Psychology* 56(1965):267–273.

Cottrell, N. B. "Performance in the Presence of Other Human Beings: Mere Presence, Audience, and Affiliation Effects." In *Social Facilitation and Imitative Behavior.* Edited by E. C. Simmel, R. A. Hoppe, and S. A. Milton. Boston: Allyn and Bacon, 1968.

Cottrell, N. B.; Rittle, R. H.; and Wack, D. L. "The Presence of an Audience and List Type (Competitive or Noncompetitional) as Joint Determinants of Performance in Paired-associates Learning." *Journal of Personality* 35(1967):425–434.

Cottrell, N. B.; Sekerak, A. J.; Wack, D. L.; and Rittle, R. H. "Social Facilitation of Dominant Responses by the Presence of an Audience and the Mere Presence of Others." *Journal of Personality and Social Psychology* 9(1968):245–250.

Courts, F. A. "Relations Between Muscular Tension and Performance *Bulletin* 39(1942):347–367.

Cowell, C. C. "The Contribution of Physical Activity to Social Develop *Quarterly* 31(1960):286–306.

Crabbe, J. M. "Social Facilitation Effects of Children During Early Stage ing." Paper presented at American Association of Health, Physical Education Recreation National Convention, April 1973, at Minneapolis.

Crasilneck, H. B., and Hall, J. A. "Physiological Changes Associated with Hypnosis: A Review of the Literature Since 1948." *International Journal of Clinical and Experimental Hypnosis* 7(January, 1959):9–50.

Cratty, B. J. *Movement Behavior and Motor Learning.* Philadelphia: Lea and Febiger, 1967.

Cratty, B. J. *Psychology and Physical Activity.* Englewood Cliffs, N.J.:Prentice-Hall, 1968.

Cratty, B. J. *Psychology in Contemporary Sport: Guidelines for Coaches and Athletes.* Englewood Cliffs, N.J.: Prentice-Hall, 1973.

Crawley, S. L. "An Experimental Investigation of Recovery from Work." *Archives of Psychology* (New York), No. 85, 1926.

Crites, J. O. "The California Psychological Inventory, I. As A Measure of the Normal Personality." *Journal of Counseling Psychology* 11(1964):197–202.

Dabbs, J. M.; Johnson, J. E.; and Leventhal, H. "Palmar Sweating: A Quick and Simple Measure." *Journal of Experimental Psychology* 78(1968):347–350.

Damron, C. F. "Two and Three Dimensional Slide Images Used with Tachistoscopic Training Techniques in Instructing High School Football Players in Defenses." *Research Quarterly* 26(1955):36–43.

Darden, E. "Sixteen Personality Factor Profiles of Competitive Bodybuilders and Weight-lifters." *Research Quarterly* 43(1972):142–147.

Darrow, C. W., and Heath, L. L. "Reaction Tendencies Related to Personality." In *Studies in the Dynamics of Behavior.* Edited by K. S. Lashley. Chicago: University of Chicago Press, 1932.

Dashiell, J. F. "An Experimental Analysis of Some Group Effects." *Journal of Abnormal and Social Psychology* 25(1930):190–199.

Davies, D., and Hockey, G. "The Effects of Noise and Doubling the Signal Frequency on Individual Differences in Visual Vigilance Performances." *British Journal of Psychology* 57(1966):381–389.

Davis, J. E. *Clinical Applications of Recreational Therapy.* Springfield, Ill.: Thomas, 1952.

Davis, J. H. *Group Performance.* Reading, Mass.: Addison-Wesley, 1969.

Davis, R. A. and Ballard, C. R. "Effectiveness of Various Types of Classroom Incentives." *Educational Method* 12(1932):134–145.

Davis, R. C.; Buchwald, A. M.; and Frankmann, R. W. "Autonomic and Muscular Responses and Their Relation to Simple Stimuli." *Psychological Monographs* 69(1955): Whole No. 405.

Davitz, J. R., and Mason, D. J. "Socially Facilitated Reduction of a Fear Response in Rats." *Journal of Comparative and Physiological Psychology* 48(1955):149–151.

459

ₐi, S. H. "An Empirical Test of Structural Balance in Sociometric Triads." *Journal of Abnormal and Social Psychology* 59(1959):393–398.

Deese, J. *The Psychology of Learning.* New York: McGraw-Hill, 1958.

Dember, W., and Earl, R. "Analysis of Exploratory, Manipulatory and Curiosity Behaviors." *Psychological Review* 64(1957):91-96.

Dember, W., and Jenkins, J. *General Psychology.* Englewood Cliffs, N.J.: Prentice-Hall, 1970.

Deutsch, M. "The Effects of Cooperation and Competition upon Group Process." In *Group Dynamics: Research and Theory.* 3d ed. Edited by D. Cartwright and A. Zander. New York: Harper and Row, 1968.

Dimitrova, S. "Concentration Attention During the Performance of Scoring in Basketball." Collection dedicated to the 20th anniversary of V.I.F. and the 80th Birthday of G. Dimitrov, 1963.

Dollard, J.; Doob, L.; Miller, N.; Mowrer, O.; and Sears, R. *Frustration and Aggression.* New Haven: Yale University Press, 1939.

Dollins, J. G.; Angelino, H.; and Mech, E. V. "With Words of Praise." *Elementary School Journal* 60(1960):446–450.

Duffy, E. "Tensions and Emotional Factors in Reaction." *Genetic Psychology Monographs* 7(1930):1–79.

Duffy, E. "The Measurement of Muscular Tension as a Technique for the Study of Emotional Tendencies." *American Journal of Psychology* 44(1932):146–162. (a)

Duffy, E. "The Relationship Between Muscular Tension and Quality of Performance." *American Journal of Psychology* 44(1932):535–546. (b)

Duffy, E. "Emotion: An Example of the Need for Reorientation in Psychology." *Psychological Review* 41(1934):184–198.

Duffy, E. "An Explanation of 'Emotional' Phenomena Without the Use of the Concept 'Emotion.'" *Journal of General Psychology* 25(1941):283–293. (a)

Duffy, E. "The Conceptual Categories of Psychology: A Suggestion for Revision." *Psychological Review* 48(1941):177–203. (b)

Duffy, E. "A Systematic Framework for The Description of Personality." *Journal of Abnormal and Social Pscyhology* 44(1949):175–190.

Duffy, E. "The Concept of Energy Mobilization." *Psychological Review* 58(1951):30–40.

Duffy, E. "The Psychological Significance of the Concept of 'Arousal' or 'Activation.'" *Psychological Review* 64(1957):265–275.

Duffy, E. *Activation and Behavior.* New York: Wiley, 1962.

Duffy, E. and Lacey, O. L. "Adaptation in Energy Mobilization: Changes in General Level of Palmar Skin Conductance." *Journal of Experimental Psychology* 36(1946):437–452.

Dunbar, F. *Emotions and Bodily Changes.* 3d ed. New York: Columbia University Press, 1947.

Dunnette, M. D. "Fads, Fashions, and Folderol in Psychology." *American Psychologist* 21(1966):343–352.

Dychkov, V. M. *Polevaulting.* Moscow: F.I.S., 1955.

Earl, R. *A Theory of Stimulus Selection.* California: Hughes Ground Systems, 1961.

Eason, R. G., and White, C. T. "Muscular Tension, Effort and Tracking Difficulty: Studies of Parameters Which Effect Tension Level and Performance Efficiency." *Perceptual and Motor Skills* 12(1961):331–372.

Edwards, A. L. *Edwards Personal Preference Schedule (Manual).* New York: Psychological Corporation, 1954.

Edwards, A. L. "A Comparison of 57 MMPI Scales and 57 Experimental Scales Matched with the MMPI Scales in Terms of Item Social Desirability Scale Values and Probabilities of Endorsement." *Educational and Psychological Measurement* 26(1966):15–27.

Edwards, A. L., and Abbott, R. D. "Measurement of Personality Traits." *Annual Review of Psychology* 24(1973):241–278.

Edwards, H. *Sociology of Sport.* Homewood, Ill.: The Dorsey Press, 1973.

Elias, J., and Dunning, E. "The Quest for Excitement in Unexciting Societies." Paper presented to the British Sociological Association, April 1970, at London.

Ellis, M. J. *Why People Play.* Englewood Cliffs, N.J.: Prentice-Hall, 1973.

Ellis, N. R., and Distephano, M. K. "Effects of Verbal Urging and Praise Upon Rotary Pursuit Performance in Mental Defectives." *American Journal of Mental Deficiency* 64(1959):486–490.

Elmadjian, F.; Hope, J. M.; and Lamson, E. T. "Excretion of Epinephrin and Norepinephrin in Various Emotional States." *Journal of Clinical Endocrinology* 17(1957): 608–620.

Endler, N.S. "Estimating Variance Components from Mean Squares for Random and Mixed Effects Analysis of Variance Models." *Perceptual and Motor Skills* 22(1966): 559–570.

Endler, N. S. "Generalizability of Contributions from Sources of Variance in the S–R Inventories of Anxiousness." *Journal of Personality* 37(1969):1–24.

Endler, N. S. "The Person Versus the Situation—A Pseudo Issue? A Response to Alker." *Journal of Personality* 41(1973):287–303.

Endler, N. S., and Hunt, J. M. "Sources of Behavioral Variance as Measured by the S–R Inventory of Anxiousness." *Psychological Bulletin* 65(1966):336–346.

Endler, N. S., and Hunt, J. M. "S–R Inventories of Hostility and Comparisons of the Proportions of Variance from Persons, Responses, and Situations for Hostility and Anxiousness." *Journal of Personality and Social Psychology* 9(1968):309–315.

Endler, N. S.; Hunt, J. M.; and Rosenstein, A. J. "An S–R Inventory of Anxiousness." *Psychological Monographs* 76(1962):Whole No. 536.

Epstein, S., and Fenz, W. D. "Theory and Experiment on the Measurement of Approach-Avoidance Conflict." *Journal of Abnormal and Social Psychology* 64(1962):97–112.

Epstein, S., and Fenz, W. D. "Steepness of Approach and Avoidance Gradients in Humans as a Function of Experience: Theory and Experiment." *Journal of Experimental Psychology* 70(1965):1–12.

Epuran, M. "Motivation Factors in Sport." In *Contemporary Psychology of Sport.* Edited by G. S. Kenyon. Chicago: Athletic Institute, 1970.

Erikson, E. H. "Youth: Fidelity and Diversity." *Daedalus* 91(1962):5–27.

Erikson, E. H. *Childhood and Society.* New York: Norton, 1963.

461

Eron, L. "Relationship of TV Viewing Habits and Aggressive Behavior in Children." *Journal of Abnormal and Social Psychology* 67(1963):193–196.

Essing, W. "Team Line-up and Team Achievement in European Football." In *Contemporary Psychology of Sport*. Edited by G. S. Kenyon. Chicago: Athletic Institute, 1970.

Evans, J. F. "A Comparison of Social and Nonsocial Competition." Master's thesis, University of Alberta, 1966.

Evans, J. F. "Components of Motivation in a Competitive Situation." Ph.D. dissertation, University of Alberta, 1968.

Evans, W. O. "A Titration Schedule on a Treadmill." *Journal of the Experimental Analysis of Behavior* 6(1963):219–221.

Eysenck, H. J. *Manual of the Maudsley Personality Inventory*. London: University of London Press, 1959.

Eysenck, H. J. "Principles and Methods of Personality Description, Classification and Diagnosis." *British Journal of Psychology* 55(1964):284–294.

Eysenck, H. J. *Facts and Fiction in Psychology*. Baltimore, Md.: Penguin, 1965.

Eysenck, H. J. *The Biological Basis of Personality*. Springfield, Ill.: Thomas, 1967.

Eysenck, H. J., and Gillan, P. W. "Hand-Steadiness Under Conditions of High and Low Drive." In *Experiments in Motivation*. Edited by H. J. Eysenck. New York: Macmillan, 1964.

Faulkner, R. R. "Violence, Camaraderie, and Occupational Character in Hockey." Paper presented at the Conference on Deviancy in Sport, 1971, at Brockport, New York.

Feather, N. "Valence of Outcome and Expectation of Success in Relation to Task Difficulty and Perceived Locus of Control." *Journal of Personality and Social Psychology* 7(1967):372–386.

Feather, N. T., and Saville, M. M. "Effects of Amount of Prior Success and Failure on Expectations of Success and Subsequent Task Performance." *Journal of Personality and Social Psychology* 5(1967):226–232.

Fehr, T. "Der Einfluss den Transzendentalen Meditation auf Personlickkeits-Variable." *Schopferische Intelligenz* 3(January, 1974):1–9.

Fenz, W. D., and Epstein, S. "Gradients of Physiological Arousal in Parachutists as a Function of an Approaching Jump." *Psychosomatic Medicine* 29(1967):33–51.

Feshbach, S. "The Drive Reducing Function of Fantasy Behavior." *Journal of Abnormal and Social Psychology* 50(1955):3–11.

Feshbach, S. "The Catharsis Hypothesis and Some Consequences of Interaction with Aggressive and Neutral Play Objects." *Journal of Personality* 24(1956):449–462.

Feshbach, S. "The Stimulating Versus Cathartic Effects of a Vicarious Aggressive Activity." *Journal of Abnormal and Social Psychology* 63(1961):381–385.

Feshbach, S.; Stiles, W. B.; and Bitter, E. "The Reinforcing Effect of Witnessing Aggression." *Journal of Experimental Research in Personality* 2(1967):133–139.

Festinger, L. E. "A Theory of Social Comparison Processes." *Human Relations* 7(1954):117–140.

Festinger, L. *A Theory of Cognitive Dissonance*. New York: Harper and Row, 1957.

Festinger, L.; Schachter, S.; and Back, K. *Social Pressures in Informal Groups: A Study of a Housing Project*. New York: Harper, 1950.

462   *References*

Fiedler, F. E. "Assumed Similarity Measures as Predictors of Team Effectiveness in Surveying." Urbana, Ill.: Bureau of Research and Service, University of Illinois, 1953. Mimeographed. (a)

Fiedler, F. E. "The Psychological Distance Dimension in Interpersonal Relations." *Journal of Personality* 22(1953):142–150. (b)

Fiedler, F. E. "Assumed Similarity Measures as Predictors of Team Effectiveness." *Journal of Abnormal and Social Psychology* 49(1954):381–388.

Fiedler, F. E. *Leader Attitudes and Group Effectiveness.* Urbana, Ill.; University of Illinois Press, 1958.

Fiedler, F. E.; Hartmann, W.; and Rudin, S. A. "The Relationship of Interpersonal Perception to Effectiveness in Basketball Teams." Urbana, Ill.: Bureau of Research and Service, University of Illinois, 1952. Mimeographed.

Fiedler, F. E.; Hartmann, W.; and Rudin, S. A. "Correction and Extension of the Relationship of Interpersonal Perception to Effectiveness in Basketball Teams." Urbana, Ill.: Bureau of Research and Service, University of Illinois, 1953. Mimeographed.

Fischer, W. F. "Sharing in Preschool Children as a Function of Amount and Type of Reinforcement." *Dissertation Abstracts* 22(1961–1962):2871.

Fisher, A. C. "Sport Personality Assessment: Facts, Fallacies, and Perspectives." Paper presented at American Alliance of Health, Physical Education and Recreation National Convention, March 1975, at Atlantic City.

Fisher, A. C., and Ahart, F. "Personality Assessment: Trait Approach, Situational-specificity Approach, or What?" Paper presented at the First Canadian Congress for the Multidisciplinary Study of Sport, October 1973, at Montreal.

Fisher, A. C., and Schoen, T. A. "Comparison of Personality Traits Between Ice Hockey Goaltenders, Team Members and General Male Population." Paper presented at the Fourth Canadian Symposium for Psychomotor Learning and Sport Psychology, October 1972, at Waterloo, Ontario.

Fiske, D. W. "Problems in Measuring Personality." In *Concepts of Personality.* Edited by J. M. Wepman and R. W. Heine. Chicago: Aldine, 1963.

Fiske, D. W., and Maddi, S. R., eds. *Functions of Varied Experience.* Homewood, Ill.: Dorsey, 1961.

Fleishman, E. A., and Rich, S. "Role of Kinesthetic and Spatial-visual Abilities in Perceptual-motor Learning." *Journal of Experimental Psychology* 66(1963):6–11.

Forlano, H., and Axelrod, C. "The Effect of Repeated Praise or Blame on the Performance of Introverts and Extroverts." *Journal of Educational Psychology* 28(1937):92–100.

Fowler, H. *Curiosity and Exploratory Behavior.* New York: Macmillan, 1965.

Fraser, D. C. "The Relation of an Environmental Variable to Performance in a Prolonged Visual Task." *Quarterly Journal of Experimental Psychology* 5(1953):31–32.

Freeman, G. L. "The Facilitative and Inhibitory Effects of Muscular Tension Upon Performance." *American Journal of Psychology* 45(1933):17–52.

Freeman, G. L. "The Optimal Muscular Tensions for Various Performances." *American Journal of Psychology* 51(1938):146–151. (a)

Freeman, G. L. "The Postural Substrate." *Psychological Review* 45(1938):324–333. (b)

Freeman, G. L. "The Relationship Between Performance Level and Bodily Activity Level." *Journal of Experimental Psychology* 26(1940):602–608.

Freeman, G. L. *The Energies of Human Behavior.* Ithaca, N.Y.: Cornell University Press, 1948.

Freeman, G. L., and Giffin, L. L. "The Measurement of General Reactivity Under Basal Conditions." *Journal of General Psychology* 21(1939):63–72.

Freeman, G. L., and Katcoff, E. T. "Muscular Tension and Irritability." *American Journal of Psychology* 44(1932):789–792.

Freeman, G. L., and Simpson, R. M. "The Effect of Experimentally Induced Muscular Tensions upon Palmar Skin Resistance." *Journal of General Psychology* 18(1938): 319–326.

Freud, S. "Triebe und Trieschicksale" (1915). In *Gessamelte Werke.* Vol. 10. London: Imago, 1946.

Freud, S. "The Loss of Reality in Neurosis and Psychosis" (1924). In *Collected Papers of Sigmund Freud.* Vol. 2. London: Hogarth Press, 1948.

Frost, R. B. *Psychological Concepts Applied to Physical Education and Coaching.* Reading, Mass.: Addison-Wesley, 1971.

Furneaux, W. D. "The Psychologist and the University." *Universities Quarterly* 17(1962).

Furst, R. T. "The Boxer and His Audience: An Empirical Assessment." Paper presented at the Scientific Congress of the XXth Olympic Games, August 1972, at Munich.

Gagaeva, G. M. "On the Psychological Preparation of Football Players for the Forthcoming Competition." *Scholarly Record* (Moscow), 1962.

Gagne, R., and Fleishman, E. *Psychology and Human Performance.* New York: Holt, Rinehart and Winston, 1959.

Gale, C. K. Quoted in "Hypnosis May Help Athletes Learn Skills." *Scope Weekly,* Upjohn, March 9, 1960.

Ganzer, V. J. "Effects of Audience Presence and Test Anxiety on Learning and Retention in a Serial Learning Situation." *Journal of Personality and Social Psychology* 8(1968): 194–199.

Gardner, J. W. "Level of Aspiration in Response to a Prearranged Sequence of Scores." *Journal of Experimental Psychology* 25(1939):601–625.

Garfield, S. L. "The Clinical Method of Personality Assessment." In *Concepts of Personality.* Edited by J. M. Wepman and R. W. Heine. Chicago: Aldine, 1963.

Garrett, H. E. *Statistics in Psychology and Education.* New York: Longmans, Green, 1947.

Gastaut, H.; Gastaut, Y.; Roger, A.; Corriol, J.; and Naquet, R. "Etude électrographique du cycle d'excitabilité cortical." *Electroencephalography and Clinical Neurophysiology Supplement* 3(1951):401–428.

Gates, M. J., and Allee, W. C. "Conditioned Behavior of Isolated and Grouped Cockroaches on a Simple Maze." *Journal of Comparative Psychology* 15(1933):331–358.

Gates, G. S., and Rissland, L. Q. "The Effect of Encouragement and of Discouragement Upon Performance." *Journal of Educational Psychology* 14(1923):21–26.

Gaylord, E. C. *Modern Coaching Psychology.* Dubuque, Iowa: Brown, 1967.

Geen, R. G. "Effects of Frustration, Attack, and Prior Training in Aggressiveness upon Aggressive Behavior." *Journal of Personality and Social Psychology* 9(1968): 316–321.

Geen, R., and Berkowitz, L. "Name-mediated Aggressive Cue Properties." *Journal of Personality* 34(1966):456–465.

Geen, R. G., and Berkowitz, L. "Some Conditions Facilitating the Occurrence of Aggression after the Observation of Violence." *Journal of Personality* 35(1967):666–676.

Geen, R. G., and O'Neal, E. C. "Activation of Cue-elicited Aggression by General Arousal." *Journal of Personality and Social Psychology* 11(1969):289–292.

Gellhorn, E. "Physiology of the Suprospinal Mechanisms." In *Science and Medicine of Exercise and Sports.* Edited by W. R. Johnson. New York: Harper and Row, 1960.

Gellhorn, E., and Kiely, W. "Mystical States of Consciousness: Neurophysiological and Clinical Aspects." *Journal of Nervous and Mental Disease* 154(1972):399–405.

Genov, F. "Emphasis on the Mental Concentration of Competitors in the Weight-lifting at the XVII Olympic Games in Rome, 1960." *Medicine and Physical Culture of the XVII Olympic Games,* 1961.

Genov, F. "Willpower in the Preparation of the Athlete." *Medicine and Physical Culture* (Sophia), 1965.

Genov, F. "Dynamics of Attention of the Weightlifter as an Indicator of Mobilized Preparedness During Competition." In *Studies of Physical Culture and Sport,* No. 3, 1966. (a)

Genov, F. "Effect of Warm-up and of Certain Psychological Factors on the Condition of Preparedness of the Athlete." In *Theory and Practice of Physical Culture,* No. 11, 1966. (b)

Genov, F. "On Mobilizing the Athlete's Readiness Before Competition." In *Theory and Practice of Physical Culture,* No. 10, 1966. (c)

Genov, F. "Questions on the Formation of Directions for Lifting Weights for Weightlifters." *Proceedings* of the G.C.O.L.I.F.K., 1966. (d)

Genov, F. "Method of Association as an Indicator of the Mobilized Preparedness of the Athlete." In *Studies on Physical Culture,* No. 9, 1967.

Genova, E. "Regularities During the Pre-starting Stage for the Track and Field Competitor." *Proceedings* from the session at N.M.S., C.N.I.I.F.K., and V.I.F., 1957, at Sophia.

Genova, E. "Certain Changes in the Summer Period of Response to the Verbal Reactions of the Wrestlers." Scholarly works of C.N.I.I.F.K., 1959.

Genova, E. "Teaching of the Maximum Continuation of Concentration of Track and Field and Field Competitors at the XVII Olympic Games." In *Medicine and Physical Culture of the XVII Olympic Games,* 1961.

Gerdes, G. R. "The Effects of Various Motivational Techniques on Performance in Selected Physical Tests." Ph.D. dissertation, Indiana University, 1958.

Gheron, E. "The Role of Concentration in Lifting Weights." Scholarly session at the C.N.I.I.F.K. and V.I.F., 1953.

Giambrone, C. P. "The Influence of Situation Criticality and Game Criticality on Basketball Freethrow Shooting." Master's thesis, University of Illinois, 1973.

Gilchrist, E. P. "The Extent to Which Praise and Reproof Affect a Pupil's Work." *School and Society* 4(1916):872–874.

Gilinsky, A. S., and Stewart, J. C. " 'Extinction' of a Success Aspiration Following Three Conditions of Reinforcement." *American Psychologist* 4(1949):222–223.

Gmelch, G. "Magic in Professional Baseball." In *Games, Sport, and Power*. Edited by G. P. Stone. New Brunswick, N.J.: Transaction, 1972.

Goldfarb, J. M. "Motivational Psychology in Coaching." *Scholastic Coach* 37(September, 1968):54–57.

Goldstein, J., and Arms, R. L. "Effects of Observing Athletic Contests on Hostility." *Sociometry* 34(1971):83–90.

Goranson, R. E. "Observed Violence and Aggressive Behavior: The Effects of Negative Outcome to the Observed Violence." Ph.D dissertation, University of Wisconsin, Madison, 1969.

Gorason, R. E. "Media Violence and Aggressive Behavior: A Review of Experimental Research." In *Advances in Experimental Social Psychology*. Vol. 5. Edited by L. Berkowitz. New York: Academic Press, 1970.

Gorton, B. E. "The Physiology of Hypnosis." *Psychiatric Quarterly* 23(1949):457–485.

Gottier, R. "The Effects of Social Disorganization in *Cichlasoma Biocellatum*." Ph.D. dissertation, Bowling Green State University (Ohio), 1968.

Gough, H. G. *Manual for the California Psychological Inventory*. Palo Alto, Calif.: Consulting Psychologists Press, 1957.

Gough, H. G., and Heilbrun, A. B. *The Adjective Check List Manual*. Palo Alto, Calif.: Consulting Psychologists Press, 1965.

Graham, J. "The Effects of Transcendental Meditation Upon Auditory Thresholds: A Pilot Study." Bachelor's thesis, University of Sussex, England, 1971.

Greene, D., and Lepper, M. R. "Intrinsic Motivation: How to Turn Play into Work." *Psychology Today* 8(September 1974):49–54.

Gregory, C. J., and Petrie, B. M. "Superstition in Sport." Paper presented at the Fourth Canadian Symposium for Psychomotor Learning and Sport Psychology, October 1972, at Waterloo, Ontario.

Gregory, C. J., and Petrie, B. M. "Superstitions of Canadian Intercollegiate Athletes: An Inter-sport Comparison." Paper presented at the American Association of Health, Physical Education and Recreation National Convention, April 1973, at Minneapolis.

Griffith, C. R. *Psychology of Coaching*. New York: Scribner's, 1926.

Griffith, C. R. *Psychology and Athletics: A General Survey for Athletes and Coaches*. New York: Scribner's, 1928.

Gross, E. A.; Griesel, D. C.; and Stull, A. "Relationships Between Two Motor Educability Tests, a Strength Test, and Wrestling Ability After Eight Weeks' Instruction." *Research Quarterly* 27(1956):395–402.

Gross, N., and Martin, W. E. "On Group Cohesiveness."*American Journal of Sociology* 57(1952):546–554.

Gruber, J. L., and Ismail, A. H. "Recent Developments in Mind–Body Relationships." *Education* 89(September, 1968):57–63.

Guilford, J. P. *Personality*. New York: McGraw-Hill, 1959.

Guilford, J. P. *The Nature of Human Intelligence*. New York: McGraw-Hill, 1967.

Gurnee, H. "The Effect of Collective Learning Upon the Individual Participants." *Journal of Abnormal and Social Psychology* 34(1939):529–532.

Gutin, B. "Exercise Induced Activation and Human Performance: A Review." *Research Quarterly* 44(1973):256–268.

Gutmann, M. C., and Benson, H. "Interaction of Environmental Factors and Systemic Arterial Blood Pressure: A Review." *Medicine* 50(1971):543–553.

Hain, P. *Don't Play With Apartheid.* London: Allen and Unwin, 1971.

Hall, C. S., and Lindzey, G. *Theories of Personality.* New York: Wiley, 1957.

Hancock, J. G., and Teevan, R. C. "Fear of Failure and Risk Taking Behavior." *Journal of Personality* 32(1964):200–209.

Hanson, D. "Cardiac Response to Participation in Little League Baseball Competition as Determined by Telemetry." *Research Quarterly* 38(1967):384–388.

Hardman, K. "An Investigation into the Possible Relationships Between Athletic Ability and Certain Personality Traits in Third Year Secondary Modern Schoolboys." Presentation, 1962, at University of Manchester.

Hare, P. *Handbook of Small Group Research.* Glencoe, Ill.: Free Press, 1962.

Harlow, H. F. "Social Facilitation of Feeding in the Albino Rat." *Journal of Genetic Psychology* 41(1932):211–221.

Harlow, H. F. "Mice, Monkeys, Men, and Motives." *Psychological Review* 60(1953): 23–32.

Harmon, J. M., and Johnson, W. R. "The Emotional Reactions of College Athletes." *Research Quarterly* 23(1952):391–397.

Harrington, J. A. *Soccer Hooliganism: A Preliminary Report.* Bristol: Wright, 1968.

Harris, D. V. "Comparison of Physical Performance and Psychological Traits of College Women with High and Low Fitness Indices." *Perceptual and Motor Skills* 17(1963): 293–294.

Harris, D. V. "On the Brink of Catastrophe." *Quest* 13(1970):33–40.

Harris, D. V. *Involvement in Sport: A Somato-psychic Rationale for Physical Activity.* Philadelphia: Lea and Febiger, 1973.

Harrison, J.; MacKinnon, P. C. B.; and Monk-Jones, M. E. "Behavior of Palmar Sweat Glands Before and After Operation." *Clinical Science* 23(1962):371–377.

Harrison, J., and MacKinnon, P. C. B. "Physiological Role of the Adrenal Medulla in the Palmar Anihidrotic Response to Stress." *Journal of Applied Physiology* 21(1966): 88–92.

Hartmann, D. P. "Influence of Symbolically Modeled Instrumental Aggression and Pain Cues on Aggressive Behavior." *Journal of Personality and Social Psychology* 11(1969):280–288.

Hartmann, H.; Kris, E.; and Lowenstein, R. M. "Notes on the Theory of Aggression." *The Psychoanalytic Study of the Child* 1949:3–4, 9–36.

Hasdorf, A. H., and Contril, H. "They Saw a Game: A Case Study." *Journal of Abnormal and Social Psychology* 49(1954):129–134.

Hase, H. D., and Goldberg, L. R. "Comparative Validity of Different Strategies of Constructing Personality Inventory Scales." *Psychological Bulletin* 67(1967):231–248.

Haskins, R. G. *The Glands and Their Functions.* New York: Norton, 1941.

Hastorf, A. H.; Schneider, D. J.; and Polefka, J. *Person Perception.* Menlo Park, Calif.: Addison-Wesley, 1970.

Hathaway, S. R. "Where Have We Gone Wrong? The Mystery of the Missing Progress." In *Objective Personality Assessment: Changing Perspectives.* Edited by J. N. Butcher New York: Academic Press, 1972.

Hathaway, S. R., and McKinley, J. C. *Minnesota Multiphasic Personality Inventory (Manual).* New York: Psychological Corporation, 1951.

Hauty, G. T. "The Effects of Drugs Upon the Components of Hand Steadiness." Report No. 5, USAF School of Aviation, 1954.

Haywood, H. C., and Dobbs, V. "Motivation and Anxiety in High School Boys." *Journal of Personality* 32(1964):371–379.

Heath, R. G. "Electrical Self-Stimulation of the Brain in Man." *American Journal of Psychiatry* 120(1963):571–577.

Hebb, D. O. "Emotion in Man and Animal." *Psychological Review* 53(1946):88–106.

Hebb, D. O. *The Organization of Behavior.* New York: Wiley, 1949.

Hebb, D. O. "Drives and the C.N.S. (Conceptual Nervous System)." *Psychological Review* 62(1955):243–254.

Hecht, E. "Football." In *Latin America and the Carribean: A Handbook.* Edited by C. Véliz. New York: Praeger, 1968.

Heckhausen, H. "Eine Rahmentheorie der Motivation in zehn Thesen." *Zeitschrift fuer Experimentelle und Angewandte Psychologie* 10(1963):604–626.

Heckhausen, H. *The Anatomy of Achievement Motivation.* New York: Academic Press, 1967.

Heckhausen, H. "Achievement Motive Research: Current Problems and Some Contributions Towards a General Theory of Motivation." In *Nebraska Symposium on Motivation.* Edited by W. J. Arnold. Lincoln: University of Nebraska Press, 1968.

Heider, F. *The Psychology of Interpersonal Relations.* New York: Wiley, 1958.

Heimburger, R. F.; Whitlock, C. C.; and Kalsbeck, J. E. "Stereotaxic Amygdalotomy for Epilepsy with Aggressive Behavior." *Journal of the American Medical Association* 198(November 14, 1966):741–745.

Heinicke, C., and Bales, R. F. "Developmental Trends in the Structure of Groups." *Sociometry* 16(1953):7–38.

Heinlä, K. "Notes on the Inter-Group Conflicts in International Sport." In *Cross-Cultural Analysis of Sports and Games.* Edited by G. Lüschen. Champaign, Ill.: Stipes, 1970.

Helson, H. *Adaptation-Level Theory.* New York: Harper and Row, 1964.

Henchy, T., and Glass, D. C. "Evaluation Apprehension and the Social Facilitation of Dominant and Subordinate Responses." *Journal of Personality and Social Psychology* 9(1968):251–256.

Hendry, L. B. "Some Notions on Personality and Sporting Ability: Certain Comparisons with Scholastic Achievement." *Quest* 13(1970):63–73.

Henry, F. M. "Reaction Time-Movement Time and Correlations." *Perceptual and Motor Skills* 12(1961):63–67.

Hess, R. D., and Goldblatt, I. "The Status of Adolescents in American Society: A Problem in Social Identity." In *The Adolescent—A Book of Readings.* Rev. ed. Edited by J. Seidman. New York: Holt, Rinehart and Winston, 1960.

Hess, W. R. *Diencephalon: Autonomic and Extra-pyramidal Functions*. New York: Grune, 1954.

Heusner, W. "Personality Traits of Champion and Former Champion Athletes." Unpublished research study, University of Illinois, 1952.

Hilgard, E. R.; Sait, E. M.; and Margaret, G. A. "Level of Aspiration As Affected by Relative Standing in an Experimental Social Group." *Journal of Experimental Psychology* 27(1940):411–421.

Hinde, R. A. "Unitary Drives." *Animal Behavior* 7(1959):130–141.

Hinde, R. A. "Energy Models of Motivation." *Symposia of the Society for Experimental Biology* 14(1960):199–213.

Hoffmann, R. L. "Homogeneity of Member Personality and Its Effects on Group Problem Solvings." *Journal of Abnormal and Social Psychology* 58(1959):27–32.

Hoffmann, R. L., and Maier, N. F. "Quality and Acceptance of Problem Solutions by Members of Homogeneous and Heterogeneous Groups." *Journal of Abnormal and Social Psychology* 62(1961):401–407.

Hokanson, J. E. "Psychophysiological Evaluation of the Catharsis Hypothesis." In *The Dynamics of Aggression*. Edited by E. I. Megaree and J. E. Hokanson. New York: Harper and Row, 1970.

Hokanson, J. E., and Burgess, M. "The Effects of Three Types of Aggression on Vascular Processes." *Journal of Abnormal and Social Psychology* 64(1962):446–449.

Hokanson, J. E.; Burgess, M.; and Cohen, M. F. "Effects of Displaced Aggression on Systolic Blood Pressure." *Journal of Abnormal and Social Psychology* 67(1963): 214–218.

Hokanson, J., and Edelman, R. "Effects of Three Social Responses on Vascular Processes." *Journal of Personality and Social Psychology* 3(1966):442–447.

Holland, J. L. "The Prediction of College Grades from the California Psychological Inventory and the Scholastic Aptitude Test." *Journal of Educational Psychology* 50(1959):135–142.

Hollander, E. P. *Principles and Methods of Social Psychology*. New York: Oxford University Press, 1967.

Holmgren, G. L., and Harker, G. S. "Characteristic Pace as Determined by the Use of a Tracking Treadmill." *Journal of Applied Psychology* 51(1967):278–283.

Holt, R. R. *Assessing Personality*. San Francisco: Harcourt Brace Jovanovich, 1971.

Holtzman, W. H. "Statistical Models for the Study of Change in the Single Case." In *Problems in the Measurement of Change*. Edited by C. Harris. Madison: University of Wisconsin Press, 1963. (a)

Holtzman, W. H. "The Robot Personality—Static or Dynamic?" In *Computer Simulation of Personality*. Edited by S. S. Tompkins and S. Messick. New York: Wiley, 1963. (b)

Holtzman, W. H. "Recurring Dilemmas in Personality Assessment." *Journal of Projective Technique and Personality Assessment* 28 (1964):144–150.

Holtzman, W. H. "Personality Structure." *Annual Review of Psychology* 16(1965): 119–156.

Holtzman, W. H.; Thorpe, J. S.; Swartz, J. D.; and Herron, ⁵. W. *Ink Blot Perception and Personality*. Austin: University of Texas Press, 1961.

Homans, G. C. *The Human Group.* New York: Harcourt, Brace Jovanovich, 1950.

Homme, L. *How to Use Contingency Contracting in the Classroom.* Champaign, Ill.: The Research Press, 1970.

Hoppe, F. "Erfolg and Misserfolg." *Psychologische Forschung* 14(1930):1–62.

Horsfall, J. S.; Fisher, A. C.; and Morris, H. H. "Sport Personality Assessment: A Methodological Re-examination." Paper presented at the North American Society for the Psychology of Sport and Physical Activity, May 1975, at Pennsylvania State University.

Hottinger, W. L. "The Effect of Waking and Hypnotic Suggestions on Strength." Master's thesis, University of Illinois, 1958.

Hubbard, A. W. "Some Thoughts on the Motivation of Sport." *Quest* 10(1968):40–46.

Hull, C. L. *Hypnosis and Suggestibility.* New York: Appleton-Century-Crafts, 1933.

Hull, C. L. *Principles of Behavior.* New York: Appleton-Century-Crafts, 1943.

Hunt, J. M. "Traditional Personality Theory in the Light of Recent Evidence." *American Scientist* 53 (1965):80–95.

Hunt, W. A. "Recent Developments in the Field of Emotion." *Psychological Bulletin* 38(1941):249–276.

Hurlock, E. B. "The Value of Praise and Reproof as Incentives for Children." *Archives of Psychology,* No. 71, 1924.

Hurlock, E. B. "An Evaluation of Certain Incentives Used in School Work." *Journal of Educational Psychology* 16(1925):145–159. (a)

Hurlock, E. B. "The Effects of Incentives Upon the Constancy of the IQ." *Journal of Genetic Psychology* 32(1925):422–434. (b)

Hurlock, E. B. "The Psychology of Incentives." *Journal of Social Psychology* 2(1931): 261–290.

Husband, R. W. "Analysis of Methods in Human Maze Learning." *Pedagogical Seminary and Journal of Genetic Psychology* 39(1931):258–278.

Husman, B. F. "Aggression in Boxers and Wrestlers as Measured by Projective Techniques." *Research Quarterly* 26(1955):421–425.

Husman, B. F. "Sport and Personality Dynamics." *Proceedings of National College Physical Education Association for Men* 72(1969):56–70.

Husman, B. F.; Hanson, D.; and Walker, R. "The Effect of Coaching Basketball and Swimming Upon Emotion as Measured by Telemetry." In *Contemporary Psychology of Sport.* Edited by G. S. Kenyon. Chicago: Athletic Institute, 1970.

Iglitzen, L. B. "Violence and American Democracy." *Journal of Social Issues* 26(1970): 165–186.

Imlach, P. (with S. Young). *Hockey is a Battle.* Richmond Hill, Ont.: Simon and Schuster, 1970.

Ingham, A. G., and Smith, M. D. "The Social Implications of the Interaction Between Spectators and Athletes." In *Exercise and Sport Science Reviews.* Vol. 2. Edited by J. Wilmore. New York: Academic Press, 1974.

Irwin, F. W., and Mintzer, M. G. "Effects of Differences in Instructions and Motivation on Measures of the Level of Aspiration." *American Journal of Psychology* 55(1942): 400–406.

Izenberg, J. "Upsurge in Violence." *Rochester Democrat and Chronicle,* February 16, 1972.

Jackson, D. N., and Messick, S. "Acquiescence and Desirability as Response Determinants on the MMPI." *Educational and Psychological Measurement* 21(1961): 771-790.

Jackson, D. N., and Messick, S. "Response Styles on the MMPI: Comparison of Clinical and Normal Samples." *Journal of Abnormal and Social Psychology* 65(1962): 285-299.

Jackson, D. N., and Pacine, L. "Response Styles and Academic Achievement." *Educational and Psychological Measurement* 21(1961):1015-1028.

Jacobson, E. *Progressive Relaxation.* Chicago: University of Chicago Press, 1938.

Jacobson, E. *You Must Relax.* 4th ed. New York: McGraw-Hill, 1957.

Jacobson, G. "Coach Endorses Transcendental Meditation for that Better Dive." *Minnesota Daily,* January 9, 1973.

James, W. "What is Emotion?" *Mind* 9(1884):188-205.

James, W. T. "Social Facilitations of Eating Behavior in Puppies after Satiation." *Journal of Comparative and Physiological Psychology* 46(1953):427-428.

James, W. T. "The Development of Social Facilitation of Eating in Puppies." *Journal of Genetic Psychology* 96(1960):123-127.

James, W. T., and Cannon, D. J. "Variation in Social Facilitation of Eating Behavior in Puppies." *Journal of Genetic Psychology* 87(1956):225-228.

Janis, I. L.; Mahl. G. F.; Kagan, J.; and Holt, R. R. *Personality: Dynamics, Development, and Assessment.* New York. Harcourt, Brace Jovanovitch, 1969.

Johnsgard, K. W., and Ogilvie, B. C. "The Competitive Racing Driver." *Journal of Sports Medicine* 8(1968):87-95.

Johnson, B. L. "The Effects of Applying Different Motivational Techniques During Training and in Testing Upon Strength Performance." Ed. D. dissertation, Louisiana State University, 1965.

Johnson, J. E., and Dabbs, J. M., Jr. "Enumeration of Active Sweat Glands: A Simple Physiological Indicator of Psychological Changes." *Nursing Research* 16(1967): 273-276.

Johnson, R. N. *Aggression in Man and Animals.* Philadelphia: Saunders, 1972.

Johnson, T. P. "Knute Rockne and Coaching." In *Motivations in Play, Games and Sports.* Edited by R. Slovenko and J. A. Knight. Springfield, Ill.: Thomas, 1967.

Johnson, W. "TV Made It All a New Game." *Sports Illustrated* 31 (December 22, 1969): 86-102.

Johnson, W. R. "A Study of Emotion Revealed in Two Types of Athletic Contests." *Research Quarterly* 20(March 1949):72-79.

Johnson, W. R. "Body Movement Awareness in The Nonhypnotic and Hypnotic States." *Research Quarterly* 32(1961):263-264. (a)

Johnson, W. R. "Hypnotic Analysis of a Case of Aggression Blockage in Baseball Pitching." *American Journal of Clinical Hypnosis* (October, 1961). (b)

Johnson, W. R., and Hutton, D. C. "Effects of a Combative Sport Upon Personality Dynamics as Measured by a Projective Test." *Research Quarterly* 26(1955):49-53.

Johnson, W. R.; Hutton, D. C.; and Johnson, G. B. "Personality Traits of Some Champion Athletes as Measured by Two Projective Tests: Rorschach and H-T-P." *Research Quarterly* 25(1954):484–485.

Johnson, W. R., and Kramer, G. F. "Effects of Different Types of Hypnotic Suggestions Upon Physical Performance." *Research Quarterly* 31(1960):469–473.

Johnson, W. R., and Kramer, G. F. "Effects of Stereotyped Non-hypnotic, Hypnotic and Post-hypnotic Suggestions Upon Strength, Power and Endurance." *Research Quarterly* 32(1961):522–529.

Johnson, W. R.; Massey, B. H.; and Kramer, G. F. "Effects of Post-hypnotic suggestions on All-out Effort of Short Duration." *Research Quarterly* 31(1960):142–146.

Jones, E. E., and Nisbett, R. E. *The Actor and the Observer: Divergent Perceptions of the Causes of Behavior.* New York: General Learning Press, 1971.

Jones, M. B. "Practice as a Process of Simplification." *Psychological Review* 4(1962): 274–294.

Jost, H. "Some Physiological Changes During Frustration." *Child Development* 12(1941): 9–15.

Kane, J. E. "Personality and Physique of Athletes." *Physical Recreation* 34(1960).

Kane, J. E. "Physique and Physical Abilities of 14-year Old Boys in Relation to their Personality and Social Adjustment." Master's thesis, University of Manchester, 1962.

Kane, J. E. "Personality and Physical Ability." In *Proceedings of the International Congress of Sports Sciences,* edited by K. Kato. Tokyo: Japanese Union of Sport Sciences, 1964.

Kane, J. E. "Personality Profiles of Physical Education Students Compared With Others." Paper presented at the First International Congress of Sport Psychology, 1965, at Rome.

Kane, J. "Personality Description of Soccer Ability." *Readings in Physical Education* 1(1966). (a)

Kane, J. E. "The Discrimination of Sports Types by Means of the I.P.F." Paper presented to the British Psychological Society Conference, March 1966, at Swansea. (b)

Kane, J. E. "Adult Involvement in Games." *Catholic Teachers Journal,* September–October, 1968.

Kane, J. E. "Personality, Arousal and Performance." *International Journal of Sports Psychology* 2(1971):12–20.

Kane, J. E., ed. *Psychological Aspects of Physical Education and Sport.* London: Routledge and Kegan Paul, 1972.

Kane, J. E. Personal Correspondence with A. C. Fisher, November, 1973.

Kane, J. E., and Callaghan, J. L. "Personality Traits in Tennis Players." *British Lawn Tennis,* July 1965.

Katchmar, L. T.; Ross, S.; and Andrews, T. G. "Effects of Stress and Anxiety on Performance of a Complex Verbal-Coding Task." *Journal of Experimental Psychology* 55(1958):559–564.

Kelley, H. H. "Attribution Theory in Social Psychology." In *Nebraska Symposium on Motivation.* Edited by M. R. Jones. Lincoln: University of Nebraska Press, 1967.

Kelley, H. H., and Stahelski, A. J. "Social Interaction Basis of Cooperators' and Competitors' Beliefs about Others." *Journal of Personality and Social Psychology* 16 (1970):66–91.

Kelley, H. H., and Thibaut, J. W. "Experimental Studies of Group Problem Solving and Process." In *Handbook of Social Psychology*. Vol 2. Edited by G. Lindzey. Reading, Mass.: Addison-Wesley, 1954.

Kendler, H. H. "Learning." *Annual Review of Psychology* 10(1959):43–88.

Kennard, M. A.; Rabinovitch, M. S.; and Fister, W. P. "The Use of Frequency Analysis in the Interpretation of the EEGs of Patients with Psychological Disorders." *Electroencephalography and Clinical Neurophysiology Supplement* 7(1955):29–38.

Kennard, M. A., and Willner, M. D. "Correlation Between Electroencephalograms and Deep Reflexes in Normal Adults." *Diseases of the Nervous Systems* 6(1943): 337–347.

Kennedy, W. A.; Turner, A. J.; and Lindner, R. "Effectiveness of Praise and Blame as a Function of Intelligence." *Perceptual and Motor Skills* 15(1962):143–149.

Kennedy, W. A., and Willcutt, H. "Motivation of School Children." Cooperative Research Project No. 1929, Department of Health, Education, and Welfare; and Department of Education, Florida State University, October 1963.

Kent, H. R. "The Effect of Repeated Praise and Blame on the Work Achievement of Blind Children." *Dissertation Abstracts* 27(1957):675.

Kenyon, G. S. "A Conceptual Model for Characterizing Physical Activity." *Research Quarterly* 39(1968):96–105. (a)

Kenyon, G. S. "Six Scales for Assessing Attitudes Toward Physical Activity." *Research Quarterly* 39(1968):566–574. (b)

Kerlinger, F. N. *Foundations of Behavioral Research*. New York: Holt, Rinehart and Winston, 1973.

Kidd, B., and MacFarlane, J. *The Death of Hockey*. Toronto: New Press, 1972.

Kimble, G. A. *Conditioning and Learning*. New York: Appleton-Century-Crofts, 1961.

King, H. E. "Psychological Effects of Excitation in the Limbic System." In *Electrical Stimulation of the Brain*. Edited by D. E. Sheer. Austin: University of Texas Press, 1961.

Kingsmore, J. M. "The Effect of Professional Wrestling and Professional Basketball Contests Upon the Aggressive Tendencies of Spectators." In *Contemporary Psychology of Sport*. Edited by G. S. Kenyon. Chicago: Athletic Institute, 1970.

Kirby, T. J. "Practice in the Case of School Children." *Teachers College Contributions to Education* No. 58, 1913.

Klein, G. S.; Barr, H. L.; and Wolitzky, D. L. "Personality." *Annual Review of Psychology* 18(1967):467–560.

Klein, J. *The Study of Groups*. London: Routledge and Kegan Paul, 1956.

Klein, M., and Christiansen, G. "Group Composition, Group Structure and Group Effectiveness of Basketball Teams." In *Sport, Culture, and Society: A Reader on the Sociology of Sport*. Edited by J. W. Loy and G. S. Kenyon. Toronto: Macmillan, 1969.

Kleinmuntz, B. *Personality Measurement—An Introduction*. Homewood, Ill.: Dorsey Press, 1967.

Klinger, E. "Feedback Effects and Social Facilitation of the Vigilance Performance: Mere Coaction Versus Potential Evaluation." *Psychonomic Science* 14(1969):161–162.

Klopfer, P. H. "Influence of Social Interactions on Learning Rates in Birds." *Science* 128(1958):903.

Kluckhohn, C. *Mirror for Man.* Greenwich, Conn.: Fawcett, 1968.

Kluckhohn, C., and Murray, H. A. *Personality in Nature, Society and Culture.* New York: Knopf, 1949.

Klugman, S. F. "The Effect of Money Incentive Versus Praise Upon the Reliability and Obtained Scores of the Revised Stanford-Binet Test." *Journal of General Psychology* 30(1944):255–269.

Klüver, H., and Bucy, P. E. "Psychic Blindness' and Other Symptoms Following Bilateral Temporal Lobectomy in Rhesus Monkeys." *American Journal of Physiology* 119 (1937):352–353.

Knapp, B. *Skill in Sport.* London: Routledge and Kegan Paul, 1963.

Knapp. B. "The Personality of Lawn Tennis Players." *Bulletin of the British Psychological Society,* October 1965.

Knapp, J. "Emotional Reactions of College Women Gymnasts as a Function of Time to Competition." Master's thesis, University of Massachusetts, 1966.

Knott, P. D., and Drost, B. A. "Effects of Varying Intensity of Attack and Fear Arousal on the Intensity of Counter Aggression." *Journal of Personality* 40(1972):27–37.

Knowles, L., and Prewitt, K., eds. *Institutional Racism in America.* Englewood Cliffs, N.J.: Prentice-Hall, 1969.

Konig, R. "Die Informellen Gruppen im Industriebetrieb." In *Organization.* Edited by E. Schnaufer and K. Agthe. Baden-Baden, 1961.

Kozar, B. "The Effects of a Supportive and Nonsupportive Audience Upon Learning a Gross Motor Skill." *International Journal of Sport Psychology* 4(1973):27–38.

Krestovnikov, A. N., and Vasilena. "On the Flow of Grey Matter Nervous Processes of Athletes." In *Theory and Practice of Physical Culture,* No. 1, 1955.

Kroll, W. "An Anthropometric Study of Some Big Ten Varsity Wrestlers." *Research Quarterly* 25(1954):307–312.

Kroll, W. "Selected Factors Associated with Wrestling Success." *Research Quarterly* 29(1958):396–406.

Kroll, W. "Sixteen Personality Factor Profiles of Collegiate Wrestlers." *Research Quarterly* 38(1967):49–57.

Kroll, W. "Current Strategies and Problems in Personality Assessment of Athletes." In *Psychology of Motor Learning.* Edited by L. E. Smith. Chicago: Athletic Institute, 1970.

Kroll, W. "Psychological Aspects of Wrestling." Paper presented at American College of Sports Medicine Symposium on Wrestling, May 1972, at Philadelphia.

Kroll, W., and Carlson, B. R. "Discriminant Function and Hierarchial Grouping Analysis of Karate Participants' Personality Profiles." *Research Quarterly* 38(1967):405–411.

Kroll, W., and Crenshaw, W. "Multivariate Personality Profile Analysis of Four Athletic Groups." In *Contemporary Psychology of Sport.* Edited by G. S. Kenyon. Chicago: Athletic Institute, 1970.

Kroll, W., and Lewis, G. "America's First Sport Psychologist." *Quest* 13(1970):1–4.

Kroll, W., and Peterson, K. H. "Personality Factor Profiles of Collegiate Football Teams." *Research Quarterly* 36(1965):433–440. (a)

Kroll, W., and Peterson, K. H. "Study of Value Test and Collegiate Football Teams." *Research Quarterly* 36(1965):441–447. (b)

Krumdeck, V. F., and Lumian, N. C. "Psychology of Athletic Success." *Athletic Journal* 44(September, 1963):52.

Kuethe, J. L., and Eriksen, C. W. "Personality, Anxiety, and Muscle Tension as Determinants of Response Stereotypy." *Journal of Abnormal and Social Psychology* 54(1957): 400–404.

Kuhn, T. S. *The Structure of Scientific Revolutions.* 2d ed. Chicago: University of Chicago Press, 1970.

Kuno, Y. "The Significance of Sweat in Man." *Lancet* 28(1930):912–915.

Lacey, J. I. "Individual Differences in Somatic Response Patterns." *Journal of Comparative and Physiological Psychology* 43(1950):338–350.

Lacey, J. I. "Somatic Response Patterning and Stress: Some Revisions of Activation Theory." In *Psychological Stress: Issues in Research.* Edited by M. H. Appley and R. Trumbull. New York: Appleton-Century-Crofts, 1967.

Lacey, J. I., and Lacey, B. C. "Verification and Extension of the Principle of Autonomic Response-stereotypy." *American Journal of Psychology* 71(1958):50–73.

Lagerspetz, K. "Studies on the Aggressive Behavior of Mice." *Annales Academiae Scientiarum Fennicae, Series B* 131(1964):1–131.

Laird, D. A. "Changes in Motor Control and Individual Variations Under the Influence of 'Razzing.'" *Journal of Experimental Psychology* 6(1923):233–246.

Lakie, W. L. "Personality Characteristics of Certain Groups of Intercollegiate Athletics." *Research Quarterly* 33(1962):566–573.

Landers, D. M., and Crum, T. F. "The Effect of Team Success and Formal Structure on Inter-Personal Relations and Cohesiveness of Baseball Teams." *International Journal of Sport Psychology* 2(1971):88–96.

Landers, D. M., and Lüschen, G. "Team Performance Outcome and the Cohesiveness of Competitive Coacting Groups." *International Review of Sport Sociology* 9(1974): 57–71.

Landis, C., and Hunt, W. A. "The Conscious Correlates of the Galvanic Skin Response." *Journal of Experimental Psychology* 18(1935):505–529.

Landy, F. J., and Stern, R. M. "Factor Analysis of a Somatic Perception Questionnaire." *Journal of Psychosomatic Research* 15(1971):179–181.

Langer, P. "Some Psychological Implications of Varsity Football Performance." *Coach and Athlete* 29(September 1966):30–31. (a)

Langer, P. "Varsity Football Performance." *Perceptual and Motor Skills* 23(1966): 1191–1199. (b)

Lansing, R. W.; Schwartz, E.; and Lindsley, D. B. "Reaction Time and EEG Activation." *American Psychologist* 11(1956):433.

LaPlace, J. P. "Personality and Its Relationship to Success in Professional Baseball." *Research Quarterly* 25(1954):313–319.

LaPorte, W. R. *The Physical Education Curriculum.* Los Angeles: College Book Store, 1955.

Lasagna, L., and McCann, W. P. "Effect of 'Tranquilizing' Drugs on Amphetamine Toxicity in Aggregated Mice." *Science* 125(1957):1241–1242.

Lawther, J. D. *Psychology of Coaching.* Englewood Cliffs, N. J.: Prentice-Hall, 1951.

Lawther, J. D. *Sport Psychology.* Englewood Cliffs, N. J.: Prentice-Hall, 1972.

Layman, E. M. "Contributions of Exercise and Sports to Mental Health and Social Adjustment." In *Science and Medicine of Exercise and Sport.* Edited by W. R. Johnson. New York: Harper and Row, 1960. (a)

Layman, E. M. "Physical Activity as a Psychiatric Adjunct." In *Science and Medicine of Exercise and Sport.* Edited by W. R. Johnson. New York: Harper and Row, 1960. (b)

Layman, E. M. "Aggression in Relation to Play and Sports." In *Contemporary Psychology of Sport.* Edited by G. S. Kenyon. Chicago: Athletic Institute, 1970.

Layman, E. M. "The Contribution of Play and Sports to Emotional Health." In *Psychological Aspects of Physical Education and Sport.* Edited by J. E. Kane, London: Routledge and Kegan Paul, 1972.

Lazarus, R. S.; Deese, J.; and Osler, S. J. "The Effects of Psychological Stress Upon Performance." *Psychological Bulletin* 49(1952):293–317.

Lazier, M. M. "Fear." *Journal of the American Football Coaches Association,* June 15, 1965.

Leavitt, E. E. *The Psychology of Anxiety.* New York: Bobbs-Merrill, 1967.

Lee, M. A. M. "The Relation of the Knee Jerk and Standing Steadiness to Nervous Instability." *Journal of Abnormal and Social Psychology* 26(1931):212–228.

Lehrman, D. S. "A Critique of Konrad Lorenz's Theory of Instinctive Behavior." *Quarterly Review of Biology* 28(1953):337–363.

Leiberson, S., and Silverman, A. R. "The Precipitants and Underlying Conditions of Race Riots." *American Sociological Review* 30(1965):887–898.

Leidermann, P. H., and Shapiro, D., eds. *Psychobiological Approaches to Social Behavior.* Stanford: Stanford University Press, 1964.

Lenk, H. "The Racing Community and Group Dynamics." *Rudersport* (1962):5–7.

Lenk, H. "Sociogram of a Club Eight." *Rudersport* (1963):5–7.

Lenk, H. "Conflict and Performance in Top Sport Teams: Sociometric Structures of Competition Eights in Rowing." *Soziale Welt* 15(1965):307–343.

Lenk, H. "Maximum Performance in Spite of Inner Conflict" *Kölner Zeitschrift für Soziologie und Sozialpsychologie* 10(1966):168–172.

Lenk, H. "Top Performance Despite Internal Conflict: An Antithesis to a Functionalistic Proposition." In *Sport, Culture, and Society: A Reader on the Sociology of Sport.* Edited by J. W. Loy and G. S. Kenyon. Toronto: Macmillan, 1969.

Lever, J. "Soccer: Opinion of the Brazilian People." *Trans-action* 7(No. 2, 1969):36–43.

Lever, J. "Soccer as a Brazilian Way of Life." In *Games, Sport and Power.* Edited by G. P. Stone. New York: Dutton, 1972.

Levitov, N. D. "On the Psychic Conditions of Man." *Enlightenment* (Moscow), 1964.

Lewin, K. "Psycho-sociological Problems of a Minority Group." *Character and Personality* 3(1935):175–187.

Lewin, K. "Self-hatred Among Jews." *Contemporary Jewish Record* 4(1941):219–232.

Lewin, K.; Dembo, T.; Festinger, L.; and Sears, P. S. "Level of Aspiration." In *Personality and the Behavior Disorders.* Edited by J. M. Hunt. New York: Ronald Press, 1944.

Lindsay, P. H., and Norman, D. A. An *Introduction to Psychology.* New York: Academic Press, 1972.

Lindsley, D. B. "Emotion." In *Handbook of Experimental Psychology.* Edited by S. S. Stevens. New York: Wiley, 1951.

Lindsley, D. B. "Psychological Phenomena and the Electroencephelogram." *Electroencephalography and Clinical Neurophysiology Supplement* 4(1952):443–456.

Lindsley, D. B. "Psychophysiology and Motivation." In *Nebraska Symposium on Motivation.* Edited by M. R. Jones. Lincoln: University of Nebraska Press, 1957.

Lindzey, G. *Projective Techniques and Cross-cultural Research.* New York: Appleton-Century-Crofts, 1961.

Littig, L. W., and Waddell, C. M. "Sex and Experimenter Interaction in Serial Learning." *Journal of Verbal Learning and Verbal Behavior* 6(1967):676-678.

Loehlin, J. C. "A Computer Program that Simulates Personality." In *Computer Simulation of Personality.* Edited by S. S. Tompkins and S. Messick. New York: Wiley, 1963.

Loew, C. A. "Acquisition of a Hostile Attitude and Its Relation to Aggressive Behavior." *Journal of Personality and Social Psychology* 5(1967);335–341.

Lorenz, K. "The Comparative Method in Studying Innate Behaviour Patterns." In Symposia of the Society for Experimental Biology. Vol. 4. Cambridge: Cambridge University Press, 1950.

Lorenz, K. *Das Sogenannte Böge: Zur Naturgeschichte der Aggression.* Wien: Borotha Schoeler Verlag, 1963.

Lorenz, K. *On Aggression.* New York: Harcourt, Brace and World, 1966. 83–93.

Lott, B. E. "Group Cohesiveness: A Learning Phenomenon." *Journal of Social Psychology* 55(1961):275–286.

Lott, A. J., and Lott, B. E. "Group Cohesiveness, Communication Level and Conformity." *Journal of Abnormal and Social Psychology* 62(1961):408–412.

Lott, A. J., and Lott, B. E. "Group Cohesiveness as Interpersonal Attraction. A Review of Relationships with Antecedent and Consequent Variables." *Psychological Bulletin* 64(1965):259–309.

Loy, J. W., Jr. "The Nature of Sport: A Definitional Effort." *Quest* 10(1968):1–15.

Lund, F. *Emotions.* New York: Ronald Press, 1942.

Lundervold, A. "An Electromyographic Investigation of Tense and Relaxed Subjects." *Journal of Nervous and Mental Disease* 115(1952):512–525.

Luria, A. R. *The Nature of Human Conflict.* Translated and edited by W. H. Gantt. New York: Liveright, 1932.

Lüschen, G. "The Social Function of Modern Sport." In *Krankengymnastik Jungend,* 1964.

Luthe, W., ed. *Autogenic Therapy.* Vols. 1–5. New York: Grune and Stratton, 1969.

Lykken, D. "Neuropsychology and Psychophysiology in Personality Research." In *Handbook of Personality Theory and Research.* Edited by E. F. Borgatta and W. W. Lambert. Chicago: Rand McNally, 1968.

Lykken, D. T. "Multiple Factor Analysis and Personality Research." *Journal of Experimental Research in Personality* 5(1971):161–170.

Maccoby, M. "A Psychoanalytic View of Learning." *Change* 3(No. 8, 1972):32–38.

Maddi, S. R. *Personality Theories: A Comparative Analysis.* Homewood, Ill.: Dorsey Press, 1968.

Maddox, D. "Losing in San Diego—With Psychiatric Implications." *The Physician and Sportsmedicine* 2(January 1974):59–61.

Madsen, R. B. *Theories of Motivation.* 4th ed. Kent, Ohio: Kent State University Press, 1968.

Maertz, R. C. "Incentive Factors for Wrestling." *Athletic Journal* 49(December 1968): 41–43.

Magoun, H. W. *The Waking Brain.* Springfield, Ill.: Thomas, 1958.

Maharishi Mahesh Yogi. *Transendental Meditation: Serenity Without Drugs.* New York. Signet, 1968.

Malinowski, B. *Magic, Science and Religion.* New York: Doubleday, 1948.

Mallick, S. K., and McCandless, B. R. "A Study of Catharsis of Aggression." *Journal of Personality and Social Psychology* 4(1966):591–596.

Malmo, R. "Anxiety and Behavioral Arousal." *Psychological Review* 64(1957):367–386.

Malmo, R. "Measurement of Drive: An Unsolved Problem in Psychology." In *Nebraska Symposium on Motivation.* Edited by M. Jones. Lincoln: University of Nebraska Press, 1958.

Malmo, R. B. "Activation: A Neuro-psychological Dimension." *Psychological Review* 66(1959):367–386.

Malmo, R. B., and Shagass, C. "Physiologic Study of Symptom Mechanisms in Psychiatric Patients Under Stress." *Psychosomatic Medicine* 11(1949):25–29.

Malmo, R. B.; Shagass, C.; Belanger, D. J.; and Smith, A. A. "Motor Control in Psychiatric Patients Under Experimental Stress." *Journal of Abnormal and Social Psychology* 46(1951):539–547. (a)

Malmo R. B.; Shagass, C.; and Davis, J. F. "Electromyographic Studies of Muscular Tension in Psychiatric Patients Under Stress." *Journal of Clinical and Experimental Psychopathology* 12(1951):45–66. (b)

Malmo, R. B., and Smith, A. A. "Forehead Tension and Motor Irregularities in Psychoneurotic Patients Under Stress." *Journal of Personality* 23(1955):391–406.

Mandler, S., and Sarason, S. B. "A Study of Anxiety and Learning." *Journal of Abnormal and Social Psychology* 47(1952):166–173.

Mark, V. H., and Ervin, F. R. *Violence and the Brain*. New York: Harper and Row, 1970.

Marquis, J. *Deep Muscle Relaxation*. Los Altos, Calif: Self-Management Schools, n.d. Cassette.

Martens, R. "Effect of an Audience on Learning and Performance of a Complex Motor Skill." *Journal of Personality and Social Psychology* 12(1969):252–260. (a)

Martens, R. "Palmar Sweating and the Presence of an Audience." *Journal of Experimental Social Psychology* 5(1969):371–374. (b)

Martens, R. "Influence of Participation Motivation on Success and Satisfaction in Team Performance." *Research Quarterly* 41(1970):510–518.

Martens, R. "Anxiety and Motor Performance: A Review." *Journal of Motor Behavior* 3(1971):161–179.

Martens, R. "Arousal and Motor Performance." In *Exercise and Sport Sciences Review*. Vol 2. Edited by J. Wilmore. New York: Academic Press, 1974.

Martens, R. *Social Psychology and Physical Activity*. New York: Harper and Row, 1975.

Martens, R., and Landers, D. M. "Coaction Effects on a Muscular Endurance Task." *Research Quarterly* 40(1969):733–737. (a)

Martens, R., and Landers, D. M. "Effect of Anxiety, Competition, and Failure on Performance of a Complex Motor Task." *Journal of Motor Behavior* 1(1969):1–10. (b)

Martens, R., and Landers, D. M. "Motor Performance Under Stress: A Test of the Inverted-U Hypothesis." *Journal of Personality and Social Psychology* 16(1970): 29–37.

Martens, R., and Peterson, J. A. "Group Cohesiveness as a Determinant of Success and Member Satisfaction in Team Performance." *International Review of Sport Sociology* 6(1971):49–61.

Martens, R., and White, V. "Influence of Win–Loss Ratio on Performance Satisfaction and Preference for Opponents." *Journal of Experimental Social Psychology* 11(1975):343–362.

Martin, B. "The Assessment of Anxiety by Physiological Behavioral Measures." *Psychological Bulletin* 58(1961):234–255.

Martin, E. D. *The Behavior of Crowds*. New York: Harper and Row, 1920.

Martin, L. "The Effects of Competition Upon the Aggressive Responses of Basketball Players and Wrestlers." D.P.E. dissertation, Springfield College, 1969.

Marx, K., and Engels, F. *Works,* 1937.

Maslow, A. *Motivation and Personality*. New York: Harper and Row, 1954.

Maslow, A. *Toward a Psychology of Being*. 2d ed. Princeton: Van Nostrand, 1968.

Maslow, A. H. *Motivation and Personality*. New York: Harper and Row, 1970.

Mason, J. W., and Brady. J. V. "Plasma 17-Hydroxycorticosteroid Changes Related to Reserpine Effects of Emotional Behavior." *Science* 124(1956):983–984.

Mason, J. W., and Brady, J. V. "The Sensitivity of Psychoendocrine Systems to Social and Physical Environment." In *Psychobiological Approaches to Social Behavior.* Edited by P. H. Leidermann and D. Shapiro. Stanford: Stanford University Press, 1964.

Mason, J. W.; Brady, J. V.; and Sidman, M. "Plasma 17-Hydroxycorticosteroid Levels and Conditioned Behavior in the Rhesus Monkey." *Endocrinology* 60(1957): 741–752.

Massey, B. H.; Johnson, W. R.; and Kramer, G. F. "Effect of Warm-up Exercise Upon Muscular Performance Using Hypnosis to Control the Psychological Variable." *Research Quarterly* 32(1961):63–71.

Matarazzo, J. D. "An Experimental Study of Aggression in the Hypertensive Patient." *Journal of Personality* 42(1954):423.

Matarazzo, J.; Ulett, G. A.; and Saslow, G. "Human Maze Performance as a Function of Increasing Levels of Anxiety." *Journal of General Psychology* 53(1955):79–95.

Matarazzo, R., and Matarazzo, J. D. "Anxiety Level and Pursuitmeter Performance." *Journal of Consulting Psychology* 20(1956):70.

McClelland, D. C. *Personality.* New York: Holt-Dryden, 1951.

McClelland, D. C. *The Achieving Society.* Princeton: Van Nostrand, 1961.

McClelland, D. C. "Achievement Motivation Can Be Developed." *Harvard Business Review* 43(November, 1965):6–8. (a)

McClelland, D. C. "Toward a Theory of Motive Acquisition." *American Psychologist* 20(1965):321–333. (b)

McClelland, D. C.; Atkinson, J. W.; Russell, A.; and Lowell, E. L. *The Achievement Motive.* New York: Appleton-Century-Crofts, 1953.

McCurdy, H. G., and Lambert, W. E. "The Efficiency of Small Human Groups in the Solution of Problems Requiring Genuine Cooperation." *Journal of Personality* 20(1952): 478–494.

"M.D.'s Frown on Hypnosis of Athletes." *American Medical Association News,* July 11, 1960.

McGrath, J. E. "The Influence of Positive Interpersonal Relations on Adjustment and Effectiveness in Rifle Teams." *Journal of Abnormal and Social Psychology* 65(1962): 365–375.

McGrath, J. E., and Altman, I. *Small Group Research: A Synthesis and Critique of the Field.* New York: Holt, Rinehart and Winston, 1966.

McKenzie, T. "Effects of Various Reinforcing Contingencies on Behaviors in a Competitive Swimming Environment." Master's thesis, Dalhousie University, 1972.

McNemar, Q. *Psychological Statistics.* 3d ed. New York: Wiley, 1957.

McNab, T. "Needs of the Budding Athlete." *Times Education Supplement* 2648(February, 1966):486.

Mech, E.; Kapos, E.; Hurst, F.; and Auble, D. "A Mathematical Description of the Relationship Between Frequency of Responding and Intertrial Interval in a Motivational Situation." *Journal of Psychology* 37(1954):251–256.

Meehl, P. E. *Clinical Versus Statistical Prediction: A Theoretical Analysis and Review of the Evidence.* Minneapolis: University of Minnesota Press, 1954.

Mefferd, R. B., Jr.; Moran, L. J.; and Kimble, J. P., Jr. "Chlorpromazine-induced Changes in Blood Constituents in Schizophrenia." In *Transactions of the Fourth Research Conference for Chemotherapy and Psychiatry.* Washington, D.C.; Veterans Administration, 1960.

Meggyesy, D. *Out of Their League.* New York: Coronet, 1971.

Metz, W. A. "The Relative Effects of Stress and Praise on Creativity." *Dissertation Abstracts* 22(1961–1962):2885.

Meyer, D. R., and Noble, M. E. "Summation of Manifest Anxiety and Muscular Tensions." *Journal of Experimental Psychology* 55(1958):599–602.

Middleton, G., and Guthrie, G. M. "Personality Syndromes and Academic Achievement." *Journal of Educational Psychology* 60(1959):66–69.

Milgram S. "Behavioral Study of Obedience." *Journal of Abnormal and Social Psychology* 67(1963):371–378.

Milgram, S., and Toch, H. "Collective Behavior: Crowds and Social Movements." In *Handbook of Social Psychology.* 2d ed. Edited by G. Lindsey and E. Aronson. Reading, Mass.: Addison-Wesley, 1969.

Miller, L. A. "The Effects of Emotional Stress on High School Track and Field Performance." Master's thesis, University of California, Los Angeles, 1960.

Miller, N. E. "Theory and Experiment Relating Psychoanalytic Displacement to Stimulus–Response Generalization." *Journal of Abnormal and Social Psychology* 43(1948):155–178.

Mischel, W. *Personality and Assessment.* New York: Wiley, 1968.

Mischel, W. "Toward a Cognitive Social Learning Reconceptualization of Personality." *Psychological Review* 80(1973):252–283.

Moede, W. "Der Wetteifer, Seine Struktur und Sein Ausmas." *Zeitschrift für Padagogische Psychologie* 15(1914):353–368. Cited in F. H. Allport. *Social Psychology.* New York: Houghton-Mifflin, 1924.

Moltz, H. "Contemporary Instinct Theory and the Fixed Action Pattern." *Psychological Review* 72(1965):27–47.

Monroe, R. R. "A Psychiatrist Looks at Medical Hypnosis." *Journal of the Louisiana State Medical Society* 112(April, 1960):148–154.

Montagu, M. F. A., ed. *Man and Aggression.* New York: Oxford University Press, 1968.

Morgan, C. *Physiological Psychology.* New York: McGraw-Hill, 1943.

Morgan, M. I., and Ojemann, R. H. "A Study of the Luris Method." *Journal of Applied Psychology* 26(1942):168–179.

Morgan, W. P., ed. *Contemporary Readings in Sport Psychology.* Springfield, Ill.: Thomas, 1970.

Morgan, W. P. "Hypnosis and the Athlete." Presentation at the Symposium on Athletic Conditioning and Sports Medicine, December 1973, at University of California, Berkeley. Cassette.

Morris, D. *The Naked Ape.* New York: McGraw-Hill, 1968.

Mosher, R., and Orlick, T. "The Overjustification Hypothesis Applied to Sport Psychology: Perspectives and Preliminary Findings." Paper presented at the Sixth Canadian Symposium for Psychomotor Learning and Sport Psychology, October, 1974, at Halifax, Nova Scotia.

Mosston, M. "Inclusion–exclusion in Education—II." A paper presented to a Symposium on Innovations in Curriculum Design for Physical Education, February 1969, at Pittsburgh.

Mowrer, O. *Psychotherapy: Theory and Research.* New York: Ronald Press, 1953.

Moyer, K. E. *The Physiology of Hostility.* Chicago: Markham, 1971.

Moyer, K. E. "A Physiological Model of Aggression: Does It Have Different Implications?" In *The Neural Bases for Violence and Aggression.* Edited by W. S. Fields and W. H. Sweet. St. Louis: Green, 1974.

Mudra, D. "Psychological Factors in the Improvement of Performance." Paper presented at American Association of Health, Physical Education and Recreation National Convention, April 1971, at Detroit.

Mumford, N. L. "Relationship Between Psychological Arousal and Women's Gymnastic Performance." Master's thesis, Ithaca College, 1973.

Mundy-Castle, A. C. "Electrical Responses of the Brain in Relation to Behavior." *British Journal of Psychology* 44(1953):318–329.

Mundy-Castle, A. C., and McKiever, B. L. "The Psychophysiological Significance of the Galvanic Skin Response." *Journal of Experimental Psychology* 46(1953):15–24.

Murphy, G. *Personality: A Biosocial Approach to Origins and Structure.* New York: Harper, 1947.

Murphy, G.; Murphy, L. B.; and Newcomb, T. M. *Experimental Social Psychology.* New York: Harper and Row, 1937.

Murray, H. A. *Explorations in Personality.* New York: Oxford University Press, 1938.

Musgrove, F. "Role Conflict in Adolescence." *British Journal of Educational Psychology* 34(1964):34–42.

Myers, A. "Team Competition, Success, and the Adjustment of Group Members." *Journal of Abnormal and Social Psychology* 65(1962):325–332.

Myslenski, S. "The Pressure Cooker." *Sports Illustrated* 31(July 7, 1969):18–22.

Neal, P. "Personality Traits of U.S. Women Athletes Who Participated in 1959 Pan-American Games as Measured by EPPS." Master's thesis, University of Utah, 1963.

Nelson, D. O., and Samuels, L. T. "A Method for the Determination of 17-Hydroxycorticosteroids in Blood: 17-Hydroxycorticosterone in the Perepheral Circulation." *Journal of Clinical Endocrinology* 12(1952):519.

Nelson, D. O., and Langer, P. "Getting to Really Know Your Players." *Athletic Journal* 39(September, 1963):88–93.

Nelson, D. O., and Langer, P. "Comments on the Athlete's Playing Performance and His Anxiety." *Coach and Athlete* 28(1965):12–23.

Nelson, J. K. "An Analysis of the Effect of Applying Various Motivational Situations to College Men Subjected to a Stressful Physical Performance." Ph.D. dissertation, University of Oregon, 1962.

Newmark, C. S. "Stability of State and Trait Anxiety." *Psychological Reports* 30(1972): 196–198.

Niwa, T. "A Methodological Study on the Group Cohesiveness of Sport Group Based on Sociometry." *International Review of Sport Sociology* 3(1968):56–71.

Noble, E. E.; Fuchs, J. E.; Robel, D. P.; and Chambers, R. W. "Individual vs. Social Performance on Two Perceptual-Motor Tasks." *Perceptual and Motor Skills* 8(1958): 131–134.

Ogilvie, B. C. "Model for General Psychological Adaptation." *Track Technique* 14(1964): 428–429.

Ogilvie, B. C. "Personality Profiles of Successful Coaches." *Proceedings* of the Sports Injury Clinic, 1965, at University of Wisconsin.

Ogilvie, B. C. "The Unanswered Question: Competition and Its Effects Upon Femininity." *Swimming Technique* 4(October, 1967):83.

Ogilvie, B. "Psychological Consistencies Within the Personality of High Level Competitors." *Journal of American Medical Association* 205(1968):780–786. (a)

Ogilvie, B. C. "The Personality of the Male Athlete." *Academy Paper* of the American Academy of Physical Education 1(1968):43–52. (b)

Ogilvie, B. C. "The Unconscious Fear of Success." *Quest* 10(1968):35–46. (c)

Ogilvie, B. C. "The Stimulus-Addicts, A Psychosocial Paradox." In *The Winning Edge.* Edited by W. C. Schwank. Washington: American Alliance of Health, Physical Education and Recreation, 1974.

Ogilvie, B., and Tutko, T. "A Psychologist Reviews the Future Contribution of Motivational Research in Track and Field." *Track and Field News,* September 1, 1963.

Ogilvie, B. C., and Tutko, T. A. "The Psychological Profile of Olympic Champions: A Brief Look at Olympic Medalists." Paper presented at First International Congress of Sport Psychology, 1965, at Rome.

Ogilvie, B. C., and Tutko, T. A. *Problem Athletes and How To Handle Them.* London: Pelham, 1966.

Ogilvie, B. C., and Tutko, T. A. "What is an Athlete?" Paper presented at American Association of Health, Physical Education and Recreation National Convention, March 1967, at Las Vegas.

Ogilvie, B. C., and Tutko, T. A. "Self-Image and Measured Personality of Coaches." In *Contemporary Psychology of Sport.* Edited by G. S. Kenyon. Chicago: Athletic Institute, 1970.

Ogilvie, B. C., and Tutko, T. A. "If You Want to Build Character, Try Something Else." *Psychology Today* 5(October 1971):60–63.

Ogilvie, B. C.; Tutko, T. A.; and Young, I. "Comparison of Medalists and Non-medalists of Olympic Swimmers," Paper presented at First International Congress of Sport Psychology, 1965, at Rome.

Olds, J., and Milner, P. "Positive Reinforcement Produced by Electrical Stimulation of Septal Area and Other Regions of Rat Brain." *Journal of Comparative and Physiological Psychology* 47(1954):419–427.

483

Oliver, C. *High for the Game.* New York: Morrow, 1971.

Olmsted, M. S. *The Small Group.* New York: Random House, 1959.

Orme-Johnson, D. W. "Autonomic Stability and Transcendental Meditation." *Psychosomatic Medicine* 35(1973):341–349.

Orne, M. T. "The Nature of Hypnosis: Artifact and Essence." *Journal of Abnormal and Social Psychology* 58(1959):277–299.

Osgood, C. E.; Suci, G. J.; and Tannenbaum, P. H. *The Measurement of Meaning.* Urbana, Ill.: University of Illinois Press, 1957.

Oslez, S. F. "Intellectual Performance As a Function of Two Types of Psychological Stress." *Journal of Experimental Psychology* 47(1954):115–121.

Otis, L. "Changes in Drug Usage Patterns of Practitioners of Transcendental Meditation (TM)." Research report, Stanford Research Institute, Menlo Park, 1972.

Oxendine, J. B. *Psychology of Motor Learning.* New York: Appleton-Century-Crofts, 1968.

Parsons, D. R. "Personality Traits of National Representative Swimmers—Canada 1962." Master's thesis, University of British Columbia, Vancouver, 1963.

Parvanov, B., and Popov, N. "Special Characteristics of the Concentrating Attention of the Volleyball Player on the Performance of the Serve." In *Studies on Physical Culture,* No. 5, 1963.

Patrick, J. R. "Studies in Rational Behavior and Emotional Excitement: The Effect of Emotional Excitement on Rational Behavior of Human Subjects." *Journal of Comparative Psychology* 18(1934):153–195.

Patterson, G. R.; Littman, R. A.; and Bricker, W. "Assertive Behavior in Children: A Step Toward a Theory of Aggression." *Monographs of the Society for Research in Child Development* 32(1967):1–43.

Paul, G. L. *Insight vs. Desensitization in Psychotherapy.* Stanford: Stanford University Press, 1966.

Paulus, P. B., and Murdoch, P. "Anticipated Evaluation and Audience Presence in the Enhancement of Dominant Responses." *Journal of Experimental Social Psychology* 7(1971):280–291.

Peatman, J. G. *Descriptive and Sampling Statistics.* New York: Harper and Row, 1947.

Peck, R., and Diaz-Guerrero, R. "Two Core-Culture Patterns and the Diffusion of Values Across Their Border." *Proceedings of the Seventh Inter-American Congress of Psychology.* Mexico City: Sociedad Interamericana de Psicologia, 1963.

Penman, K. A.; Hastad, D. N.; and Cords, W. L. "Success of the Authoritarian Coach." *Journal of Social Psychology* 92(1974):155–156.

Persky, H.; Smith, K. D.; and Basu, G. K. "Relation of Physiologic Measures on Aggression and Hostility to Testosterone Production in Man." *Psychosomatic Medicine* 33(1971):265–277.

Pessin, J. "The Comparative Effects of Social and Mechanical Simulation on Memorizing." *American Journal of Psychology* 45(1933):263–281.

Pessin, J., and Husband, R. W. "Effects of Social Stimulation on Human Maze Learning" *Journal of Abnormal and Social Psychology* 28(1933):148.

Peterson, S. L.; Ukler, J. C.; and Tousdale, W. W. "Personality Traits of Women in Team vs. Women in Individual Sports." *Research Quarterly* 38(1967):686–690.

Petrie, A. "Some Psychological Aspects of Pain and the Relief of Suffering." *Annals of the New York Academy of Science* 86(1960):13–27.

Petrie, A.; Collins, W.; and Soloman, P. "The Tolerance for Pain and for Sensory Deprivation." *American Journal of Psychology* 73(1960):80–90.

Petrie, A.; Holland, L.; and Wolk, I. "Sensory Stimulation Causing Subdued Experience: Audio-Analgesia and Perceptual Argumentation and Reduction." *Journal of Nervous and Mental Disease* 137(1963):312–321.

Petrie, A.; McCulloch, R.; and Kazdin, P. "The Perceptual Characteristics of Juvenile Delinquents." *Journal of Nervous and Mental Disease* 134(1962):415–421.

Petrovich, V. K. "Concentration of Attention Before Performing the Sports Movement." Dissertation, University of Leningrad, 1966.

Pinneo, L. R. "The Effects of Induced Muscle Tension During Tracking on Level of Activation and on Performance." *Journal of Experimental Psychology* 62(1961):523–531.

Plunkett, C. "The Effect of the Psychological Components of Competition on Reaction Time in Tennis." Master's thesis, University of North Carolina, 1967.

Potter, E. H. "The Effects of Reproof in Relation to Age in School Children." *Journal of Genetic Psychology* 63(1943):247–258.

Puni, A. C. "Towards a Psychological Characterization of the Pre-starting Condition of an Athlete." In *Theory and Practice of Physical Culture.* 7th ed., 1949.

Puni, A. C. "Immediate Preparation for Competition." *Track and Field,* No. 7, 1961.

Rao, C. R. *Advanced Statistical Methods in Biometric Research.* New York: Wiley, 1952.

Radchenko, L. I. "Study of the Preparedness of the Wrestler for Competition by the Method of Associational Experiment." In *Theory and Practice of Physical Culture,* No. 2, 1966.

Rasch, P. J. "Indexes of Body Build of United States Freestyle Wrestlers. *Journal of the Association for Physical and Mental Rehabilitation* 12(1958):91–94.

Rasch, P. J., and Kroll, W. *What Research Tells the Coach About Wrestling.* Washington, D. C.: American Association for Health, Physical Education and Recreation, 1964.

Rasch, P. J., and Mozee, G. "Neuroticism and Extraversion in United States Weight Trainers." *Journal of Association for Physical and Mental Rehabilitation* 17(1963): 55–58.

Rasmussen, E. "Social Facilitation in Albino Rats." *Acta Psychologica* 4(1939): 275–294.

Richter, C. P.; Woodruff, B.; and Eaton, B. C. "Hand and Foot Patterns of Low Electrical Skin Resistance: Their Anatomical and Neurological Significance." *Journal of Neurophysiology* 6(1943):417–424.

Roby, T. B., and Lanzetta, J. T. "Work Group Structure, Communication and Group Performance." *Sociometry* 19(1956):105–113.

Rockne, K. K. *Coaching.* New York: Devin-Adair, 1925.

Rogers, C. R. *Client-centered Therapy: Its Current Practice, Implications, and Theory,* Boston: Houghton, 1951.

Rogoff, J. M. "A Critique on the Theory of the Emergency Function of the Adrenal Glands: Implications for Psychology." *Journal of General Psychology* 32(1945):249–268.

Rohrer, J. H., and Sherif, M., eds. *Social Psychology at the Crossroads.* New York: Harper and Row, 1951.

Rosenthal, R. *Experimenter Effects in Behavioral Research.* New York: Appleton-Century-Crofts, 1966.

Rosenthal, R., and Fode, K. L. "Psychology of the Scientist: V. Three Experiments in Experimenter Bias." *Psychological Reports* 12(1963):491–511.

Rosenthal, R., and Jacobson, L. *Pygmalion in the Classroom.* New York: Holt, Rinehart and Winston, 1968.

Rosenthal, S. R. "Risk Exercise." *Polo.* (Istituo Geografico Polare) 23(1960).

Rothballer, A. B. "Studies on the Adrenaline-sensitive Component of the Reticular Activating System." *Electroencephalography and Clinical Neurophysiology Supplement* 8(1957):603–621.

Rotter, J. B. *Social Learning and Clinical Psychology.* Englewood Cliffs, N.J.: Prentice-Hall, 1954.

Roush, E. S. "Strength and Endurance in the Waking and Hypnotic States." *Journal of Applied Physiology* 3(1951):404–410.

Ruckmick, C. *The Psychology of Feeling and Emotion.* New York: McGraw-Hill, 1936.

Rudik, P. A. "Understanding, Content and Tasks of the Psychological Preparation of the Athlete." In *Psychological Preparation of the Athlete.* Moscow: F.I.S., 1964.

Rudik, P. A. "Dynamics of Psychic Functions Under Conditions of Especially Difficult Activity." Paper presented at the XVIII International Congress of Psychology, 1966, at Moscow.

Rushall, B. S. "Personality Profiles and a Theory of Behavior Modification for Swimmers." *Swimming Technique* 4(1967):33,66–71.

Rushall, B. S. "The Demonstration and Evaluation of a Research Model for the Investigation of the Relationship Between Personality and Physical Performance Categories." Ph.D. dissertation, University of Indiana, 1969.

Rushall, B. S. "An Evaluation of the Relationship Between Personality and Physical Performance Categories." In *Contemporary Psychology of Sport,* edited by G. S. Kenyon. Chicago: Athletic Institute, 1970.

Rushall, B. S. "The Environment as a Significant Source of Variance in the Study of Personality." Paper presented at the Third Canadian Psycho-Motor Learning and Sports Psychology Symposium, October 1971, at the University of British Columbia, Vancouver.

Rushall, B. S. "The Status of Personality Research and Application in Sports and Physical Education." Paper presented at the Physical Education Forum, January 1972, at Dalhousie University, Halifax, Nova Scotia.

Rushall, B. S. "A Direction for Contemporary Sport Psychology." Paper presented at the First Canadian Congress of the Multi-disciplinary Study of Sport and Physical Activity, October 1973, at Montreal.

Rushall, B. S., and Siedentop, D. *The Development and Control of Behavior in Sport and Physical Education.* Philadelphia: Lea and Febiger, 1972.

Russell, J. T. "Relative Efficiency of Relaxation and Tension in Performing an Act of Skill." *Journal of General Psychology* 6(1932):330–343.

Ryan, E. D. "The Cathartic Effect of Vigorous Motor Activity on Aggressive Behavior." *Research Quarterly* 41(1970):542–551.

Ryan, E. D., and Foster, R. "Athletic Participation and Perceptual Augmentation and Reduction." Unpublished manuscript, University of California, Davis, n.d.

Ryan, E. D., and Kovacic, C. R. "Pain Tolerance and Athletic Participation." *Perceptual and Motor Skills* 22(1966):383–390.

Ryan, T. A. "Significance Tests for Multiple Comparison of Proportions, Variances and Other Statistics." *Psychological Bulletin* 57(1960):318–328.

Sabock, R. J. *The Coach.* Philadelphia: Saunders, 1973.

Sage, G. H. *Introduction to Motor Behavior: A Neuropsychological Approach.* Reading, Mass.: Addison-Wesley, 1971.

Sandstrom, C. I., and Weinz, E. "Effects of Praise and Reproof in a Localization Experiment." *Acta Psychologia* (Amsterdam) 14(1958):137–143.

Sanford, N. "Personality—The Field." In *International Encyclopedia of the Social Sciences.* Vol. 2. Edited by D. L. Sills. New York: Crowell, Collier and MacMillan, 1968.

Sarason, I. G. "Effect of Anxiety, Motivational Instruction, and Failure on Serial Learning." *Journal of Experimental Psychology* 51(1956):253–260 (a)

Sarason, I. G. "The Effect of Anxiety and Two Kinds of Failure on Serial Learnings." *Journal of Personality* 25(1956):381–390. (b)

Sarason, I. G. "Empirical Findings and Theoretical Problems in the Use of Anxiety Scales." *Psychological Bulletin* 57(1960):403–415.

Sarason, I. G. *Personality: An Objective Approach.* New York: Wiley, 1966.

Schachter, S. "Deviation, Rejection, and Communication." *Journal of Abnormal and Social Psychology* 46(1951):190–207.

Schachter, S. *The Psychology of Affiliation.* Stanford: Stanford University Press, 1959.

Schachter, S. "The Interaction of Cognitive and Physiological Determinants of Emotional State." In *Advances in Experimental Social Psychology.* Vol. 1. Edited by L. Berkowitz. New York: Academic Press, 1964.

Schachter, S.; Ellertson, N.; McBride, D.; and Gregory, D. "An Experimental Study of Cohesiveness and Productivity." *Human Relations* 4(1951):229–238.

Schafer, W. E. "The Social Structure of Sport Groups." *Kölner Zeitschrift für Soziologie* 10(1966): 107–117.

Scheer, J. K. "Effect of Placement in the Order of Competition on Scores of Nebraska High School Students." *Research Quarterly* 44(1973):79–85.

Scheier, I. V., and Cattell, R. B. *Handbook for the IPAT 8-Parallel Form Anxiety Battery With 1962 Supplement of Norms.* Champaign, Ill.: Institute for Personality and Ability Testing, 1962.

Schendel, J. "Psychological Differences Between Athletes and Non-participants in Athletics at Three Educational Levels." *Research Quarterly* 36(1965):52–67.

Schmidt, H. O. "The Effects of Praise and Blame as Incentives to Learning." *Psychological Monographs* 53(1941):Whole No. 240.

Schnore, M. M. "Individual Patterns of Physiological Activity as a Function of Task Differences and Degree of Arousal." *Journal of Experimental Psychology* 58(1959): 117–128.

Schultz, J. H. *Das Autogenne Training: Konzentrative Selbstentspannung.* Stuttgart: Thieme, 1956.

Schultz, J. H., and Luthe, W. *Autogenic Training.* New York: Grune and Stratton, 1959.

Schwartz, G. E. "TM Relaxes Some People and Makes Them Feel Better." *Psychology Today* 7(April 1974):39–44.

Scofield, C. "Physiology of Emotion." Unpublished Chapter in *Physiological Psychology.*

✓Scott, J. *Athletics for Athletes.* Oakland: Other Ways, 1969.

Scott, J. P. *Aggression.* Chicago: University of Chicago Press, 1958.

Scott, J. P. "Hostility and Aggression in Animals." In *Roots of Behavior.* Edited by E. L. Bliss. New York: Harper, 1962.

Scott, J. P. "Sport and Aggression." In *Contemporary Psychology of Sport.* Edited by G. S. Kenyon, Chicago: Athletic Institute, 1970.

Scott, J. P. "Theoretical Issues Concerning the Origin and Causes of Fighting." In *The Physiology of Aggression and Defeat.* Edited by B. E. Eleftheriou and J. P. Scott. New York: Plenum, 1971.

Scott, M. G. "The Contributions of Physical Activity to Psychological Development." *Research Quarterly* 31(1960):307–320.

Selye, H. "General Adaptation Syndrome and Diseases of Adaptation." *Journal of Clinical Endrocrinology* 6(1946):117.

Shaffer, L. F. "Fear and Courage in Aerial Combat." *Journal of Consulting Psychology* 11(1947):137–143.

Shaw, G. *Meat on the Hoof: The Hidden World of Texas Football.* New York: St. Martin's Press, 1972.

Shaw, M. E. "A Comparison of Individuals and Small Groups in the Rational Solution of Complex Problems." *American Journal of Psychology* 44(1932:491–504.

Shaw, M. E. "A Note Concerning Homogeneity of Membership and Group Problem Solving." *Journal of Abnormal and Social Psychology* 60(1960):448–450.

Shaw, M. E. "Some Motivational Factors in Cooperation and Competition." *Journal of Personality* 26(1958):155–169.

Shaw, R. and Kolb, D. "One-Joint Reaction Time Involving Meditators and Non-Meditators." In *Scientific Research on Transcendental Meditation: Collected Papers.* Vol I. Edited by D. W. Orme-Johnson, L. Domash, and J. Farrow. Los Angeles: Maharishi International University, in press.

Sheard, M. H., and Flynn, J. P. "Facilitation of Attack Behavior by Stimulation of the Midbrain of Cats." *Brain Research* 4(1967):324–333.

Sheed, W. "This Riotous Isle." *Sports Illustrated* 30(April 21, 1969):78–95.

Sheldon, W. H., and Stevens, S. S. *The Varieties of Temperament: A Psychology of Constitutional Differences.* New York: Harper and Row, 1942.

Sheldon, W. H.; Stevens, S. S.; and Tucker, W. B. *The Varieties of Human Physique: An Introduction to Constitutional Psychology.* New York: Harper, 1940.

Shelley, H. P. "Focused Leadership and Cohesiveness in Small Groups." *Sociometry* 23(1960):209–216 (a)

Shelley, H. P. "Status Consensus Leadership and Satisfaction with the Group." *Journal of Social Psychology* 51(1960):157–164. (b)

Shepard, C. R. *Small Groups: Some Sociological Perspectives.* San Francisco: Chandler, 1964.

Sherif, M., and Sherif, C. W. *Groups in Harmony and Tension.* New York: Harper and Row, 1953.

Shore, M. F. "Perceptual Efficiency as Related to Induced Muscular Effort and Manifest Anxiety." *Journal of Experimental Psychology* 55(1958):179–183.

Silverman, H. F. "Effects of Praise and Reproof on Reading Growth in a Non-laboratory Classroom Setting." *Journal of Educational Psychology* 48(1957):199–206.

Simonson, N. R., and Lundy, R. M. "Effectiveness of Persuasive Communication Presented Under Conditions of Irrelevant Fear." *Journal of Communications* 16(March, 1966):32–37.

Singer, J. "Introduction: The Psychological Study of Aggression." In *The Control of Aggression and Violence: Cognitive and Physiological Factors.* Edited by J. E. Singer. New York: Academic Press, 1971.

Singer, R. N. "Effects of Spectators on Athletes and Non-athletes Performing a Gross Motor Task." *Research Quarterly* 36(1965):473–482.

Singer, R. N. "Personality Differences Between and Within Baseball and Tennis Players." *Research Quarterly* 40(1969):582–588 (a)

Singer, R. N. "Reaction to 'Sport and Personality Dynamics.'" *Proceedings of National College Physical Education Association for Men* 72(1969):76–79. (b)

Singer, R. N. *Coaching, Athletics, and Psychology.* New York: McGraw-Hill, 1972.

Sjoberg, H. "Relations between Different Arousal Levels Induced by Graded Physical Work and Psychological Efficiency." Unpublished manuscript, Psychological Laboratory, University of Stockholm, 1968.

Skinner, B. F. *Science and Human Behavior.* New York: Macmillan, 1953.

Skinner, B. F. "A Case History in Scientific Method." *American Psychologist* 11(1956):221–233.

Skinner, B. F. "Operant Behavior." In *Operant Behavior: Areas of Research and Application.* Edited by W. K. Konig. New York: Appleton-Century-Crofts, 1966.

Skinner, B. F. *Beyond Freedom and Dignity.* New York: Knopf, 1971.

Skubic, E. "Emotional Response of Boys to Little League and Middle League Competitive Baseball." *Research Quarterly* 26(1955):342–352.

Slusher, H. S. "Personality and Intelligence Characteristics of Selected High School Athletes and Non-athletes." *Research Quarterly* 35(1964):539–545.

Smith, C. H. "Influences of Athletic Success and Failure on Level of Aspiration." *Research Quarterly* 20(1949):196–208.

Smith, G. "An Analysis of the Concept of Group Cohesion in a Simulated Athletic Sport Setting." Master's thesis, University of Western Ontario, London, 1968.

Smith, M. D. "Aggression in Sport: Toward a Role Approach." *Journal of the Canadian Association of Health, Physical Education and Recreation* 37(January–February, 1971):22–25,47 (a)

Smith, M. D. "Some Determinants of Assaultive Behaviour in Hockey: A Theory and Causal Model." Paper presented at the Third International Symposium on the Sociology of Sport, August 1971, at Waterloo, Ontario. (b)

Smith, M. D. "Hostile Outbursts in Sport." *Sport Sociology Bulletin* 2(1973):6-10.

Smith, M. D. "Collective Violence in Sport." In *The Social Dimensions of Sport*. Edited by J. W. Loy and D. Ball. Reading, Mass.: Addison-Wesley, in press.

Smits, T. The Game of Soccer. Englewood Cliffs, N.J.: Prentice-Hall, 1968.

Spence, K. W. *Behavior Theory and Conditioning*. New Haven: Yale University Press, 1956.

Spence, K. W. "Theory of Emotionally Based Drive (D) and Its Relation to Performance in Simple Learning Situations." *American Psychologist* 13(1958):131-141.

Spence, K. W.; Bergmann, G.; and Lippitt, R. "A Study of Simple Learning Under Irrelevant Motivational-Reward Conditions." *Journal of Experimental Psychology* 40(1950):539-551.

Spence, K. W.; Farber, I. E.; and McFann, H. H. "The Relation of Anxiety (Drive) Level to Performance in Competitional and Noncompetitional Paired-associates Learning." *Journal of Experimental Psychology* 52(1956):296-305.

Spence, J. T., and Spence, K. W. "The Motivational Components of Manifest Anxiety: Drive and Drive Stimuli." In *Anxiety and Behavior*. Edited by C. D. Spielberger. New York: Academic Press, 1966.

Spielberger, C. D. "Theory and Research on Anxiety." In *Anxiety and Behavior*. Edited by C. D. Spielberger. New York: Academic Press, 1966.

Spielberger, C. D. "Trait-State Anxiety and Motor Behavior." *Journal of Motor Behavior* 3(1971):265-279.

Spielberger, C. D.; Gorusch, R. L.; and Lushene, R. L. STAI Manual. Palo Alto: Consulting Psychologists Press, 1970.

Steinhaus, A. H. "Facts and Theories of Neuromuscular Relaxation." *Quest* 3(1964): 3-14.

Steinhaus, A., and Ikai, M. "Some Factors Modifying the Expression of Human Strength." *Journal of Applied Physiology* 16(1961):157-163.

Stennett, R. G. "The Relationship of Alpha Amplitude to the Level of Palmar Conductance." *Electroencephalography and Clinical Neurophysiology Supplement* 9(1957): 131-138 (a)

Stennett, R. G. "The Relationship of Performance Level to Level of Arousal." *Journal of Experimental Psychology* 54(1957):54-61. (b)

Stevenson, H. W. "Social Reinforcement with Children as a Function of CA, Sex of *E* and Sex of *S*." *Journal of Abnormal Psychology* 63(1961):147-154.

Stevenson, H. W., and Snyder, L. C. "Performance as a Function of the Interaction of Incentive Conditions." *Journal of Personality* 28(1960):1-11.

Stile, M. H. "Motivation for Sports Participation in the Community." *Canadian Medical Association Journal* 96(1967):889-894.

Stogdill, R. *Individual Behavior and Group Achievement: A Theory, the Experimental Evidence*. New York: Oxford University Press, 1959.

Stoll, C. "Psychology and Athletics." Paper presented at American Association of Health, Physical Education and Recreation National Convention, April 1973, at Minneapolis. Cassette.

Stone, L. J., and Hokanson, J. E. "Arousal Reduction via Self-Punitive Behavior." *Journal of Personality and Social Psychology* 12(1969):72–79.

Storr, A. *Human Aggression.* New York: Atheneum, 1968.

Straub, W. F. "Personality Traits of College Football Players Who Participated at Different Levels of Competition." *International Journal of Sport Psychology* 2(1971):33–41.

Strong, C. H. "Motivation Related to Performance on Physical Fitness Tests." *Research Quarterly* 34(1963):497–507.

Stryker, S., and Psathas, G. "Research on Coalitions in the Triad: Findings, Problems and Strategy." *Sociometry* 23(1960):217–230.

Sullivan, E. "Emotional Reactions and Grip Strength in College Wrestlers as a Function of Time to Competition." Master's thesis, University of Massachusetts, 1964.

Surwillo, W. W. "A Device for Recording Variations in Pressure of Grip During Tracking." *American Journal of Psychology* 68(1955):669–670.

Surwillo, W. W. "Psychological Factors in Muscle-action Potentials: EMG Gradients." *Journal of Experimental Psychology* 52(1956):263–272.

Sutarman, and Thomson, M. L. "A New Technique for Enumerating Active Sweat Glands in Man." *Journal of Physiology* (London) 11(1952):51P–53P.

Sutton-Smith, B. "Games, Play and Controls." In *Social Control and Social Change.* Edited by J. P. Scott and S. F. Scott. Chicago: University of Chicago Press, 1971.

Taylor, I. R. "Hooligans: Soccer's Resistance Movement." *New Society* 14(August 7, 1969):204–206.

Taylor, I. R. "Football Mad: A Speculative Sociology of Football Hooliganism." In *The Sociology of Sport.* Edited by E. Dunning. London: Cass, 1971.

Taylor, I. R. "Social Control Through Sport: Football in Mexico." *Canadian Journal of Latin American Studies,* forthcoming.

Taylor, J. A. "A Personality Scale of Manifest Anxiety." *Journal of Abnormal and Social Psychology* 48(1953):285–290.

Taylor, J. A. "Drive Theory and Manifest Anxiety." *Psychological Bulletin* 53(1956):303–320.

Taylor, S. P. "Aggressive Behavior and Physiological Arousal as a Function of Provocation and the Tendency to Inhibit Aggression." *Journal of Personality* 33(1967):297–310.

Taylor, S. P., and Epstein, S. "Aggression as a Function of the Interaction of the Sex of the Aggressor and Sex of the Victim." *Journal of Personality* 35(1967):474–486.

Tedeschi, J. T.; Smith, R. B., III; and Brown, J. C. "A Reinterpretation of Research on Aggression. *Psychological Bulletin* 81(1974):540–562.

Terrell, G., Jr., and Kennedy, W. A. "Discrimination Learning and Transposition in Children as a Function of the Nature of the Reward." *Journal of Experimental Psychology* 53(1957):257–260.

"Testing Leaders." *Human Behavior* 2(October, 1973):30–31.

Thayer, R. E. "Measurement of Activation Through Self-Report. *Psychological Reports* 20(1967):663–678.

Thibaut, J. W., and Kelley, H. H. *The Social Psychology of Groups.* New York: Wiley, 1959.

Thiessen, D. D. "Population Density and Behavior: A Review of Theoretical and Phys iological Contributions." *Texas Reports on Biology and Medicine* 22(1964) 266–314 (a)

Thiessen, D. D. "Population Density, Mouse Genotype, and Endocrine Function in Be havior." *Journal of Comparative and Physiological Psychology* 57(1964):412–416 (b)

Thomas, S. E. "Hypnosis in Athletics." *Hypnosis* 1(March, 1955):11–14.

Thompson, G. G., and Hunnicutt, C. W. "Effects of Repeated Praise or Blame on the Work Achievements of Introverts and Extroverts." *Journal of Educational Psychol ogy* 35(1944):257–266.

Thorpe, J. A. "Personality Patterns of Successful Women Physical Educators." *Research Quarterly* 29(1958):83–92.

Thune, J. B. "Personality of Weight Lifters." *Research Quarterly* 20(1949):296–306.

Thurstone, L. L. *Multiple Factor Analysis.* Chicago: University of Chicago Press, 1947.

Tiber, N., and Kennedy, W. A. "The Effects of Incentives on the Intelligence Test Per formance of Different Social Groups." *Journal of Consulting Psychology* 28(1964): 187.

Tolman, C. W., and Wilson, G. F. "Social Feeding in Domestic Chicks." *Animal Be haviour* 13(1965):134–142.

Tolman, E. C. *Purposive Behavior in Animals and Man.* New York: Century, 1932.

Townsend, A. N. "The Relationship Between Parental Commitment and Certain Forms of Dependent Behavior." Ph.D. dissertation, University of Michigan, 1958.

Travis, L. E. "The Effect of a Small Audience Upon Eye–hand Coordination." *Journal of Abnormal and Social Psychology* 20(1925):142–146.

Travis, L. E. "The Influence of the Group Upon the Stutterer's Speed in Free Association." *Journal of Abnormal and Social Psychology* 23(1928):45–58.

Triplett, N. "The Dynamogenic Factors in Pacemaking and Competition." *American Journal of Psychology* 9(1897):507–533.

Tuckman, B. W. *Conducting Educational Research.* New York: Harcourt Brace Jovanovich, 1972.

Turner, E. J. "The Effects of Viewing College Football, Basketball and Wrestling on the Elicited Aggressive Responses of Male Spectators." In *Contemporary Psychology of Sport.* Edited by G. S. Kenyon. Chicago: Athletic Institute, 1970.

Turner, R. H. "Collective Behavior." In *Handbook of Modern Sociology.* Edited by R. E. L. Faris. Chicago: Rand McNally, 1964.

Tutko, T. A., and Ogilvie, B. C. "The Role of the Coach in the Motivation of Athletes." In *Motivations in Play, Games and Sports.* Edited by R. Slovenko and J. A. Knight. Springfield, Ill.: Thomas, 1967.

Tutko, T. A., and Richards, J. W. *Psychology of Coaching.* Boston: Allyn and Bacon, 1971.

Ulett, G. A.; Gleser, G.; Winokur, G.; and Lawler, A. "The EEG and Reaction to Photic Stimulation as an Index of Anxiety-Proneness." *Electroencephalography and Clinical Neurophysiology Supplement* 5(1953):23–32.

Ulrich, D., and Burke, R. K. "Effect of Motivational Stress Upon Physical Performance." *Research Quarterly* 28(1957):403-412.

Ussery, J. "Pacing a Team to the Championship in Track." *Coaching Clinic* 6(1968): 10-11.

Uznadze, D. A. *Experimental Foundations of the Psychology of Programming.* Tbilisi, 1961.

Van de Riet, H. "The Effects of Praise and Reproof on Paired-Associate Learning in Educationally Retarded Children." *Dissertation Abstracts* 24(1963):1250.

Vanek, M., and Cratty, B. J. *Psychology and the Superior Athlete.* New York: Macmillan, 1970.

Vaz, E. "The Culture of Young Hockey Players: Some Initial Observations." In *Training: Scientific Basis and Application.* Edited by A. W. Taylor. Springfield, Ill.: Thomas, 1972.

Vega, M. "The Performance of Negro Children on an Oddity Discrimination Task as a Function of the Race of the Examiner and the Type of Verbal Incentive Used by the Examiner." Ph.D. dissertation, Florida State University, 1964.

Veit, H. "Some Remarks Upon the Elementary Interpersonal Relations Within Ball Games Teams." In *Contemporary Psychology of Sport,* edited by G. S. Kenyon. Chicago: Athletic Institute, 1970.

Veller, D. "Big Question: Praise of Punishment." *Athletic Journal* 48(February, 1968): 40-41.

Vernon, P. E. *Personality Assessment: A Critical Survey.* New York: Wiley, 1964.

Veroff, J. "Social Comparison and the Development of Achievement Motivation." In *Achievement-related Motives in Children.* Edited by C. P. Smith. New York: Russell Sage Foundation, 1969.

Vogel, W.; Baker, R. W.; and Lazarus, R. S. "The Role of Motivation in Psychological Stress." *Journal of Abnormal and Social Psychology* 56(1958):105-112.

Volkamer, M. "Investigation into the Aggressiveness in Competitive Social Systems." *Sportwissenschaft* 1(1971)'68-76.

Wallace, J. "What Units Shall We Employ? Allport's Question Revisited." *Journal of Consulting Psychology* 31(1967):56-64.

Wallace, R. K. "The Physiological Effects of Transcendental Meditation: A Proposed Major State of Consciousness." Ph.D. dissertation, University of California, Los Angeles, 1970.

Wallace, R. K., and Benson, H. "The Physiology of Meditation." *Scientific American* 226 (No. 2, 1972):84-90.

Wallace, R. K.; Benson, H.; and Wilson, A. F. "A Wakeful Hypometabolic Physiologic State." *American Journal of Physiology* 221(1971):795-799.

Wallach, M. A., and Leggett, M. I. "Testing the Hypothesis that a Person Will Be Consistent: Stylistic Consistency Versus Situational Specificity in Size of Children's Drawings." *Journal of Personality* 40(1972):309-330.

Wapner, S., and Alper, T. G. "The Effect of an Audience on Behavior in a Choice Situation." *Journal of Abnormal and Social Psychology* 47(1952):222-229.

Walters, R. H., and Thomas, E. L. "Enhancement of Punitiveness by Visual and Audio-visual Displays." *Canadian Journal of Psychology* 17(1963):244-255.

493

Wankel, L. M. "The Interaction of Competition and Ability Levels in the Performance and Learning of a Motor Task." Paper presented at the Nineteenth Biennial Convention of C.A.H.P.E.R., June 1971, at Waterloo, Ontario.

Warburton, F. W., and Kane, J. E. "Personality Related to Sport and Physical Activity." In *Readings in Physical Education*. Edited by J. E. Kane. London: The Physical Education Association of Great Britain and Northern Ireland, 1966.

Warden, C. J., and Cohen, A. "A Study of Certain Incentives Applied Under School-room Conditioning." *Journal of Genetic Psychology* 39(1931):320–327.

Washburn, S. L., and DeVore, I. "The Social Life of Baboons." *Scientific American* 204(1961):62–71.

Weiner, B., and Kukla, A. "An Attributional Analysis of Achievement Motivation." *Journal of Personality and Social Psychology* 15(1970):1–20.

Weingold, U. P., and R. L. Webster. "Effects of Punishment in a Cooperative Behavior in Children." *Child Development* 35(1964):1211–1216.

Weiss, P. *Sport: A Philosophic Inquiry*. Carbondale, Ill.: Southern Illinois University Press, 1969.

Weiss, R. A. "Is Physical Fitness Our Most Important Objective?" *Journal of Health, Physical Education and Recreation* 35(1964):17–18, 61–62.

Welford, A. T. *Fundamentals of Skills*. London: Methuen, 1968.

Wells, H. P. "Relationship Between Physical Fitness and Psychological Variables." Ph.D dissertation, University of Illinois, 1958.

Welty, J. C. "Experiments in Group Behavior of Fishes." *Physiological Zoology* 7(1934): 85–128.

Wendt, H. W. "Indications of Fatigue." Paper presented at the Twentieth Congress of the German Society of Psychology, September 1955, at Berlin. (a)

Wendt, H. W. "Motivation, Effort and Performance." In *Studies in Motivation*. Edited by D. C. McClelland. New York: Appleton-Century-Crofts, 1955.

Wenger, M. A. "An Attempt to Appraise Individual Differences in Level of Muscular Tension." *Journal of Experimental Psychology* 32(1943):213–225.

Wenger, M. A. "Preliminary Study of the Significance of Measures of Autonomic Balance." *Psychosomatic Medicine* 9(1947):301–309.

Wenger, M. A., and Ellington, M. "The Measurement of Autonomic Balance in Children: Method and Normative Data." *Psychosomatic Medicine* 5(1943):241–253.

Werner, A. C. "Physical Education and The Development of Leadership Characteristics of Cadets at the United States Military Academy." D.P.E. dissertation, Springfield College, 1960.

Werner, A. C., and E. Gottheil. "Personality and Participation in College Athletics." *Research Quarterly* 37(1966):126–131.

Wertheimer, M. "Figural Aftereffects as a Measure of Metabolic Efficiency." *Journal of Personality* 24(1955):56–73.

Whalley, G. "The Mariner and the Albatross." In *Twentieth Century Interpretations of the Rime of the Ancient Mariner*. Edited by J. D. Boulger. Englewood Cliffs, N.J.: Prentice-Hall, 1969.

White, C. "An Analysis of Hostile Outbursts in Spectator Sports." Ph.D. dissertation, University of Illinois, 1970.

Whiting, H. T. A., and Stembridge, D. E. "Personality and the Persistent Non-swimmer." *Research Quarterly* 36(1965):348–356.

Whittemore, I. C. "The Influence of Competition on Performance: An Experimental Study." *Journal of Abnormal and Social Psychology* 19(1924):226–253.

Whyte, W. F. *Street Corner Society.* Chicago: University of Chicago Press, 1943.

Wiggins, J. S. "Personality Structure." *Annual Review of Psychology* 19(1968): 293–350.

Willcutt, H. C., and Kennedy, W. A. "Relation of Intelligence to Effectiveness of Praise and Reproof as Reinforcers For Fourth-Graders." *Perceptual and Motor Skills* 17(1963):695–697.

Williams, A. C., Jr.; Macmillan, J. W.; and Jenkins, J. G. *Preliminary Experimental Investigations of Tension as a Determinant of Performance in Flight Training.* Washington, D.C.: Civil Aeronautics Administration, Division of Research, January 1946.

Williams, J. M.; Hoepner, B. J.; Moody, D. L.; and Ogilvie, B. C. "Personality Traits of Champion Level Fencers." *Research Quarterly* 41(1970):446–453.

Willis, J. D. "Achievement Motivation, Success, and Competitiveness in College Wrestling." Ph.D. dissertation, Ohio State University, 1968.

Willis, J. D., and Bethe, D. R. "Achievement Motivation: Implications for Physical Activity." *Quest* 13(1970):18–22.

Wilmore, J. H. "Influence of Motivation on Physical Work Capacity and Performance." *Journal of Applied Physiology* 24(1968):459–463.

Wilt, F. *How They Train.* Los Altos, Calif.: Track and Field News, 1959.

Winer, B. J. *Statistical Principles in Experimental Design.* New York: McGraw-Hill, 1962.

Witthuhn, B. "Motivation for Winning Teams." *Scholastic Coach* 38(October, 1968):56.

Wolfgang, M. E., and Ferracuti, F. "The Subculture of Violence." In *The Sociology of Crime and Delinquency.* Edited by M. E. Wolfgang, L. Savitz, and N. Johnston. New York: Wiley, 1970.

Wolpe, J. *Psychotherapy by Reciprocal Inhibition.* Stanford: Stanford University Press, 1958.

Wood, C. G., Jr., and Hokanson, J. E. "Effects of Induced Muscle Tension in Performance and the Inverted U Function." *Journal of Personality and Social Psychology* 1(1965): 506–510.

Woodworth, R. S., and Schlosberg, H. *Experimental Psychology.* Rev. ed. New York: Holt, Rinehart and Winston, 1954.

Woodworth, R. S., and Schlosberg, H. *Experimental Psychology.* Rev. ed. New York: Holt, Rinehart and Winston, 1963.

Worrell, L. "Level of Aspiration and Academic Success." *Journal of Educational Psychology* 50(1959):47–54.

Wright, W. R. "Some Effects of Incentives on Work and Fatigue." *Psychological Review* 13(1906):23–34.

Wrightsman, L. "The Effects of Waiting with Others on Changes in Level of Felt Anxiety." *Journal of Abnormal and Social Psychology* 61(1960):216–222.

Wyrick, W. "How Sex Differences Affect Research in Physical Education." In *DGWS Research Reports: Women in Sports*. Edited by D. V. Harris. Washington, D.C.: American Association for Health, Physical Education and Recreation, 1971.

Yacorczynski, G. K. "Degree of Effort: II. Relationship to the Level of Aspiration." *Journal of Experimental Psychology* 30(1942):407–413.

Yerkes, R., and Dodson, J. "The Relation of Strength of Stimulus to Rapidity of Habit-Formation." *Journal of Comparative Neurology and Psychology* 18(1908):459–482.

Yinger, J. M. "Research Implications of a Field View of Personality." *American Journal of Sociology* 68(1963):580–592.

Yinger, J. M. *Toward a Field Theory of Behavior: Personality and Social Structure*. New York: McGraw-Hill, 1965.

Young, P. T. *Motivation of Behavior*. New York: Wiley, 1936.

Young, P. T. *Emotion in Man and Animal*. New York: Wiley, 1943.

Zajonc, R. B. "Social Facilitation." *Science* 149(1965):269–274.

Zajonc, R. B. *Social Psychology: An Experimental Approach*. Belmont, Calif.: Wadsworth, 1966.

Zajonc, R. B., and Nieuwenhyse, B. "Relationship Between Word Frequency and Recognition: Perceptual Process or Response Bias?" *Journal of Experimental Psychology* 67(1964):276–285.

Zajonc, R. B., and Sales, S. M. "Social Facilitation of Dominant and Subordinate Responses." *Journal of Experimental Social Psychology* 2(1966):160–168.

Zborowski, M. "Cultural Components in Response to Pain." *Journal of Social Issues* 8(1952):16–30.

Zander, A. "Group Aspirations." In *Group Dynamics: Research and Theory*. 3d ed. Edited by D. Cartwright and A. Zander. New York: Harper and Row, 1968.

Zander, A. F. "Productivity and Group Success: Team Spirit vs. The Individual Achiever." *Psychology Today* 8(November 1974):64–68.

Zeigler, H. P. "Displacement Activity and Motivational Theory: A Case Study in the History of Ethology." *Psychological Bulletin* 61(1964):362–376.

Zillmann, D., and Bryant, J. "The Effect of Residual Excitation on the Emotional Response to Provocation and Delayed Aggressive Behavior." *Journal of Personality and Social Psychology*, in press.

Zillmann, D.; Johnson, R. C.; and Day, K. D. "Attribution of Apparent Arousal and Proficiency of Recovery from Sympathetic Activation Affecting Excitation Transfer to Aggressive Behavior." *Journal of Experimental Social Psychology* 10(1974):503–515.

Zillmann, D.; Katcher, A. H.; and Milavsky, B. "Excitation Transfer from Physical Exercise to Subsequent Aggressive Behavior." *Journal of Experimental Social Psychology* 8(1972):247–259.

Zimbardo, P. G. "The Human Choice: Individuation, Reason, and Order Versus Deindividuation, Impulse, and Chaos." In *Nebraska Symposium on Motivation*. Edited by W. J. Arnold and D. Levine. Lincoln: University of Nebraska Press, 1969.

Zuckerman, M. "The Development of an Affect Adjective Check List for the Measurement of Anxiety." *Journal of Consulting Psychology* 24(1960):457–462.

Zuckerman, M.; Kolin, E. A.; Price, L.; Zook, J. "Development of a Sensation-seeking Scale." *Journal of Consulting Psychology* 28(1964):477–482.

Index